MOON

W9-CDN-206

# DOMINICAN REPUBLIC

LEBAWIT LILY GIRMA

# Contents

Parque
Nacional
El Morro          Playa El
                  Morro
Parque                    Monte Cristi
Nacional              El Rincón              Cabo
Monte                                        Isabela      Luperón        Playa
Cristi                                                                   Costambar          Puerto
                                                                                            Plata        Playa
                          DUARTE HWY                                                                     Dorada
Fort                                                     Reserva                 Reserva Científica                   Sosúa        Cabarete
Liberté          Dajabón            1              Científica Villa               Isabel de Torres     GREGORIO LUPERÓN
                                                    Elisa                                              INTERNATIONAL
                                          Río Yaque del Norte                                          AIRPORT                    5
HAITI                                     Cibao                        Mao                    25
                                                                                      Santiago
                          18
                    Los Almácigos                   16                                                    Moca
             45      DOMINICAN                    Valley
                     REPUBLIC                                  Janico                         San Francisco
Hinche                                       C                                                de Macorís
                                              o
                            Parque Nacional    r         Parque Nacional                 La Vega
                            Nalga de Maco       d        J. Armando                                    Reserva        Rincón
                                                 i       Bermúdez            Jarabacoa              Científica
                                                  l                                                Ébano Verde        1
                              Parque Nacional      l      e
                              José del Carmen        r           C                                             Bonao
                              Ramírez                 a           e                                                   DUARTE
                                                                   n    Pico Duarte
Laguna                                                               t  3,087m        Constanza
de                    Valle de San Juan            C                 r
Peligro                                             a                a                                              Río Haina
                    Comendador            2      San Juan de         l       Parque
Lascahobas                                       la Maguana                  Nacional
                                                                            Valle Nuevo
                          Sierra de Neyba          SÁNCHEZ                                   41
Lago                                                 HWY    Presa de
Saurnatre         La Descubierta                          Sabana Yegua                                 San José
                              Parque Nacional                                                         de Ocoa
Jimaní                        Lago Enriquillo                                                                      2
                                            Neyba              Río Yaque del Sur            Azua
             46                  Lago                                                                   Playa
                                 Enriquillo                        44                                  Monte Río
                              Reserva                                                                            Baní
                  Parque Nacional   Científica Laguna                          Bahía de Ocoa
                  Sierra de         de Cabral                                                              Playa
                  Bahoruco                       Cabral      Bahía de                                      Palenque
                     Sierra de Bahoruco                      Neyba                         Playa
                                           Barahona                                        Las Salinas
             Pedernales
                                                        Playa San
                                     Paraíso            Rafael
                              Enriquillo        Playa Los
             44                                 Patos                   C a r i b b e a n
                              Oviedo
                  Parque
                  Nacional
                  Jaragua

© MOON.COM      Isla Beata      Cabo Beata

DISCOVER

# the Dominican Republic

It's no surprise that the Dominican Republic consistently ranks as the most visited country in the Caribbean, with no signs of slowing down. The diamond-white beaches and lavish resorts, from Punta Cana to La Romana, attract millions of sun worshippers every year. And while the blue waves, swaying palm trees, and sparkling sand are worth the trip, it's the rest of the country that will make you fall in love.

Santo Domingo's restored Colonial City brims with grand Spanish-style architecture, 16th-century cathedrals, and wrought iron balconies. Outside the capital, beaches are lined with rows of *frituras* (fried-food shacks) selling the day's catch, served with red onion-spiced avocados and *tostones* (crispy fried plantains). Avid surfers and divers flock to the north, while the countryside offers enriching cultural expeditions to cacao and coffee plantations. Adventure awaits in the mountainous heart of the country, where you can hike through cloud forests and horseback ride to crisp, cool waterfalls. In the southwestern corner of the island, the possibility of sheer isolation still exists among the peaks, sand dunes, and deserted beaches.

Regardless of where you find yourself in the DR, at the center of it all are unmistakably Dominican experiences. The sound of merengue and bachata in

**Clockwise from top left**: Playa Juanillo; the Colonial City; view of Calle El Conde; countryside home; market; road to Miches.

the air invites you to dance, whether in the middle of a park or at a *rancho típico* (open-air roadside club). People gather on street corners, playing dominoes and throwing back Brugal rum or ice-cold Presidente beers from the *colmado* (corner shop). You'll find constant celebration, most notably during February's country-wide carnivals, which offer a glimpse into the country's eclectic African, Taíno, and Spanish heritage. Music mixes with laughter to create the daily soundtrack, because Dominicans enjoy every day to the fullest.

The Dominican Republic oozes life. They say New York City never sleeps, but the DR never stops dancing.

**Clockwise from top left:** view from Montaña Redonda; souvenirs along Calle El Conde in Ciudad Colonial; Salto de Jimenoa Dos; stand in Constanza.

# 10 TOP
# EXPERIENCES

**2** **Hit the Beach:** Enjoy miles of white or golden sand and clear water, for sunbathing, swimming, and playing in the waves (page 24).

**3** **Catch a Baseball Game:** Passions for baseball run deep in the Dominican Republic. Join in the fun (page 66).

>>>

**4** **Get to Know the Real DR:** Dance to merengue, snack on local cuisine, and explore the bustling markets (page 30).

**5** **Go Back in Time at Santo Domingo's Ciudad Colonial:** Stroll along cobblestone streets and admire 16th-century churches, palaces, courthouses, and statues (page 46).

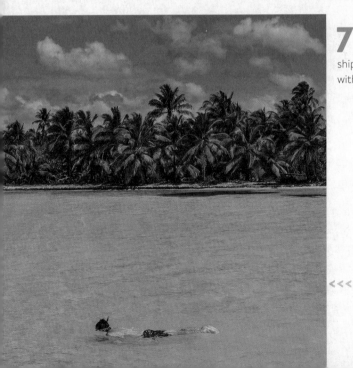

**6** **Make an Impact:** Travel with a local guide and stay in green lodging. Experience the DR with the people who live here (page 31, page 216, and page 334).

**7** **Dive & Snorkel:** Explore reefs and shipwrecks teeming with life (page 28).

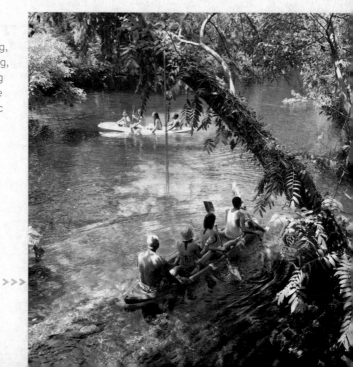

**8** **See Wildlife:** From golden swallows to humpback whales, the country's parks, sanctuaries, and reserves are home to beautiful creatures (page 170, page 258, and page 344).

**9** **Get into the Water:** Surfing, kayaking, kitesurfing, and paddleboarding are just a few of the ways to find aquatic adventures (page 242 and page 292).

**10** **Take a Hike:** Discover mountain caves, climb sand dunes, and wander through cloud forests (page 117, page 213, page 301, and page 322).

# Planning Your Trip

## Where to Go

### Santo Domingo

Santo Domingo was the first city of the Americas, and today it is the most dynamic, cosmopolitan city in the Caribbean. The **Ciudad Colonial,** declared a UNESCO World Heritage Site in 1990, displays Spanish colonial and Gothic architecture in its sprawling plazas and bustling streetscapes. The upscale **Piantini** and **Naco** districts in the center of the city offer modern, upscale hotels, sleek bistros and lounges, and shopping malls. On the weekends, city dwellers flock to the nearby beaches of **Juan Dolio, Guayacanes,** and **Boca Chica.** Santo Domingo is just a two-hour drive from Punta Cana via the Coral Highway.

### Punta Cana and the Southeast Coast

On the southeast and eastern coasts of the island are the DR's most visited regions: Punta Cana, Bayahibe, and La Romana. **Punta Cana** is the crown jewel of Dominican tourism, comprising 30 miles of powdery soft sand lined with all-inclusive resorts, with a handful of independent hotels in **Bávaro.** Inland, **La Romana** offers luxury with world-class resorts and golf courses. **Bayahibe** also boasts many resorts and tourists, though its colorful village center still provides a cultural window into the DR. Many visitors take day trips from Bayahibe to the stunning **Saona and Catalina Islands,** both of which offer beautiful beaches and great diving.

### The Samaná Peninsula

Jutting out of the northeast corner of the island is the Samaná Peninsula, with uncrowded beaches flanked by cliffs and coconut plantations. This region is a haven for European expats and independent travelers. There are three main areas: **Samaná town,** known for its seasonal humpback whale-watching; **Las Terrenas,** a funky and cosmopolitan town; and **Las Galeras,** home to top beaches like **Playa Rincón** and **Playa Frontón.** Offshore, the towering rocks of **Los Haitises National Park** are worth a boat trip for bird-watching and Taíno history. The Carretera Samaná links the peninsula to Santo Domingo in 2.5 hours, and JetBlue flies direct to Samaná's El Catey International Airport.

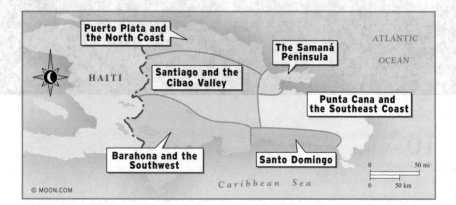

# If You're Looking For...

- **Culture:** Visit Puerto Plata province and its tour cacao farms and coffee plantations; visit the mountains of Jarabacoa and Constanza; book a homestay in Barahona.

- **Romance:** Stay in a luxury resort in Punta Cana; pick out a boutique hotel in Las Terrenas; escape to the hills of La Barbacoa on the Samaná Peninsula.

- **Nightlife:** Dance the night away in Santo Domingo, Puerto Plata, or Las Terrenas.

- **Budget Options:** Visit Bayahibe and go island-hopping; head to Las Galeras for beautiful beaches; stay at a beachfront cabin in Punta Rucia.

- **Outdoor Recreation:** Visit the Cibao Valley for waterfalls, river rafting, and mountain hiking; stay in Barahona and the southwest for national parks, lagoons, and swimming holes.

a typical countryside home in Puerto Plata Province

## Puerto Plata and the North Coast

The North Coast of the Dominican Republic is the most well-rounded destination in the country. There are historical sights in **Puerto Plata city,** water sports in nearby **Cabarete** and **Sosúa,** and cultural excursions to amber mines and coffee and cacao plantations in the province's various municipalities. Puerto Plata city is also attractive for its **Playa Dorada** resorts and beaches, but there are less crowded overnight stops along the coastline in **Punta Rucia.** If you're a wildlife lover, head west of Puerto Plata city to see manatees at the **Estero Hondo Marine Mammal Sanctuary** and mangrove swamps in **Monte Cristi.** To the west are even more beautiful beaches and offshore islands.

## Santiago and the Cibao Valley

The mountainous **Cibao Valley,** known as the breadbasket of the country, offers all kinds of adventure. There are a handful of national parks in and around **Jarabacoa**—including the tallest peak in the region, **Pico Duarte**—with freshwater rivers and lush hills for rafting and hiking. Nearby **Constanza** sits at 4,000 feet elevation, covered in pine forests, vegetable farms, and flower plantations. The **Valle Nuevo National Park** welcomes hikers to cooler temperatures and cabins with fireplaces. The Cibao Valley's major gateway, **Santiago,** is the DR's second-largest city, a commercial hub known for its cigars and active nightlife; just an hour southwest are the hot springs of the mountainous escape **San José de las Matas.**

## Barahona and the Southwest

The least tourism-developed area of the Dominican Republic straddles the Haitian border in the southwestern corner of the country. It is slowly developing, and it's best to see the region before it does. It is also unique in its geography, with a landscape that includes sand dunes, pebblestone beaches, and mountains in **Barahona** and a host of lagoons, national parks, and roads lined with cactus in **Pedernales.** The country's largest protected park, **Parque Nacional Jaragua,** is home to turtle nesting beaches and flamingos at **Laguna Oviedo.**

American crocodiles glide in the salty **Lago Enriquillo,** the lowest point in the Caribbean, while 30 endemic bird species roam the **Sierra de Bahoruco.** The southwest's highlight for many is the remote **Bahía de las Águilas,** considered one of the best beaches in the Dominican Republic.

# When to Go

The Dominican Republic is blessed with **sunny, warm weather year-round,** with average temperatures in the mid-80s. It gets extremely humid and hot in the summertime, while cooler sea breezes make mid-November through January more pleasant. The **rainy season** has become unpredictable, with more rainstorms now happening in November than in **hurricane season,** which normally peaks in September and October. In the central mountains or the Cibao Valley, days are cooler and drier, but temperatures can drop below freezing at night in December.

High **tourist season** runs from mid-December through mid-March—expect higher rates during this time. It's worth it if you're coming for the **humpback whale mating season** in Samaná (which ends mid-March), or for **Carnaval Dominicano,** which runs every Sunday in February around the island.

During Easter holidays or **Semana Santa**—Holy Week, aka the week preceding Easter Sunday—hotels fill up in popular areas from Juan Dolio to La Romana to Las Terrenas (look out for beach closures due to a high level of boozing that weekend). In Santo Domingo, the Malecón is partly turned into a pedestrian zone, and becomes a beach party in the city with games and music. It's also a dangerous time to be on the road, so be wary.

The **low tourist season** (summertime) brings with it attractive airfare and slashed hotel rates, if you can bear the heat and humidity. Catch the **rum festival** in Puerto Plata in July. November to mid-December is the best compromise between seasons, with fewer tourists, ideal weather, and good rates before the **end-of-year holidays**—not to mention the Dominican Republic Jazz Festival on the North Coast.

# Before You Go

## PASSPORTS AND TOURIST CARDS

Valid passports that won't expire for an additional six months from your travel dates are required. North American or western European travelers do not need a visa, and since April 2018 the US$10 **tourist card** fee has been incorporated into airfare, so you don't need to purchase anything at the airport. Entry is valid for a 30-day period; overstays will result in paying an exit fee at the airport

upon departure, calculated according to the amount of time extended (up to US$110 for four additional months). For complete visa requirements, visit www.godominicanrepublic.com.

## VACCINATIONS

There are no required vaccinations for entry to the Dominican Republic. However, it is recommended that you always keep up to date with routine shots for measles, mumps, and rubella. For longer stays, it is recommended that you also get hepatitis A and B, tetanus-diphtheria, chicken pox, and typhoid shots.

The CDC continues to advise that pregnant women or women who plan to conceive should postpone travel to many parts of the Caribbean, including the Dominican Republic, due to the presence of the **Zika virus.**

All other travelers should take enhanced precautions to avoid **mosquito bites.** Always be sure to use insect repellent, wear protective clothing when venturing outdoors, and keep mosquitoes outside.

## TRANSPORTATION

Transportation options abound: there's always a bus, car, bike, or coach bus heading to your destination. The DR boasts **10 international and domestic airports** at points convenient to beach resort towns and cities. **Taxis** are easy to spot, and airport fares are displayed as you exit. Around towns or cities, they have set fares, but these become open for negotiation for longer distances, especially in low season—agree on a price before entering any taxi to avoid being overcharged.

There are numerous public transportation options. Hop in the *carritos*, or **shared public taxis,** or the *guaguas*, **shared minivan buses,** that are sometimes worse for wear. These modes of transportation are dirt cheap, cramming up to 7 people in one sedan or up to 30 in a minivan, and run set routes while picking up passengers anywhere along the way. *Motoconchos* or **motorbike taxis** are popular among locals, and while they are the most cost-effective and fastest way to get to your destination, they are the least safe, especially for big cities or highways (with no helmets provided).

Two major coach **bus companies,** Caribe Tours and Metro Tours, offer convenient itineraries between major cities and hubs. Traveling to the smaller towns is easily done by *guaguas*—private vans with air-conditioning and wireless Internet on many routes. There are express *guaguas* or regular ones that stop for every passenger hollering on the roadside.

**Renting a car** is a definite possibility, with major brands present around the island and its airports. Driving offers more flexibility in your itinerary. But beware that accident rates are high in the DR due to speeding, drunk driving, and frequent road obstacles (such as cows and bikes). It is safer to invest in a local driver. Gas prices are also high.

## WHAT TO PACK

Pack any prescription drugs, sunscreen, a hat, and mosquito spray. Throw in some wipes for those long road trips, for when bathroom supplies might be lacking on the way.

Bring **lightweight clothes,** as well as long-sleeve cover-ups if you plan on taking any boat or catamaran excursions or doing some hiking. If you're heading to Jarabacoa and the beautiful mountainous central area, or even at a lodge in the hills of Puerto Plata, you'll want **warmer clothes,** as it can get chilly at night. Mountain hiking, to Pico Duarte for instance, requires proper hiking boots, while sneakers are a must for the national parks and forests you plan on exploring.

Bring **nice outfits:** at resorts, some à la carte restaurants require it, and in the cities, Dominicans dress up. Clubs can even refuse entry if you show up in shorts. Sightseeing in cities also means not dressing like you're going to the beach, especially if you plan on entering churches and cathedrals. Of course, on beaches or in beach towns, the **dress is casual,** but walking around in your bathing suit is frowned upon unless you're actually on the beach. Nudity is forbidden altogether (but often overlooked in areas like Punta Cana).

# The Best of the Dominican Republic

The Dominican Republic is the second-largest country in the Caribbean, and the most diverse geographically. This 10-day itinerary will give you a solid glimpse into the DR's beaches, culture, and opportunities for adventure. It can also be used for a 4- or 7-day trip. Mix and match as you please.

## Santo Domingo: Culture and Nightlife

### DAY 1

Arrive in **Santo Domingo** midmorning and check into **El Beaterio** in the **Ciudad Colonial.** Grab an outdoor Dominican lunch on the sidewalk terrace of **Cafetería El Conde** and enjoy the views of the **Parque Colón** and the **Catedral Primada de América** while you eat. Walk lunch off by exploring the area's stunning architecture and museums on foot, solo or guided, or rent a bike from **Zona Bici.** Make your way down **Calle Las Damas,** visiting the **Fortaleza Ozama, Museo de las Casas Reales,** and **Alcázar de Colón,** the palatial former home of Diego Colón, son of Christopher Columbus. For dinner, indulge in the seafood tasting menu at **Pat'e Palo,** the first-ever tavern in the Americas. Afterward, walk over to **La Bodeguita de la Zona** for a cocktail and live music, or to **El Patio Culinario** if you're into a karaoke-type atmosphere. If it's a Friday or Saturday, catch the free **Santo Domingo de Fiesta** folkloric dance early-evening show on the far end of **Plaza de España.** If it's a Sunday, walk over to the **Monasterio de San Francisco** for the city's most popular outdoor merengue, son, and salsa concert.

Parque Colón in Ciudad Colonial

Las Terrenas

## The Samaná Peninsula: Beaches and Seaside Landscapes

### DAY 2

Rise early and walk down Santo Domingo's **Malecón,** the waterfront promenade, to the neoclassical **Gazcue district.** Have a Dominican breakfast at **Villar Hermanos,** a cafeteria buffet with staples such as fried cheese and *mangú.* Ready for those sugary white beaches? Head north to the **Samaná Peninsula** by coach bus with **Caribe Tours** or by rental car (get your toll change ready). Enjoy spectacular views of coconut plantations on the three-hour journey before arriving in **Las Galeras.** Check into **Villa Serena** and have lunch there. Walk to the main village beach and arrange for your next-day boat ride to three of the area's most beautiful beaches, and then spend the afternoon at nearby **La Playita,** a less crowded stretch of white sand with shallow turquoise waters. If you'd rather have a little more adventure, spend the afternoon horseback riding in the hills with **Rudy's Rancho.** At sunset, walk back to the **main village beach bar** and join the locals for some rum and loud merengue

or *bachata* music. For dinner, enjoy a casual tapas meal in the village at **La Bodeguita** or salty crepes at French-run **Le BDM.**

### DAY 3

From the main beach, get whisked off to the Atlantic shores and towering cliffs of Las Galeras. You'll have an entire day for swimming, sunbathing, and snorkeling at three postcard-perfect beaches: **Playa Madama, Playa Frontón,** and **Playa Rincón.** After your excursion, have dinner at a romantic cliff-top table at **El Cabito** and take in Las Galeras one last time.

### DAY 4

Hop in a private taxi or catch a *guagua* (local bus) toward funky **Las Terrenas.** Begin with a night in the hills of La Barbacoa at **Clave Verde Ecolodge,** then move on to the chic, Bali-inspired **Hotel Mahona** and walk over to the beachfront. Stroll its length down to **Playa Las Ballenas** and have an affordable French gourmet lunch at **La Terrasse.** Spend an afternoon swimming and sunning on the beach. For dinner, grab

## PUNTA CANA AND BAYAHIBE

### Playa Bávaro (page 101)
One of the most well-known beaches in the DR, Playa Bávaro hosts many resorts, but that doesn't take away from its glorious strand. The crystal-clear water is the perfect temperature for a dip.

### Playa Macao (page 100)
The still-undeveloped Playa Macao is great for surfing or taking a stroll along the palm-studded blond sand. It also has some of the best fish shacks on the Punta Cana coastline.

### Playa Juanillo (page 118)
On the southern tip of the Punta Cana coastline, the long, shiny white stretch of Playa Juanillo is dotted with towering, leaning coconut trees—a poster-worthy sight.

### Isla Saona (page 146)
A quick boat ride off the coast of Bayahibe, Isla Saona's beaches are a brilliant white, dotted with tall coconut trees and facing a turquoise Caribbean Sea. The best of all is the uncrowded, beautiful Canto de la Playa at the edge of the island.

## THE SAMANÁ PENINSULA

### Playa Rincón (page 178)
The crown jewel of the Samaná Peninsula's beaches, Playa Rincón is a two-mile-long strip of soft white sand and leaning coconut trees, just 10 minutes by boat from Las Galeras. Visit in the afternoon for fewer crowds.

### Playa Cosón (page 189)
The most stunning beach in Las Terrenas is Playa Cosón, a long, dreamy, blond stretch dotted with a handful of luxury boutique resorts. Locals flock to the undeveloped portion on Sundays to swim and indulge in the best fish shacks in the region.

### Playa El Valle (page 168)
Tucked north of Samaná town, Playa El Valle is an ultra-remote, undeveloped golden beach, sitting at the foot of the towering, lush hills of El Valle. It is not a swimming spot due to riptides, but it makes for a lovely walk.

## THE NORTH COAST

### Punta Rucia and Cayo Arena (page 259)
Playa Punta Rucia is a jumping-off point to the off-

Playa Rincón

shore Cayo Arena, and each stuns on its own. The uncrowded Punta Rucia offers miles of unshaded white sand that sparkles even brighter in the hot sun. The tiny Cayo Arena has beautiful turquoise waters and some of the best snorkeling in the DR.

### Playa Cambiaso (page 214)
Getting to Playa Cambiaso requires a bumpy, 1.5-hour ride from Puerto Plata city, but the remoteness of this stunning stretch is what makes it unique. Locals flock here on Sundays for swimming and seafood, but on weekdays you'll have the beach to yourself—save for a couple of wild donkeys to keep you company. A close second is Playa Arroyo Salado, 10 kilometers (6 miles) south of Cabrera.

### Playa El Morro (page 262)
Hugged by El Morro, a towering limestone mesa, the eponymous reddish-blond beach offers breathtaking scenery. Soft stones shift from one half of the beach to the other with the tide.

## THE SOUTHEAST

### Bahía de las Águilas (page 345)
The remotest of them all, and often said to be the most gorgeous, is Bahía de las Águilas, a protected, undeveloped stretch facing a stunning bay and hugged by a magnificent rocky landscape.

a seafront table along the lively **Pueblo de los Pescadores** restaurant row, or you could join in a communal Dominican buffet meal at **Dan & Manty's.** Head over to **Replay** and dance the night away to Dominican and international tunes. Arrange for a taxi to El Catey Airport the next day, or continue on your trip.

## Puerto Plata and Cabarete: Cultural Tourism and Water Sports
### DAY 5
Rise at dawn and head to **Puerto Plata,** four hours by car or five hours by public bus. Admire the rustic beauty of the North Coast as you pass multiple fishing villages. Once in Puerto Plata, grab lunch at **Hyode Bistro** and then continue another 20 minutes into the countryside by taxi or car to **Tubagua village.** Drop your bags in your cabin at **Tubagua Plantation Eco Lodge** and take in the panoramic hilltop and sea views. The lodge's local guide, Juanin, will take you on a three-hour hike through Tubagua village to gorgeous falls and pools at **Charcos de los Militares.** If you'd prefer to see the DR's famous amber mines or a nearby coffee plantation, you can arrange it through your host at the lodge. Return to the lodge to enjoy the sunset while soaking in the hot pool. You could also arrange your own visit to **Chocal,** a women-run, community-owned chocolate factory in scenic Altamira.

### DAY 6
Head out early by car or taxi to explore the northwest coast, stopping first at the **Estero Hondo Marine Mammal Sanctuary.** Go on a guided hike around the reserve's mangroves and observe more than a dozen manatees from a lookout tower. Continue on to bustling **Playa Ensenada** for a Dominican lunch at one of several beachfront food shacks. After lunch, head to adjacent **Punta Rucia Beach,** where you will find boat captains ready to take you to offshore **Cayo Arena.** The boat will take you through the mangrove channels of the **Parque Nacional Monte Cristi.** Spend the rest of the afternoon snorkeling around the gorgeous corals off this tiny cay. Head back to Puerto Plata city and check into the **Boutique Hotel El Palacio.** Walk over to **Casa 40** for dinner outdoors in a funky colonial courtyard. This local favorite serves tapas, burgers, pastas, and delicious mojitos.

### DAY 7
If you're up for it, catch the sunrise along Puerto Plata's **Malecón.** Grab a morning breakfast and admire the Victorian architecture at **Heladería Mariposa,** across from **Parque Independencia.** Head to Puerto Plata airport for your flight home, or continue your trip and hop into a *carrito* (local shared taxi) heading to **Cabarete.** Check into the beachfront **Hotel Villa Taina** and grab a light sandwich at **Mojito Bar,** a short walk away. Spend the day learning how to windsurf or kitesurf at **Kite Beach.** Later, have a beachfront dinner of Dominican-style seafood at **La Casita de Papi;** burn the calories off at the two-story **Lax Ojo dance club, Onno's Bar,** or one of the other numerous beachfront dance spots.

## Jarabacoa and Constanza: Countryside Lifestyle
### DAY 8
Experience the stunning mountains of the DR in **Jarabacoa,** about a two-hour trip from Cabarete by car or bus. Check into **Jarabacoa Mountain Hostel** and head out for a casual Dominican lunch at **La Tinaja.** From there, meet up with local guide David from **Jarabacoa Eco Adventures,** who will take you on a horseback or motorbike ride to **Salto de Baiguate** for a swim in refreshingly cool waters. In the evening, hop in a taxi for dinner at the mountaintop **Aroma de la Montaña.** Pick a candlelit table on the outdoor terrace and dine with views of the **Cordillera Central.**

### DAY 9
After breakfast at the hostel, head out to neighboring **Constanza** by car or with César of

Sindi-Taxi, riding through **El Tireo village** and its vast fields of vegetable crops and flower plantations. Once there, enjoy a fresh vegetable pizza and strawberry *batida* at **Antojitos de Lauren.** Drive up to **El Divino Niño Monument,** just outside of the town center, to meet the 48-feet-high statue overlooking Constanza's hills. Head back to town for a local Ferringer brew at funky **La Esquina bar,** a local favorite. If you're able to rent an all-terrain vehicle, drive to **Parque Nacional Valle Nuevo,** one of the DR's natural wonders, and hike through its pine forests with a guide from **Villa Pajón Eco-Lodge.** Head back to Jarabacoa for the night and have dinner at **Aguas Blancas.**

**DAY 10**

Grab an early coffee and breakfast from **Super Cafetería La Tinaja** in downtown Jarabacoa before heading back to **Santiago** for your flight home. Hop on Caribe Tours (the bus terminal is a short walk from La Tinaja) or get a private taxi ride to the airport.

# Romancing the DR

## Intimate Lodgings

- **Santo Domingo:** Restored 16th-century quarters in verdant colonial courtyards await at **Hodelpa Nicolás de Ovando,** set on the first paved street in the Americas. **El Beaterio's** charming convent turned guesthouse is small and peaceful, with a tranquil rooftop terrace.

- **Punta Cana: Excellence Punta Cana** offers sexy luxurious perks, like in-room spa tubs, a butler to draw your bath at turndown, and a shower with a see-through glass wall facing the bedroom.

- **Samaná Peninsula:** Lounge poolside at the charming **Hotel Mahona,** tucked a street away from the beach in Las Terrenas, or hole up in a hilltop villa cabin at **Clave Verde**

Excellence Punta Cana's pool

Playa Esmeralda

**Ecolodge,** overlooking the coastline. You could also glam it up at sumptuous **Peninsula House,** relaxing on your private sea-view veranda. Or shack up in a cliff-top treehouse at **El Cabito,** taking in the views of Rincón Bay while the wind blows.

- **Puerto Plata:** At the hilltop **Tubagua Plantation Eco Lodge,** shower alfresco while staring at panoramic views of Puerto Plata or take a dip in the small Jacuzzi at sunset.

- **Jarabacoa and Constanza:** Stay at villa turned guesthouse **Jarabacoa Mountain Hostel** and soak in your fancy bathtub. Snuggle by the fire inside your cabin at **Villa Pajón Eco-Lodge,** surrounded by pine trees and mountains inside Parque Nacional Valle Nuevo, 2,286 meters (7,500 feet) above sea level.

- **Pedernales:** Glamp in the remote southwest of the DR at **Eco Del Mar,** with bed-furnished tents set right on La Cueva Beach.

## Candlelit Dinners

- **Santo Domingo:** Reserve a table in the cave turned dining room at **Mesón de la Cava.** For an alfresco dinner, it doesn't get more memorable than a table along **Plaza de España's** row of outdoor restaurants at dusk, facing the beautifully lit Alcázar de Colón palace.

- **Punta Cana:** Get serenaded by a Dominican guitar duo while feasting on fresh conch or curried lobster at the candlelit, waterfront **La Yola,** while the fish swim underneath the illuminated dock.

- **La Romana:** Reserve the only table for two on the lower level of the outdoor deck at **La Casita,** away from other diners, and enjoy seafood alfresco beside moored million-dollar yachts inside the illustrious Casa de Campo Marina. Indulge in fresh homemade pasta while taking in the panoramic views of the Chavón River from the romantic outdoor terrace at **La Piazetta.**

- **Samaná Peninsula:** In Las Terrenas, it's hard to beat the beachfront setting of the restaurant row in Pueblo de los Pescadores, and **La Terrasse** is the most consistent pick of all. Sit in a corner of the wooden deck and enjoy a French-Dominican menu under dim lanterns

Many resorts offer complimentary snorkeling gear, as well as introductory PADI Open Water lessons. But the best underwater marinelife in the DR is often found away from resorts and in areas that aren't visited as frequently. You'll find at least two or three reputable PADI dive shops in each of these areas.

## PUNTA CANA AND BAYAHIBE

Bayahibe is one of the best places in the DR for snorkeling as well as diving. The offshore, pro-tected Saona and Catalina Islands, part of the Parque Nacional Del Este, offer colorful 40-meter (130-foot) wall dives—the Catalina Wall is especially impressive—local reefs teeming with critters, and several neat shipwrecks to explore.

- Sign up for a trip around the islands with ScubaFun, which offers diving excursions daily, even in the slow season.

- Casa Daniel offers snorkeling excursions along the Dominicus Reef and to the Aquarium off Isla Catalina.

- Snorkel off Saona Island's stunning beaches away from crowds on a Saona Crusoe VIP day trip with Seavis Tours.

Punta Cana's best snorkeling can be found at The Aquarium, a five-minute boat ride from the Westin Puntacana Resort's beach.

- Explore with Blue Vision Adventures.

## THE SAMANÁ PENINSULA

The Samaná Peninsula offers more diving than snorkeling—particularly off Las Galeras, where you will find some of the most challenging but re-warding dives around Cabo Cabrón and Cabo Samaná. The reef facing Playa Frontón, at a depth of up to 12 meters (39 feet), is made up of tall elkhorn corals and is visited by spotted eagle rays. An advanced dive teeming with coral and marinelife is Piedra Bonita, at a depth of over 30 meters (100 feet). The reef is home to turtles, Creole wrasse, jacks, and other Caribbean critters.

Playa Frontón

- Go with Las Galeras Divers, who are experts in this region.

## THE NORTH COAST

On the northwestern coast, off Punta Rucia beach, is Cayo Arena, where you will experience some of the best snorkeling in the country amid a vibrant reef filled with tropical fish.

- Hop on a boat to Cayo Arena with local captains parked on Punta Rucia or La Ensenada beaches.

- Arrange a day trip through Bávaro Runners in Puerto Plata.

An hour farther northwest, snorkelers and div-ers will find bliss off the coast of Monte Cristi, around the offshore islands of the Cayos Siete Hermanos.

- Sign up in advance with Soraya y Santos Tours for a snorkel tour of Cayo Tuna and Cayo Montechico.

and cooling breezes. Over in Las Galeras, El Cabito's tables perched at 14 meters (46 feet) above the sea offer a memorable sunset view of this fishing village's dramatic cliffs and the Atlantic Ocean.

- **Puerto Plata and Cabarete:** Dine by candlelight in a lush garden away from the Puerto Plata city noise at **Mares Restaurant & Lounge,** where renowned Dominican chef Vasquez creates exquisite local cuisine with a twist—sit poolside and sample his Brugal rum-soaked goat stew or flambé baby lobsters. Catch the sunset and the open ocean views from the dimly lit, thatched-roof dining room of **La Otra Cosa,** and feast on seared tuna in a ginger and flambé rum sauce.
- **Punta Rucia:** Go to **Lino's** for a seaside dinner and feast on homemade pizza.
- **Jarabacoa:** It doesn't get more romantic than dining on the terrace at **Aroma de la Montaña,** perched 1,219 meters (4,000 feet) above sea level, while the night lights of all Jarabacoa flicker below.

## Sexy Beaches

- **Samaná Peninsula:** The most beautiful, romantic stretches of sand are the remote **Playa El Valle** nearest Samaná Town, and the accessible **Playa Las Ballenas** in the heart of Las Terrenas—a long shoreline with a lot of privacy.
- **Puerto Plata:** The bumpy ride to **Playa Cambiaso** will be worthwhile, particularly on the weekdays when your only company will

be wild donkeys. **Playa Arroyo Salado** is another remote but swimmable stunner, tucked between Cabrera and Nagua.

- **Río San Juan: Playa Preciosa**—adjacent to the better-known and busy Playa Grande—rewards with complete privacy and tranquility.
- **Miches:** The virgin beaches of **Miches** are far from the madding crowd of Punta Cana. Take a short drive and spend the day in bliss at **Playa Esmeralda;** bring our own snacks and drinks.
- **Punta Rucia:** Visitors primarily use **Punta Rucia** beach as a jumping-off point to Cayo Arena, but during the day it's a stunning, uncrowded white stretch with shallow turquoise waters. Sunset—complete with a fiery red ball—is not to be missed.

## Secluded Escapes

- **Bayahibe:** Book a **private sailing trip to Saona Island** on the gorgeous 51-foot *Dragonsmoke* through Seavis Tours.
- **Monte Cristi:** Go off the beaten track and charter a boat for an excursion to the remote **Cayos Siete Hermanos,** off the coast of Monte Cristi. Spend a blissful day of sunning and snorkeling with no one else around.
- **Constanza:** Experience the highest altitude in the Caribbean and bundle up in a cozy mountain cabin at **Villa Pajón Eco-Lodge,** tucked inside a protected national park. Spend the day hiking in pine forests and return to hot cocoa by your chimney.

# Roots and Rhythms

The Dominican Republic is a cultural melting pot, where numerous aspects of daily life are a blend of African, European, and native traditions or beliefs. Dance to merengue beats, snack on a plate of plantain-based *tostones,* and venture into the markets to explore the *botánicas* (herbal remedy shops). This is the real pulse of the Dominican Republic.

## Day 1

Arrive in **Santo Domingo** on a Saturday morning and sample your first Dominican lunch *cafetería* at **Villar Hermanos** in the charming **Gazcue district;** have a plate of rice and beans with chicken, or slices of *chicharrón* (pork) with sides of yucca. Walk to the **Ciudad Colonial** and check in to **El Beaterio.** Take a sunset stroll through this historic area, down **Calle Las Damas** and to the **Fortaleza Ozama.** Walk back up Calle Las Damas and indulge in a romantic dinner at one of the bistros lining **Plaza**

de España—**Pura Tasca** and **Pat'e Palo** are delicious options—imbibing *chinola* (passion fruit) sangria with a swig of mamajuana post-meal. After dinner check out the free outdoor folkloric dance performance by the **Ballet Folklórico,** also at the plaza. An alternative is to reserve a table at the lively **El Conuco** for Dominican food—try the *sancocho* stew—and a live merengue dance show, or at **Jalao,** where live merengue bands often perform. You may even be pulled onto the floor. To see Dominican recording artists perform live, check out the Monday night performances at **Jet Set Club** (Av. Independencia Km. 6 1/2, corner of Calle Proyecto, tel. 501/535-4145, www.jetsetclubrd.com, 9pm-4am, cover varies).

## Day 2

Enjoy a rich Dominican breakfast of *mangú,* fried eggs, fried cheese, and ham or sausage, with a cup of Café Santo Domingo on the outdoor terrace

merengue band in Santo Domingo

# Social Impact Tourism

You'll quickly discover a diverse country that is much more than its beaches. Where to begin? Venture beyond the tourist zones and sign up for an excursion with one of the rural cooperatives that have mushroomed around the country. These inspiring entrepreneurial groups offer visitors experiences unique to their respective villages and towns—from cacao plantation visits to off-the-beaten path hikes. The income generated helps fund jobs and is reinvested into the cooperative. This evolving, exciting concept of community tourism is a win-win for travelers looking to experience the real Dominican Republic and locals working to secure a sustainable future.

## PUERTO PLATA
(page 216)

**Take a community tour** through the **Community Tourism Network of Puerto Plata** (Red de Turismo Comunitario, https://puertoplata.do). They offer seven experiences unique to the province's various towns; check in advance for any scheduled trips if traveling solo:

Salto de Jimenoa Uno in Jarabacoa

- **Dominican baseball:** Visit Bartolo Colón's hometown and the stadium he built for his community.

- **Cacao:** Learn all about the production of organic cacao in the DR. Plant a pod, sample some chocolate, and get a chocolate mud treatment!

- **Merengue:** Spend the day immersed in all things merengue in a village that has produced generations of traditional merengue musicians.

- **Columbus's first home:** Enjoy cliff-top views and tour the ruins of Christopher Columbus's home.

- **Manatees:** Hike two trails, paddleboard among the mangroves, visit a secluded beach, and witness dozens of manatees from a lookout tower at the Estero Hondo Marine Mammal Sanctuary.

- **Amber:** Tour the only place in the world where blue amber is found and where amber is actually mined.

- **Coffee:** Learn about the production of organic coffee in the DR from bean to cup.

## JARABACOA
(page 288)

**Stay in green lodging** near the Río Yaque del Norte at the **Sonido del Yaque** (Sonido del Yaque, tel. 829/727-7413, sonidodelyaque@gmail.com), run by the **Club de Mujeres Nueva Esperanza,** a cooperative of 30 women. They offer 10 rustic cabins tucked into the lush countryside, which are off the grid, using renewable energy and water sources. They also have a riverfront restaurant that provides organic, locally sourced meals and they also provide local excursions.

## BARAHONA PROVINCE
(page 334)

Sign up with local cooperative **COOPDECI** (Cooperativa para el Desarollo de La Ciénaga, tel. 829/560-3560, www.guanaventuras.com), near Barahona, for **a range of exciting excursions,** including snorkeling in La Ciénaga's bay, hiking to the Cueva de la Virgen on an exclusive trail, river hiking, and visiting the larimar mines.

You can learn to make artisan marmalade with the women, or grab lunch at their local restaurant, Delicias Mi Siembra.

## BAGGING A PEAK

If you're a thrill seeker, hike to Pico Duarte, the tallest peak in the Caribbean at 10,125 feet. The excursion takes two days, beginning in Manabao just outside Jarabacoa. Local guide David Durán of Jarabacoa Eco Adventures is your best bet for a customized and affordable Pico Duarte trip. David can also take you on a climb to El Mogote, shorter yet more challenging than Pico Duarte thanks to its steep and rocky terrain. You'll be rewarded with a stunning panoramic view of Jarabacoa from the 3,815-foot summit.

## SPELUNKING

One of the most thrilling and remote caves to explore is Cueva Fun Fun near Parque Nacional Los Haitises. Contact Rancho Capote to book a tour. The adventure begins with a horseback ride, then a hike through a wet forest, and finally a rappel down a narrow opening 28 feet below ground. You'll spot critters while hiking past Taíno petroglyphs and pictographs. There are additional caving opportunities (with freshwater lagoons) inside the Parque Nacional Del Este. The southwest is home to the least visited caves at El Pomier and Las Caritas de los Indios.

## CANYONING

The North Coast is ideal for rock climbing and canyoning off waterfalls. Both Cabarete and Puerto Plata are solid bases for trips to Damajagua Falls and lesser-visited falls like the Big Bastard. Visit with popular outfitter Iguana Mama.

## RIVER RAFTING

Take an exhilarating rafting excursion on Jarabacoa's Río Yaque del Norte, the longest river in the DR. Contact Rancho Baiguate or Rancho Jarabacoa to book a tour.

## WATER SPORTS

Hop on a kite or a surfboard and ride the Caribbean's most sought-after waves along the North Coast of the DR from Cabarete to Kite Beach, and at Playa Encuentro. Kitesurfing and surfing outfitters abound, offering beginner to advanced classes, as well as annual kitesurfing and surfing international competitions and festivals, including the popular Master of the Ocean.

a kitesurfer walking the beach in Cabarete

## PARAGLIDING

Fly over Jarabacoa's mountains and verdant scenery, above waterfalls and valleys, with Flying Tony (www.flyindr.com). Tony takes you on a 25-minute drive from Jarabacoa to Paso Alto, where the exciting liftoff takes place. He can also take you out to Constanza.

## ZIP-LINING

Zip-lining above the hills of Samaná's dense El Valle forests and hills will have you screaming at the top of your lungs. Samana Zipline has the best-engineered zip line in the country, which will take you 122 meters (400 feet) above El Valle over 12 lines. Flip upside down or ride together as a couple—the integrated braking system means all you have to do is focus on the panoramic views.

## ATV AND QUAD RIDING

Riding at high speed down bumpy dirt roads and village tracks in an all-terrain vehicle is a fun way to get lost in nature and explore the DR countryside. In Puerto Plata, Outback Adventures offers ATV rides through the hills of Muñoz village, with visits to a local home. Samaná and Jarabacoa are also great landscapes to enjoy by ATV—rent your own from Jessie Car Rental.

of **Cafetería El Conde**. Walk to the **Mercado Modelo,** close to Chinatown, and shop for larimar or amber jewelry or Dominican-made ceramics. Don't miss the clamor of the outdoor fruit and vegetable market, where *botánicas* (traditional healers) have set up shops selling mysterious potions. Have a toasted sub sandwich and a *batida* or fruit smoothi, at **Barra Payán.** Visit nearby museums, starting with the **Museo de las Casas Reales** and the **Alcázar de Colón,** to learn about the DR's history from the colonial days, and then the **Museo de la Resistencia,** an excellent look at the DR's political journey post-independence. Grab an early dinner at **Mesón D'Bari,** serving tasty Dominican seafood and meat dishes—try the goat stew. At 7pm on Sunday, head over to the **Monasterio de San Francisco** and enjoy the best outdoor live merengue and son concert with the band **Grupo Bonyé.** Enjoy some Presidente beers and twirl away on the cobblestoned streets with the locals. Night owls can keep the party going at **Parada 77, Doubles,** or **La Cacibajagua.**

## Day 3

Rise at dawn and head north to **Puerto Plata** via Caribe Tours or Metro Tours, unless you're driving. From the city, hop in a taxi or rental car or combine *guagua* and *motoconcho* rides to reach the hilltop **Tubagua Plantation Eco Lodge.** Drop your bags and head on a three-hour afternoon hike through the village with the lodge's local guide. You'll meet the locals, sample fruit from the trees, and trek beside streams. Grab a cold Bohemia beer or soda at the village *colmado* along the way and continue until you reach the stunning blue sinkholes and falls of **Charcos de los Militares.** After the hike, drive 10 minutes up the **Ruta Panorámica** to the small community of **Yásica** and feast on *carne salada roadside*, washed down with some Brugal rum. Or stick to the lodge for a home-cooked meal in the *palapa* dining room, with panoramic starlit views of Puerto Plata.

## Day 4

In the morning, head out on a prearranged group trip to the small town of **Guananico** with Puerto Plata's local cooperative, **Red de Turismo Comunitario.** You'll first stop at **Hacienda Cufa** for a chocolate tour and tasting at a cacao farm. After a Dominican lunch, you'll head over to **Rincón Caliente,** where you'll experience an afternoon of merengue *típico* with renowned merengue artists, and learn about drum making, accordion playing, and dancing to merengue. Head back to **Tubagua** for the night.

## Day 5

Leaving Tubagua, drive south on the winding, bumpy **Ruta Panorámica,** with glorious views of the Cordillera Septentrional mountain range, lined with small villages and colorful roadside fruit and souvenir shacks. The road leads to **Santiago,** where you should stop for lunch at **Rancho Chito,** the region's best *lechonera*, a restaurant specializing in pork roasted on a pit. The *chivo* (goat) is delicious. Belly full, drive 10 minutes outside of the city to **El Higüerito,** where you'll find local potters and doll makers spinning wheels. Stop for *guineos* (bananas) roadside on your way back to Santiago. At this point, head for the airport or continue your trip to **Jarabacoa** and **Constanza**—see page 25 for more details.

# Santo Domingo

**Santo Domingo, the first city of the Americas,** is the most dynamic and exhilarating city in the Caribbean. A palpable energy blankets its multifaceted neighborhoods, from the cobblestoned streets of the Ciudad Colonial to the sleek restaurants, hotel bars, and cigar lounges of the Polígono Central, and the cacophonous inner-city *barrios*. No matter where you are, Dominican music—merengue, *bachata,* and *dembow* pours out into the streets, keeping the pulse of the city.

Beyond its quaint colonial charm lies a city with a fiercely independent spirit—thrown into relief by the statues of heroes that dot the horizon and stand for the struggle for freedom from dictatorship. The Spanish conquistadores used Santo Domingo as a base for

# Highlights

Look for ★ to find recommended sights, activities, dining, and lodging.

© MOON.COM

★ **Ciudad Colonial:** Stroll the pedestrian Calle El Conde, and wander amid restored Spanish colonial buildings and bougainvillea-shaded alleys in an area that was once Christopher Columbus's stomping grounds (page 39).

★ **Parque Colón:** Surrounded by stunning architecture, centuries of Dominican history, and boutique sidewalk restaurants, the leafy Parque Colón offers a slice of Dominican life (page 39).

★ **Catedral Primada de América:** Admire the ornate interior of the first cathedral in the New World (page 41).

★ **Museo de las Casas Reales:** Journey through the Dominican Republic's history, from the arrival of Spanish colonialists to the Trujillo years, at this museum housed in a former 16th-century royal court (page 43).

★ **Alcázar de Colón:** Immerse yourself in 16th-century royal culture by touring Diego Colón's former home—the most impressive structure in the Colonial City (page 43).

★ **Parque de la Independencia:** Pay your respects at the mausoleum of the Dominican Republic's three independence heroes (page 46).

★ **El Malecón:** Stroll down Santo Domingo's famed seafront promenade home to parks, casinos, and restaurants. Buy a fresh coconut roadside, and enjoy the Caribbean Sea breeze (page 48).

★ **Los Tres Ojos:** These ancient Taíno caves reveal a stunning ecosystem. Hike past giant caverns and stalagmites, marvel at the freshwater lakes, and look for turtles (page 53).

★ **Live Merengue, Son, and Salsa:** Head to the Monasterio de San Francisco to enjoy Grupo Bonyé's outdoor concert, held every Sunday from sunset until 10pm (page 57).

★ **Playa Boca Chica:** Relax on miles of white sand and indulge in fresh seafood at the bustling Boca Chica (page 87).

conquering the Caribbean region and parts of the Americas, as you'll note from sculptures of Christopher Columbus and his cronies around the old city. Thus Santo Domingo was home to the first cathedral, the first convent for nuns, the first university, and the first street in the New World, and it provided the first urban design template. It's a city that many fought over and occupied, including British buccaneer Sir Francis Drake, the French, and even neighboring Haiti, but it has always fought back for independence.

Today, *La Capital,* as it is affectionately called, is a bustling metropolis of 2.5 million inhabitants. It's the most cosmopolitan city in the Caribbean, with shopping malls that rival those in North America, fine dining, and more nightlife than your dancing feet could handle in one visit. Santo Domingo excels in and prides itself on promoting Dominican culture. In fact, when Dominicans speak about their country, they refer to it as "Santo Domingo" rather than República Dominicana. The city hosts festivals year-round, open museum nights, art exhibits, theatrical performances, and plenty more.

History buffs, culture lovers, shopaholics, music aficionados, and night owls—nearly every traveler will find plenty to keep them busy here. Santo Domingo is a city of contrasts; it combines the past and present, the lifestyles of a seaside town and a modern metropolis, and Dominican culture with American and international influence.

Full of surprises: that's *La Capital.*

## PLANNING YOUR TIME

Most of the city's major sights and activities are in adjacent areas or at least a short taxi ride away from one another—but like any big metropolis, expect city traffic delays in the daytime.

If you have a few days or more, your best bet is to pick one of several boutique hotels in the Ciudad Colonial as your base and spend a morning or evening checking out the nearby Gazcue neighborhood and the Polígono Central, comprising three upscale neighborhoods. You'll want to save a minimum of two days to fully appreciate the Ciudad Colonial and its parks, museums, plazas, and centuries-old architecture. Even if you're not much of an arts and culture buff, you should spend at least half a day in this area—after all, this is where the first city of the Americas took shape.

Finally, spend a day or two exploring nature—in the caves at the nearby Los Tres Ojos or at the beaches of Boca Chica or Juan Dolio. You could also opt for an excursion to a cacao farm in the lush *campo* or countryside of San Francisco de Macorís northeast of the capital, or head an hour north to Monte Plata for several spectacular waterfalls.

Only have a day? Spend the morning in the Ciudad Colonial—have breakfast at a sidewalk café on pedestrian Calle El Conde, then walk up and down Calle Las Damas to visit the Fortaleza Ozama, the Museo de las Casas Reales, and the Altar de la Patria. You could lunch on the Malecón, a 10-minute walk away, then head to the Museo del Hombre Dominicano in the city center and relax in the gardens of the Plaza de la Cultura. For a sunset cocktail, hit the swank Vertygo 101 bar in the Piantini District, join happy hour work crowds at Donde Chame Bar, or head back to the Ciudad Colonial for numerous bar options.

## ORIENTATION

Santo Domingo was the first planned urban space in the Americas, designed as a square, and is actually easy to navigate.

The Ozama River divides the city into east and west. West of the river are the main areas frequented by tourists: the Ciudad Colonial, the Malecón, and the city center—essentially the area around the major arteries of

---

Previous: the Ciudad Colonial; Parque Colón; El Malecón.

# Santo Domingo

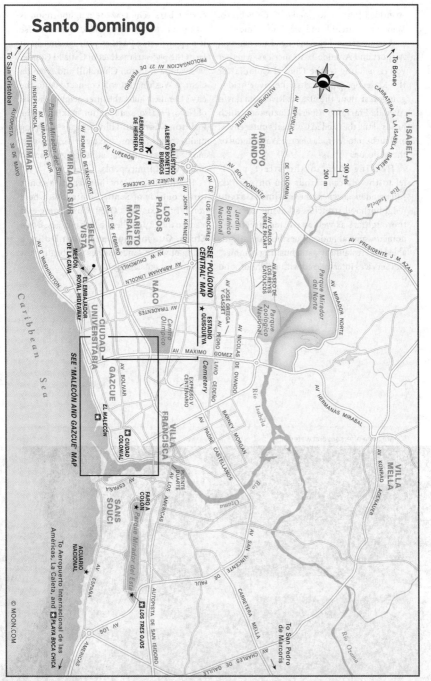

To San Cristobal
AUTOPISTA 30 DE MAYO

MIRIMAR

AV INDEPENDENCIA

AV Mirador del Sur
Parque Mirador del Sur

MIRADOR SUR

AV ROMULO BETANCOURT

PROLONGACION AV 27 DE FEBRERO

AUTOPISTA DUARTE

To Bonao

CARRETERA A LA ISABELA

LA ISABELA

Río Isabela

AEROPUERTO
DE HERRERA

GALLISTICO
ALBERTO BONETTI
BURGOS

AV LUPERÓN

AV NÚÑEZ DE CÁCERES

AV JOHN F. KENNEDY

AV DE LOS PRÓCERES

AV SOL PONIENTE

ARROYO
HONDO

AV REPÚBLICA

DE COLOMBIA

AV PRESIDENTE J M AZAR

LOS PRADOS

Jardín
Botánico
Nacional

AV CARLOS
PÉREZ RICART

EVARISTO
MORALES

AV 27 DE FEBRERO

BELLA
VISTA

MESÓN
DE LA CAVA

EL EMBAJADOR
ROYAL HIDEAWAY

NACO

AV ABRAHAM LINCOLN

AV WINSTON CHURCHILL

AV TIRADENTES

AV JOSÉ ORTEGA Y GASSET

AV PEDRO

SEE "POLÍGONO
CENTRAL MAP

AV PASEO DE
LOS REYES
CATÓLICOS

ESTADIO
QUISQUEYA

Centro
Olímpico

Parque
Zoológico
Nacional

Parque Mirador
del Norte

AV MIRADOR NORTE

AV G. WASHINGTON

Caribbean

Sea

CIUDAD
UNIVERSITARIA

GAZCUE

AV BOLÍVAR

AV MÁXIMO

Cemetery

EXPRESO V
CENTENARIO

LIVIO CEDEÑO

AV NICOLÁS DE OVANDO

GOMEZ

Río Isabela

AV HERMANAS MIRABAL

SEE "MALECÓN
AND GAZCUE MAP

EL MALECÓN

VILLA
FRANCISCA

AV PADRE CASTELLANOS

BARNEY MORGAN

PUENTE
DUARTE

Río

AV KONRAD ADENAUER

VILLA
MELLA

CIUDAD
COLONIAL

AV ESPAÑA

FARO A
COLÓN

Parque Mirador del Este

Ozama

AV LOS AMÉRICAS

SANS
SOUCI

ACUARIO
NACIONAL

AV ESPAÑA

LOS TRES OJOS

AUTOPISTA DE SAN ISIDORO

AV SAN VINCENTE DE PAUL

AUTOPISTA MELLA

CARRETERA MELLA

Río Ozama

To San Pedro
de Marcoris

AV CHARLES DE GAULLE

To Aeropuerto Internacional de las
Américas, La Caleta, and PLAYA BOCA CHICA

AV LOS
AMÉRICAS

© MOON.COM

N

0          200 yds
0          200 m

Avenidas John F. Kennedy, 27 de Febrero, Winston Churchill, and Máximo Gómez.

Arriving from Las Américas International Airport and Avenida Las Américas, whether you're heading to the Ciudad Colonial or the Malecón, you'll cross the river bridge going west along the Ozama River and down Avenida Francisco Alberto Caamaño, which heads along the Ciudad Colonial's outer edges, and turns into Avenida George Washington or the Malecón.

Heading over to the street parallel to the Malecón lands you on Avenida Independencia, where the tree-lined **Gazcue** neighborhood stretches all along the main thoroughfare as well as its side streets. It's home to several budget guesthouses, affordable local restaurants, and bustling commercial services interspersed with neighborhood corner bars. The Gazcue neighborhood is 10-minute walk to the Ciudad Colonial. Use **Independence Park** as your landmark—it faces the pedestrian street of Calle El Conde.

Avenida Winston Churchill and Avenida George Washington will connect you to the city's trendiest hubs, the three neighborhoods of Naco, Paraíso, and Piantini, making up the **Polígono Central.** Think upscale shopping malls, trendy bistros, and cigar lounges, plus movie theaters and the latest string of brand hotels with infinity pools.

Heading back east of the river and a stone's throw outside of Santo Domingo is where you'll find **Los Tres Ojos.** Continuing east leads to the city dwellers' beach escapes: **Boca Chica, Guayacanes,** and **Juan Dolio,** a string of white-sand beaches that begins just 20 minutes outside the capital.

Monte Plata offers several waterfalls.

# Sights

## ★ CIUDAD COLONIAL

The capital's historic district—the Colonial City, formally called **Ciudad Colonial**, though some locals still refer to it as "la Zona Colonial" (the Colonial Zone) or even just "la Zona"—stretches approximately 10 blocks, starting along the west bank of the Ozama River and spanning west up to Parque de la Independencia (Calle Palo Hincado), and bordered to the north and south by Avenida Mella and the Malécon (Paseo Billini), respectively. It was declared a UNESCO World Heritage Site in 1990. Sure enough, it's one heck of an architectural, historical, and visual feast. This is the section of Santo Domingo where conquistadores like Christopher Columbus, his son Diego Colón, and first governor of the Americas, Nicolás de Ovando, ruled over the first city of the Americas and plotted their growing empire in the Caribbean region. It is filled with 16th-century edifices in the form of churches (including 22 chapels), palaces, and courthouses, as well as statues of key historical figures. Most of these colonial buildings have been transformed into shops, museums, galleries, and boutique hotels.

Stroll along the cobblestoned **Calle El Conde,** recently revived with upgraded new stores and food outlets—a pedestrian haven of shops and cafés running through the heart of the area reminiscent of Barcelona's Las Ramblas. Idle away some time on a park bench alongside locals or sit at a sidewalk café with a cold Presidente and take in the seamless blend of old and new among the cathedrals and museums and wrought-iron balconies alive with flowers.

There's never a dull moment in this formerly walled historic zone. *Guagua* or local bus conductors shout and hiss as their slim bodies hang over the edge of the vans while looking for passengers. Men slam dominoes in the shade and occasionally compliment women who pass by. *Motoconchos* buzz about, while merengue echoes out of restaurants and bars. And tourists zip around in rented bikes and tricycles, while horse carriages look for customers.

In this single area, you'll find most of what is iconic to the Dominican Republic: the interplay of life at cigar shops, sidewalk cafés, larimar and amber jewelry stores, mobile vendors selling *chicharrón* or pork rinds, Helados Bon ice cream carts, and *colmados,* the DR's iconic corner stores that double as bars.

Note that the Calle El Conde's pedestrian buzz doesn't get going until around 10am, and if you head there early, you'll find the cafés open but other businesses will have their iron gates pulled down. Art vendors start wheeling out their wares later in the morning.

## ★ Parque Colón

Undoubtedly one of the best people-watching spots and most popular parks in Santo Domingo, conveniently set along the pedestrian path on Calle El Conde, **Parque Colón** (Calle El Conde, from corner of Arzobispo Meriño) is where you'll get a glimpse of Dominicans engaging in one of their favorite pastimes: taking a break with their loved ones under the shade, while indulging in sweet treats like *palitos de coco,* listening to local musicians' ballads, and watching the world go by—from tourists to vendors and artists painting on easels. Sometimes you might even catch a play in the square. At the heart of this spacious plaza is a statue of Christopher Columbus—pointing south as he did when he first spotted Hispaniola from his ship—and at his feet the beautiful and valiant Taíno chief, Anacaona, whom the Spanish colonialists betrayed and killed. Surrounding the park are notable buildings, including the first cathedral in the New World. Parque Colón, as with other parks in the area, is also where you'll find licensed tour guides in the high season in particular—look for their khaki

# Ciudad Colonial

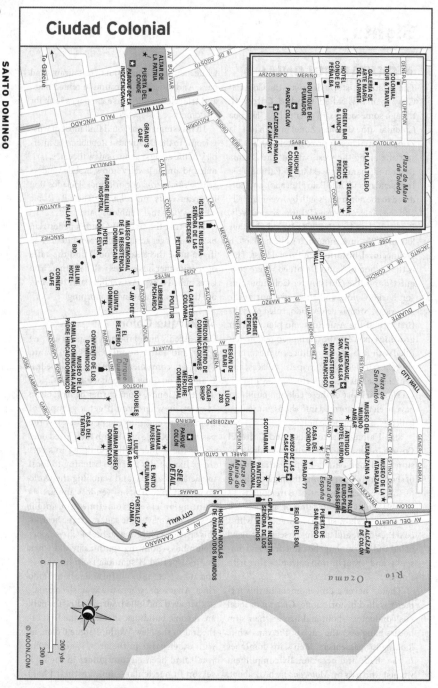

© MOON.COM

pants, blue shirts, and a badge hanging from their neck. Feel free to barter for a tour of the Ciudad Colonial on foot. At night, the park is no less lively, when couples stroll after work, rent bikes in groups for cycling around the square, and young Dominicans hang on corners with their beverage of choice. Whether it's just to laze away on a bench or to meet up with friends, there's no place in the city like Parque Colón.

## ★ Catedral Primada de América

Standing tall on the south side of Parque Colón is the first cathedral ever built in the Americas—La Basilica Catedral Santa María de la Incarnación, or **Catedral Primada de América** (Calle Isabel La Católica, 9am-5pm daily, RD$60/US$1.30, includes audio). It's worth shelling out the small entry fee to tour this architectural wonder, whether with a guide or with your English audio headphones. Construction launched in 1512 and was completed in 1540. The end result is one of the most ornate buildings in the Americas, with Gothic influence evident in its coral rock facade. It is said to have once harbored the ashes of Christopher Columbus. If you only have time for one room, look inside the sacred Chapel 12—the chapel for prayers—and prepare to gawk at the lavish designs. As a bonus, the sanctuary is nicely air-conditioned.

## Calle Las Damas

Known as the oldest and first paved street of the Americas, the **Calle Las Damas** (Street of the Ladies), is where Maria de Toledo and her 39 *compañeras* would spend the evening strolling up and down from the palace. The street has kept its charm and is one of the loveliest in the Zona Colonial. You won't see frocks and wigs, but you will still pass horse-drawn carriages. On this street you will also find venerable churches, colonial buildings-turned-upscale boutique hotels, and notable sights like the Fortaleza Ozama and the Panteón Nacional. The old-world glamour remains amid the restored colonial buildings. A walk down Calle Las Damas is a must.

## Fortaleza Ozama

The first military fortress in the Americas and the oldest military structure, the **Fortaleza Ozama** (Calle Las Damas, 9am-5pm Tues.-Sat., 10am-3pm Sun., US$1.50) was built between 1502 and 1507 by the city's first governor, Nicolás de Ovando, to resemble a medieval castle. It has a central tower, the Torre de Homenaje, standing nearly 19 meters (61 feet) on a bluff above the river. At the fort's entrance is a statue of Gonzalo Fernández de Oviedo, known for authoring "The natural and general history of the Indies"—a key document in Santo Domingo's colonial history. Climb the stairs to the top of the tower—it's more fun to use the interior spiral staircase—and take in the panoramic views of the Ozama River on one side, facing the cannons and a view of the more recent port built in 1937, and the sprawling lawns on the other. Grab a pamphlet at the entrance, if you don't need a guide—although they are usually ready and waiting for willing tourists.

## Panteón Nacional

History and architecture buffs will immediately notice the **Panteón Nacional** (Calle Las Damas, 9am-6pm Tues.-Sun, free), an impressive, towering limestone building with a neoclassical facade. This 18th-century Jesuit church turned national mausoleum is said to keep the remains of over 40 famous Dominicans and national heroes who played a big part in the struggle for independence, such as Gregorio Luperón, Eugenio María de Hostos, and María Trinidad Sánchez. A uniformed presidential honor guard holding a Dominican flag stands watch (if you want a photo, be courteous and gesture to guard if you can, they usually don't mind). Take a quick peek at the vaulted ceilings bearing a stunning mural of the Resurrection and Last Judgment by Spanish painter Rafael Pellicer. You'll also notice a giant lamp that was donated by former Spanish head of state

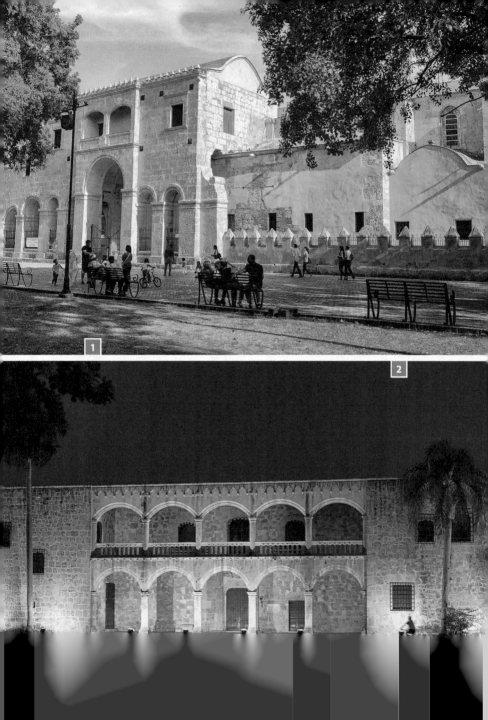

Francisco Franco. Shorts and sleeveless tops are not always allowed, so dress appropriately.

## ★ Museo de las Casas Reales

Once the Royal Court and first courthouse of the Americas, dating back to the 16th century, as well as the governors' office, the **Museo de las Casas Reales** (Calle Las Damas, tel. 809/682-4202, 9am-5pm daily, RD$100/US$2.20, includes English audio) covers the colonial history of the DR, from the arrival of Columbus's three ships in 1492—replicas of *La Pinta, La Niña,* and *La Santa María* are on display—to the mapping of the first cities founded by Columbus and the brutal days of slavery. On the second floor, the reception hall of the governors, the Gran Salón del Trono y Recepciones, is a breathtaking display of opulence. Portraits of Spanish kings look out onto mahogany floors, sparkling chandeliers, and windows opening onto the Ozama River. Directly across, the Salón de Armas houses armaments of various periods, including from Trujillo himself. Like most restored museums in the Ciudad Colonial, you'll find various open courtyards, ideal for taking a breather.

## ★ Alcázar de Colón

One of the most visited sights in Santo Domingo and the most impressive structures in the Ciudad Colonial is the **Alcázar de Colón** (Calle La Atarazana, Plaza de España, tel. 809/682-4750, 9am-5pm Tues.-Sun., US$2.25), the former and restored palatial home of Columbus's son Diego Colón and his wife María de Toledo, niece of King Ferdinand of Spain. The building of the palace—a soft coral limestone structure—began in 1510, a year after Colón became governor and viceroy of the colony. Columbus himself died before getting a chance to see his son's home, which held lavish events for the Spanish aristocracy, including the likes of Cortes, Balboa, and Ponce de León. The palace was ransacked by Sir Francis Drake and immaculately restored

in 1952. The rooms display artifacts and period furniture, as well as paintings and musical instruments. You can tour María de Toledo's bedroom, as well as Diego Colón's—with rare items like an elephant skin-covered trunk imported from North Africa in the 17th century. Don't miss the reception hall. A spiral staircase leads to a wide veranda with a lovely view of the Ozama River and the highway buzz of the modern city below. Buy entry tickets in the white building across from the museum, and avoid Tuesday and Saturday if you dislike big crowds.

## Plaza de España

At the end of Calle Las Damas and starting immediately after the Museo de las Casas Reales, **Plaza de España** (Calle La Atarazana) faces the majestic riverfront Alcázar de Colón museum and former palace and captures the old romance and the modern allure of Santo Domingo in a wide-open, unshaded square that is indeed reminiscent of Spain. Pedestrians stroll the plaza while diners relax at one of a half-dozen trendy, upscale restaurants and cafés in restored warehouses lining the square. Plaza de España is favored for live performances and holiday events, including a free folkloric dance show on Friday and Saturday evenings. It is particularly delightful to walk the space after sundown, when the gas lanterns glow over couples and dog lovers take a promenade. The sidewalk terraces fill with diners enjoying their meals al fresco with a stunning view of the illuminated palace across the way. At the center of the plaza is the obligatory statue: this time, a large bronze portrait of Nicolás de Ovando, the city's first governor, known as the founder of the new Santo Domingo, but also the man said to have been behind the extermination of the Taíno. It's incredible to think that just a few hundred years ago, Europe's most famous conquistadores occupied this same space and walked the same ground.

## Monasterio de San Francisco

The impressive ruins of **Monasterio de**

---

1: Catedral Primada de América; 2: the Alcázar de Colón at night

**San Francisco** (Calle Hostos, Calle Duarte, and Calle Restauración) tower above several blocks of the Ciudad Colonial. Walk straight up Calle Hostos, up the hill past the Calle El Conde intersection, and you'll end up there. Built in the 16th century, the first monastery of the New World was home to the first order of Franciscans to move to the Dominican Republic. Over the years, it suffered fire—at the hands of Sir Francis Drake when he took Santo Domingo—as well as devastating earthquakes in 1673 and 1751. It was then used as a mental asylum from 1881 through 1930—the chains used on inmates can still be seen scattered inside the site. Today, the ruins serve as a dramatic backdrop and stage for outdoor concerts every Sunday evening as well as performances and even weddings.

## Parque Duarte

A nicely shaded square tucked a couple of blocks away from the central hustle and bustle of Calle El Conde, **Parque Duarte** (Calle Padre Bellini, corner of Av. Duarte) is a low-key favorite among the area's older residents during the day; by night, it's a popular hangout with occasional drumming. It was once DR founding father Juan Pablo Duarte's "headquarters," where he would meet with fellow independence heroes Mella and Sánchez. The park faces spectacular colonial buildings like the first convent of the Dominican Order in the Americas, built in 1510, and the first university. At the center of the park is a statue of Duarte.

There's more buzz after sunset and later in the week, when groups of friends of all ages gather around drinks they bring from the *colmado* across the park. It's always been a popular pre-party rendezvous spot for gay Dominicans, especially on the weekends, but it's become a hangout spot for everyone, including families (even if fewer in numbers). Stick around at night instead of going to the disco and you might make some friends or end up dancing to impromptu drumming. It is a space that welcomes all to take in the beauty of the surrounding Ciudad Colonial.

You'll find local guides here as well during the day, but if you're not interested, a simple no thanks will suffice.

## Convento de los Dominicos

Set in a stunning brick and white colonial building across Parque Duarte is the church of the **Convento de los Dominicos** (Calle Padre Billini, corner of Avenida Duarte, tel. 809/683-1817, 8:30am-noon and 4-8pm Mon.-Sat., US$3.40). The Dominican friars arrived in Santo Domingo in 1510 and established the New World's oldest Catholic church as well as the first university in the Americas—one of its wings remains open, but the rest of the university was relocated. The friars were the greatest advocates for the Taíno, who were suffering at the hands of the Spaniards. One of the most outspoken was Friar Anto Montesino, whose gigantic statue you can see at the start of the Malecón. Inside, the church is a testament to Roman and Gothic architecture, with a vaulted ceiling, mahogany altar, and statue of Santo Domingo de Guzmán, the founder of the Dominican order. There are five chapels, and masses are held every morning and Sunday evenings.

## Quinta Dominica

You might miss this spot unless you walk slow and observe. The **Quinta Dominica** (Calle Padre Billini #202, tel. 809/687-5944, http://quintadominica.com, 9:30am-6pm Mon.-Sat., free) just steps across from Parque Duarte is a delightful one-floor 16th-century former home turned gallery with rotating art exhibits from notable Dominican artists. There are no English-language audio guides or labels, but the visual display is sufficient to appreciate. Most beautiful of all, however, is the open courtyard and its lush gardens at the back of the property. Grab a bench and take a respite in nature, along with a *cafecito*—you're right in the city, yet away from everything and everyone.

---

1: a fountain in the Colonial Zone; 2: Calle La Atarazana; 3: Parque de la Independencia

# Touring the Ciudad Colonial

There are numerous ways to explore the museums, churches, and cobblestoned streets of Santo Domingo's Ciudad Colonial. You can pick one of these alternatives, or combine them if you have time to spare and depending on your level of comfort. It's easy to explore on your own, but if you prefer having company, there are guided options as well. The charm of the area may have you returning more than once.

- **Take a self-guided walk:** It's perfectly safe to explore the details of La Zona at your own pace. You'll get plenty of information on the various museums via the English-audio headsets included in your entrance fee. The easiest path is to begin at **Calle El Conde,** across Independence Park, and walk all the way down the pedestrian street to admire the shops, sidewalk art, cafés, and restored colonial homes, until you reach **Parque Colón.** From there, you can head into the cathedral facing the park before continuing down Calle El Conde to **Calle Las Damas,** where more iconic sights await—including Fortaleza Ozama, the Panteón Nacional, and the Museo de las Casas Reales. After visiting the latter, walk to the edge of Calle Las Damas and you'll stumble onto the grand **Plaza de España.** Wander over to the Alcázar de Colón Museum office for tickets and then enter the actual palace museum. Take a break and enjoy cocktails and bites on the terrace at one of the outdoor restaurants on Plaza de España. It's easy to explore the entire area on foot. Don't miss seeing the area at night—it's truly romantic. Note that you should stay away from the seedier outlying parts and stick to the center of the Colonial City and its main sights, day or night.

- **Hire a private tour guide:** If you're a history buff, a writer, or someone with an insatiable thirst for an in-depth knowledge of places beyond the usual basic tourist information, contact the passionate local historian **Miguel Roman** (tel. 809/299-4906, miguelfroman@gmail. com, US$20/hour), a former college professor in the United States turned freelance guide, for a private walking tour. Otherwise, you can head to Parque Colón and find a guide by looking for blue shirts and khaki pants. These folks are licensed by the tourism board and will usually spot you before you spot them. Pick one that speaks your language well enough and bargain for your walking tour. Prices start at US$10 and may rise, depending on your haggling skills and the guide. Guides are enthusiastic about their city and full of valuable information you might not glean from an audio recording. You might need to tell them to slow down if they speak too fast, but they also don't mind stopping for your dozens of photos. If you can, tour closer to sunset—the golden light shining on the colonial buildings makes the area even more beautiful and the heat more bearable. A reliable local guide I've used and who is often on-site is **Socrates Valenzuela** (tel. 829/393-9629 or 809/407-8570)—you can ask around the park for him.

## Museo del Mundo Ambar

**Museo del Mundo Ambar** (Calle Arzobizpo Meriño 452, tel. 809/682-3309, www. amberworldmuseum.com, US$1.10) is worth the stop if you have time to spare. This lovely 17th-century colonial building turned private museum houses a jewelry store and souvenir shop on the ground floor, and up a flight of stairs is the museum. Inaugurated in 1996 by Jorge Caridad, who worked with amber from age 12, this comprehensive display of stones of various sizes from different countries is well displayed with bilingual captions and includes details on the formation of amber. Look for the Dominican Hall corner for a display dedicated to Dominican amber and its history.

## ★ Parque de la Independencia/ Altar de la Patria

Across the start of Calle El Conde, the **Parque de la Independencia** (Calle El Conde and Calle Palo Hincado, 8:30am-6pm) surrounds one of the busiest transportation hubs in the city. *Motoconchos, guaguas,* and cars are almost incessantly zipping by this intersection

- **"Trikke" your way through history:** Sign up for a three-wheeled electric scooter tour of the area—day or night—to experience one of the new fun ways to explore Santo Domingo. **Trikke Colonial** (Calle Padre Billini 54, tel. 809/221-8097, www.trikke.do, 9am-10pm Mon.-Sat., 9am-8pm Sun., US$35-45) has one-hour or 90-minute tours that come with headgear, a guide, audio, and water. Solo travelers can also show up at any time of day and get a one-on-one tour. Young and dynamic bilingual guides will lead you to the Zona's main sights—including the cathedral, Calle El Conde, and Plaza de España—occasionally stopping to take in some history and snap some photos. Soak up plenty of cultural tidbits along the way. I was nervous hopping on a motorized scooter and navigating the busy streets, but you get to warm up and practice for about 10 minutes before taking off. You'll be relieved to know that cars are more inclined to slow down for Trikke riders than for pedestrians!

- **Hop on the train:** The **Chu Chu Colonial** (Calle El Conde 60, corner of Isabela La Católica, across Parque Colón, tel. 809/686-2303, www.chuchucolonial.com, 9am-5pm daily, US$12) is a train-like wagon that may look too touristy, but it's a fun way for children in particular to imagine the lives of Spanish conquistadores as you glide past ancient buildings to the sound of hooves on cobblestone. You'll be placed in sections according to language preference for the audio recording. If you're not up for walking in the sun (or have kids) and prefer a quick 45-minute historical tour in English that you can retrace on foot another day, then this is a nice option to get the lay of the land, if a tad pricey by local standards. Tours run throughout the day, every hour on the hour.

- **Cruise on a bicycle, tricycle, or quad:** Rent a beautiful turquoise beach cruiser bicycle from **Zona Bici** (Calle Salomé Ureña, corner of Reyes, tel. 809/979-1260, 9am-1pm, 3pm-7pm daily, US$6.60/hour per bike, includes helmet and water bottle), the latest eco-friendly way to get around in this historical neighborhood. It's conveniently located in the heart of the Zona, so you can zip through the small alleys and hidden corners at your own pace, with or without a guide. They also have a tricycle for those who might be a tad nervous, and baby seats for 2- to 4-year-olds if you need them. Bike locks are included, as well as a basket for carrying any personal items. **Sunny Bike** (Calle Duarte #154, tel. 809/689-6249, 11am-9pm Tues.-Fri., 9am-8pm Sat.-Sun., US$6/hour) rents four-wheeled carts, ideal if you're towing your kids along—just know that it takes a lot of energy to cycle along the streets and cars can be impatient. Ignore them and go at your own pace.

between old and new, a park commemorating the Dominican Republic's struggle for independence. At the park's entrance, also facing Calle El Conde, is a stunning arched entrance known as the **Puerta del Conde.** It indicates the start of the Ciudad Colonial and is one of the most symbolic locations in the country's long path to freedom. It is here that Count of Peñalba defended against an invading British force in 1655. It is also here that in February 1844, independence fighters executed a coup against occupying Haiti and liberated the country to form an independent Dominican

Republic. The first Dominican flag was raised on top of Puerta del Conde.

Inside the gated park, you'll find newly installed busts of the DR's most significant heroes, male and female, before heading up a series of steps on the west end leading to the impressive **Altar de la Patria,** a white marble mausoleum. In the mausoleum are large statues of the country's Founding Fathers, each of which is holding their respective remains: Juan Pablo Duarte, Matías Ramón Mella, and Francisco del Rosario Sánchez. On Independence Day, the president stops here around 2pm to lay a wreath on the tomb of the Founding Fathers, and the surrounding scene is quite lively. Interestingly, Independence Park is considered the country's "kilometer zero" marker, or the geographical point from which all distances on roads and highways are measured.

## Museo Memorial de La Resistencia Dominicana

If you're a political buff or want to understand the key moments in history that impacted Dominicans during and after the brutal Trujillo regime, I highly recommend a visit the **Museo Memorial de la Resistencia Dominicana** (Calle Arzobispo Nouel 210, tel. 809/688-4440, 9:30am-6pm Tues.-Sun., US$3.30 or RD$150, with audio). The most striking exhibit features a wall of heroes who fought against Trujillo and perished, and the gruesome history of the dictator's regime, including the Haitian genocide of 1937 and the murder of the Mirabal sisters in 1960.

# MALECÓN AND GAZCUE

## Palacio Nacional

The **Palacio Nacional** (Av. Dr. Delgado)— often a quick roadside stop included in city tours—is a regal building in Gazcue that stretches an entire block. Inaugurated in 1947, the palace was built of roseate marble extracted from the Samaná Peninsula and designed in a neoclassical style by Italian architect Guido D'Alessandro. The building is now used as the offices of the Executive Branch of the Dominican Republic. An outside view and photo is likely all you'll get, I'm afraid, as tours are not allowed.

## ★ El Malecón

A landmark of Santo Domingo is the city's seafront Avenida George Washington, known as **El Malecón.** Facing the Caribbean Sea and dotted with large hotels, casinos, seafront restaurants, and movie theaters, this is where locals escape the heat of urban life and catch some fun when they can. It's also where you'll see them getting some exercise or dancing by the sea after sundown. It's come a long way, has been repaved and with more seating and recreational space, including food trucks on the eastern edge, just past Güibia. While there's still visible pollution along the promenade and in the sea at times—you'll see plastic, Styrofoam bits from lunch boxes, and other waste scattered in certain areas—it has seen some major improvement in that regard, with growing consciousness to keep it clean, and remains a lovely place to walk and catch the breeze. Coconut vendors set up here, and there are parks and entertainment for families—notably, Plaza Juan Barón and Playa Güibia. It's a safe area during the day, but don't wear jewelry or carry valuables; thieves have been known to jump curbs to grab unsuspecting tourists' cameras. The liveliest, and perhaps safest, stretch of the Malecón is near the Hilton Hotel, at Güibia Beach, with a playground for kids, workout machines for adults, and live Zumba classes, not to mention a stretch of beach good enough to sink your toes in. But remember: don't bathe in these parts, as the waters are polluted and the currents strong.

## Plaza Juan Barón and the Obelisk

Facing the Caribbean Sea, **Plaza Juan Barón** (Av. George Washington, Malecón, 4pm-midnight Sun.-Thurs., 4pm-2am Fri.-Sat.) is an outdoor recreational area for all, and particularly favored by local families. The kids can enjoy pizza and hot dogs, ride mechanical horses, and zip around go-kart racing, biking, and more. There are also various food stands. The cliff-top location is a dream for those seeking a break from the city madness. Events and karaoke nights are frequent, and there's an on-site bar where you can sit and drink the night away. Across the plaza is the iconic 40-meter-tall (130-foot) **Obelisk** of Santo Domingo—known locally as *Obelisco Macho* (male obelisk)—originally built by Trujillo in 1935 when he renamed the capital after himself as Ciudad Trujillo. It's one of the few dictator-built monuments to have

# Malecón and Gazcue

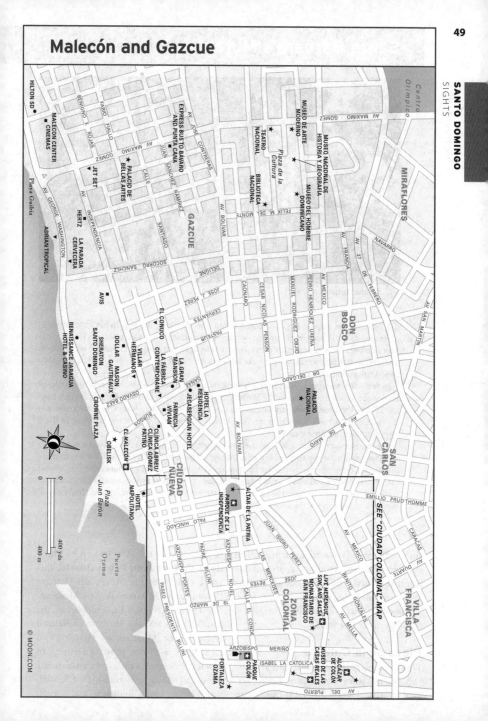

CIUDAD
NUEVA

GAZCUE

DON
BOSCO

MIRAFLORES

SAN
CARLOS

ZONA
COLONIAL

VILLA
FRANCISCA

HILTON SD

MALECÓN CENTER
CINEMAS

Playa Gaibia

ADRIAN TROPICAL

RENAISSANCE JARAGUA
HOTEL & CASINO

SHERATON
SANTO DOMINGO

CROWNE PLAZA

HERTZ

LA PARADA
CERVECERA

AVIS

DOLLAR
MASON
GAUTREAUX

VILLAR
HERMANOS

EL CONUCO

EL MALECÓN

OBELISK

HOTEL
NAPOLITANO

BENIGNO F. ROJAS

FABIO FIALLO

AV. MÁXIMO GÓMEZ

JUAN SÁNCHEZ RAMÍREZ

CALLE

AV. MÁXIMO GÓMEZ

AV. JOSÉ CONTRERAS

AV. INDEPENDENCIA

SANTIAGO

SOCORRO SÁNCHEZ

JOSÉ J. PÉREZ

CERVANTES

PASTEUR

DELIGNE

DANAE

BURGOS

OSVALDO BÁEZ

JET SET

PALACIO DE
BELLAS ARTES

AV. BOLÍVAR

FELIX M. DEL MONTE

CAONABO

CÉSAR NICOLÁS PENSON

MANUEL RODRÍGUEZ OBJIO

PEDRO HENRÍQUEZ UREÑA

AV. MÉXICO

AV. 27 DE FEBRERO

NAVARRO

AV. SAN MARTÍN

AV. FRANCIA

DR. DELGADO

AV. BOLÍVAR

AV. 30 DE MAYO

EXPRESS BUS TO BÁVARO
AND PUNTA CANA

MUSEO DE ARTE
MODERNO

TEATRO
NACIONAL

Plaza de la
Cultura

BIBLIOTECA
NACIONAL

MUSEO DEL HOMBRE
DOMINICANO

MUSEO NACIONAL DE
HISTORIA Y GEOGRAFÍA

Centro
Olímpico

AV. MÁXIMO GÓMEZ

LA GRAN
MANSIÓN

LA FÁBRICA
CONTEMPORÁNE

HOTEL LA
RESIDENCIA

JECASERGIAN HOTEL

FARMACIA
VIVIAN

CLINICA ABREU/
CLINICA GOMEZ
PATIÑO

ALTAR DE LA
INDEPENDENCIA

PARQUE DE LA
INDEPENDENCIA

EMILLIO PRUD THOMME

PALACIO
NACIONAL

SEE "CIUDAD COLONIAL" MAP

PALO HINCADO

ARZOBISPO NOUEL

PADRE BILLINI

ARZOBISPO PORTES

PASEO PRESIDENTE BILLINI

19 DE MARZO

JUAN ISIDRO PÉREZ

JOSÉ REYES

LAS MERCEDES

CALLE EL CONDE

ARZOBISPO MERIÑO

ISABEL LA CATOLICA

AV. MÉXICO

BENITO GONZÁLES

AV. MELLA

AV. DUARTE

CARACAS

AV. DEL PUERTO

LIVE MERENGUE,
SON, AND SALSA

MONASTERIO DE
SAN FRANCISCO

MUSEO DE LAS
CASAS REALES

ALCÁZAR
DE COLÓN

PARQUE
COLÓN

FORTALEZA
OZAMA

Playa Guibia

Plaza
Juan Barón

Puerto
Ozama

AV. GEORGE WASHINGTON

© MOON.COM

0        400 yds
0        400 m

HILTON SD

# Santa Bárbara's Murals

one of Santa Bárbara's murals

On the northern edge of the Zona Colonial and directly facing the port behind ancient walls and cannons is the once forgotten and neglected neighborhood of Santa Bárbara. Home to the Santa Bárbara Church, where the DR's father of independence Juan Pablo Duarte was baptized, and the Santa Bárbara Fort, which helped protect the city, it became known later as *el eslabón perdido* (the missing link).

In April 2015, the area's visibly run-down walls benefitted from a weeklong community revival art project, sponsored in part by the Ministry of Culture, called "Hoy Santa Bárbara." Artists from the DR and the Latin Caribbean—including Esteban del Valle, Vero Rivera, Dominican Natalie Ramirez, and Bik Ismo—set up shop in the streets and painted vibrant murals, most of them representative of Dominican culture.

The murals are now a bit dated and the area seldom visited by newbies, but it is still an interesting glimpse into the reality of the less affluent parts of the Colonial City. Walk all the way past the Alcázar de Colón, take the stairs down to street level and keep straight without exiting the Colonial City. Within a block and a half, on your left hand side you'll begin to spot Santa Bárbara's colorful walls. The murals can be found across a few side streets, so feel free to stroll around to view all of them—and spend a few bucks at a local store.

survived destruction after his murder. The current mural illustrations represent the Mirabal sisters, who spoke out against the Trujillo dictatorship and were murdered for it. The obelisk serves as a reminder of *la lucha*—the struggle for freedom.

## Plaza de la Cultura

This treasure trove of Dominican art, history, and museums is centered on a gated, verdant courtyard where all that is Dominican is showcased. Officially known as **Plaza de la Cultura Juan Pablo Duarte,** this space comprises the Museo del Hombre Dominicano, the Museo de Arte Moderno, the Teatro Nacional Eduardo Brito, the National Library, the Museum of Natural History, the Museum of History and Geography, a cinema showing Dominican movies, the cinema's café, and a restaurant. I like to call it the Smithsonian of the DR. With its sprawling lawns, fountains, and statues, this area is a perfect cultural and educational oasis. Expect it to be busy on Friday, when students from the various area schools are brought here on a weekly field trip. Plaza de la Cultura also hosts a popular annual book fair in the spring. The Casandra Damirón metro station is within the plaza, convenient if you want to try the first metro system in the Caribbean.

### MUSEO DEL HOMBRE DOMINICANO

If you only have time for one modern museum in Santo Domingo, make it the **Museo del Hombre Dominicano** (Plaza de la Cultura, Av. Pedro Henríquez Ureña, tel. 809/687-3622, 10am-5pm Tues.-Sun., RD$100/US$2.30). Three floors of this spacious building are filled with information on the origins of Dominicans, from the first Taíno inhabitants to present-day DR through a detailed showcase of history, culture, and religion. The first two floors house Taíno pieces and rituals displays—including body decor, ceramics, and artwork. All the labels are in Spanish, but you can follow along thanks to an English audio recording device included in your entry fee. If time is short, head straight to the 4th floor and concentrate your stay in the Ethnology Room, covering the history of the DR from its so-called discovery by the Spanish to modern-day Dominican life. The Carnival displays alone are worthwhile, with hundreds of colorful masks covering the walls and costumes from the various Carnival celebrations around the country.

### MUSEO DE ARTE MODERNO

The four-story **Museo de Arte Moderno** (Plaza de la Cultura, tel. 809/685-2154, 10am-5pm Tues.-Sun., US$2.30) hosts rotating exhibits from various parts of the world. When I visited, I stumbled on an exhibition on Ethiopia in the basement. The most impressive permanent displays are of Dominican art dating from 1844 all the way to the present. There's no coffee shop here, so bring a water bottle with you if you need it.

### Museo Bellapart

The private **Museo Bellapart** (Av. J. F. Kennedy, corner of Dr. Lembert Peguero, tel. 809/541-7721, ext. 296, 9am-6pm Mon.-Fri., 9am-noon Sat., free) is housed on the 5th floor of a Honda building and hosts rotating exhibits as well as a permanent collection of more than 2,000 pieces of Dominican art from paintings to sculptures dating from the 19th century to the 1980s. It's a great way to learn about the various stages in the country's history and about its renowned artists, including Jaime Colson, Yoryi Morel, and Celeste Woss y Gil.

### Playa Güibia

**Playa Güibia** is a seaside park and outdoor gym where you can feel the breeze as you enjoy the views of the Caribbean Sea and mingle with locals. The park livens up in the evening after sunset, particularly on the weekends, and turns into a giant entertainment center on public holidays, with street closures.

## AROUND SANTO DOMINGO

### Faro a Colón (Columbus Lighthouse)

The 204-meter-tall (670-foot) **Faro a Colón** (Av. España, tel. 809/591-1492, US$2.25) is an oddity in a desolate neighborhood. The cross-shaped memorial building commemorates the life of Christopher Columbus and was inaugurated on the 500th anniversary of his arrival to the Dominican Republic. It is said to house Columbus's remains, although Spain and Cuba have disputed that claim. Another controversial aspect of this gigantic building is its lighting mechanism, which is said to project a cross straight up into the sky that can be seen as far away as Puerto Rico. Turning it on causes a complete blackout in Santo Domingo, though, so it's never lit. The most interesting part of this sight is the various chambers displaying—ironically—indigenous artifacts and history from each country in Latin America and the Caribbean. The surrounding neighborhood isn't one to wander around in at any

time of day. The Faro a Colón is a bizarre sight at best, and not worth a special trip. But if you are going, a taxi ride from the Ciudad Colonial would cost around US$5; you can negotiate to have your taxi wait for you.

## Jardín Botánico Nacional

The largest botanical garden in the Caribbean and the fourth biggest in the world, the **Jardín Botánico Nacional** (Av. República de Argentina, corner of Av. Los Próceres, tel. 809/385-2611, www.jbn.gob.do, 9am-6pm daily, trolley departs every 30 min., US$5) is a lush 640-acre expanse of native trees, flowers, and plants from around the island. There are over 5,000 flower trees, including 360 species of orchids and over 100 species of palm trees. Founded in 1976, the full name of the garden is the Dr. Rafael Ma. Moscoso National Botanical Garden, named after the first Dominican botanist who documented and catalogued all the DR's flora in 1943. You may also see the national bird, the *cigua palmera*—or palmchat bird—nesting atop a royal palm. Entry tickets include a guided tour of the museum—worthwhile to get a quick introduction to varied topography of the DR's six regions—and a 30-minute open-air trolley ride (with a guide on loudspeaker, whose English you might not always get) that will take you through the gardens' various sections. The Japanese garden is not to be missed—the trolley stops here and you get to walk around long enough for photo ops. From there, you can hop off anywhere you like to continue wandering on your own. There's a free guided birding hike every Sunday—meet at the main entrance at 7am.

## ★ Los Tres Ojos

A trip to **Los Tres Ojos** (Parque Mirador del Este, 8am-5pm daily, US$2.30) is one of the most popular tours closest to Santo Domingo and one of the most worthwhile. Prepare to gasp as you step onto a narrow staircase that leads down into a series of three limestone caves once used by the Taíno for sacred ceremonies. Hike around giant grottoes filled with stalactites and stalagmites and dotted with three phosphorescent blue freshwater lakes (hence the name, The Three Eyes). Look closely in these waters and you'll spot turtles; they swim closer to the edge if you're lucky.

You can hop onto a hand-cranked wooden barge for US$0.50 to reach a fourth, separate cave with the most beautiful emerald lake. There's a local who stays in the cave every day who will dive into one of the lakes if you tip him. It's a gorgeous spot for photos and a lovely nature break from the city.

# Entertainment and Events

Dominicans from around the island will tell you: they love Santo Domingo at night. Whether it's the live music, the trendy clubs, or sidewalk bistros facing lantern-lit, cobblestoned plazas—there's something magical and energizing about this city after dusk. Blame it on the romantic ballads and catchy beats of the country's national music ringing all over its neighborhoods. Each day of the week in La Capital brings another "place to be," so keep an eye out on websites and social media for the latest, including happy hour specials.

## NIGHTLIFE
### Bars and Clubs

Get started by hitting up a *colmado* for some cold Presidente beers, music, and local vibes—there are some fantastic no-name ones in the Ciudad Colonial, particularly on Calle Pale Hincado, at the corner of Arzobispo Portes. Then go for a happy hour in the Ciudad Colonial, at a hotel bar on the Malecón, or

1: the Malecón; 2: Playa Güibia; 3: Museo del Hombre Dominicano; 4: Los Tres Ojos

## Barhopping Circuit

Santo Domingo has the best nightlife in the DR. Start in the Colonial City, where the happy hour buzz gets going at sunset—have a beer at a local *colmado* to warm up, and then go for some sangria at **Pura Tasca,** overlooking the lit Alcázar de Colón. Afterwards, head over to **La Bodeguita de la Zona** for tapas or dinner plates with wine, live music, and a casual but nice crowd in a cozy air-conditioned, artsy interior. You could also sit on the terrace at **Navarricos** for casual drinks and cheap tapas, in an ambience that might make you think you're in Spain. From there, walk over to **Jalao** for live merengue on the weekends, or to **Lucía 203** on Thursday nights.

Take it up a notch with a taxi ride to the Malecón and park yourself at **Parada Cerveza,** for some Brugal rum or Bohemia over loud merengue and the sea breeze blowing from across the avenue. Feel like a fancier vibe? Continue on with a taxi hop to the open-air **Vertygo 101 Lounge & Bar,** at the JW Marriott, with panoramic views over the city center.

When you're ready and warmed up for more music with your drinks, grab another taxi and head to the first drive-through bar in the Dominican Republic at **El Trompo** (Av. Tiradentes, Ensanche Naco, tel. 809/878-5827), with happy hour 6pm-10pm. Don't drink and drive though—there's seating available. You could also grab cocktails at the adjacent **Donde Chame Bar.** End your night across the street, dancing at **Miami Hot** (miamihotrd@gmail.com, noon-2am daily), as fun as its name suggests. Or go back to the Ciudad Colonial, where patrons are packed onto small dance floors under dim lights while the salsa, son, and merengue echo out onto the cobblestoned streets; start with **Onno's** or **Bio.** If you're able to leave the jam-packed crowds there, walk over to **Parada 77** for even more dancing, or grab a taxi to **Cacibajagua**—a hip and funky lounge set in a colonial building, with a DJ spinning old-school R&B to world beats—or to **Ruta 23** for a rock scene.

in the fancy Piantini District. And *then* go dancing.

In the Ciudad Colonial, you'll find a row of bars interspersed on Calle Hostos, which intersects with Calle El Conde. You'll also find bars that double as tapas restaurants on Calle Isabela Catolica, with outdoor seating. Calle Las Mercedes is for after-midnight fun, with some of the city's best alternative bars and lounges. Sometimes it feels as if a new spot opens nearly every week in the Colonial City.

For a night of seeing and being seen among the 30- and 40-something crowd, and not so much for the cocktails, dress up and head to the highly overpriced **Lulú Tasting Bar** (Calle Arzobispo Meriño 151, corner of Padre Billini, www.lulu.do, 6pm-3am daily), one of the trendiest places to hang out after work or on weekends, with a scenic outdoor terrace and dimly lit bars filled with top-shelf liquors. For live merengue music with bites, there's **Jalao** (Calle El Conde 103, tel. 809/689-9509,

www.jalao.do, no cover), conveniently located across Parque Colón.

For a chill atmosphere, with music to shake your bootie, hang at **Quintana Bar** (Calle Atarazana #13, tel. 829/788-3617, 10pm-2am Thurs.-Sat., 10pm-midnight Sun., no cover), where the party vibe and the drink discounts are at their best on Friday nights, while the latest dance tunes play both indoors and on outdoor patio. For basic drinks and a neighborhood crowd, **Sabina Bar** (Calle Isabela la Catolica #206, 7pm-3am daily) isn't a bad pick, close to the heart of the Zona.

For a more unique experience, you'll appreciate **El Vinyl Bar** (Calle Sanchez, elvinylbar@ casaquien.com, no phone, no cover) tucked to the back of an art gallery and boasting high-end craft cocktails (the best margarita to date in the Zona), a DJ spinning vinyl, and a small but cozy 2nd-floor lounge area. Another option for a more fun, eclectic vibe is **Ruta 23** (Calle Mercedes 303, tel. 809/221-0695, 8pm-midnight Wed.-Fri., 8pm-2am Sat., no cover) a rock bar, with walls covered in quotes from The Beatles and other rock icons. Tunes from the 1990s spin loudly indoors and outdoors. You'll love the British-themed space (don't miss the rooftop lounge area), with live rock bands on the weekends, as well as an outdoor grill with a full menu, including wines and cocktails.

The best spot to shoot the breeze with delish, cheap tapas and drinks is **Navarricos** (Calle Isabela la Catolica, 6pm-midnight daily except Tues., from US$3), with sidewalk terrace seating that fills up and feels almost like Madrid.

Downtown Santo Domingo boasts its own bar scene. Start at **Donde Chame Bar** (Avenida Tiradentes #5, 5pm-midnight, US$3-10) at happy hour—it gets crowded quickly—for loaded margaritas, mojitos, and other cocktails with a tasty and affordable menu of finger foods. When you've got your fix, head over to **Miami Hot** (Avenida Tiradentes, corner of Frank Felix Miranda, tel. 809/793-5202, miamihotrd@gmail.com, noon-2am, no cover), which doubles as a lounge and club—dance to merengue, salsa, or the latest reggaeton on the floor, or pick a table away from the dancing area. It's a fun and safe spot to go with friends.

For more of a chill bar-party vibe, the popular chain **Onno's** (Ciudad Colonial, Calle Hostos 57, corner of Calle El Conde, tel. 809/689-1183, www.onnosbar.com/zona-colonial, 9pm-3am, drinks US$4-10) never disappoints and attracts more foreigners. The volume and the mood rise as the clock strikes twelve, like at most watering holes in the area.

**La Cacibajagua** (Calle Mercedes #319, corner of Sánchez, tel. 809/333-9060, 10pm-2am Tues.-Sun.) is another solid bet for a laid-back and funky atmosphere, with DJs spinning rock, old-school, and alternative music in a dimly lit, cozy colonial building that spreads out into a courtyard. Expect a diverse, eclectic, 30-something crowd, and occasional live music.

You won't see a sign outside, but **El Sartén** (Calle Hostos 153, tel. 809/686-9621,

10pm-2am, no cover) is a local dance spot and bar for the older crowd, playing Latin beats in a small space that gets crowded late at night. Most head here after Onno's, just a couple of doors down. If you're up for dancing in a crowded and more hip space, the small disco **Bio Bar** (across Falafel Restaurant, Calle Sanchez 125, tel. 829/766-8122, 11pm-3am, no cover) works for after-midnight stops. The DJ spins a variety of international dance tunes while the light and smoke effects are full-on. Head to the 2nd floor and dance freely wherever you're standing.

**Parada 77** (Calle Isabela La Católica 255, one street before Plaza de España, tel. 809/221-7880, 7pm-1am Mon.-Thurs. and Sun., 7pm-3am Sat., no cover) is the preferred casual hot spot in the Ciudad Colonial, with a twenty- and thirty-something crowd dancing the night away to merengue, *bachata*, and salsa on a dimly lit open floor inside a colonial building. A back courtyard has more couples twirling under the stars on a 2nd floor. If you're solo, don't be afraid to ask a guy or gal to dance! Many also like to take a breather outside on the sidewalk with their drinks. This is a popular stop on Sundays after the outdoor Grupo Bonyé concert at the nearby Monasterio de San Francisco.

**Doubles** (Calle Arzobispo Meriño, across from Lulú Tasting Bar, doublesbar9@gmail.com, 6am-1am daily, no cover) is one of the Zona's popular clubs; it gets going late and attracts a young crowd, so be warned if you're not into crowded floors and inebriated millennials spilling their drinks on you. Otherwise, go early for drinks and enjoy the music and the colonial setting.

**Jet Set** (Av. Independencia 2253, tel. 809/535-4145, 9pm-3am daily, US$7) is the one nightclub that remains while others come and go like the wind—it's been around at least 40 years. Skyline views of the city add to excellent live merengue and salsa bands during the week, including a popular live *bachata* night on Mondays that's not to be missed.

Speaking of a jet-set crowd, mix and mingle with Dominican professionals and business travelers at the gorgeous **Vertygo 101** (JW Marriott, Av. Winston Churchill 93, Piantini District, tel. 809/807-1717, drinks US$6-20). Bring your bathing suit, if you dare, for a dip in the transparent infinity pool while you sip on cocktails and nibble from the tasty bar-bite menu. And don't forget to stand on the glass-floored terrace, where you can stare at your toes 101 feet above Avenida Winston Churchill. If you're particular about your liquor and your surrounding crew, you'll fit right in at **W Bar,** where you'll find the capital's who's who hanging out late into the night.

Adjacent to Parque Mirador del Sur, **Mecenas Café** (Av. Mirador Sur, tel. 849/206-6651, cafemecenas@gmail.com), just up from Mesón de la Cava, remains a well-kept secret known to residents seeking a beautiful space away from the crowds. This bar, art gallery, and event space boasts both outdoor and indoor space and a sophisticated ambience without the pretense. There's a complete bar, food service, and an outdoor stage for the occasional weekly live performances. You can't spot Mecenas from street level—a series of stairs take you to the subterranean venue, which adds to its charm. Check out their happy hour offerings on social media.

East of the Ozama River, across the bridge and off the beaten path from the tourist trail of the Malecón, is another favorite among young Dominicans: **Euphoria** (Calle Venezuela #15, across from Burger King, euphoritard@hotmail.com), on a street famous for its string of clubs and bars, most of which are ultra-local and play Dominican beats. Just say "La Venezuela" to a taxi driver and he'll know where to go. Leave the valuables at home and be sure to go with a local if you can; I don't recommend going alone.

If you're a salsa fan, the place to be is **Discoteca El Águila** (Av. San Vincente de Paul 20, tel. 829/578-3434, infoaguilard@ gmail.com, 9pm-4am Wed., 9pm-3am Fri.-Sat., 3pm-1am Sun., no cover), where you'll see some of the country's best *salseros.*

## Live Music

One of Santo Domingo's best features is its affinity for live music; it's a big part of the capital's culture. A number of restaurants and lounges across the city offer regular performances. Quite a few take place in the Ciudad Colonial, usually in some spectacularly romantic outdoor courtyard. From merengue to salsa and son, city dwellers love any excuse to enjoy dancing to bands all week long.

Owned by the same folks as Mesón D'Bari, **Lucía 203** (Calle Hostos 203, tel. 809/689-5546, 10pm-1am Thurs., no cover) is a must for dancing, if you're lucky to be in the capital on a Thursday. It's the most popular live music spot and evening in the Zona, and for good reason—a fantastic band performs son, as well as merengue, inside a beautiful colonial building, with seating centered on an open Spanish courtyard. The dancing usually kicks off around 11pm on a small but packed floor with a nice crowd of all ages. Reserved seating is available, but you'll find plenty of space if you arrive early. Drinks and food are available all night.

Earlier on Thursdays is the weekly **Live Jazz in the Colonial City** (Calle El Conde, 6pm, no cover), with various talents performing Afro-Caribbean rhythms, from rumba to son and samba, on the Escalinatas del Conde, or the stairs at the very end of Calle El Conde, just past the intersection with Calle Las Damas. You'll often find a young international crowd gathered here.

**Las Terrazas at Mesón de la Cava** (Av. Mirador Sur 1, tel. 809/533-2818, www.elmesondelacava.com, 8:30pm-midnight, no cover) hosts local bands Tuesday through Friday outdoors on its breathtaking, mood-lit garden dining terrace. Expect to eventually rise from your seat and burn off your meal with some hard-to-resist Latin beats.

Along the Malecón, the poolside restaurant terrace of the **Hotel Napolitano** (Av. George Washington 51, tel. 809/687-1131, reservas@ napolitano.do, 8:30pm-midnight Thurs.-Sat., no cover) hosts a live merengue band that attracts plenty of locals on the weekends.

It's hard to beat dancing al fresco amid the Caribbean Sea breeze.

Located inside a lively casino, **Merengue Bar** (Gran Casino Jaragua, Av. George Washington 367, tel. 809/221-1435, no cover) serves up plenty of cocktails and meal specials all week, but it also offers a live merengue band and an ample dance floor every evening starting at 9pm. The floor gets pretty packed with locals, pre- or post-gambling.

If you love mellow music or karaoke, **ñao** (Arzobispo Meriño #105, tel. 809/688-9277, 7pm-1am Mon.-Thurs., 7pm-3am Fri.-Sat., no cover) is a solid pick, and it also features live performances from local artists. Tucked in the heart of the Colonial City, you can enjoy drinks, live music, and tapas all in one place.

★ **LIVE MERENGUE,
SON, AND SALSA**

There are bars and dance clubs aplenty in the Ciudad Colonial, but you won't find a livelier and more exhilarating ambience than the weekly outdoor Sunday night concert and bash with popular local band **Grupo Bonyé** (Calle Hostos, 5:30pm-10pm Sun., free) performing against the backdrop of the sprawling ruins of the Monasterio de San Francisco. For four hours, city dwellers from all corners gather at this historic spot to dance to merengue, son, and salsa. This brilliant cultural event is sponsored by the Ministry of Tourism and attracts everyone out of their respective neighborhoods across the city: tourists, locals, expats, rich and poor, young and old. It's a safe environment to party in—just mind your purses and pockets. Ladies, you might be asked to dance, and it's perfectly fine to accept or decline. Plastic tables and chairs are laid out across the plaza starting around 5pm—come early if you want to save space for your group. The dance floor gets filled almost as soon as the band hits their instruments, and the neon stage lighting glowing on the ruins, under starry skies, gives the place an atmosphere unlike any other. There are food vendors on-site, and drinks flow from Presidente booths, as well as small local bars

set directly across from the event—order your jumbo Presidente bottle from the **Riconcito de Don Guillermo** for quicker service. This is one event you do not want to miss.

## Gay and Lesbian

There's a solid gay and lesbian community in the city. While clubs and bars come and go, there are a couple of favorite gathering spots.

**Parque Duarte** (Ciudad Colonial, Calle Duarte and Calle Billini) is one of the popular meeting points and pre-party hangouts for young and old gay Dominicans, particularly on weekends. One long-standing bar is **Esedeku** (Calle Las Mercedes 341, a block north of Calle El Conde, tel. 809/763-8292, esedekubar@gmail.com, 9pm-1am Wed.-Sun., 3am close on Fri.-Sat.), named after the Spanish pronunciation of SDQ, Santo Domingo's acronym. You'll find a young and lively upmarket crowd, often residents, mingling indoors and on a rooftop lounge. Be sure to dress appropriately (no T-shirts or sneakers). The Sunday karaoke nights are popular as well.

**Click Bar** (Calle Vincente Duarte, close to Plaza de España, tel. 829/449-5154, 9pm-3am Thurs.-Sun., no cover) is primarily for lesbians, but anyone is welcome to come and mingle in this trendy club setting. Occasional male and female strip shows and drink specials are offered.

For a night of loud clubbing with a young crowd, head to **Fogoo Discotec** (Calle Arzobispo Nouel 307, 10pm-4am Thurs.-Sun., US$3 cover on Fri.-Sat.), always busy with plenty of sidewalk hustle and bustle; special events or theme nights are posted on its social media channels. Adjacent is **G Lounge** (Calle Arzobispo Nouel 305, tel. 829/550-5565, 10pm-3am Thurs.-Sun., no charge), attracting crowds with fun drag shows and male strippers in barely-there thongs. Police have been known to shut the place down for noise.

## THEATER

The **Teatro Nacional Eduardo Brito** (Av. Máximo Gómez 35, tel. 809/687-3191, www.

teatro.com.do) hosts plays and musical performances year-round at the country's most prestigious facility. The stunning building is within the Plaza de la Cultura complex, with three air-conditioned halls—the largest seats 1,800 people—and excellent acoustics. Check the website for scheduled plays. There's a metro stop right by the theater, if you're feeling adventurous.

On any given day of the week, there are multiple events at the active **Casa de Teatro** (Calle Arzobispo Meriño 110, tel. 809/689-3430) in the Ciudad Colonial. It's one of the most active artistic centers in the city, founded in 1974. You'll find art and photo exhibits, movie nights, plays, and a café hosting live music most nights. The calendar is updated often, so stay tuned to social media sites.

Other smaller and reputable theaters in the city offer plays every month, including **Teatro Las Máscaras** (Calle Arzobispo Portes 56, next to Plaza de la Cultura, US$10), holding just 50 seats, and **Teatro Guloya** (Calle Arzobispo Portes 205, between Hostos and 19 de Marzo, tel. 809/685-4856, teatroguloya@yahoo.com), with plays for children and adults.

For the latest plays, check the frequently updated online schedule on http://teatro.com.do.

## CINEMAS

The **Palacio del Cine** (http://palaciodelcine.com.do) chain is your best bet—these theaters are exactly like the ones you find in the United States, with ultra-comfortable seats, air-conditioned rooms, and the typical popcorn and soda stops—except they also sell beer. The latest movies are on display and show in English, with Spanish subtitles. One of my favorite locations is inside the **Ágora Mall** (Av. John F. Kennedy, corner of Abraham Lincoln, tel. 809/732-0800, US$5.50, US$7 for 3-D). Other solid picks are the **Blue Mall's Palacio del Cine** (Av. Winston Churchill, corner Gustavo M. Ricart, tel. 809/955-3086, US$5.50-10), where there's a separate VIP section; the first IMAX theatre in the country

at **Caribbean Cinemas** on the 2nd floor of **Galería 360** (Av. John F. Kennedy, tel. 809/567-0162, www.caribbeancinemas.com.do, US$5-7); the 4-D movie theater on the 2nd floor of **Downtown Center** (Av. Nunez de Caceres, www.downtowncenter.com.do), particularly the VIP section (US$12.97); and the **Acropolis Center** (Av. Winston Churchill, tel. 809/955-1010, US$3-5).

A block away from the Fortaleza Ozama, tucked inside a restored colonial building, the **Colonial Gate 4D Cinema** (Calle Isabel la Católica and Padre Billini, tel. 809/565-0746, info@thecolonialgate.com, 9am-5pm daily, shows every 15 min., US$8) jolts you back to 1586 when Sir Francis Drake invaded the walled city of Santo Domingo. This is probably the most exhilarating five minutes I've experienced in a movie theater, from sudden seat movements to water mists in the air as pirate ships roam the seas off the island. The movie is available in both English and Spanish. There's a lovely outdoor courtyard you can enjoy after the movie, as well as a photography display of various regions of the Dominican Republic.

## CASINOS

The 24-hour **Gran Casino Jaragua** (Av. George Washington 367, www.casinojaragua.com, tel. 809/230-5383) facing the Malecón is one of the best and liveliest casinos in Santo Domingo. It's beside the Renaissance Jaragua. Here, at any time and on any day of the week, you'll find plenty of Dominicans trying their luck at slot machines, blackjack tables, roulette wheels, and in a closed-off VIP room. The atmosphere is laid back, and the nicely air-conditioned space and free drinks while you gamble are delightful after a hot walk under the sun. On the weekends, twirl to a live Dominican band at the on-site Merengue Bar (from 9pm).

The smaller **Crowne Plaza's Casino** (Av. George Washington 218, U.S. tel.

**1:** Grupo Bonyé at the ruins of the Monasterio de San Francisco; **2:** Semana Santa processions

877/859-5095 or 809/221-0000, 24 hours) is another option, located across the Malecón, and with slot machines, roulette, blackjack, and poker tables. A tad livelier is the casino at the **Hotel Napolitano** (Av. George Washington 51, tel. 809/687-1131, www. napolitano.com.do).

## FESTIVALS AND EVENTS
### Santo Domingo de Fiesta

Sponsored by the Tourism Ministry, **Santo Domingo de Fiesta** (Plaza de España, no phone, 9pm-midnight Fri.-Sat., free) is an incredibly entertaining two-hour folkloric dance show covering the history, geography, and cultural heritage of the DR—from indigenous to African and Spanish—through music and dance. This free show is held twice a week under the starry skies on the far edge of Plaza de España. The vibrant performances are ones you won't forget anytime soon—grab a seat and indulge in this visual feast. If you stay till the end, you'll see the night end with the audience—including you—pulled onto the floor for merengue with the professional dancers, until everyone goes home close to midnight. This is a real treat for those interested in the music, history, and diversity of the DR.

### Carnival and Independence Day

The Dominican Republic's biggest, most significant, and most festive celebrations take place during the month of February, with **Carnival parades** every Sunday until the first weekend of March, and **Independence Day parades** celebrated on February 27. This makes for one long week (and actually, even a month) of parties and shenanigans. In Santo Domingo, Carnival revelry takes place along the Malecón, part of which is closed off for the festivities on Sunday afternoons, and east of the city in Santo Domingo Este. The big close of carnival is the final parade (Desfile Nacional de Carnaval), held along the Malecón, usually on the first Sunday of March. It's worth attending: Show up around

4:30pm and watch from the Hilton Hotel or Güibia Park.

On **Independence Day,** head to the Puerta del Conde around 1:30pm to catch a glimpse of the president and the pomp and circumstance while he passes to pay tribute to the Founding Fathers. Otherwise, the best Independence Day event to catch is at 4pm along the Malecón: an impressive, colorful military parade begins at the Obelisco Macho and stretches all the way down the waterfront avenue. It lasts until 7pm. Expect surprises—including ships offshore blasting cannons and fighter jets and helicopters overhead—while the parade continues. It's a great time to catch the energy of this city, with tons of folks spread out along the Malecón, and plenty of vendors and local scenes. You can bring your cameras and smartphones but keep an eye on your surroundings.

### Semana Santa

The annual festivities of **Semana Santa** (Holy Week) include daily processions, starting with a street procession on Palm Sunday through the Gazcue and Ciudad Colonial neighborhoods. Good Friday has the most impressive procession of all, starting at dusk at Iglesia de las Mercedes, running through the streets of the Colonial City, and ending back at the cathedral across Parque Colón for the 8pm official mass and concert. The concert is one of the most popular events of the week; get there early if you want seats. Easter Week is otherwise quiet within Santo Domingo, as most Dominicans head to the *campo* or countryside and to nearby beaches with family. There's plenty of action and company at Playa Güibia, where the streets are closed and the seafront venue transforms into a giant outdoor pool and amusement park for the enjoyment of local families who can't afford or weren't able to travel.

### Merengue Festival

Occasionally held in late July (the past two years did not see one, but keep an eye out in case), Santo Domingo's **Merengue Festival** is a celebration of Caribbean rhythms, from the country's *bachata* and merengue sounds to salsa, reggae, and reggaeton. Major Dominican artists, as well as visiting ones, perform on a massive stage at Plaza Juan Barón over a weekend—usually Friday and Saturday—along the Malecón. But festival-related events and mini concerts can start as much as a week or two earlier, with food vendors selling Dominican fare, artisan booths, and plenty of rum to keep the merengue fever going. Book your rooms early, as this is one popular event.

### Festival Presidente

If you want to see just how much the Dominicans love their Latin music, you'll have to attend **Festival Presidente,** a three-day concert and festival held every even-numbered year in October at the gigantic Felix Sánchez Olympic Stadium. You'll gasp at the sight of over 50,000 dancing fans, clapping and screaming to lyrics as major Dominican artists perform, as well as visiting international stars like Maná and Bruno Mars. It's a jolly fun time—complete with the most amazing fireworks mid-concert, water jets splashing the standing audience in front of the stage, and green Presidente balloons to wave around with the rest of the crowd. You'll see people dancing in the aisles or from their seats, and pizza vendors will pass by with slices and drinks for sale if you'd prefer not to leave your seat to go to the downstairs food court area. Buy tickets in advance, bring small change, and don't carry anything of value—cameras are not allowed at all within the venue and security checks are strict, so stick to your smartphone.

### Colonial Fest

The celebration of all things Ciudad Colonial takes place over three days in late November at **Colonial Fest,** with concerts and ballet performances by the cathedral, artisan products, food specials, and even historical reenactments in period costumes. There are also culinary lessons at various locations within the neighborhood. Every day of the fest, the night ends with a free outdoor concert on Plaza de España. The events begin at 10am and go on until midnight, sometimes 1am.

### Noche Larga de los Museos

If you're lucky, you'll be in town when the **Noche Larga de los Museos** hits the Ciudad Colonial. During the long night at the museums held one day in each season—spring (March), summer (June), fall (September), and winter (December)—the Colonial City's major museums open their doors to the public until midnight, free of charge. Additional events are also in place at each venue to celebrate. It's a lively time to be out and about on foot.

# Shopping

Shopping opportunities are plentiful in Santo Domingo, and it's the main hub for most expats who otherwise live in other parts of the country. You'll find discount fashion shops and lots of shoe shopping all along Calle El Conde, in the Ciudad Colonial. Arts and crafts, as well as souvenir and jewelry shops, are also well represented all over this area. For American and foreign chains like Forever 21 and Zara, go to the U.S.-style malls listed below in the Piantini downtown district.

## ARTS AND CRAFTS

**Desiree Cepeda** (Calle Las Mercedes #206, 809/616-2278, desireecepedaarteint@gmail.com, 9am-6pm daily) is an artisanal store and interior decorating space, as well as a café/bistro, tucked in a gorgeous renovated colonial home. Owner Desiree is a celebrated Dominican interior decorator and florist who brings a wealth of creativity in selecting locally made items for the store, from paintings to purses, jewelry, and textiles. The back courtyard is a delight, ideal for coffee in the mornings, or lunch specials like *mondongo*, soups, and salads, as well as desserts and fresh juices and craft cocktails. Shop for souvenirs, linger with a book, or simply enjoy one of the most beautiful spaces in the Colonial City.

**Diseño Local** (Calle Isabela La Catolica, tel. 809/379-2009, disenolocalstore@gmail.com) sells fun, made-in-DR creations in a beautifully resorted colonial building. After browsing handmade bags, hand-painted mugs, art, key chains, and earrings made by a Haitian/Dominican border women's cooperative, among other unique finds, head to the back of the shop to enjoy craft beer in the Spanish courtyard or sushi on the upstairs terrace.

**Galería de Arte Maria del Carmen** (Arzobispo Meriño 207, Ciudad Colonial, tel. 809/682-7609, artemariadelcarmen.com.do, marthopm@hotmail.com, 8am-8pm daily) is a charming 30-year-old gallery, hosted in a restored colonial home, carrying original and certified works of art from Dominican artists such as Luis Oviedo and Miguel Gómez, as well as Cuban and Haitian works from Bernard Sejourne. The paintings come in all sizes and are each breathtaking, from abstract to vibrant portraits. You could easily miss this gem of a gallery; it's up a side street from Parque Colón and has no sign on the outside. Ask lovely host Nuri Jacob to show you her own paintings—they've been exhibited at the city's top museums, including Museo del Hombre Dominicano. Shipment is available by FedEx.

Tucked away from the pedestrian throngs of the Ciudad Colonial, yet a block away from the action, **Galería Bolos** (Calle Isabel La Católica 15, tel. 809/686-5073, 9am-8pm daily, http://galeriabolos.blogspot.com) is a fantastic place to get unique, handmade pieces of Dominican or Haitian art, sculpture, and crafts. From recycled wood mirrors to paintings depicting Dominican scenes, prepare to spend quite a bit of time in this colonial building. They also have Carnival devil figurines made of papier-mâché and handmade purses.

**La Placita Mercadito Colonial** (Calle Isabel La Católica 151, Ciudad Colonial, tel. 809/686-2406, carmellymorel@gmail.com, 9am-10pm) is a large, lively souvenir store where you're sure to find a classic DR gift for every member of your family, from Dominican rum to mamajuana (you can sample them), T-shirts to cups, larimar jewelry to art. Just walking through the store is sheer fun. It stretches far enough that it takes at least five minutes to get to the back, where you'll end up on a different street.

**Galería de Arte Nader** (22 Rafael Augusto Sánchez, tel. 809/544-0878, 9am-7pm Mon.-Fri., 10am-1pm Sat.) showcases work by Dominican artists.

## BOOKS AND MUSIC

The megastore **La Sirena** (Av. Mella 258, tel. 809/221-3232, 8am-8pm Mon.-Sat., 8:30am-3pm Sun. and holidays, www.tiendalasirena.com) has a book aisle in most of its locations. Offerings consist of a mix of Dominican history and education books, as well as international authors and children's tales.

In the heart of the city, **Librería Cuesta** (Av. 27 de Febrero, corner of Av. Abraham Lincoln, tel. 809/473-4020, 9am-9pm Mon.-Sat., 10am-7pm Sun., www.cuestalibros.com) is the best bookstore chain in the capital, with a two-level Barnes & Noble-style design, complete with a café and an audiovisual music listening room.

The annual **International Book Fair** (Feria Internacional del Libro, ferilibro@gmail.com) gathers all the bookstores in one place at Plaza de la Cultura. This weeklong festival celebrates all things literary, music and theater. See the website to find out when the fair will take place.

## CLOTHING AND ACCESSORIES

You'll find all of your favorite U.S. stores—including Forever 21, Zara, Mango, Nine West—at the popular **Ágora Mall** (Av.

1: Ágora Mall; 2: fruits at the Mercado Modelo

Abraham Lincoln, tel. 809/363-2323, www.agora.com.do, 8am-9pm daily), which offers the best range of affordable apparel and shoes. Another option is **Galería 360** (Av. John F. Kennedy, tel. 829/995-7360, www.galeria360.com.do, 10am-9pm Mon.-Sat. and 11am-8pm Sun.). For higher-end designer labels, head to the posh **Blue Mall** (Av. Winston Churchill, corner of Calle Gustavo Mejía Ricart, tel. 809/955-3000, www.bluemall.com.do, 10am-9pm Mon.-Sat., 11am-8pm Sun.), and **Downtown Center** (Av. Nuñez de Caceres, www.downtowncenter.com.do, 8am-midnight daily).

Pick up summer dresses and accessories with a Caribbean flair designed by Dominican Jenny Polanco at **JP Project Ciudad Colonial** (tel. 809/221-3796, www.jennypolanco.com.do, call for hours) a boutique tucked a block away from Calle Las Damas. There are also locations throughout the island.

## MARKETS

Spare at least 30 minutes for a colorful, lively Dominican experience shopping at the **Mercado Modelo** (Av. Mella, 9am-6pm Mon.-Sat., 9am-noon Sun.), originally built in 1942 by Rafael Trujillo as one of Santo Domingo's first tourist venues. On the northern edge of the Ciudad Colonial, you'll go up a flight of yellow-painted stairs and end up in an old covered market building filled with souvenir stalls selling all things Dominican—from larimar jewelry to wood carvings to Carnival masks, including some Haitian art. Be sure to bargain hard, and prepare for various vendors to call out "mi amor" and insist on you viewing their wares. Politely decline if you're not interested. Note that the prices here are some of the best you'll find after you bargain, and you would be supporting the locals. Head to the back of the market for the food section—from fish to fruits to obscure "curealls" or love potions—and watch Dominicans doing their own haggling amid the banter and passing traffic. The neighborhood isn't so safe at night, so stick to daytime hours. It's an easy walk back to the Ciudad Colonial from here, if you continue up a couple of blocks from the market's front entrance and turn right on Calle Duarte.

If you're a pro at navigating Caribbean cities and a low-key person, then it's worth a glimpse of the **market on Calle Paris**—an outdoor fruits and vegetables market where you'll really glimpse Santo Domingo's crazy but colorful side. Be sure to have a ride back and forth.

**La Sirena** (Av. Mella 258, tel. 809/221-3232, 8am-8pm Mon.-Sat., 8:30am-3pm Sun. and holidays, www.tiendalasirena.com) is the DR's version of Walmart—you can find absolutely anything here, from a fully stocked supermarket to apparel, electronics, and household items. There are at least a dozen locations throughout Santo Domingo, but my favorite is the large one across from the Blue Mall, complete with a food court.

## CIGARS

You can watch a *tabaquero* roll cigars by hand in the Dominican style at **La Leyenda del Cigarro** (Calle El Conde 161, corner of Calle Hostos, across from Mercure Hotel, tel. 809/682-9932, www.laleyendadelcigarro.com, 9am-9pm daily). Sample a variety, and sit and enjoy your cigar purchase with wine or rum at the back tables or out on the sidewalk. There are artisanal cigars you can buy as singles, if you prefer not to purchase a whole box. Hats and larimar jewelry are also for sale.

## CHOCOLATE AND SWEETS

**KahKow Experience** (Calle Las Damas 102, tel. 809/547-2166, www.cacaotour.com, 10am-7pm Tues.-Sat., 11am-7pm Sun., free entrance) offers a full Dominican cacao experience for those who don't have time to venture into the countryside. You'll learn about the history of cacao in the country through an audiovisual presentation spanning two rooms, and then move on to a display of various chocolate types (for your tasting), and into the outdoors where a small chocolate-making factory stands in the center of the courtyard. There are classes and workshops offered, as well as an on-site store and cafe where you can stock up or enjoy one of the world's most sought-after chocolate beans.

If you love sweets, you'll be like a kid in a candy store with authentic Dominican pastry and desserts at **Maria La Turca** (Calle 19 de Marzo, close to corner of Calle Mercedes, tel. 809/221-7341, 8am-8pm daily, 7pm close Sun., from US$0.50) where you'll find traditional desserts, most of which are coconut-based, as well as salty snacks like *quipes* and empanadas. The sweets alone are worthwhile—try *coconete, pan de batata, flan, dulce de coco,* or the glazed papaya slices. Ask if you're not sure what you're seeing; the ladies here don't speak English but they are friendly.

The **ChocoMuseo** (Calle Arzobispo Meriño 254, corner of El Conde, tel. 809/221-8222, www.chocomuseo.com, 10am-7pm Mon.-Sun.) is a great place to get a quick, free taste of Dominican cacao—one of the country's four largest exports. It's not a museum by any stretch of the imagination. Instead it's a store where you can get some background on organic cacao farms in the country and sample some organic chocolate made right here in the DR. Chocolate bars and other treats are for sale.

**La Casa de los Dulces** (Calle Emiliano Tejera and Arz. Meriño, tel. 809/685-0785, 9am-5pm Mon.-Sat.) displays more than 20 different types of Dominican desserts and sweet snacks on its shelves, just like a supermarket. Choose from dried fruits and blocks of *dulce de leche* and mini coconut cakes. You'll get a cultural lesson while you indulge. You can also shop for reasonably priced souvenirs.

# Sports and Recreation

## BASEBALL

You can attend a baseball game from the end of November through the end of March at **Estadio Quisqueya** (Av. Tiradentes, tel. 809/540-5772, www.estadioquisqueya.com. do, 5pm Sun. or 8pm Tues.-Sat. except Thurs., US$5-20). Purchase your tickets ahead of time or snag them at the door as the games begin. Enjoy the lively experience, complete with a marching band in the stands, fans waving flags while swigging beers, mascots and cheerleaders shaking their behinds on the field, and vendors roaming the aisles with pizza slices.

## GOLFING

One of the closest and best picks for golfing is one hour east of Santo Domingo, in the beach resort town of Juan Dolio. **Guavaberry Golf & Country Club** (Nueva Autovía del Este Juan Dolio, tel. 829/547-0000 or 809/333-4653, www.guavaberrygolf.com.do, US$95/18 holes) is a championship course designed by the legendary Gary Player. It borders a nature reserve and is famous for its signature hole played over a 15-foot waterfall. On-site are a clubhouse with pool, private beach club, restaurant, and bar. Golfers often purchase package stays with the nearby Coral Costa Caribe Resort.

## DIVING

One of the DR's best and most popular dives is a mere 12 miles from Santo Domingo's shores at **Parque Nacional Submarino La Caleta** (Autopista Las Américas Km 25, tel. 829/278-4874, info@reefcheckdr.org). It's also a popular spot for beginner PADI lessons, with a depth of just up to 20 feet and a protected bay. The chief attraction here is a 1984 shipwreck, the *Hickory,* as well as several underwater Taíno sculptures.

The more economical way to explore La Caleta is through an independent dive shop, the closest of which are in **Boca Chica.** Call ahead to check on scheduled dives

# Baseball: The National Passion

Passions run deep for baseball in the Dominican Republic, and this fervor for the sport goes back to the late 19th century. Some attribute this to the U.S. occupation of the DR in 1916, but it's more likely that it came earlier from Cuban immigrants who fled their country in the late 1890s. Either way, baseball is a sport that Dominicans took to and integrated into their culture over 100 years ago. Dictator Rafael Trujillo had a hand in modernizing and solidifying the game, building the first major stadium in the capital, which he called Estadio Trujillo (later renamed Estadio Quisqueya). The major leap and source of pride for the DR came in 1956 when Ozzie Virgil joined the New York Giants as an infielder, becoming the first Dominican to play in Major League Baseball. Since then, the DR has contributed more players to the major leagues than any other country.

From rich to poor, cities to countryside, baseball unites all Dominicans in conversation or in person at a game. In the cities and towns, the green patches where young adults train are a guaranteed sight. Beyond the fun of the sport itself, baseball also represents hope for economic salvation from a life of poverty—for the player, his family, and community—and a dream of becoming famous. It certainly was a dream come true for players like Sammy Sosa, Bartolo Colón, and Pedro Martinez, to name a few.

Six teams from around the DR make up the Liga de Béisbol Profesional de la República Dominicana, the country's professional league, and compete each season: the Águilas Cibaeñas (Santiago/Estadio Cibao), Gigantes del Cibao (San Francisco de Macorís/Estadio Tetelo Vargas), Estrellas Orientales (San Pedro de Macorís/Estadio Julian Javier), Toros del Este (La Romana), and Leones del Escogido and Tigres del Licey (both Santo Domingo/Estadio Quisqueya). Ask a local about favorite teams and it's a sure conversation starter. The winner of the season title goes on to play in the Caribbean Series.

The baseball season in the Dominican Republic runs from the end of November through the end of March, so if you're visiting during these months, you should absolutely catch a game. Purchase your tickets ahead of time, though you can also snag them at the door as the games begin.

## WHERE TO CATCH A GAME:

### Santo Domingo

- **Estadio Quisqueya** (Av. Tiradentes, tel. 809/540-5772, www.estadioquisqueya.com.do, 5pm Sun. or 8pm Tues.-Sat. except Thurs., US$5-20)

### La Romana

- **Estadio Francisco A. Micheli** (Av. Padre Abreu, tel. 809/556-6188, http://lostorosdeleste.com/estadio-franciscomicheli, US$1.11-7.80)

- **Estadio Tetelo Vargas** (Av. Circunvalación, tel. 809/529-3618, www.estrellasorientales.com.do)

### Santiago de los Caballeros

- **Estadio Cibao** (Av. Imbert, tel. 809/575-1810, http://aguilas.lidom.com/main/estadio-cibao, from RD$150 or US$3.27)

A baseball game in the DR, particularly in Santo Domingo, is livelier than any in the United States—with a marching band in the stands, fans waving flags while swigging beers, mascots and cheerleaders shaking their behinds on the field, and vendors roaming the aisles with pizza slices. Going to a baseball game is a quintessential Dominican experience.

with **Tropical Sea Divers** (Beachfront, Calle Duarte 35, tel. 829/697-9522, www.tropicalseadivers.com, 8am-5pm daily, 2-tank dive US$64 or US$150/5-dive package, plus applicable transport), because the weather determines whether or not they head out to La Caleta. If they are, hop on an early *guagua* from Parque Enriquillo and reach Boca Chica in time for the boat.

## COCKFIGHTING

Everyone tells you that baseball is the primary sport in the Dominican Republic. But lo and behold, there's another activity just as iconic: cockfighting. It remains fairly hush-hush, and those who participate are usually countryside folk who seem to just know where and when to go. If it's not your cup of tea, it's easy to ignore. Otherwise, there are cock-fighting rings *(club gallístico)* in nearly every major city and village—but some of the most authentic in decor are in Santo Domingo. Those who are interested shouldn't miss the 42-year-old **Coliseo Gallístico de Santo Domingo Alberto Bonetti Burgos** (Av. Luperón, tel. 809/563-1503, www.gallerosoy.com); the season calendar is online, with sessions running from October through August.

Another place to experience local ambience—sans sign or name, as is often the case—is just a couple of steps **adjacent to the National Zoo** (Av. Paseo de los Reyes Católicos, from 2pm Sat.-Sun., US$4.50-11). It's in a semi-dodgy area, so bring your driver. There's no charge to stand by the gate and quickly take a peek inside.

## THE CACAO TRAIL

A two-hour drive north of the city, **El Sendero del Cacao** (tel. 809/547-2166, www.cacaotour.com, year-round, from US$89) takes Santo Domingo visitors out of the city hustle and bustle and into the great Dominican *campo*—one that is lush with cacao trees in the northwestern province of San Francisco de Macorís. Hacienda La Esmeralda Garcia Jimenez, one of the oldest family-owned cacao farms in the country, is a 100-acre plantation, with 2,400 acres on yet another piece of land. It runs a chocolate factory on-site where it harvests, processes, and exports 80 percent of its product overseas to Europe, mostly France. A guide will walk you through the actual plantation, where you'll learn about cacao pods and trees, how it's harvested "family style"

cacao pods at El Sendero del Cacao

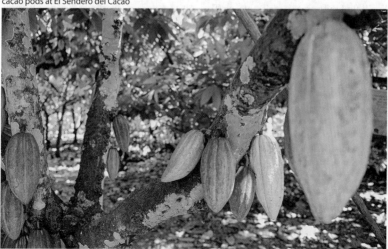

in the DR, and the three challenges facing the crop on the island. You'll get to walk through the ancient Maya way of making chocolate—including pounding a mortar and pestle to crush the beans—and the fermentation process, before ending up in the factory where modern chocolate bars are made. The obligatory gift shop is where you can purchase these rarely sold organic chocolate bars. If you visit on a Friday, you might run into school groups, but it makes for a livelier visit. It's a trip that will give you a solid glimpse into the fertile and lush Dominican countryside and one of its four most important crops.

## HIKING

Head just one hour southwest of Santo Domingo to **Dunas de las Calderas national park,** better known as **Las Dunas de Baní,** for a unique landscape not found elsewhere in the Caribbean. Hike sand dunes as if you're in the desert and take in the splendid surrounding Caribbean Sea views. It's an easy day trip, whether in your rental car or by public transportation. The buses to the town of Baní leave from Parque Enriquillo, and also pass along the Malecón for pickups anywhere you flag them down. Once in Baní, switch to a *guagua* to Las Calderas (the driver will know where to drop you off).

# Food

## CIUDAD COLONIAL
### Cafés

**El Buho Café** (Calle Arzobispo Nouel 58, tel. 809/692-3018, 8am-7pm, Mon.-Tues., 8am-9pm Wed.-Thurs., 8am-midnight Sat., 3-9pm Sun.) is one of those spots where you can linger in a tastefully decorated space with a mochaccino and a dessert, or come for breakfast or a light lunch for a taste of modern Santo Domingo in the Colonial City. You'll find salty crepes, croissants, waffles, and Dominican *mangú*. Friday evenings, locals gather for live music and happy hour (yes, there are cocktails).

The small courtyard at ★ **Desiree Cepeda** (Calle Mercedes 206, tel. 809/616-2278, 9am-6pm daily, desireecepedaarteint@gmail.com, US$5-10), an interior décor and crafts store, is all you need for a lovely morning with coffee and a book. There are also craft cocktails and a number of Dominican-inspired snacks and tapas.

**La Bodeguita de la Zona** (Calle Isabela La Catolica, tel. 809/231-2679, 7:30am-midnight Mon.-Thurs., 9am-2am Fri.-Sat., 9am-midnight Sun., www.bodeguitadelazona.com.do, US$3-10) is a welcome addition to the Ciudad Colonial, steps away from a number of hotels. It offers a comfortable café with wines, tapas, and a relaxed atmosphere away from the bustle of Calle El Conde. Breakfasts range from the traditional plate of *mangú* to omelets and croissants, as well as gourmet coffees and fresh fruit juices.

**La Cafetera Colonial** (Calle El Conde, 7am-5pm daily, from US$2), affectionately called "La Cafetera," is your historic Dominican diner. Founded in the 1930s, it was once a favorite gathering place for the country's artists, politicians, and writers. It remains a staple of the area, no matter how many trendy sidewalk digs show up. You'll find the cheapest and tastiest coffee and greasy breakfast here, from Dominican fried cheese to simple eggs on toast. Sit at the counter if you can bear the hard stools and don't mind the not-so-chatty servers, or grab a table at the back for more privacy. It's perfect if you're short on time. Right outside is the pedestrian buzz of Calle El Conde.

**Café La Moricette** (Calle El Conde, 9am-6pm daily, US$2-10) is an ideal pit stop with affordable gourmet snacks, from European-style square pizza slices to French pastries, baguette sandwiches, coffee, and fresh-squeezed juices. The cozy open-air seating area allows some people-watching without being obvious, unless you prefer to sit outdoors at one of the sidewalk tables.

Not up for crowds? **Córner Café** (Paseo Colonial, behind Calle Padre Billini, tel. 809/338-4040, US$0.50-4) is a darling spot tucked in one of the prettiest and quietest alleys in the Ciudad Colonial, directly behind the Billini Hotel's courtyard. There are two sidewalk tables shaded by pink bougainvillea, as well as indoor seating. Snacks range from mini almond croissants to pies, quiche slices, freshly baked bread, and of course, gourmet coffee, tea, and wine. The breakfast combos and prices are very reasonable.

## Dominican

Popular with locals and tourists, **Cafetería El Conde** (Calle El Conde 111, tel. 809/688-7121, www.condepenalba.com, 24 hours daily, US$3-15), at the foot of Hotel Conde de Peñalba, has the best-looking outdoor terrace and buzz in the Zona. Its umbrella-shaded tables sit smack by the Parque Colón with its constant foot traffic, musical events, and nonstop action. It's a great place to grab a Dominican meal and a beer and admire the colonial buildings surrounding the square. The affordable menu specializes in local fare, but also offers burgers and sandwiches. The Dominican breakfast here is excellent.

The other spot I love, with a delicious daily lunch buffet, is ★ **Petrus** (Calle El Conde #357, tel. 809/682-6677, from US$3-10), a gem on the Calle El Conde, otherwise overrun with fast food joints. There are also à la carte options, including juicy burgers, mofongos, yaroas, and club sandwiches. Petrus has a fun cafeteria vibe, with its open doors and a patio facing the pedestrian rush. There's also a gourmet café stand and bar where the ladies make excellent espresso, mojitos, and sangrias, and there are daily-made desserts. Lastly, there's decent Wi-Fi.

Unsurprisingly, **Paletas Bajo Cero** (Calle Isabela la Catolica #156, tel. 849/404-9935, noon-11pm daily, US$3-4) was a hit from the moment it opened its doors in the Ciudad Colonial; on Sundays, lines stretch out the door and down the block for a taste of the fruit- and natural-flavored, preservative-free *paletas.* My favorite is the coconut, but there are myriad creative flavors—Nutella-filled, passion fruit cheesecake, dulce de leche, and pineapple-mint, among others.

Offering European-style tapas with a Dominican touch, newcomer **Mercado Colón** (Calle Arzobispo Nouel 105, tel. 809/685-1103, www.mercadocolonge.com, noon-1am Mon.-Sat., closed Sun., US$2-8) is an indoor market and restaurant that has converted itself in the hottest place to eat in the Ciudad Colonial. Set in a restored colonial building with original tiles, part coral stone walls, and Dominican decor, the tavern-like wood interior is split into six stands including a Dominican dessert stop and three air-conditioned bar and seating areas (including a wine bar and imported beer stand). Hugging the outdoor patio, with 7-8 wooden tables under a covered, leafy terrace, are three windows where you can place your order for the tapas menu of your choice. To die for are the *montaditos,* units of three tapas topping house-baked bread—like the Dominican, combining osso buco, avocado, and fried plantains. There is also a wood-fired pizza station for personal-size pizzas. The later it gets in the day—particularly after 9pm Friday through Sunday—the more well-heeled city dwellers flock here to spend time "sharing good food without leaving the wallet hanging," as its co-owner describes it.

★ **Mesón D'Bari** (Calle Hostos 302, Ciudad Colonial, US$15-30), once featured on the Travel Channel, serves tasty Dominican dishes. Try the stewed goat in a *criollo* sauce, or one of the many seafood options. Set in a colonial home for over 30 years, the bar is popular with locals, but this restaurant is where you'd go for a special night out surrounded with art, dim lighting, and live merengue music on weekends. It's just a block away from Calle El Conde, yet tucked away from the crowds and the street noise.

Made famous thanks to an episode of the

# El Plato Dominicano

A common Dominican breakfast consists of fried cheese, fried salami, eggs, and a pile of *mangú*, or mashed plantains.

A blend of Taíno, European, African, and even Middle Eastern influences, Dominican food isn't complicated—it's hearty comfort food, made from fresh homegrown ingredients. Much of it is fried, stewed, and served with plenty of meats (pork and goat are favorites) and starches to fill your belly fast (like cassava bread and *batatas*, or potatoes). A great online resource on all things Dominican food is www.dominicancooking.com. Here are a few basics to get your exploration started:

- *Desayuno criollo/Dominicano:* The typical Dominican breakfast consists of fried eggs, fried salami slices, fried cheese (*queso frito*), and a couple of *mangú* mounds, topped with sautéed red onions. *Mangú* is mashed plantains, seasoned with salt, lemon, and butter. Some throw in avocado slices. You'll find these rich breakfasts sold roadside and at restaurants.

- *La Bandera Dominicana:* "The Dominican Flag" is the national dish. It's a plate of rice and beans served with meat stew (often beef or chicken). It usually comes with a side salad, like *ensalada rusa,* a creamy potato salad with eggs, peas, and carrots. It's sold cheaply at around US$3.27 and easy to find anywhere in the DR. *Note:* You can also ask for *concón*—the slightly burned, scraped crispy bottom coat of the rice in the pan.

late Anthony Bourdain's *No Reservations,* the original **Barra Payán** (30 de Marzo 140, tel. 809/689-6654, 24 hours daily, US$3) is an open Dominican diner dating back to the 1960s, complete with red stools and a silver-lined counter. It serves toasted baguette sandwiches stuffed with a choice of fillings, from chicken and cheese to ham, pork, salami, and burgers. Wash it down with fruit juice squeezed on the spot—shaken with ice or with condensed milk Dominican-style. Or do like other locals and pull into the parking

lot while a server rushes to your car window to take your order. It's perfect for those late-night snacks that soak up the alcohol after a night of dancing.

**Jalao** (Calle El Conde 103, tel. 809/689-9509, www.jalao.do, noon-1am Tues.-Sun., US$5-12), run by the same owners as popular Lulú Tasting Bar and Pat'e Palo, has an ideal location directly across from Parque Colón, where the old Hard Rock Cafe was located, and promises a menu and ambience that is *100 D'aquí*—100 percent from here. The decor is

- **Chicharrón:** These are bits of pork fat and rinds, deep-fried to perfection. You'll find street vendors pushing their *chicharrón*-topped carts or carrying them on a platter on their heads. Only the strong of stomach should try these.

- **Sancocho:** This hearty soup is the holy grail of Dominican cuisine. Often served at holidays, celebrations, and family gatherings, it's a thick concoction combining multiple ingredients seasoned and cooked in one pot: chicken, pork, potatoes, green plantain, yucca, yam, onions, and green peppers. The bowl of *sancocho* is topped with an avocado slice and a spoonful of white rice. This dish is a good cure for hangovers.

- **Pica pollo:** Deep-fried chicken with a thick, crispy skin is a popular street food, and one of the cheapest meals you'll find in the DR.

- **Locrio de pollo:** The Dominican equivalent of paella—seasoned rice mixed with chicken.

- **Quipes:** The Middle Eastern migration to the south of the island in the 19th century brought the Lebanese kibbeh—a delicious croquette snack, crispy on the outside and with mushy meat fillings on the inside. These snacks are found roadside and at restaurants.

- **Pasteles en hoja:** Frequently served at Christmastime are *pasteles en hoja*—"Dominican tamales" made with plantain dough, filled with meat, and wrapped in a plantain leaf.

- **Tostones:** Served as a side, these are plantains that are mashed, fried, and refried to make them crispy.

- **Aguacate:** Avocados are wonderfully abundant and large in the DR, making them a common side dish on menus. You'll also spot the avocado vendor on the street, selling freshly sliced portions to munch on along your route.

- **Mofongo:** Plantains mashed with garlic—the mixture can be combined with meat or shrimp (*camarofongo*).

- **Batida:** Dominicans have a sweet tooth; they love *batidas*, or fruit smoothies with a splash of condensed milk. A popular kind is the **morir soñando**—"dying while dreaming"—an orange juice smoothie with condensed milk.

- **Dulce de coco:** Crunchy bits of coconut, a popular dessert snack.

- **Palitos de coco:** Coconut balls with a caramelized outer shell.

- **Habichuelas con dulce:** Sweet creamed beans, served during Easter.

Dominican but the service slow. Dishes include the yucca croquettes stuffed with cheddar, and the Jalao Burger topped with a slice of fried plantain. A loud live band entertains on weekend nights. A better pick for food lovers is ★ **Buche Perico** (Calle El Conde #53, tel. 809/475-6451, www.bucheperico.com, US$5-20), with a covered, leafy courtyard decorated like a green room and turned into a dining terrace; giant ceiling fans rotate silently and give you the feeling of being completely outdoors. Named after a typical dish from Moca

City—a corn- and sausage-based stew—the restaurant offers a chance to dress up and sample new Dominican cuisine: ceviche with coconut, traditional *sancocho*, sweet plantain ravioli, and lobster with mashed yucca, among other delicious picks. Head there later in the week for live jazz on the terrace. Reserve ahead if you have a large group.

On a level of its own, ★ **Dos Mundos** (at Nicolas de Ovando Hotel, tel. 809/685-9955, dosmundosrd@hodelpa.com, noon-10pm daily, US$7-45, reserve ahead) is led by none other than chef Martin Omar, who returned to his homeland after many years in Spain. Sign up for his signature nine-course menu, with each plate telling a story of the old and new in Dominican culture, with influences from Omar's life's journeys.

## International

The pizza is tasty and comes in generous portions at the sidewalk restaurant and bar at **Segazona** (Calle El Conde 54, tel. 809/685-4461, 9am-1am Mon.-Thurs., later close Fri.-Sat., US$3-15), stretching along the last and most romantic block of Calle El Conde beneath trees and flowered balconies. It's a great place to throw back a Presidente or a mojito, grab a bite, and watch the crowds pass by on their way to Calle Las Damas. There is indoor seating, if you prefer, with only glimpses of the sidewalk.

Sushi fans can head to **Bamban Sushi** (Calle Arzobispo Merino #107, tel. 809/371-2009, 5pm-midnight Tues.-Sun., US$5-10 ) a romantic two-level colonial courtyard turned lounge and dining room at the back of the arts and crafts store Diseño Local. You could easily come here just for cocktails with the trendy Dominican millennial crowd, if that's your thing. A second location is in downtown, on Avenida Gustavo Ricart.

Tucked in a quiet corner close to the Ozama Fortress, ★ **El Patio Culinario** (Calle Padre Billini, corner of Isabela La Catolica, tel. 829/645-6666, 7am-midnight Tues.-Sun., US$3-10) is a relatively new concept for the Ciudad Colonial: a "street lounge," or food truck park doubling as an outdoor restaurant. It has a fun, friendly, relaxed vibe— often with karaoke nights, or a DJ spinning tunes. Waitstaff take your order from your chosen truck menu, including delicious burgers and grilled chops, as well as smaller bites like hummus and pita, with sangria and other cocktails. It's a great spot for groups.

You haven't been to Santo Domingo until you've indulged in a night of dining al fresco on the romantic terraces facing Plaza de España. Pick ★ **Pat'e Palo European**

**Brasserie** (Atarazana 25, tel. 809/687-8089, www.patepalo.com, noon-midnight daily, US$10-30) is popular with well-heeled Dominicans and serves tapas-size dishes as well as entrées like seafood pastas and steaks. Service can be hit or miss, but the view of the Alcázar de Colón at night makes that less noticeable. After all, this is possibly the first tavern in the Americas.

**Pura Tasca**'s (Calle Emiliano Tejera 51, tel. 809/333-8494, US$2.50-20) corner outdoor terrace facing Plaza de España, adjacent to a row of trendy restaurants, is where you'll find city dwellers indulging in the two-for-one sangria specials at happy hour every Tuesday, as well tapas for just over US$2 per plate. Note: The sangria special sometimes carries over to every day of the week. The restaurant offers a full menu as well, and it's quite tasty. Just remember when your bill comes that you're paying for the premium location and view.

If you want to wine and dine fabulously in a lounge atmosphere, try **Lulú Tasting Bar** (Calle Arzobispo Meriño 151, corner of Padre Billini, tel. 809/687-8360, www.lulu.do, 6pm-3am daily, US$10). There is an eclectic gourmet tapas menu, from escargot to octopus carpaccio and stuffed jalapeños, along with top-shelf liquor and fantastic cocktails. The leafy outdoor terrace surrounded by colonial buildings is certainly the major draw, but the atmosphere is no less cozy inside with the friendly bartenders and light Latin music.

Sitting on a quiet corner, ★ **Falafel** (Ciudad Colonial, Calle Sánchez, corner of Padre Billini, tel. 809/688-9714, falafelzonacolonial@gmail.com, 4:30pm-midnight daily, US$5-8) has one of the most drop-dead beautiful and romantic open-air dining rooms in the area: multilevel platforms hold tables that center on a lantern-lit Spanish courtyard decorated with plants, paintings, and masks. The falafel sandwich is good— portions are small but filling. Other Lebanese

1: restaurants in the Colonial City; 2: Lulú Tasting Bar; 3: Adrian Tropical offers breathtaking outdoor dining views.

specials include shawarma, flatbreads, hummus, and meat platters. Sit on the top level for the views, and don't forget to look up at least once to marvel at the starry skies while you dine amid colonial ruins.

## Vegan and Vegetarian

Rastafarian-owned **Kalenda** (Calle Mercedes #303 inside La Espiral, kalendaveganfood@gmail.com, 11am-5pm daily except Sat., US$5-7) is good for the vegetarian, vegan, and gluten-free crowd—as well as anyone in search of a healthy meal. The menu includes lunches at US$6.50 a plate with rice, sides, and a soup entrée. Expect to feast on flavorful falafel balls, spring rolls, sushi, and corn cakes in eggplant sauce, with world music for ambience. Menu options also include steamed or sautéed vegetables, tortillas, soups, and pastas.

# MALECÓN AND GAZCUE

## Cafés

**Benefruta** (Av. Doctor Delgado, corner of Calle Santiago, Gazcue, tel. 809/338-0907, benefruta@hotmail.com, 7am-11pm daily, US$1-5) calls itself a "fruit market cafeteria" and indeed, it's a colorful place where you can pick your fresh fruits from a vibrant sidewalk window, or go inside the diner-like setup and order a range of freshly squeezed juices—natural or sweetened—smoothies, and *batidas* along with affordable sandwiches and other healthy granola snacks.

**Villar Hermanos** (Av. Independencia 312, Gazcue, tel. 809/682-1433, 7am-11pm daily, from US$3) is a great spot for a quick morning coffee and a fresh-made pastry, whether to eat there or to go. You could also sample a Dominican breakfast, with *mangú*, eggs and all sorts of fried sausage, buffet or à la carte.

## Dominican

★ **La Fábrica Contemporánea** (Calle Danae 4, near corner of Av. Independencia, tel. 809/328-9929, lafabricacontemporanea@gmail.com, noon-4:30pm and 6pm-11pm Mon.-Sat., closed Sun., US$2-8) is a small and funky local restaurant run by Ana de León and

Angela Tavárez, two young Dominican artists. It's tucked on a side street you might otherwise not notice. This gem of a place serves succulent Dominican and Latin dishes—fajitas, burritos, *mofongo*—and daily *bandera dominicana* lunch plates (US$3). Vegetarian options are also plentiful, including roasted eggplant and salads. Nights are for à la carte and live music. Don't miss sampling the "house tea" or *te de la casa*, with or without rum. While you wait for your made-to-order meal, admire the creative bohemian space filled with recycled and repurposed furniture like barrels painted and turned into cushioned seats. Taíno masks and other art adorn the outdoor patio. If you're up for it and can sing a tune, show up at dinnertime and grab the open mic.

**Adrian Tropical** (Malecón/Av. George Washington, tel. 809/221-1764, 7am-2am daily, US$2.50-20) has a sea backdrop, with a dining terrace perched on cliffs above the Caribbean along the city's famed Malecón. Grab one of the outdoor tables and order a *mofongo* specialty—the *camarofongo* is good—or from a range of pastas, grilled meats, sandwiches, seafood dishes, and burgers. There is interior seating if you must, but that wouldn't make sense unless it's busy (or at the second location in the city center). Service can be slow and erratic, but it's a nice casual spot for a romantic lunch or dinner.

A street behind the Crowne Plaza and thus ideal if you are staying on the Malecón, ★ **Villar Hermanos** (Av. Independencia 312, Gazcue, tel. 809/682-1433, 7am-11pm daily, from US$3) is a typical Dominican *cafetería*—with food displayed buffet style—but also an à la carte casual restaurant, with a dessert section and bakery in the back. It's incredibly affordable; takeaway lunch items are charged by weight or by the lunch box if you pick the day's special (you choose three items). Come early and don't be afraid to ask the servers about the menu items.

You'll have a blast at ★ **El Conuco** (Calle Casimiro de Moya 152, Gazcue, tel. 809/686-0129, www.elconuco.com.do, 7am-midnight daily, US$5-20). This restaurant tucked in a residential neighborhood is all things Dominican, from its decor—red and blue colors, hymns and sayings painted on walls, an outdoor *fogón* (fire hearth)—to its dishes and warm service. Dominican specialties are listed on the bilingual menu, and the cocktails are divine. Some call this place touristy, but it's a great spot to get immersed in Dominican culture within your first week of arrival. A lively merengue dance show takes place starting around 9pm, with diners often pulled onto the dance floor by the attractive waitstaff. Reservations aren't required, but it might be safest to do so. The owners of El Conuco operate a similar restaurant called **Buche Perico** in the Ciudad Colonial on Calle El Conde at the corner of Calle Las Damas.

Have you ever dined in a cave? You'll long remember your experience at Santo Domingo's iconic ★ **Mesón de la Cava** (Av. Mirador Sur 1, tel. 501/533-2818, www. elmesondelacava.com, noon-midnight Sun.-Fri., noon-2am Sat., US$15-25), from a tasty menu to the stunningly romantic limestone interior. A spiral staircase leads you underground from the entrance, where tables await under stalactites. The menu offers Dominican specials—try a fish fillet in a coconut creole sauce—as well as contemporary seafood, pasta, and steak options. A wide selection of wines and champagne are available. When making reservations, which are required, be sure to specify the restaurant, and on your next visit try the adjacent outdoor La Terraza, with live music and set in a beautifully lit garden.

## POLÍGONO CENTRAL

The center of Santo Domingo is exploding with upscale gourmet restaurants, bistros, and cafés—and there seems to be a new hottest place to be every month. These are the best picks that have stuck around and are sure not to disappoint.

### Cafés

Grab a pricey but fun brunch or breakfast at the popular, Euro-chic **Julieta Brasserie** (Av. Gustavo M. Ricart 124, corner of Manuel J. Troncoso, tel. 809/475-1007, 8am-11pm Mon.-Fri., 8am-mindnight Sat.-Sun., US$5.50-10).

Expect omelets, waffles, pancakes, smoothies, Dominican-style *mangú* with fried cheese, and myriad other morning treats. Sit in an air-conditioned room or outdoors, although the traffic and noise can be a bit much on the weekdays. There's live music occasionally, and it gets crowded, so arrive as early as possible.

### Dominican

★ **Buen Provecho** (Av. Gustavo Mejia Ricart 59, tel. 809/562-4848, 7am-4pm Mon.-Sun., US$3-15) is my favorite Dominican restaurant in the city. It's set in a simple yet cozy and unpretentious dining room. There's also a shaded outdoor patio shielded from street noise with a wall of potted flowers. The tasty and authentic Dominican fare at an affordable price in an otherwise pricey and trendy area is quite the find. It's hard to say which meals are better: the Dominican breakfast (there are international breakfast options, too) or the colorful lunch buffet of all things rice, *mangú,* chicken stew, and other local specialties. Don't be afraid to ask the waiters for a menu translation on any items; they're very friendly.

### International

★ **Mitre Restaurant & Wine Bar** (Abraham Lincoln 1001, corner of Gustavo Mejia Ricart, tel. 809/472-1787, www.mitre. com.do, noon-1am daily, US$10-30) is a place to dress up and mingle among the jet set of the city or celebrate a special occasion. Nibble on foie gras before indulging in a choice of pastas, risotto, steaks, and seafood.

Inside the luxurious JW Marriott, **Winston Grill & Patio** (Av. Winston Churchill 91, tel. 809/807-1717, US$10-21) serves international and Dominican fusion plates made while you watch the chefs at work in the open, live kitchen. The shrimp risotto and filet mignon *a la parilla* are delicious. Sip it down with wine or champagne, available by the glass under the light pouring in from the floor-to-ceiling glass wall. Head out to the infinity pool-adorned terrace post-meal and take in the city views.

# Polígono Central

CALLE EUCLIDES MORILLO
HIPÓDROMO V CENTENARIO
GALERIA 360
ÁGORA MALL
EXPRESO V CENTENARIO
AV SAN MARTIN
AV MAXIMO GOMEZ
ENSANCHE PARAÍSO
AV CHARLES SUMNER
AV ABRAHAM LINCOLN
MUSEO BELLAPORT
AV ORTEGA Y GASSET
Centro Olímpico
CALLE MANUEL DE JESÚS TRONCOSO
MITRE RESTAURANT & WINE BAR
BANCO POPULAR
BUEN PROVECHO
EMBASSY SUITES
CENTRO OLIMPICO JUAN PABLO DUARTE
JW MARRIOTT SANTO DOMINGO
CAJERO SCOTIABANK
AV GUSTAVO MEJIA RICART
BLUE MALL
PIANTINI
LA SIRENA CHURCHILL
PALACIO DEL CINE
CALLE RAFAEL AUGSTO SÁNCHEZ
AV LOPE DE VEGA
ENSANCHE NACO
PLAZA DE LA CULTURA
AV MAXIMO GOMEZ
ACROPOLIS CENTER
CALLE FEDERICO GERALDINO
AV ING ROBERTO PASTORIZA
AV MEXICO
AV PEDRO HENRÍQUEZ UREÑA
WINSTON CHURCHILL
METRO/S.T. AUTOBUSES
EXPRESO 27 DE FEBRERO
Parque Iberoamérica
CALLE PASEO DE LOS LOCUTORES
CALLE FRANCISCO PRATS RAMIREZ
AV BOVILAR
AV SARASOTA
AV ABRAHAM LINCOLN
AV JOSE CONTRERAS
UASD
0       200 yds
0       200 m

© MOON.COM

Lovers of grilled fish and meats will enjoy **Victoria by Porter House** (Av. Gustavo M. Ricart, tel. 809/542-6000, www.victoria.do, noon-midnight daily, 2am close on weekends, US$6-25). The burgers and dry-aged rib eye are sure bets. There are also pasta and salad options, as well as a children's menu.

## Vegan and Vegetarian

Thanks to the active Taiwanese community in the DR, there are a few solid choices in the city for gluten-free, vegan, or vegetarian dining.

**Jardín Jazmin** (Av Núñez de Cáceres, corner of Luis F. Thomen, tel. 809/732-0701, noon-10:30pm Tues.-Sun., US$2-5) is a popular Taiwanese-owned vegan restaurant. The large menu includes everything from veggie dumplings to fried tofu. They serve excellent fruit smoothies, fresh juices (the pineapple/papaya mix is heavenly), and bubble milk tea.

**Restaurante Bambú by Meli** (Av. Rómulo Bentancourt 2064, tel. 809/482-0049, 5pm-10pm Tues.-Fri., noon-10pm Sat.-Sun., US$1.50-5) is a favorite as far as vegan eats go—so good even meat lovers won't notice. Set in what looks like someone's backyard garden with mismatched wooden tables, stools, and chairs, this off-the-beaten-track verdant spot attracts the healthy, trendy food lovers of the city. Treats here are a healthy variation on Latin eats. Think *quipes* filled with plantain and cheese, vegetable empanadas with soy, or burritos stuffed with soy meat and beans. The Vietnamese rolls are huge and delicious. Order a variety of these bites and share, tapas style.

# Accommodations

## CIUDAD COLONIAL

Staying in the Ciudad Colonial is a must if this is your first time in Santo Domingo. It's a short walk to the Malecón and Gazcue—or just about US$3.30 for a one-way taxi—and there's something to be said for being a stone's throw from the pedestrian Calle El Conde and its all-around Dominican buzz.

### Under US$50

**Island Life Backpackers' Hostel** (Ciudad Colonial, Isabel La Católica 356, tel. 809/333-9374, www.islandlifebackpackershostel.com, US$15-45) is a short walk to Plaza de España and the heart of the area. A bar and lounge welcomes you as you enter, leading to a spacious Spanish courtyard with yet another bar. Stairs head to the rooms, ranging from dorms to private. The bunk beds have thick mattresses, and all three sets of dorms share a living room and bathrooms. Travelers' favorite sayings are scattered about on the walls wherever you turn, including in the bathrooms, making you feel right at home.

### US$50-100

**Hotel Conde de Peñalba** (Calle El Conde 111, tel. 809/688-7121, www.condedepenalba. com, US$54-89, includes breakfast) was my first hotel in Santo Domingo and a perfect pick for a solo traveler and first-timer in La Capital. It's ideally located across from Parque Colón. You'll immediately notice its popular outdoor dining terrace, sharing a sidewalk with the park's passersby. Upstairs, the hotel's old, even if slightly worn, colonial charm is undeniable, with its winding staircase, period art, and wooden floors. The single rooms are small, but ideal for solo travelers spending little time in their rooms. Remember to climb the stairs all the way to the rooftop for a panoramic view of the park.

The delightful ★ **El Beaterio** (Calle Duarte 8, tel. 809/687-8657, www.elbeaterio.

fr, US$75-100, breakfast included) is a 16th-century former home turned into a cozy guesthouse you will have a hard time leaving. Situated across from quiet Parque Duarte, the value is excellent. Immaculate rooms are centered on an open courtyard and ooze romance with elegant yet simple bedding, air-conditioning, and decent-sized baths. Pick the more spacious upstairs suites, and head to the rooftop terrace for a drink and a view. The friendly Haitian staff here is a highlight.

Set in the heart of the Colonial City, **Boutique Hotel Palacio** (Calle Duarte 106, tel. 809/682-4730, www.hotel-palacio. com, US$72-111) is delightfully decorated, with rooms and suites in simple whites and dark wood colors, with air-conditioning, patio views, queen- or king-size beds, wireless Internet, and phones. The highlights are the Spanish courtyard relaxation area and the rooftop swimming pool. Free coffee and parking are additional perks. Walk in after 7pm for a one-night stay and you'll get a discounted rate of US$65.

**Hotel Doña Elvira** (Calle Padre Billini #207, tel. 809/221-7415, www.dona-elvira. com, US$50) is a small, cozy hotel ideal if you're not looking for too many frills but still want a colonial building and a central location at an affordable price. There's a pool, an on-site tapas restaurant and bar, and a rooftop Jacuzzi. Queen, double, and suite rooms feature a flat-screen TV, air-conditioning, safes, and private baths.

### US$100 and Up

The award-winning ★ **Hodelpa Nicolás de Ovando** (Calle Las Damas, tel. 809/685-9955, www.accorhotels.com, US$165) is a landmark in the Ciudad Colonial. It's grandeur is evident from the moment you step inside the famed former Santo Domingo governor's home turned luxury hotel, now managed by the locally owned and rapidly expanding

Hodelpa group. Located on the oldest street in the Americas, the hotel consists of three villas, the first of which was built in 1502. The main entrance leads to the first courtyard, but a short walk away is where the Taberna del Mojito lounge and bar awaits, with a swimming pool that attracts the majority of the clientele—I love it for its variety of Cuban mojitos. Scattered through this maze of mansions are several gardens and courtyards, ideal for strolls. Look out for the cannons that defended the mansion from invaders. The dim colonial hallways lead to rooms with arched doorways that ooze history, even if their interiors are more modern—these 7th-floor suites were recently upgraded as part of the Imperial Club Level, packed with amenities as well as a private lounge where drinks, breakfast, and appetizers await. There are a handful of presidential suites—two-story plush lofts with king-size beds and private balconies, where Brangelina stayed overnight, as well as other dignitaries like former UN Secretary-General Ban Ki Moon. On-site is **Dos Mundos,** headed by Dominican chef Martin Omar, open to the public and offering spectacular multiple-course dining menus that "tell a story" and reflect the best of the old and new in Dominican gastronomy.

**Billini Hotel** (Calle Padre Billini 256-258, tel. 809/338-4040, www.billinihotel.com, US$170-190) is the newest addition to the handful of luxurious escapes in the Ciudad Colonial. A 17th-century colonial home is now an ultra-sleek, white-and-red posh and avant-garde hotel, complete with a rooftop pool and bar, on-site restaurant, and staff in red and black uniforms. The rooms are equally bright and modern, outfitted with all the electronic bells and whistles and private patios (although the view isn't as spectacular). Perks include 24-hour room service, free airport transfers, Bang Olufsen speakers, and L'Occitane bath products.

The adults-only **Casa Sánchez** (Calle Sanchez 260, www.casasanchezhotel.com, US$90-130, includes breakfast) luxury boutique hotel has high-ceiling standard rooms and self-catering suites. Pick a poolside Colonial Room, with air-conditioning, wireless Internet, flat-screen TV, power showers, and gorgeous original tiles. The show stealer is the hotel's swimming pool set in a Spanish courtyard with powerful water jets. The multicolor pool lights are gorgeous at night. On the rooftop is a garden for more relaxation.

# MALECÓN AND GAZCUE

The Malecón has a row of high-rise brand-name hotels and casinos, which attract business travelers, while Gazcue offers extremely affordable guesthouses out of the public eye. Gazcue is generally safe to walk around, but be more cautious on the Malecón, where there are occasional peddlers, and don't display any valuables. Both areas are about a 15-minute stroll from the Ciudad Colonial west of Independence Park.

## Under US$50

Almost straddling the Malecón, up a side street behind the Crowne Plaza, is the all-white, charming colonial ★ **Maison Gautreaux** (Calle Felix Mariano Lluberes, tel. 809/412-7838, www.maisongautreaux.net, US$45, breakfast included)—an amazing deal for being just a block up from the main seafront avenue lined with pricier brand hotels and within walking distance to the Ciudad Colonial. Rooms are well appointed, with air-conditioning, wireless Internet, and cable TV. There is an on-site restaurant and rooftop Jacuzzi.

**La Gran Mansión** (Calle Danae 26, tel. 809/682-2033, johanny_v@hotmail.com, US$31) is a gated residence turned guesthouse, with clean and spacious ground-level rooms. Bedding is basic, but you have all you need for a roof over your head and a warm shower in an equally wide bathroom. There is Internet access and cable TV, and a small outdoor terrace.

The next block over, **Hotel La Residence**

---

1: Hotel Conde de Peñalba; 2: the JW Marriott Santo Domingo

(Calle Danae 62, tel. 809/412-7298, willianaresidencia@yahoo.com, US$25) welcomes you with a large covered patio where you'll find guests and locals relaxing with a newspaper. Rooms and bathrooms are visibly older, but the basics are there—including air-conditioning, wireless Internet, and small bathrooms with hot and cold water.

A much better value and the best deal in Gazcue is across the street at the hard-to-pronounce **Jecasergian Hotel** (Calle Danae 31, between Av. Independencia and Calle Santiago, tel. 809/338-9144, jecasergian@gmail.com, US$25), with 13 modern rooms that include air-conditioning, wireless Internet, cable TV, double beds, and a decent-size bathroom. You won't find this gem online, so call ahead to reserve or walk in if there are no big events in town. A stone's throw away are a handful of restaurants, including supermarkets, and roadside fruit vendors. Major hotel restaurants are a block or two away, and it's a 15-minute walk to the Ciudad Colonial.

## US$50-100

**Hotel Napolitano** (Av. George Washington 51, tel. 809/687-1131, www.napolitano.com.do, US$95-155) is an old-school Dominican favorite, but don't get the wrong idea—there's not much that's old school about its grounds. Its popularity is mostly due to its breezy, spacious seafront terrace—**La Terraza,** where a restaurant hosts live Dominican bands on the weekends for some dining and dancing al fresco and serves up a mix of Dominican dishes, seafood, pasta, steaks, and desserts. The atmosphere is laid-back, the staff friendly, and it's a great place to spend the day. Nonguests can purchase a day pass for US$20, which includes a meal with dessert, a drink, and pool and gym use. The seafront rooms are a good bang for your buck. Amenities include an on-site casino and a nightclub that goes until 6am. To top it off, you're a 10-minute walk from the Ciudad Colonial.

If you're looking for a low-key but modern, solid-value hotel on the Malecón within an easy walk of the Ciudad Colonial and Gazcue's local restaurants, the **Crowne Plaza** (Av. George Washington 218, tel. 809/221-0000, www.crowneplaza.com, US$129-198) doesn't disappoint. The staff is the highlight here, aside from the well-appointed ocean-view rooms—with air-conditioning, TV, wireless Internet, full shower tub, minibars, and stereos. There are adjoining connections for families if needed. There's an on-site restaurant with a full breakfast spread (mimosas included) and a rooftop swimming pool and lounge. To splurge, ask about the executive club and presidential suites.

## US$100 and Up

★ **El Embajador Royal Hideaway** (Av. Sarasota 65, tel. 809/221-2131, www.barcelo.com, from US$ 112), one of the most historic hotels in Santo Domingo, is an oasis in a busy city. One of the filming locations for *The Godfather Part II*, it was renovated in 2017 by the Barceló Hotel Group. Located in the Bella Vista neighborhood, it's more splendid than ever, with 298 sleek renovated suites. The Executive Level suites are well worth the splurge (think 300-thread-count cotton sheets, Bulgari toiletries, sleek technology, soaking tubs, and access to the Royal Level Lounge). The pool area sits amid beautifully landscaped grounds, and along with a new spa—outfitted with a yoga studio, Jacuzzi, sauna, and salon—it's tempting to have an afternoon of leisure in between city activities. Despite the renovations, this hotel remains the classy oasis it's been since 1956.

**The Renaissance Jaragua Hotel & Casino** (Av. George Washington 367, tel. 809/221-2222, www.marriott.com/sdqgw, from US$119), the most iconic hotel on the Malecón and open since 1942, has 300 renovated rooms and junior and presidential suites. Stay in the tower section if you can; the splurge (about US$30 a night more) is worth it. On the grounds are a renovated, spacious pool and bar-restaurant area with sea views, a fully equipped fitness center, and three restaurants, along with an often-busy casino with live music at the Merengue Bar.

**Hilton Santo Domingo** (Av. George Washington 500, tel. 809/685-0000, www.hiltonsantodomingo.com, US$159-219) is a solid pick for a modern, safe, and convenient location on Santo Domingo's waterfront. Located directly across from the water, all rooms get a sea view. But the most glorious "corner rooms"—ask for 1713 or 1715—offer a panoramic ceiling-to-floor window view of the Caribbean outside, including from the bathroom, as well as a glorious view of the coconut tree-lined avenue. The on-site, pricey **Sol y Sombra** restaurant, open to all, has stunning seafront views for a lunch or dinner rendezvous. Amenities also include a swimming pool and bar—with water views from the 7th floor—and a 24-hour gym.

The redesigned, modern open lobby and lounge seating at the ★ **Sheraton Santo Domingo** (Av. George Washington 365, 809/221-6666, US$120-800) are the property's initial draw. The hotel location is excellent, on the main drag of Santo Domingo yet walking distance to the Ciudad Colonial and Gazcue. And the rooms have all the comfort and amenities of the Sheraton brand. Food is average here at best, but the staff and the pool terrace with a view of the Malecón might just make up for it.

## POLÍGONO CENTRAL
### US$150 and Up

Inside the fancy Blue Mall and accurately boasting "unpretentious luxury," the 150-room ★ **JW Marriott Santo Domingo** (Av. Winston Churchill 93, Piantini District, tel. 809/807-1717, US$299)—the first in the Caribbean region—is a great deal for your fancy buck and is the most beautifully detailed, luxurious property downtown. It's hard to say what's more impressive here— the vertical gardens and marble wall entrances, the standard rooms with an open bathroom design and mirrors with built-in plasma TV, or the on-site **Vertygo 101 Lounge & Bar,** set on an outdoor terrace 101 feet above Avenida Winston Churchill. The bar has an infinity pool with impressive city views, and is an après-work hangout of trendy Dominicans. Don't miss the **Winston Grill & Patio** restaurant, where a Mexican-Peruvian chef and his lively open kitchen delights palates with dishes such as oriental duck tacos and shrimp risotto. The hotel is connected to the Blue Mall via three entrances, at least one of which is a private escalator, giving guests access to a multitude of shopping and entertainment options, including a full movie theater.

**Embassy Suites by Hilton** (Av. Tiradentes 32, Silver Sun Building, tel. 809/685-0001, www.santodomingo.embassysuites.com, US$159-200, includes breakfast) is housed within the tallest commercial building in the capital, along the popular Avenida Mejia Ricart, next to several trendy lounges, cigar bars, and restaurants. Sumptuous touches include marble floors, high ceilings, shining corridors, and funky light bulbs. The all-suites hotel attracts a business clientele—there are conference rooms, a bar, and restaurant on-site—and has a somewhat austere feel. Suites are spacious and furnished in brown and cream colors. Views are of unfinished high-rises across the way. The highlight, aside from location, is perhaps the fancy infinity pool on the 7th floor, with skyline views of downtown Santo Domingo.

# Safety in the City

Every Dominican you run into in the city will warn you: be careful, Santo Domingo isn't safe. Yes, there is petty theft and some distracted tourists have been known to get their cameras snatched out of their hands at sights like the seafront Malecón. But as in any big city you might visit and wander around, common sense rules. Don't flash valuables. Don't walk late at night. Taxis run 24 hours and appear within minutes of a call. This city isn't any more dangerous than Chicago or Washington DC, as long as you stick to well-frequented zones—including the Ciudad Colonial, Gazcue, and the Malecón. Downtown Santo Domingo is fine by day, and fine by night as long as you have a ride. If you're headed east of the Ozama River, *always* catch a taxi and arrange for a return pickup.

For the woman traveler: if you're going to walk around, prepare to be catcalled and propositioned for marriage every 5-10 minutes and at every corner block where men might be gathered outside. This is a frequent occurrence in Santo Domingo. If it's just a *Buen Día* greeting, then responding while continuing on your way is fine. Otherwise, your best bet is not to respond and to continue without stopping. Street talk is annoying, but in the Dominican Republic it's mostly harmless. Of course, always be sure to practice good safety habits; don't walk alone after dark or in isolated areas, and don't display valuables (including smartphones) if possible.

# Information and Services

## TOURISM

**Colonial Tour & Travel** (Arzobispo Meriño 209, a few steps from Parque Colón, tel. 809/688-5285, www.colonialtours.com. do, 9am-5pm Mon.-Fri.) is a popular travel and tour agency. It offers various full-day excursions from Santo Domingo to interesting sights including Isla Saona, 27 Charcos de Damajagua, and inland cultural tours. The website is pretty advanced, and you can book tours online. Keep an eye on their Facebook page for the latest options and departures.

**Blue Travel Partner Services** (tel. 809/200-1778, www.bluetps.com, 24-hour call center) is a destination management company offering numerous services from airport transfers to organized sightseeing tours around the Dominican Republic. Offices are located islandwide. They are reliable, friendly, and always on time.

Grab a map of the city at the **GoDominicanRepublic Tourism Booth** (Calle Las Damas, corner of Calle El Conde), which includes the downtown area by zones, and the colonial section. Feel free to ask for any other booklets and pamphlets of other regions of the DR you might be visiting. They have a *Guía Turística* magazine that is bilingual and also quite useful.

**TravelNet** (Calle Rafael A. Sánchez 102, tel. 809/534-7440, www.travelnetdr.com, 8:30am-5:30pm Mon.-Fri., 8:30am-12:30pm Sat.) is a travel agency specializing in hotel packages with excursions, flights, car rentals, and cruises to other destinations—including exclusive offers on Royal Caribbean.

## MONEY

For your banking and ATM needs, go to **Banco Popular** (corner of Calle El Conde and Calle Duarte, tel. 809/544-8917) or **Scotiabank** (Calle Isabel La Católica, across from Hotel Frances). In Gazcue, try the inside ATM at the **Crowne Plaza** (Av. George Washington 218, tel. 809/221-0000). There's also an excellent 24-hour pharmacy close to the Zona, **Farmacia Carol** (Av. Independencia 57, tel. 809/685-8165, www.farmaciacarol.com), and an Altice telecommunications desk inside if you need to purchase a SIM card (just remember to bring your passport ID).

## GROCERIES

A branch of **Supermercado Nacional** (Calle Duarte 106, corner of Calle El Conde, tel. 809/221-2224, 8am-9pm daily) is an excellent addition to the popular Ciudad Colonial area. It is stocked with full groceries, toiletry needs, wines, liquor, and a deli counter. For an even larger supermarket, if you need it, there is **La Sirena** (Av. Mella 258, tel. 809/221-3232, 8am-8pm Mon.-Sat., 8:30am-3pm Sun. and holidays, www.tiendalasirena.com)—though it is in a dodgier neighborhood. There are also smaller stores up and down Calle El Conde, including pharmacies, fashion stores, Internet cafés, and pretty much anything a traveler might need.

# Transportation

## GETTING THERE

### Air

**Aeropuerto Internacional de Las Américas** (tel. 809/947-2225, www.aerodom.com) is the main entry point into Santo Domingo, located east of the city. The drive from the airport into the metropolitan area is actually quite pleasant, with views of the Caribbean Sea. Major carriers to Santo Domingo include American Airlines (tel. 809/542-5151), Delta (tel. 809/955-1500), JetBlue (tel. 809/200-9898), Spirit (tel. 809/549-2046), Air France (tel. 809/686-8432), Lufthansa (tel. 809/689-9625), and Iberia (tel. 809/508-0288).

### Ferry

There is a ferry service from Santo Domingo to San Juan or Mayaguez, Puerto Rico, and round-trip via **America Cruise Ferries** (Puerto Don Diego, tel. 809/688-4400, www.acferries.com, US$190 adults, US$174 children). It's a 12-hour journey, departing from the port in Santo Domingo across the Fortaleza Ozama.

### Bus

**Metro Tours** (Av. Winston Churchill, tel. 809/227-0101, http://metroserviciosturisticos.com) and **Caribe Tours** (Av. 27 de Febrero, corner of Leopoldo Navarro, tel. 809/221-4422, www.caribetours.com.do) service long distances between Santo Domingo and other parts of the country. Metro Tours will take you north to Puerto Plata, with stops in Santiago and Sosúa (bring a sweater for the full air-conditioning blast), while Caribe Tours makes runs from the city to Puerto Plata, Samaná, and Barahona, among other destinations.

**Expreso Bávaro** (Calle Juan Sánchez Ramirez 31, tel. 809/682-9670 in city, tel. 809/552-1678 in Bávaro, www.expresobavaro.com, 6:30am-4pm daily, approx. US$9 one-way) takes you to the Punta Cana region, more precisely to Bávaro area hotels, north of Punta Cana airport. The trip takes just 2.5 hours along a new highway, with three departures in the morning and three in the afternoon.

You'll find numerous other express *guaguas* running frequently throughout the day that head to nearby cities such as La Romana. Head to Parque Enriquillo for more information or hop on one, but keep valuables out of plain sight.

### Car

Car rentals are easily found at the airport, as well as in the city. You'll find major brands such as **Avis** (airport tel. 809/549-0468; Av. George Washington 517, tel. 809/535-7191), **Hertz** (airport tel. 809/549-0454; Jose Maria Heredia 1, tel. 809/221-5333), **Dollar** (airport tel. 809/221-7368), and **Budget** (airport tel. 809/549-0351).

# GETTING AROUND
## Car

Unless you have nerves of steel and more than a decade of experience driving in the Caribbean—and even then—I highly recommend hopping in a taxi over driving your own car in Santo Domingo. Unlike the outskirts where highways rule and everything is well indicated, the city is a maze of mad drivers each trying to outrun the other and occasionally burning through red lights at massive intersections at night. It's nerve-wracking enough being a passenger, much less getting behind the wheel. The capital is well served with three major thoroughfares—Avenida George Washington, Avenida 27 de Febrero, and Avenida John F. Kennedy—but it can be very confusing if you're new to the city. Leave the in-city maneuvering to Dominicans. If you're heading to Boca Chica, Juan Dolio, and nearby La Romana, however, you will be better off getting your own car because taxis are expensive for long journeys, and the highways are well marked and smooth.

## Taxi

The airport ride from Las Américas to your hotel in the Ciudad Colonial or on the Malecón will cost approximately US$25-30, depending on your haggling skills, although these fares are usually standard *from* the airport to the city, and more flexible when you head back. When you get out of baggage claim with your stash, walk confidently straight toward the exit and do not go with anyone who randomly solicits you as you're walking. Once you are close to the exit doors, you'll see an official taxi booth with dispatchers ready to direct you to the right cab according to your destination. Inquire about the fare before you get in and before they grab your bags. Insist if you don't get an immediate answer, so there's no confusion at the end of your ride.

Aside from the pricey airport taxi fare for a half-hour ride, the rest is good news: taxis are incredibly cheap when exploring within Santo Domingo. There are several car companies that are on call and available 24 hours, which is handy in a spot with plenty of nightlife. The most popular of these companies, recommended the most by locals, is **Apolo Taxi** (tel. 809/537-0000, www.apolotaxi.com, 24 hours, from US$3-5). When you call, be sure to get a price quote for your destination and they will also give you the car number, color, and arrival time (they speak fast—if you need help, ask a local). Be ready before you call, as they usually have drivers within every zone of the city. There are no meters, so the price is set according to neighborhoods (usually about RD$150/US$3 from the Ciudad Colonial to Gazcue or US$4 from the Ciudad Colonial to downtown Santo Domingo, which is incredibly cheap). Prices do go slightly up at night, as expected. There may be times when you have to call twice and the cab is a no-show, but for the most part, they are on point and know all the shortcuts to get you to your destination safely. If you don't speak Spanish, hand the phone over to a local or ask your hotel to call the taxi company. Don't grab one parked right outside the Ciudad Colonial hotels or the Malecón hotels—they charge almost triple the price.

Uber operates steadily and safely in Santo Domingo, but be aware that the individual drivers who show up might not know the city or your destination well. Still, it's the most popular mode of taxi transportation.

## Guagua (Local Bus)

The most economical way to get around, safer than the motorbike taxis, is the minivan buses. They are often beat-up white Toyotas with a conductor who hauls people onto the van and hollers for the destination as the driver speeds along avenues. If you're claustrophobic, you'll likely have a panic attack at the amount of people who are crammed inside the *guagua*, at times sitting on complete strangers' laps. But the merengue beats on above the interior chatter, and the van always gets you to your destination. While *guaguas* can be safe on longer distances—to say, Boca Chica and nearby beaches—the local, in-city *guaguas* are rougher and I don't recommend them for novice travelers. But if you're traveling light and looking for a cultural experience, by all means, be my guest. And save some money while you're at it.

### Motoconcho (Motorbike Taxi)

They are all over the Dominican Republic: *motoconchos*, or motorbike taxis. They'll take you at similar taxi distances or shorter for far less. They usually park on street corners and will holler at pedestrians within their view (much like the *guagua* conductors and shared taxi drivers). They don't provide helmets, however, and they also cram several passengers onto one bike—some of whom may have big bags or other items to carry—so be aware of the risks you are taking. I don't recommend them in Santo Domingo's insane traffic and aggressive driving shenanigans. Shelling out five bucks for a cab is worth it.

### Metro

Clean and sleek, Santo Domingo's **metro** (www.metrosantodomingo.com, 6am-10:30pm daily, US$1.30 for a rechargeable metro card, US$0.90 round-trip)—the only one in the Caribbean—opened in 2008 under President Leonel Fernández and with an initial outlay of US$700 million (to the dismay of many, at least at first). It now consists of two lines, with more on the way. Before you get excited: it doesn't yet connect all of the areas that are relevant to tourists, but it has been useful to daily workers commuting from the suburbs to the city center. It's still a fun way to experience this large city and get a sense of just how much more modern it is than its Caribbean counterparts. The first line consists of 16 stations, named after historical Dominican figures, and begins at Centro de Los Heroes, passes through downtown, and ends in Villa Mella, with an exit along the way at the National Theater and Plaza de la Cultura. The second line has 14 stops. Rides cost RD$20 one-way (approximately US$0.50), and no food or drinks are allowed.

# East of Santo Domingo

## BOCA CHICA

Twenty-five minutes' drive from Santo Domingo—and less than 10 miles from the international airport—is a beautiful, swimmable, white-sand Caribbean beach, and the average city dweller's number one escape: Boca Chica. Once a free-spirited fishing village, tourism has long since discovered Boca Chica. Dotting the nearly two-mile-long stretch are al fresco cafés, thatched-roof restaurants, *frituras* (fried-fish shacks), dive shops, and mid-size resorts, with plenty of music echoing along the way. Dominican families, lovers, friends, teenagers, toddlers: everyone loves a day's escape to Boca Chica from neighboring Santo Domingo.

Boca Chica gets a bad rep for its high prostitution levels, but it's more in your face at night. Everyone just keeps about their business and plenty of families frequent Boca Chica. If you're a Caucasian male, you'll be approached more often by the working ladies, but you are free to say no and keep your eyes on your pockets and belongings. If anything, Boca Chica's beach is clean, well maintained, and safe for kids. The town has become a lot more tourist-oriented over the years.

It is safe to walk around the main drag and the beach during the day, as well as the main drag of Calle Duarte at night. Just remain vigilant and bring few valuables to the beach. At night, the beat moves over to Calle Duarte and a handful of outdoor bars and clubs. A portion of the main drag is blocked off every night after sundown, and tables are placed in the middle of the street for those who want to dine amid all the nighttime action.

Weekdays are ideal if you seek a less crowded scene, while Sunday is the

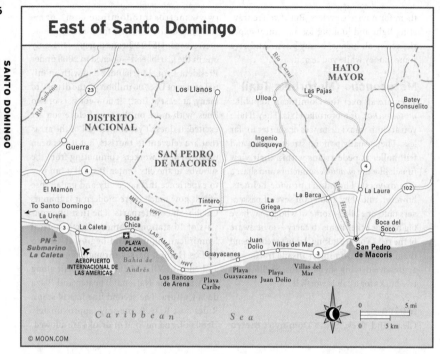

## East of Santo Domingo

liveliest day to experience Boca Chica in all its Dominican glory.

## Orientation

Arriving from the main highway, the Autopista de las Américas, you'll turn right at the traffic light onto Avenida Caracoles, which curves right and turns into Calle Duarte after you take another right. This is the main drag where you'll find most of the restaurants, shops, bars, pizzerias, *colmados*, local *pica pollo* restaurants, a central park—across from Banco Popular—and small hotels. Take any side street on foot from Duarte, and end up at the beach. Along Avenida San Rafael, parallel to Duarte, are a few more local sidewalk cafés and the north side of the park, where buses run all day long, as well as guesthouses nearby.

Knowing where to relax on the beach and where to mingle won't take long to figure out. On the far eastern end is a quiet pocket by the casual seafront terrace at The Boat House

restaurant, where you can sit and watch paddleboarders and boats pass in the distance. Going west, past the restaurant and Tropical Sea Drivers, is a lively stretch of locally owned beach restaurants serving everything from pizza to fresh fish. Eventually you'll hit the Don Juan Beach Resort, which sits at about the halfway point.

Across the resort is a tranquil dockside restaurant and lounge, as well as a stone pier where kids gather to jump into the water. Past this area farther west, a wide-open expanse of beach is a refreshing break from the crowded restaurants. This is where the Sporting Club crowd relaxes with lunch and private beach chairs. Beyond them, the local decibel goes up, and soon at the very western edge of the beach, you'll find yourself amid larger crowds of Dominicans. They gather around a table and under the shade playing dominoes, while others are closer to the beach with their coolers, Tupperware, and boom boxes sharing lounge chairs. Vendors make their way

# Playa Boca Chica

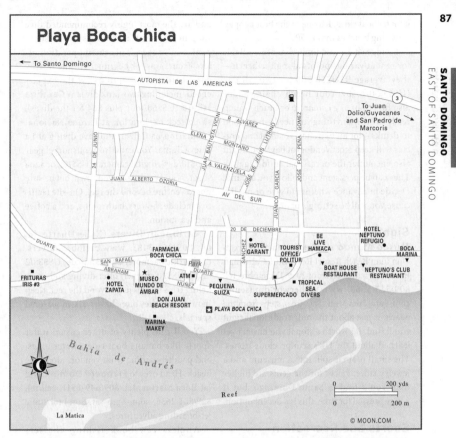

through the beachgoers, offering everything from massages to plates of food and beer from the nearby row of *frituras*.

Back on the far eastern end of Boca Chica, past the beach, is the glamorous side: three overwater dock restaurants—Neptuno is the best pick—where well-heeled Dominicans come to spend their Saturday or Sunday afternoons away from the public beach to indulge in gourmet meals, pricey cocktails, soaking in Jacuzzi tubs, and swimming right off the dock.

## ★ Playa Boca Chica

Part of the reason **Playa Boca Chica** is so popular, aside from its powder-soft sand, is that it faces a coral reef in Caucedo Bay that catches the waves and thereby creates a

natural lagoon that is safe for all to enjoy. The water is still a glorious island turquoise hue and shallow. It's less than one meter (four feet) deep, so you can wade out from the beach over to La Matica, a mangrove and bird cay across the way.

The daily scenes on Boca Chica beach are typically Caribbean and Dominican. The merengue and *bachata* music waft on the sea breeze. There is a constant stream of activity as locals play dominoes in the shade, frolic with their infants in the water, play beach football and volleyball, and throw back their mixed Brugal cocktails while standing in the sea together at sunset. Vendors hawk pretty much everything: sunglass racks, floaties, candy, ice cream, coconut, fruits, massages, and more. Still others are in the water, selling banana boat rides. It's one of the best people-watching beaches in the DR.

Lounge chairs and umbrellas are available for rent at various points along the beach—they average RD$250-300 for two, all day (US$5.50-6.50). Your beach chair vendor also functions as a *camarero* or beach waiter, ready to bring anything you need—from food to drinks—for an extra fee. A simple *no gracias* will keep most vendors at bay. You might also encounter the occasional child begging. They can be persistent and follow you around. Decide in advance whether to give or not because you will be setting a pattern.

## Sights

**Museo Mundo de Ámbar** (across from Don Juan Beach Resort Reception, Calle Juan Bautista Vicini, corner of 20 de Diciembre, tel. 809/523-5668, www.amberworldmuseum.com, 9am-5pm Mon.-Sat., free), steps from the beach, is just about the only traditional sight you'll find. It's worth a stop if you haven't yet learned about the DR's semiprecious stones. The small room is split into a museum and a jewelry store. Prices for the gems are higher than you'll find in Santo Domingo, but if you're pressed for time, this is a decent option.

## Sports and Recreation

Although it's as easy as parking yourself on the beach to feel entertained by the crowds and the people-watching, there's also plenty to do for those who love to be active on the water. And the good news is, most tour operators and dive shops in Boca Chica are bilingual, even trilingual thanks to a solid North American and European expat community.

Boca Chica's calm waters, as well as its closeness to a reef, make it an ideal place to get into water sports. There are over 20 local dive spots less than 10 minutes from shore. Check in with Swiss-owned **Tropical Sea Divers** (Beachfront, Calle Duarte 35, tel. 829/697-9522, www.tropicalseadivers.com, 8am-5pm daily, 2-tank dive US$64 or US$150/5-dive package, plus applicable transport). They have three PADI-licensed dive instructors

and are the most highly recommended dive shop in Boca Chica as well as the most organized I've seen. This small operation offers excursions for beginners to the nearby coral gardens and options for the experienced, including two-tank dives at **Catalina Island** (US$68/tour plus $64 for the dives), shipwreck exploration at Parque Nacional Submarino La Caleta, and cave diving at La Cueva Taína. You can also rent snorkel gear (US$10/day), digital cameras (US$10), or aqua scooters and explore on your own, but be sure not to venture beyond the reef. On-site facilities include showers, bathrooms, and a coffee and tea station.

**Caribbean Divers** (Calle Duarte 44, tel. 809/854-3483, www.caribbeandivers.de, markushaemmerle2@yahoo.de, US$88/2 dives, US$20 snorkel) offer diving and snorkeling trips to sites just beyond the reef. Keep in mind that they often have walk-in seasonal specials.

You'll find plenty of other casual water sports like banana boat rides, water bikes, and paddleboarding from vendors along the beach. Head over to **Flyboard Dominicana** (at Boca Marina, tel. 809/649-8511, cell tel. 829/861-2636, noon-6pm Sat.-Sun.) for some jet-boarding adventures.

Anglers can book fishing charters through **Don Juan Beach Resort** (Calle Abraham Nunez 4, tel. 809/687-9157, www.donjuanbeachresort.com). Trips depart from **Marina Makey** across from the resort.

For a day of golf, you're in luck: only a 15-minute drive away is one of the country's top golf courses at **Guavaberry Golf & Country Club** (Nueva Autovía del Este Juan Dolio, tel. 829/547-0000 or 809/333-4653, www.guavaberrygolf.com.do, US$95/18 holes) in the beach town of Juan Dolio.

## Food

The handful of restaurants and cafés in Boca Chica, whether facing the beach or on Calle Duarte, offer seafood, shellfish, and plenty of Italian food. You'll find numerous casual dining options on the beach—feel free to experiment—but these few selections will set you on the right path.

**The Boat House** (Calle Duarte 34, next to Tropical Sea Divers, tel. 809/523-6986, lawrencederijk@gmail.com, 8am-11pm daily, US$3-15) is ideal for a morning coffee and breakfast with glorious sea views—or any meal for that matter, and anytime you want to escape the crowds. Although directly on the beach, it's tucked in a corner away from the noise of the main strip and a favorite among U.S. expats and locals. Meal prices are reasonable, and choices include Dominican specials as well as tasty pizza. Look out for the daily lunch offer at just US$3.50. There's a giant screen that comes on in the evening for the sports fanatics, but it isn't disruptive to those who aren't. Portions are generous, and the atmosphere is laid-back. Friday evenings are the liveliest here, when happy hour specials and free *bocas*—mini plates of the chef's choosing, like pasta carbonara—kick in at 6pm and attract a loyal crowd of local characters as well as residents from nearby Juan Dolio.

**Makey Bar & Grill** (across from Don Juan Beach Resort, Marina Makey, tel. 809/687-9157, 10am-9pm daily, US$5-25) is set over the water on a dock and marina a stone's throw from the beach. It's a tad pricier than the beach restaurants, but you're paying for those gorgeous views. Besides, the food is worth it, from the chicken croquettes to the seafood paella. The breeze and jazzy music lull you into that relaxed Dominican pace.

**Pequeña Suiza** (Calle Duarte, tel. 809/523-4619, pequenasuiza@bocachicaplaya. com, 9am-10pm daily, US$5-20) offers a delightful lunch or dinner respite from the sun, with tables set in a leafy, romantic courtyard (there's even mosquito repellent provided on the tables). There's an air-conditioned dining room as well, if you prefer. But the best things about this place are the Italian menu of delicious pastas and fish and the staff. There's an outdoor breakfast counter for some morning action, and tables set directly on the street when the strip closes to traffic after dark.

Get your beach glam on and spend the day on the overwater deck of **Neptuno's Club Restaurant** (Calle Duarte 12, tel. 809/523-4703, 11am-midnight, US$10-20) on the eastern tip of Boca Chica. One of three upscale waterfront restaurants on this end, it doubles as beach club where you'll find all an all-white decor with curtains, plush seafront couches and beds, sunning platforms, and Jacuzzi tubs smack in the middle of the restaurant where you can get served your cocktails. There are even steps directly beside your dining table for a pre- or post-meal dip in the Caribbean Sea. All these bells and whistles come at a hefty menu price, of course. The food is decent—including lobster linguini and lasagna—though not quite as impressive to your taste buds as a casual meal from the local fry fish shack.

## Accommodations

Just a couple of blocks from the beach, **Hotel Garant & Suites** (Calle Sánchez 9, tel. 809/523-5544, www.hotelgarant.com, US$57-77) is a no-frills, safe place to stay in a convenient location. The basic amenities include a spacious room with satellite TV, refrigerator, air-conditioning, hot water, and wireless Internet. The "luxury rooms" aren't lavish; they just have access to a shared veranda and a view of the small swimming pool below. There's an outdoor patio facing the street for morning coffee and breakfast. A street up from the hotel is Calle Duarte and its central park, bank, and convenience stores.

The 224-room **Don Juan Beach Resort** (Calle Abraham Nunez 4, tel. 809/687-9157, www.donjuanbeachresort.com, US$150) is right at the heart of the beach strip and offers an all-inclusive escape in the middle of the local action. The rooms are basic—request one with a beachfront balcony—and the buildings are old, but the location is ideal. Particularly if you'd rather not eat out every day, this could be an option. There are specials year-round, so be sure to ask if you are walking in without reservations.

## Information and Services

There's a Banco Popular branch and ATM

across from Central Park, and you'll find all you need—from groceries to a pharmacy and phone stores—along Calle Duarte, the main street in Boca Chica, one block from the beach.

## Getting Around

Getting around Boca Chica's main drag and the beach is a breeze: use your feet, as the locals do. It's generally safe at reasonable hours. Don't walk alone late at night. *Motoconchos* or motorbike taxis are another mode of transportation, though I don't recommend these, particularly on the highway. You'll see them parked by the central park or along various street corners off Calle Duarte.

# JUAN DOLIO AND GUAYACANES

Approximately 40 minutes from Santo Domingo and a mere 15 minutes from Boca Chica is the small and quiet resort town of Juan Dolio, favored by the wealthier Dominicans of Santo Domingo. The chief attraction here is a six-mile-long stretch of powdery, thick white sand, dotted with just a handful of restaurants, beach bars, condominiums, and resorts.

The area remains safe and the beach is as pretty as ever. Santo Domingo residents with a bit more buck flock here on the weekends or on a free weekday. The president keeps a vacation house along the stretch just beside the Coral Costa Caribe Resort. In March 2015, Juan Dolio became the home to Pinewood Studios' largest underwater film studio in the Caribbean and Latin America, and with that comes the hope that this beachside community will soon see a tourism boom.

The resort side of Juan Dolio runs all along Calle Principal. The western side, facing the more public beach areas, is known as Old Juan Dolio and home to some of the longer-lasting small hotels and resorts. On the eastern end of the drag is Juan Dolio Nuevo,

starting with the Banco Popular branch and a string of mini shopping plazas, with supermarkets, hair salons, and more of the higher-end restaurants and condominiums along Calle Principal. The beach on this end—also referred to as Villa Real—is also cleaner than the main public stretch (you won't see piles of trash tossed at the back of the beach). You can access it even if you're not staying at the resorts here—all beaches in the DR are public. There's a passage right beside Club Hemingway. Be on alert when swimming here: stay close to shore, as there are strong currents.

It's easy to get up and down Juan Dolio's main beach. You'll find entry points—and two separate parking lots—on Calle Principal running parallel to the main highway. The more "public" side of the beach is dotted with chairs and umbrellas for rent as well as a handful of restaurants. Walking west, the stretch becomes more deserted for a good while—facing gated apartment buildings or abandoned hotels—before you reach the Coral Costa Caribe Resort. Continuing farther takes you all the way to Club Hemingway. Don't walk it alone.

You'll find everything you need on the main drag of Calle Principal, which is easy to get around. Walking is an option but it does get superhot. Using a bicycle—ask your host—or taking a *motoconcho* ride is recommended to get to Juan Dolio Nuevo.

Barely a 10-minute ride west from Juan Dolio is the fishing village of Guayacanes, also blessed with a white-sand beach and sufficient facilities for the day-tripper: lounge chairs and umbrellas, *frituras*, changing facilities, and the gorgeous Caribbean Sea to dip in. You'll see fishers and their canoes along the beach, going back and forth with their catches. It's a low-key, daytime-only escape, with fewer hustlers bothering you. The main beach entrance is where you'll find most locals relaxing on lounge chairs on the weekends. On the far eastern end of the beach is a row of food shacks, restaurants, and thatch umbrellas.

Another five minutes west of Guayacanes

---

1: Playa Boca Chica; 2: Boca Chica style fried fish; 3: the beach at Guayacanes; 4: Playa Caribe

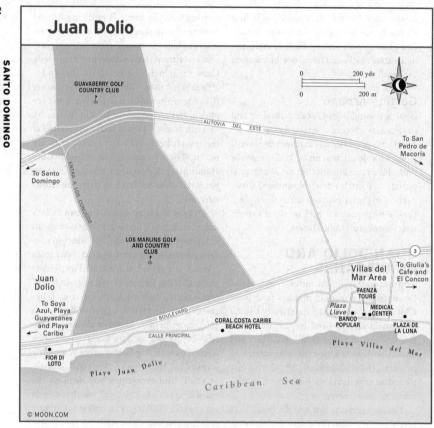

## Juan Dolio

GUAVABERRY GOLF COUNTRY CLUB

AUTOVIA DEL ESTE

To San Pedro de Macorís

To Santo Domingo

ENTRA A LOS CONUCOS

LOS MARLINS GOLF AND COUNTRY CLUB

Juan Dolio

To Soya Azul, Playa Guayacanes and Playa Caribe

BOULEVARD

CORAL COSTA CARIBE BEACH HOTEL

CALLE PRINCIPAL

FIOR DI LOTO

Playa Juan Dolio

Villas del Mar Area

To Giulia's Cafe and El Concon

FAENZA TOURS

Plaza Llave

BANCO POPULAR

MEDICAL CENTER

PLAZA DE LA LUNA

Playa Villas del Mar

Caribbean Sea

© MOON.COM

0   200 yds
0   200 m

---

before reaching Boca Chica, you'll see signs for **Playa Caribe**—this beach faces a small cove offering waves that attract surfers and boogie boarders on the weekends. During the week, it's as tranquil as it gets, and the scene is breathtaking. Yuri and Rai are the attendants here (cell tel. 829/926-9891, 7am-6pm daily), providing lounge chairs and umbrellas (RD$300/US$6.70 for two chairs and an umbrella all day). There are surfboards for rent (RD$100/US$2.25/hour) if you want to give the waves a twirl. Yuri can give you a lesson if you ask. He doesn't charge, but tip him what you wish. There's a restaurant on-site, but call ahead to make arrangements for a plate of fried fish (US$6.70), or bring your own snacks.

## Sports and Recreation

**Los Delfines Water and Entertainment Park** (Autovía del Este, Km 15, tel. 829/520-8481, www.losdelfinespark.com, US$19 adults, US$16 children 4-12 years) is fun for the family and worthwhile if you're looking to keep your kids entertained away from the beach. The largest water park in the Caribbean, it counts up to 17 roller coaster-like waterslides, a children's pool, and average restaurants good enough for an afternoon's trip. Bring your own towels, and save by catching a *guagua* or public bus from the highway. They will stop for you directly in front of the park.

If you're a golfer, you've come to the right town. Juan Dolio is home to the stunning

**Guavaberry Golf & Country Club** (Autovia del Este Km 55, tel. 829/547-0000 or 809/333-4653, www.guavaberrygolf.com.do, US$95/18 holes), a par-72 course designed by the legendary Gary Player and bordering a nature reserve. The entire course blends seamlessly with its surroundings—one of the course's signature holes is played over a 15-foot waterfall and indigenous coral rock formations.

Inquire about hopping on dive trips with **Juan Dolio Divers** (Calle Principal, U.S. tel. 888/774-0040 or 809/526-1948, www. juandoliodiversrd.com, US$40/dive or US$16/ snorkel equipment) at Coral Costa Caribe Resort. There are over 20 sites to explore up and down the Juan Dolio coast less than a 10-minute boat ride away.

Independent operator **Faenza Tours** (Calle Principal, Villas del Mar area, tel. 809/526-1713 or cell tel. 829/292-5000, faenzarentacar@yahoo.com) offers reasonably priced excursions from Juan Dolio, including ATV tours to San Pedro de Macorís (US$50, 2 persons min.) and Isla Saona (US$60).

## Entertainment and Events

There is very little entertainment in Juan Dolio. It's not a party town like Boca Chica. The chief activity after dark is to barhop.

Among the watering holes, **Bar Cacique** (Beachfront, Calle Principal, noon-midnight daily) is good for a cold beer or local mixed drinks with a view. The bar attracts a usual cast of characters, with plenty of local women and older expat men. Other popular haunts include **Paladart** (Carretera Nueva, tel. 809/526-1855, 11:30am-midnight Tues.-Sun., closed Mon.), an Argentinean tapas bar on the roadside.

You can have drinks while trying your luck at the small **Dreams Casino** (Coral Costa Caribe Resort, tel. 809/526-3318, 7pm-midnight); ask about their free shuttle service.

## Food

You can get a cheap buffet lunch of rice and beans with stew at **La Differencia Pica Pollo** (Calle Principal, across from Bar Cacique,

US$2.25). They also have fresh-squeezed juices daily.

**Giulia's Cafe and Sports Bar** (Plaza Hispaniola, Calle Principal, tel. 809/526-1492, 7am-5pm Thurs.-Tues., US$6-12) is a convivial place to grab a traditional Dominican breakfast, as well as omelets and pancakes. Lunchtime offer burgers, sandwiches, pasta, and steak. It's located on the street side, but the atmosphere makes up for the lack of a sea view. You can watch sports, access free wireless Internet, and, when you're ready for the beach, cross the street and walk south for a couple of minutes.

A long-timer in the area, **El Mesón** (across from Club Hemingway, Calle Principal, tel. 809/526-2666, 11am-11pm daily, US$8-15) offers Spanish specialties, including paellas and imported sausages.

It is my hope that **Soya Azul** (Calle Principal, going west from Fior di Loto, tel. 809/526-2101, 11am-6pm daily, occasional evenings, US$6-15) will be around for a long time to come. This Asian restaurant sits on a gorgeous, calm portion of Juan Dolio Beach facing beautifully tranquil waters ideal for a swim. The food is a wonderful change from local fare, and ranges from Thai fried rice to spicy tuna rolls, ceviche, and conch with Thai curry.

## Accommodations

By the time you leave ★ **Fior di Loto** (entrance to Juan Dolio, first turnoff after the Shell gas station, Calle Principal 517, tel. 809/526-1146, www.fiordilotohotels.com, US$15-40), you will have gained a friend in the lovely Mara Sandri, owner and longtime expat from Italy. Her budget hotel, decorated in all things India in honor of the nonprofit school for girls that she single-handedly launched in Pushkar, shines with its stunning murals, paintings, colorful daybeds in the reception area, and plenty of Indian and astrological motifs. Rooms range from a shared dorm to double beds and apartments. There's a gorgeous gymnasium on the top floor where Mara teaches yoga three times a week for free (4:30pm-6:30pm Mon.-Wed.). Basic breakfast and coffee are available for a small fee, as well as sodas and beer. Mara is a wealth of DR knowledge and her all-Dominican staff is equally charming. It's a great place for independent solo or couple travelers and attracts guests of all ages, as well as plenty of Europeans and Peace Corps volunteers. There's a 24-hour front desk for added security.

**Coral Costa Caribe Resort** (Calle Principal, tel. 888/774-0040, US$80) is an average all-inclusive at best, although it faces a clean and swimmable part of Juan Dolio's beach. There are a couple of swimming pools, three restaurants—Mexican, Italian, and Dominican—and an on-site dive shop. Kayaking and snorkeling gear are provided. The nightclub **Boom** occasionally opens to the public on the weekends for a cover charge. Across the street from the resort, you'll find tennis courts and a casino. If you are looking for an affordable weekend resort escape close to Santo Domingo, this would be a decent pick.

**Emotions Beach Resort** (U.S. tel. 800/801-1971, www.hodelpa.com, US$134-186), a Hodelpa property, is a standout on Juan Dolio Beach and was the first sign of the area's revival. This already popular boutique hotel is set in the heart of Juan Dolio's main white-sand stretch, as well as roadside, and has intimate and immaculate grounds with sleek superior or deluxe rooms and suites. There are three swimming pools with in-water loungers and five restaurants, including options for Dominican fusion, seafood, Italian, and organic for the health-conscious. There's also a spa on-site, bicycles, tennis courts, and a billiards room. For a notch up, get an Essential Club beachfront room with an exclusive beach and pool space and other perks thrown in, such as a free tour to Santo Domingo's Ciudad Colonial.

## Information and Services

There aren't a ton of services in this area, but you'll find the basics. There's an ATM at the Banco Popular branch (Calle Principal), halfway between the old and new Juan Dolio, as well as a couple of supermarkets and plazas along the way. Right in Old Juan Dolio is the sparsely stocked Naito supermarket. Farther down the main drag in Juan Dolio Nuevo is **Plaza Llave** for Internet access, beauty salon services, and a supermarket.

For car rentals, head to **Faenza Tours** (Calle Principal, Villas del Mar area, tel. 809/526-1713 or cell tel. 829/292-5000, faenzarentacar@yahoo.com, US$49/day, discounts for longer-term). They also rent scooters (US$25/day or US$100/week).

## Getting There

If you're driving from Santo Domingo, take Avenida George Washington going toward the bridge and port, leading outside the city. Go right along Avenida España, where you'll begin to enjoy gorgeous views along sea. Take the exit for Boca Chica and keep straight. You'll hit a tollbooth (RD$30/US$.065 per car), and past that will be Boca Chica signs. You'll see *colmados,* shops, and casual restaurants on both sides of highway, until you reach the light at Avenida Caracoles where you'll turn right toward Calle Duarte and the beach.

To catch a *guagua* to Boca Chica, head to Parque Enriquillo in the Chinatown neighborhood, within walking distance from the Ciudad Colonial if you don't have heavy bags. You'll see them parked all around on the street parallel to Calle Duarte. Ask anyone where to catch the Boca Chica buses heading east, as it can be confusing to find them. If you'd prefer a private ride to Boca Chica, call **Apolo Taxi** (tel. 809/537-0000).

To catch a *guagua* heading back to Santo Domingo (RD$70, every 15 minutes from 6am to 11pm), head to the north side of Parque Central, along Avenida San Rafael. Some of them are marked "express" and only require one terminal switch. You'll see these minivans stop and the conductor coming out.

Heading back to the city or to Boca Chica from Juan Dolio, you can hail a *guagua* along the highway, going west. If you're headed to the airport, let the conductor know to drop you close to it. You'll have to walk the remainder of the way to the terminal, or catch a *motoconcho* down.

## Getting Around

The heart of Boca Chica consists of the main strip running all along the beach and the main road (Avenida/Calle Duarte), where all the hotels, restaurants, and activities are strung from west to east. You won't need more than your feet to get around.

There are taxis or motorbike taxis available if you plan to go out at night from one end to another; they are usually parked at the main entrance to Boca Chica. You can also find private taxis at the intersection of Avenida San Rafael and Avenida Caracoles, or even parked outside your hotel. Alternatively, call the **Sindicato Transporte Turístico de Boca Chica** (Sitratubochza, tel. 809/523-5313). Fares include Aeropuerto Internacional Las Américas (US$25), Santo Domingo (US$40), and Juan Dolio (US$30).

If you want to continue on your adventures from Boca Chica going east, wait for the *guaguas* at the intersection of the highway and Avenida Caracoles. They go to Juan Dolio (RD$30, 20 minutes), San Pedro de Macorís (RD$60, one hour), La Romana (RD$140, one hour), and Higüey (RD$250, two hours). *Guaguas* pass from dawn until about 6pm. There aren't any at night.

# Punta Cana and the Southeast Coast

Diamond-white beaches, infinite blue skies,
and a slew of five-star all-inclusive resorts draw millions to postcard-perfect Punta Cana. This area is largely responsible for making the DR the crown jewel of Caribbean tourism destinations.

There are actually two distinct areas to "Punta Cana": Bávaro, north of the Punta Cana Airport, and Punta Cana proper, south of the airport. Either way, as locals and residents will tell you any chance they get, "this isn't the Dominican Republic, it's *Punta Cana*." The area's relatively high prices and exclusive resorts echo this. For those who want to venture outside and look past the Punta Cana resorts, there are small, local beach enclaves in Bávaro, such as Los Corales and Cortecito, which welcome the independent explorer.

# Highlights

Look for ★ to find recommended sights, activities, dining, and lodging.

★ **Playa Macao:** A popular spot for surfers, development-free Macao is one of the most beautiful beaches in the DR (page 100).

★ **Playa Bávaro:** The many resorts don't detract from its glorious beach—ideal for lying in the sun or swimming in temperate, crystal-clear waters (page 101).

★ **Scape Park:** Hike through subtropical forest on this natural park, once home to the indigenous Taíno people. Explore underground caverns filled with fresh water, swim in a cenote tucked beneath limestone cliffs, horseback ride, or zipline over a thick canopy (page 117).

★ **Playa Juanillo:** With iridescent white sand and luminous blue ocean, this uncrowded beach makes for a perfect photo op (page 118).

★ **Altos de Chavón:** Marvel at the architectural wonders of this Mediterranean village replica, perched 91 meters (300 feet) above the majestic Río Chavón (page 131).

★ **La Punta de Bayahibe:** Sample life in a Dominican fishing village—stroll down alleys lined with colorful wooden homes, fish with locals, and watch the sun go down over the bay with a cocktail in hand (page 141).

★ **Sendero del Padre Nuestro:** Explore the beautiful forests and freshwater Taíno caves of the Parque Nacional Cotubanamá on this hiking trail (page 145).

★ **Isla Saona:** You'll find it difficult to put down your camera as you journey from one diamond-white beach to another on the largest offshore island of the DR (page 146).

# Punta Cana and the Southeast Coast

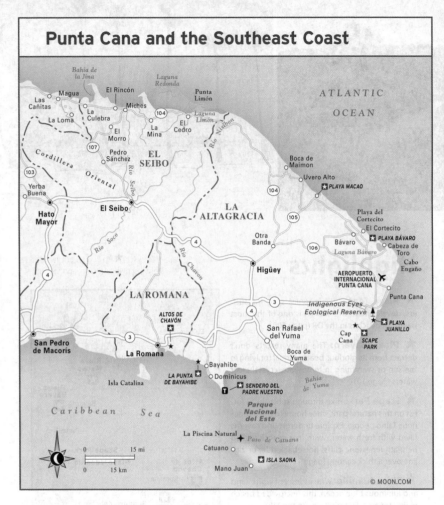

The area jutting south of Punta Cana is more typically Dominican. The seaside fishing villages of Boca de Yuma and Bayahibe are a stone's throw from the Parque Nacional Cotubanamá (formerly Parque Nacional del Este) and offer easy access to hiking, birding, diving, snorkeling, and cave exploration for Taíno pictographs. Hit the links at the renowned Teeth of the Dog at Casa de Campo, shop for Dominican art in La Romana, catch a baseball game, or dine at the riverfront Altos de Chavón. And Bayahibe's most special attractions are offshore: the protected Saona and Catalina Islands, which offer unbelievably beautiful beaches and incredible snorkeling opportunities.

## PLANNING YOUR TIME

It's obvious that most who head to Punta Cana and La Romana do it for one reason: the

**Previous:** Playa Dominicus; Río Chavón and its thick jungles; Playa Juanillo.

beaches. Sure enough, there are more white-sand stretches and corresponding beachfront resorts here than in any other portion of the country. It's tempting to kick back and relax for the entirety of your trip, with all the pampering you could imagine available just a couple of steps away from your lounge chair.

Still, save a half day at least to wander up and down Bávaro's Los Corales and Cortecito beaches, both in the day and at night, for a glimpse of the remaining local vibe in this touristed part of the DR, as well as much better dining options and some dancing Dominican-style. While in Punta Cana, also make time for a countryside excursion to visit Higüey's basilica, its roadside butcher shops in La Otra Banda, and its cacao and sugarcane plantations. Plenty of safari tours are around, and most offer a solid glimpse of *campo* life in the DR. If you can spare another day, or a few hours on the way to Bayahibe, stop in the fishing village of Boca de Yuma and explore this untouristed part of the south. Birders, nature lovers, and pirate enthusiasts will enjoy their time here; you can also sample the freshest fish there is and visit one of the largest caves within the Parque Nacional Cotubanamá.

For those who crave nice beaches but love culture, adventure, and water sports even more, make time for at least a one- or two-night stay in Bayahibe. You'll get a good feel for a small but bustling Dominican fishing village, while also having easier (and more affordable) access to prime snorkeling and dive sites and the offshore islands of Saona

and Catalina. These islands are an incredibly long day trip from Punta Cana—something that tour operators in Bávaro don't always make clear. The bonus is enjoying some of the prettiest sunsets on this side of the Dominican Republic.

## ORIENTATION

The Punta Cana Airport is your point of reference when deciding where to stay or how far to head along the long Punta Cana/Bávaro main drag. Whether you decide to set yourself up on the southern tip of the area in Cap Cana or north in Üvero Alto will make an impact on your stay in terms of what activities will be closest to you or how often you'll dip into your wallet for gasoline refills.

North of the Punta Cana Airport is the **Bávaro** area, with most of the all-inclusive resorts as well as a couple of hideaways for independent travelers. A portion of Bávaro is home to small beach communities like Cortecito and Los Corales, where you can come and go from your hotel as you please. *Guaguas* running along the main drag in Bávaro are another advantage to staying in this area, as well as local restaurants and beachfronts that are easily accessed at various intervals. North of Bávaro is **Üvero Alto.**

South of the Punta Cana Airport is the area labeled **Punta Cana** proper, and south of that, **Cap Cana.** These two exclusive regions don't have any public transportation running along the main road and are more isolated than Bávaro.

# Bávaro

The neighborhood north of Punta Cana Airport is called Bávaro, after its biggest beach stretch, Playa Bávaro. Here you'll find a concentration of resorts, small hotels, a multitude of local and international restaurants, the pedestrian-friendly beach villages of Los Corales and Cortecito, and a local atmosphere in an area that is sufficiently connected by public transportation.

## SIGHTS
### Aqua Park
Every year seems to bring with it a new recreational park in Punta Cana, and this time it's **Aqua Park** (Carretera Veron-Bávaro km 38, tel. 829/760-1076, www.aquaparkdr.com, 11am-6pm Mon.-Sun., US$75/3 hrs, US$90 full day), promising "action-packed family adventure." Set over a natural lagoon in Cabeza de Toro, families will find plenty of entertaining water activities here. You can wakeboard, flyboard, paddleboard, or join your kids in a variety of tube rides, as well as navigate a pool inflatable obstacle course.

### Bávaro Adventure Park
**Bávaro Adventure Park** (Entrada Boulevard Turístico km 8.5, tel. 809/933-3040, www.bavaroadventurepark.com, 8am-6pm daily, US$99 for package of three activities) offers a host of activities in one gated park. Fly over the landscape up high on a zip line or skim it on a mountain bike or Segway. You can even try "zorbing" (rolling downhill inside a giant ball). It's not so much a trip into nature as it is an outing for those seeking an adrenaline rush close to the hotel.

### ChocoMuseo
Located inside the Mundo Auténtico tourism complex, which also houses a store with Dominican coffee and the renowned Don Lucas Cigar Factory, the **ChocoMuseo** chain (Downtown Punta Cana, tel. 809/480-3104, www.chocomuseo.com, 9am-6pm daily) is more a shopping complex than a museum. However, if your time is limited and you can't go to a countryside cacao plantation, stop here for a free 10-minute introduction and walk through on the making of organic Dominican chocolate from bean to bar, followed by tastings. Don't miss the mamajuana and chocolate-blended drinks.

### Don Lucas Cigar Factory
The president of the Dominican Republic, Danilo Medina, has been spotted smoking the handmade Don Lucas cigar brand, among the oldest and most respected cigar brands in the country. There's only one place where a Don Lucas cigar is rolled and sold, and this **Don Lucas Cigar Factory** (Av. Barceló, tel. 809/200-0129, www.donlucascigars.com.do, 9am-6pm daily, free resort pickups and tour) location is it. Watch the men methodically creating each cigar before heading into the shop to buy your own, if you so choose.

## BEACHES
### ★ Playa Macao
**Playa Macao** is one of the most beautiful beaches in the Dominican Republic. Even UNESCO agrees this spot is a jewel—they declared it one of the best beaches in the Caribbean. Prepare to gasp as you approach the top of the hill and get an initial glimpse of the deep blue ocean, golden sands, and coconut trees ahead. There are no hotels or buildings here or anywhere near the beach, and that's what makes it special. There have unfortunately been rumors for several years now that a US$35 million investment purchase has been made and a resort might be in the works. Beach vendors, local businesses, and concerned citizens have held periodic strikes and protests in the past, and the development is yet to begin. If you're feeling adventurous, ride all the way down to Playa Macao's eastern

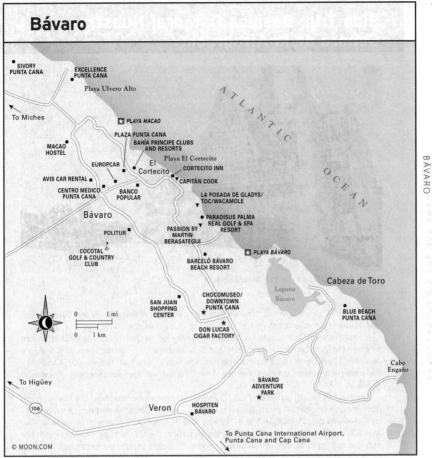

edge, then hike a visible dirt path beside the last parking lot, follow the trail, and climb down a rock to reach a tranquil cove flanked by cliffs. It's a delightful swim away from the crowds and big waves.

Macao is also a popular surf spot. You'll get to see some serious wave action here. You can rent equipment and get lessons on-site with **Macao Surf Camp** (Üvero Alto, beachfront, tel. 809/430-9017, www.macaosurfcamp.com, 8:30am-5:30pm daily, US$115 two-hour class, US$300 three-day course). Beware of rip currents while in the water, however. Drownings have occurred when people have gone too far out from shore, so if you decide to take a dip,

stick close to the shore but don't venture out alone or at off-hours.

If you want to avoid the bulk of the crowd, head to the beach in the morning and stay for lunch. One of the highlights at Macao is the fresh seafood restaurants on the beach, where you can indulge in fried fish, Dominican-style.

## ★ Playa Bávaro

One of the most well-known beaches in the Dominican Republic is **Playa Bávaro.** Its stunning miles of white sands are the most developed in this area, dotted with all-inclusive hotels, but that doesn't take away from this

# Side Trip: Basílica Catedral Nuestra Señora de la Altagracia

Basílica Catedral Nuestra Señora de la Altagracia

The town of Higüey is an agricultural and transportation hub with the hustle and bustle, traffic, and modern conveniences of a big city. One of the only reasons you'd venture here, other than making a bus transfer, is to visit the basilica of Higüey, or the **Basílica Catedral Nuestra Señora de la Altagracia** (8am-6pm Mon.-Sat., 8am-8pm Sun., mass 6:30am, 8am, and 6pm Mon.-Fri., 10am, noon, and 5:30pm weekends). The basilica was built between 1954 and 1971. Pope John Paul II visited in 1992. This is one of the most important religious sites in the Dominican Republic.

Designed by French architects Pierre Dupré and Dovnoyer de Segonzac, the basilica is imposing inside and out. The exterior, including royal palms along the entrance, encompasses a 69-meter-high (225-foot) arch and a bronze-and-24-karat-gold entrance. Inside is an altar with a framed painting of the Virgin Mary dating back to the 16th century. Believers get in line and wait as long as it takes for a chance to say their prayers and requests before her. There are several stories of how this painting got here; the most commonly told is that a sick child was healed after seeing the Virgin Mary appear at this site close to an orange tree. Under that tree, the child found the painting.

Within the compound the **Altagracia Museum** (US$10) is well worth a stop for some religious history of the DR, as well as an outdoor candle-lighting prayer area.

Every **January 21,** Dominicans and Catholics from around the world descend on the basilica to pay their respects. The day turns into a party in the streets, with the usual music, food—including plenty of oranges—and drinks.

Many tours from Punta Cana include a brief stop and tour of the basilica. If you're not appropriately dressed and are showing skin above the knees, you will be handed a long skirt cover-up at the entrance to the church.

glorious stretch. You'd have to stay here to truly enjoy this beach, sought after for its calm and temperate reef-protected turquoise waters. You won't be alone here, unless you head to the beach early in the morning or stay on at lunchtime while everyone crowds the restaurants.

## Other Beaches

Also in the Bávaro area, a stone's throw north of Playa Bávaro, are two public stretches offering a more cultural beat than the others: Playa Los Corales and Playa El Cortecito. Both of these beaches and their small communities are ideal for independent travelers who want space to throw their towel, with or without a rented chair, and enjoy some people-watching, local restaurants, and an ultra-local vibe. **Playa Los Corales** is dotted with small restaurants and resorts. You'll spot tourists parasailing above boating activity, jogging, or floating in the Caribbean-flat waters. The stretch is home to a small number of trendy beachfront lounges and restaurants, but it still has a less overwhelming feel than farther south on the Punta Cana trail. Rising sea levels and poor land-use planning have caused erosion to a portion of Los Corales's beach, with the water line uncomfortably close to hotels, but a series of sand-filled structures in the sea are helping, and they add to the scenery with pelicans and tourists swimming around them.

You'll know you've reached the end of Los Corales and entered the Blue Flag Certified **Playa del Cortecito**—one of my favorites—when you spot more foot traffic and more mobile vendors hollering out their offerings. This area has a bustling Dominican vibe. It is one of the only two truly public beach communities left on this eastern coast. Playa del Cortecito is home to some favorite local and expat haunts both by day and night, including Capitán Cook and Onno's. There are newly rebuilt souvenir shacks, small hotels, and dive and glass-bottom boats waiting to scoop you up. But the atmosphere is authentic, the beach wide and clean with impossibly tall coconut trees, and water that makes it all postcard-worthy. Don't miss posing by the "I heart RD" sign at the first souvenir shack on the beach.

# SPORTS AND RECREATION
## Diving and Snorkeling

There are three main PADI dive shops in the Bávaro area, and they offer similar dive excursions: local, in the Atlantic, or in the Caribbean Sea with an excursion all the way south. Options south include diving off Calatina Island (US$209 all-inclusive, 9am-5:30pm) or local dives off the fishing village of Bayahibe, as well as cave diving in the Parque Nacional Cotubanamá (for those certified for cave diving). Call by 4pm the day before to see what's available and to reserve a space. One place to try is **Global Divers** (Barceló Dominican Beach Resort, tel. 809/618-9092, www.diving-idc-bavaro-puntacana-bayahibe. com, US$135 3-dive package, Discover Scuba US$225 2-tank dive). **VIP Divers** (Cortecito Beach, Hotel Vista Sol, tel. 809-763-0752, vipdivers@gmail.com, US$60/dive, US$200 Catalina 2-tank dive) are popular for certification classes, and **SeaPro Divers** (Los Corales, next to Barceló Dominican, tel. 809/754-3632, www.seaprodivers.com, US$100 2-tank dive) gets rave reviews for both its diving and snorkeling excursions to Saona and Catalina Islands, with two-tank dives every morning.

You can hop on glass-bottom boat snorkeling trips with **Global Divers** (US$45 pp) right off the coast, followed by a trip to a natural pool on the tip of Playa Bávaro. The excursion lasts a couple of hours.

### Parasailing

Happiness is floating 46 meters (150 feet) above the Coconut Coast with **Global Divers** (Barceló Dominican Beach Resort, tel. 809/618-9092, www.globaldiverspuntacana. com, 8am-4pm, US$45 pp or $85 for two). You'll be airborne for about 10 minutes. It's quite memorable to see all those miles of pearl-white beaches from above. Another option is the independent **SeaPro Divers**

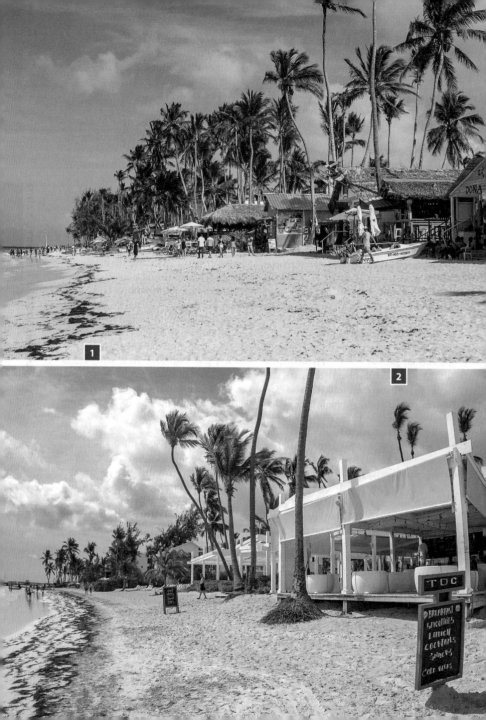

(Los Corales, next to Barceló Dominican, tel. 809/754-3632, www.seaprodivers.com, 9am-5pm Mon.-Sat., US$100 for two).

## Sailing

For a private or more exclusive snorkeling and sailing experience, **Side by Side Adventures** (tel. 829/761-3464, www.sidebysidepuntacana.com, US$109, lunch included) is an excellent choice, with professional staff and up to three stops along the most beautiful stretch of Punta Cana's coastline.

Sailing with **Ocean Adventures** (next to Huracán Café, Corales Beach in Bávaro, tel. 829/754-3632, www.oapc.com.do, US$90) takes you aboard a FreeStyle III catamaran to explore the popular (and often crowded) "natural pool"—a sandbank in shallow waters—off the beach of Bávaro. For a party boat, look up **SeaPro Divers** (sailing locations at Now Larimar and Occidental Grand resorts, tel. 809/754-3632, www.seaprodivers.com, US$55), which has an all-inclusive run with a stop at the natural pool for more merriment.

## Surfing and Kitesurfing

Run by surf enthusiasts and pioneers of the sport in the DR, the **Macao Surf Camp** (Üvero Alto, beachfront, tel. 809/430-9017, www.macaosurfcamp.com, 8:30am-5:30pm daily, US$115 two-hour class, US$300 three-day course) offers surfing classes for all levels off the beautiful, public Playa Macao. They take everyone from beginners to competition-level surfers and nearly all ages (4 to 76). Lessons can last a couple of hours or nearly an entire week. You can rent boards (US$10/hour or $25/day) and surf solo if you already know what you're doing.

North of Bávaro, check out **KBS Kite Boarding School** (Zoetry Agua Punta Cana, tel. 829/672-6133, www.kbspuntacana.com, 8am-6pm daily, US$224 three-hour beginner, pickup available).

---

1: Playa del Cortecito; 2: TOC's beachfront location

## Golfing

The combination of golf and beaches with the courses facing the sea is part of this area's claim to tourist fame. There are several excellent options for some early tee times. Within Bávaro, you'll find the popular **Cocotal Golf & Country Club** (Bávaro area, tel. 809/687-4653, www.cocotalgolf.com, US$119/18 holes, golf lesson US$86, shuttle service), conveniently close to the major resorts and offering 27 holes set around lakes and coconut trees, inside a residential community.

## 4x4 Safaris

**Colonial Tours' Super Truck Safari** (tel. 809/688-5285, www.colonialtours.com.do, US$95) has knowledgeable local guides who will give you as much insight into local life as possible as you ride through the streets and down dirt roads from La Otra Banda to Higüey and into farms and sugarcane plantations. The day ends on the gorgeous beach of Macao, where you'll have time to swim at your leisure and bask in the glorious Dominican sun. Pickups are available from resorts on the Bávaro or Punta Cana coastline. **Bávaro Runners** (tel. 809/833-0260, www.bavarorunners.com, US$55-135) is also popular for its safaris, albeit they are a tad more crowded because of this. Whether from Bávaro or Punta Cana, you'll head to well-known sights—including the Higüey Basilica and cacao and coffee farms.

## Horseback Riding

To ride in a natural theme park through forest and past Taíno caves, sign up for a couple of hours with **Scape Park** (Cap Cana, tel. 809/469-7484, www.scapepark.com, US$69 adults, US$41 children, pickup included). They offer a full equestrian center with an introduction to horseback riding before you head out for two hours into its forests and shaded trails. Horseback riding on the beach was prohibited in 2017 by the DR Ministry of Environment (whether that will remain enforced is unclear, but my advice is to refrain from such activities.).

# ENTERTAINMENT AND EVENTS
## Bars and Nightclubs

If you're looking to throw back some delicious daytime cocktails on the beach, head to ★ **TOC** (beachfront, Los Corales, tel. 809/864-2359, www.playaturquesaoceanclub.com, 10am-8pm daily, US$10), part of the Turquesa Ocean Club vacation condominium complex, where the motto is "don't worry, beach happy." The vacay-classic cocktails are excellent and worth the higher price tag (US$10); enjoy coco locos, mojitos, and original cocktails like the Saona (pineapple, watermelon, and coconut) or the Happy Island (ginger, lime, and mint). Go on Sundays for live music at 3pm, and check the weekly schedule.

Bavaro's bar scene is all grown up and sexy now, with a row of establishments lining a side street known as Calle Aruba, in the heart of Los Corales behind Plaza Turquesa. Each offers a variety of live music or DJ entertainment. Hanging out away from the sand, city-style, seems to be the latest trend. **The Living Room** (Calle Aruba, tel. 809/972-7124, daily 9pm-3am, from US$5) attracts locals who work in the area, as well as its fair share of travelers, with its lively, small outdoor terrace where a talented live soloist or band performs on the weekends. Go for the music, but not for the cocktails (stick to beer), and order your drink at the bar before proceeding to the terrace. There's limited indoor seating with cozy red lights and air-conditioning. Directly next door, on the same elongated terrace, is **Coyote Bar & Lounge** (Calle Aruba, tel. 829/712-3618, from US$7), also a popular pick, offering food and better, if pricier, cocktails. Wednesday nights are popular at **Wacamole** (Calle Aruba, tel. 829/750-1777, 11am-2am daily, from US$5), the hottest Mexican hangout, where the margaritas and mezcal flow and the tacos (and other Mexican favorites) might make you consider returning during your stay. Wednesdays are 2-for-1 for the ladies on mojitos and margaritas, and there are daily happy hour specials, as well as live music—check the latest on social media.

The open-air **Onno's** (Playa del Cortecito, tel. 809/552-0376, www.onnosbar.com, 11am-5am daily, US$5-15) is a well-known chain in the DR, consistent in providing decent food (especially pizza), DJs from 10pm, and merriment directly on the beach until the wee hours of the morning.

**Soles Chill Out Bar** (Playa Los Corales, tel. 809/910-4371, solesbar@gmail.com, 10am-2am daily, US$5-20) continues as a trendy beachfront hangout for the young, the mature, and the fabulous, with lounge beds and tables directly on the beach. A live DJ spins electronic lounge music all day and in the evening. Just a five-minute walk along the wide beach is **Huracán Café** (Playa Los Corales, tel. 809/552-1046, www.huracancafe.com, 9am-11pm daily, US$5-20) with a similar setup, but a somewhat less pretentious vibe and tasty meals to boot.

The **Pearl Beach Club** (Cabeza de Toro, next to Catalonia Bávaro Beach Resort, tel. 809/933-3171, www.pearlbeachclub.com, 9am-midnight Sun.-Thurs., 9am-1am Fri.-Sat., no cover except for events) is the latest Miami-style beachfront club addition to Punta Cana, with plush sofas, poolside live music, or DJ themed parties (the foam type). It's an all-day and evening hangout. There's a Caribbean-themed restaurant on site, a sushi bar, and of course, fancy cocktails.

One of the most distinctive nights out in Punta Cana can be had at **Coco Bongo Show & Disco** (Downtown Punta Cana, Av. Barceló, tel. 809/466-1111, www.cocobongo.com.do, 9pm-4am Thurs.-Sun., from US$75, drinks included), a part nightclub, part Vegas-style show with performances that begin close to midnight and run until early morning. Prepare to be stunned by nonstop entertainment once you enter this small but impressive club, from the exhilarating lights, smoke, and visual effects of the nightclub during intermission to dancers and acrobats flying across the room as well as on a giant stage. Performances include tributes to Michael Jackson, Madonna, and the Moulin Rouge. There are fun moments throughout, including "kiss cams" putting patrons on the spot for a public smooch shown on two screens. Local drinks are all-inclusive, and there are tables available at an extra cost if you don't want to stand all night long. There's also an outside bar as you arrive, if you want to have a couple of preshow drinks alfresco.

Past a glamorous fountain pool entrance, bats welcome you to **Imagine Club** (Cruce Carretera Coco Loco, no phone, www.imaginepuntacana.com, 11pm-4am Tues.-Sun., US$30 regular, US$50 all-inclusive local drinks). Dancing inside an ancient limestone cave is what makes Imagine Disco a must-see-at-least-once. There are two separate cavernous chambers where DJs spin a variety of music under disco lights—from techno to merengue to R&B—as well as random dancers performing various stunts. If you're in the mood to let loose and party all night, while occasionally getting bumped by a 20-something spring break-type of crowd, that's what you will get. At the very least, it makes for great photos.

**Drink Point** (Av. España, corner of Av. Francia, tel. 809/552-0920, 9pm-2am Thurs.-Sun., no cover), across from the Texaco station, is an open-air bar and nightclub that had a nice crowd when it started out. It is now a hit-or-miss dance spot with a less than stellar audience. Still, it's good for a quick beer and casual merengue or *bachata* dancing during the week (avoid Sunday). A couple of blocks north is a better option at **El Kan Drinks House** (Carretera Bávaro Veron, tel. 809/762-1200, 6pm-4am daily, no cover), with a similar lounge and club setup but a better DJ, nicer crowd, and plenty of seating space. That includes outdoor tables on the sidewalk. Keep in mind that clubs come and go like the wind, so when in doubt, ask a local about the latest place to dance.

Looking for a more laid-back spot for cheap drinks and more Dominican vibes close to your hotel in Los Corales or Cortecito? Head to the **Colmado El Billar** (Los Corales, Avenida Alemania, across from Posada de Gladys, no phone, 8am-10pm), a place to throw back some beers and people-watch from picnic tables, all to the sound of *bachata* music.

## SHOPPING

Newcomer **BlueMall** (Boulevard Turístico, corner of Carretera Juanillo, tel. 809/959-0900, 10am-10pm Mon.-Sat., 10am-8pm Sun.), a sister location to the same-named shopping center in Santo Domingo, has raised the ante in the area with its luxurious designer boutiques, from brands such as Zara to niche European labels. A food court offers fast-food options as well as cafes, and nearby in its own corner, the highlight of the mall: Bachata Rosa, famed Dominican and Latin music legend Juan Luis Guerra's new restaurant.

The **Palma Real Shopping Village** (Av. Alemania 57, tel. 809/552-8725, www.palmarealshopping.com, 10am-10pm daily) is on the main drag running along Bávaro, just past the Cocotal Golf & Country Club, and offers a range of American and international brand stores, centered on a romantic Spanish courtyard complete with fountains. You'll find apparel, perfume, and cigar shops. There are also banks with ATMs, a movie theater (Palacio del Cine, shows begin 4pm-10pm), and an open-air food court nicely ventilated with powerful fans, with a Hard Rock Cafe. Stop by **The Organic Caribbean** (tel. 849/815-4523, 10am-10pm daily, from US$6) to browse shelves and tables beautifully laid out with organic bath-and-body products made right in Punta Cana from homegrown natural fruits and spices, including coconut, almonds, cinnamon, aloe, and passion fruit. Head to the back of the store to sample fruit, cacao, and chocolate liqueurs—bottles come in various sizes and make for great gifts. You can easily get to this mall by *guagua* from your resort if you're within the Bávaro area. Just step outside onto the main avenue and hail the bus, usually a white minivan. Expect to wait longer on the way back, as there's no telling when the bus will appear.

Also on the main drag and in the Los Corales area of Bávaro, **Plaza Turquesa** is

a strip mall with a couple of welcome conveniences. Check out fashion store with cute bikinis at **Fashion by Cusie** (tel. 809/455-7346, 9am-9pm daily), also selling reasonably priced contemporary shoes and beachwear accessories. A short walk away on the same strip is Bazar Pharmacy, where you can pick up your beauty, hair, or sun protection products, as well as other beach trinkets.

You'll find the biggest mall at **San Juan Shopping Center** (Carretera Barceló Km 9, tel. 809/466-6000, www.sanjuanshoppingcenter.com, 9am-9pm daily). Several of the big hotels offer free scheduled pickup and drop-off. If you're driving, you can get your parking ticket validated. Here you'll find the **Super Pola Supermarket** stocked with everything from groceries to a deli counter, as well as wine and liquor sections. Boutiques include amber jewelry stores, cigar shops, and plenty of American designer apparel boutiques on the 2nd floor. Caribbean Cinemas and arts and crafts stores are also on-site. At the far western end of the strip, you'll find Noah Restaurant and ATMs. On the eastern edge are a new row of shops, as well as an outdoor amphitheater for concerts and festivals.

There are plenty of local souvenirs and Dominican cigars in the beachfront shopping alley at **El Galeón del Pirata** (Los Corales, Bávaro, next to Solas Cafe).

# FOOD
## Cafés
If you're looking for that cup of java first thing in the morning, head to **Dalias** (Plaza Turquesa, Los Corales, tel. 809/466-1009, reposteriadalias@gmail.com, 7am-10pm daily, US$1.50-5) and sit on its outdoor patio (though street-side) or in its cool interior. Enjoy fresh-baked French pastries, omelets (including a Dominican *mangú* option), and quiche, in addition to gourmet coffee. If you're just in search of a cheap dollar coffee

1: Palma Real Shopping Village's open-air food court; 2: Dalias

and affordable local breakfast, try **Fast Chef** (Av. Alemania, Los Corales, tel. 829/774-8883, 10am-2am daily, US$1.50-2).

For fresh fruits and fruit smoothies made fresh while you wait—or batidas, made Dominican-style with milk added—find the delightful **Tropical Fruit** shack, one block behind Plaza Turquesa (Calle Las Olas, corner of Avenida Alemania, no phone, 9am-5pm daily, US$3 for large cup).

## Dominican
**La Posada de Gladys** (Av. Alemania, Los Corales, no phone, 8am-10pm daily, US$3-10) offers your basic rice and beans plates, served under a thatched open-air *palapa* with old wicker chairs and tables. It's not as delicious as it used to be, though Sunday offerings tend to be better and fresher. If you don't have a car and are staying in this area, you'll have few other choices to eat Dominican. If you can, head to the downtown area for better options. Expect *bachata* and merengue echoing in the background, and random people shuffling in and out of the dining room and bar area.

Across the street is **Fast Chef** (Av. Alemania, Los Corales, tel. 829/774-8883, 8am-midnight daily, US$1.50-5), where budget travelers converge outdoors on the casual restaurant's communal picnic tables to enjoy orders of *mofongo* (a Dominican mashed plantain specialty), fried chicken, burgers, nachos, or the local rice and beans menu of the day.

Downtown at the crossroads between Bávaro and Punta Cana, **El Pollo Boracho** (across from Sunix gas station, Cruce Blvd. Aeropuerto, tel. 809/754-4401, 11am-11pm Mon.-Sat.) is easily the cheapest meal in this area of resorts, serving Dominican food, served cafeteria-style. Ask for the *plato del día*—usually priced at RD$150 or US$3.35—consisting of rice and beans with a choice of chicken or beef. Another option is **La Casita de Yeya** (next to Coco Bongo, Downtown Punta Cana, casitadeyeya@gmail.com, noon-1am daily, from US$5-17) offering all the Dominican specialties such as sancocho or fried fish Sosúa-style, and others with a twist like *chivo al ron* or goat in a rum sauce.

## Caribbean and International

Occupying an intimate corner of the BlueMall Puntacana, facing a large fountain pool, the glass-walled ★ **Bachata Rosa** (Boulevard Turístico, corner of Carretera Juanillo, tel. 809/784-4047, bachatarosapc@gmail.com, noon-2am daily, US$10-25, reserve a week ahead) is the toughest place to get a table in the DR at the time of writing. It's owned by Dominican and Latin music legend Juan Luis Guerra, the man credited with taking merengue and *bachata* onto the world stage. Named after his famous love song and Grammy-winning 1990 album, the restaurant is a long-planned partnership between Guerra and Dominican restaurant group SBG, which owns seven of the country's finest dining establishments. The sensory experience begins as you stroll down Bachata Rosa's dimly lit, cobblestoned exterior corridor, leading towards the restaurant's two entrances: one towards the SBG Salon for lunch, and the other for dinner in the Bachata Rosa Salon, a red-lit, colonial-style dining room where live merengue performances take place at night. The entrance hallway murals will plunge you into a colorful visual tribute to Dominican culture with typical scenes of Dominican life in the Colonial City: a local bus, a hair salon, a street painter's stand, a *colmado* (or *bodega* in Dominican-speak), and balcony railings with clothes hanging out to dry. The menu and indoor dining area is no less impressive. A series of open or glass-framed kitchens sit in view of diners, including a smoke pit grill to smoke veggies, fish, and meat; tandoori ovens at the back making fresh naan bread; and an outdoor terrace with a pizza oven. The Dominican, Latin, and international fusion menu includes lamb samosas, mini *arepas*, Peruvian ceviche, pit grill-roasted chicken (a popular pick), and bamboo-steamed whitefish. It's like a fine tour from the DR to the world, and back.

Walk one block west and you'll find the Plaza Turquesa strip, also in the Los Corales section of Bávaro, lined with trendy but laid-back cafés and restaurants attracting locals and expats. It's particularly lively at night, when folks come out to dine with live music or grab drinks on sidewalk terraces. Try **Dalia's** (Av. Alemania, tel. 809/466-1009, reposteriadalias@gmail.com, 7am-10pm daily, US$3-10), a European bistro with gourmet sandwiches, quiche slices, and wine that you can enjoy on the terrace or in an air-conditioned interior. There's a flat-screen TV in the all-white interior for those who prefer air-conditioning, a couch, and some football.

**Citrus** (Plaza Turquesa, Los Corales, tel. 809/455-2026, noon-11pm Mon.-Sat., closed Sun., US$5-12) serves excellent bacon cheeseburgers alongside seafood options. It fills up quickly in the evening; get there around 6pm to avoid a long wait.

★ **Wacamole** (Los Corales behind Playa Turquesa, Calle Aruba, tel. 829/750-1777, 11am-2am, US$5-15) is a huge hit thanks to its tasty Mexican fare, excellent margaritas, selection of mezcal and tequilas, and laid-back, thatch-roofed outdoor terrace. The latest music videos play on a giant flat screen above the bar, while diners fill up on guacamole served in a Mayan ceramic bowl, churrasco or shrimp quesadillas, tortillas, and tacos. All tortillas are made in-house with Mexican-imported masa flour (you'll taste the distinction). There are daily happy hour specials to boot, including live music.

The beachfront lounge **Huracán Café** (Playa Los Corales, tel. 809/552-1046, giacomo.zatti@yahoo.it, 10am-11pm daily, US$5-15) is popular with the young and trendy, from residents to visitors. A DJ spins on the beach while you lie back on an all-white daybed or sofa and sip on cocktails. The restaurant serves a basic menu of pastas and salads.

A two-minute walk from the noisy restaurant row, tucked down a quiet alley, **Pranama** (Plaza El Dorado, Los Corales, behind Cicolello Supermarket, tel. 809/552-6767, pranamapc@hotmail.com, 5am-11pm

Mon.-Sat., US$5-10) started out strong in Bávaro's incredibly diverse cuisine scene, with authentic homemade Indian meals courtesy of chef Krishna Duddukuri, who hails from South India and moved to the DR after training in Geneva. The quality has dipped a notch, but it's decent if you are craving Indian food. Order the coconut rice, which is blended with shaved coconut bits and peppers. Soak it in the ghost vindaloo—a spicy, tender goat stew with potatoes—or the tikka masala, among other options. Wash your meal down with a *lassi*—mango, rose, or passion fruit flavored.

To take it up a notch for a special occasion, dress up and splurge on dinner at ★ **Passion by Martin Berasategui** (Paradisus Palma Real, tel. 809/688-5000, US$65pp tasting menu), the AAA 4-Diamond restaurant ranking among the best in the Caribbean. The chef, winner of seven Michelin stars, puts out a creative menu that will surprise, from monkfish to perfectly seared steaks to herb-crusted tuna. Go for the seven-course tasting menu for a fun food lover's experience.

## Pizza

The best thin-crust, wood-fired pizza you'll have is at **Venezia** (Av. Alemania, Plaza Costa Bávaro, tel. 829/912-6969, 7am-midnight daily, US$5-10), a small, Italian-owned spot reached by car on a road with otherwise no other attractions. Still, it's worthwhile and only a short motorbike ride from your Bávaro digs. There are 36 pizza combinations, baked fresh while you wait, as well as pasta, risotto, and seafood dishes. The small, leafy outdoor terrace fills up quicker than the inside air-conditioned space.

## Seafood

★ **TOC** (beachfront, Los Corales, tel. 809/864-2359, www.playaturquesaoceanclub.com, 10am-8pm daily, US$10-15), part of the Turquesa Ocean Club vacation condominium complex, is a perfect stand-alone beachfront bar and restaurant, encouraging you with a "don't worry, beach happy" sign. Select dishes include a popular seafood ceviche, red snapper, grilled octopus, and fish burgers. Their beach cocktails are excellent, if pricey. Go on Sunday for live music at 3pm.

**Capitán Cook** (Cortecito Beach, tel. 809/552-0645, capitancook@live.com, noon-11pm daily, US$3-15) is well known for its freshly caught fish and attracts plenty of Dominicans. Pick your table alfresco, followed by a short walk to a giant wooden trunk filled with ice and the latest catch of the day. Your choice will be weighed to determine price—pick a size you can afford—and then you sit back and relax at your table with views of Cortecito Beach and watch the world go by. You'll spot the entrance from the beach thanks to a fishnet hanging over the gate. You can also access it from the main road in Cortecito.

**Noah Restaurant** (San Juan Shopping Center, Av. Barceló, tel. 809/455-1060, www.noahrestaurant.com, noon-midnight daily, US$10-25) is popular for its sushi, pizza, and Sicilian pasta, among other options. The food is decent, though not outstanding, and there's both indoor and outdoor seating. Across from the restaurant, **Quicksilver Surf and Crepes** (tel. 809/466-1726, 9am-11pm daily, US$3-10) doubles as a surf apparel store and a crêperie/café. It's convenient if you're hanging out at the mall.

## Vegan and Vegetarian

Vegans will find unique offerings at **AmaLuna Food Vibration** (Los Corales, tel. 809/552-0664, www.amalunarestaurant.com, 7:30pm-10:30pm Mon. and Wed.-Sun., US$12-28), set inside a delightful garden turned restaurant. Pricey five-course organic tasting menus (US$28 pp) are offered with a choice of Japanese, Indian, Italian, and Spanish cuisine options. There are also more affordable single-plate pasta dishes. The presentation is creative though the flavors might be lacking for the non-vegan. Note that boxing up food is not favored; only order what you can finish. **Balicana Asian Restaurant** (Cocotal Golf & Country Club, tel. 809/455-7432, www.balicana.com, 10am-4pm Mon.-Sat., US$5-20) offers a taste of Thailand in the Caribbean. They keep changing their location every year; they've most recently set up inside Cocotal condominium complex, still in Bávaro. You'll need a car or taxi to reach it.

You'll find vegetarian options at **Pranama** (Plaza El Dorado, Los Corales, behind Cicolello Supermarket, tel. 809/552-6767, pranamapc@hotmail.com, 5am-11pm Mon.-Sat., US$5-10), including chickpea curry, spinach curry, and lentils, along with coconut, mango or lemon rice, salads, and potato sides.

## ACCOMMODATIONS

Note that all prices listed are for double occupancy during high season. Rates can drop dramatically during low season, and hotels regularly list their specials online. Bávaro hosts more affordable resorts closer to the small beach towns of Cortecito and Los Corales, while Üvero Alto, the more remote area north of Bávaro, is home to a handful of luxury resorts catering mostly to couples.

### Under US$50

Backpackers flock to rustic **Macao Beach Hostel** (Calle Los Coquitos, tel. 829/913-6267, www.macaobeachhostel.com, US$15-29), located adjacent to a farm, where it's all about communing with fellow travelers. A series of basic, blue zinc-roof cabins offer double rooms, or a shared five-bed dorm (US$15), all outfitted with nets, centered on a fire pit. Showers and bathrooms are outdoors. Camping is also available (US$12/night for one tent, US$20/two tents, with tents and mattress/linen provided) The hostel is approximately a 15-minute walk to the beach, and near local shops serving daily meals. Bring insect repellant and towels.

### US$50-150

One of the few affordable and small hotels in Bávaro, ★ **Cortecito Inn** (Calle Pedro Mir 1, tel. 809/552-0639, US$50, includes breakfast) is a decent spot to lay your head while staying a stone's throw away from Cortecito Beach. It sits on the active main drag of this

small beach community, steps from popular restaurants and bars like Onno's and Capitán Cook. The hotel's courtyard features a pool surrounded by tall coconut trees. Rooms are clean and basic but offer air-conditioning, as well as pool-facing balconies if you choose.

The beachfront **Los Corales Villas & Apartments** (Calle Marcio Veloz Maggiolo, tel. 809/891-5915, from US$110) are off the main drag yet still close the beach and offer a range of studios and apartments for those who wish to enjoy self-catered, spacious accommodations where you can come and go as you please. Restaurants and entertainment are nearby. There's a pool on-site, and amenities include free wireless Internet and 24-hour security. The only nuisance is the additional daily US$7 electricity fee and the music from surrounding resorts at night.

**Barceló Dominican Beach Resort** (Av. Alemania, U.S. tel. 800/227-2356 or 809/221-0714, www.barcelo.com, dominicanbeach@barcelo.com, from US$150) is probably the most affordable of the all-inclusive resorts and of all the Barceló hotels for couples and families. It's also super convenient, which is its greatest strength. It sits smack in the heart of Los Corales, facing its beautiful beach, and therefore within easy on-foot access to local restaurants, nightlife, shopping, and water sports. Over 700 rooms attract a young international crowd, and the resort offers seven à la carte restaurants, three buffets, and three pools. The all-white rooms are clean and basic and have terraces, mini fridges, and coffeemakers. You can easily hop on the local *guagua* and cheaply go up and down the Bávaro drag to San Juan Shopping Center. That also means there's plenty of noise and little privacy.

A good value for families or traveling friends, **Whala!Bávaro** (Los Corales, tel. 809/688-1612, www.whalabavaro.com, US$130-172) is a small classic beachfront all-inclusive with a lively vibe. It offers 150 double or superior rooms and suites, three bars (closing by midnight), three pools, and two restaurants. Superior rooms have

# Beyond the Resort

If you're staying in Bávaro or Punta Cana, you'll notice that every other white van or safari truck running down the main road is a tour company hauling its next bunch of tourists to a number of popular and often crowded excursions. But escaping the hotel and creating your own adventures is a definite possibility. Rent a compact car (Nelly RAC, Carretera Higuey-Miches, near Petromovil gas station, tel. 809/687-7797 or 809/959-1241, www.nellyrac.com, from US$20/day, 8am-11pm daily) and drive at your leisure to some of the natural sights, shopping malls, or restaurants in the area, from Bávaro to Punta Cana to Cap Cana. Venture this region and you'll be rewarded richly with culture and country scenery. But even if it's just to shop and wander to sights on your own, it's a more authentic experience.

- Drive to Scape Park (page 117) and purchase tickets on-site (or online to save some bucks).
  Palma Real, BlueMall, and San Juan Shopping Center are all easily accessible, with ample parking space and shopping, food, and movie theaters. You can also head solo to El Mundo Auténtico to shop for Dominican coffee, cacao, and cigars.

- To sample the excellent international food options that Punta Cana is known for, drive to Punta Cana Marina for a nice meal on the water at La Yola. Or go for breakfast, drinks, or lunch in Cap Cana (you'll need a solid GPS to find your way around the maze; and take your passport to show at the security gates to this private zone). Sanctuary Cap Cana is a good option, or head one block to Juanillo Beach for some food directly on the beach.

- Beach clubs offer a worthy day escape as well, and you'll be able to make your way solo to Pearl or Playa Blanca for additional sand-and-sea days with excellent food and cocktails away from the resort.

- For a bit more adventure, rise early and head on a day trip north to Miches (page 124), an easy drive up a smooth highway, and glimpse rural scenes and spectacular, sometimes undeveloped, Esmeralda and Limon beaches. Another day trip is to head south to Boca de Yuma (page 121), where you can hike dry caves inside the Parque Nacional Cotubanamá,
  lunch in town over the water, or go on a riverboat ride around this historic fishing village where Ponce de León once roamed. If you'd rather tour with a small group, history lovers with solid Caribbean driving skills should head west to Higuey to tour the basilica and get a glimpse of a typical hectic, industrial Dominican town.

- If you're decided on hopping on a tour, then opt for Colonial Tours (tel. 809/688-5285, www. colonialtours.com.do, US$95) which offers a packed Super Truck Safari tour that offers good bang for your buck as far as organized tours are concerned. You'll ride in military-style off-road trucks blasting merengue out into the countryside of the Altagracia province. In just about 30 minutes outside of Punta Cana, you'll find yourself plunged into the real Dominican *campo* after first driving through the bustling iconic town of La Otra Banda, where the meat shops hang flesh outside, and Higüey, home to the most important shrine and basilica in the DR. Past these urban hubs, the day involves bumpy roads, pastureland with grazing cows and horses, a herd of bulls holding up traffic, coffee and cacao farms in El Bonao for tastings in a Dominican yard, and sugarcane fields and horseback riding at Rancho Valencia, among other exhilarating activities and sights on this full-day trip. The day ends with a stop at the breathtaking Macao Beach, where you'll have enough time to swim and watch the surfers and boogie boarders trying their luck. Another solid option is Mike's Punta Cana Tours (tel. 809/981-7989, www.puntacanamike.com, US$89-120), albeit pricey like most group excursions out of Punta Cana. Tours visit places such as Boca de Yuma or out for a day at Playa Macao. Tours begins in a lower-income neighborhood in Friusa, just a 10-minute drive outside of the all-inclusive enclave of Punta Cana, where you get an inside glimpse of the Haitian immigrant life as well as background on the Dominican Republic's geography and educational system before touring the local school. The second part involves a lengthy stop at El Mundo Auténtico, which could be done solo, but if you're intent on going with others, you'll still get some value from the main destination of the day that you choose.

balconies, and suites have Jacuzzis. All amenities are included—full bath, satellite TV, air-conditioning, and mini fridge. But wireless Internet and the safe are an additional fee. The daily buffet restaurant provides tasty Caribbean dishes. A second, à la carte restaurant rotating Mediterranean and Dominican food is at your expense (though, as you are close to a handful of excellent local restaurants around the hotel, you should skip it).

## Over US$150

With 272 rooms facing a glorious stretch of Playa Bávaro, the adults-only **Iberostar Grand Bávaro** (U.S. tel. 888/774-0040, www.iberostargrandbavaro.com, from US$250-330 pp) stays true to the brand's luxurious offering. Enjoy butler service, upscale furnishings and linens, and marble baths. The oceanfront luxury suites are worth the splurge—they come with reserved poolside cabanas. Equally tempting are the pool suites with walkout access from your terrace for a private dip at all hours. The resort provides free wireless Internet for guests—a rare perk among all-inclusives—and there's an 18-hole golf course on-site. There isn't much of a party scene, but you'll want to ask about the Ship Bar.

An innovative option awaits at ★ **Blue Beach Punta Cana** (Carretera Cabeza de Toro, tel. 809/468-2583, www.bluebeachpuntacana.com, from US$140), boasting ultra-spacious, self-catering luxury junior and master suites, as well as rooftop suites (ideal for honeymooners), hugging a gorgeous series of lake-like swimming pools that run through the heart of the complex. Located in the fishing village of Cabeza de Toro, the resort reflects a new trend to offer independent travelers more options in the area than the typical all-inclusive. The suites are fully furnished, counting even dryer and washer, full kitchen equipment, espresso machines, rainfall showers, and spacious terraces outfitted with a Jacuzzi tub. There are two restaurants on-site—the beachfront open terrace at Blue Wave serves tasty beach-type fare or seafood (the burgers and ceviche are excellent)

for lunch and dinner, while La Caracola is for buffet meals (an all-inclusive option is possible, for an added fee). Perks include 24-hour room service, poolside drink service, and random snack offerings. Although the beachfront isn't as scenic as Bávaro Beach, it's uncrowded and good for a swim, plus the resort's intimate size and the ample parking space directly beside your suite means you can come and go as you please in your rental. There's on-site water sports entertainment and a kids club, or you can hop on the shuttle at night to Kviar disco. A spa was being built at the time of writing.

Ideally located adjacent to the Palma Real Shopping Village and across from the Cocotal Golf & Country Club (unlimited rounds included), the luxurious ★ **Paradisus Palma Real Golf & Spa Resort** (Bávaro Beach, tel. 809/687-9923, www.paradisus.com, paradisus.punta.cana@melia.com, from US$600) oozes romance with its central courtyard opening onto the pool, sea, and towering coconut trees. Restaurants are a highlight here, notably the AAA 4-Diamond restaurant Passion by Martin Berasategui, a seven-time Michelin-starred chef. For ultra-luxurious pampering, ask about "the Royal Service experience."

Sited north of Bávaro, the luxury boutique all-inclusive **Zoetry Agua** (Üvero Alto, U.S. tel. 888/496-3879, www.zoetryresorts.com/agua, US$235-715) has a beautiful stretch of beach and is popular with couples looking to pamper themselves and decompress away from it all with the help of an assigned butler. The grounds are immaculate and include 96 thatch luxury suites with wooden floors, soaking tubs, and all the bells and whistles. Think 24-hour in-suite dining, two infinity pools, four restaurants, three bars with top-shelf liquor, and an on-site spa. The "endless privileges" perks are free wireless Internet, 20-minute massages, and a 45-minute horseback ride.

Another great pick for a honeymoon escape is ★ **Excellence Punta Cana** (Playa Üvero Alto, U.S. tel. 866/540-2585, www.excellenceresorts.com, US$280-570). The five-star, adults-only resort, on the northern tip of the whole Punta Cana area, sits along 48 kilometers (30 miles) of golden beach and is ideal if all you want to do is eat, drink, bask in the sun, and indulge in some of the most beautiful resort suites you'll experience. Think in-room jet tubs and marble bathrooms, see-through glass rain showers and a fully stocked bar. The pool snakes around the resort and is a primary attraction—floaties provided. The restaurants are decent for an all-inclusive, including the Grill and the Market. Whatever you do, don't miss experiencing the two-floor luxury spa, especially the hydrotherapy circuit. For an extra fee, Excellence Club members get additional perks: a private butler, access to a private beach with drink service, and a lounge with hot foods and top-shelf liquor. Wireless access is free throughout the property.

**CHIC Punta Cana by Royalton** (Playa Üvero Alto, U.S. tel. 800/558-7414, www.chicpuntacanahotel.com, US$420-900) is one of the newest adults-only boutique resorts in the ever-growing Üvero Alto area north of Punta Cana. It offers 323 luxury suites, all of them facing the Atlantic Ocean. It truly delivers on its promise of an all-exclusive experience, from neon purple-lit rooms to rain showers to reservation-free fine dining—including a unique Moroccan restaurant—to free international calls home. The ultimate in exclusivity is the CHIC Mansion: a 1,068-square-meter (11,500-square-foot) villa with six luxurious rooms and seven baths, a breathtaking pool and bar area, a wine cellar, and a lounge fully stocked with premium liquor.

## INFORMATION AND SERVICES

### Money

You won't find ATMs in the Cortecito or Corales areas unless you are staying inside a resort. There are machines in Friusa town (you'll need a taxi ride or car), but your closest bets are the ATMs inside **Palma Real Shopping Village.** There's also one inside Super Lama supermarket on the edge of the shopping complex. Another good location

is at **San Juan Shopping Center,** inside the supermarket as well as on the edge of the mall next to Noah Restaurant. You'll find a **Scotiabank** branch in Plaza Brisas, in Bávaro.

### Groceries

**BAM Market** (Plaza Turquesa, Los Corales, tel. 809/455-7344, bammarket@hotmail.com, 8am-10pm daily) sells groceries, a wide variety of wines, and over 50 imported beers. They even deliver. A few steps over on the adjacent block is **Plaza El Dorado,** where you'll find **Supermercado Cicollela** (tel. 809/552-0143, 9am-10pm daily) with a small selection of groceries and drinks.

### Laundry

Next to Plaza El Dorado, the **Punta Cana Laundromat** (Plaza Arenal Caribe, tel. 809/552-9970, 7am-8pm daily, US$2.23/load, US$4.50 to dry, additional US$2.23 for dropoff) can meet your needs for clean apparel. Call ahead before heading over because the owner tends to close on a whim when he needs to run an errand or have breakfast. There's open Internet access for customers if you want to wash and surf.

### Health and Emergencies

For serious concerns aside from the quick clinic visits—usually available on-site at resorts—head to **Hospiten Bávaro** (Carretera Higüey-Punta Cana, tel. 809/686-1414, bavaro@hospiten.com), about a 15-minute drive north from Punta Cana Airport, with a 24-hour emergency room, multilingual medical staff in various departments ranging from pediatrics to cardiology, and high-end medical equipment, including an ICU and X-ray machines. Another solid option is **Centro Médico Punta Cana** (Av. España 1, Los Corales, tel. 809/552-1506, or for emergencies tel. 809/473-7283, www.centromedicopuntacana.com), with 24-hour emergency care. There are **pharmacies** in both Los Corales—at Plaza El Dorado—and in Cortecito. Resorts also carry first aid kits and often have supplies of pain medicine and aspirin; or you can buy such over-the-counter drugs from the supermarket or local stores.

A branch of the tourist police, **CESTUR** (Av. Estados Unidos, Esq. Friusa, tel. 809/754-3082 or 809/552-1060) is open 24 hours next to the Bávaro Express bus terminal. There is another near the airport at Puntacana Village.

## GETTING THERE
### Air

The private **Punta Cana International Airport** (PUJ) serves most passengers who are flying into the southeast region. With two terminals, it's the second largest in the Caribbean, receiving over two million passengers a year on direct flights from at least 96 cities. Check with your hotel on whether they offer a free shuttle transfer. Otherwise contact the responsible and friendly **Juan** from **Lillian Tours and Transfers** (tel. 829/570-4810), the driver I use when in the area. **Dominican Plus** (tel. 809/481-0707, www.dominicanplus.com) has reasonably priced nonstop transfers for US$32 one-way to Bávaro-area hotels. You can also book online.

### Bus

Those flying into Santo Domingo can hop on buses run by **Expreso Bávaro** (Calle Juan Sánchez Ramírez, corner of Av. Máximo Gómez, Gazcue, tel. 809/682-9670, www.expresobavaro.com, departures every two hours 7am-4pm, US$8; in Bávaro, Cruce de Friusa. tel. 809/552-1678). Buses are the large coach type and nicely air-conditioned, with the occasional movie showing during the 3- to 4-hour journey, but there is no Wi-Fi on board. When loading luggage, let the driver know your hotel name or destination area (such as Los Corales) so they will tell you where to get off to connect with a taxi. The bus makes multiple spots to accommodate travelers (expect a four-hour journey with those additional stops).

Hard-core backpackers might want to skip the fancy coach and hop on a series of *guaguas* from the capital; you'd have to switch again in Higüey, the major hub in these parts, for a second bus to the Bávaro area. It's cheaper (about US$5 to Higüey, US$2 second leg) and you'll get a full cultural experience, but if you have a lot of luggage and/or don't speak Spanish, I don't recommend it.

### Car

The smooth **Coral Highway** linking Santo Domingo to the Punta Cana area has cut a 4-hour journey down to just 2.75 hours. The road bypasses Higüey, which helps. There are three tollbooths along the way, at RD$100 each. The drive is easy and pleasant, past sugar-cane fields, grazing cows, and open landscapes. This same highway will take you to La Romana in just 45 minutes.

## GETTING AROUND
### Taxis

Taxis are a lot more expensive in Punta Cana. You'll notice this when you start paying US$10 each way within Bávaro no matter how short the ride is. Most resorts post prices to sample destinations; consult the list and agree on a fee before entering a taxi. Alternatively, befriend a local driver and negotiate a price for taking you around during your stay. Try **Juan** from **Lillian Tours and Transfers** (tel. 829/570-4810).

Another way to save yourself a lot of money: hop on a *guagua* or local bus. They travel up and down the main drag in Bávaro to any shopping center, resort, or restaurant you want to reach in Cortecito or Los Corales. You just need the occasional dose of patience because you never know if you'll wait 5 minutes or 30 on the side of the road, but the low fare of RD$30 (under a dollar) will remind you of that. There are numerous tour operator minivans passing along the main road too, so don't get confused. The *guagua* will have a sign that reads "Traumabapu," on the front of the bus, as well as "Transport Higüey-Bávaro-Punta Cana" on the side. Just hail it from anywhere along the main road going in the direction you're headed. They pass every 15-20 minutes.

Note that they don't travel south of the airport to Punta Cana hotels. That's considered a private-access road and used only by licensed tour and taxi drivers.

## Car

Most visitors choose to stick to their resorts and hop on tours to explore the vicinity, but you can get a better feel for the country by getting your own vehicle and roaming around the countryside. Rates are usually better when booked online—they start around US$35— than once you are in Punta Cana. You must be over 25 and have a valid driver's license. Try **Budget Rental Car** (PUJ airport, tel. 809/480-8153, www.budget.com.do, 7am-9pm daily), **Avis** (Av. Barceló Km 6.5, tel. 809/688-1354, 8am-5pm daily, or at PUJ airport, tel.

809/959-0534, www.avis.com.do, 8am-9pm daily), **Europcar** (Carretera Friusa-Melia, tel. 809/686-2861, www.europcar.com.do, 8am-6pm, or at PUJ airport 8am-10pm), or the local **Melo Rent Car** (Los Corales, tel. 829/669-2723, rentcarmelo@gmail.com).

## Air

Charter flights are now more popular for getting from Bávaro to other remote parts of the island such as Samaná and Puerto Plata. Contact **Dominican Plus** (tel. 809/481-0707, www.dominicanplus.com, from US$539 one-way for 1-3 to Samaná, or US$879 to Puerto Plata). Another option is **Dominican Shuttles** (tel. 809/931-4073, www.dominicanshuttles.com, from US$369 to Samaná).

# Punta Cana

South of the Punta Cana Airport is the area labeled Punta Cana proper, and south of that, Cap Cana. This area is known for its beaches and exclusive resorts. But Punta Cana also offers plenty of outdoor activities, including hiking in natural parks, dipping in sinkholes, and golfing.

## SIGHTS
### Indigenous Eyes Ecological Reserve

On private property owned by the Puntacana Ecological Foundation, the **Indigenous Eyes Ecological Reserve** (tel. 809/959-9221, www.puntacana.org, 8am-5pm daily, US$50 entrance fee, US$67 Segway tour, US$10 for Puntacana Resort & Club guests) is a protected 1,500-acre lowland subtropical forest with a verdant, shaded trail leading to 12 freshwater lagoons. The most popular of those lagoons is the freshwater **Ojos Indígenas**— or Indigenous Eyes, as the Taíno called these pools for their oval shape—which is open to the public for a swim in its turquoise and emerald water. The 20-minute hike to reach the

lagoon is easy, but requires closed-toe shoes to avoid stubbed toes on stones and other protruding bits of wood. Expect to stop several times to see the various lagoons on your path, and the flora surrounding the narrow trail. There are maps indicating your whereabouts as you progress on your hike.

Once you reach the main deck over the lagoon and are ready to swim, walk a few steps farther up the trail where a jumping platform awaits. Leap just a few feet into the crisp, cool waters.

TOP EXPERIENCE

## ★ Scape Park

Comprising nearly one million square meters, **Scape Park** (Cap Cana, tel. 809/469-7231, www.scapepark.com, 8am-6pm daily, US$149 full day includes meals, US$69 Hoyo Azul, transport included) is a green escape ideal for a half day out of your gated Punta Cana hotel and into the great outdoors. This natural theme park—at least a 40-minute ride from Bávaro and 20 minutes from downtown Punta Cana—is set up and landscaped beautifully. Marked trails and gardens lead to various activities. The cenotes are one of the highlights here. The most visited is the **Hoyo Azul** sinkhole, 14 meters (45 feet) deep and sitting below a 75-meter-high (246-foot) limestone cliff. Locals discovered it only recently. The **hike** to the mineral waters of Hoyo Azul is a mere 15 minutes from the park entrance, taking you past medicinal plants, endemic species and orchids, and an impressive suspension bridge. It can get a tad crowded when tour groups arrive in the morning and afternoon, so visit here either very early or at lunchtime.

The second sinkhole on a shorter hike is a stunner: **Cenote Indígena Las Ondas** is a cool pool buried deep in an ancient Taíno cave and with only a sliver of sunlight reaching it. Blue underwater lights give it an eerie feel. The trail to this sinkhole is lined by informative boards on Taíno history and culture, complete with mystical sounds (courtesy of hidden speakers) and an impressive winding wooden staircase that leads to the water. So beautiful is the scenery that it beats any upscale spa you've ever visited. Look out for Taíno pictograms on rocks, possibly the face of a Taíno god.

The park also offers the longest **zip line course** in Punta Cana, with platforms atop cliffs. The **equestrian center** is home to 30 horses and probably the most professional setup I've seen, complete with a training ring, video tutorials, and trails taking you through the forest's winding paths. **Buggies, mountain bikes,** and **caving** are available as well. Meals are included with a combo of two excursions, and shuttles are provided to all the major hotels up and down the coast. To add some sea to your inland excursions, ask about Scape Park's Juanillo VIP catamaran cruise, taking you along the glitzy Cap Cana coast and marina for a cool US$200.

## BEACHES
### ★ Playa Juanillo
**Playa Juanillo** is absolutely breathtaking. Perhaps its allure is that it isn't overdeveloped and only supports a couple of restaurants. Or maybe it's that the sun shines particularly bright in this area, causing the sand to literally sparkle and the sea to turn a phosphorescent blue. With incredibly tall coconut trees, it's one of the most memorable beaches in the DR. It's worth coming here if only for a cocktail or a fresh coconut and the view.

Indigenous Eyes Ecological Reserve

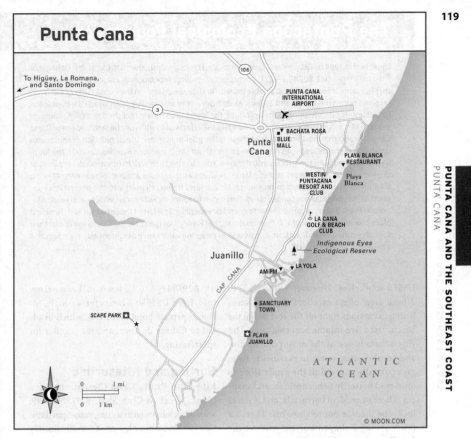

# Punta Cana

## Other Beaches

The sargassum issue has spread to the Punta Cana coastline, so don't be surprised to see this particular seaweed floating in the water or piled along the shores despite daily efforts to clean up. It doesn't change the beauty of the place, but is a slight nuisance. In addition to your resort's beachfront, you'll find two additional stretches, where you can escape for more food options and more brilliant white sand in your toes.

**Punta Cana Beach,** in the area south of the Punta Cana Airport known as "Punta Cana proper," is actually not as impressive or long as you'd expect, but it still offers white sand and pretty Caribbean views facing the private Westin Puntacana. Next door next to the Westin is **Playa Blanca,** a small and more charming white-sand stretch delighting a blend of locals and visitors thanks to the on-site kitesurfing and paddleboarding shop, a dive center, and the excellent open-air **Playa Blanca Restaurant.** Sundays and long weekends find this beach particularly busy with Dominicans visiting from other parts of the coast and La Romana. Expect to see the young and fabulous socializing here.

## SPORTS AND RECREATION

### Diving and Snorkeling

On Playa Blanca in Punta Cana south of the airport, PADI dive shop **Blue Vision Adventures** (Playa Blanca, tel. 809/455-0833, www.bluevisionadventures.net, US$80/dive,

# The Puntacana Ecological Foundation

Launched in 1994 by Grupo Puntacana and located on its grounds, the **Puntacana Ecological Foundation** (tel. 809/959-9221, www.puntacana.org, fepc@puntacana.com) is a nonprofit that has been a pioneer in sustainable tourism and development on the Punta Cana coast. It has received numerous grants and awards. Aside from an organic garden, from which the Puntacana Resort hotels procure some of their produce, the foundation runs established and pilot programs in a constant effort to conserve and to mitigate the effects of tourism on the land and sea of Punta Cana. Among the most important of these is the goal to increase the population of rhinoceros iguanas, a prehistoric species once found throughout the Dominican Republic. In 2002, the foundation reintroduced the species into the area. You can visit their walled home on the grounds of the foundation and marvel at these large creatures as they roam around in near-natural living conditions that allow them to reproduce, before later being released into the natural environment. Other projects run by the foundation, open to tours, include coral gardens and rehabilitation off Playa Blanca, worm composting, and beekeeping. The last of those has earned them first place more than once in the DR's annual National Honey Competition. Be sure to ask about their lionfish women's handicraft project, as well as other initiatives such as community recycling and a biweekly farmers market.

US$60 snorkeling, Discover Scuba US$220 2-tank dive) offers excellent dive and snorkeling excursions right off the reef facing the beach, just a five-minute boat ride away. **The Aquarium** is one of the most popular dive and snorkel sites, home to marinelife from rays partially covered in the sandy floor to four-eyed butterfly fish, angelfish, and snapper. There's a resident barracuda, and if you're lucky, he'll come out to show off. There's a fairly strong J-shaped current around the Aquarium, so you'll need a life jacket and solid fins to help with your swim. Adjacent to the Aquarium, the **Museum** is an underwater display of Taíno god sculptures, dropped into the sea as some sort of tribute to the first rulers of the island. It makes for fun photos. Dive excursions with Blue Vision include 18-meter (60-foot) or deeper shipwrecks all close to shore. You can also book banana boat rides, fishing trips, and wakeboarding here.

## Fishing

**Blue Vision Adventures** (Playa Blanca, tel. 809/455-0833, www.bluevisionadventures.net, US$850 half day up to 6 people) has deep-sea fishing excursions. Book a catch-and-release excursion with the long-running **Mike's Marina Fishing Charters** (tel. 809/729-5164 or 829/649-6408, www.mikesmarina. info, from US$650 4 hours for 4 people, includes private hotel transfers), which heads out to Cabeza de Toro, an area popular for sportfishing.

## Surfing and Kitesurfing

**Kite Club Punta Cana** (Beachfront Playa Blanca, next to Club Med, 829/576-6399, www.kiteclubpuntacana.com, 9am-6pm daily, US$390 three-hour lesson, US$830 two-day private lessons) offers kitesurfing classes with IKO instructors right off Playa Blanca south of Punta Cana Airport.

## Parasailing

Soar 46 meters (150 feet) above the stunning Punta Cana coastline for 10 minutes—it will seem like longer—with **SeaPro Water Sports** (tel. 809/754-3632, www. seaprodivers.com, US$60 pp or US$100 double). Transportation is provided to select hotels in the area; check listings ahead of time.

## Sailing

Explore the beautiful southern tip of the coast at Cap Cana on the **Juanillo VIP** luxury catamaran trip (tel. 809/469-7231, www. scapepark.com, Mon.-Fri., US$169, includes

# Beyond the Resort:
# Day Trip to Boca de Yuma

A 45-minute drive south from Punta Cana, the fishing village of Boca de Yuma is a picturesque escape for the day, far from the madding tourist crowd. This place is an Italian expat favorite; you'll find Italian seafront restaurants perched atop cliffs, with a view reminiscent of an Italian seaside town. Home to approximately 3,000 people, Boca de Yuma is more steeped in history than you might think on first glance. Where the Yuma River meets the sea, you'll see locals sit on towering rocks for a cool breeze, fishers linger along riverbanks, and undeveloped white-sand beaches where pelicans fly about. But it's also where pirates and conquistadores once roamed and launched adventures. There isn't a whole lot happening in this once-favorite Dominican weekend getaway, but it makes for an educational and relaxing day away from your resort, while offering a glimpse of local fishing life—some of the country's best fishing is right here—and the DR's past. Head to the river close to sunset and hire a fisher to take you on a small motorized boat up and down the water (approximately US$20). Pirate Cofresí, one of the longest-lasting pirates who was caught and later executed by the Americans in 1825, often navigated along the Yuma River. You'll see his impressive original ship on display on a dry dock as you cruise along the Yuma River, placed there in honor of the pirate after locals discovered it in the water in the late 1990s. Crossing to the other side of the river lands you on a small, deserted white-sand beach.

For more inland adventure, drive to the entrance of the Parque Nacional Cotubanamá—right in Boca de Yuma—and hike the dry and impressive Cueva de Berna (RD$100/US$2.30 entry fee). You'll see a number of Taíno pictograms, particularly of Taíno faces, as you spelunk higher on the left-hand side after entering the cave. This makes it one of the most significant caves on the eastern coast, and it was recently studied by researchers from the University of Indiana.

If you'd rather explore Boca de Yuma with a tour guide, look up Mike's Punta Cana Tours (tel. 829/981-7989, www.puntacanamike.com, US$120). The trip begins in Punta Cana with a couple of hours at a local school and shopping for cigars and chocolate in town, after which you head to Boca de Yuma for a cliff-side Italian meal, a hike through Cueva de Berna, and a boat ride down the Yuma River.

Those driving or catching the guagua—you'll have to transfer in Higüey—can head over to the town of San Rafael de Yuma and visit the former home of Spanish explorer Juan Ponce de León, turned into the Museo Casa Ponce de León (7am-5pm daily, US$1.50). The conquistador arrived on the island in 1493 and fought the Taíno who lived inside what is now Parque Nacional Cotubanamá before heading out from Boca de Yuma—then known as the Port of Higüey—in 1508 to conquer Puerto Rico and discover Florida. In the museum you can view 16th-century furniture, utensils, and other artifacts that he used.

pickup). Spend all day on the blue seas, stopping for swims and a lobster lunch as well as cocktails on the diamond stretch of Playa Juanillo. The day ends at Scape Park with a dip in the Hoyo Azul sinkhole.

## Golf

In Punta Cana proper, La Cana Golf & Beach Club (Puntacana Resort & Club, tel. 809/959-2222, www.puntacana.com/golf/la-cana-golf-course, US$175, par 72, 27 holes) was designed by the celebrated Pete Dye and offers signature Caribbean Sea views—14

holes face the water—along with the most sustainable greens in the area. The hybrid grass can be irrigated with salt water. There's a clubhouse on-site, and nearby are beaches and excellent restaurants that are part of the resort.

## Horseback Riding

Scape Park (Cap Cana, tel. 809/469-7484, www.scapepark.com, US$149 full day includes meals, US$59 Hoyo Azul, transport included) offers a full equestrian center, complete with introductions to and training in horseback riding, and a stable full of gorgeous horses. If you're not up for an all-day "safari" out of town, this is the perfect choice. The dry forests and shaded paths make for an ideal place to take an hour-long ride in the bush past ancient Taíno caves. Pickups from all the major Punta Cana resorts are included.

The **Puntacana Resort & Club's El Rancho** (www.puntacana.com/to-do/horseback-riding) provides both riding classes for adult guests and horseback rides.

## Caving

This region was once the center of the Taíno civilization and the area is blessed with a handful of ancient caves previously used for Taíno ceremonies and rituals. Spelunkers will find their bliss at the **Parque Nacional Cotubanamá** (southeast entrance off dirt road after Carretera 4, 8am-5pm daily, US$2.20), at least a 1.25-hour drive south of the Punta Cana region. There, at the eastern entrance of the park in the fishing village of Boca de Yuma sits the cavernous and dry **Cueva de Berna,** one of the most important caves in the area due to its great number of petroglyphs. Along with hundreds of bats and small birds, you'll see Taíno *caritas* (little faces) carved on the walls and rocks—climb with care—on the right-hand side of the entrance. You don't need a guide to accompany you, but if you're solo, it's always best to have company.

**Scape Park** (Cap Cana, tel. 809/469-7484, www.scapepark.com, 9am-4pm daily, US$59) offers a two-hour dry cave expedition on its grounds, reached after a hike through dry forest and along an informative plant trail. The cave is equipped with a wooden staircase to lead you down into its chambers and tunnels filled with stalagmites, stalactites, and resident bats.

Take it up a notch with a full-day trip north to **Cueva Fun Fun** (pronounced "foon-foon," in Spanish), located in the lush and hilly province of Hato Mayor, at the mouth of **Parque Nacional Los Haitises** (tel. 829-909-6027, www.ambiente.gob.do/ambienterd/ecoparque/parque-nacional-los-haitises, 8am-5pm daily, US$2.20). Excursions to the cave are only out of Punta Cana; book your trip with **Rancho Capote** (Calle Duarte 12, 809/553-2656, info@cuevafunfun.net). The cave is approximately a three-hour drive from Punta Cana, but the journey is well worth the experience of exploring the largest cave in the Dominican Republic and the longest in the Caribbean region. Fun Fun—previously known as the Devil's Cave, but renamed to

La Cana Golf & Beach Club

describe the sound bats made flying around together—is filled with exhilarating moments not for the faint of heart or the unfit.

The adventure begins with a 20-minute horseback ride or hike across the private Rancho Capote's wide forestland, past fruit trees, to the trailhead. From there, it's 3.2 kilometers (2 miles) uphill on foot to the southeastern entrance of Parque Nacional Los Haitises, and then another 45 minutes through the park's wet forest to the mouth of the cave. You'll rappel 9 meters (28 feet) down into a narrow cave opening in one of the most heart-pumping moments of the trip. From there, spelunking for the mile-long journey is fairly moderate and will include wading through parts submerged by the Almirante River. Along the way you'll spot various fauna, including crabs, insects, bats, and perhaps even a stranded grass snake, as well as view pre-Columbian rock art from petroglyphs to pictographs. Bring a waterproof camera.

### 4x4 Safaris

Your best bet among the multitude of safaris being sold left and right in Punta Cana and Bávaro is to go through **Colonial Tours' Super Truck Safari** (tel. 809/688-5285, www.colonialtours.com.do, US$95), with local guides who will give you as much insight into local life as possible as you ride through the streets and dirt roads, from La Otra Banda to Higüey and into farms and sugarcane plantations. The day ends as it should: on the gorgeous beach of Macao, where you'll have time to swim at your leisure and bask in the glorious Dominican sun.

**Bávaro Runners** (tel. 829/599-7444, www.bavarorunners.com, US$55-135) is popular for its safaris as well, although they are a tad more crowded because of this. You'll head to well-known sights, including the Higüey Basilica and cacao and coffee farms.

### Spa

Almost every all-inclusive resort offers on-site spa services. But if you can spare the time,

make the drive to Punta Cana proper and the **Six Senses Spa** (Puntacana Resort & Club, tel. 809/959-7772, 9am-8pm daily, US$110), the only option in the Americas for proper pampering with an authentic Thai massage, centering your body using the Tibetan method. From the treatment rooms to the staff, this is no ordinary spa.

## ENTERTAINMENT AND EVENTS
### Bars and Nightclubs

**Oro Nightclub** (Hard Rock Hotel, Blvd. Turístico del Este Km 28, Macao, tel. 809/687-0000, www.oronightclub.com, US$70 with unlimited drinks from a set list) offers Vegas-style nightlife—complete with exorbitant prices for entry or for private tables. But then again, this isn't the place for those who want to feel like they are in the Dominican Republic.

A much better option is **Mangú** (Hotel Occidental Flamenco, tel. 809/221-8787, 11pm-4am Tues.-Sat.), a nightclub with a mix of Dominican music as well as international, and a down-to-earth, good-looking crowd.

**La Taberna de Charlo** (Cap Cana, by entrance of Al Sol Resort on 2nd floor, 6pm-midnight, US$5-10) offers a hip tavern-lounge vibe with a rooftop terrace, on the 2nd floor of the same building as AM PM Café (it's a day/night concept, so if you see the name AM PM, you're at the right spot). This is where locals gather after work for cocktails and bites—tapas, fondues, salads, subs—and live music or a DJ spinning. It's a fun spot to hang out if you're in the area.

### Casinos

The majority, if not all, of the all-inclusive resorts in this area have an on-site casino, usually located beside the nightclub. There are two popular options for those who want to try their luck outside their own resort. At 4,181 square meters (45,000 square feet), the **Hard Rock Casino** (Boulevard Turístico del Este Km 28 #74, Macao, tel. 809/687-0000, www.hardrockhotelpuntacana.com) is the largest gaming facility in the Dominican Republic and

# Beyond the Resort: Day Trip to Miches

Miches offers a perfect escape.

For a full day's beach escape close to Punta Cana yet away from the crowds, head to the beautiful coastal town of Miches, just a 1.5-hour drive north of the Üvero Alto area of Punta Cana via a newly finished highway. Settled in the late 19th century as a fishing and agricultural community, Miches and its surroundings offer stunning scenery: white-sand stretches, the rolling mountains of the Cordillera Central, and lagoons teeming with mangroves and wildlife. Punta Cana visitors have slowly started heading north to this piece of paradise, now on the radar of developers, to enjoy one of the most breathtaking mountaintop views in the DR at **Montaña Redonda** (Carretera Miches-Uvero Alto km 56, tel. 829/233-4994, www.montanaredonda.com, US$2 pp). This third-generation family-owned property, long popular with locals and increasingly so with tourists, is well worth glimpsing.

Rent a car and drive to the entrance of Montaña Redonda—there's a sign directly off the highway, approximately one hour north of Bávaro but before the village of Miches—where you'll park your car in the lot before being transported up the mountain by all-terrain trucks (US$16 ride up for group of four, US$25 for three—do not pay more). The ride up is quite excit-

has won Best of Caribbean awards. You'll find 40 unique gaming tables as well as over 400 slots here, and when you're done, you can head over to the on-site Oro Nightclub. Another popular choice is the spotless **Princess Tower Casino** (Bávaro Princess Hotel, tel. 809/552-1111, http://towercasinos.com), offering Texas hold'em poker, blackjack, and roulette. The atmosphere is lively with music and there's a free shuttle to and from the casino.

## Festivals and Cultural Events

**Jazz en el Este** (year-round, quarterly, Downtown Punta Cana) is an exciting initiative for the east coast area's musicians. Pioneered by local jazz artists, the event has grown to include Dominican and international bands of various jazz genres, from Punta Cana, La Romana, and surrounding areas. The one held in 2018 had a fantastic jazz-rock band, as well as an a capella one, among many others.

**Carnaval Punta Cana** (www.puntacana. com/to-do/carnaval-punta-cana.html, second Sunday March, dates vary, free entry in general area or VIP seated area at US$40 pp) ing, as you bump your way up to what seems like the sky. Once there, take a few minutes to take in the spectacular 360-degree panoramic views over the mountain, lake, and greenery as vultures flock overhead. Then line up to get your shot on one of various swings, strategically placed to face the views and appear as if you were swinging right into the landscape (though if you're afraid of heights, don't swing too high up). Ask for El Don, an older gentleman who works here and enjoys helping people getting the perfect angle and position—tip him at least US$2 before you depart. There are also hammocks and broomsticks for a "witch flying over the DR" postcard. Arrive by 8am so you can have the place relatively to yourself. After 9:30am, tour groups invade.

After Montaña Redonda, drive up to the small town of Miches and find its public beach; there's a sign off the main road on the right-hand side going into town indicating Playa Arriba Miches. On a good day, this stunning, nearly mile-long stretch of white sand is ideal for a dip and time away from the masses (except on Sundays).

The crème de la crème of Miches beaches, Costa Esmeralda awaits at the end of a bumpy but drivable dirt road (avoid rainy days, however) winding through lush forest. The highway turnoff is well indicated; ensure your car is at least a four-wheel drive. Pack sandwiches and a cooler before heading here. For now, there is no development on this stretch and you'll wonder why when you see just how mesmerizing this near two-mile strand is, framed by coconut trees and with water in layers of blue hues. (Head there now before tourists reach it when a luxury Club Med opens here in 2019, though even then it will still be worth it.) Otherwise, head back on the highway, going towards Punta Cana, and find Comedor Lourdes (Carretera Bavaro-Miches, across from La Topora Restaurant, near Montaña Redonda) for a lunch plate of homemade Dominican rice and beans (US$3.50) and cold sodas and beer.

Up for more nature? Head toward Playa Limon to see yet another stunning beach, or for a scheduled tour with the recently renovated Hotel La Cueva (tel. 809/519-5271, facebook.com/rancholacueva), which offers horseback rides (and more recently, quad-bike tours) down a dirt path from the lodge to Playa Limon, a postcard-perfect stretch with nothing but white sand and blue (albeit rougher) waters. From there, you'll hop on a motorboat to the freshwater Laguna Limon, exploring mangroves and birdlife. Back on shore, you'll ride your horse back to Rancho La Cueva for your return to Punta Cana. You can go on your own to the ranch, or you can arrange your trip with El Cedro Eco Tours (tel. 829/659-1756, pickups for groups of up to 15); drive to their office and the charge is just US$6 per person to Montana Redonda and Laguna Limon from El Cedro, or US$13 per person to Limon. They can also arrange trips to Playa Esmeralda.

is organized by the Puntacana Group and is set up in Puntacana Village. Around 15 carnival troupes attend from around the country, sometimes joined by groups from neighboring islands such as Aruba, Haiti, and St. Martin. It's not the same as the authentic in-the-street carnival parades in other parts of the Dominican Republic, but if you're in the Punta Cana area for a while and have cash to spare, it could be worth it. The event includes post-carnival concerts with merengue, *bachata,* and reggaeton artists.

## SHOPPING

Aside from shopping options in town or in Bávaro, within the Punta Cana enclave is Puntacana Village (809/959-5006, www.puntacanavillage.com), your one-stop shopping center with the Galerias Puntacana mall for souvenir shops and an on-site supermarket. The upscale BlueMall Puntacana (tel. 809/784-4001, www.bluemallpuntacana.com.do, 10am-9pm Mon.-Sat., 8pm close Sun.) is lined with designer boutiques and imported apparel, jewelry, and home store brands, as well as familiar stores such as

Zara. It's a quieter spot to shop and eat, if more expensive.

## FOOD

Although not as diverse as the independent restaurant options in Bávaro—which you can still go to, with your own car or a pricey taxi—the resort areas of Punta Cana and Cap Cana hold a few of the best upscale restaurants in the area, if not the country. Some may require digging a little deeper into your pockets than you are used to in the DR, while others are reasonably priced. For breakfast, ★ **AM PM** (entrance of Fishing Lodge by Al Sol, 8am-noon, US$5-10) is a standout for serving fresh coffee by the carafe alongside delicious omelets with sides of cassava bread, hearty cheese-avocado or salami sandwiches, and other options—all presented on cutting boards rather than plates. Expect a surprise as well when you're served your cup of coffee (I'm not ruining it for you.). Ask to be seated upstairs on the rooftop terrace, with a partial water view. Note that the place turns into a tavern at night, with the name Taberna de Charlo.

The casual-chic **Playa Blanca Restaurant** (beachfront, tel. 809/959-2714, ext. 2234, noon-2pm and 7pm-10:30pm daily, US$6-40) is one of my favorites. This beachfront restaurant has a lovely open view of the beach and sea, and its menu offers both Dominican and beachside foods with a twist. Opt for a bowl of shrimp ceviche, yucca empanadas, or a plate of spicy goat stew with coconut rice, all washed down with the best margarita in town. The mango mojito is also to die for.

Playa Juanillo is home to a couple of spendy beachfront restaurants that double as beach clubs—with lounge chairs for a post-meal nap and beach day. The more popular one is **Juanillo Beach, Food and Drinks** (Cap Cana, tel. 809/469-7727, www.juanillo.com.do, 9am-6pm Mon.-Sun., US$6.50-21), which has a real beach bar feel, decent burgers, wraps, pizza, and seafood. The "beeritas" are refreshing and huge.

Designed by Oscar de la Renta, the romantic open-air setting of AAA Three-Diamond Award-winning ★ **La Yola** (tel. 809/959-1010, www.puntacana.com/dining/item/la-yola-restaurant, noon-3pm and 7pm-10:30pm daily, US$10-30) on a white-draped bamboo deck perched over Punta Cana Marina is only surpassed by chef Luis's Mediterranean menu with a Dominican twist. Try the sautéed shrimp in a coconut sauce with *moro de guandules* or pigeon peas rice or the baked eggplant layered with sweet plantain and mozzarella cheese. Pick a table beside the glass floor panels and look down into the turquoise sea while a trio of Dominican musicians serenades you.

Inside **Puntacana Village** (www.puntacanavillage.com) are small, reasonably priced restaurants, though they do tend to change over time. **La Casita de Yeya** is your pick for Dominican dishes, while **El Burrito** taqueria offers an all-Mexican menu, from taco salads to enchiladas and margaritas. **La Cava Kitchen & Bar** is for cured meats and cheese, but also pastas, catch of the day, and flatbreads, among others.

If you're near Playa Juanillo and looking for a different setup than the beach, stop at nearby **Sanctuary Town** (inside Sanctuary Cap Cana Resort but accessible roadside, www.sanctuarycapcana, 6pm-11pm daily except Mon.), offering a series of nine small dining establishments with varying cuisines and ambience, from tapas to Italian, Dominican, desserts, and an Irish pub with imported brews. Fusion, Sense, & Flavors is all the rage for its Asian fusion cuisine cooked in front of you, matched with a live musical choreography set from the staff.

## ACCOMMODATIONS
### Over US$150

In Punta Cana proper, 10 minutes' ride south from the Punta Cana Airport, the **Westin Puntacana Resort & Club** (beachfront, tel.

**1:** spicy goat stew with coconut rice at Playa Blanca Restaurant; **2:** the beach at the Westin Puntacana Resort & Club

809/959-2262, www.westinpuntacana.com, US$275-640), part of the Puntacana Resort & Club community where the likes of Julio Iglesias and Oscar de la Renta have homes, has 200 rooms with ocean views facing Punta Cana Beach. The open lobby entrance will draw your attention to the infinity pool in the near distance. Rooms are all-white, comfortable, and feature all the modern bells and whistles, but do retain a hotel feel.

Adjacent to the resort is the small but gorgeous **Playa Blanca,** popular for its excellent on-site restaurant with Dominican fare, water sports shops with nearby snorkeling, and a relaxed beach club vibe that welcomes outside guests. There's a fee for wireless Internet at the hotel, as with most resorts, unless you're a Starwood Preferred Guest. The convenience of amenities included is what brings families and groups here—including a nearby equestrian center, the P. B. Dye-designed La Cana Golf Course, an on-site ecological reserve with lagoons for a cold swim, the Puntacana Village shopping and restaurant area, and some of the best fine-dining à la carte restaurants in the area (guests only), such as **Anani** and **The Grill.** The hotel offers shuttles to these various locations. Note that there isn't any nightlife at the resort, save for a cigar lounge, and you will be quite a distance from the Bávaro area and north of the airport with no public buses passing through. Prepare to stick to your immediate surroundings unless you don't mind splurging on local taxis.

## INFORMATION AND SERVICES

Each resort will offer its own services, including shopping strips—but be aware that prices are super inflated. Make your dollars count and shop responsibly with local vendors whenever you are able. Most local services and shops are located in the Bávaro area, in Cortecito and Los Corales. If you're staying in the Punta Cana area south of the airport, it will cost more to get up there, so factor that in when picking a hotel.

### Money

For ATMs, head to the **Puntacana Village** complex (www.puntacanavillage.com). Check with your hotel if they provide complimentary rides to this shopping center.

### Health and Emergencies

For serious concerns aside from the quick clinic visits—usually offered on-site at resorts—head to **Hospiten Bávaro** (Carretera Higüey-Punta Cana, tel. 809/686-1414, bavaro@hospiten.com), about 15 minutes' drive north from Punta Cana Airport, with a 24-hour emergency room, multilingual medical staff in various departments ranging from pediatrics to cardiology, and high-end medical equipment including an ICU and X-ray machines. Another solid option is **Centro Médico Punta Cana** (Av. España 1, Los Corales, tel. 809/552-1506, emergency tel. 809/473-7283, www.centromedicopuntacana. com), with 24-hour emergency care. There's a pharmacy inside **Puntacana Village** (www. puntacanavillage.com). Resorts also carry first aid kits and often have supplies of painkillers and aspirin.

A branch of the tourist police, **CESTUR** (Av. Estados Unidos, Esq. Friusa, tel. 809/688-8727) is open 24 hours next to the Bávaro Express bus terminal. There is another near the airport at Puntacana Village.

## GETTING THERE
### Air

The private **Punta Cana International Airport** (PUJ) serves most passengers who are flying into the southeast region. It recently expanded with a second terminal, the second largest in the Caribbean, receiving over two million passengers a year on direct flights from at least 96 cities. Check with your hotel on whether they offer a free shuttle transfer. Otherwise, taxi costs vary according to the area of Punta Cana you're headed to, with Üvero Alto north of Bávaro being the farthest out at around a 45-minute drive. You can also contact **Dominican Plus** (tel. 809/481-0707, www.dominicanplus.com), which offers reasonably priced nonstop transfers door-to-door for US$32 one-way to Bávaro-area hotels. You can book online.

## Bus

**Expreso Bávaro** (Calle Juan Sánchez Ramírez, corner of Av. Máximo Gómez, Gazcue, tel. 809/682-9670, www.expresobavaro.com, departures every two hours from 7am, last bus at 4pm, US$8; in Bávaro, Cruce de Friusa. tel. 809/552-1678) takes you from Santo Domingo to the major resorts in Bávaro. From there, you'd have to take another private taxi to your Punta Cana resort. This option would be for those who started their journey elsewhere on the island—such as the capital city—but then it might make more sense to hire a driver from Santo Domingo and split the fee with your traveling group.

## Car

Inaugurated in 2012, the relatively new, smooth **Coral Highway** linking Santo Domingo to Punta Cana has cut a four-hour journey to just under three hours by private car. The road bypasses Higüey, which helps. There are three tollbooths along the way, at RD$100 (US$2.20) each. The drive is easy and pleasant, past sugarcane fields, open fields, and grazing cows. This same highway will take you to La Romana in just 45 minutes.

# GETTING AROUND
## Taxis

Taxis are a lot more expensive in Punta Cana. Most resorts post prices to sample destinations; consult the list and agree before getting into a taxi. Alternatively, befriend a local driver and negotiate a price for taking you around during your stay. Try the friendly and responsible **Juan** from **Lillian Tours and Transfers** (tel. 829/265-4621 or 829/570-4810); tell him Lily the travel journalist sent you.

## Car Rental

Car rental rates are better when booked online (starting around US$35) than at the Punta Cana Airport. You must be over 25 and have a valid driver's license. Try **Budget Rental Car** (PUJ airport, tel. 809/959-1005, www.budget.com/en/locations/do/punta-cana, 8am-10pm daily), **Avis** (PUJ airport, tel. 809/959-0534, www.avis.com.do, 8am-9pm daily), or **Europcar** (PUJ Airport, tel. 809/688-2121, www.europcar.com.do, 8am-10pm).

## Bus

Note that there is no public transportation traveling up and down the Punta Cana resort area (the section south of the Punta Cana Airport). Public *guaguas* (small minivans shared with other passengers) only travel up and down the main road in the Bávaro area.

## Air

Charter flights can take you from Punta Cana to other remote parts of the island such as Samaná and Puerto Plata. It makes sense when you are traveling in a group. Contact **Dominican Plus** (tel. 809/481-0707, www.dominicanplus.com, from US$539 one-way for 1-3 to Samaná, or US$879 to Puerto Plata). Another option is **Dominican Shuttles** (tel. 809/931-4073, www.dominicanshuttles.com, from US$660 to Samaná).

# La Romana

An entirely separate destination from Punta Cana, and yet barely a 1.25-hour ride south of the Coconut Coast, La Romana province is home to some of the most well-known luxury escapes and grand sights in the Dominican Republic and in the Caribbean. Casa de Campo Resort opened in 1973 and kicked off golf tourism in the DR, and the architectural wonder of Altos de Chavón provides a unique experience.

The city of the same name, the third largest in the country, is a bustling commercial center offering a taste of Dominican life away from the tourism hubs. The Parque Central's baseball statues tower over coconut vendors and gritty pastel-colored buildings. *Motoconchos* and *guaguas* buzz past shops with grilled windows, lottery shacks, and fabric stores. Quieter streets harbor Dominican art galleries and boutiques. Along the edges of the city are La Romana's small marina as well as the glamorous Casa de Campo and Altos de Chavón.

If anything, the La Romana region is the laid-back and more independent sister to Punta Cana, with fewer beaches but a slew of other natural adventures on the Parque Nacional Cotubanamá trails and offshore islands teeming with mangroves and marinelife.

## SIGHTS

### El Obelisco

**El Obelisco** (Av. Libertad) is one of the first sights you'll spot as you arrive into La Romana, standing tall in the middle of a shaded and sadly abandoned-looking small park and square away from the main traffic noise of Parque Central. A few seniors hang out here on the benches. The hand-painted structure is a smaller replica of the U.S. Washington Monument and depicts images of historical and modern-day Dominican life.

### Parque Central

A quick walk through La Romana's **Parque Central** (Calle Duarte) is worthwhile just to see the gorgeous steel baseball statues, symbolizing the importance of the game in the DR but especially in this town. La Romana is home to local team Los Toros del Este. Indeed,

boat cruising the Río Chavón

# La Romana

To Estadio Francisco A. Michell

HOTEL OLIMPO

JOAQUIN SUAREZ
PADRE ABREU
CALLE B
CALLE A
CALLE PRIMERA
JULIO A GARCIA

PEDRO
SANTA ROSA
LLUBERES
CREALES

GARCIA DICKSON
DOLORES TEJADA

FRANCISCO DEL CASTILLO MARQUEZ

Río Dulce

TENIENTE AMADO GARCIA GUERRERO

GASTON FERNANDO DELIONE
TIBURCIO MILAN LOPEZ
ESPAILLAT

ENRIQUILLO
HECTOR RENE GIL
G. LUPERON

DR. TEOFILO FERRY
TRINITARIA

FRANCISCO RICHEZ

SCOTIABANK
JUAN DE UTRERA    BUS STOP
POST OFFICE
CYBERNET CAFÉ

EUGENIO A MIRANDA
IGLESIA DE SANTA ROSA DE LIMA
DUARTE

Cemetery

PEDRO A LLUBERES
SANTA ROSA
TEOFILO HERNANDEZ

Parque Central    PICA POLLO RODRIGUEZ
SHISH KABOB    ALTAGRACIA
BIBI LEON

To Higüey and ALTOS DE CHAVÓN

30 DE MAYO
HERIBERTO PAVAN
AVENIDA LIBERTAD

JUMBO SUPERMARKET

To El Obelisco

0    200 yds
0    200 m

© MOON.COM    Caribbean Sea

it has produced numerous U.S. Major League Baseball players, such as Fernando Abad, Edwin Encarnación, Antonio Alfonseca, and Samuel Deduno. There might be a couple of undesirable characters hanging out in the park, as in any city, but this is a place frequented by all and by no means unsafe. Keep valuables to a minimum and make sure you get shots of those impressive statues.

## ★ Altos de Chavón

Perched on cliffs 91 meters (300 feet) above the majestic Río Chavón and bordering the

east side of the prestigious Casa de Campo Resort and its Dye Fore golf course, **Altos de Chavón** (tel. 809/523-5318, www.casadecampo.com.do/altos-de-chavon, open daily) is a model 16th-century European Mediterranean village unlike anything you'll find in the Caribbean. Designed by Dominican architect Jose Antonio Caro and created by Italian designer Roberto Coppa, the village was completed in 1982 after six years of construction. No details were spared, from handcrafted stone paths to ironwork, custom doorframes, and period furniture. The place oozes the feel of a medieval town, with its cobblestoned streets and narrow, leafy alleys.

Aside from being an architectural wonder, the compound is home to museums, shops, and restaurants. Central features not to miss include the **St. Stanislaus Church,** built in 1979; the **Altos de Chavón School of Art and Design,** which hosts frequent cultural and art events and has an exchange program with New York's Parson School of Design; the **Art Gallery,** which features Dominican artists; and the breathtaking 5,000-seat **Altos de Chavón Amphitheatre,** which hosts big-name artists year-round. The amphitheater and the entire village were inaugurated with a concert by Frank Sinatra.

Behind the church is the stunning **Museo Arqueológico Regional** (tel. 809/523-8554, www.altosdechavon.museum, 9am-8:30pm daily, US$4.50 or free for Casa de Campo guests), displaying the most comprehensive pre-Columbian and Taíno collection in the country. Exhibits at the archaeology museum date from 4000 BC to AD 1492 with over 3,000 pieces and the best labeling I've come across, in both English and Spanish. Dominican archaeologist Don Samuel Pion assembled them all over the course of 40 years of research in the DR. There are also displays covering the history of the DR and of Altos de Chavón. Expect to spend a good 30-45 minutes here; the room on the history and culture of the Taíno is especially captivating.

You'll also find high-end specialty boutiques selling premium cigars, apparel from Dominican designer Jenny Polanco, amber jewelry, and organic chocolate. For drinks, the open-air **Dye Fore Bar** has fantastic river views you can enjoy with a cocktail even if you're not a golfer. Dinner is excellent at the Italian **La Piazzeta;** the antipasti spread alone is worth it, as is the outdoor dining terrace overlooking the river.

If you're staying at the Casa de Campo Resort, then you'll have easy, free access to Altos de Chavón. Otherwise, area tour operators usually offer daytime excursions to the compound. **Colonial Tours** (tel. 809/688-5285, www.colonialtours.com.do, US$35) has a half-day tour, which is just enough time to take it all in.

### Estadio Francisco A. Micheli

Inaugurated in 1979 and renovated in 2013, **Estadio Francisco A. Micheli** (Av. Padre Abreu, tel. 809/556-6188, http://lostorosdeleste.com/estadio-francisco-micheli) is home to La Romana's baseball team, Los Toros del Este (The Bulls of the East) and has an audience capacity of 10,000. The gorgeous renovated facilities are comparable to Major League stadiums in the United States. The impeccable new field makes it one of the country's best venues. Practice begins in October for the November season. You can show up to take a sneak peek while you are in town. Sign your name on the entrance wall beside the hundreds of other fan signatures, and purchase some paraphernalia while you're at it in the on-site boutique.

## BEACHES

As an inland city, La Romana doesn't have any natural beaches but there are stretches nearby in Bayahibe. Hop on Expreso La Romana (Av. Padre Abreu, tel. 809/550-3328) direct to Bayahibe, lined with quiet and small beaches (after boats have left on excursions), or sign up for a boat ride to Saona and Catalina Islands.

## SPORTS AND RECREATION

Aside from snorkeling and diving excursions that head to Bayahibe and its offshore islands, most of the inland activities and sports are found at **Casa de Campo** (tel. 809/523-3333 or a.concierge@ccampo.com.do for inquiries). It has the largest sports-oriented complex in the Caribbean. While not all the activities are open to nonguests, you'll find enough that are.

### Golfing

One of the chief reasons visitors come to La Romana is to play the world-renowned **Teeth of the Dog** course (Diente de Perro in Spanish, Casa de Campo, tel. 809/523-3333, http://casadecampo.com.do/golf, 7:30am-6pm Mon.-Sun., US$255 for nonguests), ranked among the top 50 courses worldwide and first in Latin America. It is one of three Pete Dye courses at Casa de Campo. Built in 1971, this par-71 championship course stretches 6,721 meters (7,350 yards) and faces the Caribbean Sea on seven holes. It's on the bucket list of any avid golfer in the Caribbean, but even if you don't golf, take a tour of the course and you'll see what all the fuss is about—the views are unparalleled. Request your tee times well in advance.

If you're up for learning from top-notch instructors and staying at Casa de Campo, you're in luck: the resort launched a Golf Learning Center in late 2017 for its guests and members, featuring two hitting bays outfitted with TrackMan and BodiTrak technology.

Renovated in 2014, **Dye Fore** (Casa de Campo, tel. 809/523-3333, http://casadecampo.com.do/golf, t.times@ccampo.com.do, US$255/18 holes for nonguests) hugs Altos de Chavón and has dramatic views of the river below, the village, and the Caribbean Sea. There are seven cliff-side holes. It's a challenging course; relax afterward at the riverfront Dye Fore Bar. **The Links** (tel. 809/523-3333, http://casadecampo.com.do/golf, t.times@ccampo.com.do, US$180 for nonguests), an 18-hole, par 72 course, was built five years after Teeth of the Dog; Dye

# A Land of Sugarcane

a sugarcane field in La Romana

If there were no sugarcane industry, there might not have been a Casa de Campo, an airport, or a modern seaport here. And tourism—particularly cruise tourism—wouldn't be synonymous with La Romana. The two primary industries or this province are historically linked. It all began in 1911, when La Romana started booming after the establishment of the largest sugar mill in the country. It became a primary driver of the area's economy as sugarcane prices rose steadily over the years.

In the late 1960s, Alvaro Carta, who had fled Communist Cuba to live in Miami, headed to the Dominican Republic to help run the financially troubled South Puerto Rico Sugar Company in La Romana. Later, with the financial backing of Gulf & Western, he formed a new division known as Gulf & Western Americas. The sugar mill became the largest producing mill in the world. Carta then used the millions in revenue flowing from the operation to invest in a new industry in La Romana that would improve the town and the condition of its people: tourism. This eventually led to the six-star Casa de Campo complex and its world-renowned golf courses.

Despite the obvious bitterness that comes with the history of abuse of the Taíno, the African slave trade, and the harsh treatment of Haitian workers on sugarcane plantations in the Dominican southeast, the industry helped the town thrive and survive. Today, the sugar-producing Central Romana Corporation employs about 25,000 people, and aside from cruise tourism, sugarcane is La Romana's most important source of income.

originally called it "La Barranca," or the little hill. At 6,309 meters (6,900 yards), it's an inland course featuring undulating hills and lagoons.

## Snorkeling and Diving

If you're into snorkeling or any type of diving, from wall to cave diving, you're in luck. There are more dive sites than you might have time for in this area. The various dive shops in nearby Bayahibe offer snorkeling trips to offshore islands Saona, Catalina, and Catalinita. If you are based in a La Romana hotel, **Isla Catalina** is closest and might be the best option when time is limited. But none of the other sights are too far out, though they might require a full-day excursion. The closest dive shop is also one of the most attentive: **UWESCUBA** (Paseo de Mar 8, tel. 809/804-9445, www.uwescuba.com, US$110/2-tank

# Best Golf Courses in the DR

The Dominican Republic ranks among the top golf destinations in the Caribbean. It's also number 15 worldwide, according to the Ministry of Tourism and the Association of Golf Tour Operators. A combination of constant warm weather, varied landscapes, Caribbean Sea views make it hard to beat. The country counts 27 courses and 300 holes—52 of which front the Caribbean Sea. The majority are located on the east coast thanks to its spectacular scenery. They center on Santo Domingo's beachside escapes as well as the vacation haven of Punta Cana.

Golf tourism is big business, drawing in US$200 million in revenue a year. Resorts support courses designed by the likes of Pete Dye, Gary Player, Nick Faldo, and Jack Nicklaus and attract many a luxury traveler. Hot spots include Tortuga Bay, Eden Roc at Cap Cana, and Casa de Campo. Below is a summary of five of the best courses around the country outside of Santo Domingo. Note that rates listed are for winter season and only include greens fees.

- The world-renowned **Teeth of the Dog** (Diente de Perro in Spanish, Casa de Campo, tel. 809/523-3333, 7:30am-6pm Mon.-Sun., htp://casadecampo.com.do, US$190) is ranked among the top 50 worldwide and one of three Pete Dye courses at the exclusive Casa de Campo. Built in 1971, this par-71 championship course stretching 6,721 meters (7,350 yards) is on the bucket list of any avid golfer in the Caribbean. Seven holes face the Caribbean Sea.

- The **Cocotal Golf & Country Club** (Bávaro, tel. 809/687-4653, www.cocotalgolf.com, US$119, golf lesson US$86) is convenient to the major Punta Cana resorts and offers 27 holes set around lakes and coconut trees inside a residential community. It has a clubhouse and cafeteria. Opened in February 2000, the course was designed by six-time Spanish champion Jose Pepe Gancedo. Ask about shuttle services.

- The seafront **La Cana Golf Course** (Puntacana Resort & Club, US$180) is a beauty with panoramic views and 14 holes around the Caribbean Sea. There's a clubhouse on-site, and nearby are restaurants that are part of the Puntacana Resort & Club.

- **Corales Golf Club** (Puntacana Resort & Club, tel. 809/959-4653, www.puntacana.com/golf, US$180) hosted the PGA Tour in 2018, the first time the event has been held in the Dominican Republic. Its 18-hole course boasts cliff views with six oceanside holes, inland lakes, and coralina quarries. There's a clubhouse, bar, and grill on site.

- The 18-hole, par-72 **Playa Grande Golf Course** (Río San Juan, tel. 809/582-0860, golf@playagrande.com), part of the Playa Dorada 14-resort complex, was designed by the celebrated Robert Trent Jones Sr. It has 10 holes facing the Atlantic Ocean and offers amazing vistas over its 6,400-meter (7,000-yard) course. It was renovated under the direction of Rees Jones, the son of Robert Trent Jones Sr., in 2015.

- Another Trent Jones Sr. design, **Playa Dorada Golf Course** (Playa Dorada Resort Complex, tel. 809/320-4262, www.playadorada.com, US$75/18 holes) is an 18-hole, par 72 on the northern Puerto Plata Atlantic coast. It's surrounded by 19 restaurants as well as casinos and beaches. The complex is just a 20-minute ride from the Puerto Plata airport.

dive) based at Casa de Campo's Marina. Award-winning instructor Uwe Rath and his staff offer all the PADI courses you might need, including cave diving and wreck diving courses. Dives will take you to nearby Bayahibe's waters and caverns.

In Bayahibe, just a 15-minute ride south of La Romana, **ScubaFun** (Calle Principal 28, Bayahibe, tel. 809/833-0003, www.scubafun.

info, 2-tank dive US$80/half-day) is your best bet, with a fun diving crew who will take you on dive or snorkeling excursions to Catalina or Saona, a shipwreck exploration, and cave diving for the advanced.

## Kayaking and River Boating

Those staying at Casa de Campo will benefit from the single or double kayaks provided to explore the Caribbean off the shores of Minitas Beach. Or better yet, paddle over to the stunning Chavón River—featured in major movies like *Apocalypse Now*—and get a different view of the medieval village from the water. For a speedboat ride down the river, including a tour of Casa de Campo's Marina, contact **ProExcursions Bayahibe** (tel. 829/659-4688, www.proexcursionsbayahibe. com, US$55 pp), based in the nearby beach village, for a 2.5-hour Rio de Chavón Speedboat Journey.

### Sailing

Have you always wanted to charter your own boat and live it up? Casa de Campo's office at the **Casa de Campo Marina** (tel. 809/523-8646, www.marinacasadecampo.com.do, US$600-3,555 for 51 ft./15 people) has a wide selection for your dream excursion out at sea from speedboats to luxury yachts. They can find a match for all budgets and groups.

### Fishing

Deep-sea and freshwater river fishing trips are available through **Casa de Campo** (tel. 809/523-3333, www.casadecampo.do, from US$700 half-day), departing from the marina. The fishing season goes from February through May, with peak months being March, April, and May. The main fish hooked include wahoo, kingfish, sailfish, marlin, and barracuda, or snooker in the river. It's a great day out for those who fish and their families.

### Baseball

There's baseball everywhere in the DR. during the season is from mid-October through January. If you're visiting during baseball season (mid-October-January), you'll be able to catch a game right here in La Romana; you may even catch the ball fever that hits residents when it comes to their home team, Los Toros del Este. **Estadio Francisco A. Micheli** (Av. Padre Abreu, tel. 809/556-6188, http://lostorosdeleste.com/estadio-francisco-micheli, US$1.11-7.80), close to the center of town, is the only privately owned and funded baseball stadium. Practice sessions run in October, and regular play starts in November.

About a 45-minute drive west, the **Estadio Tetelo Vargas** (Av. Circunvalación, tel. 809/529-3618, www.estrellasorientales.com. do) in the industrial town of San Pedro de Macorís is home to the Estrellas Orientales and one of the major hubs for baseball in the Dominican Republic, even though it is also the smallest facility with a capacity for only 8,000.

Estadio Francisco A. Micheli is home to Los Toros del Este.

Inaugurated in 1959 in the days of Trujillo, the stadium is named after Dominican baseball great Juan Esteban Vargas, nicknamed Tetelo. He was known for his speed and strong throwing arm, which earned him the title *El Gamo Dominicano* (The Dominican Deer). His successful career took him overseas to Puerto Rico, Venezuela, Cuba, Canada, and the U.S. Negro Leagues. In 1953 at age 47, he was the league-batting champ with a .353 mark. The team won the Dominican League championship in 1954. The stadium is dubbed as the home of the Dominican Big Leaguers, because the province is the birthplace of some of the most famous Big League players out of the DR. If you're lucky to catch a game here, you will have experienced a big piece of Dominican history and culture.

## Tennis
Dubbed the "Wimbledon of the Caribbean," Casa de Campo's tennis center at **La Terrazza** (tel. 809/523-3333, 7am-9pm, US$31/hour daytime, US$39 after 6pm) boasts a glorious Caribbean Sea view and features 13 fast-dry Har-Tru clay courts supported by a staff of more than 70. You can play during the day or at night, as you choose. This is a full-service luxury tennis center: there are ball boys, a spectator deck, and an onsite pro shop. Sign up for lessons if you're a newbie (US$61-76/hour); racquets are also available for rent (US$10/hour). After a game, relax with a drink or take a dip in the pool. Every year on the Thursday before Labor Day weekend, the center hosts the international Casa de Campo Cup, attracting over 200 players from 14 countries.

## Tours
**Runners Adventures** (tel. 809/833-0260, www.runnersadventures.com/tours/bayahibe-runners, US$85) offers a Bayahibe Runners excursion that takes you on a horseback safari into the La Romana countryside, touring a sugarcane plantation and learning about the rum-making process. Next you'll be on to coffee and cacao farms, before ending

with a visit to Higüey's Basilica La Altagracia. Runners also offers a Hispaniola Explorer VIP excursion, which includes a city tour of La Romana with a stop at the Micheli Baseball Stadium and a trip to Altos de Chavón, where you'll also get to cruise down the river. It's not so much a shopping trip as it is an opportunity to see beyond the resort for those short on time.

### CIGAR FACTORIES
If you're into cigars or even just curious about this prime Dominican export, visit a cigar factory and witness the rolling process firsthand. In the Punta Cana and Bávaro area, head to **Don Lucas Cigar Factory** (tel. 809/200-0129, www.donlucascigars.com.do, free tour and pickup), said to be among current DR president Danilo Medina's favorites. Remember to wear appropriate clothing when visiting factories: closed toe shoes and no bathing suits. In the La Romana area, you should tour **La Flor Dominicana** (La Estancia, Autopista del Coral, tel. 809/550-3000, www.laflordominicana.com, 8am-7pm daily) or **Tabacalera de García** (Industrial Free Zone, tel. 809/556-2127, http://cigarcountrytours.com, free factory tours Tues. and Thurs., reservations required).

## ENTERTAINMENT AND EVENTS
### Bars and Clubs
If you find yourself in the city for a night for whatever reason, you can grab drinks and get a taste of the nightlife at the trendy **Bar Marinelli and Lounge** (Av. Santa Rosa, tel. 809/556-1891, consorciomarinelly9@gmail.com). They pour premium liquor and entice with the sounds of merengue, *bachata,* and other genres. Ask locals for the latest city dance spot, as these fluctuate as often as the wind, but be careful roaming around at night unless you are with a local.

Over at Altos de Chavón, **Onno's** (tel. 809/523-2868, www.onnosbar.com/altos-de-chavon, noon-2am daily) is a good bet for happy hour drinks and late-night dancing,

# San Pedro de Macorís and the Cocolo Festival

Less than an hour west of La Romana in the baseball-famous town of San Pedro de Macorís, an annual festival celebrates the unique Afro-Caribbean Cocolo culture of the Dominican Republic. The Cocolos are the descendants of enslaved Africans who emigrated to the DR in the late 19th century from the all over the British Caribbean—including Anguilla, Barbados, St. Kitts, Nevis, Tortola, Turks and Caicos, and St. Croix—to work in the sugar industry. It is estimated that about 6,000 initially immigrated to the DR.

Dominicans first gave them the name *Tortolo*—assumed to have derived from Tortola in the BVI—which later evolved into *Cocolo*, initially used in a derogatory manner. But these workers were valued for their technical know-how, and were hired as experienced drivers, chemists, and machinists. Cocolo is now a reclaimed term used with pride in this community.

The Cocolo presence resulted in a unique cultural evolution in this corner of the DR, and every year the Cocolos' descendants celebrate their Afro-Caribbean heritage through dance troupes and plays between December 25 and the first week of January, and again on June 29 to coincide with the feast of San Pedro (the town's patron saint). The performances include African-inspired folkloric dances and characters, mixed with plots and legends from medieval British literature and the Bible. The *Guloyas*, or dancers, wear vibrant costumes and feathery hats. The musical support beats various types of drums as they all celebrate and twirl through the streets. It's well worth venturing to San Pedro to witness this unique expression of Caribbean heritage. In 2005 UNESCO classified it as a masterpiece of the Oral and Intangible Heritage of Humanity.

with river views and breezes. But the current hotspot is **Living Room by Good Vibe** (Altos de Chavon, 6pm until the good vibe lasts, Wed.-Sun., from US$5) with a killer terrace overlooking the Chavón River, cozy couches, hammocks, and a cool bohemian lounge vibe with cocktails and bites. They also host happy hours, outdoor cinema nights, tango shows, and other innovative fun nights (check their social media).

## Festivals and Cultural Events

The **ProCigar Festival** (third week of February, tel. 809/580-4754, www.procigar. org, US$895 for full program) celebrates the premium tobacco grown in the Dominican Republic, also known as Cigar Country. The ProCigar association, formed in 1992, includes the country's top cigar manufacturers such as La Flor Dominicana, Tabacalera de García, and Tabacalera Fuente, among others. The festival has been held in several areas at once, including in La Romana, Santiago, and Puerto Plata (the 2016 edition will begin in Punta Cana). Over 400 people visit from around the world and indulge in dinners, excursions, local cuisine, and nightlife, along with, of course, cigars. Events also include cigar factory tours, and a charity auction is usually part of the event, with all proceeds donated to a nonprofit organization assisting children and the elderly. Check the website for each year's schedule of activities, full program, and cost.

Keep your eyes and ears open for the annual **Carnaval de La Romana** (every Sunday in February)—ask for location and times as these may vary, but the parades usually kick off around 4:30pm. It's a good time to see the diversity in the region, with plenty of elaborate Taíno chief costumes.

## SHOPPING

You'll have access to a variety of stores in La Romana city, from high-end designer boutiques and a new shopping mall to side-of-the-road pottery and crafts stands. But the most authentic finds are the art by local creators, from paintings to vibrant handmade items.

**El Artístico** (Km 3 1/2 Carretera La

Romana, elartisticord@gmail.com, tel. 809/349-7198, 10am-6pm Mon.-Sat.) is a name everyone knows in these parts and across the DR: it's the nickname of Dominican artist Jose Ignacio Morales Reyes. Born in La Romana, the artist began playing with metal cans of tomato paste when he was a kid, and would transform them into decorative pieces he would eventually sell. Today, his lamps can be found even in the U.S. White House, among other prestigious world venues. At his headquarters a shopping arcade is filled with El Artístico handmade items: lamps, furniture, steel structures, and metal sculptures. The metals he uses the most are iron, aluminum, bronze, and copper. But a more fascinating and worthwhile sight is his actual workshop across the street, where the creations take shape. You can go inside and watch employees at work (don't show up at lunchtime—between noon and 1pm—when it will be deserted), as well as admire some of his original works. One standout is a tree-shaped stand of the molded hands of visiting celebrity artists. El Artístico himself may be there, unless he is busy in meetings with his latest clients, which have included the president of the Dominican Republic; he has commissioned exclusive pieces to be displayed in the DR and overseas.

**Tina Bambu's Mercado Artesanal** (Calle Prof Juan Bosch, tel. 809/550-8322, 9am-6pm daily) is a popular pit stop for tourists, offering souvenirs as well as handmade pottery at a reasonable price.

If you're looking to purchase coffee or rum at the local price, the area's largest supermarket is **Jumbo** (Av. Libertad, corner of Doctor Gonzalvo, tel. 809/813-5033, www.jumbo.com.do, 8am-10pm Mon.-Sat., 9am-8pm Sun. and holidays). Look for the big red letters—you can't miss them when passing through the heart of town. Locals drive from as far as Punta Cana to shop here for better prices. Much like in the La Sirena chain, you'll find everything under the sun here, including groceries, banks, a food court, an electronics store, and lockers.

**Multiplaza La Romana** (tel. 809/556-4446, www.multiplaza.com.do/romana, 8am-8pm) will keep you busy for a few hours browsing its clothing, home décor, electronics, and craft stores. It also has a pharmacy, an ATM, and phone stores. There's also a food court and a movie theater, and La Sirena store is on-site.

**Altos de Chavón** (tel. 809/523-2045, www.casadecampo.com.do/altos-de-chavon, open daily) offers a handful of high-end shopping opportunities, from cigars to jewelry to designer clothing.

# FOOD
## Dominican

A cheap meal can be had at the Dominican-owned **Pica Pollo Rodríguez** (Calle Duarte, tel. 809/813-3493, 11am-9pm daily, US$3-5), whose signature is fried chicken and fries. The meal is quite tasty and not super greasy. There's a convivial outdoor veranda if you have time to sit and eat.

## International

In the city, **Shish Kebab** (Calle Castillo Marquez #32, tel. 809/556-2737, jgiha@hotmail.com, 10am-11pm Tues.-Sun., US$7-17) is such an iconic restaurant in these parts that Dominicans from as far as Santo Domingo will tell you that it's a sin to pass through La Romana without eating here. And they do have a point. The meat here is succulent—order ahead if you don't want a 45-minute wait for your kebabs—and you'll find all the Middle Eastern specialties, from tabbouleh to baklava desserts. The menu also includes steaks, salads, and seafood. Try one of their fresh fruit juices or Dominican *batidas* with your meal. Seating is indoors in a more formal air-conditioned room with white tablecloths or outdoors on a shaded veranda facing the street. There is open wireless Internet, and the service is friendly.

Casa de Campo's presence near the city means a host of excellent meal options, for which it's worth dipping into your pockets. For fine dining, indulge in a magical evening at **La Casita** (U.S. tel. 866/860-5472, www.casadecampo.com.do/restaurants/la-casita, 6pm-11pm Tues.-Sun., dress casual-elegant, US$10-39) at the Casa de Campo Marina. You can enjoy waterfront dock seating beside pricey yachts. The menu is popular primarily for its seafood, including the paella. There are also steaks, salads, and chicken entrées. The service and atmosphere are excellent, as is the light jazz that flows gently past the billowing white drapes. There's a special, more private table for two below the main platform edging the water.

Treat yourself to lunch by the beach at the swank, newly redesigned ★ **Minitas Beach Club and Restaurant** (Casa de Campo, U.S. tel. 855/877-3643, www.casadecampo.com.do/restaurants, noon-4pm and 7pm-11pm daily, US$10-60). Dine on Mediterranean and Latin American cuisine, and then go relax along the 23-meter-long infinity pool deck.

Inside Altos de Chavón, ★ **La Piazzetta** (tel. 809/523-3165, noon-3pm in high season, 6pm-11pm Fri.-Mon., US$10-26) is a cut above the rest. The charming, dimly lit dining room's wooden tables and stone floor win you over immediately, or choose the outdoor terrace facing the river and the evening breeze. But the authentic, homemade Italian dishes are what truly delight. The antipasti buffet is to die for, with imported cheeses and cuts, while entrées range from chicken and beef fondues with mustard and blue cheese to a succulent and classic lasagna Bolognese. You'll have trouble finishing because of the huge portions. Service is excellent, and there's often a nice trio of musicians to serenade you with Latin ballads while you wait on your meal.

A couple of cobblestone paths away, the chain **Onno's** (tel. 809/523-2868, www.onnosbar.com/altos-de-chavon, noon-10pm daily) doesn't disappoint with its usual hip and lively atmosphere and a casual and expansive menu of burgers, pizzas, and seafood. The bar, which offers hundreds of cocktails, gets rowdier by the hour and turns into a dance spot after dinner hours (10pm-3am Fri.-Sat.).

Wednesdays are ladies night. Happy hours are 6pm-8pm daily.

# ACCOMMODATIONS

In truth, there's very little reason to overnight in La Romana, unless you are headed to the Casa de Campo Resort, which is at the entrance of La Romana rather than in the city center, or you are in transit during a long-term stay.

## Under US$50

The three-story **Hotel River View** (Calle Restauración 17, tel. 809/556-1181, hotelriverview@gmail.com, US$44, includes daily breakfast and dinner) is basic and dated. Expect tiled floors, thin bedding, and a shower and worn tub. But it's clean if you must spend a night in La Romana town. There are more spacious rooms at this property for the same price, if you're lucky enough to get one (or ask ahead of time).

A notch better, **Hotel Olimpo** (Av. Padre Abreu, corner of Pedro Lluberes, tel. 809/550-7646, www.olimpohotel.com, US$36-43) looks impressive from the exterior, and the interior is acceptable for the price. A cool air-conditioned lobby and wrought-iron staircase lead to basic and clean rooms with double beds, peach walls, and mini fridges. There are lounge areas and inviting hallways.

## US$50-100

On the western side of the Río Chavón and formerly a sugarcane plantation surveillance post, **Hotel Vecchia Caserma** (Km 12 Carretera La Romana-Bayahibe, tel. 809/556-6072, www.hotelvecchiacaserma.com, US$89-125, includes breakfast and wireless Internet) offers 14 rooms, as well as four triples, with air-conditioning and satellite TV. There's a small pool and an Italian restaurant on-site. The hotel is isolated so you'd need a car to get around, but it's a decent pick for a night or two.

## US$100 and Up

Jet-set favorite and Leading Hotels of the

World property ★ **Casa de Campo** (8.9 kilometers/5.5. miles from La Romana Airport, Carretera La Romana, U.S. tel. 866/860-5472 or 809/523-3333, www.casadecampo.com. do, from US$200, or US$624 all-inclusive) is one of the most prestigious properties in the Caribbean, let alone the Dominican Republic. This is where you're likely to spot celebrities from athletes to musicians to heads of state relaxing on a championship golf course or sipping cocktails at La Caña Restaurant's outdoor lounge—a Le Cirque collaboration—with views of a sprawling cascade pool. The immense 28-square-kilometer (7,000-acre) compound, immaculately landscaped, is an escape from everything mundane.

There are 173 rooms and 12 suites within the hotel itself. Each comes with a four-seater golf cart for exploration and faces either the gardens or the golf driving ranges. Private villas are also available for rent. The property includes six excellent restaurants. There is also a spa, three Pete Dye-designed golf courses, including **Teeth of the Dog,** a new Golf Learning Center, an equestrian center, three polo fields, a sailing school, movie theaters, and 13 Har-Tru tennis courts. Don't miss riding a golf cart through Teeth of the Dog for its breathtaking sea views, dining at **La Piazetta** or at **La Casita,** and getting a full, free entry and tour of **Altos de Chavón,** where outdoor movies are periodically shown. The revamped **Minitas Beach Club** is also worth a stop to enjoy the poolside restaurant with infinite sea views.

**Casa de Campo Marina** (tel. 809/523-8646, www.marinacasadecampo.com.do) within the Casa de Campo grounds has capacity for 350 yachts, in addition to being home to a handful of waterfront restaurants and shops. It has its own yachting club, sailing school, shopping mall, and movie theater. There are several pathways through the plazas ideal for an evening or daytime stroll.

## GETTING THERE

To reach La Romana from Santo Domingo, hop on Highway 3 and take it all the way. Highway 3 will turn into Avenida Padre Abreu once you enter the city limits. Turn right onto Santa Rosa Street, which leads to the Parque Central close to restaurants, banks, and services. If you plan to continue on to Bayahibe, once you arrive into La Romana follow the signs for Casa de Campo, which will take you onto Avenida Libertad. This turns into Carretera La Romana-Higüey, and from there follow along the signs to Bayahibe, just 15 minutes away.

**Aeropuerto Internacional La Romana** (tel. 809/813-9000, www.romanaairport. com) is just under a 20-minute drive from the center of La Romana city, as well as Casa de Campo or Bayahibe and Dominicus resorts. Flights arrive daily on carriers such as American Airlines, American Eagle, JetBlue, and Air Canada. A host of charter flights arrive from Europe. Taxi rates from the airport to area resorts including Casa de Campo begin at US$35, and of course depend on your final destination. Prices are set and will be posted once you get past customs; double-check the rate with the driver before you depart.

From Santo Domingo, you can catch a local *guagua* (about US$5) headed to Higüey from Parque Enriquillo. Ask around to make sure you hop on the right one that makes a stop in La Romana. There's also an express to La Romana, if you're lucky enough to catch it. It leaves every half hour until 5pm. You will likely get dropped off at the Parque Central, where you can catch a taxi or a bike taxi. If you're with a group, it may be a better value to pay a taxi to drive you to La Romana; rates are usually around US$135 for up to four passengers—contact **Apolo Taxi** (tel. 809/537-0000, www.apolotaxi.com) and get an instant quote and ride.

If you're coming south from the Punta Cana Airport or the Punta Cana area, note that there aren't any direct public buses and you'll have to take a taxi. Contact **IBK Servicios** (tel. 829/926-0707, http:// ibkservicios.com, US$105 one-way, 1-4 pp) for a private transfer.

## GETTING AROUND

Exploring downtown La Romana is easily done on foot, but in-city taxis are also affordable. Call **Santa Rosa Taxi** (tel. 809/556-5313). If you choose to rent a car from La Romana, the airport has a branch of **Budget** (tel. 809/813-9111, 9am-5pm daily, from US$45), and there is an **Avis** (Francisco Castillo Marquez 35, tel. 809/813-9099, 8am-11pm daily) in town.

To go from La Romana to Bayahibe by public transportation, find the central bus gathering spot on Avenida Libertad across from the public jail. And if you're heading to Santo Domingo, there's a **SICHOEM bus terminal** (RD$150/US$3.40 express)—you can also ask for *la salida de La Romana*—on Avenida Abreu, which leads into Autopista del Este, next to the Shell gas station. You catch an air-conditioned bus to the capital and reach it in 1.5 hours. You can also just head to the Parque Central and catch a free bus ride in front of the church to the SICHOEM terminal.

# Bayahibe

One of the last Taíno strongholds in the country, Bayahibe was founded as a fishing village in 1874, when Juan Brito and his family arrived from Puerto Rico. Fishing and the traditional wooden sailboat building were primary trades. The tiny *pueblo* has since transformed into a tourist destination as more resorts realized the beauty of Bayahibe and all of its assets. The calm, crystal-clear waters of its Caribbean coastline make it perfect for water sports and beachcombing. The protected national park nearby offers hiking and freshwater-filled caverns with some of the best cave diving in the Caribbean. And then there are always stunning offshore islands for day trips to paradise.

Despite the crowds of tourists and buses shuffling in and out daily on day trips from neighboring Punta Cana, Dominican village life still rules in Bayahibe. Alarm clocks are 4am rooster calls, followed by birdsong and music. The streets are dotted with colorful, traditional wooden homes and eateries. The bay, filled with boats and facing small white-sand beaches, is clean and postcard-worthy. The sunsets here are some of the most spectacular in the country.

Bayahibe is *tranquilo,* as most European and Haitian expats will tell you when explaining why they made their home here decades ago. The community way of life means that this is a very hospitable and welcoming place to stay. There's little crime here, and it is considered to be one of the safest parts of the country. Even late at night, walking is the norm (though I always advise not to do so or to carry valuables).

The main road into the village ends at a giant parking lot where tourist buses park for the day while their customers hop on boats from Bayahibe to the nearby islands. Fishing still holds a key place in the village's identity, even if it isn't the primary income earner. If you're lucky, you'll arrive on the last weekend in May when the fishing tournament is on.

## DOWNTOWN
### Casas Típicas

Stroll around the main street in the village to enjoy the visual feast of vibrant, pastel-colored **Casas Típicas,** the traditional wooden homes of Bayahibe. You'll also spot them on side streets off the main drag. Prepare to snap lots of pictures of these photogenic structures.

### ★ La Punta de Bayahibe

**La Punta de Bayahibe,** or **La Ensenada,** is a rugged peninsula jutting out into the sea from the western edge of the village just after the main dock area. This area is the most historic part of the village. A pleasant trail, La Ruta La Punta Bayahibe, leads you to three of

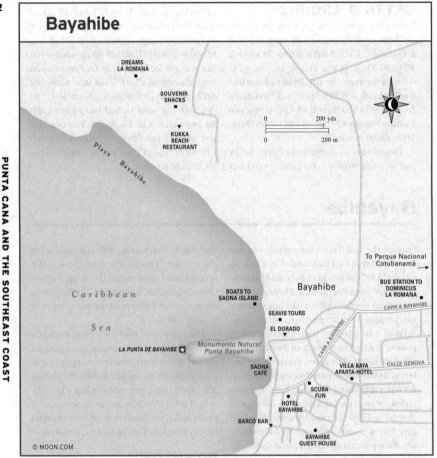

## Bayahibe

DREAMS LA ROMANA

SOUVENIR SHACKS

KUKKA BEACH RESTAURANT

Playa Bayahibe

Caribbean

Sea

0      200 yds

0      200 m

To Parque Nacional Cotubanamá

BUS STATION TO DOMINICUS LA ROMANA

Bayahibe

CARR A BAYAHIBE

BOATS TO SAONA ISLAND

SEAVIS TOURS

EL DORADO

CARR A BAYAHIBE

CALLE GENOVA

VILLA BAYA APARTA-HOTEL

LA PUNTA DE BAYAHIBE

Monumento Natural Punta Bayahibe

SAONA CAFÉ

SCUBA FUN

HOTEL BAYAHIBE

BARCO BAR

BAYAHIBE GUEST HOUSE

© MOON.COM

its significant points: a church, archaeological ruins, and a botanical trail. The short hike eventually leads to a glorious deck overlooking the sea and the bay ahead.

Walk up the front street, continue past the big central parking lot (behind Café Saona) and continue on that road until you reach a gate. It will be open, even if it doesn't seem so at first. As you get past it, you'll see the beautiful **Parroquia Divina Pastora** (tel. 809/833-0654, ptmariadenazaret@hotmail.com) with its entrance directly facing the sea. It was built from wood brought over from Florida and without any architectural

or engineering assistance. It was the first religious institution in the area, and the oldest building in the village, and was consecrated on March 25, 1925, by Archbishop Monseñor Nouel. In 2015, the church celebrated its 90th anniversary. The most venerated item inside the church is a framed painting of the Divina Pastora (the Virgin Mary), dating from 1954. It was a gift from a Brazilian Franciscan monk who was visiting the village and was moved by its *fiestas patronales*. The church has received prominent visitors over the years, including former president of the DR Monsignor Adolfo Alejandro Nouel y Bobadilla.

After touring the church, ask to see resident Padre Antonio Villavicencio's garden at the back of the church, where he has created **La Ruta de Las Virgines:** a garden where he has planted a trail of all the matron saint figurines he has received from guests from around a dozen countries, including Portugal, Spain, Cuba, Italy, Chile, Costa Rica, Brazil, Mexico, France, and Puerto Rico. There is also one from Higüey. Each one of the figurines is labeled.

Beside the church entrance is a **Bayahibe rose garden.** The cactus trees carrying this national flower *(Pereskia quisqueyana)* are found only in this village. Past the church, look closely and you will spot archaeological ruins left behind from the first inhabitants of the village and dating back to 2000 BC buried under overgrown shrubs. The area awaits better upkeep. Continue walking down and you'll run into a bigger garden of Bayahibe roses. The pathway eventually leads to a covered lookout cabana and deck with breathtaking 180-degree views of Bayahibe's waters and coastline. You can walk past the lookout point along the water and circle back to the church without retracing your steps.

## PARQUE NACIONAL COTUBANAMÁ

At the southeastern tip of the country and accessible on foot from Bayahibe or via a short drive from La Romana town, the magnificent **Parque Nacional Cotubanamá** (formerly known as Parque Nacional del Este, 9am-5pm daily, entry fee US$2.20) has been a protected nature reserve since 1975 and is the crown jewel of the southeastern coast. Approximately 790 square kilometers (305 square miles) of reserve encompasses both land and sea. On land there is a subtropical rainforest and a dry forest that can be explored via a 2-kilometer (1.24-mile) trail known as the **Sendero del Padre Nuestro.** It will take you to Taíno caves with pictographs and the springs around which the Taíno once lived. The sea portion of the park includes the popular offshore islands of **Saona, Catalina,** and **Catalinita,** as well as the natural pool area of **La Palmilla.**

The park is home to at least 539 species of flowers. It also makes a great birding excursion. It is home to 144 types of birds, including brown pelicans, the red-footed boobies, barn owls, and the Hispaniolan parrots. A large frigate bird colony convenes at Bahía de las Calderas, a bay on the southern coast of

a view of the bay from La Punta de Bayahibe

# Best Tours in Bayahibe

## TOURING ISLA SAONA

With a focus on ecofriendly tours, the multilingual-staffed Seavis Tours (beachfront, between Dreams Resort Bayahibe and town, Calle Eladia 4, tel. 829/714-4947, www.seavisbayahibe.com, US$95) offers the "Saona Crusoe VIP"—an excellent insider's take on Isla Saona. They are conscious of the fact that you'd rather not be crowded in with other speedboats and tourists and find ways to avoid them (although it's a tall order). Plenty of information is provided along the way, making the trip both cultural and educational—particularly at Mano Juan, the only inhabited portion of Saona, where Seavis subsidizes a turtle nesting center. The stop at the *piscina natural* will be uncrowded because the boat heads to an area of the natural pool that is a bit more removed from everyone else. The last stop is Canto de la Playa, which is completely deserted by 3pm. It's a great time with lively guides, plenty of drinks, and a fun and mature crowd. Snorkeling gear is provided, as are drinks, snacks, and lunch.

The best way to go—and to really escape the daily crowds—is to rent your own small speedboat and hire a captain to customize your Saona day trip. It can include lunch at Playa Bonita, where you can pick your own quiet corner of beach, and enjoying the Piscina Natural all to yourself. Bring your own booze if you wish. An excellent boat captain who has navigated these waters his whole life is Captain Nicola or Nico ($100 for two, approx. 5 hours, 8-seater covered speedboat).

To sail in style to Isla Saona on your own charter, contact Dragonsmoke Sailing Charters (Casa de Campo Marina, tel. 829/272-9069, www.dragonsmokesailing.com, US$250 pp, four people minimum) for a blissful day drifting across the Caribbean. You can fish, snorkel, and sun yourself on a 16-meter (51-foot) yacht with fully furnished cabins and private bathrooms. The trip includes lunch, snorkeling gear, and stops at Catuano Beach and the natural pool on Isla Saona.

## HIKING THE JUNGLE AT SENDERO DEL PADRE NUESTRO

Another unique excursion in the Bayahibe region is to explore the former Taíno grounds and caves at the protected Padre Nuestro Trail within the Parque Nacional Cotubanamá. The only tour operator specializing in an extensive guided hiking trip—aside from the Spanish-speaking local

the park. You can also expect to see sea turtles on Isla Saona. This is the most important nesting site in the country, attracting hawksbill, green, and leatherback species; nesting season is March through November. Spotted and bottlenose dolphins roam the seas surrounding the islands, as do humpback whales and manatees. On dry land, the endangered rhinoceros iguana ranges up to 1 meter (4.5 feet) in length and as heavy as 9 kilograms (20 pounds).

To tour the various areas of the park, whether the trail or the islands, you must be accompanied by a licensed guide. The park's own guides are available at both park entrances (from either the Boca de Yuma side or from Bayahibe). Note that camping is not permitted. The best way to tour the sea portion of the park is to hop on a boat excursion

with one of the tour companies in Bayahibe. If you have time, or if you're a cave diver, throw in the Padre Nuestro Trail.

If you're arriving by car, you'll use the western entrance to the park, in Bayahibe. You can reach the entrance by taxi or on foot from downtown Bayahibe also. If you're coming from the east (Punta Cana), the entrance is at Boca de Yuma, and will need to be reached by car.

### Caving

There are over 400 caves within the park. The most well known is Cueva del Puente, easily hiked on foot. The Cueva de Chicho contains a crystal-clear *manantial*, or freshwater spring, around which you can spot over 20 original Taíno petroglyphs. Divers with open water or advanced certifications can guides by the park entrance—is Seavis Tours (beachfront, between Dreams Resort Bayahibe and town, Calle Eladia 4, tel. 829/714-4947, www.seavisbayahibe.com, US$95). You learn about the flora and fauna of the park and its prior inhabitants before exploring stunning Taíno freshwater caves. What makes this tour even more special is that it's designed to help the local community as well. You'll visit the settlement of Benerito, just outside Bayahibe, where the locals who once lived in the park relocated and the women are now running an arts and crafts cooperative financed by USAID. The trip ends with a river excursion down the Chavón. It's a great day of local history and culture with outdoor adventure. Call ahead to check on the status of the trail and to find available tour dates with an English-speaking guide.

## DIVING AT ISLA CATALINA

The popular PADI five-star dive center ScubaFun (Calle Principal 28, Bayahibe, tel. 809/833-0003, www.scubafun.info) is your best bet for exploring the reefs and critters off the Bayahibe coast and some of the best diving in the DR. The two-tank dive off Catalina (US$80 2-tank dive plus half-day Catalina US$55 excursion) includes a 40-meter (130-foot) wall dive, which you can cruise between 9 and 12 meters (30-60 feet) to see the best portions. The lunch isn't stellar but the surroundings make up for it, along with plenty of time to relax on the white-sand shores and snap photos. There are also shipwreck dive excursions to the Coco wreck and St. George wreck. Also up to 130 feet, it's for advanced divers.

## FISHING IN BAYAHIBE

Fishing is still a primary activity in this village, so much so that there's even an annual fishing tournament in the summer. Bayahibe Fishing Centre (Bayahibe Beach 2, tel. 809/833-0009 or 829/914-4162, www.bayahibefishingcentre.com, US$175 half day or US$260 full day, four people min.), and one of the best fishermen in this area, Captain Pepe, take you deep-sea fishing to catch marlin, mahi-mahi, barracuda, and more. All fishing gear, bait, and guides are included, as well as drinks and snacks.

indulge in waters ranging in depth from 9 meters (30 feet) to over 30 meters (100 feet), filled with the larger Caribbean critters along with stalactite and stalagmite formations. Contact ScubaFun (Calle Principal 28, Bayahibe, tel. 809/833-0003, www.scubafun. info, single-tank dive, US$84pp) for more information; they specialize in cave diving in this area.

## ★ Sendero del Padre Nuestro

While the islands get the most tourist attention, the Sendero del Padre Nuestro, also known as Ruta Ecológica y Arqueológica de Padre Nuestro (Carretera a Bayahibe, tel. 829/521-3398, senderopadrenuestro@ explorelaromana.com, 9am-4:30pm Mon.-Sun., RD$200/US$4.45), is also an integral and informative part of the Parque Nacional Cotubanamá. The trailhead is on the main road leading to Bayahibe and Dominicus, right after you pass Hilton La Romana on the corner of Avenida Wayne Fuller. It's a long walk in to reach the actual entrance of the park—you'll need to take a taxi (US$20 one-way) or horseback ride your way to reach the trailhead.

The trail is a 2-kilometer (1.24-mile), easy-to-moderate hike that takes two hours. You are required to be accompanied by one of the accredited park rangers (if you speak a little Spanish you will get the most out of the informative tour). You can also tour the park by horse with one of the rangers. Seavis Tours (beachfront Bayahibe, between Dreams Resort Bayahibe and town, 4 Calle Eladia, tel. 829/714-4947, www.seavisbayahibe. com, US$95) also offers a hiking excursion

## Isla Saona

To La Piscina Natural

Isla Catalinita

*Paso de Catuano*

Cueva Cotubanamá

Catuano

Playa Bonita

Cayo Ratón

**SHARK POINT** ★

Punta Roca

*Laguna Secucho*

*Laguna los Flamencos*

**Parque Nacional del Este**

Punta Laguna

Mano Juan

*Laguna Canto de la Playa*

0    2 mi

0    2 km

Canto de la Playa

*Caribbean  Sea*

Punta Cana

© MOON.COM

down the Padre Nuestro Trail with English-speaking guides.

After arriving at the Parque Nacional Cotubanamá reception area, you'll first spot several boards explaining the park's history, flora, and fauna, as well as Taíno past. The history behind the trail itself is equally interesting and plays a role in what the park has to offer today. This area was originally called Padre Nuestro, formerly a village of up to 180 families attracted by the freshwater springs—the park has an abundant underground lake and spring system—and the weather. They subsisted in the indigenous forest through hunting, beekeeping, and burning wood for coal production. Eventually, pollution from waste, deforestation, and hunting led to serious environmental impacts, not to mention water contamination (the aquifer supplies most of the eastern portion of the DR). This was compounded by damage caused by Hurricane George. As a result, the majority of individuals were moved to modern housing about 13 kilometers (8 miles) away in the village of Benerito, and in 2002, eight square kilometers of the land were legally transferred within the national park's boundaries. The trail was developed starting in 2007 with the help of USAID and inaugurated in early 2008. A new tour guide association provides jobs to displaced families,

who also maintain the trail, as a means of sustainable development.

Today, a hike through Padre Nuestro takes you through areas supporting some of the DR's native plants. The guayiga plant is a root vegetable used by the Taíno to make bread. Some of the Rose of Bayahibe cacti—the national flower, endemic to this region—are over 6 meters (20 feet) tall. Charcoal sites provide a replica of what villagers once used to produce coal.

## ★ Isla Saona

Simply put, **Isla Saona** is a sight for sore eyes. The island sits approximately 19 kilometers (12 miles) south of Bayahibe within the Parque Nacional Cotubanamá. Its numerous beaches, turquoise waters, glorious starfish-filled sandbanks, and towering coconut trees bring approximately 3,000 visitors to the island daily via speedboat or catamaran. It's an excursion you might be tempted to repeat. Once there, visitors can snorkel, swim, and beach-hop Saona's gorgeous shores until about 4pm. Besides being the largest offshore island of the DR at 24 kilometers long (15 miles) and 5 kilometers wide (3.3 miles), it's also the most important sea turtle nesting site in the country.

A tour of the island includes stops at the **Caves of Peñon, La Piscina Natural,**

**Mano Juan Village,** and if you're lucky, **Canto de la Playa** on the southeastern tip of the island.

## THE CAVES OF PEÑON

Excursions often stop along the western coastline of the Parque Nacional Cotubanamá, where you'll cruise along a series of dramatic cliffs and water-filled caves, the **Caves of Peñon.** Certified divers can explore underwater and discover an incredible amount of marinelife, including spotted eagle rays, sharks, and vibrant corals. Contact **ScubaFun** (Calle Principal 28, Bayahibe, tel. 809/833-0003, www.scubafun.info, single-tank dive, US$84 pp) if you're interested in exploring these caves underwater.

## LA PISCINA NATURAL

Said to be the longest or largest sandbank in the world, **La Piscina Natural,** also referred to as **La Palmilla,** offers brilliantly turquoise warm and shallow waters lined for miles with coconut trees, mangroves, and underwater seagrass patches where starfish laze at your feet. The view of this coastline is simply breathtaking and makes it a sheer paradisiacal stop worth the entire trip alone. There will be other boats along the sandbank, but it's also long enough that yours could get away from the crowd and find its own pool area. Brown pelicans fly over this idyllic spot, and you can see, in the distance, the first beach on Saona a 5- to 10-minute ride away.

Past the natural pool as you travel along the Catuano Channel separating the main island and Saona, you'll notice bird nests in mangroves. The Catuano Channel is teeming with numerous species of algae, coral sponges, fish (over 100 types), turtles, manatees, and dolphins. Keep your eyes peeled.

## MANO JUAN

The most culturally interesting stop in Parque Nacional Cotubanamá is **Mano Juan**—another 10-minute boat ride from Catuano Beach on the south end of the island. This is Saona's sole settlement. The first inhabitants came to Mano Juan during World War II, when dictator Rafael Trujillo sent them to guard the island. Today, approximately 300 people live in pastel-colored traditional wooden houses dotting sandy streets facing the beach. It is a typically Dominican fishing village. Tourism and fishing are the main occupations here, though it's mostly vendors hawking their wares or foods to visitors. Children go to school for about four hours a day because there aren't enough teachers. The village finally got electricity in 2014, thanks to solar panels. There's still no plumbing inside the homes; they pump well water instead.

On the very back end of Mano Juan, past an open field, is a turtle sanctuary. This project was established with the help of a local fisherman and funded by Seavis Tours (so, of course, they always make a stop here). Check with your chosen tour operator to make sure you get to visit the sanctuary if you're interested in conservation. About 120 to 150 eggs are laid on the beaches of Saona during turtle nesting season. Eggs were under threat due to locals eating or selling them—the belief is that this works like a drink of mamajuana—but thanks to the conservation project, preservation has improved and beaches are monitored regularly to protect the nests.

You can now have a Robinson Crusoe experience on this dreamy slice of Isla Saona by staying overnight in the protected area. **Casa Rural El Paraíso de Saona** (contact Bayahibe Fishing Centre, tel. 809/833-0009 or 829/914-4162, bayahibefishingcentre@ yahoo.com, US$60 with breakfast and dinner) offers 10 rooms in a colorful, simple single-story wooden house on the beach a stone's throw from the sea. Rooms 1 and 2 have shutters with direct a sea view. Private bathrooms, linens, fans, and mosquito nets are provided (bring repellent and long sleeves for the evenings). You'll get to enjoy Isla Saona before and after all the tourists have come and gone—and that's pretty special. Meals are provided at half or full board (breakfast and dinner only or breakfast, lunch, and dinner), with full board costing extra, and served on

the beach. There are usually fish, chicken, and lobster options. The local *colmado* also sells affordable meals. Just don't expect to be connected to the Internet or to have cell phone coverage (though you might get a signal near the police station). Reserve ahead and arrange for pickup from Bayahibe village; you could also combine your ride with a tour of Isla Saona.

### CANTO DE LA PLAYA

One of the beaches on the far southeastern tip of Saona, often deserted, is an absolute stunner: **Canto de la Playa** (the song of the beach). If you were ever to take sexy photos of yourself anywhere, this would be the beach to do it on. It's lined with taller, thinner coconut trees than the other beaches at Saona, and they continue along the shoreline as far as the eye can possibly see. The diamond-white sand is near perfection, as are the calm blue waters. If you're lucky, your tour will stop here for a swim. There's only one structure on the island: the summer home of Dr. Francisco Antonio Gonzalvo, which former president Joaquín Balaguer gifted to him for curing him of a serious illness. The house sees visitors only at Easter, when the physician's daughter descends on it with her friends.

## Isla Catalina

Directly off the shore at La Romana, **Isla Catalina** is part of the Parque Nacional Cotubanamá and closer to La Romana than Bayahibe—although both are possible starting points. The island is a stunner lined with thin, soft white sands and has a more rustic, undeveloped feel than Saona. On day trips you'll get to lunch and swim here at your leisure. There are some sketchy bathroom facilities. Portions of the beach are also used for cruise ship excursions during the winter season, and by resorts such as Casa de Campo, which often dock along a more "cleaned

up" section of the beach. The highlight of Catalina, aside from its pristine sands, is the diving and snorkeling off its shores. Two of the prettiest dives are at the 30-meter-plus (100-foot) **Catalina Wall,** with hard and soft corals and colorful Caribbean fish species. On the other side of the island is the gorgeous **Aquarium,** a 9- to 12-meter (30- to 40-foot) dive where you'll spot sea horses, black urchins, and more Caribbean critters in deep blue waters.

## Isla Catalinita

The smallest of the islands, **Isla Catalinita** is popular for snorkeling and diving. Visibility is excellent year-round, and you'll spot big Caribbean critters here including eagle rays, sharks, and sea turtles. The coral reefs are equally impressive. Check with **ScubaFun** (Calle Principal 28, Bayahibe, tel. 809/833-0003, www.scubafun.info) about an all-day snorkeling and diving trip out to Catalinita combined with Saona. You'll dive at Shark Point, snorkel off Catalinita, and continue on for lunch on Saona, before returning to the Piscina Natural and a last dive at the Caves of Penon on Saona (US$79/excursion).

# BEACHES

There are essentially two separate beaches in Bayahibe: **Playa Bayahibe,** beginning at Hilton La Romana as you enter the Bayahibe village area and continuing into the village; and **Playa Dominicus,** occupied in large part by all-inclusive hotels (also called the "hotel zone") just south of Bayahibe. Portions of both—just 100 kilometers (62 miles) from Punta Cana Airport—have earned a European Blue Flag certification. Dominicus was the first to do so in the Caribbean region, a prestigious accolade for keeping up cleanliness and environmental standards. You'll see their certified parts designated as "Playa La Laguna."

Playa Bayahibe and Playa Dominicus are public, like all beaches in the Dominican Republic, meaning that the first 60 meters (197 feet) of shoreline are accessible and you can easily stroll past seaside hotels or even

---

**1:** Mano Juan Village on Isla Saona; **2:** There are local vendors on the public end of Playa Dominicus.

swim in the water fronting the resorts as long as you're not using their lounge chairs or going inside.

Bordering the Parque Nacional Cotubanamá on one end and the Viva Wyndham on the other, the nearly mile-long **Playa Dominicus** is easily the more stunning and longer beach of the two. The most beautiful part isn't the one facing the hotels actually, but rather the fully open, unbuilt section just past the Be Live resort. It's accessible from two parking lots: one just past the Catalonia Dominicus and the other beside the Anani Beach Restaurant. Walking the entire Playa Dominicus isn't easy in the hot sun; the beach is heavily sloped in some places and the sand is thick and coarse. Prepare for a workout, and wear plenty of sunscreen and a hat. You'll find souvenir shacks along the start of the resort-free stretch, but after that are quiet parts where you can stroll to your heart's content and swim with less company. The water at Dominicus is blissful. There are gentle rolling waves that make you feel like you are on a floatie, and the turquoise is perfectly iridescent. Alongside some of the resorts, as well as a small portion of the public area, you'll find some rocks upon entry, but they are easily avoided. You can lay your towel and relax like a Dominican or opt for a lounge chair at Anani while enjoying an Italian lunch. The far eastern end of the beach leads to an entrance into the Parque Nacional Cotubanamá, but I don't recommend wandering there on your own without a guide.

**Playa Bayahibe** is smaller, yet no less picture-perfect with its gorgeous bay, even if it isn't as continuous a stretch as Dominicus. Parts of the beachfront are occupied by numerous excursion boats, and in the distance, fancier catamarans. Still, there are portions where you can lay your towel and marvel at this fishing village's postcard-worthy scenery on the stretch past Hilton La Romana and before reaching town. Want a quieter, more exclusive section where you could easily be alone on a weekday? Walk all the way west of the main street, past Mare Nostrum, and once

you reach Barco Bar, make a right. You'll find idyllic white sands as well as an adjacent cove-shaped stretch.

Both Dominicus and Bayahibe beaches get rowdier on "Dominican Sundays," when locals flock from neighboring La Romana, as well as Santo Domingo, to bathe and relax.

# SPORTS AND RECREATION
## Diving and Snorkeling

Whether you're a beginner or looking for a fun time under the waters of Bayahibe, the American-owned **ScubaFun** (Calle Principal 28, Bayahibe, tel. 809/833-0003, www.scubafun.info, 2-tank dive US$80/half day) is your best bet, with excellent staff from the desk to the dive masters. Dives head to all the offshore islands with a range of wall dives, and there are the popular Bayahibe shipwrecks *Coco* and *St. George* and the caves of Padre Nuestro to explore. An excursion fee will be tacked onto the tank-dive cost when you head to the islands, so be sure to inquire what it is and allocate funds for it.

In addition to making trips to the offshore islands, **Casa Daniel** (Calle Principal, bayfront, tel. 809/833-0083, www.casa-daniel.com, US$156-162/two-tank dives to Catalina or Saona) goes on local dive trips to coral-rich areas in the national park and along Dominicus Reef, a five-minute boat ride from Bayahibe's shores. Shipwrecks such as the *Atlantic Princess* and *St. George* are also options, as well as cave diving. You can do a combined diving and snorkeling trip (US$48-54) if you only have one diver in your group and others want to explore on the surface before getting to the islands to relax together.

## Sailing

You'll be spoiled with options when it comes to sailing along Bayahibe's bay and on to its nearby islands. Nearly all of the tour operators in town will be seeking you out to sign up. Thousands descend on the village every day from nearby Punta Cana to sail these dreamy Caribbean waters.

# Diving for Treasures

Off the coast of Bayahibe, divers not only get to explore the colorful reef, walls, and fascinating caves of the Parque Nacional Cotubanamá, but also historic shipwrecks turned underwater archaeological and marine museums. These living museums play an important role in the preservation of history as well as supporting biodiversity. Whichever wreck you end up exploring, remember to always take care not to touch or remove anything. These are fragile ecosystems; a reef environment is very easily affected by the presence of humans.

A half-mile off the coast of Dominicus Beach, the *St. George* Shipwreck is the most popular dive and certainly one of the most colorful. Built in 1962 in Scotland to transport wheat and barley between Norway and the Americas, the 73-meter-long (240-foot) cargo ship—originally known as *M. V. Norbrae*—was later abandoned in Santo Domingo after 20 years of service. After it was destroyed by Hurricane George, which hit the DR in 1998, the ship was renamed after that disaster and eventually moved and purposely sunk off Dominicus's shores on June 12, 1999. It is now an artificial reef with sponges and corals, attracting all sorts of Caribbean critters, particularly large barracudas. Experienced divers can literally go in and out of the ship during their dive.

Opened in July 2002, the 1724 Guadalupe Underwater Archeological Preserve is directly across from the Viva Dominicus Beach Resort. The 1,000-ton, 74-gun Spanish galleon *Nuestra Señora de Guadalupe* originally set sail in 1724 from Spain to Mexico, carrying mercury (used in Spain's gold and silver mines) and passengers. A hurricane caused her to get stuck near Samaná Bay and sink off a reef along the coast of the DR. The majority of the passengers survived, while the mercury remained stuck in the hold. In 1976, the Dominican government hired a salvaging firm to recover any artifacts and prevent looting. They pulled up cannons, crystals, and religious objects. In 2002, Indiana University suggested that the artifacts be put back underwater as an exhibit for divers and snorkelers. The school developed the preserve in about 8 meters (26 feet) of water just 0.4 kilometers (0.3 miles) off Dominicus. Today you'll spot several cannons, an anchor, cannonballs, and a deadeye from the shipwreck. These substrates attract all of the coral and marinelife you see.

Off the shores of Isla Catalina is the Captain Kidd Shipwreck: Living Museum of the Sea, opened in 2011. The wreck lies under 3 meters (10 feet) of water and wasn't discovered for almost three centuries. A snorkeler spotted the cannons in 2007. The infamous pirate captured this ship in 1698 in the Indian Ocean and later abandoned it off the southwest coast of the DR. With the help of Charlie Beeker, director of Indiana University's Office of Underwater Science, and his colleagues, the wreck was confirmed as Captain Kidd's. It held guns and anchors. Today, it helps the underwater sealife thrive, particularly coral.

At 13 meters (41 feet) deep, the *Atlantic Princess* is an easy wreck to navigate and swim through, therefore a good choice for PADI Open Water divers. The former tourist boat from Bayahibe is home to numerous species of sponges, corals, and fish, schools of sergeants major, trumpetfish, and the invasive lionfish.

Among your best options is **ProExcursions Bayahibe** (tel. 829/659-4688, www.proexcursionsbayahibe.com, US$195, includes all gear, meal, and drinks) and their Saona Prestige trip. You'll sail to Isla Saona on a 23-meter (75-foot) luxury catamaran. A notch up, and the way to explore the Caribbean Sea the way it was meant to be, is to contact **Seavis Tours** (beachfront, between Dreams Resort Bayahibe and town, Calle Eladia 4, tel. 829/714-4947, www.seavisbayahibe.com, US$1,200/day charter,

includes lunch). Their private 16-meter (51-foot) Dragonsmoke sailboat accommodates up to 10 people and will head to multiple islands, if you wish, and stay as long as you like.

## Paddleboarding

**Bayahibe SUP** (Bayahibe Beach, tel. 809/609-4045, www.bayahibesup.com, 9am-5pm Tues.-Sun., US$50 two hours with instruction or US$20/hour) operates out of a simple shack and will take you on SUP excursions. They have everything from a "Surfari" two-hour trip along the coastline (US$50) to a paddle and snorkeling combo (US$40).

## Fishing

**Bayahibe Fishing Centre** (tel. 809/833-0009, www.bayahibefishingcentre.com, US$175/half day pp, 4 people minimum) goes out on affordable half-day morning deep-sea fishing trips with popular Captain Pepe. You'll catch sailfish, marlin, king mackerel, mahi-mahi, and other big fish trolling 3-16 kilometers (2-10 miles) offshore. You can share the boat or charter it, with a minimum of 4 and maximum of 8 people per boat. Fishing trips can also be combined with excursions to Saona and Catalina. **ProExcursions Bayahibe** (tel. 829/659-4688, www.proexcursionsbayahibe.com, US$195, includes all gear, meal, and drinks) offers a leisurely sailing, deep-sea fishing, and snorkeling trip aboard a 12-meter (38-foot) catamaran that takes you from the village shores all the way to Isla Saona.

## ENTERTAINMENT AND EVENTS

Bayahibe is a tiny village. What little nightlife there is centers on a couple of bars. The ones that aren't frequented by too many working ladies are listed here.

### Bars and Nightclubs

Bayahibe's **Super Colmado** gets going every day around 5pm when employees of hotels hang here after work. They are joined by guides, fishers, and, as the night goes on, the ladies of the evening. You'll get a feel for an authentic, small-town Dominican *colmado* here. Couples will dance both inside the bar/store and outside on the sidewalk as the music blasts and the beer flows all night, including spillover across the street. It's the liveliest local spot in the village, where all the usual suspects can be seen daily.

Tucked away at the western end of the main road, and yet a minute's walk from the center of the village, **Barco Bar**'s (Calle La Bahía, tel. 849/875-5081, info@barco-bar. com, 8:30am-12:30am daily, US$3-15) ambience and views are hard to match. The casual, open-air bar and restaurant is not much more than wooden tables and chairs but offers the best cocktails-at-sunset scene as well as a beach stretch right in the *pueblo*. Sit on the wooden swings if your bottom fits and take in the breeze and the bay. The food is decent, ranging from pasta to fish dishes. Wednesdays are poplar for karaoke, and weekends (particularly Sundays) are busy as Dominican families come from nearby La Romana to relax.

**Café Saona** (Calle Principal, bayfront, tel. 809/349-5164, www.saonacafe.com, 10am-11:45pm Tues.-Sun., 10am-2am Fri.-Sat.) is a good spot to mingle. It serves up cheap but potent cocktails to the latest tunes from happy hour on. **The Pit Stop** (Carretera Bayahibe-Dominicus, tel. 809/272-8933, thepitstopbayahibe@hotmail.com, 10pm-4am Thurs.-Sun.) is where everyone ends up late at night, after a few drinks at the Super Colmado. The vibe and the music are Dominican, and the dancing goes on late. Note that Fridays get wild with a bar-top strip show of near-naked men and women doing all sorts of nasty acrobatics.

**Kviar Show Disco** (Boulevard Dominicus-Americanus, www.kviar.com.do, 10pm-4am, free except during special events) offers the area's first full-on modern club experience. Check with your hotel for a shuttle to the venue, and to purchase cover ahead of time for special events.

### Festivals

The **Bayahibe Torneo de Pesca** is an annual fishing tournament that makes for a great visit. Running Thursday to Sunday during the second or third week of May, up to 30 teams—mostly from Bayahibe, but a handful from Boca de Yuma, Isla Saona, and La Romana—head out to sea each day in search of the biggest and heaviest catch. I've seen catches weighing up to 14 kilograms (30 pounds), including mahi-mahi. The catch is weighed right in town at the entrance of the bay where the boats come in, in full view of the cafés and a highly excited local crowd of families and children. There are picnic tables set up above the bay in the grassy area, where folks go to buy a plate of freshly caught fish from the tournament, as well as chicken. A DJ blasts merengue, *bachata,* and reggaeton all day long throughout the tournament.

## FOOD
### Cafes
**Café La Marina** (tel. 809/260-1426, lamarinacafe@yahoo.com) is your best bet for a cup of coffee and breakfast right in the village, especially before you head out for the day's adventures. **Waikiki Café** (slightly behind and across from Saona Café) makes thick breakfast sandwiches and strong coffee.

### Dominican
**Comedor Criollo Amarillis** (off main street, Calle Los Manantiales, across from Supermercado La Defensa, noon-9pm daily, US$3-5) serves up homemade Dominican food amid local *comedor* experience, with all the special characters that entails. Try *la bandera dominicana*, a plate of rice and beans with a meat stew (always on offer at lunchtime) or a bowl of *sancocho,* a traditional meat and vegetable soup. There's an outdoor terrace if you want to enjoy your meal with views of Bayahibe.

    **Saona Café** (Calle Principal, bayfront, tel. 809/833-0541, www.saonacafe.com, 10am-11:45pm Tues.-Sun., 2am close Fri.-Sat., US$3.90-14.40) remains my favorite stop after a long day of exploring the village or its Caribbean waters. The food is cheap and tasty, and the service is friendly. There are all the usual choices from sandwiches to seafood. Be sure to ask about the lionfish, their specialty, and the fish-and-chips is to die for. The wide selection of mojitos and caipirinhas don't disappoint. It also has the best views for people-watching across the bay.

    The laid-back yet tastefully decorated ★ **El Dorado** (beachfront Bayahibe, tel. 809/214-8792, 11am-11pm daily, US$5-10) is a must when in Bayahibe thanks to its tastefully

prepared and affordable seafood dishes, bursting with Dominican flavor. Ideally situated in the heart of the village yet away from the foot traffic, facing a gorgeous stretch of the public beach and anchored boats, the outdoor patio and white-painted wooden chairs and tables sit under a giant tree, with steady breezes from the sea. Opt for the fried or stewed fish, among other options, with sides of rice, *tostones,* or salad. The lobster pasta is also a solid pick. Portions are huge (two fish on a plate for a single order), the presentation delightful, and the freshly squeezed juices are just right, not too sweet like most Dominican restaurants. It's the perfect spot for a nice lunch or dinner out.

### International
If you're up for a good steak dinner, **Perlita Morena** (off the main street, tel. 829/919-5296, 11am-3pm and 6pm-11pm Tues.-Sun., US$10-20) serves up tasty imported Texas beef, grilled to your liking. **Mamma Mia** (next to Perlita Morena, off the main street, tel. 829/664-1694, noon-9pm Tues.-Sun., US$3-5) is probably the best deal in town for cheap but tasty Italian, served out of a small corner building you might otherwise miss, one street behind the bay. Homemade dishes come out of a tiny kitchen, but portions are generous and flavorful.

    For a romantic dinner table perched directly over the rocks and the Caribbean sea, yet right in the village, head to the laid-back **Doña Clara** (Calle Principal, no phone, 8am-10pm daily, US$5-15). The food is decent enough though not spectacular, but the views delight, especially at sunset. On offer are various types of pasta dishes and seafood.

    **Mare Nostrum** (Calle Principal, tel. 809/833-0055, www.marenuestro.com, noon-10:30pm Tues.-Sun., US$10-30) is a decent spot for fine dining and the only upscale option. It has the best view in town from an open terrace perched above the Bayahibe waters. The service leaves a little to be desired, but the ultra-long menu offers a wide choice of salads and especially seafood. Try the seafood

carpaccio or lobster ravioli. There are endless pasta options, including risotto, as well as meat-free dishes.

Facing the public section of Bayahibe Beach, adjacent to Hilton La Romana, **Kukka Beach Restaurant** (beachfront, Av. Laguna, tel. 849/655-1608, 8am-midnight Fri.-Wed., US$5-10) serves up more Italian favorites, including fresh seafood. Meals and service are decent, but the location and privacy alone are worth the price of a meal. Funky yet soothing Latin beats accompany your meal, while the constant roll and crash of iridescent turquoise waves carries on a few steps away from your table. Swimming here is simply heavenly; take a dip pre- or post-meal. The restaurant also allows use of its beach chairs and showers for around US$3.

## ACCOMMODATIONS

Bayahibe is pretty much divided into two zones, so you'll have two choices of where to stay: at a hotel in the *pueblo* itself or at one the all-inclusive resorts lining Playa Dominicus, ranging from Iberostar to the Catalonia. Keep in mind that getting from one side of Bayahibe to the other will require a bus or an overpriced taxi. Those who stay in an all-inclusive might end up having to stick to their area or only come out once to visit the village. They do have the advantage, however, of being on the longest and prettiest beach stretch in Bayahibe. The exception among the all-inclusive resorts is Hilton La Romana, which is just a two-minute walk down the beach to the village. When you stay at Dreams or in the village proper, you'll have easy access to all the excellent local restaurants and nightlife.

### Under US$50

**Hotel Bayahibe** (tel. 809/833-0159, www. hotelbayahibe.net/home.html, US$37) is your classic beachside hotel, with an art-decorated lobby and hallways cheerfully painted in tropical island colors. Rooms are equally spotless

and bright, and have tiled floors and double beds, air-conditioning, mini fridges, TV, and phone. There are appealing open-air balcony lounge areas on every floor. It's a good deal for the money.

The Italian-Dominican family-owned **Villa Baya Aparta-Hotel** (Calle Tamariando 1, U.S. tel. 888/790-5264 or tel. 809/833-0048, www.apartahotelvillabaya.com, US$40-50) offers a range of six well-appointed rooms, three suites with kitchen, and eight apartments inside a residential compound that is just two minutes off the main drag and another two to the beach. The rooms are split across three-story peach buildings named after the islands off the coast of Bayahibe. There's a budget room for the solo traveler, but note that it's tiny, removed from the wireless Internet signal, and can get hot (it has just a fan). There's a central courtyard with a seating area, and continental breakfast and coffee are served daily with fresh fruits. Amenities include free wireless Internet and ample parking. They can also help arrange excursions. It can get very noisy in the neighborhood, but that's what happens when you stay smack in the village.

A better deal is the quaint **Bayahibe Guest House** (1 Calle Los Manantiales, tel. 829/642-6243, www.bayahibeguesthouse. com, US$48-93), a white villa turned into a series of boutique apartments and six comfy double rooms (US$48), decorate with care, that hug a charming and verdant garden (look out for hummingbirds and wake to birds singing). The housekeeper's towel art and fresh flowers in the room will surprise you daily. Rooms include a mini fridge, flat-screen cable TV, air-conditioning, a fan, safe, coffeemaker, rain showers, and fast Wi-Fi. There's a security guard on-site all night. It's a five-minute walk to the heart of the village.

### US$100 and Up

The laid-back yet upscale ★ **Hilton La Romana** (Bayahibe Beach, tel. 809/221-8880, www.dreamsresorts.com, US$101-266) is located in Bayahibe, not in La Romana as its

1: food at El Dorado; 2: Hilton La Romana on a beautiful section of Bayahibe's beach name suggests. Its most recent addition includes an Adults Only Preferred Club section, worthwhile for those who want the perks of an all-inclusive and then some with private access to a stunning pool area, club lounge, two restaurants, a private beach section, and wireless Internet (otherwise not included). The resort is immaculately clean, spacious, and pleasant to the eye. Rooms are cozy, with comfortable beds, strong air-conditioning, flat-screen TVs, glass showers and soaking tubs, and a stocked mini fridge. The portion of Playa Bayahibe facing the resort is small but charming, although it can get crowded with lounge chairs. The farther right toward the dock you go, the quieter it is. Alternatively, you can walk a bit past the resort beach going toward the village and lay your towel there. The resort's several restaurants are quite good for an all-inclusive, and you don't need reservations for any of them. The best are Portofino and Olio. Other amenities include nightly entertainment with live music, a disco, and merengue dance classes on the beach during the day. If you're going to stay at an all-inclusive in Bayahibe or in La Romana province, this would be your best pick for a relaxing, pampered stay, only a stone's throw from the fishing village of Bayahibe with its own excellent local restaurants, shops, and bars.

Sandwiched among a row of beachfront resorts, **Iberostar Hacienda Dominicus** (Playa Dominicus, tel. 809/688-3600, www. iberostar.com, from US$169) is on the Dominicus side of Bayahibe, about 5 kilometers (3 miles) south of the village. It has a popular black-and-white-painted lighthouse bar right on the beach that you can spot from miles away. The five-star resort is spotless and offers impressive comforts, à la Iberostar: fountains amid manicured grounds, three pools, seven restaurants, a fitness room, and nightly entertainment.

**Whala!bayahíbe** (Calle Corales la Magdalena, Dominicus, 809/468-1619, www. whalabayahibe.com/en, US$108, deals online) is for those who want a more intimate experience than the all-inclusive. A former condominium complex turned resort, it is perched at the start of Dominicus's clifftop area, just five minutes' ride from Dominicus Beach. The resort's highlight is its series of three big infinity pools directly over the cliffs and the Caribbean Sea. There are steps that take you down to dip in the sea if you choose (avoid days of rough sea, even if you see others daring it). The double seafront view rooms boast gorgeous panoramic views from your king-size bed or from your spacious balcony—watch the sailboats and catamarans going to and returning from Isla Saona—and offer flat-screen TV, phone, mini fridge, and spacious shower-equipped baths. There are two restaurants on-site, but the buffet is surprisingly the better pick. You can opt to pay an extra fee to include all your meals. A free shuttle shuffles guests to Dominicus Beach all day long, every 30 minutes from 9am until 6pm.

## GETTING THERE AND AROUND

**Expreso La Romana** coach bus service (in Bayahibe, local bus station near village parking lot; in Santo Domingo, Calle Caracas, corner of Calle Jacinto de la Concha, near Parque Enriquillo, tel. 809/596-6765, US$5pp one-way) now connects travelers directly to Bayahibe from Santo Domingo. Take the "express" with a grain of salt during earlier weekdays (when the bus tends to fill up, and drop-offs are frequent in La Romana), but on weekends it tends to be a speedier journey of about 2.5 hours. The set departure schedule—whether from Santo Domingo to Bayahibe or vice versa—as of publication time is 7am, noon, and 5pm.

Getting to Bayahibe from La Romana is a mere 15-minute ride. If you're coming from La Romana Airport, expect to pay around US$30 for a taxi ride for up to five people. It's a lot cheaper to reach Bayahibe from downtown La Romana, where you can hop in a *guagua* from the Parque Central for about 60 pesos (US$1.33). If you'd rather invest in a taxi ride, contact **Cesar Avila** (tel. 809/392-8685), a taxi driver based in Bayahibe, and try to negotiate.

He can also take you from Bayahibe village to the Dominicus side (RD$500 one-way).

If you're up for a day of sightseeing in La Romana city, find the local bus station in Bayahibe village: an orange-painted open garage labeled "ASODEMIROBAM Parada Bayahibe-Romana" located across from the giant parking lot where tourist buses park (ask anyone if you don't spot it). This will get you to La Romana for just 60 pesos (US$1.60) one-way.

Getting around the village of Bayahibe itself is super easy: just walk. No cars needed. It's a small place and you'll want to slowly wander its colorful streets and alleys and take photos of its traditional wooden homes. If you're interested in getting around by scooter or rental car, try **Dominican Emotion** (tel. 809/897-9270 or 809/452-5698, www.dominicanemotion. com, US$13/day scooter, US$33/day sedan, also offers discounted tours).

## Information and Services

You'll find the answer to all of your needs right in Bayahibe village. If you're on the Dominicus side, there are plenty of small markets and services—just a tad pricier perhaps, because of the location.

In the village, there's an **Internet center** (25 pesos or US$.50/30 min., 8am-9pm Mon.-Sat.) with four or five desktop computers in a blue building on the main drag across from **CESTUR** (tel. 809/200-3500).

**Supermercado La Defensa** (Calle Juan Brito, tel. 809/833-0504, 7:30am-9pm daily), the local supermarket, is a few steps up from ScubaFun, next to the town's Super Colmado bar/corner store.

You'll find a **BanReservas ATM** beside Hotel Bayahibe—keep your wits about you anytime you are withdrawing money on the street.

# The Samaná Peninsula

Sticking out of the northeastern coast like an outstretched arm, the Samaná Peninsula is one big showcase of tropical splendor. Towering bluffs and lush green hills stand in contrast to the deep blue Atlantic. Rustic and uncrowded beaches stretch out against the horizon. Waterfalls cascade and coconut trees sway.

This coast is home to some of the country's top-rated beaches, including Playa Rincón and Playa Frontón in Las Galeras, and Playa Cosón in Las Terrenas. The rugged landscape of the peninsula, particularly in Los Haitises and El Valle, offers a lot of recreation options for those who like the outdoors. There are hard-to-reach corners, mysterious caves, glistening rivers, and far-flung beaches like Playa Morón and Playa El Valle.

# Highlights

Look for ★ to find recommended sights, activities, dining, and lodging.

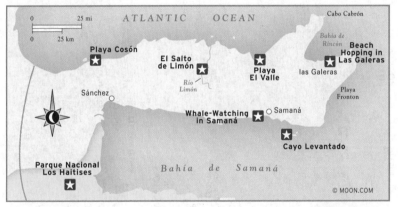

★ **Cayo Levantado:** Five kilometers (three miles) off the shore of Samaná, this dazzling island was once the site of a major Bacardi commercial—giving it the nickname "Bacardi Island" (page 165).

★ **Parque Nacional Los Haitises:** Take a boat tour to see giant mangroves and towering bluffs, teeming with birdlife and insights into the Taíno past (page 166).

★ **Playa El Valle:** The bumpy journey to this spectacular beach will reward you with cliff views, authentic fishing scenes, and delicious seafood (page 168).

★ **Whale-Watching in Samaná:** Witness the 40-ton humpbacks during their mating season from mid-January through March (page 170).

★ **Beach-Hopping in Las Galeras:** Take a boat tour to three of the most beautiful beaches in the DR: **Playa Rincón, Playa Frontón,** and **Playa Madama.** You'll spend an entire day swimming, sunbathing, and snorkeling (page 180).

★ **El Salto de Limón:** Horseback ride or hike through lush forests to reach the peninsula's most spectacular waterfall, towering more than 27 meters (90 feet) high (page 187).

★ **Playa Cosón:** Bury your toes in spongy sands and take a dip in warm waters at the most stunning beach in Las Terrenas. When you get hungry, indulge in some of the best fresh fish in the region (page 189).

# The Samaná Peninsula

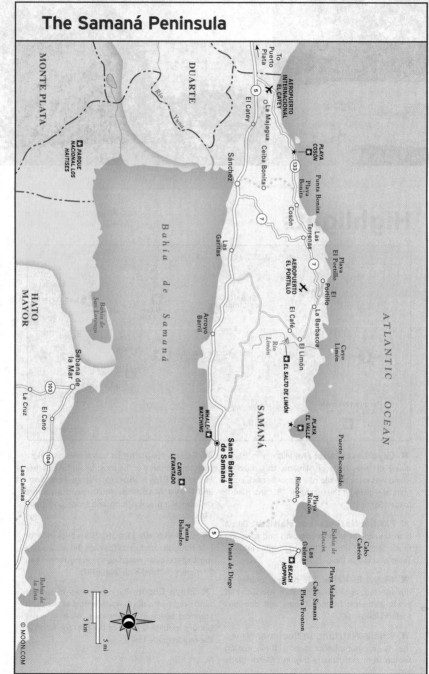

© MOON.COM

The peninsula was an isolated escape before the opening of El Catey International Airport in 2006, followed by the installment of a scenic highway linking the peninsula to Santo Domingo in 2011. But Samaná's charm holds fast despite the growth. The vibe on the peninsula remains laid-back. The melting pot of history, food, and cultures attracts independent and international visitors. Las Terrenas, a funky beach haven with a lively European beat, is particularly international, with boutique hotels, trendy cafés, and French bakeries. Opportunities to immerse yourself and mingle with locals abound amid the peninsula's Afro-Euro Caribbean beat.

## PLANNING YOUR TIME

There are three main areas you'll want to consider when planning a trip to Samaná Peninsula: the town of Santa Bárbara de Samaná, Las Galeras, and Las Terrenas. The peninsula as a whole remains quite a distance from the rest of the island, but getting there has been made easier by an international airport at El Catey and a highway linking the peninsula and Santo Domingo in just 2.5 hours.

Las Galeras and Las Terrenas are your best bets for overnight stays. Samaná town doesn't have much happening unless it's humpback whale season. Passing through this scenic town to enjoy the gorgeous bay views and the nearby El Valle region is worth it, however, even for just a day. Explore the town on foot to visit La Churcha, the Malecón, and its peculiar Bridges to Nowhere. Or head directly north to El Valle, where you can take in some of the most splendid scenery in the country at Playa El Valle.

From there, continue northeast until you reach the end of the road—literally—and you'll hit Las Galeras, a rustic and quiet fishing village blessed with amazing beaches, tucked between the Atlantic and a cliff-hugging coastline. Spend at least two days here to hike, dive, beach hop by boat, and indulge in the freshest seafood.

Head east for two more days to the more developed and trendier Las Terrenas, with its own funky, international beach vibe, where you can indulge in French cuisine, breathtaking beaches, and plenty of nightlife.

# Santa Bárbara de Samaná

The Samaná Peninsula's capital, Santa Bárbara de Samaná—called Samaná for short—is a small, scenic bayfront town of 15,000 inhabitants and a quiet hub where tourism, construction, and fishing are the main industries. Samaná's big moment comes once a year—from January through March—when the humpback whales make their entrance into the bay and stay there to mate and calve.

Much of the day-to-day activity in town centers on the Malecón, which offers scenic strolls with views of bluffs and sea. Everyday life is simple yet authentic, with fishing and sailing boats floating in the bay, children playing soccer and baseball nearby in the center of town, and others resting up in the shade by the water. At night, the Malecón—nicely updated with more green spaces and benches—echoes with merengue, and locals congregate by the sea for a twirl and a cold beer, particularly on the weekends. Past the small-town atmosphere, Samaná has made efforts to keep with the times, with modern European-style outdoor cafés and fine-dining options lining the main drag. Revamped waterfront *casetas* have given older haunts a facelift and are offering a variety of snacks, from ice cream to Italian-style pizza.

**Previous:** Las Terrenas Beach; Cayo Levantado; Parque Nacional Los Haitises.

It's true that not much goes on in this town when the whales aren't passing through and attracting thousands of cruise ship visitors and other nature lovers in the first quarter of the year. But Samaná offers easy access to Los Haitises National Park, and if you're passing through in the summer, you might get to enjoy the unique harvest festivals celebrated by Samaná's African American descendants—complete with ginger beer, johnnycakes, and coconut treats.

Up in the hills, more guesthouses are tucked away in the neighborhood of Samaná Heights. Drive just a bit farther—past blankets of coconut trees and a string of uncrowded local beaches—and enjoy towering views over the Bahía de Samaná.

## SIGHTS
### El Malecón

Samaná's waterfront faces one of the most beautiful bays you'll see in the DR. It's decorated with sailboats and, in the distance, mangrove cays connected by the town's famous Bridges to Nowhere. Like most *malecón* areas across the DR, it's quiet during the day as most folks relax on grassy areas under the trees away from the harsh sun yet close to the sea breeze, while the kids are jumping off the dock into the water. El Malecón comes to life at sunset with various kiosk bars and restaurants offering snacks, from ice cream to authentic Italian pizza, and plenty of outdoor seating and merriment along the water as well as the avenue across from it. **La Ballena Blanca** is a bar on the bay open most of the day and night, with tables literally steps from the water below, under a tree (heads up, Wednesdays are karaoke nights). Across the street are more bars street side, such as **Tronco Móvil,** where locals play dominoes, throw back beers, and twirl to music late into the night.

### Los Puentes (The Bridges to Nowhere)

Looking out from the waterfront avenue,

you'll immediately notice a long bridge—in actuality, two bridges, linking two small offshore cays that look like deserted mangrove isles. Soon you'll wonder just where exactly the bridges lead, because they seem to just stop at one point in the middle of the water. The answer is, nowhere! Samaná's iconic, dated bridges are a sight in and of themselves. They do lead from town—there is public access to the stairwell to begin hiking the bridges adjacent to the Cayacoa resort—to two small cays. The first stretch alone is 200 meters (655 feet) long and takes you to the first and most frequented plot on Cayo Linares with a small beach where locals hang out and swim.

These bridges were a project of former DR president Joaquín Balaguer, who was inspired by and misread an architectural plan once put together by Napoleon. He saw Samaná's bay and surrounding hills as an ideal base for his own conquering ambitions and ordered the bridges' construction in the 1970s. Balaguer's grandiose plan included turning Samaná into a resort town, despite the difficulty of access at the time, and adding a restaurant on the first cay. Unfortunately, nothing but its shell remains. Be careful climbing up those steps to the top of the first cay.

The dilapidated condition of the bridges and steps is evident as you make your way across them, and you might wonder how they've lasted this long. But they remain sturdy and safe for now to cross and hike for stunning views of the bay. The sunrise from here is well worth it.

### The Market

Samaná's small but lively covered market reveals the abundance of the area's fresh produce, as well as its primary cultivation: the coconut. You'll find everything you need here, from local fruits and vegetables—including yams, plantains, green bananas, sweet potatoes, and glandules—to fish to a butcher's shop where the meat hangs in plain view. Locals are friendly here and don't mind photos—just ask first.

# Santa Bárbara de Samaná

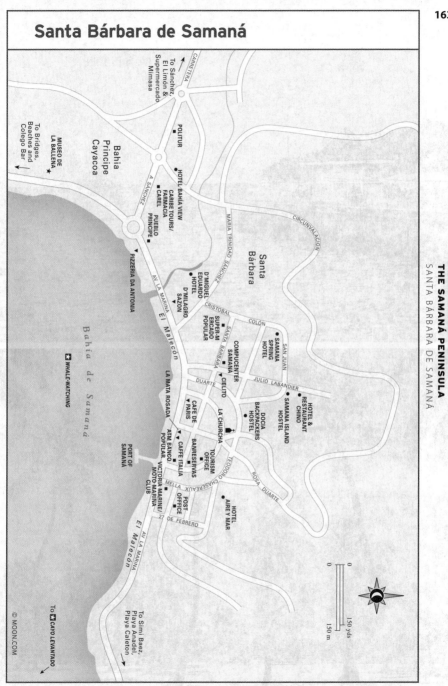

To Sánchez,
El Limón &
Supermercado
Mimasa

CARRETERA

POLITUR

To Bridges,
Beaches and
Colego Bar

MUSEO DE
LA BALLENA

Bahía
Príncipe
Cayacoa

HOTEL BAHIA VIEW

CARIBE TOURS/
FARMACIA
CAREL
PUEBLO
PRÍNCIPE

A SÁNCHEZ

CIRCUNVALACIÓN

MARÍA TRINIDAD SÁNCHEZ

Santa
Bárbara

PIZZERIA DA ANTONIA

AV LA MARINA

D'MIGUEL
EDUARDO
HOTEL

D'MILAGRO
SAZÓN

El Malecón

CRISTOBAL

COLÓN

SUPER-M
ERCADO
POPULAR

SANTA BÁRBARA

SAMANA
SPRING
HOTEL

SAN JUAN

Bahía de Samaná

WHALE-WATCHING

COMPUCENTER
SAMANA

CIELITO

JULIO LABANDIER

HOTEL &
RESTAURANT
CHINO

LA MATA ROSADA

DUARTE

CAFÉ DE
PARÍS

LA CHURCHA

DOCIA
BACKPACKERS
HOSTEL

SAMANA ISLAND
HOSTEL

PORT OF
SAMANA

ATM BANCO
POPULAR

CAFFE ITALIA

BANRESERVAS

TOURISM
OFFICE

TEODORO CHASSEREAUX

ROSA DUARTE

MOTO MARINA
CLUB

MELLA

VICTORIA MARINE

POST
OFFICE

HOTEL
AIREY MAR

27 DE FEBRERO

AV LA MARINA

El Malecón

0      150 yds

0      150 m

To CAYO LEVANTADO

To Simi Baez,
Playa Anadel,
Playa Caletón

## Museo de la Ballena (Whale Museum & Observatory)

A bit hidden from plain view, the town's **Museo de la Ballena** (tel. 809/538-2042, 8:30am-3pm Mon.-Fri., RD$100 or US$2.20) is dedicated to the visiting mammals that bring in tourists three months out of the year. It's a small space, exhibiting a handful of informative billboards and photos about the history of Samaná and on the humpback whale species. It also showcases the full skeleton of Nima, found dead in February 1993 amid rocks off the coast of the peninsula between Samaná town and Las Galeras.

## La Churcha

The oldest and most significant structure in Samaná is the 18th-century **La Churcha**—a Dominican play on the English word *church*—officially known as the Iglesia Metodista de San Pedro. It's a beautiful gothic structure brought over from England in 1901. Its red corrugated iron roofing stands out against a sea of modern buildings. The story behind this place of worship, still in regular use today, goes back to its founding in 1824 by freed African Americans who moved here from Philadelphia and New York at the invitation of Haiti, then-ruler of the entire island of Hispaniola. The new residents came here with their spiritual leader, Reverend Isaac Miller—his tomb remains on-site, with his wife's.

From the beginning, the denomination was the African Methodist Episcopal Church (Metodista Episcopal Africana). Its historical importance led La Churcha to be declared a *patrimonio cultural,* or part of the DR's cultural heritage. If you get the chance, meet the current pastor Albert Moses James Cuello, who comes from Barahona, south of the DR, and is a descendant of the *cocolos,* yet another group of African descendants who came from various parts of the English-speaking Caribbean to work in the sugarcane fields of the south. The mass at La Churcha—called *culto*—is held in Spanish, with some English hymns and chants.

Inside you'll find parts from the original structure, as well as refurbished and replaced pieces. The altar is an original, as are the side pews and the two stained glass windows. At the back of the church you will find a photo of the first structure erected before the current one was brought over from England. There are schedules posted on a notice board, as well as events. This is also where you'll find information on the harvest festivals, held from June through October on the church grounds, celebrating all things agriculture—as their ancestors did—with African-influenced foods including *pan inglés,* coconut dishes, and ginger beer. The church maintains additional chapels in different parts of the Samaná Peninsula in Limón and Las Galeras.

## ★ Cayo Levantado ("Bacardi Island")

This large cay off the coast of Samaná, about 10 minutes or 6 kilometers (3.7 miles) away by boat, has one of the most stunning white-sand beaches on the peninsula. Known as "Bacardi Island" because it was the site of a popular Bacardi commercial in the 1970s, it's an idyllic spot to spend a day. The island is part private—the all-inclusive Grand Bahia Principe Levantado occupies two-thirds of the island—and part public. The beach is spacious, and the turquoise waters are shallow near shore, if rocky in parts. The views of the bluffs and the bay in the distance are stunning.

Walk to the back of the beach and you'll find a sort of "beach food court" where all the various fish shacks and local restaurants tempt customers with fried catches, from snapper to lobster, along with all the typical Dominican sides and fresh piña coladas (US$5).

To get to Cayo Levantado, you can opt for an organized tour—most operators include a stop here along with a boat excursion to Los Haitises National Park, or whale-watching when in season. If you'd rather just head here solo, you can catch a boat from the Samaná

1: El Malecón; 2: Cayo Levantado

# Samaná's African American Heritage

Between 1824 and 1825, around 200 families came from the East Coast of the United States—specifically from Philadelphia and New York—at the invitation of then-president Jean-Pierre Boyer of Haiti. At this time Haiti had control over the entire island of Hispaniola including the DR. As one of the first leaders of Haiti after the Haitian Revolution of the 19th century, the president established a pro-African immigration policy with the aim of welcoming those of who had been stripped from their native lands and sold into slavery, offering them a form of repatriation to a better place (Africa was considered too far and expensive to achieve, as well as dangerous healthwise). These families reached Samaná by boat, bringing along their traditions as well as their AME religion. Once here, they were given land.

Although the Samaná population includes many nationalities from various parts of the world, these *Americanos de Samaná*, as locals call them, had more influence on Santa Bárbara de Samaná's culture than any of the others. They inspired a cuisine with typical African foods, including *pan ingles*, coconut-based meals, and ginger beer. They established their own church—La Churcha, as it's famously known, now a *patrimonio cultural*—and still hold African Methodist masses. Various pastors came to serve there from Jamaica to Puerto Rico; those who spoke Spanish brought their Latin influence along.

Today, descendants of those African Americans speak Spanish and have adopted Dominican culture, but many still celebrate their own tradition of the harvest festivals, a religious celebration in which farmers give thanks to God for water, land, and agriculture, and bring fruits and produce to the church. There's plenty of outdoor cooking, and ginger beer and coconut fish are popular. The festivals take place every Sunday from July to October. A calendar is published and posted inside La Churcha for those interested in attending. The last Sunday of October is the biggest celebration of all the harvest festivals and recognized as an official holiday by the Samaná City Hall.

Port (the main dock on the waterfront) for about US$33 round-trip or RD$1,500 for up to three people; the larger the group, the more room you have to bargain. You'll find additional boat captains outside of Samaná town, on the road to Las Galeras, on Playa Carenero, in the village of the same name; they offer rides to the cay at a reasonable price. You can bring your own snacks; ice is sold on the island. Guests of the Grand Bahia Principe Levantado get a free boat ride from the resort's private marina just outside of town.

Tour excursions flock to this island, and during the high season it can be crowded with the addition of cruise ship visitors. Avoid weekends or visit in the slow season to really enjoy this gorgeous stretch.

## ★ Parque Nacional Los Haitises

A protected area since 1974, **Parque Nacional Los Haitises** is undoubtedly unique among the parks and landscapes you'll see in the Caribbean. Just 15 kilometers (9.32 miles) out from Samaná Port are a series of towering rock mounds—their heights ranging between 40 and 335 meters (130 and 1,100 feet)—blanketed in vegetation and stretching over an area of 1,598 square kilometers (617 square miles). Birds flock overhead as fishers navigate the surface to and from the beaches where they camp out. Farther out, mangrove tunnels hiding ancient Taíno caves await exploration.

From a Taíno word meaning highland or land of mountains, Los Haitises covers 3,217 square kilometers (1,242 square miles) and has elevations of up to 40 meters (130 feet), and can only be reached by boat. The ecosystem of the park ranges from rainforest to coastal wetlands, and there's approximately 2,000 mm (79 inches) of rainfall every year. Mangroves cover an area of about 98 square kilometers (38 square miles), and this is one of

1: Parque Nacional Los Haitises; 2: Playa El Valle

the only spots in the country to have all four species of mangrove: red, black, white, and button. The diverse environment allows for a great deal of flora and fauna within the park, spanning over 700 species of plants and 230 species of birds, including Ridgway's hawk and the magnificent frigate bird. Underwater are coral reefs supporting fish, crustaceans, and mollusks, not to mention marine mammals such as dolphins and manatees.

The most common way to tour Los Haitises from Samaná town is to sign up for a boat excursion. If you're visiting in the off-season, you can sail to the park, and from there, hop into kayaks to get farther into the mangrove channels. There's also access to Los Haitises National Park through Sabana de la Mar, across the Samaná bay; an unofficial ferry makes daily runs from the town's main dock at 7am, 9am, 11am, 3pm. From there, you can hop on a 15-minute bike taxi to Caño Hondo, where two lodges sit within the protected area and offer boat trips daily (call ahead to reserve, tel. 829/259-8743). It's a longer way to travel and see the park from Samaná, but it shows you a different angle.

Boat tours from Samaná take you along the park's various points of interest and past the area's spectacular scenery, from the various cays with bird colonies to beaches that lead to cave access. Among the more distinctive cays are the **Boca del Infierno** and the **Isla de las Aves** or **Cayo de Pájaros**—the birds' isle—where brown boobies, pelicans, and frigates circle continuously overhead. The various caves are often visited on foot; all are easy to hike, with handrails and interiors that are well lit. The **Cueva del Ferrocarril**, or **Cueva de la Línea**, is considered the most significant due to having the highest number of petroglyphs and rock art. The name of the cave, which translates into "railway cave," refers to the previous existence of a railway line that ran through this area, used to carry the area's rice harvests to the dock. There's a giant opening in the ceiling of the cave 600 meters (1,969 feet) up, letting light into the chambers. Many of the drawings represent animals, especially birds, along with deity masks, though many remain skeptical as to the authenticity of the drawings and what really is of Taíno origin.

## BEACHES
### ★ Playa El Valle

**Playa El Valle,** 30 minutes north of Samaná town, is a sight for sore eyes. As its name suggests, this 2-kilometer (1.2-mile) stretch of golden beauty sits at the foot of a lush valley, flanked on three sides by towering cliffs. The beach is development-free and uncrowded, and the water is a turquoise green. Rocks separate the two sides of the beach, but there are openings easily crossed on foot. Playa El Valle is as rustic as Samaná itself and reflects the peninsula's true natural splendor.

The road to get here is bumpy along the second half, and it's quite a trek, which is why the beach is so uncrowded with tourists. Swimming here is dangerous during the winter season. Stick close to shore—there have been drownings in recent years—and do not go out alone. On-site are a few local seafood restaurants, all of them decent; seek out the one on the far edge, **Clarissa's** (tel. 809/667-0213), a cozy *palapa* facing the most gorgeous part of the beach.

To get to this beach by car, head toward Dominican Tree House Village, then continue around the resort down a dirt road, crossing a dry riverbed along the way, and eventually you'll end up at the stretch. On the far western edge of the beach—cars can drive down this dirt path—you'll spot the mouth of the river El Valle.

### Other Beaches

**Playa Los Cayos** is a lovely golden stretch facing part of the Grand Bahia Principe Cayacoa with warm waters and gorgeous views of the bridges, Samaná Bay, and Cayo Levantado in the distance. The public entrance is from town, by the bridges. Driving past the main entrance to the Grand Bahia Principe Cayacoa, you'll end up going downhill to **Playa Escondida**—also facing the hotel, from the lower level. There, you can lay

# Best Tours on the Samaná Peninsula

A handful of tour operators across the Samaná Peninsula offer similar excursions at competitive rates. Below are a handful of the best trips and companies. Note that if you're here in high season (winter), you might be sharing the sights with cruise ship visitors. Most operators run hotel guest excursions on different days, but check to make sure you're not booking on one of these days.

## WHALE-WATCHING IN SAMANÁ BAY

Kim Beddall is your best bet for whale-watching tours, through her operation **Whale Samaná** (Av. La Marina, tel. 809/538-2494, www.whalesamana.com, US$64pp, includes Marine Mammal Sanctuary fee). The marine mammal specialist hails from Canada and has observed and studied Samaná's humpback whales since 1983, as they faithfully return to give birth in Samaná's waters every year from mid-January through late March. Observe the humpbacks with Kim and her crew from a spacious, two-deck 17-meter (55-foot) boat with 360-degree views. Excursions

Explore Las Galeras's beaches by boat.

leave at 9am or 10am, but from February through mid-March there are also 1:30pm outings.

## ECOTOURS ON THE PENINSULA

**Flora Tours** (Calle Duarte, tel. 809/240-5482, www.flora-tours.net, US$75 pp half-day) offers nature-focused excursions. The highlight is a half-day kayak excursion down the mangrove channels of the Cosón River, just off the coast of Las Terrenas. The kayaking, good for all levels, ends at Playa Cosón. The full-day boat trip to Los Haitises National Park is also comprehensive, taking you through the unique ecosystem to get close-up views of birds and mangroves and making multiple stops at the various Taíno caves tucked inside this natural wonder.

## BOAT TOUR OF LAS GALERAS'S BEACHES

Exploring Las Galeras's top four white-sand beaches, reached most easily by boat, is a bona fide adventure. Head to the main public beach where all the boats and captains are waiting in the morning, between 8am and 9am, and let them know you'd like to see Playa Frontón, Playa Madama, and Playa Rincón. You'll need to know some Spanish to bargain, but your guesthouse can give you an idea of prices. You'll hop into a 24-foot panga-style boat and pass by gargantuan cliffs and impressive waves. The first stop is at Playa Frontón; there's an incredible view as the boat turns the corner and the beach appears, with its coral-filled turquoise waters. A beach stop with snorkeling—you must pack fins to avoid stepping on sea urchins—and coconut water is in order. Next you'll head back out to Playa Madama, another small, white-sand stunner. Following that is the renowned Playa Rincón, where you'll have a lobster lunch, and plenty of time to swim, snorkel, or sun yourself on a paradisiacal, 3.2-kilometer (2-mile) white-sand stretch. If it rains in particular the week you head there, don't be surprised to see sargassum on some of the beaches; this is a phenomenon that has hit the Caribbean hard in the last few years. It comes and goes.

## HORSEBACK RIDING IN LAS GALERAS

Go deep into the rustic countryside of Las Galeras with Rudy from **Rudy's Rancho** (La Caleta, tel. 829/305-3368, rudysrancho@yahoo.com, www.rudysrancho.com, from US$20-50). Born and raised in this corner of the DR, Rudy knows the area inside out. Now in charge of his family's horse farm, Rudy offers rides through the countryside of Las Galeras to reach its best beaches, including Playa Madama, Playa Rincón, and the less crowded La Playita. Beginners and advanced riders are welcomed.

your towel in the sand on the far right of the beach, on the other side of the hotel lounge chairs, and do as locals for a dip in the sea.

In town and facing part of the bay before you reach the bridges is a public stretch that is barely worth mentioning; it's visibly neglected and there's litter scattered about the shores. That said, you can enjoy the views of boats in the bay and grab a drink at the onsite Colego Bar.

The Bridges to Nowhere lead to two small cays, **Cayo Linares** and **Cayo Vigia.** The first has a small strip of beach, accessed by a flight of stairs after walking the bridge. The scenery is as rustic as the bridges themselves, but the water is good for swimming. This is where Samaná's locals hang out and cool off on Sunday and public holidays. The unofficial name of this beach, according to those who grew up here, is *playa de los cueros* (lovers' beach)—couples come to this out-of-the-way spot for some memorable romantic activities.

Just five minutes outside Samaná on the road to Las Galeras is **Playa Anadel,** popular with locals. It's not the prettiest, save for the palm trees that provide some shade, but there are a couple of local restaurants and you can swim off the dark sands. Five minutes farther east, in the direction the Simi Baez Marina and immediately past its entrance, you'll find the slightly hidden **Playa Caletón** populated with dozens of tall coconut trees. Just drive right onto the beach and park anywhere (except under a coconut-bearing tree). It's a dark golden stretch where a few locals and fishers come to relax. An equally pretty and rustic beach is **Playa Los Grayumos,** accessible through the marina or by making a right turn before you reach the marina entrance.

## SPORTS AND RECREATION

### ★ Whale-Watching

The number one reason to stay in the town of Santa Bárbara de Samaná, and what brings thousands of tourists here every year from mid-January through end of March, is the humpback whales that make their way to Samaná's bay to mate. There are several operators in town offering a whale-watching tour, but there's little argument about the best one: You'll learn the most from marine mammal specialist Kim Beddall, owner of **Whale Samana** (Av. La Marina, tel. 809/538-2494, www.whalesamana.com, US$62, includes sanctuary fee). From aboard the *Pura Mia,* a 17-meter (55-foot) whale-watching vessel, you'll see these spectacular creatures flipper and tail lob, among other surprising moves. There's enough space on the boat that you'll be able to move around comfortably, and the wealth of information is shared in several languages when needed. If you get seasick, take some pills; if you're not sure, there will be bags available on board.

Another popular tour operator is the long-running **Moto Marina** (Av. La Marina 3, tel. 809/538-2302, www.motomarinatours-excursionsamana.com, from $65 pp), which offers a combo trip to the nearby island of Cayo Levantado after the whale-watching, where you'll have plenty of swim and beach time. Trips depart at 9am.

### Kayaking

Those staying at the Grand Bahia Principe Cayacoa will have access to complimentary kayaks from the water sports shack. Just hop in and explore the bay. Around the Bridges to Nowhere, stop for a break on the beaches and a swim. In the off-season, **Whale Samana** (Av. La Marina, tel. 809/538-2494, www.whalesamana.com) offers kayaking trips to Parque Nacional Los Haitises. You'll sail over first and then explore the park's stunning mangroves up close.

If you're fortunate enough to stay at **Paraíso Caño Hondo** or **Altos de Caño Hondo** (tel. 829/259-8743, www.paraisocanohondo.com), twin lodges located within the Parque Nacional Los Haitises boundaries, you can hop on their kayak tour

# Samaná's Humpback Whales

For the three months from January through March, Samaná Bay on the extreme northeast of the DR is graced with humpback whales, or *ballenas jorbadas*. The humpback whales (*Megaptera novaeangliae*)—called this because of the way they hunch their back when diving—begin their journey months earlier, migrating from the North Atlantic to the Caribbean to mate and calve in the warm and protected shallow waters off Samaná.

As early as the 17th century, whales were commercially hunted for their oil and for making flexible materials. Their numbers had dropped dramatically by the 1930s, until the International Whaling Commission imposed a moratorium in 1966. More threats to these mammals include human activity like marine pollution, entanglement in fishing gear, and boat activity. In 1996, the Bay of Samaná was declared part of the 1,180-square-kilometers (12,700-square-feet) Marine Mammal Sanctuary of the Dominican Republic and whale-watching regulations were imposed. The Marine Mammal Sanctuary itself, comprising Banco de la Plata, Banco de la Navidad, and Bahía de Samaná surrounding Samaná, was established in 1986, prohibiting any kind of harassment of marine mammals. These regulations limit the number of vessels allowed in the bay, and there are specific guidelines on surface whale-watching and direction and speed of approach.

Every year, the whales return like clockwork, as do over 35,000 tourists who come to see them. It's a show you cannot afford to miss if passing through the area at this time. Adult humpbacks can reach up to 12 to 15 meters (39 to 49 feet) in length and weigh up to 40 tons. They feed on fish—crustaceans when they are in the North Atlantic—and can consume up to a ton in just a day. Once they reach Samaná's waters, they no longer need to feed and focus only on mating and growing their calves. The warm water helps the calves to grow fast and gain weight while they feed on mother's milk—yes, they produce a thick, rich-in-fat milk—and prepare for their migration back to the North Atlantic.

The whales' return to the bay is so regular that some have been named—including Salt, who has been visiting since 1976, and has birthed 12 calves over the last 35 years. Remember that whether or not you see the creatures making amazing dives or moves will depend on how lucky you are, but spotting their presence in the waters is guaranteed.

To learn more about these creatures, you can visit the whale museum in town, **Museo de la Ballena** (tel. 809/538-2042, www.samana.org.do, 8:30am-3pm Mon.-Fri., weekends by appointment only, US$2.20 or RD$100), a small space with informative text displays about the mammals, or better yet, sign up for a whale excursion with expert Kim Beddall and **Whale Samana** (Av. La Marina, tel. 809/538-2494, www.whalesamana.com, US$62, includes sanctuary fee). There's also an annual **Festival de las Ballenas Jorbadas** in mid-January, which officially launches humpback whale-watching season.

along the Cano Hondo River and the bay of San Lorenzo within the park. The trip departs at 3pm and lasts a couple of hours.

## Zip-Lining

Just outside of town, 30 minutes up a long and occasionally bumpy road, Dominican Tree House Village offers the popular **Samana Zipline** (tel. 809/542-3005, www.samanazipline.com, 8am-3pm daily except Tues., US$105 pp, US$52 under 12), probably the best engineered zipline in the country. It sends you towering over a waterfall and 122 meters (400 feet) above the verdant hills of El Valle. Getting to the starting point of the zipline itself is a challenge on a steep 20-minute hike, but you'll soon forget that when you're soaring above the mountains. There are 12 lines and 13 stations, the longest line reaching 366 meters (1,200 feet), for a total of 2,256 meters (7,400 feet) of zipline. Lines have an integrated brake system. If you're an adrenaline junkie, this one is for you! If you sign up with **Tour Samana with Terry** (tel. 809/538-3179, www.toursamanawithterry.com, from US$100 pp), after the two-hour experience you'll stop at El Valle beach and/or swim in a waterfall, among other options.

To get to the Samana Zipline on your own, follow Route 5 through town until you come to the turnoff on the left to El Valle (there's a big sign and you can't miss it). Then follow the road all the way north. It turns into a bumpy dirt road, and soon you'll see the entrance to the zipline, which is well indicated. You can also take a motorbike taxi (about US$5) or a taxi (US$20 up to 3 persons) to get there.

## ENTERTAINMENT AND EVENTS
### Bars and Nightclubs

The little nightlife there is in Samaná is enough to bring the town alive. You'll find most of it along the bars on the waterfront avenue, both directly facing the sea and across the main road. They are your typical Dominican-style, open-air spaces where you can get your drinks and dance to merengue, *bachata*, and other Latin tunes on a small floor all night. One of the most popular ones is **El Tronco Móvil** (across Malecón, tel. 809/232-0000, from 10pm Thurs.-Sun.). Follow the sound; you won't miss the action.

**Cielito Disco** (Calle Rosa Duarte 2, tel. 809/849-3024, free for ladies, 9pm-4am Tues. and Fri.-Sun., US$1.10 men) is where the hardcore partygoers continue after midnight. There's almost always a time to party. Tuesday means drink specials, while Friday is ladies' night, with three free drinks 9pm-11pm.

### Festivals and Events

Besides Samaná's main event of the visiting humpback whales, there are a couple of cultural celebrations worth noting. In June, a small annual **Marisco Ripao Festival** takes place in the neighboring town of Sánchez, celebrating all things seafood, along with music, of course.

The African American descendants of Samaná celebrate an annual **Harvest Festival**—*fiestas a la cosecha*—every Friday starting in July through October,

## Samaná's Traditional Dances

Santa Bárbara de Samaná's African-influenced culture is evident during the *fiestas patronales,* or town patron saint festival, in the first week December, when the African drums come out. The beats and chants echo through the small town's narrow streets and seafront avenue while couples perform traditional African-influenced dances. There's the *bambula* (known as *la bambula de Samaná*), danced by both men and women. They hold hands while shaking their hips from side to side and dancing in circles as the drummers chant. The women wear long, traditional dresses. You can also see this dance being performed at the church harvest festivals. Another dance, considered erotic (and obscene by some) for its suggestive movement, is the *chivo florete* or the *chivo de Samaná* (goat dance), in which the man is standing behind the woman and they both jump forward together...simulating the sexual act performed by goats.

held outdoors in the yard of the historic La Churcha in town. The last Sunday of October—an official holiday in Samaná—is the biggest harvest festival celebration of all. Expect plenty of outdoor cooking, coconut seafood, and ginger beer.

### Casinos

The casino at **Grand Bahia Principe Cayacoa** (Puerto Escondido, U.S. tel. 866/282-2442 or tel. 809/538-3131, 8pm-midnight daily) is tiny, but it's the only one in town. It is a viable option if you're really desperate to gamble the night away. The views from the hotel entrance are an added bonus.

## SHOPPING

The shopping isn't mind-blowing in Samaná town. The **Plaza Pueblo Principe** (Av. La Marina, 9am-9pm Mon.-Sat.), in a row of colorful Caribbean-style shacks across the Malecón, is home to a couple of souvenir stores with your usual trinkets and beach accessories. You'll also find a pharmacy here. For souvenirs, you're better off continuing up the same road for more local souvenir stores and more choices.

## FOOD

On the way to Samaná from Santo Domingo, off the Autopista del Nordeste and past the first toll, you'll spot ★ **Gran Parador Bellamar** (next to Petronas gas station, Carretera Samana Km 1, tel. 809/741-6069, 6am-11pm daily, US$6.50). Affordable, clean, and friendly, this outdoor grill and restaurant cooks a variety of meats. Patrons pull over to fill their stomachs before continuing their journeys. Pick among their baby back ribs, sausage, pork, or goat, with tasty sides such as mashed cassava and plantain. Wash it down with a cold Presidente.

In Samaná town, grab a cup of coffee and a croissant at **Cafe Italia** (Av. La Marina 3, tel. 809/538-2742, US$1.50-4), a cute, shaded café and restaurant with an outdoor terrace along a central stretch of the seafront boulevard, near the departure dock. It's a good spot to start the day with wireless Internet, French pastries, or an omelet. A more basic option for a pre-excursion sandwich and coffee is **Royal Snack Bar** (Avenida La Marina 3, tel. 829/994-2951, 7:30am-7:30pm daily, except Mon., US$3).

If you're going to try just one of the food shacks directly on the Malecón, make it ★ **Pizzeria Da Antonio** (Kiosk #5, Malecón, tel. 829/665-6545, 5pm-11pm daily, US$5-10), baking delicious Italian-style pizzas, with meat and veggie topping options, as well as house specials with Italian sausage and gorgonzola. There are sandwiches as well, and a variety of drinks from juices to wine to whiskey. The small size is huge for one person, and the seating directly by the sea.

★ **D'Milagro Sazón** (Av. Maria Trinidad Sanchez, next to Tierra y Mar, no phone, 11am-8pm daily) is popular for affordable and tasty local fare, including the Samaná specialty *pescado al coco* (coconut whole fish). A daily dish of rice, beans, and chicken is just US$3.30 (RD$150). There's an open-air shaded seating area, and takeout is possible.

Steps from the Malecón, under a giant and spacious *palapa* with ceiling fans, old dining room chairs, and tables on a stone covered floor, the local **Tierra y Mar** restaurant (Av. Maria Trinidad Sanchez, tel. 809/538-2436, 9am-10pm daily, US$2.25-14) offers, as its name suggests, surf and turf options. Also on the menu are pastas, local salads, soups, and a daily *bandera dominicana* lunch special—the typical plate of meat, rice, and beans (US$3.30). Service is slow but friendly; if no one comes to your table, don't hesitate to call out to the server as locals do.

Tucked up in the hills, a short and steep walk from town, **Restaurante Chino** (Calle San Juan 1, tel. 809/538-2215, restaurant_chino@hotmail.com, 11am-11pm daily, US$3-20) is a longtime favorite thanks to its spacious outdoor terrace with bay views. Service can be slow, but the excellent and reasonably priced menu ranges from Americanized Chinese options—from fried rice to lo mein dishes—to Dominican favorites like *chicharrón de pollo* (fried chicken). Portions are large.

**Taberna Mediterranea** (Av. La Marina, tel. 829/994-3634, 10am-11pm Tues.-Sun., US$5-20, cash only) has a rustic, Spanish tavern feel on its outdoor terrace across from the Malecón. Expect tasty seafood dishes, as well as paella, tapas, steaks, and pizza. The wine selection is ample, and the sea breeze and view complete the experience.

A surprisingly sophisticated dining experience in Samaná, and a favorite among well-heeled Dominicans, is ★ **La Mata Rosada** (Av. La Marina, tel. 809/538-2388, 11am-3pm and 7pm-11pm Thurs.-Tues., US$5-15). A romantic all-white and bamboo interior draws you in immediately with its open shutters, flowing drapes, mood lighting, and a breeze that sweeps in from the sea on the other side of the street—with the occasional outside clamor. The menu, specializing in seafood, is filled with tantalizing dishes, starting with the fish and mango tartare in vanilla oil. Ask for the *pescado al coco,* not on the menu but served if you ask; it is to die for. Pastas and turf options are also available.

## ACCOMMODATIONS
### Under US$50

Across from La Churcha, **Docia Backpackers Samaná** (Calle Theodore Chasereaux, tel. 809/538-2497, US$22) is a decent spot for those seeking a basic, clean place to stay. The Dominican American-owned hostel offers four-people dorms (US$10) as well as 12 private rooms with either fan (US$22) or air-conditioning (US$31); all have hot water. Rooms on the top floor have air-conditioning and a veranda to themselves. Walk-ins are likely to get a lower rate. A communal kitchen and an outdoor veranda are available to all guests. There's wireless Internet in the reception area.

A better option is ★ **Samana Island Hostel** (Calle San Juan 8, corner of San Juan and Duarte, www.tropicalislandbb.com, US$20-24 pp), offering basic rooms with bunk beds accommodating up to four people, or fully furnished one-bedroom studio apartments (US$40) with kitchenette, just a couple of blocks from the Malecón (if a bit tricky to find at first). Amenities for all include wireless Internet, Netflix, fridge, microwave, and coffeemaker. The owner's daughter also runs a lovely hostel (that looks more like an upscale B&B) in Jarabacoa.

**Hotel D'Miguel Eduardo Hotel** (Calle Maria Trinidad Sanchez 5, tel. 809/538-2195, dmigueleduardohotel@outlook.es, from US$17) is just one street up from the waterfront, and you'll get what you pay for—a place to sleep. Bright orange and lime walls on the 2nd floor of the building hug 13 rooms with private baths. Rooms with air-conditioning are pricier (US$28.79); some have double beds. Be prepared for the noise from bars around the corner, particularly starting midweek and running through the weekend.

One block farther up is the 16-room **Hotel Samana Spring** (Calle San Cristobal 94, tel. 809/538-2946 or 829/763-2048, US$35) remains the go-to for a typical hotel stay in rooms that are basic but clean, with strong air-conditioning, hot water, cable TV, and weak wireless Internet. A stone's throw from restaurants and Samaná's waterfront, with friendly staff, it's a solid pick for those on a budget. Don't be alarmed by the loud bell that goes off was you enter the hotel.

Directly next door, the brand-new, turquoise-and-white-painted boutique **Hotel Nilka** (Calle Santa Bárbara, tel. 809/538-3174,

Hotel Nilka

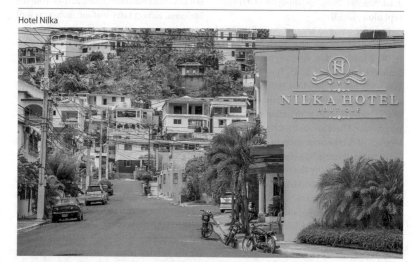

www.nilkahotelboutique.com, US$72-108, breakfast included) sticks out in a town with older buildings and budget hotels. Its pricing for similar amenities is a bit hard to justify, particularly when only staying a night or two, unless you just want that sleek contemporary feel. Sliding doors lead to a chic lobby with a fountain, and sea-tones throughout the furnishing. The 18 rooms are tastefully furnished as well, with king or double options and glass showers. Wi-Fi, air-conditioning, and cable are included. Room 217 has a balcony onto the street side. There's a restaurant in the works.

## US$50 and Up

**Hotel Chino** (Calle San Juan 1, tel. 809/538-2215, hotelchino.samana@hotmail.com, US$85-103) is a 15-minute walk uphill from the waterfront, but its panoramic terrace views of the bay and town, tastefully decorated rooms, and on-site restaurant perhaps might justify the high price for this area. The spacious rooms offer air-conditioning, king or double beds, wireless Internet, and breakfast.

The **Grand Bahia Principe Cayacoa Hotel** (tel. 855/350-5535, www.bahia-principe.com, from US$95-145) has inarguably the best views of the bay and town. The 295-room all-inclusive hugs the Bay of Samaná and faces the town's two beautiful beaches. Any direction you look from its entrance, rooms, or its various terraces offers great scenery. The elevator bridge to the beach might be slow and annoying to some, but it affords a stunning view of the Atlantic Ocean as the glass elevator carries you down. If you can, stay in the oceanfront suites, which have private balconies and 180-degree views over the beach and Cayo Levantado beyond, with the boats moored in Samaná Bay on the left. Rooms are cozy, ranging from standard to junior suites, with minibars, air-conditioning, cable TV, and spacious baths. Three pools allow for less crowded areas, and a second beach below the main hotel building is less crowded and quieter. Restaurants are decent for an all-inclusive—the à la carte seafood restaurant is especially good—and service is friendly. Every hour, a shuttle takes guests back and forth from the Pueblo Principe shopping plaza in town.

**Dominican Tree House Village** (El Valle, tel. 829/542-3005 or U.S. tel. 800/820-1357, www.dominicantreehousevillage.com, US$245) is adjacent to the most exciting zipline in the country, but it also holds its own with its dramatic jungle tree house setting just a 30-minute drive outside of town. The lodge is a green escape from Samaná's beaches set amid a rainforest backdrop. Coffee and lime trees lead to a swimming pool, and suspension bridges take you to open-air tiki huts suspended in the forest, where your bedroom awaits. The cabin you pick—all 20 of which have wood floors, flowing curtains, fans, mosquito nets, and mini hammock chairs—will depend on your comfort with heights, because it is not for the faint of heart. Electricity is available all night. Breakfast and dinner are included, shared in the communal dining space. A 10-minute ride away is the stunning Playa El Valle, where you can enjoy a local seafood lunch.

Occupying two-thirds of Cayo Levantado is the 268-room **Bahia Principe Cayo Levantado** (U.S. tel. 855/350-5535, www.bahia-principe.com, from US$240), a five-star all-inclusive resort that's a favorite among honeymooners for its seclusion from the mainland and its white-sand beaches. To be honest, it isn't as uncrowded or idyllic as it might seem to be on a private portion of an island; the hotel is often booked solid, and the beach stretch isn't large enough to be isolated. Well-appointed rooms are divided into "villages" of deluxe suites with garden or sea views, and each gets a butler. There are two large pool areas, one of which is the quiet corner. The Orquidea buffet has decent options, and four additional restaurants offer Italian, Mediterranean, and à la carte options. Guests are transferred to the island from the resort's private Simi Baez Marina, a short distance outside Samaná town.

## INFORMATION AND SERVICES

A branch of **Farmacia Carol** (Av. El Malecón, tel. 809/538-2543, 9am-11pm daily) is located within the Pueblo Principe shopping row on the main drag.

**Supermercado Mimasa** (Av. Francisco del Rosario Sanchez 26, tel. 809/538-2217, or 809/538-2448 for delivery, 8am-10 pm daily), going west on the Malecón, is a place to stock up on groceries or bathroom toiletries, and includes a bakery. Closer to the hotels, you'll find **Mini Market La Mazorca** (Calle Maria Trinidad Sanchez, corner of Malecon across D'Milagro restaurant, no phone, 8am-11pm daily).

**Centro de Especialidades Médicas** (Calle Coronel Andrés Díaz No. 06, tel. 809/538-3999 or 809/539-3888, www.cmes.com.do) is a respected medical facility with Cuban doctors on hand and 24-hour emergency service. There's also a branch in Las Galeras.

## GETTING THERE AND AROUND

Samaná's **El Catey International Airport**—also called Aeropuerto Internacional Presidente Juan Bosch—has service from various airlines including JetBlue, WestJet, and Air Canada. The airport is approximately 40 minutes' drive from Samaná town. You can hop in a taxi outside the airport or you can schedule your pickup online through **Tour Samana with Terry** (www.toursamanawithterry.com, US$85 one-way/1-4 people).

**Caribe Tours** (Av. El Malecón 5, Samaná, tel. 809/538-2229, US$7.80 or DP350) offers daily service between Samaná and Santo Domingo, a direct route via the new highway, with various departures. The trip is just 2.5 hours, part of it along winding roads offering spectacularly verdant scenery.

Aside from the *boletería* or ticket booths, inside the Caribe Tours Samaná terminal is a bank teller and *cambio* for currency exchanges. The bus terminal is also just a two-minute ride away from the Grand Bahia Principe Cayacoa. Taxi drivers and bike taxis will be approaching you from the moment you begin to step off the bus.

Taxis can be costly, as is the case across the DR, and prices are set by the Samaná taxi cooperative: US$40 to Simi Baez Marina round-trip, US$80 to Las Galeras round-trip, US$120 to Playa Rincón round-trip, US$80 El Limón round-trip, US$120 Las Terrenas round-trip. One friendly and professional licensed taxi driver is **Miguel Angel Samboy** (tel. 809/827-5470); you can set up your own custom day trip with him if you wish.

*Motoconcho* taxis (or *conchos*, as locals like to say) are popular in these parts, because of their affordability and the small size of these fishing villages. Also the intense afternoon heat makes them somewhat more bearable to hop on than in big cities. If you want to catch one, step out and look for the neon jacket-wearing men on the corners of main thoroughfares. Rides often cost 50 pesos for a basic trip in town.

*Moto-carritos* or *motoconchos de carreta* are another typical option in Samaná—motorbike drawn carriages. You can easily spot them parked along the Malecón, especially by the main dock, waiting for passersby. They cost approximately US$5 for a ride and a quick tour around town—a cheaper alternative to taxis, but not as cheap as the *motoconchos*.

# Las Galeras

Located 30 minutes outside of Samaná town, at the end of the road running northeast, Las Galeras is as remote as it gets on the peninsula, yet it's one of the most touristed areas because it's the departure point for renowned beaches such as Playa Rincón. This forever rustic corner of the DR—it remains so for a reason, as it's purportedly a known drug trafficking area—has a breathtaking Atlantic coastline and a daily *pueblo* scene where all there is to do is shuffle tourists to beaches, play dominoes under the shade, and throw back beers after-hours. Fruit and veggie shacks sit on the road next to horses and donkeys munching on grass off the beach. Despite the crowds, taking delight in the nature that surrounds could mean hiking in the village (stick to groups with a local guide), horseback riding through the *campo,* going fishing, or taking a boat ride to the area's spectacular Atlantic-facing beaches.

Las Galeras is known for being home to some of the most beautiful beaches in DR—including Playa Rincón, a popular excursion offered from all points on the peninsula. Despite the hordes of tourists who descend on it for a day's beach escape, it's still less frequented overnight than neighboring, trendy Las Terrenas. There's just one main drag in town, dotted with most of the guesthouses, restaurants, and cafés. Beneath the scenic beauty, however, is a seedy underbelly, mostly visible at night or in isolated areas during the day; if you steer clear of illicit activities, and just beach hop in groups, you'll be fine. Beware of heading to isolated areas solo; it's best to avoid carrying valuables, as there have been robberies of individuals and even the occasional group in these parts.

## BEACHES

For a small village, Las Galeras is blessed with stretches that will have you gasping. There are numerous ways to get to them—consider

hiking, horseback riding, or the most popular of all, boat excursion.

Please remember that when visiting any of these beaches or sights in Las Galeras, you should not go alone or at deserted times—opt for a *motoconcho* ride or sign up for a group excursion to avoid isolation and possibly robbery, which has happened in the past (the downside of beautifully isolated locations). Also, ask the locals about the weather and current conditions before you jump in—better safe than sorry.

## Playa Las Galeras

The plainest of the beaches is the one right in the village where the excursion boats and fishers park themselves, but even **Playa Las Galeras** holds its own. There's seagrass in parts, but the water is delightful for a swim—walk the beach all the way east to the Grand Paradise Samaná resort, where you can swim even if you can't lounge on their chairs. Sunsets are lovely here, and the echoes from the village's main bar give the stretch a fun vibe.

## La Playita

A favorite of mine, the perfectly white **La Playita** is 10 times more beautiful than the main beach of Las Galeras, and it's just a 10-minute walk from there. Look for the sign for La Playita just off the end of the main road before you reach Las Galeras beach. Walk down the path until you hit an iron gate. Ignore the "private" sign and push open the gate, then take the first right and walk along the pathway past some private vacation homes, down until you see a beach up ahead, past a wooded section. This pathway from town can seem a bit isolated and eerie, but it's generally safe—just don't wander here at night, and use common sense. There are a couple of good restaurants on La Playita beach as well as chairs and kayaks (US$11/

# Las Galeras

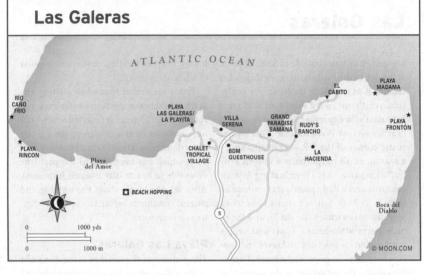

ATLANTIC OCEAN

RÍO CAÑO FRIO

PLAYA LAS GALERAS/ LA PLAYITA

VILLA SERENA

GRAND PARADISE SAMANÁ

RUDY'S RANCHO

EL CABITO

PLAYA MADAMA

PLAYA FRONTÓN

PLAYA RINCON

Playa del Amor

CHALET TROPICAL VILLAGE

BDM GUESTHOUSE

LA HACIENDA

★ BEACH HOPPING

Boca del Diablo

5

0    1000 yds
0    1000 m

© MOON.COM

two hours) for rent. Palm trees line the shore, and there are lovely views of Rincón's bay in the distance, shade under almond trees, and water in varying hues of blue. Entry is shallow and easy—follow the path that is free of seagrass. In the evening, large frogs come out to play on the beach path. To drive to the beach, take the turn off the main road marked Chalet Tropical and keep straight until you hit the end and the beach parking lot.

## Playa Rincón

The famous **Playa Rincón,** consistently ranked as one of the DR's best beaches, is a brilliantly white, soft sandy strip located just 10 minutes by boat from Las Galeras village, flanked by **Cabo Samaná** and **Cabo Cabrón.** You can walk the length of the beach, from the frequented side (with calmer waters and local restaurants) to a deserted stretch (don't walk it alone), before arriving at the end favored by locals, where the river meets the sea. At this end there is more wave action and bordering cliffs. There are kayaks for rent (US$20/hour) on the restaurant side.

Most arrive at Playa Rincón from Las Galeras's beach by boat, approximately US$77 for up to five persons. (Head to the main

beach and you'll find plenty of captains ready to negotiate.) Those with sturdy cars can arrive on the other end—look for the turnoff on the road south to Samaná. The beach can feel touristy in high season; if you're not one for crowds, take a boat ride here around 3pm on a weekday after most of the tourist groups have left. Walk with your guide (not alone) to the far eastern end of the beach, or better yet, ask for a motorbike ride (for about US$5) to where you can dip in the Caño Frío River—going down the sandy roadway that runs parallel to this gorgeous beach is an amazing experience—and perhaps even sample local food cooked over an open fire.

## Playa Madama

**Playa Madama** is an approximately 15-minute boat ride on choppy Atlantic waters from Las Galeras's beach. It's an isolated and small crescent-shaped stretch, hiding a cave and sitting at the foot of a dense forest that some reach by hiking here (do not attempt this alone due to robbery risk). The sand is pristine, unless you arrive on a day there's sargassum piled up, and the location

1: Playa Rincón; 2: La Playita

romantic for two. But look out for the white urchins on the beach. Some hike here from La Hacienda or get here on horseback. The clifftop views of the beach and scenery below are more breathtaking that way if you have the time.

### Playa Frontón

Formerly a *Survivor* filming location, **Playa Frontón** rivals the beauty of Playa Rincón. If you ask me, it has a greater wow factor, hugged along its coastline by gigantic cliffs made out of *roca de mármol*—metamorphic rock with marble characteristics. The sight of this easternmost beach as your boat turns the curve on approach is breathtaking. Locals consider Playa Frontón the jewel in Las Galeras's crown. It not being readily accessible means it has maintained its beauty. Picture the color contrast of iridescent emerald waters reflecting the corals below, against a white sand layer ahead, and, beyond it, ebony rocks. You'll want to jump right in from the boat, but beware: there are small and large black sea urchins and corals teeming below, which also make this one of the best sites for snorkeling. Wear fins if you're swimming anywhere beyond the immediate shoreline.

Behind the reef, humpback whales can be spotted from shore as they make their way to Samaná Bay during the mating season from mid-January to mid-March. Walk on the far east of the beach, hiking through a wooded path, and you'll come across a small cave— where the *Survivor* series also filmed—and another stretch and cove where it's a lot easier to swim away from the corals. You used to be able to hike to this beach, and some still try, but I highly discourage it for safety reasons, and even the tourist police—who are occasionally along the path in busy times— will ask you to turn back if you try it (this has happened).

### Playa del Amor

If you ever get there, you'll likely be the only one at **Playa del Amor**—a beach only reachable by boat. As romantic as its name suggests, it's a teeny yet delightfully deserted golden stretch with white shells scattered about on the beach and sea floor. Bring your picnic cooler to spend the day. There's a lot of wave action so stick close to shore. And leave all valuables at home.

### ★ Beach-Hopping

The best way to experience Las Galeras's beaches is by taking a boat tour to three of the most beautiful in the DR: **Playa Rincón, Playa Madama,** and **Playa Frontón.**

The most affordable option is to contact the local **Asociación de Lancheros de Las Galeras** (Playa Las Galeras, tel. 809/916-7591, US$75 for up to 4-5 persons), headquartered on the beach and offering set rates for boat tours. You can also just walk up to Las Galeras beach in the village and negotiate your boat ride with one of the captains. They don't speak a lot of English, but if you name the beaches you want to see, they'll understand. There's always one or more of them in the early morning, when tours depart, and at the end of the day between 3:30pm and 4:30pm.

For an organized all-day tour of the three beaches, with lunch and snacks included, contact **Tour Samana with Terry** (tel. 809/538-3179, www.toursamanawithterry.com, US$100 pp), owned by longtime expat and Samaná resident Terry.

## RÍO CAÑO FRÍO

On far end of Playa Rincón you'll find the **Río Caño Frío,** a river feeding into the Atlantic and dotted with mangroves. It is a local favorite on weekends for families seeking a cool swim in hot weather. The farther back you walk away from the beach, the more breathtaking the river: the water turns bright turquoise, and you find yourself swimming while surrounded by denser woods and mangroves. On this beach end of the river are a row of open-air shacks where Dominican women fry up fresh fish and plantains (US$9 for a

1: Río Caño Frío; 2: horseback riding in Las Galeras

plate, or US$15 for lobster) on open wood fire. Meals are served on shaded picnic tables, and the mood is jovial and ultra-Dominican, a far cry from the western end where your typical tourist beach chairs await.

## BOCA DEL DIABLO

The **Boca del Diablo** (Mouth of the Devil) is a well-known and simple natural attraction: a blowhole that on a windy, clear day sees the sea shoot its waves straight up into it, splattering loudly above the rocks at almost 10 meters (33 feet) high. It almost sounds like a devil's roar. The surrounding wild tropical and cliff scenery is no less breathtaking. Catch a *motoconcho* if you can, and leave valuables behind. The road leading up to Boca del Diablo is well past the sign for Playa Rincón in an isolated area.

## SPORTS AND RECREATION
### Snorkeling and Diving

**Las Galeras Divers** (Main Street, Plaza Lusitania, tel. 809/538-0220 or cell tel. 809/715-4111, www.las-galeras-divers.com, from US$85/two-tank dive) sits along the main road steps from the beach, offering excursions to several of the peninsula's dive spots, including Piedra Bonita and Puerto Malo, off Cabo Cabrón, or off Playa Frontón. Two-tank dives are offered every morning in high season; stop in or call a day prior to see what's available. The shop also offers PADI certification and cave diving excursions north to Lake Dudú in Cabrera for the experienced.

**ScubaLibre** (Grand Paradise Samaná, tel. 809/958-9119, US$70/two-tank dive) takes you snorkeling right off Las Galeras beach or diving off Cabo Cabrón and Cabo Frontón. Pickups are free for off-resort guests. You can also snorkel at the **Kaio Natural Aquarium** (on Grand Paradise Samaná beach, tel. 809/883-6118, US$15), an artificial reef created to protect marinelife. You can observe Caribbean critters right off this beach facing Grand Paradise Samaná resort.

### Windsurfing and Kayaking

You'll find a windsurfing shack on the beach at **Grand Paradise Samaná** (Playa Las Galeras, U.S. tel. 888/774-0040 or tel. 809/538-0020, $30/one-hour class); kayaks are also available for rent for nonguests ($10/hour).

### Fishing

**Casa Dorado** (Casa Dorado B&B, Calle Playa Colorada, tel. 829/933-8678, casadorado@ gmail.com, from US$280/half day) offers some of the best deep-sea fishing in the DR. Year-round excursions take you to catch your own mahi-mahi, red snapper, grouper, or yellowfin tuna in 7- to 9-meter (22- to 28-foot) *pangas* or sportfishing boats.

### Horseback Riding

You'll have a better day and stay, and even gain a friend, just from meeting Rudy from **Rudy's Rancho** (La Caleta, tel. 829/305-3368, rudysrancho@yahoo.com, www.rudysrancho.com, from US$20-50), a mile from the village or a 10-minute walk from the end of the Grand Paradise Samaná's beach. The dynamic young Dominican quit his resort job of four years to realize his dream since being a teenager: turning his family's farm—his grandparents were among the first to move to the DR and Las Galeras 60 years ago—into a 10,000-square-meter (2.5-acre) horse ranch and escape for those who not only love to ride but also want to experience a taste of Dominican *campo* life. It's the only Dominican-owned horse farm in Las Galeras, all the more reason to support this wonderful man's efforts. Rudy takes you on horseback rides through the gorgeous countryside to experience a taste of Dominican life. Rudy's 15 horses, with names like Medialuna and Chuco (warrior), aren't too huge. The farm is set up like a typical Dominican countryside home, with an outdoor chicken coop, goats roaming, and an outdoor wood-fire kitchen.

Also a little over a mile from the village, past Grand Paradise Samaná resort, **La Hacienda Hostel** (Camino al Faro, tel.

829/939-8285, www.lahaciendahostel.com, US$75 full day) is at the entrance of hiking as well as horseback riding trails into Cabo Samaná National Park. Owner Karin is a horse lover and can pick the right mounts and trail for your group, as well as take you on some unique back roads to the area's beaches. You can take a motorbike taxi to get here if you don't want to walk in the sun. It's a great spot for young, independent, and active travelers.

## ATV Riding

You can bump and ride your way through the countryside and onto Playa Rincón in your own ATV with **Tauro Tours** (tel. 849/658-8997, http://taurotours-excursionsamana.com, US$86/four hours).

# FOOD

**La Bodeguita** (Calle Principal, tel. 809/907-5111, 4pm-midnight daily except Tues., US$5-10) is a safe bet for reasonably priced tapas and drinks in the evening. **Boulangerie La Marseillaise** (Main Rd., no phone, 8am-8pm daily, US$1-11) has French croissants, baguettes, and espressos; that's when you're not tempted to stay for lunch or dinner to sample their seafood dishes. It's close to a number of guesthouses and within walking distance from the main beach. Farther up the drag is **Comedor Rossy** (Main Rd., tel. 809/477-0168, 11am-8pm daily), serving local fare, especially seafood, at good prices under a giant *palapa*. The specialty there is *camarones al ajillo* or *a la criolla*—shrimp in a garlic or tomato-based sauce (US$11). They also have your usual rice and beans with stewed chicken.

The beachfront **La Playita Restaurant** (La Playita, tel. 849/627-2514, 9am-8pm daily, US$3-15) is a safe bet for a day on the sands, with a menu ranging from local rice and beans dishes to sandwiches and burgers.

★ **El Cabito** (tel. 809/697-9506, www.elcabito.net, 11am-9pm Tues.-Sun., US$5-15, cash only) is one of Las Galeras's gems, and where you'd go to treat yourself to a spectacular sunset dinner with equally satisfying view of the Atlantic Ocean from your cliff-top table. The restaurant specializes in seafood—if you can, opt for the paella. A motorbike ride here shouldn't cost more than 100 pesos (US$2.20) one-way, or 500 pesos (US$11) round-trip for two in a taxi. It's a popular spot so reserve ahead.

Another idyllic restaurant with stunning panoramic views and a lounge feel perched high above the ocean is **El Monte Azul** (La Gazuma, tel. 849/249-3640, 10am-9pm daily, US$7-15, reservations recommended), run by a French and Laotian couple. It is an adventure from the moment you begin to make your way here, particularly the last stretch getting to the top of the mountain—catch a *motoconcho* or a taxi with all-terrain wheels. The food is equally satisfying—once you get over the view (you might not), order the tenderloin steak, the lionfish, or a pad thai.

Treat yourself to lunch at **Villa Serena** (Playa Las Galeras, www.villaserena.com, 9am-2pm daily, US$5-15), where the salads in particular are delicious.

# ACCOMMODATIONS

A stone's throw from the main village beach, ★ **BDM Guesthouse** (formerly El Pequeño Refugio, Main Rd., tel. 849/267-5848, www.elpequenorefugiodesamana@gmail.com, US$35) is ideal for solo travelers on a budget who end up at this "Bout du Monde," or end of the world in French. The small, funky, partly thatch hotel offers basic, dated rooms—mosquito-netted double beds, private baths, wireless Internet (spotty on the top floor). There's shaded courtyard seating in the restaurant area, allowing a peaceful respite from the sun. Note that the loft can get very hot and the furnishings and ceiling fan were outdated at publication time. On the ground level is a friendly bar and restaurant with a tasty menu of crepes, grilled fish, and salads.

A block away, set off from the main road, **La Isleta** (Main Rd., tel. 829/887-5058, www.laisletasamana.com, from US$82) has seven self-catering units inside a gated residence.

The overpriced, slightly dated lofts have full kitchens, but the layout isn't as comfortable as you'd expect; there's a steep staircase to the bedroom and lofts have fans only (no air-conditioning). The location is the best asset—it's just a two-minute walk to Las Galeras public beach.

**Chalet Tropical Village** (Calle Chalet Tropical, tel. 809/901-0738, www.chalettropical.com, US$75-155) is off the main drag and down a side road, far enough that you'd need a bike. The hotel's setup is unique: three "chalets," or individual thatch-roofed huts, that fit up to five people—with a single bathroom, except for Chalet 3, which has two—as well as two chalet guesthouses where rooms share the villa's amenities, ideal for solo travelers. Everything is made of local wood and bamboo, while the verdant yard separating each cabana is dotted with hammocks and flowers. The hotel can arrange for whale-watching tours to Samaná in season, and it's a short distance to La Playita or Las Galeras beach.

**Grand Paradise Samaná** (Playa Las Galeras, U.S. tel. 888/774-0040 or tel. 809/538-0020. www.grandparadisesamana.com, US$104-192) is the only all-inclusive traditional resort in Las Galeras. Tucked at one end of Las Galeras beach, rooms range from superior to deluxe, but your best bet will be the bungalows, which have a loft design for a second bedroom, a full kitchen, and a spacious outdoor terrace. Room perks include minibars, air-conditioning, satellite TV, safes, and hair dryers. The food across the various restaurants is average at best, but the bartenders make stiff drinks and there are two pools available, with one tucked away from the crowds. The highlight here is undoubtedly the beach—the best stretch of Las Galeras Beach—peppered with ultra-tall coconut trees and facing calm turquoise waters. There's a sandy path that takes you directly from the beach onto the more public side of Las Galeras Beach. Note that on the eastern end of the beach, you'll find several locals renting

horses, as well as a snorkel shack for trips to the Aquarium, just a mile offshore. Rudy's Rancho is also a 10-minute walk east of Grand Paradise Samaná.

The all-white, green-roofed ★ **Villa Serena** (beachfront Las Galeras, tel. 809/538-0000, www.villaserena.com, US$110-150) feels more like a friend's dreamy Victorian beachfront home than a hotel. It's also as serene as its name suggests, facing a quiet stretch of Las Galeras Beach, yet just a three-minute walk down to the village or to La Playita in the other direction. The boutique hotel has a sophisticated, old-school feel with grand staircases, wicker furniture, and four-poster beds in 21 rooms facing the sea and pool, views of which you can enjoy from a terrace. There's a small and excellent restaurant on-site, which, although pricey, serves some of the best food I've had in Las Galeras. Rooms include air-conditioning, wireless Internet, phone, and a separate, spacious bathroom. Bikes are complimentary. It's a great spot for a romantic weekend getaway or for families seeking a restful escape after excursions.

## INFORMATION AND SERVICES

You can find tourist police on Las Galeras beach and near Grand Paradise Samaná resort. **Banco de Reservas** has a 24-hour ATM on the main drag. There's also an ATM at Grand Paradise Samaná resort.

The **pharmacy** (Main Rd., 9am-8pm Mon.-Sat., no working phone) is next to Las Galeras Divers. For medical services, contact **Centro Médico Las Galeras** (Main St., tel. 809/538-0134, lasgaleras@cmes.com.do).

## GETTING THERE AND AROUND

The closest airport to Las Galeras is the **Samaná International Airport El Catey** (also known as Aeropuerto Internacional Presidente Juan Bosch, AZS, tel. 809/338-5888), about 72 kilometers (45 miles) west. You'll have to find your way to Santa Bárbara de Samaná town first if you're taking public transportation—from there a local mini-van bus runs east to Las Galeras (US$2.20 or RD$100). Alternatively, an airport taxi ride costs approximately US$100 one-way for up to five passengers.

There's no direct coach or bus service to Las Galeras from Santo Domingo or even from Las Terrenas. You'll have to transfer through Samaná town first. **Caribe Tours** (Av. 27 de Febrero, tel. 809/576-0790, www.caribetours.com.do, RD$270/US$5.88 one-way) offers departures from Santo Domingo; from Samaná town you'll catch a local **bus** leaving from the market (as you enter the market compound, turn left and look for parked minivans). You can also hire a **taxi** driver if you prefer (US$60 round-trip to Samaná town); it's a 30-minute drive from Samaná town to Las Galeras.

If you choose to rent a car and drive from Santo Domingo, the smooth **Samaná Highway** (also called DR 7 Autopista del Nordeste) takes you on a leisurely two-hour drive to Las Galeras. The route begins with Autopista de Las Americas or Highway 3 (about 30 kilometers/18.6 miles east of Santo Domingo) and continues via toll roads (have change ready of about five 100-peso bills) through Samaná town. If you're coming from Puerto Plata, take the coastal Highway 5 all the way to Samaná (be wary of turning off into Santo Domingo when reaching Nagua). Getting around Las Galeras is easy: it's small and everything is centered in one area. Walking is your best bet if you're just in the village. You can also use a bicycle from your hotel—it's fairly safe because there's only so much traffic down the main road or the side country roads. Motorbike taxis and taxis are also plentiful. The taxi drivers are parked by the beach entrance, at the end of the main drag in town. Prices are set to destinations, but in the low summer season you might have more room to bargain. *Motoconchos* are easy to spot, just a block before you reach the end of the main road to the beach, waiting in the shade.

# Las Terrenas

With one foot in the Caribbean and the other in Europe, Las Terrenas—or *La Terrena* as Dominicans like to pronounce it—is one of those multicultural beach towns in which you could picture yourself spending your winters. This town is a 24/7 flip-flop kind of place, yet trendy and cutting-edge in its cuisine and nightlife. There's something to be said for its scenery—the main road hugs the coastline and white-sand beaches all the way through town, stretching from Playa El Portillo to Playa Bonita and the palm-studded Playa Cosón. Erosion resulting from storms over the past couple of years has prompted the shutting down of bars that once lined the water, but it's opened up the town's views even more. After sunset, it's time to wine, dine, and eventually dance the night away on the Pueblo de los Pescadores row of beachfront bars, or off the beaten bath at local bars.

The village prides itself in being multicultural and multigenerational. Expats will tell you that this is some sort of magical place outside of social norms, where age and class don't matter. What's for sure is that each year Las Terrenas attracts more and more beach-seeking tourists, jet-setters from Santo Domingo, and backpackers in search of a lesser touristy and more affordable corner of the DR. Various languages can be heard while wandering around the village. There's a large French enclave in particular, as evidenced by the number of French restaurants and cafés around town, as well as the French *tabac* (tobacco shop) and newsstands inside the main shopping center, Plaza El Paseo. The transportation is

# Las Terrenas

© MOON.COM

0
200 yds
0
200 m

as diverse as the residents; motorbikes, cars, and ATVs all fill up the streets.

## PUEBLO DE LOS PESCADORES

You might forget you're in the Caribbean when you're hanging out at **Pueblo de los Pescadores,** the main drag of Las Terrenas. This area used to be a fishing village, as the name suggests, and now houses lively sea- and beachfront bars and restaurants. These places light up at night, attracting residents and visitors alike—in particular the international crowd. The range of cuisine represents the diverse nationalities of the town's residents, though the restaurants change with the wind. Here you can have a gourmet meal blending European, American, and Dominican specialties, all while enjoying the sound of waves rushing to shore.

A fire destroyed the heart of the Pueblo de los Pescadores in May 2012, and its rebuilt version is less rustic and more modern—but while development continues to add shiny buildings, the laid-back attitude of Las Terrenas remains.

## ★ EL SALTO DE LIMÓN (EL LIMÓN WATERFALL)

One of the crown jewels of Samaná, if not the entire DR, is the near 30-meter-tall (100-foot) **El Limón Waterfall.** Recognized as a natural monument in 1996, it is tucked inside a humid subtropical forest, with a cascade that gushes down moss-covered rocks into a stunning emerald-turquoise pool. The water is cold and refreshing, but not unbearable. Most excursions offer horseback riding all the way to the start of the steps leading down to the falls—a 45-minute journey on a pathway that's mostly stone and dirt—but you also have the option to hike. The walk is of moderate difficulty and allows you to fully appreciate the various plants, fruit trees, and fauna of the park at your own pace, as you wander past guava and mango trees, pineapples, and hummingbirds, with more streams and honeybees humming along the way.

The last portion of the hike includes an easy series of steps that lead down to El Limón's cascade. There, you can carefully enter the pool and swim—if you are a strong swimmer, head to the back of the pool to the right of the falls and you'll find a small cavern, where you can sit for a few minutes behind the nearby rush of the falls. Since 2015, the water levels have been low due the serious decline in rains (others say it's due to environmental abuse from extraction from riverbeds). You might see a local or two jump from the top, but don't do it! There are rocks and only locals know exactly where to land on which particular day, depending on the water levels.

There are various *paradas*—local horseback tour operators—along the main road in the town of El Limón, 30 minutes' drive from Las Terrenas. They are the departure points for the excursion to the waterfall. You can save a chunk if you find your own way to El Limón town by bus or car to one of these *paradas*. Among the most recommended of these are **Rancho Parada La Manzana** (tel. 829/931-6964 or 809/916-0892, alcalanuez@gmail.com) and **Santi Rancho** (tel. 829/342-9976, www.cascadalimonsamana.com, US$15 pp to hike, US$20 horseback); prices include guides, lunch, and park fees. Santi also offers a unique canyoning excursion to El Limón, via the river and its nine falls. Whichever outfitter you choose, be sure to call ahead of time so they know to expect you, and so that no hustlers deviate you from your route (it's been known to happen when tourists are spotted walking around in El Limón; tell them you're heading to Samaná). To go with tour operators and get picked up directly from your hotel, contact **Tour Samana with Terry** (tel. 809/538-3179, www.toursamanawithterry.com, US$55 pp on Tues.).

After your waterfall tour, if you want to cool off some more, stop at **Manantial de Limón,** a roadside freshwater spring where locals love to cool off, especially on the weekends. It's also known as El Arroyo after the

name of the bar beside the pool. Across the street are livelier *colmados* and drinking spots, blasting merengue and *bachata*. The whole block turns into a fun spot to park yourself in the afternoon and weekends.

## BEACHES
### ★ Playa Cosón

Playa Cosón is easily the most stunning beach in the area. The stretch is so long that it transitions from a wild, rustic side where the river runs in the background to a perfectly golden shore. Sundays are a lively time for seafood shacks—Luis's is the best—and families enjoying *la playa* Dominican-style. There's a kitesurfing shack on-site, as well as plenty of lunch tables and lounge chairs for spending the day. A 10-minute ride up the road from Playa Cosón and a half-mile along the Boulevard Turístico del Atlántico is Mirador Cosón, a scenic stop offering panoramic views of the coconut tree-filled hills and Cosón beach below. It's probably one of the best photo ops in Las Terrenas.

### Other Beaches

Las Terrenas's beaches begin at Playa El Portillo, where the Grand Bahia Principe El Portillo sits, and continue along the main road and through various parts of town all the way up to Playa Bonita, which then links to Playa Cosón. As if on purpose, the beaches go from the least attractive to the most stunning. Playa Punta Popy is peppered with palm trees and was once the hub of social activity, until the Ministry of Environment came along and forcibly removed the beachside bars that were too close to shore in an attempt to prevent further erosion. Today some of those bars have crossed over to the street side, like the popular Mojito Bar, where they retain the views of kitesurfers and paddleboarders on the open water. The sunsets here are gorgeous.

Playa Las Terrenas, in the heart of town, is decent enough, but certainly not the best

1: El Limón Waterfall; 2: Playa Cosón; 3: Pueblo de los Pescadores

for swimming or sunning all day given the choices you have. It faces the noisy village and sees plenty of passersby on the roadside. Continue a tad west and you'll hit Playa Las Ballenas, beginning beyond the Pueblo de los Pescadores and across from Hotel Alisei, fronting that strip's vacation villas and other small hotels. The name comes from a set of three rocks jutting out of the water a few miles offshore—they resemble the humpback whales that visit the peninsula every year. It's ideal for a swim, for a nice long beach walk or jog, and picnicking all day. It's shallow enough upon entry, which makes it good for families, and there isn't much wave action. The sunsets here are lovely, particularly across from Hotel Playa Colibri. Locals say Playa Las Ballenas is the best one in town, and I have to agree, even if recent storms have pushed back the beach a bit. There are no constant pestering vendors, either—save for the occasional men on bikes yelling out for fried fish or drinks, and a mobile masseuse. You'll find a handful of excellent and small beachfront restaurants scattered along the way, as well as a sailing club renting kayaks and Hobie Cat. At the edge of Las Ballenas is the stream that feeds into the ocean, a local favorite for cooling off as if in a swimming pool and hanging out with drinks, food, and music.

A 10-minute scooter ride from the center of town is Playa Bonita—a nice, long stretch that is less crowded during the week and attracts those who want to spend the day away from the village on a beautiful golden-white strip lined with boutique hotels, villas, and a couple of excellent restaurants. The sand has receded in parts, but it's still a gorgeous beach, with leaning coconut trees and a few almond trees providing shade for your towel. Continue walking to the far western end of the beach and you'll find the Hotel Atlantis and its famous French restaurant, and beyond that, at a sandbank-like corner, Punta Bonita—the point where Bonita joins the stunning Playa Cosón.

Playa Morón is quite the trek—it's approximately 40 minutes out of Las Terrenas by motorbike—but it's a nice ride into the countryside. The bumpy gravel road passes farmlands and kids collecting mangoes from the trees. Once there, you'll appreciate the golden beach with its turquoise waters and tall palm trees, and the complete seclusion. Locals with horses for rent might harass you a bit to go on a ride, but just refuse politely if you're not interested. Stay close to shore because the waves can get strong here.

## SPORTS AND RECREATION
### Snorkeling and Diving

Snorkel or dive with **The Dive Academy** (Beach Garden Plaza, 2nd floor, tel. 829/906-9618, www.tdalasterrenas.com, US$90/2-tank dive, US$375 Open Water Certification, US$70 snorkel). Dives take you to various shipwrecks, like the *The Aquarium* in Samaná or *The Dolfin in Las Terrenas,* as well as lake diving at Dudú in Cabrera. Over at **Profundo Blue** (next to Hotel Playa Caribe, Calle 27 de Febrero, cell tel. 829/349-1913, www.profundoblue.com, US$400/Open Water), a longtime PADI center, you can get certified at all levels; local dives take you right off the beaches of Las Terrenas (US$44/one-tank dive).

Snorkel, beachcomb, stuff yourself with barbecue—it's a formula that **Cap Caraïbes** (Playa Las Ballenas, tel. 829/707-9298, johnnygodin49@gmail.com US$70-80 pp) has perfected on its full-day catamaran excursion, which takes you to several uncrowded beaches like Playa Jackson, and a natural sandbank at Puerto Escondido. You can charter the boat through them if you wish (US$600-700/day).

### Sailing

At the end of Playa Las Ballenas is **Las Terrenas Sailing Club** (next to Sol y Mar Restaurant, tel. 829/580-3065, www.lasterrenassailing.com, US$13/hour double kayak or SUP), where you can rent kayaks and Hobie Cats or get a sailing lesson. Just look for the equipment parked on the beach near the stream. Catamaran sailing trips to area beaches are offered through **Cap Caraïbes** (Playa Las Ballenas, tel. 829/960-9722, www.capcaraibes-catamaran.com, US$100 pp), with plenty of food, drinks, and snorkeling equipment.

### Kitesurfing and Surfing

**Carolina Surf School** (Playa Bonita at Hotel Acaya, tel. 809/882-5467, carolinasurfschool@

Punta Bonita

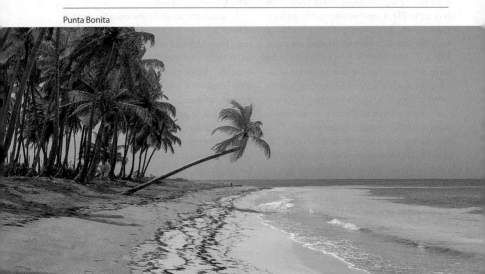

gmail.com, 9am-5:30pm Tues.-Sun., US$50/ two-hour lesson), owned by a Dominican pro kitesurfer turned entrepreneur, offers surfing lessons for adults and kids, as well as surfboard rentals (US$13/hour) and paddleboard rentals (US$25/hour). Mornings are a good time for SUP lessons, when the waters are calmer. Ask about the surf trips to Nagua and Río San Juan on the north coast.

To see kitesurfers, head to Playa Punta Popy or Portillo Beach, where you'll spot them enjoying the sweeping winds that grace this area from December through September. For lessons, there's **LT'Kitesurf** (Calle 27 de Febrero, tel. 809/801-5671, www.lasterrenas-kitesurf.com, US$300/six hours); you can also rent equipment if you're certified (US$70/day).

## Horseback Riding

The French and Swiss duo running **Rancho Playa** (in Limón, tel. 829/868-5233, ranchoplaya.lt@gmail.com, 10am-6pm daily, US$35/hour) offer beach and forest rides to off-the-beaten-track spots at an affordable price. **Flora Tours** (Calle Duarte, tel. 809/240-5482, www.flora-tours.net, $55 pp/1.5 hours) offers beach horseback rides along Playa Cosón.

## Whale-Watching

You can hop on a whale-watching tour with the one and only Kim Beddall of **Whale Samana** (Av. La Marina, tel. 809/538-2494, www.whalesamana.com, US$62, includes sanctuary fee), which now offers pickups in Las Terrenas.

## Fishing

For a fun day out sportfishing, call **CoCokite Fishing** (Calle Duarte, tel. 829/380-8449, www.cocokite-fishing.com). **Cap Caraïbes** (tel. 829/960-9722, US$700/half day with max of five) is another top-notch operation, taking you to Puerto Escondido and other spots where you can bag your own wahoo, tuna, and other critters. Trips depart at 7:30am and return at 1pm.

## Dancing

Las Terrenas is home to a couple of popular dance and entertainment groups, as well as dance studios. This town is for those who love to shake it. You'll get a great workout and make friends at the same time. Learn how to merengue, salsa, son, cha-cha, or *bachata* and partake in the village's active nightlife Wednesday through Sunday. Ask about the *noches de animación*, nights when dance groups head to a particular bar or restaurant and "host" the evening by entertaining guests with their dance routines, as well as inviting them to the floor and showing them a few steps. There's usually a small cover (less than US$5). If you'd rather have formal lessons first, you have several options.

**By Bolivar Escuela de Baile** (Calle Duarte 250, tel. 809/977-9938, www.bybolivardanceschool.com/contact) offers private "original Dominican *bachata*" classes individually (US$32-37) or by couple (US$52). Packages are also available if you're staying awhile. The school hosts a new annual Bachata Paradise Festival in Las Terrenas in May.

## Cockfighting

You don't hear anyone talking about it, but look closely and in every town in the Dominican Republic, you'll spot a *club gallístico*—an enclosed ring where, away from plain view, men gather and bet on cockfights. It's even more of a culturally entrenched sport than baseball. If you happen to be here on a Sunday, particularly in the midmorning hours, head out on the road to Playa Cosón from Las Terrenas town, and you'll see hundreds of bikes parked in the area of La Ceiba, outside an enclosed ring where cockfighting takes place. If you're comfortable with the content, it's quite a cultural experience. Tickets start at RD$200 (US$4.40) depending on your chosen seat.

## Spa

**Janyra** (tel. 809/426-4901, RD$1,200/ US$26.20/hour or RD$600/US$13.10/half hour), the beach masseuse, will bring her table to your favorite corner of Playa Las Ballenas, across from the row of hotels and villas. Call ahead to set up a meeting spot; she also can often be found in the morning at the restaurant across from Hotel Playa Colibri. Soak in a Turkish bath or hammam at **Alisei Spa** (tel. 809/240-5555, www.aliseihotelspa.com, from US$65) or opt from a range of massages, Vichy showers, and other full spa services.

## ENTERTAINMENT AND EVENTS

### Nightlife

**La Bodega Bar** (Calle 27 de Febrero, corner of Calle Duarte, 9pm-2am Wed.-Sun., no cover) has the best setting in town for a club—a grand open dance floor, plenty of seating, and a large bar. It's also a regular hangout and meet-up point for prostitutes and their customers, but it's a good place to watch professional *bachata* and merengue dancers take over the floor—they host various nights here—and try a few steps while you're at it. The best nights are Thursday through Saturday. Start here before heading to the next dance spot like Son Latino or Replay.

If you're looking for a spot to park yourself with good cocktails and music late into the night, **El Mosquito Art Bar** (Francisco Alberto Caamaño Deño, Pueblo de los Pescadores, 5pm-2am, later close Fri.-Sat., midnight Sun.) is a popular pick. There's a lounge side facing the beach as well. With a mixed tourist and local crowd, things get rowdier as the hours pass. For sunset, or a swim with cocktails, **Eden Bar** (beachfront, Playa Las Ballenas, no phone, 11am-10pm daily) has a dream location for mojitos and beers directly on Playa Ballenas, with food if you're in need of a snack.

The international crowd of Las Terrenas hangs out mostly in Pueblo de los Pescadores—a row of lively beachfront bars and restaurants, ranging from French to American, that light up at night with outdoor decks. Sandwiched amid this row is **Replay** (tel. 829/717-1293, 9pm-3am Thurs.-Sun., no cover), your classic beach town dance club, with a DJ spinning everything from thumping house music to the latest R&B and some local tunes. The inside floor gets jammed after midnight, and the crowd spills over into the outdoor seafront deck.

**Gaia Nightclub** (Pueblo de los Pescadores, tel. 809/914-1023, www.gaialasterrenas.com, cover US$7-10) is across the street from Replay. This fancy three-level nightclub is impressive for a small place like Las Terrenas. It costs more to party here, so you won't see it as crowded on weekdays, except perhaps on Saturday when the well-heeled come here to feel exclusive.

**El Son Latino** (behind gas station, Calle Carmen, tel. 809/879-2135, 9pm-2am Thurs.-Sun., US$2.30) has the best Dominican party vibe in Las Terrenas by far, with a mixed crowd of locals and a few expats who love to dance on the spacious, second-level floor. Thursday is the night to go—it used to be mostly karaoke but has since turned into a DJ spinning various tunes from Latin to rap. Portraits of famous Dominican artists grace the walls above the few tables reserved for bottle service. When the night here ends at 2am, the crowd moves over to the adjacent bar and club, or spills out around the gas station.

**El Patio Tropical de Juampi** (Calle Duarte, no phone, 6pm-midnight Thurs.-Sun., no cover) is ultra-local, with its Dominican car wash feel—a spacious thatch-roofed open-air bar, dance floor, and pool tables. Just another couple of blocks up is the similar **El Almendro Car Wash** (Calle Duarte, tel. 809/240-5478, 6pm-midnight, Thurs.-Sun., no cover) where you can enjoy a live merengue band on Sunday. The floor here is smaller and somewhat slippery, but the atmosphere is just as great, if not better because the crowd is a bit more mature.

## SHOPPING

On the main street of Calle Duarte, you'll find a string of small plazas with souvenir shops, starting with Plaza Taína, as well as art and artisan boutiques with carefully selected items from both the DR and Haiti. Note that most stores close their doors at lunchtime for a good two hours, European style.

**Nativ'Arte** (Calle Duarte 270, tel. 829/262-3406, perla90@gmail.com, 9am-7pm Mon.-Sat., 1pm-close Sun.) carries artisan works from various parts of DR. You'll find unique items like candles in coconut shells, hand-woven beach bags, and Taíno ceramic deity figures.

**Haitian Caraibes Art Gallery** (Calle Duarte 159, tel. 809/240-6250, 9am-noon and 3pm-7pm Mon.-Sat., noon-close Sun.) is owned by a French journalist who resides in Haiti and shuffles back and forth across the island. Collections showcase Haitian paintings, as well as Dominican items like cigars and a series of sarongs.

Inside the brightly colored Plaza Casa Linda is **Côté Soleil** (cell tel. 809/869-0160, 10am-4pm Mon.-Sat., hours vary), carrying some funky summer clothes including silk tunics, linen dresses, and accessories. Owner and longtime resident Chantal hails from St. Tropez and her French fashion flair is all over this boutique. She designs the clothes herself and has them manufactured in Italy. Ask her about her favorite places in Las Terrenas and you'll be hanging out here for a little while.

**Puerto Plaza** (Francisco Alberto Caamaño Deño, tel. 809/240-5544, www.puertoplazalasterrenas.com, 8am-6pm daily, lunchtime close until 3pm) is the gargantuan, new boat-shaped shopping mall in town (word is, a second boat is being built right behind the first). Locals call it Los Barcos, and you'll find a few upscale fashion stores with beachwear, as well as a 24-hour Farmacia Carol.

## FOOD

You might forget you're in the Caribbean when you're out for food in Las Terrenas. There might be as many dining spots as there are nationalities. **Pueblo de los Pescadores** is where you'll find a string of restaurants offering prime beachfront seats

and meals blending European, American, and Dominican specialties. As many options as there are, most stand out less for the food than for the setting. In Las Ballenas there are casual beachfront bistros, some now directly on the beach, while Punta Popy has its own restaurant row across the sea at the entrance of town. This list below is by no means comprehensive.

For morning coffee and a pastry, head to the street-side **La Boulangerie Française** (Calle Duarte, Plaza Taína, tel. 809/876-4709, 7am-7pm Mon.-Sat., from US$2), a popular Parisian-style bakery that wins rave reviews. The java is good, but the croissants are average. Baguette sandwiches are also available among other sweet treats. The small outdoor terrace has wicker chairs reminiscent of a Paris sidewalk café and faces the main drag's continuous traffic and pedestrians. Note that there's no wireless Internet here. Another bakery-style pick is **Pan/Am** (Plaza Colonial, near Puerto Plaza Hotel, tel. 809/514-5024), offering a choice of delicious fresh-baked breads and pastries (try the brioche) consumed outdoors on the terrace, steps from the main road facing a parking lot. For a typical plate of eggs with coffee, there's **Bar Bruno** (Plaza Taina, across public park), with an outdoor terrace facing a busy street where quads and bikes zoom past, but at least there's a slight breeze coming across from the nearby sea.

Sandwiched amid the Pueblo de los Pescadores, longtime favorite ★ **La Terrasse** (on Pueblo de los Pescadores, 809/240-6730, 11:30am-2:30pm and 6:30pm-11pm daily, US$20-40) has a beach-chic atmosphere, with its beige and white colors, swaying lanterns, and wooden deck steps from the sand. The menu offers fish, meats, and pastas, with a blend of French and Caribbean specialties. The *salade niçoise* is excellent, as is the *dorado al coco* (coconut stewed fish, a specialty in these parts). It's a lovely spot for a romantic, relaxing meal on a hot afternoon.

You can pick up a pizza any day from **Pizzeria El Pescador** (Francisco Caamaño

Deñó St., tel. 809/240-6202). **Bar Bruno** (Liberty Street, 8am-4pm daily, from US$5) makes paninis of various fillings at a decent price, with fresh-squeezed fruit juices and beers.

**Le Tre Caravelle** (Punta Popy, Av. 27 de Febrero, tel. 809/917-6639, simone.mura@ yahoo.it, US$5-20) serves seafood in all its forms; try the risotto. The outdoor terrace has a view of the sea and beach across the road, but there's also interior dining if you tire of the mosquitoes at sunset. It's a nice spot for a fancy dinner.

★ **Le Thalassa** (Francisco Alberto Caamaño Deñó St., tel. 829/847-3568, www. thalassabymaeva.com, 3pm-midnight Mon.-Sun., closed Mon. in low season) is one of the few constants in Las Terrenas's ever-changing restaurant world, thanks to its level of service and quality seafood dishes, from creole crab to ceviche to seafood salad.

A sign of Las Terrenas's diverse expat population, **Zubr Beer House** (Pueblo de los Pescadores, across Puerto Plaza, tel. 829/828-5152, www.zubr.do, 8am-10pm daily except Mon., Sunday 3pm close, from US$2) offers Czech cuisine—handmade sausages, burgers, and chicken schnitzel prepared by a Czech chef, downed with Czech beers (Zubr, Litovel, Holba). You'll also find crepes and flan, among other options. The place gets crowded in the morning, no doubt for the cheap breakfast special with a serving of eggs, fruits, and bread at just US$2.60. Facing the long pedestrian boardwalk on Las Terrenas Beach, **El Cayuco** (Pueblo de los Pescadores, tel. 809/240-6885, noon-midnight daily, US$4-15) is a great spot for breakfast or for dinner when you feel like snacking from their tapas menu along with a glass of sangria. They also offer reasonably priced entrées.

**Paco Cabana** (Calle Libertad 1, tel. 809/240-5301, pacocabana@hotmail.com, US$12-20) has a small thatch-roof *palapa*, white tablecloths, and chandelier atmosphere that's enough to draw you in. But the equally small menu is decent, offering a range of seafood, pasta, and meats.

Also on the beachside of Las Terrenas, right in town, you'll find a row of shacks facing fishing canoes where locals cool off and sell fresh-catch meals every day. For fresh fruits and veggies, try the **Mini Market** (Caamaño Deñó Francisco St., near Hotel Marilar, 9am-5 pm daily). There are fresh fruit and coconut vendors around town—just keep your eyes peeled.

Up for some fresh fried fish on the beach, Dominican-style? The best in the area is the open-air **Restaurant Luis** (no phone, 11am-6pm daily) on gorgeous Playa Cosón, where you can watch them cook outdoors on open wood fires. Pick your fresh catch and size (about US$8/pound of red snapper) and order it grilled, steamed, or fried. Head for a swim until the food is brought to your table; expect heaping sides of rice and beans, *tostones,* and avocado.

★ **L'Atlantis Restaurant** (tel. 809/240-6111, www.atlantis-hotel.com.do, noon-9pm Wed.-Mon., US$11-30) is a treat, and not to be missed when you spend the day on Playa Bonita. Sit at one of a handful of tables set in a *palapa* facing the sea or on a covered outdoor terrace by candlelight. The restaurant—helmed by Chef Gerard, former private chef to former French president Francois Mitterrand—dishes out fresh seafood picked by Gerard himself, French specialties, and delights like fish ceviche in a coconut sauce or grilled lobster in a butter sauce. Pastas and steaks are on offer as well. With the backdrop of the artsy hotel, the atmosphere is sophisticated yet intimate and casual.

Take it up a notch at the all-white **The Beach** (Playa Cosón, tel. 809/962-7447, US$10-25) for a decadent meal, whether as a long lunch or dinner. Dine on the small terrace of this seafront restaurant with an old-world charm, where house specialties include shrimp with passion fruit sauce or crab cakes with mango chutney. Sample the coconut shavings while you wait on your meal.

---

**1:** the boat-shaped Puerto Plaza shopping mall; **2:** Hotel Mahona

## ACCOMMODATIONS

Just like restaurants, rooms abound in Las Terrenas, ranging from budget accommodations to hotels offering self-catering apartments and exclusive villas. Prices have gone up in recent years, and while it's not as cheap as staying in Las Galeras, it's cheaper than staying in Punta Cana.

### Under US$50

Off the beaten track in the town of Limón, yet easily found down a path directly beside the Manantial de Limón (the popular freshwater pool on the main Limón road), **Samaná Eco-Lodge and Hostel** (tel. 849/357-1481, samanaecolodge@gmail.com, US$35) is the latest addition to the peninsula's growing list of independent traveler haunts. Solar panels provide power, while water is pumped from the freshwater river nearby and filtered by the owners for the front pool, the toilets, and the al fresco showers. A main thatched *palapa* serves as the chill-out lounge and breakfast area, surrounded by banana trees and lush grounds, while a series of four spaced-out, private wooden cabanas share two bathrooms. There's a large dorm room ("the barn") with 10 mattresses on wooden slats arrayed around a common space, and mosquito nets (US$15). Dinner is available daily ($6) in high season.

A brisk 10-minute walk south from the heart of Las Terrenas will plunge you into a scene reminiscent of the Dominican campo at ★ **Dan & Manty's** (Calle del Carmen 105, near Calle Duarte and across from Pan de Antes bakery, tel. 849/873-5742, topdeckgames@yahoo.com, US$16), with children playing by a creek facing the home turned hostel. The friendly Dominican-American couple running this hostel are committed to creating a community atmosphere, and it shows immediately as you enter their large, welcoming veranda transformed into a vast open kitchen on one side, and a lounge on the other with wall-couches, tables, and plenty of communal seating around two murals of the Samaná map. Dan and Manty's love story alone will make you fall for this place

that gathers international travelers in one of four dorms, with bunk beds and attached bath (US$16). There are also two private apartments (US$24-30) on the ground floor, with double beds for local families or groups who wish to stick together. Breakfast is offered for a small fee (US$3). Manty's daily all-you-can-eat Dominican-style dinner buffet kicks off at 8pm and is open to guests and the public for US$7. I can't say I've come across a hostel quite like this one yet in the DR, oozing pure Dominican hospitality.

**Casas del Mar Neptunia** (Calle Emilio Prud'Homme 1, tel. 809/240-6884, www.casasdelmarneptunia.com, US$46, includes breakfast) boasts 10 basic rooms in Dominican-style cottages set in a tropical garden. Rooms have outdoor porches, king-size beds, a refrigerator, safe, fans, hot water, and backup power supply. It's good enough for solo travelers, if you're not up for being social (though the latter is what's great about the DR), and a short walk from the main drag in town.

### US$50-100

★ **Hotel Mahona** (Calle Italia 3, tel. 849/651-3078, US$70-80, full breakfast included) is Las Terrenas's newest but still-hidden gem, though probably not for long. This newly renovated boutique hotel boasts exquisite suites—king or double, with private verandas—hugging a lush, tropical, and flowery garden. There's an intimate pool with shaded seating and an open dining room (also to be renovated and enlarged). The owners, a delightfully welcoming French couple who are well traveled and have an architectural background, have transformed this place into an Asian-inspired oasis that's just a five-minute walk down an alley from the heart of the village's lively Pueblo de los Pescadores. Suites are decorated in earth tones, with decorative shells for art, white drapes casually thrown over four-poster beds, romantic Asian-style lampposts, and open brick showers. The highlight, aside from the tasteful tranquility, is the included breakfast fit for French royalty—house-made croissants and marmalade, French toast, eggs cooked any way you wish, fresh fruits, and a coffee carafe that's all yours. You might not even want to leave for the day afterwards. Families should inquire about the gorgeous, hidden-from-view self-catering loft suite that resembles a villa, with its own private pool and garden. The only downer here may be the weak Wi-Fi.

**La Residencia del Paseo** (Calle Juan Pablo Duarte 272, tel. 809/240-6778, www. residenciadelpaseo.com, US$72-90) sits smack in the middle of the action on the main street in town, surrounded by hotels, shopping, restaurants, and some nightlife. It's a bit dated, although it is two minutes' walk to the closest beach; there are better alternatives (see above) at that price or if you can splurge for a few more dollars a day. The resort has a pool, wireless Internet, and cable TV, and the self-catering apartments—kitchens and baths are dated—have balconies, fan if you pick a studio, or air-conditioning for duplexes. It's safe and a good spot if you're just passing through for a night or two. There's access from the back of the hotel to the Paseo Plaza, as well as the Pueblo de los Pescadores restaurants.

## US$100-150

For an eco-chic lodge experience near Las Terrenas, head approximately 15 minutes east into the countryside and spend a couple of nights at ★ **Clave Verde** (La Barbacoa, tel. 809/802-1146, www.claveverde.com, US$100-475, breakfast included), perched in the gorgeous hills of La Barbacoa. Owned by a warm Dominican-British couple from Santo Domingo, you'll find a lodge with four cozy villas, studios, and rooms across comfortable wooden cabins named after trees, boasting private porches and verandas with panoramic views onto the tropical forests below and the coastline ahead. It's a haven for nature lovers—all sorts of bird species, lizards, and butterflies scurry around the lodge—and couples looking to disconnect, with a salt-mineral capsule-filtered infinity pool, and delicious meals worthy of a top restaurant (some fruits come directly from the garden). The lodge is adamant on being ecoconcious, and runs on 90 percent solar electricity. There's a recreational room with Ping-Pong tables if you're up for it. You'll need a car to stay here, or a taxi. Nearby beaches are virgin, and hour-long hikes from the beach into Las Terrenas are possible.

If you're looking for a quiet getaway for two, lazing on the beach, the whimsical yet classy **Hotel Atlantis** (Playa Bonita, tel. 809/240-6111, http://hotel-atlantis-lasterrenas.com, US$135-185) is hard to miss as you walk along Playa Bonita's shore. Flanked with palm trees, 18 artsy and cozy sea-facing rooms are tucked in white buildings with funky architectural shapes that look straight out of a fairy tale. Stay in Jamaica, Quito, or Malaga, among other picks—each room offers its own decor. On-site is the excellent L'Atlantis Restaurant. The hotel is tucked away from the main beachgoers at Playa Bonita, and at least 10 minutes' ride from town.

★ **Hotel Playa Colibri** (Calle Francisco Camaaño Deño, tel. 809/240-6434, www. hotelplayacolibri.com, US$99-119) is a solid pick for families with little ones, and I love the beach vacation hotel feel it has. It is barely 10 steps across the street from a lovely stretch of Playa Ballenas. The staff is friendly, and the self-catering apartments have full kitchens, cable TV, air-conditioning, wireless Internet, separate living rooms, and en suite baths. Some are a bit dated, but the place is spotless. There's a pool at the center of this small collection of privately owned units, and the reception desk is staffed 24 hours, with security. The small restaurant shack on the beach serves up breakfast and lunch, and the sandwiches are decent. It's just a 15-minute walk from the hotel to the village, yet away from the city noise.

★ **Hotel Alisei** (Playa Las Ballenas, tel. 809/240-5555, www.aliseihotelspa.com, from US$130, includes breakfast) has a location that's hard to beat, steps from town, and within seconds of the beach. It's a clean and beautifully laid-out property, with 54 self-catering apartments, but also on-site are a full-service spa, a restaurant, swim-up bar, pool, and gym. Rooms are tastefully decorated and have terraces, satellite TV, air-conditioning and fans, phone, and wireless Internet. It's a solid pick for families.

Hugged by a forest of coconut trees, the boutique **Casa Cosón** (www.casacoson. com, US$140-220) appeals to honeymooners or couples seeking a dreamy escape in Las Terrenas. Facing the gorgeous Playa Cosón, the gated villa-looking hotel has an immaculate yard where you can relax on loungers with a good book, or wander to the beach. It would be easy to not leave; the meals on-site are enticing. Rooms all include air-conditioning and a mini fridge, while others also have oceanview terraces. If you're up for a lazy stay, this is yet another excellent choice.

## US$200 and up

The boat-shaped **Puerto Plaza** (tel. 809/240-5544, www.puertoplazalasterrenas.com, from US$400) gets raves for its sleek, tastefully furnished self-catering one- and two-bedroom apartments with multiple baths in the heart of the village. Though the property sits roadside, the private hot tubs, pool, and partial ocean views make you feel as if you're on a cruise. It's ideal for families, as you can fit up to four people by using the large modular sofa beds. There are better deals in the summertime.

The hilltop ★ **Peninsula House** (Calle Cosón, tel. 809/962-7447, www. thepeninsulahouse.com, from US$550, breakfast included) is straight out of a movie. This dream vacation mansion/colonial palace is as opulent as it gets, if only because of its antique and art-filled rooms—each item would tell a story if it could. The open Spanish courtyard as you enter the house is as charming as the staircase leading up to the six junior suites with private terraces that reveal spectacular garden and sea views above Playa Cosón. The family-run property, which has a driveway that is unmarked, is for those who seek complete exclusivity, whether for a weekend of romance or for a special family celebration.

No details are spared in providing personalized five-star (or is it six?) service, whether it's the 19th-century ivory closets, the china service used for meals, or the turndown while you're downstairs enjoying dinner al fresco. You could easily spend hours inside exploring the various trinkets and decorative furniture pieces—I stumbled on a wooden Ethiopian cross—accompanied by jazzy old-school music.

There's an on-site pool with views of the ocean, and a darling beach house where you can relax, read a book, grab towels, or marvel at the African-themed decor complete with masks. Breakfast and dinner are offered, while lunch can be enjoyed at The Beach, the property's excellent restaurant directly on Playa Cosón (you'd need a car to get there or hitch a ride). Before you leave, ask to see the view of the Cosón Bay from the helipad.

The sleek **Sublime Samaná** (tel. 809/240-5050, www.sublimesamana.com, US$200-350) has for its centerpiece a series of narrow pools with sunbeds facing each private villa or suite and leading from the entrance of the hotel all the way to the beach. Set on one end of Playa Cosón, the all-white resort has a posh Miami atmosphere. Meals at the on-site beach restaurant are surprisingly good, albeit pricey. There's also a small spa. Note that you'd want to have a car if you stay here, as taxi rides are to Las Terrenas town start to add up, unless you're set on unwinding in Cosón your entire stay.

# INFORMATION AND SERVICES

If you're stocking up your villa for the week, head to **Super Pola** (Calle Duarte, tel. 809/472-4444, 8am-10pm Mon.-Sat., 9am-8pm Sun.). **Supermercado Lindo** (tel. 809/240-6003, Calle Juan Pablo Duarte, 8:30am-8pm Mon.-Sat., 9am-1pm Sun.) carries imported French and Spanish goods, including wines, champagne, and deli meats. They also offer free delivery. Get your fresh catch directly from the fishermen at the daily **fish market** (7am-1pm) in Las Terrenas, on the beach where all the fishing boats are parked. Choices range from oysters to mahi-mahi.

**Banco Popular** has a branch and ATMs on the main Avenida Duarte; you'll find **BanReservas** across from it, while **Progreso Bank** has an ATM inside El Paseo shopping plaza.

You can reach the **police** at 809/240-6022. The specialized tourism police **CESTUR** (Liberty Street, tel. 809/754-3017) share headquarters with the police and have a visible presence throughout Las Terrenas. Look out for these uniformed men and feel free to ask them for directions or even to escort you at night if you need.

For medical care, there's **Centro Galeno Integral Las Terrenas** (Calle Duarte No. 242, next to Banco León, tel. 809/240-6817, www.clinicalasterrenas.com) and the public **Hospital Las Terrenas** (Calle Mella Ramon, tel. 809/240-6474). There's a 24-hour **Farmacia Carol** in town, inside the **Puerto Plaza** (Pueblo de los Pescadores, tel. 809/240-6688 or 809/240-5000, www.farmaciacarol.com).

## GETTING THERE AND AROUND

Various airlines fly directly from North America into Samaná's **El Catey International Airport,** including WestJet and Air Canada. From the airport, the Boulevard Turístico del Atlántico takes you directly to Las Terrenas (you can stop in Cosón for the scenic viewpoint).

**Caribe Tours** (Av. 27 de Febrero, tel. 809/576-0790, www.caribetours.com.do, RD$270/US$5.88 one-way) has daily departures from Santo Domingo to Samaná town in big coach buses. You can then hop in a local bus or take a taxi to Las Terrenas. **Transporte**

**Las Terrenas** (tel. 809/687-1470 in Santo Domingo, 809/240-5302 in Las Terrenas) is a regular private minibus service with various departures from Santo Domingo (5am, 7am, 9am, 2pm, 3:30pm), as well as from Puerto Plata (6:30am). Call to check the latest pickup times and locations.

If you're driving from Santo Domingo directly to Las Terrenas, there are two options: taking the **Boulevard Turístico del Atlántico** (Route 133; bring toll money, about RD$400/US$8.70), which connects to **Autopista del Nordeste** (Route 7) from the Santo Domingo Airport; or the scenic, winding Sanchez-Las Terrenas road, with breathtaking twists and views of the Cordillera Samaná below. Drive slowly, and take your time going around bends. The road will eventually turn into Las Terrenas's main drag of Duarte, which hugs the coastline and beaches.

Getting around on foot is easy and safe in this beach town in daylight and evening hours (just don't walk around past midnight if you have a distance to go). Still, you can rent a scooter (US$30/day), quad (US$50-55/day) or a car (US$50-75/day) from the reputable **Jessie Car Rental** (Pueblo de los Pescadores, tel. 809/240-6415, www.jessiecar.com). **Motorbike taxis** are also plentiful all over Las Terrenas and are a convenient and cheap way to reach Playa Bonita or Playa Cosón, or anywhere you need to go in town—look for the neon yellow jacket-wearing lads.

As in most parts of the DR, there's a **tourist taxi association** with expensive set prices. In Las Terrenas, **ASOCHOTRATUTENA** (tel. 809/240-6391 or 809/240-6339) takes you to popular destinations including El Portillo (US$10), Punta Bonita (US$15), Playa Cosón (US$25), Playa Morón (US$30), Samaná (US$70) and Las Galeras (US$100).

# Puerto Plata and the North Coast

**Puerto Plata is lovingly called** *la novia del Atlántico*, or the Atlantic's darling, for its sea-hugged landscape. Nearly 80 kilometers (50 miles) of pristine beaches stretch east to west along the Atlantic and beg for a stopover. Inland, verdant fields and mountains beckon with waterfalls, manatee lakes, and mangrove swamps tucked away in national parks.

This province was the birthplace of tourism in the DR, before its sunshine was eclipsed by the rapid rise and mega development of all-inclusive beach haven Punta Cana in the southeast. Since 2015, Puerto Plata and its eponymous province have experienced a revival, thanks in part to community-driven sustainable tourism initiatives, the renovation of the city's historic center and parks, and

# Highlights

Look for ★ to find recommended sights, activities, dining, and lodging.

★ **Pico Isabel de Torres:** Ride a cable car 793 meters (2,600 feet) above the Atlantic to get a closer look at Puerto Plata's symbolic landmark: a replica of the giant Christ the Redeemer statue in Rio de Janeiro (page 206).

★ **El Malecón de Puerto Plata:** Strolling down the city's waterfront boulevard at sunset is as local as it gets (page 209). End the walk with a stop at the waterfront Parque La Puntilla.

★ **27 Charcos de Damajagua:** These 27 waterfalls are the number one attraction in the DR—worth every slip, slide, jump, and spelunk (page 211).

★ **Charcos de Los Militares:** In Tubagua, hike past village scenery to reach a series of three stunning waterfalls beyond tourist crowds (page 213).

★ **Social Impact Tourism:** The Community Tourism Network offers seven unique tours in Puerto Plata, each of which has a positive impact on local communities (page 216).

★ **Water Sports in Cabarete:** Appreciate the North Coast's sought-after winds and waves by taking a surfing class on world-famous Encuentro Beach, a windsurfing class on Cabarete Beach, or a kitesurfing class on Kite Beach (page 242).

★ **Playa Arroyo Salado:** Just 10 kilometers (6 miles) south of Cabrera, this stunning beach boasts a gorgeous coastline and an eponymous freshwater river, which makes for a great two-for-one recreational space, along with seafood shacks, bars, and a lively familial ambience (page 257).

★ **Estero Hondo Marine Mammal Sanctuary:** Visit this breathtaking lagoon and stand on its lookout tower to spot manatees, mangroves, and over 30 species of bird and fish (page 258).

★ **Playa El Morro:** The dramatic limestone cliff of El Morro in Monte Cristi hugs this red-gold beach, making it one of the most unusual landscapes in the DR (page 262).

★ **Cayos Siete Hermanos:** It doesn't get more idyllic than this series of seven cayes amid the turquoise waters off the coast of Monte Cristi (page 264).

# Puerto Plata and the North Coast

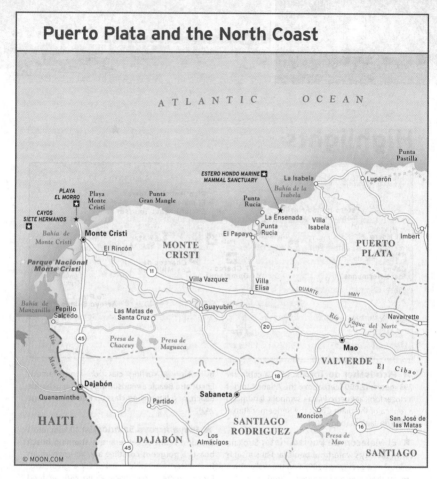

the opening of the new Amber Cove cruise port. But in truth, the North Coast, home to Christopher Columbus's second settlement in the Americas, has always packed in a lot to see and do along its breezy Atlantic shoreline.

Puerto Plata stands out for offering a window into the authentic DR, whether it's Puerto Plata city's stunning Malecón and its incessant buzz of *motoconchos,* the laidback and revived beach community life in Costambar, the multicultural restaurants of Sosúa, the wind sports hub of Cabarete, the

cacao farming in Guananico, or just the merengue ringing out of bars and car washes. At the heart of it all are the North Coast's residents, who are some of the most hospitable and charitable people you'll find in the DR.

## PLANNING YOUR TIME

The North Coast is an explorer's dream and a vacationer's dilemma in terms of determining how to fit in all the fun. If you love road trips, there's no more diverse and all-encompassing spot in the Dominican Republic. In one drive,

**Previous:** Parque Independencia; North Coast sunsets are breathtaking; water sports along the North Coast.

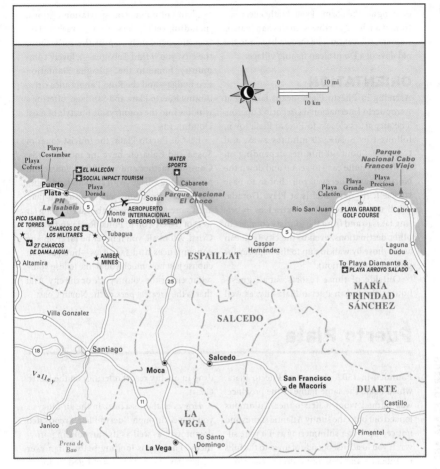

you'll experience everything from beaches to lagoons, mangrove swamps to offshore islands, water sports to hiking mountains and parks, plush resorts to jungle lodges. You won't be able to do it all, but if you plan your time right, you'll get a solid glimpse of the region and its offerings.

Determine your preferred activities and then pick a base. If you want a taste of it all, begin in the historic city of Puerto Plata. Save a couple of days to enjoy the city's museums and architecture, the beaches at Playa Dorada, and the water sports at Playa Chaparral. From there, you can head to the hills of Tubagua to hole up at Tubagua Plantation Eco Lodge,

where you'll experience authentic Dominican *campo* culture and explore surrounding scenic villages. A day trip will take you to the amber mines in La Cumbre or to Guananico to make coffee or to learn how to dance merengue.

You'll want to save a couple of days to travel northwest to the paradisiacal Estero Hondo lagoon and the beaches in Punta Rucia and offshore Cayo Arena. End your journey in wild and mountainous Monte Cristi, home to gloriously uncrowded beaches.

Still have time? A jaunt to Cabarete is worth it to see this lively water sports haven of a beach village, where kites fill the sky, surfers tumble, and beachfront barhopping and dancing are the norm. If you'd rather get away from it all, head northwest to Río San Juan or Cabrera, where you'll be thrown back into the old days of a Dominican fishing village.

## ORIENTATION

Arriving in Puerto Plata means landing at Aeropuerto Internacional Gregorio Luperón. The airport is closest to Puerto Plata town, followed by Sosúa, 20 minutes away, and Cabarete, about 40 minutes depending on traffic. It's quite easy to get up and down the North Coast wherever you choose to base yourself. If your hotel is at Playa Dorada, you'll want to account for extra fees in getting taxis to and from the touristy complex to other destinations, even to the city (you can avoid those by walking up to the highway for public transportation).

Outside of those resorts, small guesthouses abound in Puerto Plata city, as well as plenty of public transportation options, including rental cars if you'd rather day-trip independently. Up in the hills above the city, you'll find Tubagua—a lovely community, home to the Tubagua Plantation Eco Lodge—and the Ruta Panorámica drive linking Puerto Plata and Santiago, offering a window into the countryside lifestyle of most Dominicans.

East of Puerto Plata, the tourist zones of Sosúa and Cabarete have the most crowds. Continue farther and you'll find yourself in more fishing villages with glorious landscapes or natural attractions, such as Río San Juan and Cabrera. The same can be said heading far west of the city, on to Punta Rucia and Monte Cristi. All in all, you'll never be far from any conveniences and facilities—but you can choose just how much you'd like to lose yourself in either the countryside or the city. And that is the greatest perk of the North Coast.

# Puerto Plata

Founded in 1502, the city of Puerto Plata, which bears the same name as the province, was named when Christopher Columbus looked out onto the sunny Atlantic shores and noticed the water shimmering as if it were silver. If you head just outside of town to the hills of Tubagua and look out onto the coastline, you'll see the sea does indeed resemble a silver blanket under the hot sun. Others say the silver illusion came from the sight of clouds hanging above Mount Isabel. Puerto Plata has earned numerous nicknames, including "the amber coast," for the area's richness in the precious stone. Residents affectionately call it *la tacita de plata,* or "a silver cup."

Puerto Plata was the first major tourism destination in the DR in 1974. The region thrived up until the 1990s, with tourism income surpassing that of the sugar, tobacco, and cattle industries. Sadly, the decline of Puerto Plata tourism began with the development of the Punta Cana coast, as well as the drop in quality resort offerings on the North Coast.

However, there's a buzz in the air today as you travel through Puerto Plata's renovated downtown, as well as its surrounding provinces. The city is looking better than ever with repaved streets and renovated Victorian buildings in its scenic town square—there are over 100 altogether, the largest number in the Caribbean—as well as new hotels and international restaurants. Off-the-beaten-track cultural activities are more within reach than ever before thanks to sustainable tourism initiatives, making this destination even more attractive for independent travelers.

The most well-known area of Puerto Plata city remains the gated, all-inclusive resort and beach complexes of Costa Dorada and Playa Dorada. But there's plenty to see and do apart from them: visiting the main historical sights and museums (including a significant fortress), strolling down the stunning seafront

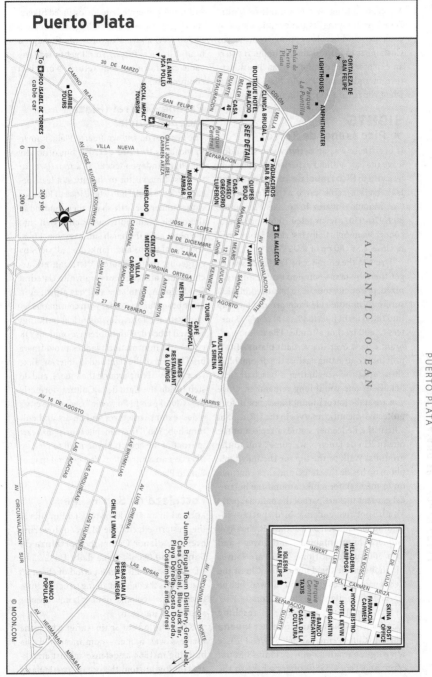

# Puerto Plata

To Pico Isabel de Torres cable car

To El Anafe Pica Pollo

30 DE MARZO

CAMINO REAL

CARIBE TOURS

SOCIAL IMPACT TOURISM

SAN FELIPE

IMBERT

VILLA NUEVA

AV JOSE EUGENIO KOUNHART

BOUTIQUE HOTEL EL PALACIO

CASA 40

BELLER

DUARTE

RESTAURACION

CLINICA BRUGAL

MELLA

AV COLON

Bahía de Puerto Plata

LIGHTHOUSE

FORTALEZA DE SAN FELIPE

Parque La Puntilla

AMPHITHEATER

SEE DETAIL

Parque Central

SEPARACION

CALLE JOSE DEL CARMEN ARIZA

MUSEO DE AMBAR

MERCADO

AQUACEROS BAR & GRILL

QUIPES BOJO

CASA MEARS

MUSEO GREGORIO LUPERON

MARGARITA

JOSE R. LOPEZ

20 DE DICIEMBRE

CARDENAL

CENTRO MEDICO

DR. ZAIRA

VIRGINA ORTEGA

JOHN F. KENNEDY

12 DE JULIO

SANCHEZ

AV CIRCUNVALACION NORTE

JAMY'S

EL MALECON

A T L A N T I C   O C E A N

VILLA CAROLINA

EL MORRO

ANTERA MOTA

SANCHA

JUAN LAFITE

27 DE FEBRERO

METRO

16 DE AGOSTO

TOURS

CAFÉ TROPICAL

MULTICENTRO LA SIRENA

MARES RESTAURANT & LOUNGE

PAUL HARRIS

AV 16 DE AGOSTO

LAS ACACIAS

LAS BROMELIAS

AV LUIS GINEBRA

AV CIRCUNVALACION SUR

LAS ORQUIDEAS

LOS TULIPANES

CHILEY LIMON

LAS ROSAS

SEBASTIAN LA PERLA NEGRA

BANCO POPULAR

AV HERMANAS MIRABAL

AV CIRCUNVALACION NORTE

To Jumbo, Brugal Rum Distillery, Green Jack, Casa Colonial, Blue Jack Tar, Playa Dorada, Costa Dorada, Costambar, and Cofresí

© MOON.COM

0
0   200 yds
0   200 m

## Detail

PROF. JUAN BOSCH

IMBERT

BELLER

JOSE DEL CARMEN ARIZA

12 DE JULIO

IGLESIA SAN FELIPE

HELADERIA MARIPOSA

HYODE BISTRO

FARMACIA CARMEN

SKINA

POST OFFICE

TAXIS

Parque Central

HOTEL KEVIN

BERGANTIN

BANCO MERCANTIL

SEPARACION

CASA DE LA CULTURA

DUARTE

Malecón, hiking to the summit of Mount Isabel or enjoying its panoramic views by cable car, and beach-hopping from nearby Costambar to Cofresí and Maimón. If you're an explorer, you're in for a treat. The adventure in and around Puerto Plata only ends when you realize you've run out of time.

## SIGHTS
### ★ Pico Isabel de Torres

If ever there was an activity you shouldn't leave the city without experiencing, it would be a visit to **Pico Isabel de Torres** on Mount Isabel via a cable car on the **Teleférico** (Av. Manolo Tavárez Justo, Las Flores, tel. 809/970-0501, www.telefericopuertoplata. com, 8:30am-5pm daily, last ride 15 min. prior to close, US$7.80 pp or RD$350).

Drive to the entrance of Teleférico solo or get there by taxi—you don't need an organized, pricey city tour. It's a breathtaking, leisurely 10-minute ride from ground level up into the skies of Puerto Plata, at over 793 meters (2,600 feet) of altitude. The iconic panoramic view over the verdant plains of this province contrasting against the distant blue, shiny Atlantic—including a baseball field below—is one you'll long remember. Once you are at the top of Mount Isabel, one of four protected scientific reserves in the DR, a giant Christ the Redeemer statue, a replica of the one in Rio de Janeiro, welcomes you to the grounds. Walk to the top for the inevitable photo op beside the statue, and then continue on to the back for a hike around the botanical gardens that are part of the national park. You'll spot five endemic bird species—including the national bird of the DR, the *cigua palmera,* hummingbirds, and doves—and over 500 species of flora. There are souvenir shops inside the dome by the Christ the Redeemer statue; go in and browse, but be warned of the slightly pushy vendors.

Want another perspective in reaching Pico Isabel? Top adventure outfitter **Iguana Mama** (Calle Principal, tel. 809/654-2325, www.iguanamama.com, 7:45am-3:30pm Mon. and Fri., US$80) offers a hike to the summit for intermediate to advanced hikers, starting at sea level and ending at 823 meters (2,700 feet) above after crossing through a humid tropical forest. You'll get to ride the cable car down on your return. Not a bad compromise!

### Parque Central (Plaza Independencia)

The heart of downtown Puerto Plata, known to locals as **Parque Central** but officially the Plaza Independencia, is a must-see for the first-time visitor to the city, not least because it's the social hub where Puerto Plateños gather under the little shade they can find in the daytime and idle on benches well into the night after the harsh sun has gone. Lined with royal palms and flanked on all sides by gorgeous, pastel-colored Victorian-era architecture and the towering white Catedral San Felipe Apóstol, the area has grown even more beautiful every year with continuous revitalization efforts. Key historical buildings are well labeled, with impressive outdoor QR codes and information plaques providing a brief history of the sight and its interior. Take your time walking around the square, and do step inside the Casa de la Cultura, formerly the "Club Fe en El Porvenir," one of the city's oldest extant structures and an art and cultural hub. You'll find a mobile tourist info cart in front of the church, if you need to pick up flyers on area attractions or a general map of Puerto Plata.

### Fortaleza de San Felipe

Located in an area known as La Puntilla at the western edge of the Malecón, towering over the Atlantic Ocean, the **Fortaleza de San Felipe** (9am-4:30pm daily, US$2.25 or RD$100) was built over a period of about 13 years and is the *only* remaining structure from Puerto Plata's colonial days. It is now open as a historical museum.

King Philip II of Spain—after whom the fortress was named—commissioned the building in 1564 as defense against attackers coming in from the ocean, particularly

# Downtown Puerto Plata Walking Tour

Plaza Independencia is a popular meet up spot both day and night.

Santo Domingo has its Colonial Zone, and Puerto Plata has its Victorian architecture-filled city center. History spreads from the Parque Central (or Plaza Independencia, as it's formally known) and into the characterful side streets and alleys. A handful of the 19th-century buildings have been renovated and are open for visitors. They add a unique charm to the city, not to mention making great photo ops for architectural buffs. Meandering your way around the city on foot for even a half day will give you the true pulse of Puerto Plata.

- On an early morning, head out to the **Plaza Independencia,** better known to locals as Parque Central, and start the day with a cup of Dominican coffee and breakfast at **Heladería Mariposa,** a great example of renovated Victorian building.

- Afterward, cross over to the park, sit on a bench for a selfie, and take in the buildings hugging the square and the passing morning traffic buzz, before you start exploring the various museums.

- Start with the **Casa de la Cultura** to walk all of its levels and admire the exhibit rooms and their architectural details.

- When you're done, head back out and make a left onto **Calle Duarte,** where a couple of blocks down is the **Museum de Ámbar,** which provided stones for Stephen Spielberg's *Jurassic Park*

- Two blocks from the square, go for a visit of the beautiful **Casa Museo General Gregorio Luperón**—one of the most stunning renovated Victorian buildings in town. Enjoy the courtyard before you leave, then head two blocks west to **Hyode's** for a Dominican lunch.

- From there, walk it off on the Malecón—just a five-minute walk toward the sea—with a glorious breeze sweeping in from across the boulevard. You'll blend in with the residents who are often found relaxing here, whether they be fishers, guides, or retired expats.

- Take a seat at **La Carihuela** for *una fría*—a cold Presidente—before taking a dip at the beach.

- Still have energy? Head back up to the central square to browse the handcrafted, locally made gifts at **Casa 40,** before heading to its colorful courtyard for happy hour mojitos. Stay later in the week and you'll enjoy live jazz.

the pirates who preyed on Puerto Plata because of all of the gold and silver mined in the area at the time. Construction of the fortress ended in 1577. Over time, the purpose of the fortress changed: In the 19th century, Dominican Republic founding father Juan Pablo Duarte was imprisoned here by General Pedro Santana; he was one of many to suffer that fate, all the way through the Trujillo years. In 1965, the fortress was turned into a museum. It appears small, but inside are several informative displays of 19th-century weapons in the low-ceilinged chambers. The ramparts, which hold the original cannons, offer an impressive panoramic view of the Atlantic and the surrounding areas. It's a key piece of Puerto Plata's history.

## Parque de La Puntilla

Adjacent to the fortress, boasting the same Atlantic Ocean views, is **Parque de La Puntilla,** which, after renovation now comprises a beautiful, Grecian-inspired open-air amphitheater for outdoor concerts (similar to the one in Altos de Chavón), paved bike trails, landscaped lawns, and plenty of bench seating. It's a favorite place for local families and lovers to stroll or bike around at sunset. While some bemoan the old rustic park, the new and modern one is a welcome addition to a city where there's little urban recreation.

## Casa de la Cultura

Housed in the only three-story Victorian-style wood building in downtown Puerto Plata, **Casa de la Cultura** (in front of Parque Independencia, Calle Separación, 809/261-2731, 9am-noon and 3pm-5pm daily, free), formerly called Club Fe en el Porvenir (you'll see that label outside), hosts art exhibits and musical events year-round on its three floors. The building itself is worth a look while you're meandering in the downtown area. It was rebuilt in 1908 as a recreational and cultural center and is one of four original buildings facing the park at the start of the 20th century. It once served as a gathering place for the intellectuals who fought against the

dictatorship of Ulises Heureaux, who fell from power in 1889. On the 2nd floor is a veranda overlooking the park and square, and on the 3rd you'll find a library of Spanish literature. You are welcome to have a seat and consult the collection.

## Museo de Ámbar

**Museo de Ámbar** (Calle Duarte 61, tel. 809/586-2848, www.ambermuseum.com, 9am-6pm daily, includes guided tour, US$1.10 or RD$50), housed in a gorgeous restored Victorian building, opened its doors in 1982 thanks to the Costa family. It is a small yet informative museum on the history of the Dominican stone. The fun parts include the 2nd-floor gallery, with displays set in a cave to mimic an amber mine setting and fossilized amber pieces containing prehistoric insects, one of which was used in Stephen Spielberg's *Jurassic Park.* The movie was filmed in part in the Dominican Republic, and the museum played an important role in providing amber. The stones displayed here come from the Septentrional Mountain Range in the central highlands of the North Coast. There's a jewelry store as you exit with some unique pieces.

The **Galería de Ámbar** (Calle 12 de Julio, tel. 809/261-2000, www.ambercollection.itgo. com, 8:30am-5pm Mon.-Fri., 2pm close Sat., from US$10) sells more larimar and amber jewelry and has one of the largest selections in town outside of the Museo de Ámbar.

## Casa Museo General Gregorio Luperón

Easily the prettiest museum in town, and a short walk from the Parque Independencia, **Casa Museo General Gregorio Luperón** (Calle 12 de Julio 54, corner of Padre Castellanos, tel. 809/261-8661, museogregorioluperon@claro.net.do, 8:30am-6:30pm Tues.-Sun., US$2.25 or RD$100) is a grand tribute to the beloved Dominican military hero's life and times, set in yet another Victorian home that was restored in 2012 for upwards of US$2 million. The museum is actually his daughter's abode, which he gave

# A Dominican Hero: General Gregorio Luperón

A national hero of the Dominican Republic and son of Puerto Plata, General Gregorio Luperón (1839-1897) is loved and respected as the country's greatest leader and a key player in the restoration of the DR after its annexation to Spain in 1861. He is also admired for his incredible story of rising from humble background to the rank of general and later provisional president of the DR for 11 months from 1879 to 1880.

His foray into politics began when he was 18, when he was named assistant commander. And he was just 22 when Spain once again took over control of the territory on March 18, 1861. The annexation was at the request of General Pedro Santana, who feared another attack from Haiti. Luperón joined in rebelling against the Spanish and was eventually arrested. He escaped into exile to Haiti, Mexico, Jamaica, and New York. He returned to the Dominican Republic to continue the fight, and led the famous El Grito de Capotillo rebellion on August 16, 1863, after which he rose to the rank of general.

Forever a symbol of perseverance, patriotism, and national fervor, Luperón succumbed to cancer in his beloved Puerto Plata city at just 58 years of age. He is buried at the National Pantheon in Santo Domingo's Colonial Zone. His life and achievements, as well as relics from his home and his family, are beautifully displayed at the Casa Museo Luperón in Puerto Plata city, a restored Victorian building well worth a stop for more information on this important Dominican figure. A small village outside the city is named after the hero, as is Puerto Plata's international airport.

her when she married and where he eventually died, across the street from his own home. It is said that Luperón used to love looking out onto Mount Isabel through the 2nd-story windows. The turquoise and white museum building has perfectly polished wood floors, and displays period items. Some are original, including swords, trunks, costumes, and a model 19th-century kitchen. Luperón's life and history are on display in Spanish, but a guide is on hand to tour with you and explain it all in English for up to a full half hour if you so choose. Highlights include an outdoor courtyard facing a colorful mural depicting the life of Luperón, an upstairs photo gallery with images of Puerto Plata centuries ago—such as the Central Park area and the House of Culture—and period costumes.

## ★ El Malecón de Puerto Plata

Puerto Plateños will quickly tell you how much prettier their Malecón is compared to Santo Domingo's. Some things are for sure—the beaches are cleaner, the traffic less daunting, and yes, the sea is a prettier, striking baby blue, not to mention swimmable—making

the long stretch a lovely walk in the constant fresh breeze. You can grab some fresh catch at a fraction of a restaurant's price, right by Las Yolas fishermen co-op—the boats usually start rolling in around noon. Or you can stroll down the various beaches, including **Playa Cosita Rica** and **Long Beach,** and grab a cocktail and a meal at a number of bars or *casitas* dotting the Malecón; La Carihuela and Big Lee's Beach Bar are good options. Puerto Plata's Malecón certainly has a livelier and laid-back feel—though residents say it's less active than it used to be—and it's safe to cross the main avenue. In the morning and at sunset, the health-conscious jog or bike up and down the pedestrian lanes. This main drag is also where major events take place, including the Merengue Festival.

## Brugal Rum Distillery

The **Brugal Rum Distillery** (Carretera Playa Dorada, no phone, www.brugal.com.do, 9am-noon and 2pm-5pm daily for tours) is the largest producer of rum in the DR. You can hop on one of several daily tours offered to observe the manufacturing process—the rum is aged

# Dominican Amber

In 1492, when Columbus first landed at La Isabela, he was gifted with a piece of Dominican amber, but the conquistador didn't think much of it and preferred to continue the hunt for gold deposits. It wasn't until the mid-1900s that interest grew in the rich amber deposits of the DR. Today, one of the unique and most popular gifts brought home from the Dominican Republic—alongside cigars, cacao, and coffee—is amber jewelry.

American entomologist George Poinar Jr. was one of the first scientists to discover the value of the Dominican stone, because of the insects and plants that were found trapped within the gems. In 1993, the scientist extracted DNA strands from a prehistoric insect found in an amber stone, making it possible to study DNA dating back to the early days of the dinosaurs. The movie *Jurassic Park* was based on the idea that dinosaurs could be re-created from extraction of dinosaur DNA found in amber. Dominican amber was thus made famous in Hollywood.

raw amber from the land

There are four types of amber found in the DR: yellow, red, green, and blue. The rarest of them all, found nowhere else in the world, is blue amber. Blue amber isn't always blue to the sight after it's been polished; it appears as yellow under natural light yet blue under ultraviolet. It is a gorgeous stone, even worth buying unpolished, when it takes a deep royal hue.

Until recently, you could only visit any of several amber museums (and their adjacent amber jewelry stores), found in every major destination of the country, from Santo Domingo to La Romana to Punta Cana and all the way up north in Puerto Plata, where the stone originates. And while that's always informative, the better alternative, now offered right here in Puerto Plata province, is to **tour the actual amber mines** of the community of La Cumbre (contact UMPC, tel. 809/696-6932, www.popreport.com/turisopp, 9am-5pm Mon.-Fri.)—that is, hike the private land on which the mines are located, including peeking inside a previously mined hole or two that aren't too deep for the average person, where you will be shown how the presence of amber is spotted as the rocks are scraped—usually a vertical line, revealing veins of black shale.

La Cumbre is known as the birthplace of Dominican blue amber, and where the best-quality stones are mined. The tour is part of a community tourism project described in this chapter, and benefits the community visited. It's a gorgeous, green drive up the Ruta Panorámica to reach La Cumbre, passing through villages while taking in views of the Cordillera Septentrional and colorful roadside shacks, stopping at local fruit shops if you like. The road gets quite bumpy and run-down at one point, but the sights and a slow pace will easily distract from the discomfort. The area visited includes peeking down into the active 61-meter-deep (200-foot) mines where workers continue to dig daily with high hopes of unearthing brilliant stones. It's much more exciting than a museum visit, if you ask me. Miners dig without a set wage, but the stones found are worth all the hard work: the income is divided between the miners and the private landowner.

Don't forget to buy blue amber once you get up to the on-site workshop—whether it's a polished bracelet or in rock form at just US$5/gram (price varies according to the density of the amber). It's a unique souvenir that is authentically Dominican, right from the source, and found nowhere else in the world.

in American white oak barrels right in Puerto Plata. The tour lasts about 20 minutes; what's more fun is ending up in the adjacent store where tastings take place and you can purchase reasonably priced bottles.

## La Ruta Panorámica

Up for a scenic drive and cultural excursion you'll long remember? Rent a car, grab a guide for the **Ruta Panorámica** (tel. 809/696-6932, www.rutapanoramica.com), and travel the Santiago-Puerto Plata Panoramic Route (also known as the Carretera Turística Gregorio Luperón)—a 30-kilometer (18.6-mile) drive uphill along a winding road that will take you past local villages and scenes of Dominican rural life. There are stunning views of the Cordillera Septentrional mountain range. The route begins about 12 kilometers (7.4 miles) east of Puerto Plata, going up from the Gran Parada Junction. From Gran Parada all the way to La Cumbre, the highway rises to 671 meters (2,200 feet) above sea level and connects the North Coast with the verdant Cibao Valley. You can tour a cacao farm or amber mines on the way, or just stop for local fruits, cheese, souvenirs, or drinks at a shack. Part of the road has deteriorated and is bumpy, with ongoing repair work, but that means it's less traveled as a result and therefore you can take your time. Roll down the windows, take in the fresh air and views, and immerse yourself in a true slice of Dominican countryside. You can download a map of La Ruta Panorámica directly from the website or drop by Tubagua Plantation Eco Lodge on your way up the highway and pick up a local guide there. Call ahead to schedule.

## Monument to the Mirabal Sisters

This symbolic sight was inaugurated in 2008 and is worth a stop while you're in the area of the Ruta Panorámica linking Puerto Plata and Santiago. Located in the community of La Cumbre, the guarded **Monument to the Mirabal Sisters** pays tribute to the three heroines—Maria Argentina Minerva,

Patria Mercedes, and Antonia Maria Teresa Mirabal—in the location above the hills where their bodies were found dumped in a wrecked car, along with that of their driver, on November 26, 1960, during the Trujillo dictatorship. The sisters were known for their efforts to overthrow Trujillo, creating a resistance movement against his regime. Their murder caused indignation and catalyzed efforts to put an end to Trujillo's tyranny, leading to his assassination six months later in 1961. The Mirabal sisters symbolize the struggle for freedom for all Dominicans. Look closely at nearby homes in the area and you'll notice the symbol of three butterflies painted or pinned beside doorways—the sisters' code name in the secret movement was *Las Mariposas*, or The Butterflies.

## ★ 27 Charcos de Damajagua

One of the top sights in the Dominican Republic with over 115,000 annual visitors— it's no surprise, you won't find anything like it in the Caribbean—the **Charcos de Damajagua** (www.27charcos.com, 8am-3pm daily, US$6.25-10, includes gear and guide) are a series of 27 waterfalls cascading down boulders and emptying into gorgeous pools in hues from emerald to blue. The adventure begins with a moderately steep hike of about 40 minutes, after which you should prepare to get wet: swimming, spelunking, jumping into the water from heights up to 6 meters (20 feet) (optional), and sliding your way to and from the falls—with a guide, of course. The average two-hour excursion is filled with surprises and a lot of fun, giggles, and screams. Declared a Natural Monument and therefore a protected area, since 2007 a percentage of all entrance fees (a dollar per fee; the fee varies according to how many waterfalls you climb) collected at the park goes directly into the community fund and helps support the surrounding villages.

As the tour begins, you'll be fitted with a life jacket and a helmet for safety, and a mandatory guide will accompany you. If you don't have water shoes, they can be rented on-site

for less than a dollar (bring small change). Wear your swimsuit, and if you get cold easily, put on clothes you don't mind getting wet while swimming. There are bathrooms, albeit not always clean.

You'll find options to either leap off the waterfall, at your on risk, or slide down the rocks on natural slides. If you don't feel like doing either, there are staircases to bypass and continue on your merry way (some will call it "the chicken route"—peer pressure is a pest). The tours usually only take you up to the seventh fall—but if you're moderately fit, that is plenty, trust me. To venture beyond the seventh, arrange for a group of at least five to do the 4- to 5-hour adventure, or sign up with **Iguana Mama** (www.iguanamama.com, Tues. and Sat., US$89 plus tax, 10 percent online discount), the only outfitter authorized to go up to the 27th fall.

The throngs of visitors who descend on this North Coast gem come on safari excursions, usually in the mornings through lunchtime. But the site is easily accessed solo by public *guagua* (bus) or by taxi—they will drop you at the main highway entrance, and from there it's a short walk down a driveway to the main ticket office and the attraction. A local, trained guide will be assigned to you once you pay your ticket. Come either as the doors open or after lunch to avoid the crowds, and most definitely avoid the weekends. If you choose to visit with a tour operator, look up their various offerings and decide which works best for you.

TOP EXPERIENCE

## ★ Charcos de Los Militares

In the community of Tubagua is **Charcos de Los Militares,** a series of three small waterfalls and glorious freshwater pools, ranging from jade to pure turquoise. This area is accessible to the village's residents and to guests of Tubagua Plantation Eco Lodge, or independent visitors who can sign up for a hike here with the lodge's local guide. The starting point for this hike is at the lodge. You can opt for either a 1.5-hour or 2.5-hour route one-way across the *campo,* past gorgeous pastureland, once-upon-a-time sugarcane fields, traditional 1970s pastel-colored Dominican wooden homes with zinc roofs, grazing cows and horses, numerous fruit trees, the village corner store, and women cooking outdoors in wood-fired ovens.

The longer route is easily one of the most distinctive and memorable hikes you'll experience here on the North Coast, and even in the Dominican Republic, in its authenticity and in the opportunity it gives to expose you to a Dominican village and its inhabitants. Once you reach the falls and pools—the last 30 minutes are the most intense of the relatively flat hike, including climbing rocks while holding on to a cable—you'll instantly know it was worth the effort. The first pool looks like a cenote, at about 10 feet of depth. Hiking farther up will take you to a cooler, shallower emerald pool and falls. You can stay as long as you like and the lodge's certified guide, Tubagua native Juanin Valbuena, is one of the best you'll find.

## BEACHES
### Playa Dorada

**Playa Dorada** is indeed a beauty. The blond sand, crystal-clear water, and views of Mount Isabel make this beach a worthwhile place to visit. Playa Dorada is Puerto Plata's renowned gated complex just five minutes' drive from the city center. You'll find a handful of resorts ranging from all-inclusive to boutique luxury, such as five-star Casa Colonial, facing the golden Playa Dorada shoreline. Also within the compound are excellent restaurants, all open to the public—Green Jack Tar, La Tarappa, and Lucia—as well as a small shopping mall, a nightclub, a movie theater, and the Robert Trent Jones-designed Playa Dorada Golf Club. Catamaran trips also depart from these shores, and water sports are available including kitesurfing and banana

---

**1:** Pico Isabel de Torres; **2:** Fortaleza de San Felipe; **3:** Charcos de Los Militares boat tubing. Parking is free for patrons at the mall, and the beach is accessible to the public.

## Playa Costambar

A mere 10-minute drive west of Puerto Plata town or an easy motorbike ride away, the beach community of **Costambar** (emphasis is on the second syllable) is its own getaway—with villas, shops, and casual restaurants surrounding one of the most beautiful beaches in the area. If you ask me, the white-sand Playa Costambar is even prettier than Playa Dorada. The Costambar area was once hugely popular in the mid- to late 1990s, until the arrival of the Smith Enron power plant built directly behind the then Bayside Hill Hotel. Besides being a serious eyesore for guests and beach dwellers, the plant brought about significant pollution from fumes and caused respiratory problems for residents. Throw in intermittent electricity in Costambar, and villa owners slowly began to desert the area. As a result, Costambar had an abandoned feel for a long while.

In 2012, the plant finally shut down. Community residents are advocating for its complete removal, but in the meantime, Costambar not only has 24-hour power, but this beach escape is on the rise again, with new expat residents moving into renovated or new villas and businesses sprucing up their wares. CESTUR (the tourism police) has an outpost here, and Los Mangos's nine-hole course and full wellness and spa center are bringing more traffic to the beach. The beach is as pretty as ever, and it's a great spot to spend the day, whether solo or with the family. You can reach Playa Costambar by public transportation (the shared taxi passes down Gregorio de Lora Avenue, US$0.55) or by taxi (US$6.50 one way).

## Playa Cambiaso

Not up for crowds? You'll find your bliss at **Playa Cambiaso,** a well-kept secret among locals and long-time residents. This absolute stunner of a white-sand stretch is tricky to reach—you'll need an off-road vehicle and a local driver (contact Antonio, tel. 809/252-3508). An hour's drive will lead you to a long, romantic beach, where you can swim (remain close to shore and beware of the waves), relax, and not be bothered by anyone but donkeys. There are a handful of seafood restaurants and bars on-site, and it gets livelier on Sundays. Don't forget your camera and try not to tell all your friends.

Playa Costambar

## Other Beaches

The North Coast of the Dominican Republic, both west and east of Puerto Plata and along the Malecón, is blessed with a string of beaches, each with its own character and beat. From surfing havens to frenzied party stretches to deserted white sands, it's easy to get in the car or local *guagua* or taxi and head out to spend your days exploring these glorious *playas*.

Beginning with the Malecón, there are several stretches worth a swim. **Playa Camacho,** a short walk east of La Sirena, is popular with the locals for its wide space, white sands, and fun waves. You'll spot locals of all ages, lovers and families, picnicking and bathing close to sunset or napping in the shade of the trees. There are chairs for rent, but you can just lay your towel and keep it simple. Another favorite, smack in the middle of the Malecón, is **Playa Cosita Rica,** one of best for swimming, with fine sands, slightly calmer waters, a couple of decent restaurants, and a view facing the Neptune Rock out at sea, past which kitesurfers zoom from neighboring **Kite Beach.** There's a volleyball net and families flock here in late afternoons. **Long Beach** is at the very eastern end of the Malecón and the most popular stretch with local crowds.

Sandwiched between Playa Dorada and the Iberostar Costa Dorada and lined with multicolored umbrellas and beach chairs, **Playa Chaparral**—better known to locals and taxis as El Pueblito—is a wide white-sand stretch facing the local Orange Market with a series of souvenir and beach accessories shacks and a kitesurfing school. You'll also find a local bar and restaurant, and the fancier Le Petit François, good for romantic dining in the evening. If you continue past the restaurant—which you should for the scenery—you'll spot apartments, more shops, and eventually the river running into the sea from below the *punto verde del pueblito,* a rusty but scenic green bridge. Playa Chaparral gets lively here on Sundays when locals and tourists mingle. Note that there's also a roadside public entrance for Playa Chaparral off the highway, just before you reach the Playa Dorada entrance gates.

Next up is the small **Playa Cofresí** within the Cofresí compound by the Lifestyle Resort and Ocean World. Named after pirate Robert Cofresí, it isn't the most attractive stretch on the North Coast (the sand is a dark blond color). But the public, resort-free side is nice for a quieter swim and sits across from the seafront Los Charros Mexican restaurant, alone worth a hop to this area. The nearby Ocean World Terrace is also decent for drinks or the occasional live Dominican concert.

## SPORTS AND RECREATION
### Diving and Snorkeling

**SeaPro Divers** (tel. 809/586-1239, http://caribbeanoceanadventures.com/diving.htm, dive.pro@codetel.net.do, US$90 two-tank dive) out of Sosúa is popular with beginner divers. They will take you out into the shallow Sosúa Bay and along relatively shallow wall dives such as the Point, at 12 meters (40 feet). Puerto Plata and its neighboring areas aren't exactly the best spot in the Caribbean for diving or snorkeling, so keep your expectations in check. Sadly, much of the reef you'll see at **The Point** is brown, having died due to the sheer volume of tourists trampling on live coral. Still, you'll spot colorful Caribbean critters—including yellowtail snapper, trumpetfish, blue-striped grunts, four-eyed butterfly fish, spotted drums, and the invasive lionfish, against a beautiful, deep blue ocean.

Snorkeling stops are right off Sosúa's beaches—including in front of the new Gansevoort Playa Imbert—but you'll see only a few fish, less than if you were to dive. However, the water is spectacular for swimming: it is incredibly clean and is the turquoise color that brings everyone to the Caribbean. Head out on a beautiful 16.5-meter (54-foot) catamaran with **Freestyle Catamaran Sailing Tours** (tel. 809/586-1239, http://caribbeanoceanadventures.com/catamaran.htm, US$79), part owned by a longtime Puerto Plateño who first came here to surf decades

# ★ Social Impact Tourism in Puerto Plata

The **Community Tourism Network of Puerto Plata** (Red de Turismo Comunitario de Puerto Plata, https://puertoplata.do) was born in 2009 with the aim of creating jobs and opportunities for the surrounding rural communities of Puerto Plata, all while redefining the region's tourism offerings.

Today, the Community Tourism Network has not only built an exciting new tourism model combining sustainability and community involvement, but has also identified experiences for travelers that aren't offered anywhere else, through their **Social Impact Tours.** All of the proceeds from the tours and crafts are reinvested directly into communities to continue their growth and development.

At this time, only groups of 10 are easily accommodated, at a cost of about US$7-8 per person. Contact them through the website (https://puertoplata.do/index.php/contact) to book and connect with like-minded travelers looking to participate. Some of the tours can be combined when in the same or neighboring area. Social Impact Tours also welcomes those who are interested in volunteering in these communities during their stay.

- **Baseball at Bartolo Colón's Stadium in Altamira** (9am-5pm daily): Visit the birthplace of baseball great Bartolo Colón, who became the leader in wins by a Latin American pitcher in 2018. Tour the gorgeous stadium he built for the children in his community. There's an on-site gallery that has information about the cultural importance of baseball in the DR, and you can even see some of Colon's first uniforms and a handful of his luxury cars. Try your hand with the community boys training in the hopes of becoming the next Bartolo. And if you're lucky, the baseball great will be visiting, as he does in the off-season.

- **The Cacao Trail in Guananico** (9am-3pm Wed.-Sun.): The drive to reach **Hacienda Cufa** chocolate plantation is itself worth the 1.5-hour journey. You'll learn all about the production of organic cacao, its importance to the DR's economy, and you'll even get to plant your own pod, all before moving on to the fun part: sampling! Run by multiple generations of the Mercado family, the trip includes a Dominican lunch, and if there's time, ask for a chocolate mud treatment in the outdoor jungle spa.

- **Merengue Workshop in Guananico** (10am-4pm Tues., Thurs., Sat.): Spend a day immersed in all things merengue in the village known as the **Rincón Caliente,** or the "hot corner"—the birthplace of generations of traditional merengue (*merengue típico*) musicians from the award-winning Peña family. It's a super-fun, high-energy day where you'll not only learn about the three instruments that make up the genre, but you'll also get to give them a

ago and made the DR his home. The boat leaves out of Playa Dorada and heads toward Sosúa for a two-snorkel day trip from 8:30am to 2:30pm.

## Catamaran Sailing

The two popular choices for sailing down the Puerto Plata and Sosúa coasts are **Freestyle Catamaran Sailing Tours** (tel. 809/586-1239, http://caribbeanoceanadventures.com/catamaran.htm, US$79), taking you to Sosúa on a 54-foot cat with a couple of swim and snorkel stops, or **Tip Top Catamaran Tours**

(tel. 809/710-0503, www.catamarandomrep.com, US$79), offering a regular sailing trip or a VIP option complete with masseuse on board. Both make similar snorkel stops, and whichever you choose, you'll likely cross paths along the way.

## Kiteboarding and Surfing

Adjacent to Playa Dorada's beachfront offerings—technically sandwiched between Playa Dorada and Costa Dorada—is **Kite Legend School** (Playa Chaparral, Orange Market, a few steps before Blue Jack Tar, try (musician Facundo Peña will show you how to play the accordion). You'll tour the workshop room where drums are made and repaired by renowed drummer Isabel Trejo Peña, who crafts instruments on demand for musicians around the country. Finally, you'll take to the dance floor across the street for lessons. The half-day workshop takes place in a couple of the families' homes, which were transformed just for this experience.

- **History in Luperón** (8am-4pm Mon.-Sun.): Christopher Columbus built his very first home in La Isabela in 1493, and you can tour the house's ruins at Parque Nacional Histórico y Arqueológico de La Isabela, along with the ruins of the first church and replicas of his men's homes. There's a museum on-site, and you'll hike to the nearby rebuilt church, Templo de las Américas. The cliff-top views in this seafront community are stunning.

- **The Manatee Trail in Villa Isabela** (9am-5pm daily): This nature excursion will show you just how diverse the DR's landscape, flora, and fauna can be. The Estero Hondo Reserve is a sanctuary for manatees and offers breathtaking scenery from deserted white-sand beaches to coastal lagoons. You'll hike two trails at the sanctuary, accompanied by a guide, but the highlight is getting on a paddleboard and gliding across the vast, tranquil waters as you explore four species of mangroves and many different species of birds—including the Hispaniolan woodpecker, green herons, cattle egrets, and the *cigua palmera*. You'll even swim in a "natural pool" beside the mangroves while taking a break from paddling. At the end of the tour, there's a lookout tower, from which you can watch the manatees rising to the surface. If time permits, ask to squeeze in a lunch stop at nearby Playa La Ensenada.

- **The Amber Route in Yásica Arriba** (8am-5pm Mon.-Sun.): Forget the museums—you can now head to the only place in the world where amber is actually mined, in La Cumbre, and the only place where blue amber is found. You'll hike the family-owned land where the mines are located, set against the backdrop of the Cordillera Septentrional. You'll meet workers who are in the midst of mining, and they might even show you the stones they've discovered that day. You will also enter previously mined terrain and learn how amber deposits are spotted. Lastly, you'll get the unique opportunity to buy the gems on-site, polished or raw by weight, at a fraction of the price you'd find in stores. Near the mines is the Monument to the Mirabal Sisters, also worth a stop if possible.

- **The Coffee Trail in Pedro Garcia** (8am-5pm daily): Learn about reforestation and the harvesting of organic coffee in Pedro Garcia. You'll even get to make your own—from the bean to the cup.

tel. 809/603-5860, www.kitelegendschool. com, 10am-6pm daily, US$60/hour), where IKO instructor Bibby Burgos teaches beginners out of his small kitesurfing shack. Two assistants and four freelance instructors are on standby when the shop gets busy. You can also rent or purchase quality gear here if you're already a pro. In town, on the Malecón, **Pauhana Surf School** (tel. 809/304-4835, www.pauhanasurfcamp.com/surf-puerto-plata, US$45 for two hours) offers lessons for those who can't make it to Cabarete, as well as board rentals.

## Golfing

Designed by Robert Trent Jones Sr., the **Playa Dorada Golf Club** (tel. 809/320-4262, www. playadoradagolf.com, US$190 3 rounds, US$60/hr lesson) opened in 1976 within the Playa Dorada complex, a stone's throw from the beach, restaurants, and hotels. The course is fairly flat, and some holes are near the ocean and have pleasant views. It makes for a good morning or afternoon golf break.

**Los Mangos Golf & Country Club** (Playa Costambar, Calle Kennedy 2, tel. 809/970-3110, ext. 104, or 829/679-3184, US$25 greens fee) is an average nine-hole course set within Los Mangos residential complex, part of the Playa Costambar beach community. Redesigned by Pete Dye in 2010, it's a stone's throw from the glorious white sands of Costambar and all of its beachside community conveniences. A clubhouse with a restaurant, a pool, a gym, and a full-service salon and spa are all on-site. It's not as fabulous a course as Playa Dorada, but if you're staying on Costambar's beach, it's close.

## Horseback Riding

One of the longest-running safari tour companies, **Mega Trucks** (Plaza Turisol, tel. 809/586-3611, www.topaciotours.com, US$89) offers a half day of horseback riding on its ranch a five-minute ride from the Damajagua Falls. The ride takes you across the property's acres of forest, past river and jungle for about 40 minutes. If you're lucky, you'll get to cool off in the river at the end. Ask about their secret little oasis where you can sip on coconuts and bathe in a freshwater pool.

**Rancho Lorilar** (tel. 809/320-0498 or cell tel. 809/885-9642, lorilar@gmail.com, 9am-4pm Mon.-Sat.) gets rave reviews for its beginner to advanced horseback riding options, as well as its beautiful location near Maimón. It is less than an hour's ride from downtown Puerto Plata.

## Zip-Lining

**Mega Trucks** (Plaza Turisol 60, tel. 809/586-3611, www.megaadventuresdr.com, US$89) has an incredible, nearly two-mile-long course on its private ranch near the Damajagua Falls and the small town of Imbert. It takes you across parts of its hundreds of acres of verdant hills and forests, even above a river, on a double-cabled zipline. Besides the course, there's a 27-horse stable, a garden trail with Dominican fruit trees and plants, and an open-air restaurant area with stunning mountain views. Most zipline adventures are packaged into the Zip 'n' Ride half-day excursion, combining horseback riding for beginners or pros. Before you leave the ranch, ask for a dip

at the "secret garden," where you'll find a gorgeous turquoise-colored natural pool.

Up in Yásica, about 30 minutes outside of Puerto Plata along the scenic Ruta Panorámica, **Yásica Adventures** (Carretera Turística Gregorio Luperón, tel. 809/320-0000, www.yasicaadventures.com, 9am-4pm Mon.-Sat., US$84, discounts online) offers a zipline that takes you across 10 platforms, at a height ranging from 100 and 300 meters (328-984 feet) and speeds of up to 48 kph (30 mph). Speeding across this stunningly verdant, hilly part of the North Coast is a memory you'll hold long after you leave. Safety is taken seriously, and there are practice runs before you take off.

## ATV Terra Cross

A fun way to get deeper into the countryside of the northern province is by riding your own ATV on a fun, half-day Terra Cross excursion with **Outback Adventures** (Plaza Turisol, tel. 809/320-2525, www.outbackadventuresdr.com, US$89). You'll get to ride a four-wheel ATV buggy from Puerto Plata—the headquarters are close to Playa Dorada—into the nearby village of Muñoz, dominating all sorts of terrain, from rocky paths to dusty roads, past horses, cows, pastureland, and spectacular countryside scenery. Stops are made at a traditional Dominican home, where you'll refresh with coconuts, and the Muñoz River for a swim. Come here on a Sunday to witness an authentic Dominican "Sunday fun day" at the river, with plenty of frolicking and swimming, and outdoor cooking in big pots. Prepare your camera for the view of Puerto Plata's gorgeous coastline from the hills of Muñoz.

## Ocean World Park

It's hard to miss the gigantic sign off the highway, but **Ocean World** (809/291-1000, 9am-6pm daily, US$69 adults, US$54 children 4-12) is your typical water park where dolphins and sea lions are on display for the

**1:** horseback riding with Mega Trucks; **2:** Explore the hills of Muñoz in an ATV with Outback Adventures.

entertainment of families and their kids. I neither recommend nor support such attractions where animals are sequestered. A better time is spent on the Ocean World Terrace restaurant and bar for the adults, where you can enjoy the weekly Bravissimo dance show or occasional live merengue or *bachata* concert.

## Birding

Birders will find their bliss heading out of Puerto Plata and venturing either west or far east of the North Coast. The most beautiful birding areas include the **Estero Hondo Marine Mammal Sanctuary** (tel. 829/492-3362, 9am-5pm daily, US$5.55 or RD$250), where you can paddleboard or kayak on the lagoon and explore the birdlife amid the mangroves. You'll find up to 20 species, including the *cigua palmera*, Caspian tern, cattle egret, green heron, white ibis, red-tailed hawk, brown pelican, and Hispaniolan woodpecker. You can also hike the reserve via a couple of trails for more sightings, and you can spot manatees as well.

Río San Juan is a veritable bird sanctuary. The small fishing village is surrounded with birdlife, but you can find them in highest concentration while cruising down the **Laguna Gri Gri**—the highlight in Río San Juan—where cattle egrets and vultures fill the mangroves and trees surrounding the lagoon. There's also a **bird sanctuary** on the other side of the Gri Gri Lagoon, heading east of Hotel Bahia Blanca and facing Playa de los Guardias. You can see plenty of egrets, including babies barely walking, as well as vultures roaming. This is the part of the lagoon that you miss when doing a boat tour; it's even better observed on foot. The collective sound of the birds echoing through the sanctuary, even as you walk past, is incredible. They tend to come out of the mangroves and trees a bit more in the early mornings or at sunset.

## Cacao Tour

**Chocal** (Chocolate de la Cuenca de Altamira, tel. 829/308-5852, chocolatedealtamira@ hotmail.com) is a small chocolate factory owned and operated by a women's cooperative, in the town of Altamira. You can arrange for a half-day visit, where you'll hike the plantation and join the women in making chocolate from bean to bar (go home with yours, or shop on-site). Another option is **Hacienda Cufa** (tel. 809/756-4806, by appointment), a beautiful family-owned cacao plantation located in the small town of Guananico, west of Puerto Plata, where you'll get a full tour of cacao production, from tree to tastings; a post-tour Dominican lunch is offered. Ask about their rooms if you feel like staying longer.

## Spa

The luxurious, 929-square-meter (10,000-square-foot) space at **Baguá Spa** (Casa Colonial, Playa Dorada, tel. 809/320-3232, www.casacolonialhotel.com/spa, from US$65) is your best bet for an all-around pampering experience. There are 10 treatment rooms indoors with ocean views, including couples rooms. Outdoor massage gazebos overlook the sea and beach, surrounded by ponds and soothing fountains. Ask about the indigenous spa therapies using amber gems, honey, and ocean water.

**Los Mangos Golf & Country Club** (Costambar, Calle Kennedy 2, tel. 809/970-3110 or 829/679-5049, US$35 60-min. massage) has a small spa complete with a full-service salon. Options include hyperbaric oxygen therapy, steam and sauna rooms, a gym, and free use of the swimming pool.

# ENTERTAINMENT AND EVENTS
## Nightlife

In Puerto Plata, as in much of the DR, nightlife kicks off in earnest starting on Thursday, from local bars to dance clubs to *rancho típicos* along the highway where merengue blasts all night long. The most popular spot in town for late-night hangouts for the young (or old) and restless is the Malecón, lined with various local or expat bars or *casetas* (they also serve bar food). The younger and older generations often park their cars or their chairs on the far

# At the *Bomba* or the Car Wash

In any city or town you end up in, it doesn't get more local in the Dominican Republic than starting the night by heading to the *bomba,* or gas station, for drinks and music. There's a culture of throwing back beers and rum and sometimes even being served like at a drive-through while fueling up or just parked at the gas station. In Puerto Plata, the place to begin a night of weekend partying is **La Isla Gas Station** (Av. Luis Ginebra, off La Sirena). You'll find plastic chairs and tables on ground level—directly across from the pumps—or upstairs in the open-air lounge where you can comfortably order your bottles and mixers and sit back and watch music videos playing (loudly, of course) on a big screen above the station. The entire area surrounding the gas station is abuzz with motorbikes, partygoers, and all-around merriment. If you're in a town and you're not sure where the party is, start with the central gas station. Another popular hangout is at the **car wash.** You'll often see them as a thatch-roofed building with a giant attached parking lot. The place goes from car wash and bar—drink while you wait!—to a full-on open-air dance spot at night, often with live merengue and *bachata* bands on the weekends. In Puerto Plata, **Automatic Carwash** (Av. Manolo Tavares Justo Km 1, tel. 809/261-0152, 6pm-midnight Thurs.-Sun.) is a good example. Travel in a group, and take a taxi home.

eastern end by Long Beach and blast out music from their mega speakers while the crowd relaxes seaside or dances on the boulevard.

Facing the Malecón, **Big Lee's Beach Bar** (tel. 829/868-0017, www.bigleesbeachbar.com, 9am-midnight daily) is popular among expats and tourists for its weekly karaoke Thursday and live music on Friday. A short walk over is **Tropical Bar,** where you can sit back and relax while chugging beers from all over the world. If you're up for a local beat, head to **La Casona.** These are good spots to try before you move on to more serious jamming. Also on the Malecón is **La Carihuela,** with an eclectic crowd and a lovely beachfront terrace where a DJ occasionally spins at night. The drinks here are stiff! A few steps away on the boulevard, streetside, is **Zona Acapella Club,** an open-air Dominican joint blasting out salsa and merengue; it's especially crowded on Sunday nights when there is a live merengue band. Farther west on the Malecón, you'll find a yellow open-air terrace on the corner of Calle Separación, at **Chicharrón Light** (next to D'Angel Restaurant). It's popular, and a live *merengue típico* band turns the place out on Sunday nights.

Over in town, the casual but artsy place to be for cocktails is **Casa 40** (Calle Duarte no. 40, corner of Calle Imbert, tel. 809/434-0072,

10am-11pm Thurs.-Mon.), where every drink—try the mojitos—and bite is made with love and some French-Dominican influence. Check their social media pages for evening specials, including live soloists. **Lust AfterWork** (Av. Manolo Tavarez Justo 104, tel. 809/261-8078, lustafterwork@gmail.com, 6pm-2am Wed.-Sun.) is a staple in the city, offering an outdoor lounge with live musicians and DJ dance nights on the weekends.

At **La Casona** (Calle 27 de Febrero, corner of 12 de Julio, 8pm-midnight Thurs.-Sun.), a small bar and club space, there are enough glass walls, neon lights, and seating areas to make it seem a notch trendier. Merengue, salsa, reggaeton, and *bachata* dominate here. Couples love to twirl away in the tight space. Because of its early close, most head over to the next club at midnight.

Once the local bars and gas station shut down at midnight, the crowd shifts to nearby **La Esquina de Chalo** (Calle 16 de Agosto, corner of Calle Sanchez, tel. 809/586-1414, 10pm-3am Thurs.-Sun.) in an area known for its bars and not-so-shiny street scene. But the fancy club is as popular as ever and gets supercrowded on the weekends, including Sunday nights. There's no dance floor per se, but rather small tables where most sit and sway or get up and dance against passing crowds. It's not the most comfortable setup, but it's a good place to party if you're in the mood. Ladies, beware—there's a meat market vibe here.

A better pick and less pretentious, always-packed spot is the recently renovated **El Furgón** (Av. Luis Ginebra, no phone, Thurs.-Sun. 10pm-2am, no cover), a cozy, single-floor nightclub with spinning disco lights and a DJ playing merengue, salsa, and *bachata* tunes all night while patrons gather around bottle-filled tables or on the small, square dance floor. If you want to see a typical Dominican club, this is a good bet.

**Ocean World Terrace** (Ocean World, Cofresí, 8am-midnight daily, later close Fri.-Sat.) facing the sea is a favorite of locals, who gather here after work during the week for drinks, karaoke, and dancing. Saturdays are for the Bravíssimo Show, a Vegas-style costumed dance extravaganza with all-inclusive drinks. An all-night party follows. They also host live Dominican concerts; check the online schedule for the latest.

### Festivals and Cultural Events

Puerto Plata puts on its own **Carnival** (http://www.discoverpuertoplata.com/es/que-hacer) in February, when parades and fanfare take place every Sunday afternoon along the Malecón and Parque Independencia. It's a colorful time to be in the city and a great way to experience the importance of carnival culture in the DR. Costumes are vibrant and showcase African and native Taíno influences. Various characters are represented, such the Diablo Cojuelo or the limping devil, inherited from Spanish culture. Each carnival year, a new King Momo is crowned, symbolizing the person who has helped preserve tradition, along with a carnival queen. A final grand parade takes place on the fourth and last Sunday of the month (sometimes the first week of March).

The **Annual Cultural Festival** takes place the third week of June and celebrates both Dominican and Puerto Plateño culture with traditional folk music, merengue, African

dances, and of course, plenty of local arts and crafts, food, and all-around merriment.

The first edition of the **Dominican Rum Festival** launched in July 2018 and was a fun two-day event held on the Puerto Plata Amphitheater grounds, showcasing the DR's major rum houses with free tastings, cash bars with craft rum cocktails, a food truck area, and several presentations. Each day wraps up with live performances from local and international stars.

Playa Dorada's **Caribbean Cigar Night** (www.cigarnightpop.com, US$100 pp) is in March with all the major tobacco-producing brands in attendance. The evening is for wining, dancing, and dining at one of the resorts. It's a night to dress up and rub elbows with Puerto Plata's elite while celebrating all things cigar.

Held the third week of October, the annual **Merengue and Caribbean Rhythms Festival** brings all of Puerto Plata down to the Malecón for four days of merengue dancing to various live bands.

## SHOPPING

**Playa Dorada Plaza** (Av. Manolo Tavarez Justo, tel. 809/320-6645, www.playadorada.com.do, 8am-10pm daily) has a variety of stores and kiosks spread across two levels, although only about two or three are worth a visit. But if you're pressed for time and don't have other options, you'll find all the Dominican souvenirs you're looking for, including cigars, rum, coffee, and cacao, as well as your usual beach apparel. There's a BanReservas ATM on-site. Haitian art and random clothing stores are on the 2nd floor.

**La Canoa** (Calle Beller 18, tel. 809/586-3604, 9am-6pm Mon.-Sat., 9am-1pm Sun.) is one of the city's oldest jewelry stores and has larimar and amber for sale. Prices are on par with other boutiques in town. For beachside souvenir shopping, look no further than the local vendor shacks of **Orange Market** in El Pueblito-Playa Chaparral area, immediately adjacent to Playa Dorada. They sell sarongs, totes, and all the usual Dominican items, ranging from rum to cigars. Your purchases will go a lot further for the local families running their own businesses.

Get fresh fruits and vegetables from this fertile region at the lively **Mercado Viejo** (Calle Ureña and Separación, 8am-6pm), which spills out onto the streets and is a real cultural experience. Over at the adjacent concrete and less appealing **Mercado Nuevo** are souvenirs and handmade crafts.

For the food or wine items you can't find at the local **Supermercado Jose Luis** (Av. Manolo Tavarez Justo 20, tel. 809/586-3347, 8am-9pm Mon.-Sat., 8am-1pm Sun.) grocery store, there's a new branch of **Jumbo** (Av. Manolo Tavarez Justo, tel. 809/261-1118, wwww.jumbo.com.do, 8am-10pm daily, except Sun. 9pm close) in town, and as its name implies, it's a Walmart-type store that's even larger than **Multicentro La Sirena** (Av. del Malecón, tel. 809/586-6066, 8am-10pm Mon.-Sat., 8am-8pm Sun.). Both stores offer full supermarket options, as well as beauty products, electronics, discount apparel, and any other items you might have forgotten along your travels. Inside these stores are other mini outlets, including dry cleaning and laundry, artisan ice cream, Domino's pizza, a food court with upstairs seating, cell phone companies, and outdoor/indoor Banco Popular and Scotiabank ATMs.

The fishing cooperative **Las Yolas** (Malecón, across from Tam Tam Café, US$1.25-4.45) sells fresh fish daily; catches are brought in starting around lunchtime and throughout the afternoon. Prices are listed right by the beachfront fish cleaning station. A fun option is to eat at one of the famous fish shacks in Maimón, serving up fresh catch roadside. Among them, **Los Primos** (tel. 809/272-8168) is a solid pick.

Get a unique Puerto Plata experience with an hour at **La Pulga** (across from the market, 8am-7pm Tues. and Thurs.), the biggest flea market in the city and what looks like the entire Caribbean! Endless rows of both new and used clothing, shoes, fashion jewelry, and household items are busy with locals of all walks of life searching for that great bargain.

# FOOD
## Cafés

Start your day with the sunrise, ocean views, and a hearty breakfast on the beach at **Margo's Beach Bar** (Malecón Caseta 9, margotdr@yahoo.de, 8am-10pm daily, US$3-5). Service is friendly and portions generous. It's as great a spot for families as for couples. For a spot near the central park, head to **Herdman's Chocolate Bakery & Café** (tel. 809/261-9478, 8:30am-11:30pm Mon.-Sat., 2pm-10:30pm Sun.), a coffee and chocolate shop located on the 2nd floor of the turquoise-painted Paseo Del Parque building, with a panoramic view over Parque Independencia. Sit on the outdoor terrace, or indoors with air-conditioning, and enjoy your hot drink with a pastry. Pizzas and burgers are also available.

Facing the Parque Independencia, you can't miss the jolly pastel yellow exterior and orange furnishings at **Heladería Mariposa** (Calle Beller 38, tel. 809/970-1785, www.heladosmariposa.com, 8am-10pm Mon.-Fri., 8am-11pm Sat.-Sun., US$3-10), a solid option for a quick cup of java any time of day or a breakfast sandwich. It's also popular for its homemade ice cream in various local fruit flavors, pastries, cakes, and brownies. You'll want to linger at the nice location facing the Victorian square—which makes up for the service being slow.

One street away, **Kaffe** (Calle Profesor Juan Bosch 42, tel. 809/261-3440, comunicaciones@kaffeweb.com, 8:30am-11pm Tues.-Sun.) was one of the first fancier spot to have coffee and desserts in town. It's set in a beautifully renovated Victorian mansion filled with funky decor. The back veranda is the highlight, along with the breezy garden terrace it faces, shaded by mango trees. Colorful tables, mosaic floors, hanging potted plants, and plenty of interesting art pieces keep your attention when it's not drifting away with the soothing sounds of Latin ballads. The coffee is either Lavazza gourmet Italian or regular Nescafé.

You'd come here for the setting more than anything else.

A bit off the beaten tourist track, yet worth a trip for coffee or dessert lovers, is cozy **Café Atlántico** (Av. Luis Ginebra 56, tel. 809/320-8629, info@cafedelatlantico.com, 9am-9pm daily, US$3-6), serving delicious combinations of tall iced or hot java or chocolate drinks, complete with whipped cream. The drink creations are pure works of art, and the churros are to die for. They occasionally host DJs and live music.

## Dominican and Latin

The beautiful ★ **Hyode Bistro** (Calle Jose Carmen del Ariza, tel. 809/739-9790, noon-midnight daily, US$4-10) is one of the most popular newcomers to the city's food scene. Located just steps from the central square, its promise is to bring you high-quality homemade food, served either indoors or outside on a gorgeous outdoor Victorian veranda. Dishes burst in Dominican and Latin flavors from the Dominican chef-owner, trained in New York. Try the shrimp paellas, the seafood ceviches, or a filet of steak covered in passion fruit sauce. Vegans fear not—you can make requests and the chef is likely to accommodate you. There are live music performances from Thursday through the weekend.

A good lunch pick near the Parque Independencia is longtime favorite **Skina** (Calle Separación, corner of 12 de Julio, tel. 809/979-1950, charodeventura@gmail.com, US$3-10), set outdoors on a beautiful terrace with a leafy garden and shaded with trees. Latin sounds fill the air, with videos displayed on a giant screen—the owner himself is a musician—but at soft volume. Specialties are Dominican and Latin; the *mofongo* and fajitas are excellent. And there are options such as burgers and grilled chicken sandwiches. Portions are generous and the staff friendly. It's a romantic, casual spot tucked away from foot traffic yet smack in the city center, popular with Puerto Plata's professionals. They occasionally have live music. A short walk towards the sea is the open-air **Aguaceros Bar**

**& Grill** (Malecón, tel. 809/586-2796, US$6-11) a longtime landmark on Puerto Plata's Malecón, serving up affordable, convenient options for the starved such as burritos, nachos, and fajitas.

**La Leña** (across from Scotiabank, Calle 27 de Febrero 12, tel. 809/970-1013, 8:30am-11pm daily, US$2-4) is a Dominican cafeteria offering a buffet or boxed lunch to go, but there's also plenty of open-air seating for those who have time to chow down on a burger, chicken sandwich, pizza, pasta, and more. There's wireless Internet on the premises, and the coffee is decent. A much better bet is ★ **Café Tropical** (next to Supermercado Jose Luis, Calle 27 de Febrero, corner of Beller, tel. 809/586-6667, cafetropical@claro.com.do, 8am-9pm Mon.-Sat., 8am-3pm Sun., US$5-6). The setting and Dominican lunch buffet here are attractive, and there are other buffet picks like lasagna or fried chicken. The à la carte menu is no less appetizing, with delicious sandwiches and desserts. It's conveniently close to the Metro Tours bus headquarters.

The picaderas, or Dominican snacks, are so good and cheap at **Amparo Delicatessen** (Calle Antera Mota 15, corner of José del Carmen Ariza, tel. 809/660-3085, from US$1.10) that the small window shack used to get jammed with waiting customers late into the night. The spot recently expanded into a lovely outdoor terrace with seating and an indoor counter space in a restored Victorian building, ideally located just one street behind Puerto Plata's central square. Locals flock here for empanadas, quipes, and other starchy treats, which they enjoy on the terrace or to go. They also have batidas and sodas to wash it all down. It's a classic Dominican joint, and the service is pleasant.

Mexican cuisine fans will love ★ **Chile y Limón** (Av. Luis Ginebra, tel. 829/864-9742, Tues.-Sun. 5pm-midnight, US$3-10) for happy hour bites or dinner. Located on the first floor of the new Galerias del Atlantico plaza downtown, it serves up all the Mexican favorites, from quesadillas to tostadas, in a delightfully artsy interior featuring colorful murals.

Tuesdays are 3-for-2 tacos, washed down with buckets of Dos Equis or 2-for-1 margaritas.

Another popular and casual evening spot is the Mexican and Dominican fusion **Tostacos** (Calle Presidente Vásquez 3, tel. 809/261-3330, 4pm-11pm Tues.-Sun., US$5-10), popular for tacos, burgers, mofongo, and margaritas.

Fast, cheap, and tasty describes the **Pizzata food truck** (Malecón roadside, tel. 809/586-7272, US$1-2.45), dishing out empanadas and quipes (they also deliver). This roadside stop—with plastic chairs and table seating—is ideal for filling hungry beachgoers showing up here barefoot or on scooters from across the Malecón. If you're close to the waterfront and want a satisfying, fried snack to go at über-cheap prices, this is it.

Snack on some delicious, melt-in-your-mouth Dominican *quipes*—a twist on the Lebanese kibbeh—sold out of a family home at ★ **Quipes Bojo** (Calle Margarita Mears, 4pm-7pm Mon.-Sat., US$0.66-0.78 each). You'll see the sign as you arrive—just walk in and order the amount you'd like and whether you want meat-stuffed or chicken-stuffed. Take your snacks to the Malecón or the fort as the sun goes down. This place is an institution in Puerto Plata.

## International

Run by a Dominican-French pair, **Casa 40** (Calle Duarte #40, corner of Calle Imbert, tel. 809/434-0072, 10am-11pm Thurs.-Mon., US$3-10) is a delightful celebration of art and creativity, from the menu to the colorful terrace furnished with recycled items. The on-site gift shop features local artisan-made purses, jewelry, art, handpainted hats, and a variety of souvenirs well worth the purchase. Out in the courtyard, you can indulge in a fruit-flavored mojito and delicious pastas, burgers, and other daily inventions. Check their social media pages for a schedule of live music on the weekends.

The beautiful colonial décor of **El Bergantín** (Calle Beller, across Parque Independencia, tel. 809/261-5860, www.elbergantin.com.do, 9am-11pm daily, US$5-15), both exterior and interior, sadly doesn't match the food—the beautiful restored Victorian building, once a ladies' social club, boasts the perfect view of the central park, with a wraparound veranda and ample interior seating. The pricey menu ranges from pastas to ceviche to steaks, but the full meal I had, which included fish, was not flavorful in the least, which is a darn shame. Come here for drinks and the setting, but keep it moving over to better options nearby, such as Hyode Bistro and Casa 40.

**Tam Tam Café**'s (Av. Gregorio Luperón 4, tel. 809/970-0903, tamtamcafé2012@gmail.com, 8am-1pm daily, US$4-15) sidewalk terrace, across the Malecón's glorious breeze, is a good place to take a breather, with average meals ranging from salads to steaks to seafood to pasta. There might be a few vendors passing by, but service is friendly the vibe is good. There's indoor seating if you prefer.

You can relax on the open-air terrace at the casual **Kilómetro Zero** (Av. Luis Ginebra 6, tel. 809/244-4346, 10am-midnight Thurs.-Tues., US$5-15) with any dish from its delicious menu, which includes steaks, ribs, pastas, and sandwiches.

**Las Palmas** (Av. Luis Ginebra 47, tel. 809/586-7065, noon-11pm daily, US$8-25) has a delightful setting for a nice dinner out or special occasion. Set in a residential home turned restaurant, the seating is indoors as well as on a veranda that continues all the way to the back of the property to a second outdoor terrace. The pizzas are baked in a wood-fired oven and are delicious, as are the pastas—with pick-your-pasta-and-sauce options—and seafood plates. Make reservations on weekends, as it fills up quickly.

**Il Giardino**'s (Av. 27 de Febrero 55, tel. 809/320-7469, 11am-10pm daily, US$4-30) small open-air terrace is framed by plants and enough foliage to distract from the fact that you're steps away from the constant traffic of the main road. Dishes here are also good, from Italian staples like lasagna to tasty wood-fired oven pizza. If you're staying at nearby Villa Carolina, it's a worthwhile hop, and they also deliver. Ask about the list of daily lunch specials, available from 11:30am to 3pm, for just US$4.45 with sides. A bit more on the romantic side yet equally welcoming, ★ **Sebastian La Perla Negra** (Av. Luis Ginebra #62, tel. 809/320-8818, 4pm-10pm daily except Tues.) serves all your pasta and pizza favorites. Here you'll find more residents than tourists; the owner himself will be on the floor working. The place has a trendy, dim-lit vibe and the drinks and desserts are excellent.

Italian favorite **La Tarappa** (Calle Privada 2, corner of Av. Hermanas Mirabal, tel. 809/261-2423, www.latarappa.com, 9am-11:30pm Tues.-Sun., US$3-15) serves wood-fired pizza, pastas, salads, steaks, calzones, and giant sandwiches in a convivial, open dining room. There's a second location inside the Playa Dorada shopping mall.

Inside the Playa Dorada resort area, ★ **Green Jack** (At Blue Jack Tar hotel, Playa Dorada, www.bluejacktar.com, noon-11pm daily, later close on Fri.-Sat., US$7-20) has one of the most creative menus in Puerto Plata and is reasonably priced. Whether you pick the beef carpaccio, the plantain-and-bacon-stuffed burger, or the creole seafood, it's all finger-licking good.

Just before you reach the Playa Dorada you'll hit the Playa Chaparral (known locally as El Pueblito) complex, where longtimer **Le Petit François** (tel. 809/320-9612, noon-midnight Wed.-Sun., US$16-45) serves seafood specialties and a variety of French entrées on a romantic 2nd-floor terrace where you can dine al fresco facing the beach or indoors. The lobster thermidor is a highlight, as are the cordon bleu and fondue options. Service is solid, and the dimly lit atmosphere, away from the tourist crowds, makes it a decent pick for a quiet evening.

The best Mexican food in the DR is at ★ **Los Charros y Los Pinches Chaparros** (Cofresi Beach 5, close to Ocean World, tel. 809/970-3332, eat@charros.co, noon-10pm daily, closed Mon. during low season, US$5-18). Originally from Acapulco, Mexico, Juanita uses her mother's and grandmother's recipes to fill her menu with tempting choices. Don't miss the Taquisa Los Charros, a "culinary trip through Mexico" with a plate that includes a choice of tostada, flauta, taco de cochinita pibil, and taco los charros. Wash it all down with a margarita—there are premium tequilas to pick from, of course. As for the meaning of the fun alliteration in the restaurant's name, you'll have to ask Juanita.

If you're going all out for an occasion, **Lucia** (Casa Colonial, Playa Dorada, tel. 809/320-3232, www.casacolonialhotel.com, US$10-30) is the place to do it. The all-white setting—in a dimly lit dining room with cozy corner booths and stand-alone tables—complements the outstanding Mediterranean-Dominican fusion menu. Don't miss Los Dos Chivos, with lamb simmered in an organic cacao and red wine sauce on one side of the plate and in a creole sauce on the other. There are also vegetarian options and an extensive wine list.

For a romantic night, reserve a poolside table at ★ **Mares Restaurant & Lounge** (Calle 6 Francisco Peynado, tel. 809/261-3330, www.maresrestaurant.com, noon-3pm and 7pm-11pm Tues.-Sun., US$10-25), set in a delightful garden. Chef Rafael Vasquez Heinsein serves a creative menu he whips up from his kitchen, which he describes as Dominican but global. Dishes include T-bone steak, lobster tail, and Dominican goat with Brugal rum. It's a culinary treat and one of Puerto Plata's gems.

## ACCOMMODATIONS
### Under $25

A pick for location, cleanliness, and price is **Hotel Victoriano** (Calle San Felipe 33, corner of Calle Restauracion, tel. 809/586-9752, US$13-16), a three-story hotel with 25 rooms, with or without air-conditioning, and free wireless Internet.

In a residential area about a 15-minute walk from the central park of Puerto Plata, the family-owned **Villa Carolina** (Calle Virginia Elena Ortega 9, tel. 829/908-2200, www.villacarolina.hostel.com, US$20-30) is a solid base for solo and independent travelers on a budget. Tucked at the back of a lush yard (bring mosquito spray), past the owner's home, the dated white colonial building offers nine simple but immaculately clean rooms with queen-size beds, wood closets, and spacious bathrooms. The furniture is basic, but the low rates include a daily continental breakfast in the main living room, daily maid service, and wireless Internet (albeit spotty). Francia is a warm Dominican host who delights in helping her guests select excursions and ensuring they get around safely. The guesthouse is conveniently located just a couple of blocks from the Metro Tours bus terminal, the local fruit and vegetable market, and a handful of local restaurants.

## US$25-50

Set in a Victorian residence, ★ **Hotel Kevin** (tel. 829/253-0083, hotel-kevin@hotmail. fr, US$30) is ideal for solo travelers or couples looking for a clean, simple place to crash with a location smack in the city center, just steps from the central park, restaurants, and the waterfront Malecón. Rooms are basic, but come with air-conditioning and wireless Internet. There's also a boho-artsy lounge area with green plants and a shared kitchen with

daily (free) coffee. Water is available free on various floors. If a roof over your head is all you're after, this is a good choice.

Along the seaside boulevard, **Aparta-Hotel Lomar** (Av. Malecón 8, tel. 809/320-8555, from US$30) offers both short- and long-term stays in one of its double rooms or studio apartments. It's a safe place to reside with 24-hour security. Rooms come with wireless Internet, TV, and optional air-conditioning.

**Sunshine Hotel** (Av. Manolo Tavarez Justo No. 78, tel. 809/586-1771, hotel. sunshine@outlook.com, US$31) is a decent budget spot for those who have transportation and don't mind being a little away from the city center, yet just a 10-minute drive out. White-tiled rooms are spacious and clean, and come with a small balcony, air-conditioning, and wireless Internet, while suites have a kitchenette. There's a popular local restaurant on the ground floor, offering an à la carte menu or an affordable daily local lunch.

## US$50-100

A place like ★ **Tubagua Plantation Eco Lodge** (tel. 809/696-6932, www.tubagua.com, US$50-140, meals at additional cost) comes around once in a blue moon. Just a 30-minute

the panoramic views of Puerto Plata from the Tubagua Plantation Eco Lodge ride out of the city center, the lodge is perched at the top of a hill at the heart of the Tubagua community in the central highlands of Puerto Plata. The open-air main dining room has a show-stopping panormaic view of Pico Isabel, Playa Dorada, and the Atlantic Ocean—even as far as Sosúa.

While the panoramic views steal the show, the cabins and surrounding natural environment are what make this a laid-back escape. There are two private cottages or "casitas" with private baths, two *palapa* cabins with a shared bathroom with a view, and a longhouse, all on multiple levels like a traditional Dominican *campo* yard. Drapes, wooden doors, and funky shutters open onto the verdant landscape. The main dining room is under a thatch-roofed wooden structure where flavorful communal meals are shared in a convivial space. A small soaking pool facing the hills is there for a cool dip or to relax beside on a lounge chair with a good book. The lodge blends seamlessly with its environment, and your daily companions will range from roosters waking you early for the glorious sunrise views to resident dogs Mariposa and Tonta.

The local community tours offered to guests are among the best in the area, created by lodge owner and 30-year resident Tim Hall to help travelers immerse themselves in local culture, including an on-site cacao demonstration. Don't miss the hike to Charcos de los Militares waterfalls with guide Juanin Balbuena, who will take you through the Tubagua community or on a drive down the Ruta Panorámica (in your car) on visits to amber mines or a coffee plantation.

A gem in downtown Puerto Plata, worth the slight splurge and a short walk from both the Central Park and the Malecón, the ★ **Boutique Hotel El Palacio** (Calle Prof. Juan Bosch 14, tel. 809/261-0942, www. hotelelpalacio.com, US$60) sets the bar for guesthouses in the area. Six spacious rooms and a suite are set on the 2nd floor of a gorgeous 1920s colonial building with original floors. The hotel is delightfully decorated in antique furniture and trinkets—the owner's antiques store is next door—set against modern details like sliding-door showers and air-conditioning. The Dutch owners have spared no detail, including an outdoor terrace with a movie screen and a pool for cooling off from the hot Puerto Plata sun. Breakfasts and other meals can be included upon request.

**Hotel KMA** (Calle #2 Urb. Reyes Caminero, tel. 809/244-4237, www.kmahotel. com, US$60) is popular with long-termers, but families or groups might appreciate its humongous apartments—1-3 bedrooms—with full kitchens and appliances, air-conditioning, and basic furniture. There's a small pool by the entrance and parking lot and laundry facilities, but that's about all for amenities. You'll need a car to stay here, or prepare to taxi to the city for dinner and entertainment.

## Over US$100

Those looking to stay on the beach and enjoy a touch of luxury won't go wrong at one of Playa Dorada's resorts inside the gated complex, facing the golden beach yet a stone's throw from town. But the real star here is an exclusive five-star boutique property and my own favorite, ★ **Casa Colonial** (Playa Dorada, tel. 809/320-3232, www.casacolonialhotel.com, US$195-235). It's worth every penny you shell out. The stunning grounds include a lush garden hugging a mangrove lagoon, a quiet golden stretch of sand where you're free to have breakfast or lunch daily, and a 3rd-floor infinity pool with four Jacuzzi tubs directly facing the sea ahead—the highlight for sure. The rooms come with seafront balconies and plenty of lavish treats, including daily turndown service with a dessert or snack. Last but not least, the on-site **Lucia Restaurant** is a delight for both its Zen ambience and its Mediterranean-Caribbean fusion menu of dishes made from organic, homegrown ingredients as well as unique takes on Dominican specialties.

**Gran Ventana VH** (Playa Dorada, tel.

809/320-2111, www.granventanahotel.com, from US$138) is a classic family-friendly all-inclusive property inside Playa Dorada. If you have small kids, this is a reasonably sized resort where the main pool is the highlight, along with a nice beachfront. The rooms are in pastel beach colors and have comfortable beds, air-conditioning, and cable TV. Note that it gets really loud at the main resort, with music and entertainment during the day and nightly outdoor shows that are a stone's throw from the rooms. Couples might prefer the separate hotel wing across the parking lot, with a "quiet" pool and bar.

The new ★ Emotions by Hodelpa (U.S. tel. 809/320-6226, www.granventanahotel. com, US$138) filled a need on Playa Dorada by offering a beautiful, compact resort with something for everyone, from the adults-only private section to the two children's pools, and the ground-floor suites with private swim-up pools. The food is generally excellent, from the buffet to the Dominican-themed Oregano restaurant. You'll also find a café, a sports bar, a beachfront grill and bar, a baseball batting cage, and nighttime music live on the pool terrace. Avoid staying here during Easter or DR public holidays, when it gets quite crowded.

For an intimate, medium-sized resort set on the gorgeous Playa Dorada, with a great on-site à la carte restaurant, stay at ★ Blue Jack Tar (Playa Dorada, tel. 809/320-3800, from US$154). The standard ground-floor guest rooms have a tropical feel with baby-blue colors, and have all the amenities you need, including air-conditioning, TV, mini-bar, and full bath. There's a pool on-site, a few steps away from the ocean where beds and loungers await.

Set inside the small Cofresí compound, Lifestyle Holidays Vacation Resort (Cofresí Beach 1, tel. 809/970-7777, www. lhvcresorts.com, US$100-400) attracts plenty of tourists for its yearlong all-inclusive deals, but probably more for its party vibe. The resort is average—its beach is one of the least attractive on the North Coast—and includes eight separate sections, such as Cofresí Palm, The Tropical, Crown Suites, Villas, and Presidential Suites. It's not close to the city. You'll need transportation to venture anywhere outside of the compound, but plenty of tours are offered. There are a couple of restaurants within walking distance, including the authentic Mexican restaurant Los Charros. Most travelers who are members rave about the Lifestyle, while those visiting on a discount coupon often leave disenchanted. If you're going to opt for an all-inclusive or boutique resort, go for one at Playa Dorada.

# INFORMATION AND SERVICES

You'll find plenty of supermarkets in Puerto Plata town. Try the locally owned Supermercado Jose Luis (Av. Manolo Tavares Justo 20, corner of Calle Beller, tel. 809/586-3347, 8am-9pm Mon.-Sat., 8am-1pm Sun.) for decent groceries, fruits, and on-site ATMs. The new Jumbo (Av. Manolo Tavarez Justo, tel. 809/261-1118, wwww.jumbo.com. do, 8am-10pm daily, except Sun. 9pm close) has everything from food to clothes. Casa Nelson (across Parque Independencia, Calle Separación, 8am-8pm Mon.-Sat.) is a Puerto Plata institution. The locals' favorite discount department store, this is where you'll find everything from beauty products to school supplies, men's and women's apparel, and a shoe department popular for its low prices.

For anything else you can't find, head to Multicentro La Sirena (Av. del Malecón, tel. 809/586-6066, 8am-10pm Mon.-Sat., 8am-8pm Sun.), where there are additional ATMs, as well myriad on-site services, including phone companies, a pharmacy, dry cleaning, and a cafeteria.

If you're staying in Playa Dorada, you'll find basic needs and shopping at Playa Dorada Plaza (Av. Manolo Tavarez Justo, tel. 809/320-6645, www.playadorada.com.do, 8am-10pm daily), located a short drive past the main entrance. Expect prices to be a tad higher than in the city.

## Health and Emergencies

Puerto Plata has plenty of health care services. For clinic care, go to **Clínica Brugal** (Jose del Carmen Ariza 15, tel. 809/586-2519), with 24-hour emergency service, or **Centro Médico Dr. Bournigal** (Calle Antera Mota, tel. 809/586-2342), which also has a pharmacy. The public hospital is **Hospital Dr. Ricardo Limardo** (tel. 809/586-2210). Inside the Playa Dorada complex is the **Urgent Care Clinic** (tel. 809/320-2222).

The tourism police, **CESTUR** (Hermanas Mirabal, tel. 809/320-4603 or 809/320-0365), has a solid presence in Puerto Plata by Long Beach and is open 24 hours. You'll find plenty of CESTUR officers patrolling downtown areas frequented by tourists, such as Independence Park and the Malecón.

## Money

**Banco Popular** (across from the Central Park, Calle José del Carmen Ariza, corner of Duarte, tel. 809/586-2121) has a 24-hour ATM, and you'll find more ATMs outside La Sirena supermarket. **Scotiabank** (across from La Leña, Calle 27 de Febrero, tel. 809/200-7268) is smack in town with outdoor ATMs, and Banco Progreso outlets can be found outside the supermarket Jose Luis, across the street from Scotiabank.

## Tourist Information

The **Oficina de Turismo** (Calle José del Carmen Ariza 45, close to Banco Popular, tel. 809/586-3676, 9am-3pm daily) has multilingual staff ready to assist you across from Independence Park. They have plenty of area brochures and maps to help with your trip. Note that as of publication time, the office has plans to relocate, so be sure to check ahead before going there.

## Communications

There's a **post office** (Calle 12 de Julio, tel. 809/586-4545, 7am-5pm Mon.-Fri., 8am-noon Sat.) in town, if you care to send only postcards and nothing of value—but don't fully rely on it getting to your addressee.

# GETTING THERE

## Air

If you're staying on the North Coast, in Puerto Plata, Playa Dorada, Sosúa, Cabarete, or Río San Juan, you should fly into **Aeropuerto Internacional Gregorio Luperón** (tel. 809/291-0000, ext. 221, or 809/586-0175, www.aerodom.com), sandwiched between Puerto Plata town and Sosúa, and just 18 kilometers (11 miles) east or 15 minutes from Puerto Plata town and Playa Dorada. Taxi fares to and from the airport are usually posted on a board as you exit customs; as of publication time they are US$30 to Puerto Plata or US$35 to Playa Dorada. Airlines that fly here include American Airlines, Delta, United, Air Canada, Spirit, JetBlue Airways, and Copa.

## Car

Coming up north from the south, take Autopista Duarte toward Santiago, then take the exit for Puerto Plata. If you're coming from Samaná, take the scenic Highway 5, all the way toward Sanchez, then to Nagua, and on to the north.

## Bus or *Guagua*

Getting to Puerto Plata from Santo Domingo or Santiago is easy with the in-town branch of **Metro Tours** (Calle Beller, corner of 16 de Agosto, tel. 809/586-6063, http://metroserviciosturisticos.com). There are fairly punctual departures throughout the day starting at 6:30am. Check the website for the latest scheduled departures. You'll travel in a large air-conditioned coach bus and reach the capital in about four hours, passing through Santiago. It can be freezing cold on board, so bring a jacket and thank me later for that tip. **Caribe Tours** (Calle Camino Real, tel. 809/586-4544) also offers daily bus service to Santo Domingo—they have more frequent stops during the journey—departing every hour on the hour 6am to 7pm. Both bus companies promise wireless Internet on board, but it's hit-or-miss.

If you're coming from the Samaná

Peninsula, there's a small *guagua* that runs from Las Terrenas to Puerto Plata called **Transporte Las Terrenas** (tel. 809/240-5302, or RD$300 or US$6.55 pp) departing at 6:30am (though it has been known to show up at 6am, so get there early to be safe) on the main road across from Plaza Taína and Plaza del Paseo. It's a straight shot for the most part, with one break in Nagua for coffee and food, then the occasional passenger drop-off along the way. You'll reach Puerto Plata between 11:30am and noon. I've done this route, and while it wasn't always comfortable, it was safe and had views of the lovely fishing villages as we made our way up. The reverse route is also possible, from Puerto Plata to Las Terrenas. A bus departs daily across from the hospital around 1:30pm, passing through Sosúa. Always inquire a day or two ahead of time, in case schedules and departure locations have changed.

If you're heading to Puerto Plata from Río San Juan or Cabrera, the smaller local *guaguas* are the only option—unless you've rented a car or a taxi, both of which are pricey. The *guaguas* take you north passing through Sosúa and Cabarete. They'll pick up and drop off anywhere along the routes, and they are an economical way of getting around. Do be aware they are also often involved in accidents due to speeding, but for the most part it's like anywhere in the world when it comes to public or private transportation—there are no guarantees.

## GETTING AROUND

Puerto Plata city and its surroundings are well connected by public transportation, and that's good news if you're traveling on a budget or would rather not drive. Like most parts of the DR, traveling by private taxi will cost you significantly more than braving a ride on a *motoconcho* or in a *carrito (carro)*. Both of these modes of transportation dominate on this side of the island. Whichever method you choose, **look for licensed modes of transport.**

## Car Rentals

The big rental car companies are here, including **Avis** (tel. 809/586-4436), **Budget** (tel. 809/320-4888), and **National/Alamo** (tel. 809/586-1366). You can find them at the Puerto Plata international airport. For a local rental shop in the city with a good, affordable selection of SUVs, contact **Pionia Rent Car** (Av. Malecón, a block from La Sirena, tel. 809/586-3809, pioniarentcar@gmail.com, 8am-6pm Mon.-Sat., from US$35/day).

## Taxis

Always ask the rate *before* you get in the car, because taxis aren't metered; they follow fixed rates from the taxi association. You don't want to find yourself at your destination and cornered into paying an exorbitant price. A good rule of thumb is to remember that in-town destinations are usually no more than US$3.50 (or RD$150), while rides to Playa Dorada, Costambar, and Cofresí range around US$7-10, and to Cabarete US$30. In Puerto Plata, contact Antonio Perez (tel. 809/252-3508), who can drive you pretty much anywhere on the north coast, as well airport runs. For in-town rides, ask your hotel to call the 24-hour **taxi central dispatch** (tel. 809/586-5335); they will give you the time estimate and you can ask for the rate. Always carry small change, as drivers will rarely have it.

## Carros Públicos (Shared Taxis)

The originating and final destinations of the *carro público*, or shared taxi, are usually indicated at the top of the car, often a Toyota sedan. Most go back and forth between Puerto Plata and Sosúa (RD$50 or US$1.10)—where you can then switch to Cabarete—and stop anywhere you need along the main highway, including Playa Dorada (RD$30 or US$0.66). The main *carrito* hub for departures to Sosúa is on the street corner adjacent to the Ricardo Limardo Hospital; they also pass along Calle Separación beside the Parque Central and go down Beller Road on their way to Sosúa. Ask anyone for "*la parada de carros de Sosúa*." They also pass through town, so ask where the closest street is where you can hail one down. A good guess is Independence Park.

If you have luggage or are going to Cabarete, it's a better bet to go to the main exit hub by the hospital to load your suitcase and get a better seat. In general, the *carro público* is a safer alternative to *guagua* minivan buses, which can get even more crammed.

### Motoconchos (Motorbike Taxis)

Sometimes abbreviated to *conchos*, **motorbike taxis** can take you to places in town or to Costambar (RD$80 or US$1.75) and Cofresí. Locals often prefer to catch a ride from a motorbike taxi, despite that they are more dangerous, to avoid being squashed inside a shared taxi car or van. Motorbike taxis—riders wear **neon traffic vests**—are parked on street corners around the city's main avenues. You'll also find them outside most major supermarkets, including La Sirena's parking lot. Current fares are usually displayed on a board beside their stop. They also zoom along most main streets and will likely spot you before you spot them and whistle or call out—their job is to find pedestrians. A simple "no gracias" or an index finger wag indicating "no" will suffice if you're not interested.

### Guaguas (Public Buses)

*These* public white minivans also go to Sosúa and Cabarete with stops at Gran Parada, where you can catch a motorbike taxi to Tubagua. From there they continue past Cabarete as far as Río San Juan and Cabrera.

# Sosúa

Sosúa's history is undoubtedly unique among the Dominican Republic and the Caribbean. The town was first settled by Jewish refugees offered a place to escape Nazi persecution during World War II. The Dominican Republic was the only country in the world to offer to take up to 100,000 Jews as refugees in what is known as the Luperón Agreement. Between 1940 and 1945, five thousand visas were issued for displaced Jewish refugees, but only six hundred came. Most were single men from Austria and Germany, but some traveled from China and the Caribbean as well. They became Dominican citizens immediately and used this freedom to raise families and start a community in Sosúa. As Sosúa resident and descendant Joe Benjamin states, "The Luperón Agreement shows that even in those days, the DR was a country that accepted diversity and compassion." The Jewish Museum in town commemorates the settlers, who founded the meat and dairy industries of Sosúa before tourism came along, and others who left their mark here. Today about four of the original families remain, while most others have left for mainland North America.

Today, this beachside community is unfortunately mostly known for its well-earned rep of being the epicenter of heavy prostitution. I'll admit that it's one of my least favorite tourist hubs in the DR. It's still a decent quick spot for some beach fun in the daytime, and for some history and snorkeling if you're nearby. You'll also find a multicultural spot where expats from around the world have made their homes and opened businesses—the variety of cuisine alone is testament to this.

## ORIENTATION

Sosúa is very small; you'll be able to get around on foot between the two main beaches with no trouble at all. The main drag of Pedro Clisante is where most of the restaurants and bars are located, aside from the ones lining Playa Sosúa and facing Playa Alicia. The main street turns pedestrian as the sun goes down and the nightlife ramps up. Note that the

# Sosúa

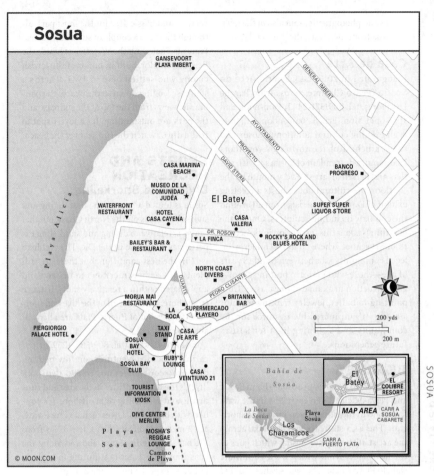

scene might not be your cup of tea, as prostitution is obvious here.

You'll find most of the hotels and guesthouses around the streets of Pedro Clisante, Dr. Alejo Martinez, and Dr. Rosen, and there are a couple of entrances from the highway into Playa Sosúa as you approach from Puerto Plata or Cabarete or across from Supermercado Playero. You can find your way on foot between Playa Sosúa and Playa Alicia by taking the staircase up or down across from the artist alley and navigating Sosúa's small side streets.

## SIGHTS
### Museo de la Comunidad Judía

A great place to learn the history of the town of Sosúa and its unique cultural legacy is the Jewish Museum, or **Museo de la Comunidad Judía** (Calle Dr. Alejo Martinez, next to Casa Marina Hotel, tel. 809/571-1386, call to arrange visit, US$4), created to commemorate the Jews who were welcomed by the Dominican Republic and settled in Sosúa in the 1940s. The single-floor gallery displays the entire history of not just the families who made their home here—including names and photographs—but also of the town of Sosúa from then until the present day.

### Casa de Arte

Inaugurated in 2013, **La Casa de Arte de Sosúa** (Pedro Clisante, across from Parque Las Flores, tel. 809/571-2442, 9am-noon and 1pm-6pm Mon.-Fri., 8:30am-noon Sat., free) is an exciting cultural addition to Sosúa and the brainchild of the town's mayor, Ilana Neumann, a descendant of Sosúa's Jewish settlers and herself an artist. Every month on the 1st floor, the cultural house hosts a rotating exhibit of Dominican artists from all around the country, including sculptors. One of the best things about this institution is its second-floor art school, where up to 200 underprivileged community kids between 8 and 18 years of age—those who perform best in school—get instruction in a range of free classes, from painting to ballet, jewelry making to choir singing. It's an incredible resource for the community and a shining light for Sosúa's future generations.

## BEACHES

There are two beaches in Sosúa—Playa Sosúa and Playa Alicia. It's an easy, 20-minute walk from one to the other if you know the shortcuts. There's a staircase you can take across the artist alley by Playa Sosúa, which goes to the hotel side, from which it's a 10-minute walk to Playa Alicia. The two beaches couldn't be more different from each other. **Playa Sosúa** is a beautiful golden stretch protected by a reef, making it ideal for swimming with kids and nearby snorkeling. But the beach is also more crowded and filled with vendors, cafés, bars, casual restaurants, and all-around social activity and music. Come here early in the morning if you want a quiet swim before the rush begins, or stay on and join into the upbeat beach vibe.

Flanked by towering cliffs and away from the mayhem of the main drag, **Playa Alicia** is wide open—it formed over the last decade when the sea receded—and offers glorious, unobstructed views of the water. It's

vendor- and hassle-free for the most part, although there are a couple of surrounding restaurants, including the Waterfront beside the Parque Mirador, built in honor of the Jewish colony who settled here in 1941. There's a staircase leading down to the beach; the panoramic views from the top of the staircase and the park are outstanding. It's a lovely spot to take a dip or watch the sun set over the beach.

## SPORTS AND RECREATION
### Diving and Snorkeling

Sosúa is touted as one of the best diving and snorkeling areas off the North Coast, but that praise is relative to diving and snorkeling experiences elsewhere in the DR. The reef here isn't in the best condition, but there are still plenty of Caribbean critters to be seen and appreciated within a relatively short distance from shore. Note that all of the dive and snorkel offerings out of Puerto Plata are all available from Sosúa.

**SeaPro Divers** (tel. 809/586-1239, http://caribbeanoceanadventures.com/diving.htm, dive.pro@codetel.net.do, US$90 two-tank dive) is the main outfitter in the area and runs diving and snorkeling right offshore. It's popular with beginners. Dives include **The Point,** at 12 meters (40 feet), just a few miles from the bay. Snorkeling stops abound along the coastline—the water is stunning to explore, but don't expect a multitude of fish.

You could haggle for a **glass-bottom boat ride** from the beach, usually around US$20 per person. They take you to some of the popular snorkel spots, albeit in wooden boats that are less spacious. Look for the captains along Sosúa Beach.

## ENTERTAINMENT AND EVENTS

There aren't major annual events in Sosúa save for the small multicultural festival that takes place in August, celebrating art, music, and the town's international food scene. For a

---

**1:** Playa Sosúa; **2:** Playa Alicia

drink and some dancing, you'll find most of the bars and clubs along Pedro Clisante Street, which closes to traffic after dusk. The scene isn't likely one you'd want to linger around too long, but there are a couple of places you can have a drink in peace and enjoy the evening if you'd rather not head to nearby towns like Cabarete or Puerto Plata. One is **Rocky's Rock & Blues Bar** (Calle Dr. Rosen 24, tel. 809/571-2951, www.rockysbar.com, 9am-11pm daily), an expat favorite and a nice spot to mingle and have a few cocktails or beers. The other is **The Finish Line** (Ayuntamiento 5, half a block off Pedro Clisante, tel. 829/678-2975, sosua.finish.line@gmail.com, 9am-midnight daily), also a North American haunt with a live rock band on Saturday afternoons from 4pm to 7pm.

## SHOPPING

Located down an alley now known as the artist street of Sosúa, make sure you stop at **571 Art Gallery by Leo Diaz** (tel. 809/712-3632, www.leodiazart.com, 10am-9pm daily, hours vary), where the talented self-taught Dominican sells paintings, sculptures, and other unique souvenirs bearing his art. Ask him about the story behind his "Las señoritas de Sosúa" collection of paintings, inspired by the personal stories of Sosúa's ladies of the night. Leo also teaches a painting class to community kids every week at La Casa de Arte de Sosúa.

For premium cigars, head to **Café Cubano** (Calle Pedro Clisante 27, tel. 809/571-3493 or 829/921-1763, http://sosuacigars.com, 8am-11pm Mon.-Sat.). If you're looking for sarongs, beachwear, and DR-printed totes, you'll find plenty of souvenir shops along Pedro Clisante as well as around Playa Sosúa, which is filled with mobile vendors selling trinkets.

## FOOD
### Dominican

A good pick among the hundreds of casual, average food shacks dotting Playa Sosúa is **The Mofongo King** (Playa Sosúa, 9am-9pm daily, US$3-10), serving its namesake dish in a variety of ways including with chicken and pork. It's a casual spot that's just as great for a cup of coffee and some people-watching. There are also beach chairs across from the café when you're ready to pass out after all that mashed plantain.

Grab some Dominican and Mexican fare on the main drag at **Bistro Típico Alberto** (Calle Pedro Clisante 12, tel. 809/571-4975, 8am-1am daily, US$3-6). Enjoy lunch or post-party grub on this sidewalk terrace.

### International

**Jolly Roger Bar & Grill** (Calle Pedro Clisante 11, tel. 829/299-0753, www.jollyrogersosua.com, US$3-7) is popular with Canadian expats mostly thanks to its lively bar with sports screening, weekly events (including bingo), and cold beers, but it also serves decent sandwiches—try the bacon chicken burger. It's a short walk from the beach and a good setting for all, including families with kids.

Another great chill-out spot on the beach, with tasty Jamaican fare from jerk to curried goat, is ★ **Mosha's Reggae Lounge** (#85 Playa Sosúa, noon-9pm daily, no phone). The food is cooked fresh, so relax on the beach while your meal is prepared.

The extensive, consistently good menu and service at **Scandinavian Beach Bar** (Playa Sosúa, 9am-11pm daily, US$3-15) make it a standout on the beach. The ribs in particular win rave reviews. The spot is ideal under the shade, with free wireless Internet and a convivial atmosphere backed with music.

**Captain Bailey's** (Calle Alejo Martinez, 8am-midnight daily, US$5-20, cash only) has a thatch roof and sits a few steps from Banco Popular along the sidewalk. This casual open-air spot is decent if you're tired of walking in the heat and want a quick sandwich or coffee near your hotel. The food is average, with options ranging from burgers to Dominican specials and seafood. Note that it can get quite smoky here, and mostly foreign men congregate at the bar.

**Casa Valeria** (Calle Dr. Rosen 28, tel. 809/571-3565, hotelcasavaleria@gmail.com,

8am-11pm Thurs.-Tues., 8am-1pm Wed., US$5-15) is set in the leafy, cozy courtyard of its hotel. The menu offers decently priced entrées, including excellent steaks, burgers, and pastas. You can "bring you own wine" (there's no corkage fee) and if it's your birthday, the discount is your actual age—pick the better deal betwen the two!

Enjoy top-notch cigars and gourmet coffee at **Café Cubano** (Calle Pedro Clisante 27, tel. 809/571-3493 or 829/921-1763, http://sosuacigars.com, 8am-11pm Mon.-Sat., US$2-20), a popular hangout for residents and visitors alike. The menu also offers plenty of sandwiches—from breakfast croissants to burgers to Cubanos—as well as desserts and cocktails. If you're a cigar aficionado, it's a good spot to learn about the various Dominican brands and find your favorite or a gift to take home.

**On The Waterfront** (Calle Sin Salida, tel. 809/571-3024, www.waterfrontrestaurantdr.com, noon-midnight daily) has a glorious open-air dining terrace facing Playa Alicia and the Atlantic at the end of a cul-de-sac. The menu, albeit pricey, offers a wide range of entrées, but excels in grilled meats and seafood. Caesar salads are made fresh tableside. Happy hours kick in 5pm-7pm, and there are steps leading down to the beach, making it an ideal spot to catch sunset with a drink.

**Baia Lounge** (Gansevoort Playa Imbert, tel. 849/816-2436, noon-10pm daily, US$10-30) faces the private beach and the infinity pool at this new luxury resort in Sosúa and offers a decent, varied menu ranging from Italian to Asian fusion. There's a separate sushi menu, and the wine list is extensive—ask to see the cellar on the lower level where you can dine in groups and enjoy cigars for special occasions.

Another fine dining option is at the trendy, all-white **Infiniti Blu Restaurant** (Calle Alejo Martinez/Helipuerto Sosúa, tel. 809/571-2033, 7:30am-11pm daily), serving Mediterranean, Italian, and Middle Eastern specialties, as well as breakfast treats and lunch bites from pizza to sandwiches. There's live music every Friday evening.

## ACCOMMODATIONS

The all-white ★ **Casa Veintiuno 21** (Calle Piano 1, tel. 829/341-8551, www.casaveintiuno.com, US$119-152) is an elegant, small B&B—it has just three rooms, of which two are suites—ideal for those seeking luxury away from the Sosúa strips but close enough to walk to the beach and the in-town action. Suites offer plenty of pampering, from the Egyptian cotton linens to espresso machines, plush robes, and all the electronics you need—but if you pick the 21 package, you can also get your clothes packed and unpacked for you, among other perks. There's an on-site restaurant open five days a week, as well as a lovely courtyard with a pool and plenty of loungers. The only company you'll find are the owners' two dogs.

**Hotel Casa Cayena** (Calle Dr. Rosen 25, El Batey, tel. 809/571-2429, www.casacayenahotel.com, US$91-101, cash discount) is a bit dated with its peach walls, but it's a longtimer, located just a block from Playa Alicia. There's an on-site restaurant facing the hotel pool. Rooms worth booking offer king beds, mini fridges, and pool-facing balconies.

A few steps away, **Casa Valeria** (Calle Dr. Rosen 28, tel. 809/571-3565, www.hotelcasavaleria.com, US$55-80, breakfast included) is a small hotel that delights from the moment you reach the entrance courtyard. The tastefully decorated rooms—red and white hues dominate—face the swimming pool and have air-conditioning, TV, wireless Internet, and kitchenette options. There's a good restaurant on-site as well. It's a solid pick for solo travelers as well as couples who want to be away from the prostitute-and-client scene of Sosúa.

The **Piergiorgio Palace Hotel** (El Batey 1, tel. 809/571-2626, www.piergiorgiopalace.com, US$95-115) is a staple in Sosúa and is like a faded palace, but its wide, cliff-top seafront terrace still has the most breathtaking view over the Sosúa bay and beach. That alone makes it worth staying here if you're just passing through for the night, as well as the waterfront restaurant and the rooms facing La Puntilla, causing you to fall asleep to the hush of the ocean.

## INFORMATION AND SERVICES

You'll find most services on the main streets of Calle Pedro Clisante and Calle Duarte. This is the main intersection in the tourist part of Sosúa, an area known as "El Batey." For groceries and other such needs, **Supermercado Playero** (Carretera Sosúa-Cabarete Km 1, tel. 809/571-1821) has a larger branch on the main highway; the smaller one is closer to the hotels and the main drag.

### Health and Emergencies

For emergencies in the DR, you can dial 911, just as in the United States. You'll find the 24-hour **Centro Médico Bella Vista** (Carretera Sosúa-Cabarete, tel. 809/571-3429, 8am-9pm Mon.-Sat., 8am-8:30pm Sun.) on the road between Sosúa and Cabarete. Pharmacies are on Calle Pedro Clisante—try **Farmacia Sosúa** (tel. 809/571-2350, 8am-7pm Mon.-Sat.).

### Money

There's a **Banco Popular** (Dr. Alejo Martinez 1, tel. 809/571-2555, 9am-4pm Mon.-Fri., 9am-1pm Sat.) as well as **Banco Progreso** (Calle Pedro Clisante), both with ATMs.

## GETTING THERE

Most fly into Puerto Plata's **Aeropuerto Internacional Gregorio Luperón,** then catch a *guagua, carro público,* hotel shuttle, or taxi for the 20-minute ride to Sosúa. Cab fare is around US$35. Check the boards as you exit customs at the airport for the latest official fare.

**Caribe Tours** (Autopista Puerto Plata-Sosúa, tel. 809/571-3808) has a station in the nontouristy area of Sosúa, known as Los Charamicos. Buses head out to Santo Domingo daily, leaving every hour starting at 5:20am and running until 6:20am, or try **Metro Tours** (Calle Dr. Rosen, tel. 809/571-1324).

## GETTING AROUND

It's easy to walk around Sosúa and get to the beaches on foot. That's the good news. If you need to go farther, all of the public transportation options abound from motorbikes—there are many in these parts—to private taxis, which often park on Calle Pedro Clisante.

You can flag down a *carro público* heading to either Cabarete or Puerto Plata (RD$50 or US$1.10); they pass up and down along the highway. To head to Puerto Plata (RD$50 or US$1.10), stand in front of the big Playero Supermarket on the main road or go to the main departure hub one block up, which is a gas station across from the Texaco. The *carritos* to Cabarete are immediately adjacent to the ones heading to Puerto Plata. Ask anyone for help, and they'll point you in the right direction. If you'd rather take an expensive taxi, call **Taxi Sosúa** (tel. 809/571-2797). To rent a car for road trips to neighboring towns like Cabarete or Río San Juan, contact **Pionia Rent Car** (Av. Malecón, Puerto Plata, a block from La Sirena, tel. 809/586-3809, pioniarentcar@gmail.com, 8am-6pm Mon.-Sat., US$35).

# Cabarete

Cabarete is referred to as the water sports capital of the Dominican Republic, and sometimes even of the Caribbean. It is indeed one of the world's top windsurfing and kitesurfing hubs. Thousands descend on this beachfront town throughout the year from around the world to spend their days splashing in the sun along the glorious white sand and skimming over incessant waves amid constant trade winds. Yearly competitions like the Windsurf Classic and Master of the Ocean keep Cabarete at the top of the world's water sports scene. By night, the adrenaline rush is tempered with plenty of libations and dancing in outdoor bars lining the beach. It's the perfect vacation for the young and restless—or the young at heart and restless. Yes, it is touristy, but you'll also find a solid expat community of all ages, many of whom have made their homes here in search of the perfect beach life.

## ORIENTATION

The Cabarete area is essentially split into three main parts: Cabarete proper, Kite Beach, and Encuentro Beach. If you want to stay close to the action—the heart of town with bars, restaurants, clubs, and Parque Nacional El Choco—stay in **Cabarete.** In Cabarete, you'll find all your needs from windsurfing schools to swimmable beaches to fine dining along the main drag, both roadside and beachfront. As you continue west, it gets less and less crowded. **Encuentro** is far more isolated, and it's where you'll find boutique resorts. **Kite Beach** has more hotels and kitesurfing schools, as well as boutique resorts. The waves are rough here, and erosion has become a serious issue; it's really not a leisurely spot for swimming. Going east in Cabarete, you'll find an area known as **La Punta,** where the sunsets are lovely and there are romantic hotels and restaurants that form an ideal escape from the noise, but still walking distance from the heart of Cabarete.

## SIGHTS
### Parque Nacional El Choco

It's pretty amazing that just a 10-minute drive from the main strip of Cabarete and its water sports-jammed beaches is a 77-square-kilometer (30-square-mile) national park and protected area where you can hike, ride horses, mountain bike, or bathe in jade-colored waters. Set in the local neighborhood Callejón de la Loma, **Parque Nacional El Choco** (Callejón de La Loma, tel. 809/454-3072, 9am-5pm daily, US$1.10) greets visitors with a beautiful freshwater lagoon by the entrance, a popular swimming spot for locals on the weekends.

Over 100 families once inhabited El Choco, until the government decided to turn it into a national park and relocated many. Today there are only a handful of inhabited homes that remain within the park, closer to the entrance, and they offer insight into traditional Dominican living. Hiking through El Choco takes you past various fruit trees, including cacao and coffee, medicinal plants, birds, and tropical jungle foliage. Along the way are two water caves—known as **Las Cuevas de Cabarete**—entered by means of ladders and wooden steps and home to incredible stalactite formations. These are said to be the deepest water caves on the entire island of Hispaniola, and certified cave divers can explore them. The entire park feels like one big jungle, virtually untouched and waiting to be discovered.

The easier, main entrance to the park is close to town. Get there by taking the Callejón de la Loma down from La Roma Restaurant and continuing all the way to the end; it's about a 20- to 25-minute walk from the center of Cabarete. I recommend you visit the park with **Iguana Mama** (www.iguanamama.com) for a more informative 2.5-hour hike (US$35 pp, US$25 children). If you head there solo, ask for one of the bilingual local guides

# Cabarete

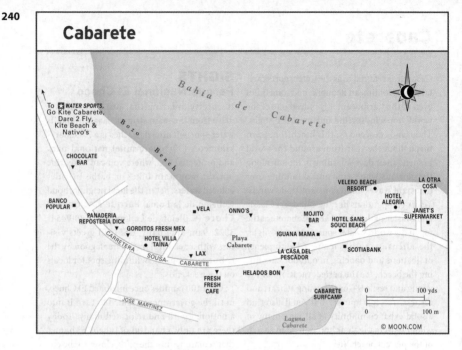

at the entrance of the park when you pay your entrance fee—**Levi Martinez** (tel. 809/972-1162) is a good one.

Zipline and animal lovers will appreciate **Monkey Jungle and Zip Line Adventures** (Carretera El Choco, tel. 809/649-4555, www.monkeyjungledr.com, 9am-4pm daily, US$50 zipline only or US$70 combo, cash only, with own transport, or US$90 Runners Adventures excursion). This nature sanctuary is tucked 9 kilometers (6 miles) into the lush forest of El Choco. The 1.1-square-kilometer (280-acre) farm is also home to a 1,372-meter (4,500-foot) certified zipline with seven stations, a five-acre botanical garden, and 45 squirrel monkeys you'll get to feed and watch crawl over you. All profits from visits go directly to an on-site medical and dental clinic for locals, where health care teams have volunteered since 2009 and treated over 21,000 patients.

## BEACHES

There are three main beaches in the Cabarete area, each with its own atmosphere. **Playa Cabarete,** on the eastern end and facing the Cabarete bay, is the social beach, with a fun row of bars, restaurants, and water sports shacks. It's popular for windsurfing, but there's plenty of space to swim and relax as well. It's wide, allowing for plenty of lounge-type setups. You won't see any kiting on this main portion of Cabarete Beach, for the safety of all swimmers, particularly kids. At night, it's even prettier with colorful lights and island ambience as folks come out to eat and dance in flip-flops.

On the eastern edge of the beach, about 15 steps from the heart of the stretch, you'll begin to spot kitesurfing school after kitesurfing school, and plenty of kites resting on the beach or up in the air—this is where beginners take their lessons. This beginners' area is known as **Bozo Beach.** It can get supercrowded so

**1:** Parque Nacional El Choco; **2:** beachfront restaurant at Playa Cabarete; **3:** kitesurfing in Playa Cabarete

watch your feet (and sometimes your head) as you walk along the stretch.

Continue walking west and you'll hit **Kite Beach**—with more kitesurfers, although fewer beginners. The waves are stronger and this isn't really a swimming beach like Cabarete. The shoreline has also eroded quite a bit, so you may end up wading through water in some parts when walking from the Cabarete end. There are a couple of nice bars out this way, along with more small hotels and resorts.

**Playa Encuentro** is the farthest from Cabarete town on the western end. It's the surfer's beach—one of the best in the country for its water and wind conditions. It was at the center of controversy in 2018, when authorities blocked the public access road leading to the beach and forcibly removed all of the surf schools' shacks on the site, evicting them as a result of it now being private property. As of September 2018, the court in Puerto Plata ruled that vehicular access to the beach must remain open, and that use of the beachfront is allowed up to the 60 meters allowed by law. While no longer having shacks on-site, surf schools do bring their clients here regularly; call ahead to arrange this. The beach is rocky—you can't enter the water without water shoes—and not for relaxed swims.

## SPORTS AND RECREATION

**TOP** EXPERIENCE

### ★ Water Sports
#### KITESURFING

If you're heading to Cabarete specifically to kitesurf by day (and party by night), you'll find excellent schools lining the shore with multilingual instructors and often on-site hotels offering packages. Start with **Go Kite Cabarete** (Extreme Hotels, Kite Beach, tel. 829/644-8354, www.gokitecabarete.com, 9am-6pm, US$550/7 hours), locally owned and operated by native Richard Diaz. The school gets rave reviews for its ideal location on the premises of an adventure hotel and with plenty of space for beginners to learn off its beach. Another solid pick on Kite Beach for a laid-back lesson away from the crowds is **Dare 2 Fly Cabarete** (Agualina Resort, tel. 809/571-0805, www.daretofly.com, 9am-6pm, US$520/9 hours), one of the first kiteboarding schools in the area.

surf shacks at Playa Encuentro

## WINDSURFING

**Vela Windsurf Resorts** (beachfront, tel. 809/571-0805, www.velacabarete.com, 9am-6pm daily, US$45/hour private or US$140/6-hour group lesson) is the popular choice for windsurfing classes. It's right on Cabarete Beach, tucked amid all the lounges and restaurants where you can come and go as you please.

## SURFING

**Playa Encuentro** is the place to be for surfing. The schools now operate independently and don't maintain shacks on the beach any longer (as it's now private property), but at of publication time they are allowed to bring their clients here for surfing classes and have continued to do so. Call the surf schools ahead of time to schedule your sessions.

## Fishing

**Captain Freddy** (tel. 809/613-4177, www.dominicanfisherman.com, US$25-125) offers reef trolling along the reefs of Sosúa, Cabarete, and Sabaneta, as well as deep-sea fishing—think mahi-mahi and marlin—shore fishing, and family trips for freshwater fishing in remoter villages.

## Diving and Snorkeling

**Dive Cabarete** (Calle Principal, tel. 809/915-9135, www.divecabarete.com, 10am-6pm Mon.-Sat., US$100/2-tank dive) offers PADI scuba lessons (US$456 Open Water) as well as dive excursions, the majority of which are off the coast of Sosúa. There's also cave diving possibilities at El Dudú Blue Lagoon in Río San Juan for the experienced. Two-hour snorkeling trips (US$35 pp) take you to Sosúa Bay, where you can see a variety of Caribbean critters.

## Stand-Up Paddleboarding

**Kayak River Adventures** (Calle Principal, Cabarete, tel. 829/305-6883, www.kayakriveradventures.com, US$59-89) takes you on guided SUP tours down Cabarete's Jamao and Yásica Rivers, for a half or full day. Beginners are welcome, as are children eight years old and up. Dominican outfitter **Jamao Eco Tours** (tel. 809/743-5523, jamaoecotours@gmail.com) also offers kayaking and hiking along the gorgeous Jamao River.

A handful of kitesurfing and windsurfing schools on Cabarete Beach also rent out SUP boards. In town, try **Vela** (Calle Principal, tel. 809/571-0805, www.velacabarete.com, 9am-6pm daily, US$20/hour or US45/half day).

## Yoga

Yoga classes abound in Cabarete. Find weekly 90-minute sessions on Encuentro Beach at **Natura Cabana** (Paseo del Sol 5, Perla Marina, tel. 809/571-1507, info@naturacabana.com, US$10, no reservations required); contact them for the latest schedule. Closer to town, at Kite Beach, **Rogue Fitness Yoga Loft** (Extreme Hotel, tel. 809/571-0330, http://yogacabarete.com/schedule, US$15) offers beachfront sessions.

## Canyoning, Waterfall Rappelling, and Caving

**Iguana Mama** (Calle Principal, tel. 809/654-2325, www.iguanamama.com, 7:45am-3:30pm Mon. and Fri., US$80-159) is the DR's top adventure company and the longest-running one on the North Coast. You can't go wrong with any of their adrenaline-inducing activities and friendly guides. Try the full-day **Big Bastard** adventure, where you'll test your endurance canyoneering in a stunning river valley, with rappels of up to 160 feet and jumps of up to 60 feet. You'll likely be the only ones on-site. Other waterfall trips head to 27 Charcos de Damajagua, the Magic Mushroom, and Ciguapa Falls. Iguana Mama also offers hiking trips to Parque Nacional El Choco in Cabarete, where you can spelunk in two water caves.

The smaller eco-adventure company **Kayak River Adventures** (Calle Principal, tel. 829/305-6883, www.kayakriveradventures.com, US$89-129) also takes you hiking and canyoning to the Magic

# Kitesurfing Schools

The hottest and fastest-growing water sport in the Caribbean is kitesurfing. The sport first made its appearance in Cabarete in the 1990s, introduced by a couple of adventurous Frenchmen, and it soon captured attention as the popularity of windsurfing slowly declined. Less wind is needed to kitesurf than to windsurf, which provided more days of the year to practice. With perfect wave conditions, and a growing number of IKO-certified schools, this northern piece of the DR has established its dominant position in the kiting world.

Cabarete's sought-after kitesurfing schools line the beachfront from Cabarete town to neighboring Kite Beach. What school you choose to kitesurf with, as a beginner in particular, will depend on your language ability—there are schools catering to the French-, or German-, or English-speaking. It isn't so much a question of expertise, since all schools are IKO certified, as it is a matter of comfort and fit for the student. Here are recommended schools that will offer you a great jump-start into this adrenaline sport, with a focus on both safety and fun.

Kitesurfing schools abound on the western end of Playa Cabarete.

Dominican-owned and operated **Go Kite Cabarete** (Extreme Hotels, Kite Beach, tel. 829/644-8354, www.gokitecabarete.com, 9am-6pm daily, US$550/7 hours) is one of the best on the stretch. It specializes in beginners and has experienced Dominican instructors, including the popular Richard Diaz. The school has a laid-back atmosphere and is ideally located on an all-adventure hotel's premises—with on-site gym facilities, a yoga studio, and even a circus school. There's plenty of space for everyone's equipment on the beachfront, where training begins. Advanced kiteboarding lessons are also offered.

A hip and lively female pro kiteboarder-owned school, **Laurel Eastman Kiteboarding** (tel. 809/571-0564, www.laureleastman.com, 9am-6pm daily, US$71/hour or US$630/10 hours) is where the cool kids hang out—including from the neighboring Millenium Resort. The atmosphere is fun throughout the day, with music and kitesurfers going to and from the beach. Beginners are welcome, and you're only charged for the minutes actually spent learning from your coach. Kiteboarding for kids is offered (over age 8) as well as advanced lessons.

From beginners to pros, **KiteClub Cabarete** (tel. 809/571-9748, www.kiteclubcabarete, 11am-6pm daily, US$240/3 hours) has a solid, long-running reputation thanks to owner Jon Dodds, who is an IKO examiner. Aside from the usual beginner lessons, the school offers two-way radio helmets, whereby students stay in contact with their instructor while kitesurfing. The vibe is social and there's an excellent on-site cafeteria.

The friendly, multilingual instructors and staff at **Dare 2 Fly Cabarete** (Agualina Resort, tel. 809/571-0805, www.dare2fly.com, 9am-6pm daily, US$190/3 hours) teach on a beautiful stretch of Kite Beach, beside the popular VacaBar.

Mushroom or Ciguapa Falls. Also on tap is caving at one of their "off-the-beaten-track" caves called La Cueva, which requires four rappels before you even start spelunking in chambers ranging from 10 to 50 meters (32 to 165 feet) in height. Once you reach the cave floor, the caving continues: you will make your way through the cavern for two hours, give or take, guided only by your headlamp and your experienced guides. The cave is huge! The ceiling of the cave is between 10 and 50 meters high (33-164 feet).

## Kayaking

You'll experience the real DR by kayaking or SUPing downstream 10 kilometers (6 miles) along jungle and farmland with **Kayak River Adventures** (tel. 829/305-6883, www.kayakriveradventures.com, US$59-89). It's a half-day excursion on the Jamao and Yasica Rivers, at the foothill of the Cordillera Septentrional. A great trip for families—you'll learn about a variety of Dominican flora and fauna, including birds, on this ecotour. Impromptu stops allow for dipping into fresh river water, of course. There's also a full-day version.

Alternatively, get it touch with **Jamao Eco Tours** (Carretera Duarte Km 1, Jamao Norte, www.jamaoecotours.com, US$28 pp), a locally run initiative with Dominican guides who take groups kayaking down the Jamao River and offer reasonable prices, as well as a true Dominican ambience. They also offer more adrenaline-packed adventures like canyoning at Cola de Pato (US$32), jumping down a series of cascades.

You can also rent single or double kayaks from **Vela Windsurf Resorts** (beachfront, tel. 809/571-0805, www.velacabarete.com, 9am-6pm daily, US$10-15/hour) and go exploring on your own; just beware of the busier kitesurfing end.

## Zip-Lining

The closest zipline is within El Choco at the 1.1-square-kilometer (280-acre) **Monkey Jungle and Zip Line Adventures** (9 km up Carretera El Choco, tel. 829/649-4555, ww.monkeyungledr.com, 9am-4pm daily, US$50 zipline, cash only). There are seven stations and a certified 1,372-meter-high (4,500-foot) zipline. If you choose to continue the adventure, on-site are a botanical garden where squirrel monkeys reside and a cave. All profits go to charity. You can venture here in your own car, or you can sign up with **Runners Adventures** (tel. 809/320-1061, www.runnersadventures.com) for US$35 more, which usually includes all these attractions.

## Horseback Riding

Go horseback riding in the Dominican countryside with **Bávaro Runners** (tel. 809/320-1061, www.bavarorunners.com, US$120), out of nearby Puerto Plata. They offer a "triple adventure day" with waterfalls, horses, and zip-lining.

## Cultural Tours

**Cabarete Coffee Company** (Bahia de Arena, between Kite Beach and town, tel. 809/571-0919, www.cabaretecoffee.com, 8:30am-2pm every Tues. and Thurs., US$75) offers tours of an organic cacao farm, as well as a coffee plantation—two of the DR's major exports.

## Spa

**N Day Spa** (Plaza El Patio, Calle Principal, across from Panadería Repostería Dick and across from Friends, tel. 809/905-6510, www.cabaretespa.com, 9am-6pm Mon.-Sat., US$45-95), short for Naomie Day Spa, is in the center of town, but its facility is tucked away from the traffic noise on the main street. This full-service spa is small but cozy, offering two treatment rooms, with options for a couples massage. The staff here is friendly and bilingual.

**Attabeyra Spa** (Natura Cabana, Paseo del Sol 5, Perla Marina, tel. 809/571-1507, info@naturacabana.com, 10am-6pm daily, US$30-80) is set amid the quiet oasis of a boutique resort on Encuentro Beach. Treatments range from after-sun wraps and Turkish baths to chocolate exfoliations and various kinds of massage, including hot stone and reflexology. Mani-pedis and waxing services are also offered.

# ENTERTAINMENT AND EVENTS

## Nightlife

Cabarete is the place to be for all-night partying and boozing like you're forever young, if that's your fancy. Cover-free lounges, bars, and discos line the beach, which becomes one big outdoor *va-et-vient* of partygoers from tourists to local out-of-towners, shuffling in the sand as they hop around their favorite venues. Others lounge by the water with treats bought at the liquor store. Whether you prefer a game of pool or an all-out rave, you'll find your fun in Cabarete. Prostitution isn't as prevalent or as in your face as it is in Sosúa, and the scene is international. Here are a few spots to check out.

**Mojito Bar** (Cabarete beachfront, tel. 809/571-9327, www.mojitobar-cabarete.com, 11am-11pm Wed.-Mon.) is a great pick to start the night off with some freshly made mojitos on the beach. It's hard to beat this affordable, lively spot. There are daily happy hours 4pm-8pm with two-for-one mojitos, Cuba libres, margaritas, piña coladas, and more, as well as a drink special every day of the week. Green Friday is popular, with local bands performing on a small stage inside the open-air restaurant. Nearby, **voyvoy!** (Cabarete beachfront, tel. 809/571-0805, www.voyvoycabarete, 9am-2am daily) has friendly bartenders and a cozy space serving excellent happy hour specials, starting at US$2.25 a cocktail.

**Havana Club** (Cabarete beachfront, tel. 809/882-3144, 9pm-2am daily) is a bit of a dive, with no air-conditioning or fans, but the DJ spins excellent Latin sounds and drinks are cheap. If you're willing to sweat it out, it's not a bad spot. Just don't expect a stellar crowd.

The open-air **Lax Ojo** (beachfront Cabarete, tel. 829/745-8811, www.laxojo.com, 10pm-2am Sun.-Wed., later close Thurs.-Sat.) is the largest and most packed nightclub on the strip, featuring two large floors where DJs spin a variety of music. Thursdays are Latin night and attract locals from neighboring Puerto Plata. It can get unbearably packed on the weekends, especially on the ground floor. **Onno's** (beachfront, tel. 809/571-0461, www.onnosbar.com, 9am-3am daily) is another favored dance spot, especially among the locals; its smaller space gives it more of a lounge feel. Music ranges from R&B to *dembow* and merengue. Thursday is ladies' night, with half-price drinks. You can also hop over to **Bambú Bar** (beachfront, tel.

809/982-4549, 10pm-2am daily) for more dancing.

**Arriba Bar** (Av. Principal, tel. 809/571-9592, noon-2am daily) is a great chill-out spot where you can play pool with locals and expats, throw back some drinks, and listen to a DJ spinning music, at times with videos on screen. When it isn't busy you can find enough space to dance on the floor beside the bar. It's a place to wind down after the madness of Cabarete Beach across the street.

**Voodoo Lounge** (entrance of Callejón de La Loma, tel. 809/874-0615, 5pm-midnight Wed.-Sun.) is a casual, unpretentious local spot to mingle with Dominicans and expats away from the tourist club strip on the beach. Wednesdays are popular for open mic, and there are occasional live music nights on Saturday—keep an eye out on social media pages.

## Festivals and Cultural Events

Every January around the middle of the month, over 30 master sailors from both the DR and abroad gather to compete at the **Caribbean Laser Midwinter Regatta,** an ISAF grade 3 event consisting of nine races and organized by the Laser Training Center in Cabarete. Entering its 17th edition as of 2019, the race takes place a week prior to the Miami Olympic Regatta, in which many also participate. Cabarete has also hosted the **World Cup of the Windsurfing Association** for several years.

**Cabarete Kite Festival** (www.cabaretekitefestival.com) is in full swing in July, taking place in front of Millenium Resort and the Laurel Eastman Kiteboarding School. It's a great time to see the DR's top kitesurfers competing alongside big international names from as far as Brazil and Europe.

One of the most popular annual events in all the Dominican Republic is the **Dominican Republic Jazz Festival** (www.drjazzfestival. com) held the first week of November, with performances from both Dominican and international jazz artists taking place in Puerto Plata, Sosúa, and Cabarete. It's a great time to be on the North Coast and enjoy the mix of both Dominican and international vibes that this area represents so well.

The annual **Master of the Ocean** competition (tel. 809/856-4798, www.masteroftheocean.com) launched in 2003 on Playa Encuentro and brought even more international attention to the North Coast of the Dominican Republic. The brainchild of Marcus Bohm, owner of 321 TakeOff surfing school, it had to pause for a year due to Encuentro's property status, but was back in full swing in Cabarete in February 2019. Teams come from around the world as well as across the DR to compete for the title by mastering four water sports: windsurfing, surfing, stand-up paddleboarding, and kiteboarding. It's a fun time to be in Cabarete.

## SHOPPING

**Kana Rapai Art Studio** (Calle Principal, across from Onno's, tel. 809/852-0757, www.kanarapai.com) is very Cabarete in its original, handmade gifts made out of recycled material. You'll find casual jewelry, purses, and magnets, among other items. A few steps away, across the street, is the more traditional **Taina Joyería Shop** (Calle Principal, tel. 829/678-3595, 10am-7pm daily), a small boutique with locally made wood carvings, larimar and other handmade jewelry, Taíno and Haitian art—including statues of Taíno gods—and run-of-the-mill souvenirs like mugs. Get your cigars at **D'Angel Cigar Lounge** (Calle Principal, facing Scotiabank, tel. 809/571-9761, angelcigarlounge@hotmail.com, 9am-5pm Mon.-Sat.), where you'll find a humidor and a couple of chairs where you can cool off while enjoying your purchase.

For groceries, you'll find all your need to stock your fridge at **Janet's Supermarket** (Calle Principal, tel. 809/571-9774, www.janetssupermarket.com, 8am-8pm Mon.-Sat., 8:30am-1pm Sun.) in Cabarete town, or closer to Kite Beach there's the smaller, local **Supermercado La Rosa** (tel. 809/571-0361, 8am-10pm daily).

## FOOD
### Cafés

Breakfast on the beach never looked so good as at the open-air, casual beachfront **voyvoy!** (next to Vela Windsurfing School, tel. 809/571-0805, www.voyvoycabarete, 9am-2am daily, US$1.50-4), facing Cabarete's beautiful stretch with crowds walking past and windsurfers dotting the sea. The menu ranges from omelets to coconut pancakes to fresh smoothies. Of course there's coffee as well. Bury your toes in the sand and enjoy the moment.

For a Brooklyn-type spot, head to **Vagamundo Coffee & Waffles** (5700 Calle Principal, across from Supermercado La Rosa, tel. 809/739-3081, www.vagamundocoffee.com, 7am-5pm Mon.-Sat., 9am-3pm Sun., from US$2.50-7.50). This coffee shop is affiliated with a nonprofit organization that works with street kids from the DR and from the Cabarete area in particular; their graduates work as staff here. Serving up gourmet coffee—including beans from Ethiopia—the menu consists of salty or sweet waffles, topped with a world of different ingredients, including smoked ham, spinach, bacon, and jalapeno with maple syrup. The outdoor patio offers table or lounge-type seating. The only thing missing is a sea view.

On the main drag, a traditional breakfast can be had at **Panadería Repostería Dick** (Calle Principal 31, tel. 809/571-0612, panarolfdick@yahoo.com, 6:30am-5pm daily, US$2-10), be it English, French, or Dominican. This popular casual café has a sidewalk terrace on the main drag. The service and atmosphere are authentically Cabarete.

The **Belgium Bakery** (Plaza Popular, next to Banco Popular, tel. 829/571-8198, US$3-10) boasts a shaded outdoor terrace blessed with the delicious aroma of freshly baked pastries, quiches, cakes, and other artisan desserts, to be washed down with coffee or a Belgian beer. The glass display alone is enough to make you grab a seat. Aside from breakfasts, there's a daily coffee and dessert special for under

US$4 (RD$150) and two-for-one happy hour hamburgers noon-2pm.

**Cabarete Coffee Company** (Bahia de Arena, between Kite Beach and town, tel. 809/571-0919, www.cabaretecoffee.com, 7am-3pm daily, US$3-10) organic coffee is grown in the mountainous Madre de las Aguas region, considered to be the most important watershed on all of Hispaniola. Try the dark roast "Surfer's Blend" to take home, or stay in and enjoy a healthy breakfast or lunch with your java or smoothie. Choices range from sandwiches to bagels to salads. **Chocolate Bar** (across from Banco Popular, Calle Principal, tel. 809/603-8354, chocolatebardr@gmail. com, 8am-6pm Mon.-Sat., 8am-2pm Sun., US$2-10) is good whether you need a cacao fix or healthy fruit juices and smoothies.

## Dominican

**Casa Mami** (Carretera Principal, next to police station, Kite Beach, tel. 809/618-6987, casamamicabarete@gmail.com, 9am-10pm daily, US$3) serves daily Dominican dishes at local prices, including fish fillets, barbecue chicken, salad, and rice and beans.

★ **Nativo's Café** (Calle Principal, across from Ocean Dream Plaza, tel. 809/571-0126, noon-10pm daily, except Tues., US$4-10) sits on Cabarete's main strip. It's a cozy, friendly, and reasonably priced Dominican sit-down restaurant serving daily luch plates, as well as a menu with classic Dominican dishes, such as mofongo, sancocho, goat, and fried fish, among other picks.

**La Parilla Luis** (across from Ocean Dream Plaza, Callejón de La Loma entrance, tel. 809/857-5527, 5pm-10pm Fri.-Wed., closed Thurs., US$4-8), affectionately known as the Chicken Shack, doesn't disappoint. It serves up one of the cheapest meals and tastiest grilled barbecue chicken in town, with yucca, rice, plantains, or sautéed veggies for just over US$2.

**La Casita de Papi** (Cabarete beach-front, tel. 809/986-3750, noon-10pm Tues.-Sun, US$7-20) is one of the busiest dining spots on the beach, and for good reason. Its signature seafood dishes, Shrimp a la Papi and Langostino a la Papi, are finger-licking good, as are the desserts—try the banana flambé, lit at your table. There's a cozy interior with a couple of white linen-covered wooden tables, facing an open kitchen, but the best setting is under the blue sky or stars along the white-sand beach.

Reached by boat, ★ **Wilson's La Boca Restaurant** (Camino del Sol, tel. 809/571-9594 or 809/667-1960, noon-3pm daily, US$7, boat ride provided) offers fresh fish Dominican-style with an ambience to match. Hop in a taxi from Cabarete town (US$10 one-way) and head to the south side of the beach, about 4 kilometers (2.5 miles) away, at the mouth of the Yásica de Sabaneta River. There, you will hop in a small motorboat to reach the rustic, open-air shack of a restaurant. In a town that sometimes feels like it has more tourists than locals, it's a nice escape and reminder of the real DR. Options for lunch are the catch of the day—lobster when in season, mahi-mahi, or crab—with typical sides of rice and beans, salad, and plantains.

## International

On the road between Cabarete and Sosúa, stop by **Parada Típico El Choco** (across from Ocean Village, Carretera Sosúa-Cabarete, tel. 809/854-5562 or 809/571-3534, paradaelchoco@diconti.com, 8am-11:30pm daily, US$5-10) is a solid pick for meals any time of day and a popular expat haunt. Try the omelets for breakfast, or the steaks, barbecue, or burgers at lunch or dinner. Portions are huge, and the atmosphere is convivial under a cozy thatched roof.

You could quickly become a regular at the lagoon-facing casual restaurant inside **Ali's Surf Camp** (Calle Bahia 11, ProCab, tel. 829/548-6655, www.cabaretesurfcamp.com, 7:30am-9:30pm daily, US$4-10). Tucked in the back of the ProCab expat neighborhood an easy walk from town, the romantic candlelit tables on the thatch-roofed wooden deck are matched with a flavorful menu. You'll find it written on small chalkboards pinned around the dining area. Juicy grilled steaks or *parillada*, seafood, and finger-licking side dishes (the spiced, sautéed potatoes and rice are some of the best I've had in Puerto Plata) will keep you returning, as will the cocktails. Bring mosquito repellent.

★ **Mojito Bar** (Cabarete beachfront, tel. 809/571-9327, www.mojitobar-cabarete.com, 11am-11pm Wed.-Mon., US$3-10) has the best drink specials (two for one at happy hour) and the most affordable sandwich deal in town with its daily "combo" special: grab a mojito and a sandwich for under US$5. There's interior seating but the beachfront is delightful, with a perfect view of windsurfers on the water.

With a cozy beachfront setup of sofas and chairs, **Onno's** (beachfront, tel. 809/571-0461, www.onnosbar.com, 9am-3am daily, US$5-7) is a classic, with its burgers, sandwiches, pizza, and seafood entrées. The food is decent but the local atmosphere is great. Happy hours last 5pm-9pm, with mojitos for US$2.

For a taste of Mexico on the go, the local favorite ★ **Gordito's Fresh Mex** (Plaza Ocean Dream Plaza, tel. 809/571-0128, www.gorditosfreshmex.com, 11:30am-8:30pm Mon.-Sat., US$3-10) doesn't disappoint, serving up scrumptious tacos—the fish ones are especially delicious—burritos with veggie options, rice bowls, and even margaritas.

For tasty Italian-style pizza or pasta, **Pomodoro** (Cabarete Beach, tel. 809/571-0085, pomodoropizzacabarete@gmail.com, 4pm-11pm Wed.-Mon., 11:30am-11:30pm Sat.-Sun., US$10-15) is the long-standing, consistent pick. Add some wine and gelato to your order. They also deliver.

Want an unforgettable dinner? Head to ★ **La Otra Cosa** (La Punta de Cabarete, tel. 809/571-0607, www.otracosarestaurant.com, 6:30pm-10pm daily, US$10-35), especially at sunset. Located on a scenic spot in La Punta just past Velero Beach Resort, you'll walk past the main entrance and suddenly come upon a stunning open-air, thatched-roof multilevel dining room with panoramic views of the Atlantic below. As if the scenery isn't

romantic enough, the menu is a delight. Try the tuna tartare tempered by mango chutney, or the seared tuna in a ginger and flambé rum sauce. It's a real treat to dine here to the sound of world music beats.

**Miro's** (Cabarete beachfront, tel. 809/571-9345, mirobeach@hotmail.com, 11am-11:30pm Tues.-Sun., US$10-30), though slightly pricey, is a standout amid restaurants serving similar fare for its sophisticated ambience on the beach and its Mediterranean and seafood menu including paella, tuna tartare, and sushi.

On the street side, the small but übermodern **Yalla** (next to Panadería Dick, Calle Principal, tel. 809/571-9357, noon-11pm Thurs.-Tues., US$7.65-12) impresses with its creative tapas and sandwiches. Try the pineapple pork, diced chorizo, manchego cheese croquettes, or chicken skewers, among other tapas options. The chocolate churros are a must for dessert.

Go for steaks and seafood at the beachfront **Chez Arsenio** (Hideaway Beach Resort, tel. 809/571-9948, lagan.anne@gmail.com, 11am-10pm Mon.-Fri., 9am-10pm Sat.-Sun., US$5-20), even if the slow service might taint your experience on a busy night. Options also include curries and pastas. Set under a thatched *palapa* flanked by the beautiful and breezy Encuentro Beach and the resort swimming pool, it's a good choice for a romantic meal al fresco, away from Cabarete's busy beachfront.

## Vegan and Vegetarian

Vegans and even non-vegans will enjoy ★ **Fresh Fresh Café** (Calle Principal, tel. 809/571-0283, freshfreshcabarete@gmail.com, 8am-9pm daily, US$3-10). The most popular items, savored on the covered terrace or indoors with air-conditioning, are their breakfast bagels and their healthy detox smoothies and salads. You'll also find veggie burgers and wraps. The meat eaters can enjoy the fish bowls or chicken sandwiches, or veggie curries, yucca fries, and grilled fish for dinner. Don't miss sampling the coconut brownies. There's also a Sosúa location.

On the Kite Beach end, the seafront **Vitamin D Cafe** (at Agualina Kite Resort, tel. 829/204-4360, US$2-7.55) maintains a strictly healthy menu, entirely gluten-free, serving "raw, vegan, and vegetarian plates," from muesli bowls to veggie omelette to salads to lentil bowls. Note that everything is cooked with no salt, no sugar, and no hot oil. It's not for everyone (nor this author), but that's the point. There's a single burger-and-fries option for the meat eaters, however, cooked with pink salt. Smoothies, coffee, sodas, and green juices are available.

## ACCOMMODATIONS
### Under US$50

**Casa Blanca Hotel** (Calle Principal, tel. 809/571-0934, www.casablancacabarete. com, US$25-55) offers a range of rooms, albeit dated, ranging from single-bed hostel types to larger, self-catering apartments. There's a small pool on the grounds and a restaurant for guests.

The budget **Hotel Alegría** (tel. 809/571-0455, www.hotel-alegria.com, US$40, air-conditioning additional) has an ideal location on the eastern edge of Cabarete beach, steps from Janet's Supermarket and a stone's throw from the sand and its activities, yet away from the mayhem. Standard rooms are basic, with wireless Internet, fans, and small TVs, but if you're just looking for a safe and relatively clean roof over your head, they'll suffice. Those who wish can upgrade to oceanview rooms, with optional air-conditioning for an extra fee. There's a restaurant on-site that is good for breakfast, although you're so close to the beach you might as well venture out.

Get a feel for a local neighborhood and stay at **Casa Carmen** (Callejón de La Loma, tel. 809/879-2415, h.perez@hotmail.com, US$25). This hostel-style accommodation is ideal for the unfussy, light traveler who wants to immerse. Rooms are basic, with fans and a communal kitchen. You'll be around plenty of local shops, fruit markets, and a mixed Dominican and expat population. The main Cabarete Beach is a 10-minute walk away.

**Kite Beach Hotel** (Carretera Sosúa-Cabarete, tel. 809/571-0878, www. kitebeachhotel.com, $50-160, includes breakfast) offers a range of rooms to fit every budget, from basic pads with no air-conditioning to superior rooms and deluxe apartments. A beach-facing pool and restaurant complete the setting. You'll be a bit isolated from the town's social corner, but it's an easy shared taxi hop away.

### US$50-100

**Cabarete Palm Beach Condos** (beachfront Cabarete, tel. 809/571-0758, www. cabaretecondos.com, US$85-198) offer a range of beachfront apartments, studios, and penthouses with delightful summer furniture, oceanfront patios, full kitchen facilities, and an on-site swimming pool. To top it off, you're a stone's throw from all of Cabarete's amenities from restaurants to kitesurfing schools, yet set back enough from the beach to get some tranquility. It's a great spot for families and groups.

★ **Hotel Villa Taina** (Playa Cabarete, tel. 809/571-0722, www.villataina.com, US$97-163, includes breakfast) is a solid pick for families, with 57 rooms facing Cabarete Beach, conveniently close to restaurants and activities on the main drag, as well as on the beachside. Options range from standard to partial oceanfront suites, all of which are tastefully decorated in tropical colors–the 3rd-floor king suites have gorgeous views of kitesurfers and windsurfers in the distance. Expect in-room fridges, TVs, air-conditioning, and free wireless Internet. Other amenities are Serenade Restaurant—with a popular all-you-can-eat Mongolian barbecue dinner on Wednesdays for US$15—a swimming pool, wind sports school, and soon a full-service spa. Yoga, a gym, and volleyball are offered as activities.

**Extreme Hotel** (Kite Beach, tel. 809/571-0330, www.extremehotels.com, US$59) is everything its name suggests: a nontraditional eco-friendly (solar-powered) escape where you'll find an active vacationer's playground, including kitesurfing lessons, an on-site gym with regular Zumba and yoga classes, and the Kaiceitos Circus, where you can learn how to swing from a trapeze like a pro. Rooms are clean and basic, yet just right for a fun, active beachside vacation. With a solid restaurant on-site serving Dominican and Spanish specialties, Extreme Hotel is its very own getaway.

On the beginning edge of Playa Encuentro is **Natura Cabana Boutique Hotel & Spa** (Paseo del Sol 5, tel. 809/571-1507, www. naturacabana.com, US$90, breakfast included), popular for its *palapa* bungalows—doubles and triples are available—with kitchenettes and beachfront setting, as well as its on-site yoga classes. The rooms are fan-only (an eco-friendly measure, although there is 24-hour generator power), with full baths, a couple of water bottles a day, and wireless Internet. There is a breakfast *palapa*, as well as a separate, pricey gourmet restaurant; unless you're cooking in your apartment or take a taxi to town, you will have to dine here, as the resort is remote. Note that the ocean is rough and rocky so you can't swim, but you can still relax beachside and read a good book in the breeze or take a dip in the small swimming pool. Don't walk the deserted beachfront trail to the surf school area by yourself or even as a pair—opt for a quick taxi or bike ride on the roadside instead.

## Over US$100

★ **Velero Beach Resort** (Calle La Punta, tel. 501/571-9727, www.velerobeach.com, US$135) is my favorite in Cabarete—a gorgeous, immaculately clean boutique-size resort close enough to the action but set apart from the madding crowd. The infinity swimming pool is the main draw, with all the rooms' balconies facing it and the Atlantic. The view from the on-site restaurant is equally stunning. Rooms are cozy and include all the comforts, from air-conditioning to flat-screen TVs, without being over the top.

**Ultra Violeta Boutique Residences** (next to Cabarete Coffee Company, tel.

829/931-5555, http://ultravioletacabarete.com, from US$165) takes the boutique resort up a notch. Tucked on a quiet corner of Kite Beach, this white-and-purple escape has 21 one- to three-bedroom seafront apartments facing an infinity pool and looking out over the beach. No amenities are spared, from the gourmet kitchens to music equipment, outdoor showers, and Jacuzzi tubs.

**Millenium Resort & Spa** (tel. 809/571-0407, www.millenniumcabarete.com, US$120-200) is the favorite hideout of kitesurfers, ideally located next to Laurel Eastman Kiteboarding School and facing some of the best waves on the strip. Junior, ocean, and one-bedroom suites are all-white, ultramodern, and outfitted with full kitchens, flat screen TVs, Wi-Fi access, and balconies, as well as spacious baths. There's a pricey beachfront restaurant on-site and a swimming pool with weekly workout activities.

# INFORMATION AND SERVICES

## Health and Emergencies

**The tourist police, POLITUR** (Gaspar Hernandez, tel. 809/571-0713), has a presence in town, but the office itself is actually outside of town. To reach the police, you can call 809/571-0810 or simply dial 911.

In town, **Servi Med Cabarete** (tel. 809/571-0964, 24 hours) has various multilingual staff doctors. You can also contact **Centro Médico** (tel. 809/571-4696).

## Money

There's a branch of **Scotiabank** right in Cabarete town (Calle Principal, tel. 809/571-0292, 8:30am-4pm Mon.-Fri., 9am-1pm Sat.) with 24-hour ATMs. You'll also find a **Banco Popular** (Calle Principal, 809/571-0903, 9am-5pm Mon.-Fri., 9am-1pm Sat.).

## Laundry

If you've been on the road for a while and need clean clothes, head to **Family Laundry** (across from Janet's Supermarket, 8am-6pm Mon.-Sat., US$5.50/load).

## GETTING THERE AND AROUND

To get to Cabarete from Puerto Plata, you can take an airport taxi for US$35 (for 1-4 people, one-way) or you can hop in a *carrito* or shared cab for less than a dollar, and get an interesting cultural experience while you're at it.

Once there, getting around Cabarete and its various beaches is easy on foot, but there may be times when you'd rather take a break from long walks in the hot sun. When that happens, you have a few choices. The shared taxis go up and down the main drag and are easy to flag down anywhere. You can go between Cabarete and Kite Beach for 30 pesos (US$0.65), for instance. The cars usually read "Sosúa Río San Juan" top, but it's not always visible from a distance, so just keep a close eye on the road as they approach.

If you need to get from Cabarete to Sosúa or Puerto Plata, it's equally simple to catch a *carrito*. You'll have to switch in Sosúa to continue on to Cabarete, but the switch takes place immediately adjacent to the last stop in Sosúa, at a gas station across from the Texaco. Fares range between 45 and 50 pesos (US$0.98-1.09) for each leg, before dark.

If you'd rather pay a lot more to go by taxi to nearby towns or destinations farther afield, contact **Taxis Cabarete** (tel. 809/571-0767 or 809/571-0824), or the reliable Gabriel Polanco (tel. 809/602-6568), who might be willing to negotiate with you if you're a solo traveler. Rates range from 300 pesos (US$6.55) from Cabarete up the drag to Encuentro Beach to US$100 to Río San Juan.

# East of Cabarete

## RÍO SAN JUAN

About 100 kilometers (62 miles) east of Puerto Plata, or just an hour's drive east from Cabarete, Río San Juan is a stunning, refreshing little corner of the North Coast. A fishing town where nature is still splendid, Río San Juan has a Mediterranean-like rocky coastline, diamond-white beaches, and mangrove lagoons home to herons and vultures. Aside from having the most breathtaking daily sunsets, it's a place that has retained its Dominican authenticity with fishing as its main industry. You'll see more Dominicans out and about enjoying their beach, while others drive here on weekends for a peaceful family getaway. The electricity shortage is an issue here—power cuts take place almost daily from 11am to about 4pm—and there isn't a whole lot to do. But who needs indoor activities or organized tours when you're surrounded with natural sights to enjoy? Río San Juan's slow pace and natural beauty are likely to change soon. Several resorts are being furiously built along the coast. A seven-star Aman Resort opened at Playa Grande in December 2015.

My advice? Visit now and enjoy this gift of nature before the secret's out.

Getting around Río San Juan and finding your way around the small town is super easy, as most of the town, including its three beaches, is centered on a couple of main streets. The highway links Río San Juan to Playa Grande, Cabrera, and Laguna Dudú to the east. Calle Duarte is the main road in town, where restaurants, shops, and the Gri Gri Lagoon can be found.

### Sights
#### LAGUNA GRI GRI

A peaceful, small lagoon sitting between the heart of Río San Juan and the Atlantic Ocean, the **Laguna Gri Gri** flows through dense, mazelike rows of red mangrove trees. Turkey vultures soar above the gri gri trees during the day. The lagoon is brackish, made up of part saltwater and part fresh water.

Steps going down from the main street of Calle Duarte in town take you to the entrance of the lagoon. This is where locals hang out on benches and plenty of wooden motorboats

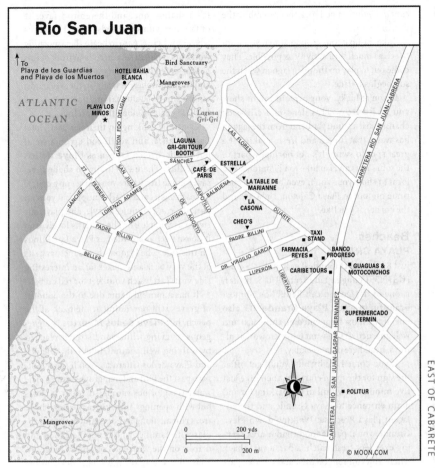

## Río San Juan

To Playa de los Guardias and Playa de los Muertos

ATLANTIC OCEAN

Bird Sanctuary

Mangroves

HOTEL BAHIA BLANCA

PLAYA LOS MINOS

Laguna Gri-Gri

GASTON FDO DELIGNE

LAGUNA GRI-GRI TOUR BOOTH

LAS FLORES

SANCHEZ

ESTRELLA

CAFÉ DE PARIS

LA TABLE DE MARIANNE

27 DE FEBRERO

SAN JUAN

BALBUENA

CAPOTILLO

16 DE AGOSTO

SANCHEZ

LORENZO ADAMES

MELLA

RUFINO

LA CASONA

CHEO'S

DUARTE

PADRE BILLINI

TAXI STAND

PADRE BILLINI

BELLER

DR. VIRGILIO GARCIA

FARMACIA REYES

BANCO PROGRESO

LUPERON

LIBERTAD

CARIBE TOURS

GUAGUAS & MOTOCONCHOS

CARRETERA RIO SAN JUAN-CABRERA

CARRETERA RIO SAN JUAN-GASPAR HERNANDEZ

SUPERMERCADO FERMIN

POLITUR

Mangroves

0    200 yds
0    200 m

© MOON.COM

park on the western side. Kids like splashing about in the water on the eastern corner where the fresh water is. The on-site office, **Sindicato de Boteros de la Laguna Gri Gri** (tel. 809/589-2277, 8:30am-5pm daily, US$18 for 1-3 persons or RD$800, US$26.60 for two or RD$1,200), is where you pay for the boat ride down the lagoon—a handful of captains are always on standby. The excursion will take you past the mangroves and along various scenic stops like the **Cueva de las Golondrinas,** a natural turquoise sandbank or *piscina natural,* and **Playa Caletón,** where you're free to stay until sunset if you choose. Snorkeling (US$40) and

fishing (US$75) can be added. Enjoying the view of the lagoon or bathing in it is free—it's fun to do as the local kids do and engage in backflip contests.

Although cruising down the river is a short 10-minute ride, the sight of the dense trees and vultures coupled with the hissing sound of white herons passing above calm waters is a mesmerizing experience. Soon enough, the river opens up onto the Atlantic Ocean, and the stunning cliff coastline and turquoise sea of Río San Juan. Don't miss spotting the white rock sculptures set on the cliffs, created by artist Persio Checo in honor of the DR's first Taíno inhabitants. There's also a natural *cara del indio*-shaped rock that resembles the face of a native.

Take the boat tour around 4pm if you want to see as much bird activity as possible. They come out to play on the open lagoon when the sun begins to fade.

If you're lucky, your captain might show you **El Pontón.** This dead-end cliff-side channel just around the bend from the lagoon has water that is cold and fresh, making it a great spot to swim. It's not normally part of the tour. You can also hike to El Pontón; ask a local to show you. You'll even be able to continue on foot to Playa Caletón, right around the corner, if you like.

## Beaches
### PLAYA GRANDE
Just 8 kilometers (5 miles) east and a 25-peso (US$0.55) *guagua* ride from Río San Juan is one of the Dominican Republic's 10 most beautiful beaches: **Playa Grande.** It's also one of the most frequented on this coast and well guarded. If you want fewer crowds, as always, head here on a weekday.

If you come here by bus, you'll get off at the sign for the main entrance, then hike just five minutes downhill to the parking lot and main entrance to Playa Grande and the adjacent Playa Preciosa. Walking down Playa Grande, you'll pass a food vendor area serving excellent fresh catch, a bar, a surf shack where you can rent boards, and a rocky part of the beach before you see its full grandeur: the wide, mile-long golden expanse stretching into the distance. The tides have created a thick and tall slope of sand before you step down and into the water. Entry is smoother on the eastern end of the beach. Chairs are about 100 pesos (US$2.18) each. The waves at Playa Grande are real—this beach is known for its swells and undertows—so be sure you're a good swimmer and don't venture too far from shore.

### OTHER BEACHES
**Playa Los Minos** is one of three beaches in town, and right beside Hotel Bahia Blanca.

It's a shallow one, and therefore a favorite of families with small kids, as well as adults who come here at 6am to begin their morning workouts. The sun sets directly in front of this beach—a red ball sinking into the horizon—and the atmosphere is lively on the weekends, with a small on-site bar and merengue and *bachata* echoing along the shoreline.

Continue walking on the road past Hotel Bahia Blanca, and you'll end up on a small but idyllic stretch known as **Playa de los Guardias.** There's virtually no shade here, save for one tree where you can set up a couple of beach chairs and a barbecue pit, but you can park the car, Dominican-style, and play your stereo as you please. The water is lovely, and it doesn't get as crowded as Playa Los Minos on this side. The lagoon's bird sanctuary sits at the very back and makes for an interesting side visit. Just watch your feet for red crabs.

It has a morbid name due to the handful of graves still remaining at the back of the beach, but **Playa de los Muertos** is a gorgeous, curving white-sand stretch reached by walking well behind Hotel Bahia Blanca and Playa de los Guardias. You'll see a footpath past the bird and mangrove swamps. The water is a glorious turquoise, rocky in parts but with openings allowing easy entry. Shade trees run all along its edges and make it popular with families who bring their food and drinks on the weekends or after a long day. Kids like to leap off the small rocks on the edges of the beach.

Reached by road via public bus or by boat—you can ask to include this stop on your tour of the Laguna Gri Gri—**Playa Caletón** is within Río San Juan. This lovely small crescent is flanked by cliffs, covered in sponge-like sands—though its rocky in parts—and is idyllic during the week. At the back of beach you'll find a series of *casitas* selling fresh fish and drinks, including your regular beachside piña colada in a pineapple. Not surprisingly, it is supercrowded on Sundays when Dominicans descend with their coolers and hot lunches dished out of big pots, while a DJ with mega speakers blasts the area.

A two-minute walk down a narrow pathway to the far right of the Playa Grande parking lot leads to **Playa Preciosa,** a deserted white-sand beach that's a sight for sore eyes. There are no guards or facilities here, so if you're solo, don't stay too long by yourself and leave your valuables at home. It's a gorgeous blond and turquoise scene and good for strong swimmers, with stronger waves than Playa Grande. Don't venture out far alone.

## Food and Accommodations

You won't find another place with as spectacular a view or location as **Hotel Bahia Blanca** (Gaston Fernando Deligne, off Calle Duarte, tel. 809/589-2563, US$31), flanked by two stunning bays. It's a five-minute walk from the main drag, and equally close to each of Río San Juan's three beaches, as well as the Laguna Gri Gri. The friendly French Canadian owner, a resident of the DR for over 30 years, manages the hotel. It's true that the rooms are dated; don't expect great mattresses or locking windows, and there are only fans. And there's no power every day 11am-5pm: The generator comes on at 5pm and lasts through the night until midmorning. But it's decent for a night or two, and frankly, you'll forget about any minor inconveniences when you're out and about enjoying all the beaches or sitting on one of several wide terraces facing the glorious panoramic view of the ocean and the daily sunset. There's a small restaurant here that serves breakfast and dinner with a view and cold beers or sodas when you need them.

The French restaurant **Estrella** (Calle Duarte 7, tel. 809/589-2303, 8am-11pm daily, US$4-20) has a casual bakery and pizzeria on one side and a formal open-air dining room on the other. Conveniently set on the main street, it's one of the few consistent dining spots in town. Choices range from burgers to pastas to seafood.

**La Casona** (Calle Duarte 6, tel. 809/589-2597, lacasonarsj@gmail.com, 9am-10pm daily, US$3.30-5) cafeteria-style restaurant is the best in town for affordable and tasty Dominican food, served from a buffet.

Portions are generous for rice and beans, your chosen stew of the day, and yucca chips. They also have cheap and finger-licking good empanadas stuffed with chicken or fish. There's inside seating or you can pop up on the counter and watch the news from a distance.

**Café de Paris** (Calle Duarte, tel. 809/778-0687, 9am-11pm daily, US$4-6) serves a full menu ranging from seafood to steaks, and its terrace facing the lagoon is a lively spot to mingle.

## Getting There and Around

Shared taxis run the highway east from Puerto Plata to Río San Juan. You'll have to make a couple of transfers, but it's easy. Getting around the main sights in town only requires walking or taking the public bus off the main highway to head to Playa Grande or in the direction of Cabrera and Laguna Dudú.

**Caribe Tours** (tel. 809/589-2644, www.caribetours.com.do, US$7) has a terminal on the main highway close to the entrance to town and offers daily departures from Río San Juan to Santo Domingo. Check the online interactive map for the latest schedule.

# CABRERA
## Laguna Dudú

The **Laguna Dudú,** or **El Dudú** (8am-6pm daily, US$3.32 or RD$150) is one of the most beautiful natural sights on this North Coast. Three stunning freshwater blue lagoons of varying depth and surrounded with caves and a verdant tropical forest have been turned into a park. As you pass the front gate, you'll be amazed at the well-manicured gardens dotted with hammocks, benches, and thatch-roofed seating areas. There are signs directing you to the various lagoons. Two require taking a staircase down to the lower level. The screams you hear will likely be coming from **El Dudú Blue Lagoon,** the biggest pool of all, which is composed of 90 percent freshwater and 10 percent salt on the eastern end. There's a zipline directly above the gorgeous emerald and turquoise expanse 8 meters (25 feet) deep and 1,900 square meters (0.5 acres) wide, and you

can hang on to a tiny bar, with no other supportive gear, and zip your body down the line until you reach a point of no return and have to let go, jumping approximately 10 meters (33 feet) down into the water. It's a real adrenaline rush. Not to worry: you can bypass the madness and go down the stone staircase to bathe in the lagoon below instead.

On the other side of the park, you'll find two more lagoons. One is a shallow sinkhole with fish swimming beneath a near-crystal surface reflecting stalactites and bats scurrying at the back of the cave. There are more rocks and the water is shallow, but it's a gorgeous sight and the water is cold. A few steps over is my favorite of the pools, a gem of an emerald lagoon sitting at the foot of a towering limestone cliff, surrounded by wild trees and with a rocky entrance. The view is breathtaking, as is taking a swim in this cold freshwater body. There are kayaks for rent (US$2.21 or RD$100) if you want to circle the lagoon. (There's no exit, but it can be fun for two to four people per kayak.) There's also a wooden platform with seating overlooking the lagoon, usually busy on the weekends when the on-site outdoor bar is open.

Besides all the refreshing water, you'll find a dry cave that you can explore solo. Cueva Taína isn't much to see beyond its interesting arched entrance and some giant stalactite formations. There's an enclosure with ostriches and turkeys, and an on-site restaurant with restroom and very basic shower facilities serving lunch during park hours.

The park, east of Cabarete and Rio San Juan in the town of Cabrera, can be reached easily by hailing the *guaguas* (US$70 pesos from Río San Juan) running up and down the highway between Río San Juan and Cabrera. The trip is about 45 minutes from Río San Juan and 10 minutes from Cabrera.

## Playa Diamante

**Playa Diamante** is of the most unusual beaches in the country because a river flows almost into the sand as you approach the beach. Walk from east to west on this small stretch and you'll go from warm to cold water. The sand is sticky and wet, the water super-shallow out for miles. It makes for a favorite Dominican spot to talk, throw back some drinks, and bathe with the kids. There's a sign for the turnoff right off the main highway in Cabrera, and it's a short drive from there.

## ★ Playa Arroyo Salado

Less than a 15-minute drive south of Cabrera's attractions, listed above, you'll find Playa Arroyo Salado, located where the eponymous river empties into the ocean. The scene is one of the most spectacular in the DR, with large freshwater pools lined with mangroves on one end, and, a five-minute walk away, a near two-mile-long golden beach with towering trees. Seafood restaurants abound, serving everything from fried fish to octopus, and there are plenty of drinks. It's a fun, lively familial atmosphere on the weekends.

**1:** Hotel Bahia Blanca; **2:** Zip-line into one of Laguna Dudú's freshwater lagoons. **3:** Laguna Gri Gri

## PARQUE NACIONAL HISTÓRICO Y ARQUEOLÓGICO DE LA ISABELA

Located in Luperón and hugging the Atlantic shoreline, Parque Nacional Histórico y Arqueológico de La Isabela (9am-5pm daily, US$2.21 or RD$100)—not to be confused with the Villa Isabella municipality farther south—comprises a museum and archaeological site preserving the ruins of the first European settlement in the New World. It's where Christopher Columbus's second voyage landed him in 1493, and he named it after the Spanish queen Isabel La Católica, who funded his voyages. The small museum displays the history of Columbus's times, the Taíno people, and details on the ruins left behind by Columbus that are on display in the park. The hike begins just past the museum, and takes you to a beautiful oceanfront display of replica Spanish homes and original stones from the church where the first mass was held in 1494, and, perched on a bluff, Columbus's first home here.

Farther up from the park, you'll find the rebuilt Templo de las Américas, a replica of the original church. Walk up the winding interior staircase and admire a view of the deserted white sands of Castillo Beach in the distance. If you're already in the area, it's worth a quick stop here; if not, you can skip it.

TOP EXPERIENCE

## ★ ESTERO HONDO MARINE MAMMAL SANCTUARY

If you only make it to one natural sight on the North Coast, I highly recommend the natural wonder and protected area at the Estero Hondo Marine Mammal Sanctuary (tel. 829/492-3362, 9am-5pm daily, US$5.54 or RD$250, includes guided tour), consisting of a lagoon and park covering nearly 49 square kilometers (19 square miles) and located approximately 69 kilometers (43 miles) west of Puerto Plata. This is 10 kilometers (6 miles) west of where Christopher Columbus first landed in the DR. The drive to this northwestern edge of the Puerto Plata province is one of the country's loveliest, passing through fishing villages and farming communities where local scenes abound: small colmados, passing cows, men on donkeys or horses, pastel-colored homes surrounded by hills and subtropical landscape. Arriving to the park, your first sight will be a wide, stunning, and often-deserted turtle-nesting beach—Playa Marisa—to the left, stretching all the way to the entrance and hugging the lagoon.

Your tour will begin at the main park ranger office where you pay your entrance fee and explore a small indoor and outdoor display about the sanctuary, with information on its three mangrove species and its birdlife. Read about manatees and look at a glass-enclosed skeleton of a 1,300-kilogram (2,866-pound) male manatee found dead of old age (approximately 70) in 2011. There are over 50 manatees that are a constant presence within this protected lagoon. Knowledgeable head guide Freddy Garcia will lead you through the first trail, known as El Sendero del Cangrejo because of all the crab holes in the ground. Hermit crabs are a common sight, while blue crabs only come out at night or when it rains. This 20-minute hike goes through an incredibly rich landscape that includes all three types of mangroves found in the Dominican Republic—red, white buttonwood, and white—one of only two sites in the country to have them in one place. The hike will also take you past medicinal and native Taíno trees and plants like the saladillo, which the Taíno used to spice their food. The second hike, known as the Sendero del Manatí, requires a one-minute ride to the other side of the park just 1 kilometer (0.62 miles) away, where an observation deck awaits and you are guaranteed to spot manatees rising to the surface every few minutes. Bring your camera.

While you can visit the park solo and hike with a guide, the best way to appreciate the splendor of Estero Hondo is to explore the lagoon on a 1.5-hour kayak or paddleboard jaunt as part of a full-day Paddle Manatee Adventure tour with **Bávaro Runners** (Puerto Plata, tel. 809/320-1061, www. runnersadventures.com, US$95). You'll get to paddle off the beach and cruise along the waters, appreciating the park's grandeur and its breathtaking landscape while heading toward the *"palo de la Garza,"* a dense maze of mangroves that's home to cattle egrets. Beside it is a natural pool where you can park your kayak and hop into the delightful water. There's a small beach and hut beside the natural pool where you can also take a rest if you wish, and if you're lucky, a manatee might come close to shore. In the mangroves, you'll see birds soaring and spider crabs crawling, with beautiful seashells covering the bottom.

You'll then head to the mouth of the lagoon where it meets the sea, closer to where the majority of manatees reside, and glide around from a safe distance (absolutely no motorized boats are allowed on the protected lagoon). You might also spot barracuda leaping out of the water as they consume the small fish inhabiting the lagoon.

## LA ENSENADA

A 15-minute drive farther west past Estero Hondo will bring you to the beautiful beach of La Ensenada. The stunning **Playa Ensenada** has soft, white sand and super-shallow, calm waters—you can literally walk out several miles—making it a favorite of families coming from Santiago, Puerto Plata, and other northern towns. The beach is lined with the usual plastic chairs and tables, as well as dozens of local *frituras,* all offering the traditional fried or steamed fish meals. The atmosphere is busy and lively, in true Dominican fashion.

The beach has shower and bathroom facilities. As always, come on a weekday if you're not into crowds and rowdiness.

This is also one of the jumping-off points for speedboat excursions to Cayo Paraíso or Cayo Arena. For snorkel trips to Cayo Arena, contact **Capitán Josy** (tel. 829/712-2835, US$75 for two, but less with up to 13 people, three-hour tour). There are facilities here, including showers for 25 pesos or US$0.55.

## PUNTA RUCIA

Just past the beach at La Ensenada, barely a five-minute drive west and up a long and dusty dirt road, begins the beachfront community of **Punta Rucia.** This village is an ideal spot to get away from it all, especially midweek before locals descend on the area from Santiago, Puerto Plata, or even as far as Santo Domingo. The first sign you'll see is for the upscale Punta Rucia Lodge on the right-hand side. Again, the highlight here is a beautiful, uninterrupted white-sand beach—prettier than La Ensenada and with fewer, if any, crowds—with gloriously flat turquoise waters and floating fishing boats. There's seaweed and corals in some parts on the eastern end of the beach, but entry is easy. Dotting this coastline are quite a number of B&Bs and guesthouses, fish shacks, and a couple of Italian and French restaurants.

An option to overnight and get away from it all is **Lino's Beycaribi** (end of main road, right after Paradise Island Tours), with fan-only (US$60) or air-conditioned rooms (US$70), a two-minute ride down to the village center. For food, two decent choices are **Restaurant Damaris** (tel. 849/251-2709, US$6.55 for buffet) for local fare and fish, and **Lino's** (tel. 809/704-3045, US$8-12.30) for homemade pizza and freshly baked bread overlooking the water on the far end of Punta Rucia's strand. You can also rent kayaks and bicycles from **La Cueva d'Ali-Boubou Gift Shop** (beachfront, US$6).

### Cayo Arena

Punta Rucia is a primary jumping-off point to

# Side Trip: Kitesurfing in Buenhombre

An isolated beach community less than a two-hour drive west from Punta Rucia, Buenhombre boasts a kitesurfing school, kite camp, and a handful of fish shacks. It's worth coming here to get a slice of the old DR in a true fishing village. If you have a day to spare, kick back and spend it around local fishers and the occasional kitesurfers who come here to try new waters with Kite Buenhombre (tel. 829/325-5250, www.kitebuenhombre.net, US$65/class or US$500 for full course/12 hours, day trips from Cabarete also offered). Beware of the beach—there's coral, including deep sinkholes with occasional currents, especially closer to the eastern side where the fishing boats are moored. It isn't always as shallow as it seems close to shore. There have been accidents in the recent past with weak swimmers.

The quickest way to get to Buenhombre is along a very poorly indicated route that begins past Punta Rucia along a gravel road. You'll have to ask directions at every point because there are literally no signs for this shortcut to Buenhombre, but it's the most interesting and picturesque route, taking you past villages and countryside scenes. Locals are used to it so don't fret. Go a couple of kilometers on the gravel road until you hit what seems like the top of a hill where you'll see a paved road; turn right. Keep going until you spot a gas station—*la bomba*—but ask locals because it will otherwise be harder to find. On spotting the gas station, make a left toward it but at its corner, turn clockwise (like a u) to continue on the road. It will wind into a coastal roads with stunning panoramic views as you descend to Buenhombre's coastline and bay.

Cayo Arena (also called Cayo Paraiso), and there are various hotels and outfitters offering excursions from Punta Rucia or Puerto Plata. Cayo Arena is essentially a sandbank sitting about 7 kilometers (4.35 miles) off the coast; it's where you'll experience some of the best snorkeling in the DR. The corals, critters, and waters glow in true Caribbean fashion. Cayo Arena is part of the Parque Nacional Monte Cristi, and thus a protected area. A series of thatch huts line the small island, where outfitters lay out their gear and entertain their respective day-trippers. It's a fun day out surrounded by a gorgeous island landscape, but don't expect to have a solo *Robinson Crusoe* experience unless you head out here very early in the morning to avoid all the tour groups and various boats that end up docking here by 11am. Still, it's an excursion that is absolutely worthwhile. Contact the local fishermen's association, Cooperativa de Pescadores Punta Rucia (Cesar, president, tel. 809/866-4079 or Captain Francisco, tel. 829/943-7457, US$78 1-4 persons), for a

reasonably priced excursion. The tour includes all of the regular offerings of snorkeling stops, park entry fees, a ride along the mangroves of the Parque Nacional Monte Cristi, and a full day out on Cayo Arena (or as long as you'd like to stay). The association also offers fishing trips, from spearfishing to deep-sea fishing (half day 6am-1pm, US$112 for two).

At the far western end of Punta Rucia beach, Paradise Island (tel. 809/320-7606 or in Punta Rucia tel. 809/841-7606, www. paradiseisland.do, US$50 pp for 1-5 persons, US$40 pp for more) also offers an all-day excursion to Cayo Arena with lunch, snacks, drinks, and the usual mangrove and snorkeling tour stops. They also have seven rooms if you decide to overnight, slightly tucked at the back of the beach but just a few steps away, with air-conditioning, breakfast, hot and cold water, and balconies if you choose, but no TV. From Puerto Plata, you can also hop on a catamaran cruise to the cay with Bávaro Runners (tel. 809/320-1061, www. bavarorunners.com, Tues., Thurs., and Sat., US$95 pp).

---

1: Estero Hondo Marine Mammal Sanctuary;
2: Playa Ensenada

# Monte Cristi

Most visitors don't go farther west than Punta Rucia on their adventures on the North Coast. In doing so, they miss a unique landscape and one of the most authentic parts of the Dominican Republic, just an additional hour's drive west. It's a ride that will take you past mountainous and wild rocky scenery. This cactus-filled landscape—dotted with banana plantations, rice fields, and salt mines—is an ecotraveler's dream tucked on the western edge of the North Coast and within view of Haiti. It's an entirely different DR: one where rural life dominates and massive resorts with vendor-filled beaches are far away.

Staying overnight is the best way to fully take in the unique preserved landscape of this authentic part of the North Coast. This is also one of the best spots to indulge in the freshest seafood or traditional spicy goat stew (*chivo picante*), a specialty of this region. Monte Cristi is the last town on the northwestern coastline, and sits just outside the boundary of the national park bearing the same name.

## SIGHTS

As you enter town, you'll spot piles of salt on either end of the main road—look out for a **Salt Interpretation Center,** a quick stop where you can learn how salt is made—before you arrive at the small but picturesque Malecón with a long dock where locals like to take in the breeze in this hot town. In the near distance is a view of El Morro, Monte Cristi's iconic landmark.

### El Morro

**El Morro** is a majestic 242-meter (793-foot) mesa—the tallest in the DR. Some might say it resembles Table Mountain in Cape Town, if a smaller version. It features prominently from almost anywhere in Monte Cristi town and the surrounding area. As you enter the **Parque Nacional Monte Cristi** boundary, located a 10-minute ride from the Malecón,

the rather deserted landscape will make it seem as if it's just you, the sea, and the mountains. You'll eventually reach a dead end with a parking lot, and an adjacent ranger cabin. From there, you can hike down to the gorgeous **Playa El Morro.**

Although you used to be able to hike to the top of El Morro, it's highly inadvisable (as of publication time) due to unstable, rubble-strewn terrain and a neglected, makeshift trail. There's another, safer option, however: hike on the opposite (eastern) end for a panoramic view of the beach and the mesa. An obscured sign across from the ranger station indicates the start of the ascent, but ask the rangers before you head up to ensure safety.

### ★ Playa El Morro

You'll reach **Playa El Morro** by driving to the end of the road, where there will be a parking lot. You'll have to hike a few easy steps down the rocks below the parking lot to reach the beach. With its reddish-brown sand on one end, a blondish stretch on the other, and a dramatic spray of waves crashing against towering rocks, Playa El Morro is a sight for sore eyes. The cliffs of El Morro hug the shore on the northwest—be sure to prepare your camera for this stunning landscape.

Before you descend, take in the spectacular view of the sea, sand, and El Morro's imposing presence—there are no vendors here, no man-made structures of any kind. Get here during the day before the shadows fall and the sun begins to lower, shedding a true golden light on the sand. On one end of the beach, you'll see piles of soft stones covering the sand—sometimes they move to the left, sometimes to the right, according to how the tide shifts them.

### La Playita

Sandwiched between the end of the Malecón and the road to El Morro (and nearly directly across from El Morro Eco Lodge), this public

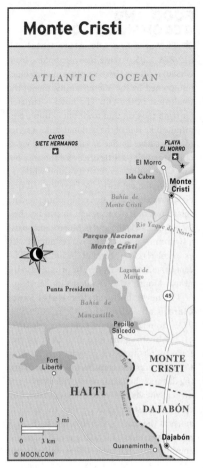

## Monte Cristi

ATLANTIC OCEAN

CAYOS SIETE HERMANOS

PLAYA EL MORRO

El Morro

Isla Cabra

Monte Cristi

Bahía de Monte Cristi

Río Yaque del Norte

Parque Nacional Monte Cristi

Laguna de Marigo

Punta Presidente

Bahía de Manzanillo

Pepillo Salcedo

45

Fort Liberté

MONTE CRISTI

HAITI

DAJABÓN

0      3 mi
0      3 km

Dajabón

Quanaminthe

© MOON.COM

beach has a lovely local pulse, with just a bar shack perched on the rocky edge, and below, a shallow beach ideal for families with roaming kids. The *bachata* and merengue blast from the bar, and it's a nice spot to cool off for an afternoon.

### Casa Museo Máximo Gómez

In the town center, make a stop at the historic **Casa Museo Máximo Gómez** (8am-noon and 2pm-5pm daily, free), once the home of Gómez and where, more importantly, he and José Martí met as they drafted and signed Cuba's declaration of independence. It's said that Martí stood at the doors and shouted:

"Here begins Cuba's independence!" There are various portraits of independence heroes, as well as family memorabilia, and a copy of the declaration. There's no signage in English, but if you speak Spanish, the museum attendant, an older gentlemen, is quite the source of information.

## TOURS

The only tour operator in the area is the long-time, family-run **Soraya y Santos Tours** (Malecón, tel. 809/961-6343 or 829/221-0453, www.sorayayleonardotours.com), a solid pick specializing in eco-friendly excursions around natural gems and offering a variety of day trips to snorkel, swim, and explore Monte Cristi's gorgeous waters, including offshore Cayos de Siete Hermanos.

### Ruta El Morro y Los Caños

Touring the park's waters and mangrove swamps can only be done by boat. An overview tour of the Parque Nacional Monte Cristi, known as the **Ruta El Morro y Los Caños** (Soraya y Santos Tours, US$204/four people), begins with cruising along the mangroves for a good 15 minutes or so, followed by swimming stops at two natural pools where the waters turn into a clear turquoise and you'll find it hard to leave. One is known as **the platform** (*la plataforma*); it's just a half-mile boat ride into the park, and there is literally a wooden platform set up beside the swimming area and mangroves where you can dock and jump in to enjoy fresh water. There's a picnic table and a grill that locals use on the weekends. The second natural pool is known as **La Avena,** translated as "oats", because its floor is covered with an oatmeal-textured sand. Locals bottle up this sand to use it as a body scrub—or you can scrub away right there. It's the only place in the Dominican Republic where you'll find this. The tour continues onto the open water of the Atlantic Ocean, and you'll cruise across a spectacular Mediterranean-like landscape past Playa del Morro and its towering rocks. You'll stop next at an offshore island across from Playa El

Morro known as **Isla Cabra.** There's an old lighthouse here and a small shaded stretch of white sand where you can picnic, swim, and pretend you're on your own deserted island. The water is a gorgeous clear turquoise, and you'll even see the fish scurrying past your feet.

### ★ Cayos Siete Hermanos (Seven Brothers Cays)

Starting one kilometer (0.6 mile) off the shores of Monte Cristi is a set of islets that few get to experience. The Seven Brothers Cays, or Cayo Siete Hermanos, are seven tiny cays where deserted, idyllic beaches are home to various migratory birds and sea turtles: **Tururu, Cayo Muerto, Montechico, Monte Grande, Cayo Tuna,** and **Cayo Arena** (not to be confused with the Cayo Arena in Punta Rucia, which, by the way, got that name as a marketing ploy—it's not the island's original name, as the original Cayo Arena is the one in Monte Cristi). Surrounding the islands are some historic shipwrecks ideal for diving excursions, although there are no longer any dive shops in Monte Cristi.

Trips to the cays are costly, but that's the price of seeing one of the unique spots of the DR. Particularly if you have a large group, it's money well spent (US$410 for 1-8 persons) to arrange for a day out to the cays. While you'll get to see all the cays around you from the boat, the two main stops are **Montechico,** the first caye, and **Cayo Tuna,** which sits almost smack in the middle of the group. The farther cayes are too close to the Haitian border and Haitian fishermen often come over to camp or fish, leading to safety concerns.

Montechico boasts a beautiful white-sand beach with calm turquoise waters ideal for swimming and snorkeling right offshore (make sure you have fins to avoid urchins). Cayo Tuna is a stunner thanks to the numerous colonies of migratory birds, including boobies, which reside here, sitting atop bushes and flying overhead behind a white-sand beach—it's quite the showstopping scene.

## FOOD AND ACCOMMODATIONS

★ **El Morro Eco Adventure Hotel** (tel. 849/886-1605, www.elmorro.com.do, from US$80) is Monte Cristi's newest upscale hideout, owned by the Vicini family, one of the wealthiest in the DR. The hotel is situated far from the center of town but within a ten-minute bike ride of the national park. A series of casitas have double or king beds and views of El Morro. It's a little pricey for the area, but that's the point—exclusivity—and while it's not quite the definition of "eco" (you'll find plastic water bottles, air-conditioning, and no solar power), it's convenient to two beaches, including La Playita and El Morro, and boasts a swimming pool, as well as a restaurant with excellent à la carte breakfast (included) and decent chivo. You can fly here by private jet at the nearby Monte Cristi Osvaldo Virgil airstrip.

The newly built, modern **Hotel Santa Clara** (Calle Mayobanex #8, tel. 809/579-2433, from US$30) stands out on a side street off the bustling main road of Monte Cristi town thanks to its all-glass facade. It's close to restaurants and transportation—not walking distance, but a motorbike ride away—and owner Sylvia is a friendly, bilingual expat host ready to assist with advice. Pick the spacious suites at the front of the building, with every amenity included, including mini fridge, air-conditioning, and cable TV, as well as ample space for a couple to move around. Check-in prior to 3pm is not allowed.

**Chic Hotel** (US$26) is the favorite budget pick in Monte Cristi, and if anything, its restaurant alone is worth the stay, serving one of the best goat stews in town, and boasting a convivial dining terrace frequented by visitors and residents alike.

For meals, you can't go wrong with the prices or the taste at ★ **Lilo's** (across from Lilo supermarket, tel. 809/579-3169, 7am-midnight daily, US$2-10), from breakfast omelets to the rice and beans plates of the day, or à la carte menu with everything from pastas to crabs to steaks. The chivo guisado is quite good, as is the seafood pasta. Fresh fruit juices are also popular here. To catch a stunning red sunset from your table and through the open shutters beside you, head to **Coco Mar** (Malecón de Monte Cristi, noon-10pm, tel. 809/579-3354) a longtimer in Monte Cristi, perhaps more for its location than its seafood. The conch and seafood is decent, but set your expectations low on the rice and beans, which are sometimes reheated. It's pricey for the area, but that's what you get for a table with an all-around water view.

Pre-meal, head over to the Malecón at sunset for drinks from a number of bars or "shacks" lining the boulevard, as locals flock with families to have a drink and a swim while the sun goes down. For a bar near the action but set off a bit from the loud speakers competing at every shack, go to **D Classic Beach Bar** and have a proper sit-down drink.

## TRANSPORTATION

From Puerto Plata, Monte Cristi is an approximately three-hour drive, depending on traffic. The most common route is to take the Navarrete-Puerto Plata highway (still undergoing construction but passable, so look out for road signs), going past Los Hidalgos and onto Autopista Duarte, which goes straight to Monte Cristi.

If you're looking to travel by local bus from Puerto Plata to Monte Cristi, there's no direct route—your best bet is to head to Santiago first (via Caribe Tours or Metro Tours), and from there hop on a Caribe bus to Monte Cristi. Be aware that if one of the stops includes Dajabón, after Monte Cristi, there may be multiple military checkpoints, particularly returning from Monte Cristi, to check for illegal Haitians and contraband. It's nothing to worry about, other than delays; keep your passport close.

Once in town, taxis are very sparse—in fact, there are only two guys in town making runs, both of whom can be reached by calling **Boli** (tel. 809/351-5373, US$8 one-way from town to the Malecon). Otherwise, motorbike taxis are the only way to get around; there are no local buses.

# Santiago and the Cibao Valley

## This region is often called "the Dominican Alps"

because it's hugged by the Cordillera Septentrional and central mountain ranges. It's a delightful and surprising departure from the stereotypical image of the DR as a sun, sea, and rum destination. Affluent locals escape the heat and buzz of Santiago to the peaks and valleys of El Cibao, as Dominicans refer to it. El Cibao, which means "mountain rock" in Taíno, is blessed with the highest mountain in the Caribbean: Pico Duarte, at 10,125 feet above sea level. Pico Duarte is the crown jewel of the region, and the most intrepid explorers will opt to spend a night on the peak.

The country's most important national parks, such as Valle Nuevo, are also found in the highlands where the most valuable rivers supply

# Highlights

Look for ★ to find recommended sights, activities, dining, and lodging.

★ **Monumento a los Héroes de la Restauración:** Climb to the top of Santiago's most famous landmark to learn more about the heroes in the War of Restoration and take in 360-degree views of the city (page 272).

★ **Carnival in La Vega:** Buy a devil's mask and join in the frenzy at the country's largest and most colorful carnival, which takes place every weekend in February (page 286).

★ **Saltos de Jimenoa:** Used as the filming location for the opening scene in *Jurassic Park,* these two stunning waterfalls are not to be missed (page 288).

★ **La Confluencia:** Bring your picnic fare and take a dip in swirling freshwater pools at this park, where three of Jarabacoa's rivers meet (page 290).

★ **River Rafting on the Río Yaque del Norte:** Get soaked tumbling down the DR's longest river (page 292).

★ **Manabao and La Ciénaga:** Experience the beauty of the real Dominican countryside in these villages where you can visit agricultural farms and swim in the Río Yaque del Norte (page 299).

★ **Hiking Pico Duarte:** Visit the Parque Armando Bermúdez for a two-day hike to the highest point in the Caribbean. At the top you can proudly take a selfie with a statue of Juan Pablo Duarte, father of Dominican independence (page 301).

★ **Parque Nacional Valle Nuevo:** Escape civilization at one of the most impressive and biodiverse parks in the DR. Spend a night at Villa Pajón Eco-Lodge to truly appreciate the park's landscape (page 307).

# Santiago and the Cibao Valley

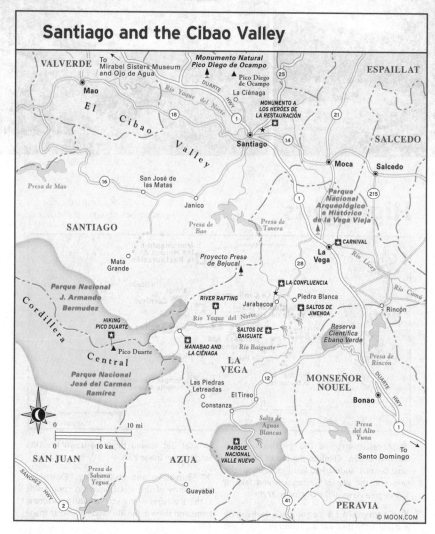

the country with water. A handful of them are even classified as scientific parks for their biodiversity. These parks are home to mountainside villages that offer prime material for outdoor and photography enthusiasts. The Cibao's land makes it the breadbasket of the Dominican Republic; over 90 percent of the country's vegetables are cultivated and produced in the stunning, green, cool hills of Constanza, dubbed "the Switzerland of the Caribbean" for its stunning views of rolling farmlands and cabins. This area is surrounded by imposing, mist-covered mountains up to 2,134 meters (7,000 feet) above sea level—easily the highest inhabited elevation across the Antilles. The Cibao Valley is also made

**Previous:** view of the city and mountains from Santiago's Monumento a los Héroes de la Restauración; La Confluencia park; the Río Yaque del Norte.

up of rolling tobacco hills, where the world's best cigar leaves are grown and hand rolled to perfection.

As if its natural gifts weren't enough, culture is plentiful in these parts, too. The largest and most vibrant carnival in the country takes place in La Vega. Roadside *lechoneras,* or roast pork eateries, are here in abundance. And the DR's second-largest city, Santiago—possibly the least touristy part of the country—is a sweet spot for night owls, cigar aficionados, and baseball enthusiasts.

As the birthplace and home of the Mirabal sisters, from Salcedo, it's no wonder Cibaeños are so proud; there's a bold claim that the most beautiful Dominican women come from this region. If you haven't been to the Cibao, the cultural heartland of this country, you haven't been to the Dominican Republic. Squeezing in this side of the country, if only for a day or two, will give you a better view and understanding of this stunning island's incredible topography and friendly inhabitants.

## PLANNING YOUR TIME

If you're coming to the heartland of the Dominican Republic, it's to experience outdoor adventure, scenic rides, and the country's most spectacular landscape. You can easily skip Santiago—unless you're a cigar and nightlife lover, in which case one night is the minimum, or you only have time for a day's escape to San José de las Matas. Otherwise, make Jarabacoa your base, where there's enough to do that you could be busy for well over a week. From Jarabacoa, explore the mountains—hike El Mogote, if you dare— waterfalls, rivers, and *campo* villages. Save at least three full days for this place. From your Jarabacoa base, you could go to nearby Manabao and La Ciénaga, which easily have the most showstopping scenery. These two villages are also departure points for the hike to Pico Duarte. If you are braving the tallest peak in the Caribbean, you'll need to put aside at least three full days—two for the hike and one to rest. Plan your trek ahead of time by contacting one of the major organizers; it will save you a lot of effort and precious vacation time.

Put aside at least a day and a night for Constanza, an hour and 20 minutes south of Jarabacoa, where you'll find little tourism but more stunning landscapes across flower plantations and vegetable and strawberry fields. Hike the pine forest-filled Parque Nacional Valle Nuevo, which has the coolest temperatures in the Caribbean, and spend the night by a chimney fire for a unique Caribbean experience.

The Cibao Valley, as you'll soon realize, is its own getaway. If you're combining it with a beach stay, split your days and spend three on this side, at a minimum.

# Santiago de los Caballeros

The Dominican Republic's second-largest city after Santo Domingo, Santiago de los Caballeros—which citizens call *la Ciudad Corazón,* or "heartland city"—is a massive, sprawling, scorching-hot, traffic-filled maze. It isn't much of a destination for tourists, except that it's a primary gateway to the mountainous, adventure-filled towns of Jarabacoa and Constanza. It's an industrial city for the most part. Because of its location in the fertile Cibao region, it's a leading exporter of major Dominican products such as rum, cigars, and textiles. Tobacco aficionados will find their pleasure here at premium cigar outlets like La Aurora.

With attractive mountain towns like Jarabacoa and Constanza just over an hour away, Santiago's primary use for the visitor is as a public transit stop en route to those regions. It's just good enough for a day's visit, perhaps to see the Monumento a los Héroes, tour a couple of museums, and buy what you

# Santiago de los Caballeros

© MOON.COM

need at the mall. It doesn't have much more to offer unless you're a major cigar lover, a baseball fan (this is home to the Cibao Eagles), or a night owl.

The city's main shopping drag, Calle del Sol, is easily explored on foot. Lined with Chinese fashion apparel and American fast-food chains, as well as the pedestrian bustle of hawkers and shoppers, when you're here you'd almost think you're on one of New York City's streets, except for the security guards with shotguns standing outside of jewelry stores. There's a local sidewalk market tucked at the back of this area with much more local color. Here Dominican and Haitian vendors hawk fruits and vegetables. The Monumento a los Héroes is the main landmark, and surrounding it are numerous restaurants, bars, and lounges. It and Calle del Sol are the city's only pedestrian-friendly areas; the rest of the city is spread out, with large avenues and plenty of traffic, so you'll need a car or a taxi to get around, especially in the scorching Santiago heat.

Established in 1495 and named by Columbus in honor of 30 Spanish aristocrats who helped found the city, Santiago's history bears mentioning because of its important role in the country's independence movement. It was once the capital of the Dominican Republic during the War of Restoration between 1863 and 1865, and it was also the site of the Battle of March 30, 1844, when the Dominican Republic fought for and won independence from Haiti.

# SIGHTS

## Parque Duarte

Parque Duarte, the city's most popular park, is a wide, shady expanse, noisy during the day but a favorite respite from the hot sun. It's surrounded by gorgeous architecture from the Palacio Consistorial to the cathedral, but it's also on the end of busy Calle del Sol. Expect plenty of foot traffic and keep an eye out while walking in these parts, day or night.

## Parque Central

Opened in 2017, Parque Central de Santiago (Av. Bartolome Colón, tel. 809/583-9581, parquecentralsti@gmail.com, 5am-10pm daily, free) is a massive sports complex for outdoor recreation that Santiago needed badly. It boasts multiple designated areas for sports, including lanes for cycling and walking, a series of basketball courts, a soccer field, and a boxing ring, all hugged by a dense forest. You will find plenty of picnic areas and bench seating along the way, as well as a separate baseball-training zone. It's ideal for families as well. Head there after 5pm, when most locals go after the sun becomes less intense.

## Catedral de Santiago Apóstol

Set in the heart of the city, Catedral de Santiago Apóstol (Calle 30 de Marzo) is an all-white gothic and neoclassical building from the late 19th century. Its most impressive feature is its stained glass windows. Also on site are the marble tombs of former Dominican dictator Ulises Heureaux and General Jose Maria Imbert. Opening hours vary, as there are often special masses held here.

## Palacio Consistorial

Across from Parque Duarte is the two-story Palacio Consistorial (Calle Benito Monción, corner of Calle del Sol, free). Built between 1895 and 1896, this renovated neoclassical building once served as city hall. The most interesting room here is the Salon del Carnaval de Santiago on the ground floor, with displays of life-size mannequins decked out in carnival costumes and masks explaining the importance of carnival culture in this part of the Dominican Republic. Unfortunately for the monolinguals, all labeling is in Spanish and there aren't any audio translations. The 2nd floor hosts rotating photography and art exhibits. Head up here if only to enjoy the outdoor balcony views onto the Parque Duarte and the cathedral.

# Cigar Country

It's no exaggeration to say that the DR is the number one exporter of premium cigars in the world. In fact, Dominican cigars account for over half of the cigars sold in the United States alone. These fine, hand-rolled products have been judged to be superior in quality and flavor to those made in Cuba.

The history of tobacco cultivation and cigar making in the country goes back centuries. The indigenous inhabitants used tobacco in religious ceremonies, before the arrival of the Spaniards. During the 20th century, Cuban tobacco growers threatened by the Castro regime, which was seeking to nationalize their operations, moved over to the Dominican Republic. Thanks to the DR's fertile soils and ideal temperatures, the seeds were here to stay and thrive.

Some of the best tobacco is grown outside of Santiago in the Cibao Valley, particularly in the Yaque Valley and Villa Gonzalez, home to tobacco fields from which sought-after, award-winning cigars are made: Davidoff Nicaragua Toro, Arturo Fuente Don Carlos, and Fernando Leon Family Reserve Belicoso, among others. The ideal breezy and sunny climate, along with good drainage and fertile lands, have helped production. Today, cigar brands of various strengths come out of such respected factories as Tabacalera de García, Tabacalera La Aurora, and La Flor Dominicana, where they are hand rolled and assembled by artisans who are passionate about and meticulous in their application of traditional craftsmanship.

In 1992, the country's top cigar manufacturers created the Asociación de Fabricantes de Cigarros de la República Dominicana—currently at 11 members, each of whom produce at least six or more cigar brands—to establish and help maintain high-quality production standards. Every year, they put on a prestigious ProCigar Festival, a weeklong cigar retreat celebrating the product and taking visitors across some of the most visited regions from Punta Cana to La Romana.

To experience a Santiago cigar factory—a must while in the DR if you partake—be sure to visit one of the top outlets in the country and purchase directly from them, as counterfeit cigars are all too frequent in tourist areas. It is an easy ride from downtown Santiago to the renowned La Aurora (Av. Tamboril-Santiago, Parque Industrial Tamboril, tel. 809/575-1903, www.laaurora.com.do, free, reservations required), offering one-hour tours of the oldest cigar factory in the country (it was established in 1903). You'll learn how to smoke a cigar, observe the rolling process, and perhaps even try your hand at making your own. For a smaller boutique factory, visit PDR Cigars (Pinar del Río Cigars, no phone, www.pdcigars.com, 8am-noon and 2pm-4pm Mon.-Fri., free tour) in the town of Villa Gonzales, about 14 kilometers (9 miles) northwest of Santiago, producing four Dominican *puro* (made with DR tobacco) cigars, as well as blends with Brazilian tobacco. Across the street visitors can watch the process at the popular Tubano's (Villa Gonzales, no phone, 8am-noon and 2pm-4pm Mon.-Fri., free tour). Besides simply having access to quality products, prepare to be impressed with how quickly and yet precisely cigar rollers make and finish each piece. The sampling that ensues isn't too bad, either.

## ★ Monumento a los Héroes de la Restauración

Atop a hill on the eastern side of the city, the 67-meter-tall (220-foot) white marble Monumento a los Héroes de la Restauración (Av. Coronel Juan Maria Lora, tel. 809/241-1391, http://monumentomhr.com, 9am-6pm Tues.-Sun., RD$60 or US$1.30) is the most impressive and recognizable building in Santiago. Locals simply call it El Monumento de Santiago. It's worth a stop if you have a couple of hours in the city. This structure was completed in Trujillo's time, and the dictator himself named it the Monumento a la Paz de Trujillo. When his regime fell, it was rededicated to the Heroes of the War of Restoration (or Guerra de España, 1863-1865). The statue at the very top of the monument represents the Ángel de la Paz, the peace angel, facing what is considered to be the center of Santiago.

Designed by architect Henry Gazón Bona, the monument's construction began in 1944 on the centennial of the DR's independence, and was completed in 1952. There are five floors in the monument, each of which recounts the history of the Dominican Republic and its major battles, depicted in various glass displays, as well as the most significant players in the War of Restoration. You'll also see large paintings by Spanish artist Vela Zanetti, created while he was in exile during the Spanish Civil War.

If you manage to traverse the 347 steps to reach the 5th floor (bring water), you'll enjoy the **Mirador Santiaguero,** a wraparound terrace with glorious views of the city below. There are telescopes you can use for 10 pesos (US$0.22). The outdoor area at the base of the monument is perhaps even more impressive, with life-size statues of Dominican heroes hugging the building. It is also of more use to residents, with sprawling lawns and benches that have a 360-degree view over the city and the distant Cordillera Central. Lovers and families take a moment out of their busy day to relax here or enjoy a Sunday afternoon.

There are unfortunately no English audio devices available, and the elevator is often out of service.

## Fortaleza San Luis

Originally built in 1804, Santiago's **Fortaleza San Luis** (Calle Duverge, 9am-5pm daily, free) is close to the center of town and has a gorgeous, imposing, yellow-walled entrance with two cannons facing the city. This fortress is one of the city's most historic sites; it is where numerous battles took place during the War of Restoration. It's also where over 1,000 U.S. Marines took over the city during the United States occupation of the DR in 1916, which lasted until 1924.

The entrance is always open, if guarded, and leads into a spacious parking lot after you pass the three busts of independence heroes Sanchez, Melia, and Duarte, and, behind them, a whole row of statues of important historical figures. It makes for an interesting walk, but don't do it in the hot Santiago sun.

On the other side of the parking lot, opposite an impressive display of army tanks, the **Museo de la Fortaleza** (donation suggested RD$150 or US$3.27, with guide) might surprise you when you see just how spacious and well stocked it is. Opened in 2005, its displays show off Taíno items dating back 500 years, including items used in everyday life and in rituals, containers, and carvings of witch doctors' faces. At the back are items dating from World War II. Between you'll see shotguns and swords used by conquistadores like Drake and Columbus and pirates. The first U.S. Marine occupation of the DR in 1916 is documented in black-and-white photographs taken at the fortress. There are gorgeous paintings, as well as displays of various carnival and folklore figures. The museum's well-informed guide, **Etnaras Sarante** (tel. 829/871-6478, etnaras39@hotmail.com), speaks enough English to explain various items in the museum and their historical context.

## Casa del Arte

You'll find Dominican artists' works displayed at the **Casa del Arte** (across from Parque Duarte, Calle Benito Monción, 3pm-8pm daily, free), a renovated Victorian building in this historic part of downtown Santiago. You'll recognize it by the colorful mural that covers its front walls and entrance. The opening hours can be random and the curator isn't the friendliest chap you'll meet, so prepare to just wander around alone and take in the drawings. There are paintings by Luis Jimenez and Ofemil Abreu, among others.

Directly across from Casa del Arte is **La 37 por Las Tablas** (Benito Monción 37, tel. 809/587-3033, www.la37porlastablas.blogspot.com, from US$1), a renovated cultural space dedicated to Dominican performing arts. It's ideal for those who speak Spanish and want to catch some theater. Even if you don't, you can call ahead for some historical background on Dominican arts and drama before grabbing drinks on the patio at adjacent sidewalk bars. Check the hours before you go because they vary.

## Centro Cultural León Jimenes

The **Centro Cultural León Jimenes** (Av. 27 de Febrero 146, tel. 809/582-2315, www.centroleon.org.do, 10am-7pm Tues.-Sun., RD$150 or US$3.27) was built by the tobacco empire that is the León Jimenes family. There are three permanent exhibit rooms on the ground floor. The Sala de Antropología displays Taíno artifacts, ceramics, and deities, as well as background on the sugarcane industry and its African origins. An adjacent exhibit room displays Dominican cultural items and lifestyle photos. The Sala de Artes Visuales showcases creations of Dominican artists who participated in the León Jimenes art contest, which goes back to 1964 when Eduardo León Jimenes created the event in the hopes of promoting art and creativity in new generations of artists in the DR.

Walk through the cafeteria and cross over the patio to the second building to find out more information on the León family on the 2nd floor. On display are old machines and tools used for cigar making.

Unfortunately, the center isn't as informative if you're not a Spanish speaker: there are no bilingual guides on permanent staff (you'd have to call ahead to book one) and there were no English audio devices available as of the time of writing. The souvenir shop, however, has a few worthwhile items authentic to the area and the DR, including *merenguero* hats, cigars, coffee, and history books.

A taxi to Centro León or other major sights within the city shouldn't cost more than RD$150 (US$3.27). There are also shared taxis—catch the one labeled Route A and be sure to confirm your drop-off location.

## Fábrica de Cigarros La Aurora

A free one-hour factory tour at the oldest cigar factory in the country is a must for cigar smokers or anyone curious about one of the country's main exports (the DR is the number one producer and exporter of premium cigars in the world). Founded in 1903, **La Aurora** (Av. Tamboril-Santiago, Parque Industrial Tamboril, tel. 809/575-1903, www.laaurora.com.do, free, reservations required) exports to at least 64 countries, and imports about 20 percent of the tobacco used. On the tour you'll get a history of the founding León family and see the various factory floor rooms where cigar rollers turn around about 200 cigars by hand every day (for RD$5,000 or US$100 a week salary), as well as the humidor and the vintage cigar gallery, among other sections. While you tour, you'll get a complimentary cigar, and learn how to light, hold, and smoke in true cigar smoker swag (the guide Eugenio Hernandez is quite amusing in his demonstrations). Classes are offered on how to roll your own cigar, so be sure to inquire if that's of interest. Pick up a box of Aurora Preferidos or León Jimenes Prestige from the shop for the tobacco lovers in your life. Tours are complimentary, as are pickups, but you must call ahead and make a reservation.

## Jardin Botánico de Santiago

Santiago's new botanical gardens, officially called **Jardin Botánico de Santiago Profesor Eugenio de Jesús Marcano Fondeur** (Av. del Botánico Dr. Jose de Jesus Jimenez Almonte No. 1, tel. 809/489-2400, botanicodesantiago.com, 8am-7pm daily, free), opened in April 2018 and are a work in progress, with signs lacking, but the park is already a popular escape among residents seeking a green escape. Stretching 600,000 square meters and with a beautiful mountainous backdrop, the park boasts brand-new cycling and hiking lanes, butterfly and rose gardens, and nurseries. A towering statue of Christ the Redeemer was being completed when I visited. The place might give Santo Domingo's botanical garden a run for its reputation in a few years when more plants have bloomed.

## Estadio Cibao

Home to the Cibao Eagles (Águilas Cibaeñas), one of the most successful of the six baseball

---

1: Monumento a los Héroes de La Restauración;
2: Fortaleza San Luis; 3: rolling cigars at Fábrica de Cigarros La Aurora

## Santiago's *Cabaña* Culture

one of Santiago's infamous *cabañas*

You can't miss the big, bold, and flashy signs for *cabañas turísticas* (some call themselves *aparta-hotel* officially, but if you're paying by the hour, there's no confusion as to what the place is and the highway signs are clear). By-the-hour hotel rooms for trysts and other illicit encounters are common throughout the DR, but Santiago takes them to a whole new level. Some of these *cabañas* are so fancy and fabulous—complete with themed executive spa suites—they make Punta Cana's most luxurious suites seem standard. You will want to move in immediately.

Just for kicks—or heck, for real—visit a couple of them and stay for a few hours to get a sense of just how big this market is and how huge of a cultural trend it reflects. The way they operate is all part of the fun: there is no reception check-in; just drive straight into the private garage, which shuts down after you enter (so no one sees you arriving or exiting). Enter your suite, lock the door behind you, and escape for four hours at a time or up to a week! Everything is provided: food, condoms (from a secret swinging box in your suite, accessible immediately after you turn over the cash), spa tubs, full kitchens, disco lights, and outdoor patios with cascading swimming pools. You name it, it's all here.

One of Santiago's most luxurious and popular *cabaña* complexes is **Bora Bora** (Autopista Duarte Km 5 1/2, tel. 809/570-7000, www.borabora.com.do, US$40/4 hours). Like its name, the interior of each presidential suite is exotic and themed (I loved the Samurai Suite) with varying features, including bedroom balconies looking down into the hot spa tub on the ground floor. **Horus** (Carretera Las Palomas, off Autopista Duarte, tel. 809/241-0606, www.horusapartahotel. com, US$50/4 hours) is another to offer fancy digs. **Fenix Aparta-Hotel** (Carretera Canabacoa, tel. 809/612-5999, US$77/4 hours) has a ridiculously lavish driveway featuring giant, cast-iron animal figures. Its executive suites feel like a penthouse, with a disco-lit floor and pole in the living room and a swimming pool outdoors.

Illicit love is not mandatory: you can share the suite with friends, stock up on food and drinks, and have one heck of a private party.

teams in the country, the **Estadio Cibao** (Av. Imbert, tel. 809/575-1810, http://aguilas. lidom.com/main/estadio-cibao, from RD$150 or US$3.27) is the largest baseball facility in the DR, seating at least 18,000. It hosts pro baseball games two to three times a week from mid-October to late January. Dubbed "el valle de la muerte" (the valley of death), it was built in 1958 and expanded in 1974. In 2014, the stadium suffered a major fire; luckily it was closed at the time.

## Gran Teatro del Cibao

Across from the Monumento a los Héroes, the two marble and mahogany halls of the **Gran Teatro del Cibao** (Calle Daniel Espinal, corner of Av. Las Carreras, tel. 809/583-1150, 9am-4pm Mon.-Fri.) play host to national and international artists. Check the theater's social media pages for the latest events. Dominican architect Teofilo Carbonell designed the building in 1995 and is said to have modeled it after Santo Domingo's national theater. It has a capacity of 1,600.

## Monumento Natural Pico Diego de Ocampo

Outdoors enthusiasts should visit the **Monumento Natural Pico Diego de Ocampo** (tel. 829-799-7839, lisandromichael1998@hotmail.com, US$10)—declared a biological reserve in 1996—to make the two-hour hike up the 1,249-meter-tall (4,097-foot) peak. Named after a maroon who fought against Spanish colonialists from these mountains back in the 16th century, it's the highest point on the Cordillera Septentrional and a perfect way to get your body ready for the peaks of Jarabacoa, especially if you're going to climb Pico Duarte later in your journey. The 15-kilometer (9.3 miles) ride north of Santiago to the entrance of the monument takes 45 minutes and is quite a challenge—you'll need an all-terrain vehicle—but the vistas are gorgeous and the countryside life you see make it worthwhile.

Get on Highway 1 from the city and continue onto the Carretera al Pico Diego. After about 40 minutes, when you reach yellow Colmado Checo (good place for a water stop), you'll know you're just a minute away from the start of the hike. The trick: guides are only around on the weekends, Friday through Sunday. There's signage to the entrance of the hike; the guides sit and wait at the top of the hill during that time. The view from the top of Pico Diego over the Cibao Valley is spectacular, taking in the Septentrional range, part of the Cordillera Central, and Santiago in the distance. To arrange for a car and a ride to take you up to the peak, contact the local taxi dispatch **Santiago Taxi** (tel. 809/581-8888).

## Mirabal Sisters Museum

The heroines of Dominican history, the Mirabal sisters—Patria, Minerva, Maria Teresa, and Bélgica, also known as the Butterflies—were from Salcedo and fought to overthrow former dictator Rafael Leonidas Trujillo before three were eventually murdered by his men on their way back home from visiting their husbands in prison. Their killing triggered a revolt that ultimately led to the assassination of Trujillo in 1961.

The surviving sister, Bélgica Adela Mirabal, affectionately known as Doña Dede, founded the **Mirabal Sisters Museum** (Av. Duarte, tel. 809/587-8530, www. casamuseohermanasmirabal.com, 9:30am-4:30pm Tues.-Fri., call ahead, US$2) in 1994 in her native city of Ojo de Agua, near Salcedo, to commemorate her family. She passed away in 2014 at the age of 88. The museum is in the sisters' former second home. Sitting amid immaculate gardens, the home contains displays of the family's personal effects, from handkerchiefs to dresses to teacups. The kitchen and other rooms are kept in their original condition. The most moving showcase is of the items recovered from the murdered sisters' bodies—including a bloodstained handkerchief, shoes, and a braid from Maria Teresa's head that her sister cut and kept. There's a gift shop on-site, as well as a bookstore.

# SPORTS AND RECREATION

## Hiking

If you're not headed to Jarabacoa, then your best bet for some outdoor activity is to hike the Pico Diego de Ocampo. It's a tricky spot to find; get a local taxi to drive you up the hills from the city, on a 45-minute, part-paved and part-bumpy ride to the trail entrance at Monumento Natural Pico Diego de Ocampo (tel. 829-799-7839, lisandromichael1998@hotmail.com, US$10). At least that is clearly marked with a giant sign. Follow the trail on foot to meet up with the guides that wait here on weekends, before starting your two-hour journey that will give you a feel for the glorious mountainous landscape of this Cibao region and the city of Santiago's backdrop. There isn't much else to do here, so begin the hike in the morning, and return by early afternoon in time for lunch.

## Horse-drawn Carriage Tour

Tour the city while shielding yourself from the harsh sun for a couple of hours in a traditional horse-drawn carriage tour. You'll find the carriages outside or around the Monumento a los Héroes, as well as around Parque Duarte, waiting to whisk visitors away. Don't pay more than RD$400 (US$8.72).

# ENTERTAINMENT AND EVENTS

Santiago is known to have one of the most active nightlife scenes in the country. There are certainly more clubs, bars, and corners to hang out in than are listed below, but these are the safest for first-time visitors, especially those who aren't bilingual. Even this fearless traveler recommends that you don't venture into local neighborhoods and clubs unaccompanied.

## Nightlife

You'll find the majority of popular, trendy bars surrounding the Monumento a los Héroes, an area that comes alive at night. The largest outdoor lounge is Puerta del Sol (but note they don't serve Presidente beer), which fills up beginning in late afternoon. Under a royal poinciana, the best ambience is at the outdoors Ahí Bar (Calle Tolentino, corner of Calle Restauración, tel. 809/581-6779, www.ahi-bar.com, 4pm-2am Mon.-Fri., noon-4am Sat.-Sun.). It is a popular stop for a cold drink any day of the week with music, video screens, and smaller space that's tucked away from the main streets. An indoor Ahí nightclub opens across the street from the bar on the weekends.

A few blocks north of downtown Santiago, Típico Monte Bar Las Colinas (Av. 27 de Febrero, across Direccion General de Impuestos Internos, no sign, look for merengue concert posters on its outside walls) hosts live merengue on the weekends and the occasional Dominican recording artist. Pasión (Autopista Duarte Km 7 1/2, 809/612-6411, 10pm-3am daily) is the fancier club option.

Tabú Room Club (tel. 809/724-4671, 8pm-8am daily) and Trio are both located within the Matum Hotel & Casino (Av. Las Carreras) grounds. Tabu is the more popular and packed one, despite its smaller size. If you're up for a night of gaming, head to the on-site casino.

## Festivals and Events

The grandest outdoor show in the city is Carnaval de Santiago. And it gets more elaborate and popular every year, despite competition from neighboring La Vega for title of the biggest carnival destination in the country. Santiago's Carnival is one of the most colorful and culturally authentic you can attend. If you're here in February, every weekend of the month you can enjoy watching Dominicans from all walks of life celebrating in the streets of the city and revelers in colorful folkloric costumes and handcrafted masks with spiky horns representing Santiago's *lechones* (devils), as well as other popular Dominican carnival personalities.

The celebrations take place around the city's most popular sight, the Monumento a los Héroes de la Restauración (Monumento de

Santiago), giving the already-colorful event a gorgeous, green backdrop. Everything kicks off on Sundays between 3pm and 4pm and lasts until 8pm. Crowds spread out either along the barricades of the parade route or up on the lawns of the monument to watch from above. You can show up as early as 2pm if you like and enjoy the sponsoring rum company's bar slinging mixed drinks for 50 pesos (barely over a dollar) while a DJ spins the latest Dominican and Carnival tunes. Once the parade begins, look out for those *lechones* and the long sisal rope whips they swing at high velocity. As long as you're standing behind the barricaded sidewalks you will be safe. Security is plentiful all along the parade route and around the monument, and food vendors are numerous. It's a fun time to visit this otherwise hectic city.

**ProCigar Festival** (third week of February, tel. 809/580-4754, www.procigar. org, US$895 for full program) is celebrated during one week across several locations across the DR. It includes a stop in Santiago, the birthplace and capital of the world's best cigars. Over 400 participants come from around the world to indulge in a fun time that includes cigar factory excursions, local cuisine and nightlife, and plenty of entertainment. Check the website for each year's schedule of activities, full program, and cost.

## SHOPPING

**Calle del Sol** is the main shopping street in Santiago, where you'll find fast food, electronic junk, Chinese fashion stores, and plenty of street vendors trying to sell you something, anything. Don't be surprised to see security guards with shotguns in front of jewelry stores. In the heart of Calle del Sol, the **Mercado Modelo** is a bit less hectic than the rest of the street and offers locally made souvenirs. Inaugurated in 1942 by Trujillo, the covered yet bright market complete with a fountain and rest area hosts over 400 vendor shops, ranging from jewelry and Dominican larimar and amber stones to merengue instruments you can take home.

For a colorful food market experience, and a look into why this area is known as the breadbasket of the DR, head to the sprawling, outdoor **Mercado Hospedaje Yaque** (Calle Capotillo, off Calle del Sol), where you'll find all the local vegetables and fruits you can think of and might not know, herbal shops with over a dozen *botánicas* where locals buy healing potions (believer beware), cafeteria shacks for cheap lunches, and men playing dominoes in corners while waiting to make a sale. It's a noisy, busy, crazy corner of the city, but a wonderful peek into daily Dominican life.

You'll find your fair share of shopping malls in Santiago with the requisite shoe stores, movie theaters, and food courts, but they're not terribly impressive compared to Santo Domingo's. Try the popular **Plaza Internacional** (Av. Juan Pablo Duarte), home to Caribbean Cinemas and decent fashions, **Bella Terra Mall** (Av. Juan Pablo Duarte, near corner of Estrella Sadhala, tel. 809/336-2903, www.bellaterra.com.do), or **Las Colinas Mall** (Av. 27 de Febrero, corner of Av. Imbert, tel. 809/576-6555, www.colinasmall. com.do).

The gift shop inside **Centro León** (Av. 27 de Febrero 146, tel. 809/582-2315, www. centroleon.org.do, 10am-7pm Tues.-Sun.) carries typical Santiaguero and Dominican items worth checking out, including La Aurora cigars and *merengue típico* hats.

Just 15 minutes outside of Santiago, in the village of **El Higüerito** (off Carretera 1/Autopista Duarte towards Ortega, after Rancho Chito restaurant), you'll find some delightful pottery, hand-made by Dominican artisans who use a potter's wheel. You can sit and watch them if you like, and it's an easy stop on the way from or to the airport. These potters and artisans are unique to this area. The vases and other household items are painted in vibrant colors and make a beautiful addition to any home. Visit the small, Dominican-owned ceramic workshop **Arte en Barro Jimenes** (Calle Bonagua Abajo 145, tel. 809/409-1006 or 829/655-9982,

## The Faceless Dolls of El Higüerito

You've probably spotted and been intrigued by them in souvenir shops: ceramic dolls with hats and zero facial features. The concept was born right here, in the village of El Higüerito, just 15 minutes outside of Santiago south of the airport. The Jose Marte Polonia family, which still runs its own workshops, has manufactured the *muñecas sin rostro* since 1983, after a woman from the neighborhood came up with the idea of producing a doll representing the average Dominican woman. That is to say, one who could be of many diverse roots—Dominicans have African, Spanish, and Taíno blood in their veins—so that it would be impossible for her to have any distinct facial features. The dolls act as a reminder that this is an all-inclusive culture, a melting pot that is embraced. For the past 35 years, the Marte family has been just one of a handful that make these dolls right out of their homes turned ateliers, and you can walk right in and watch **"Jose muñequito"** (Calle Camboya, tel. 809/216-5955, 8am-5pm)—as the workshop is also known in the village—spinning the wheel as he begins to shape each

one of El Higüerito's faceless dolls

one, later turned over to their painter to apply the colorful shades. The earth used to make the dolls comes from Bonao, mixed with El Higüerito's own.

There used to be up to 100 doll makers in this village, but competition and recessions proved tough and now only five remain. The Marte family's dolls sell in major tourist zones, including Punta Cana. A small doll costs about RD$100 (US$2.18), and a larger one is RD$600 (US$13.08).

7:30am-12:30pm and 1:30pm-5:30pm daily). The main potter, Guancho, has worked here for 22 years and uses earth brought in from nearby Bonao to make the pots—about 150 pots are made by hand daily. You can walk to the back and watch the kiln where they fire the pots. Across the street, the painter decorates and covers them in various colors and patterns. This is also where you can purchase the finished items.

## FOOD

If you're in the city center, grab coffee and dessert at **Pan y Galletas Piki** (across from Parque Duarte, Calle del Sol, tel. 809/582-2334, 6:30am-7:30pm daily, US$2-4), set on the corner of a pedestrian-only alley lined with historic buildings. You can enjoy your treats in the Parque Duarte.

An even better option, away from the madness of Calle del Sol, is **La Campagna**

(Av. Duarte 21, tel. 809/581-5056, www.lacampagna.com.do/panaderia, 7am-10pm daily, US$3-10), a coffee shop with a nicely shaded open terrace. It serves gourmet java as well as sandwiches, burgers, and small bites. The quiet atmosphere is perfect for those who want to bring their laptops and surf the Net. There's an adjacent restaurant if you need more options.

Set amid a row of trendy bars and restaurants across from the Monumento de Santiago, **El Tablón Latino** (Calle del Sol 12, tel. 809/581-3813, 11am-11pm daily, US$5-12) serves up a wide range of Latin dishes—think Peruvian ceviche, Dominican pork *chicharrón*, or Spanish risotto—in a casual-chic atmosphere. Eat on the outdoor terrace or indoors with tightly spaced seating and freezing air-conditioning. They also offer a solid range of salads, flatbread sandwiches, and desserts. Portions are large, and you can't go wrong with much of their menu. Wash it all down with a fresh juice. Service can be slow when it's busy.

**Max's Delicias** (pronounced "Mas," Calle del Sol 28, tel. 809/971-5574, 9am-10pm daily, US$3-10) is a casual Dominican cafeteria where you can eat well and cheaply. It's a one block walk up from the monument, yet hidden because a giant tree hangs over the restaurant's sign. Keep your eyes peeled when walking or driving there.

On par with Dominicans' love for hanging out by a gas station, **Square One** (Av. Estrella Sahlada, by Shell Gas, tel. 809/241-5384, www.square1rd.com, US$5-15) is the most popular diner in the city, open 24 hours with a decent, affordable menu of breakfast treats, sandwiches, burgers, and more. The 20- to 40-something crowd is hip and urban, and you might think you're back in the United States.

In the city center, **Pizzeria Monti** (corner of Duarte and Beller) serves a decent, large slice of pizza for just RD$60 (US$1.09). The small, cozy restaurant also has a second floor for additional space.

Situated across from the city's popular shopping malls, the tree-shaded ★ **La Parillita** (Av. Juan Pablo Duarte 162, tel. 809/583-1925, noon-midnight daily, US$5-10) is perfect for a post- or pre-shopping meal, with tasty grilled meats and other Dominican specialties (mashed yucca, plantains, rice and beans) served outdoors or inside, with open views to Santiago's never-ending traffic. Prices are affordable and service speedy.

A longtime favorite in Santiago and popular spot for business folks and groups, **Pez Dorado** (Calle del Sol 43, tel. 809/582-2518, noon-11pm daily, US$5-12) specializes in Chinese cuisine, as well as Dominican seafood dishes and steaks. It has a more formal atmosphere than most of Santiago's restaurants.

An excellent alternative for seafood is ★ **Marisco Caribeño Restaurant** (Calle del Sol 1, corner of Av. Francia, tel. 809/971-9710, www.mariscocentro.com, 10am-midnight daily, US$6-15), close to the Santiago Monument. There's an excellent seafood buffet on Sundays (RD$600), as well as an à la carte menu. On Saturdays you can listen to live music while you dine.

For a secluded, upscale restaurant to celebrate birthdays or simply sit on a terrace with cocktails, away from downtown, head to **Saga Restaurant & Cigar Club** (Av. Benito Juarez #24, tel. 809/276-7900, noon-midnight Tues.-Sun., from US$10-20). It has multiple rooms to suit different tastes, including one for cigar smokers. Famous for its meats, from pork chops to goat stews and steaks, you'll also find seafood and an extensive wine list. Try the Tomahawk rib eye, which feeds two and is served sizzling on a salt block.

★ **Camp David Ranch** (Carretera Gregorio Luperón Km 7.5, tel. 809/275-6400, 7am-midnight daily, US$5-15) has the nicest setting of the area's restaurants, reached via a 10- to 15-minute drive out of town and up into the hills. The panoramic mountain view from the outdoor dining terrace is just one of the reasons to dine here. (There's also cozy indoor seating.) The menu delights with appetizers like pork belly *taquitos* or shrimp soaked in a passion fruit sauce and served with spicy guacamole. Entrées could be yucca gnocchi stuffed with beef or paella. It's popular among Santiagueros on Sundays, so come early (or reserve ahead) if you want to find space.

## ACCOMMODATIONS

Hotel accommodations are surprisingly pricey in Santiago—perhaps because it's primarily a business travel destination.

Newcomer ★ **El Palmetto** (Av. Juan Pablo Duarte, corner of Puerto Rico #132, tel. 809/241-4821, from US$50, includes full breakfast) is a wonderful addition to the otherwise average hotels in Santiago. Ideally located smack on the busiest entertainment avenue of Santiago, it sits on the 2nd floor of a modern building and is flanked by malls and restaurants. It's just a short drive to nearby parks. Rooms are secure—each floor has a separate locked door—with modern, sleek furniture, working tables, flat-screen TVs,

## Santiago's *Lechoneras*

*Lechoneras* specialize in pork.

Meat lovers alert: Santiagueros love their pit-roasted pork. There are three renowned *lechoneras*, as they're called, in the city. All are casual, open-air restaurants right off a main road or highway and serve foods other than pork (in case you're only interested in seeing the setup). Note that this isn't food for the poor: roasted pork is a Dominican delicacy. A plate goes for about RD$200-300 (US$4.36-6.54) for a quarter, or RD$600 (US$13.08) for a pound. Go early if you want to see how the meat is made (as early as 6am); after lunchtime it's all gone.

**Lechonera Milito** (Av. Hispanoamericana, tel. 809/626-0140, 7am-6pm daily) is perhaps the farthest out from downtown and used to be a much bigger restaurant before the owner passed and the business moved to its current location. Still, it's a popular pit stop, offering casual restaurant seating or counter service. A second option is **El Embrujo** (Av. Rafael Vidal, across from the Century Plaza Hotel, tel. 809/581-4099, 7am-midnight). Santiagueros agree that **Rancho Chito** (Autopista Duarte Km 12 1/2, tel. 809/276-0000, www.ranchochito.com, US$3.65-20) is the best option of the three, and the more modern, fancier setting certainly proves it. The spacious thatched-roof restaurant offers cafeteria-style dishes, where you can pick your pork cuts among numerous other local options, or from an extensive à la carte menu. It's a family favorite and fills up on Sundays for its buffet option (RD$230 or US$5).

hot and cold water, air-conditioning, Wi-Fi (though it drops occasionally), and glass showers.

The two-person operation at **Via Emilia B&B** (Calle Estado de Israel 16, tel. 809/820-6609, www.viaemiliasantiago.com, US$35-39) is a find in a city filled with big hotels. A stone's throw from the main bus stations and Calle Duarte yet out of plain sight, this small guesthouse provides all you need for a safe, comfy place to stay.

Small, immaculately clean rooms include private bath, flat-screen TV, fan and air-conditioning (though not strong), and wireless Internet. There's an on-site dining room offering meals at an extra charge. Staff are friendly and accommodating. Look for the Italian flag on the front door when you're first trying to locate the place. You'll need a car or taxi to get here.

**Hodelpa Centro Plaza Hotel & Casino** (Calle Mella and Sol, tel. 809/583-6666, www.

hodelpa.com, US$90-130, includes breakfast) is right at the heart of the city's main commercial shopping street, Calle del Sol. It's good for those who want to be in the middle of the action and near the city's few sights. You'll find all the classic hotel room furnishings and comfort here—though rooms are small—including minibars and coffeemakers. Perks include a free airport shuttle and an on-site casino and restaurant.

Hotel Platino (Av. Estrella Sadhala, tel. 809/724-7576, www.hotelplatinord.com, US$53-130) gets rave reviews for its staff and provides good value for those passing through the city but not looking to stay in the center. The slightly dated rooms are clean and have mini fridges, TVs, and wireless Internet. If you want to take it up a notch, go for the suites.

Those who want to escape or bypass Santiago for the day while transiting can head to Camp David Ranch Hotel (Carretera Gregorio Luperón Km 7.5, tel. 809/276-6400, www.campdavidranch.com, US$90-115, includes breakfast), sitting 457 meters (1,500 feet) above sea level overlooking the bustling city. The hotel's 17 modern rooms are well appointed with king beds, neutral wall colors, wood furniture, flat-screen TVs, air-conditioning, irons, wireless Internet, safes, and outdoor verandas with views onto the valley. The bathrooms, while small, have marble sinks and glass showers. On display in the lobby—attached to the on-site restaurant's glorious outdoor terrace—are original vintage cars belonging to former dictator Rafael Leonidas Trujillo, including his black 1956 Cadillac Fleetwood.

## INFORMATION AND SERVICES

You'll find plenty of shopping on Calle del Sol, the main commercial street in the city. Avenida Duarte is home to shopping malls, restaurants, cafés, and various stand-alone stores, including La Sirena (Calle España, 8am-10pm). Parallel Avenida 27 de Febrero houses numerous services from banks to bus stations.

For 24-hour medical care, the in-town options are Centro Medico Semma (Padre Francisco Bono, tel. 809/688-6646 or 809/226-1053) or Hospital Jose Maria Cabral y Baez (Av. 27 de Febrero, tel. 809/724-7555), close to the center. If you have the time to spare, a better bet is on Autopista Duarte, at Hospital Metropolitano de Santiago (Autopista Duarte Km 2.8, tel. 829/947-2222, www.homshospital.com).

## GETTING THERE AND AROUND

### Air

Aeropuerto Internacional del Cibao (www.aeropuertocibao.com.do) is just a 20-minute drive out of the city, and serves airlines such as American, Delta, JetBlue, United, Copa, and Spirit. Airport taxis to the city cost around US$25.

### Bus

Getting to Santiago is quite easy from Santo Domingo or Puerto Plata. Caribe Tours (Av. 27 de Febrero, tel. 809/576-0790, www.caribetours.com.do, US$2.39-5.88) sends a bus nearly every hour from Santiago to Santo Domingo; check the website for departure times. Get off at the second and final stop in Santiago in the city center, as there are two. Metro Tours (Av. Duarte, tel. 809/587-3837, http://metroserviciosturisticos.com, US$2.39-5.88), just a block away, also has departures throughout the day, even if not every hour like Caribe. Whichever bus you opt for, bring a scarf or jacket of some kind because the air-conditioning can be frigid. Other possible destinations from Santiago by bus include Puerto Plata, Sosúa, and Monte Cristi. Arrive at least 45 minutes prior to your bus departure.

A third way of reaching Santiago from Puerto Plata, particularly if you plan on connecting to other small towns such as La Vega or San Francisco de Macorís, is to hop on a Javila Tours minibus. It's popular with the locals and comfortable, with air-conditioning and wireless Internet on board.

# Day Trip: Sajoma

If you're up for a unique drive into the deep, green mountains of the Cibao region, devoid of other tourists, head to San Jose de Las Matas, affectionately known as "Sajoma." This little-known, remote town in the province of Santiago, in the vicinity of Parque Nacional Armando Bermúdez, is growing thanks to a number of surrounding natural parks turned recreation centers. Here is where you should make a stop and spend the day.

- **Aguas Calientes** (Los Montones, tel. 809/691-4090, US$2.50 pp, 9am-6pm daily): Boasting a small pool fed by mineral-rich sulfur springs, this park has been developed into a recreational escape. A boardwalk leads you along the small thermal tub with infinity views, and onward to a pedestrian suspension bridge and the Bao River, where you can also swim. To escape any visiting local groups, head to the other side of the park, across the parking lot, where you'll find another long boardwalk and additional areas to relax and swim by the river. There are snacks, bars, and a local lunch lady selling meals daily. Avoid coming here on Sundays, as it gets quite crowded with families.

- **Hacienda Campo Verde:** This family-friendly spot boasts a swimming pool your kids will appreciate, as well as the river below, with plenty of lounge chairs shallow parts for swimming. There's a restaurant on-site as well, with a daily lunch buffet. It's a casual atmosphere; don't expect any fancy amenities. The key is to enjoy the natural surroundings.

The more adventurous can extend the trip to dine at Mirador de Arte (San Jose de las Matas Km 7, tel. 829/649-6487, noon-midnight daily), if only to have your meal on a terrace boasting spectacular views of Sajoma's mountains.

The vans depart every 15 minutes from 6am through 5pm. The fare is just RD$120 or US$2.60, and you can hop off at Parque Los Chachases in Santiago for the next round of connections.

## Taxi

Santiago's taxis charge a set fare of about US$3.27 (RD$150) for one-way rides within city limits. You'll usually see them parked outside major supermarkets, sights, and bus stations. You can call **Santiago Taxi** (tel. 809/581-8888) or request an Uber—the app-based service is active and reliable in Santiago.

## Car

Getting around Santiago isn't hard if you remember the key drags: Calle del Sol, the main shopping street, runs east into the Monumento a los Héroes. The main avenues are 27 de Febrero and Duarte, where you'll find all the malls, movie theaters, and supermarkets. You can rent a car from the airport (booked online to ensure better rates) through **Avis** (tel. 809/233-8154, www.avis.com), **Alamo** (tel. 809/233-8163, www.alamo.com), **Europcar** (tel. 809/233-8150, www.europcar.com), or **Honda Rent-a-car** (tel. 809/233-8179, www.nationalcar.com).

# La Vega

A hot, dusty city, and the third largest in the DR, La Vega is essentially a transportation and commercial center. There's no reason to visit—*unless* it's February, when you can witness one of the most vibrant and traditional carnivals in the country. Despite the fact that it doesn't have much going on, La Vega is home to two historically significant sights: the Holy Hill of Santo Cerro and the archaeological ruins of La Vega Vieja, the original city founded by Columbus himself in 1494 as a gold mining base. An earthquake leveled it in 1562, and the population relocated to the town's current spot along the Río Camú.

## SIGHTS

In the city itself, Casa de la Cultura (across from Parque Duarte, tel. 809/573-1021, casadelaculturadelavega@gmail.com, 8am-5pm Mon.-Fri.) displays local art every month; there was no schedule when I visited, so don't expect too much if you happen to stop in here. Within the Parque Duarte compound a few steps north is the city's well-known and imposing Catedral Inmaculada Concepción. This towering, odd, faded gray stone building is a serious eyesore on the outside. It's much more attractive on the inside, with an impressive 15-foot-tall statue of Jesus. The ceiling, lit up to look like a starry sky, took 15 years to complete (1977-1992). The cathedral has a 1,000-person capacity.

### The Holy Hill of Santo Cerro

Whether you're into history or religion or neither, if you're lucky enough to pass through Santo Cerro northeast of La Vega and Highway Duarte and indulge in the views over the Valle de La Vega, you will not be sorry. It's absolutely breathtaking. But Santo Cerro is also one of the holiest sites in the country and one of the most historically significant. This was one of the first three dioceses in the New World. A major pilgrimage takes place every

year on September 24 to the Nuestra Señora de Las Mercedes Church (mass 6:30am and 5pm Mon.-Fri., 7am and 4pm Sat., 6:30am, 9am or 11am, and 4pm Sun.) following nine days of *fiestas patronales* (patron saint celebrations) that begin around September 16. Thousands of Dominicans come from all corners of the country and from abroad.

Legend has it that Santo Cerro was the site of a miracle in the Spanish colonial days. Columbus had received a cross from Queen Isabela of Spain when he set sail, and he planted it on this hill overlooking the Cibao upon arriving. When the Taíno fought the Spaniards in 1495, they attempted to burn the cross, but it wouldn't take fire and the Virgin de las Mercedes appeared before them on the cross. The Taíno are said to have fled in fear, and it brought an end to the war with the indigenous population (you can tell whose version of the story this was). The original cross, made of níspero wood, is no longer here. It is thought to have ended up in private hands in Rome, among various stories which can't be verified, but you can still see the Holy Hole or *Santo Hoyo* where it was originally planted inside the church. Before reaching the church, look out for a fenced-off *árbol de níspero*—a tree originally planted by Columbus in 1495.

Be sure to walk behind the church to the lookout terrace for unbelievable views over the valley. Take the staircase down to admire the 14-meter-high (46-foot) cross from up close. Built in 2013, its base hugged by a giant rosary, its mosaic tiles are covered in depictions of the passion of Christ. Look down at the steps and observe the intricate verses sculpted into each one. On your way out, buy some local *croquetas de maís* snacks—sweet corn crackers—from vendors.

### Parque Nacional Arqueológico e Histórico de la Vega Vieja

At the Parque Nacional Arqueológico e

Histórico de la Vega Vieja (Carretera Juan Bosch, 8am-5pm daily, US$2.18 pp), you can walk amid the 500-year-old ruins of the old city, named Concepción de La Vega, that Christopher Columbus founded as a gold mining base and turned into one of the most prosperous cities in the Americas. Declared a national park in 1976, it's tucked off the highway before La Vega's center (there's a hard-to-spot sign for the turnoff to the park). A young, Spanish-speaking guide will show up as you arrive at the parking lot to collect your entrance fee and take you through the ruins. He will tell you the story of Columbus's old fort, now in ruins, where he kept his precious gold, and show the old sentinel towers. It's pretty incredible to think that you're standing on one of the oldest colonial settlements in the Americas. If you position yourself in front of the fort facing west, you can spot the new Santo Cerro cross in the distance.

The first archaeological studies of this site began in 1994, with the help of researchers from the Florida Museum of Natural History. These determined the size and location of the original city, along with cataloging over 200,000 items recovered from excavations. It was later found that it was the largest settlement in the New World until at least 1520. At the back of the park is a museum—more of a room, really—filled with ancient Taíno artifacts and tools, Franciscan stones and early Spanish tools, telescopes, and random items from various periods.

## ENTERTAINMENT AND EVENTS

### ★ Carnival in La Vega

Dating back to the 1500s, **El Carnaval de La Vega or Carnaval Vegano** (www.carnavalvegano.do) is the biggest, oldest, most vibrant and culturally authentic Carnival celebration in the Dominican Republic. Every Sunday in February, no detail is spared in this party in the third city of the DR. Any other time of year it is a noisy, dusty place with not much happening other than day-to-day commerce. But for those six weekends of the year, culminating with independence weekend at the end of February, the heart of the city along Parque Duarte and the main avenues surrounding it transforms into the most exuberant scene you'll witness in the Caribbean. La Vega's celebrations reflect the DR's mixed African, Taíno, and European heritage.

the view from the Holy Hill of Santo Cerro

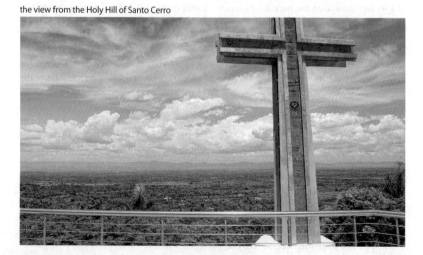

Expect music and drumming, parades of colorful costumes with signature devilish masks with horns—the making of which is true art and begins months prior—pageant contests to crown a king and queen of Carnival, and large concerts. This is also one of the most commercially sponsored Carnivals in the country.

Arrive by noon in front of Parque Duarte along a block of Calle Juan Bosch to catch La Vega's smaller, lesser-known **Carnaval de La Boa**—a traditional version celebrating how Carnival used to be feted 50 years ago—with plenty of families and kids and costumed devils. This smaller carnival lasts until about 2pm. The bigger La Vega carnival celebrations with tents stretching down Calle General Juan Rodriguez and parallel streets kick off around 3pm, but the crowds are already streaming through from 1pm. You'll see the various *cuevas* (headquarters) of each devil group, as well as bars where you can purchase drinks and dance. If you mingle on the sidewalks with the crowd, look out for those devil whips or *vejigazos!* Carnaval de La Vega is one massive street party worth seeing at least once.

## FOOD AND ACCOMMODATIONS

**El Zaguán** (Av. Pedro Rivera, tel. 809/573-5508, 9am-10pm daily, US$2-3) is a favorite for its *mofongo* and its generous portions of Dominican and creole dishes. On **El Naranjo**'s (Calle Padre Adolfo, tel. 809/573-7751, elnaranjocafe@hotmail.com, 8am-11:30pm daily, US$3-10) outdoor patio, you can enjoy a small menu of tacos, burritos, and sandwiches, ideal if you're in a rush and on the go. Directly across the street is a **Pollo Licey** (tel. 809/242-3090, 11am-10pm daily, US$1.50-3) for a cheap box of rice and beans.

Hotels are scarce in La Vega. If you must stay here, which would be for Carnival, **Hotel**

**El Rey** (Calle Don Antonio Guzmán 3, tel. 809/573-9797, US$50) is the best option, a straight 10-minute walk to the city's parks and area restaurants. There is also a restaurant on-site (closed Sunday). Rooms include double or queen beds, as well as flat-screen TVs, fridges, decent air-conditioning, and private baths with shower. The surrounding area is a bit run-down, but walking it in daylight hours is fine. A block south is the budget **Hotel Zitro** (Av. Antonio Guzmán Fernández, tel. 809/573-7731, US$15), offering spacious rooms but no air-conditioning or restaurant.

## GETTING THERE AND AROUND

There are various transport options to La Vega. **Caribe Tours** (Av. Pedro Rivera 37, tel. 809/573-6806, www.caribetours.com.do) provides transport to or from Santo Domingo, as well as the northern cities of Puerto Plata and Santiago. There's also service—at 8:30am, 11:30am, 3:30pm, and 6pm—from La Vega to the more tourist-ready Jarabacoa (RD$70 or US$1.53). Check the website for current times and prices. From Santiago, **Expreso Quito Patio** minibus line departs throughout the day (5am-5pm) for La Vega (across from Parque Los Chachases) and offers regular service between the two cities. The ride is just 20 minutes with light traffic. Purchase your RD$75 or US$1.65 ticket at the window before boarding.

The north-south running **Autopista Duarte** linking to Santo Domingo is always a good bet for catching a *guagua* off the main road, going in either direction. Stay in the center of the city and you'll be able to get around on foot; alternatively, you can hire a taxi to get you around La Vega and Jarabacoa. Ask your hotel for referrals.

# Jarabacoa

Easily one of my favorite parts of the DR, Jarabacoa (pronounced HA-ra-bah-ko-ah) takes your breath away with its mountainous landscape, rolling hills, fresh air, and friendly people who live in colorful villages along three rivers—the Río Yaque, the Baiguate, and the Jimenoa. After all, the city name is Taíno for "place of waters." You won't tire of the sweeping *campo* fields where goats, turkeys, and birds roam and chew, and where wooden shacks dangle on mountain edges, attached to the earth with wooden footbridges. Roads are lined with flowers and fields of fragrant cilantro, *tayota* (chayote), and other natural delights. Fresh water, fresh food, fresh and cool mountain air: it's hard to beat the center of the Cibao Valley, and Jarabacoa is a wonderful introduction to it.

There's no shortage of social activity either. *Parilladas* (steak houses) are packed with folks enjoying the grilled meats the area is known for. Kids are always jumping off the handful of cascades that bless Jarabacoa. Weekends mean tubing down rivers in old tires while families barbecue riverside. When the sun goes down, bars blast merengue and *bachata* out under the starry, chilly skies.

On the flip side, Jarabacoa is also where you'll spot some of the country's most extravagant mountain vacation homes, perched so high you'll wonder how amazing the view is from the inside. This town is indeed the rich Santiaguero and Santo Domingo *capitaleño's* weekend escape. There are numerous privately owned cabins and villas, some with pools and infinite mountain vistas.

Downtown Jarabacoa is an intimate, pedestrian-friendly town easy to explore in a day. Whatever you do, don't leave without getting a motorbike ride through some of the most scenic areas outside the center of town, including Pinar Quemado, Manabao-La Ciénaga, and the neighborhoods lining the Río Yaque del Norte. The "City of Eternal Springs" was made not just for freshwater bathing, but also exploring on motorbike or mountain bike, the wind blowing through your hair.

## SIGHTS

One of the landmarks here, as in most Dominican towns, is the **Parque Central** or **Parque Duarte,** a small but clean space with a bust of the independence hero, plenty of benches, and lovely mountain views in the distance. Locals hang out here in the day as much as the nighttime. Traffic, especially motorbikes, is always whizzing around.

### ★ Saltos de Jimenoa

It is said that if you haven't been to the Jimenoa waterfalls, you haven't been to Jarabacoa. There are two **Saltos de Jimenoa:** Jimenoa Uno and Jimenoa Dos. Jimenoa Dos is easy to reach from town and doesn't require much of a hike thanks to a series of bridges. The entrance to the **Salto de Jimenoa Dos** (8am-5pm, RD$50 or US$1.09), just outside Jarabacoa, is reached after a gorgeous ride through the Pinar Dorado community, past chayote fields, grazing cows, and gorgeous green hills dotted with cabins. You'll need a car, taxi, or bike to reach it.

After paying the park fee at the entrance, you'll begin your hike along the river on footbridges and steps until the last portion where the waterfall is located. Along the way, you'll spot riverbanks where you can descend and sit if you choose (no benches) before continuing your hike. The views of the suspension and wooden footbridges against towering rocks make for great photo ops. You can't swim in this 40-meter (131-foot) waterfall's pool, unfortunately. The currents below the falls are strong, and there have drownings here. The lookout point is fenced off and quite high, but allows admiring the waterfall from a close

## Jarabacoa

LA CONFLUENCIA

HOTEL GRAN JIMENOA

Residential Don Mon

Urb. Jackeline

La Rueda

JARABACOA GOLF CLUB

**SEE DETAIL**

La Javilla

CASA DE TIA YESI

Colina Los Pomos

CAFE MONTE ALTO

Jarabacoa

JARABACOA MOUNTAIN HOSTEL

Pinar Dorado

Elias Santana

HOTEL CALIFORNIA

28

SALTOS DE JIMENOA

Salto Jimenoa Uno

Salto de Baiguate

SALTOS DE JIMENOA

28

0    1000 yds
0    1000 m

EL TAINO/ PICA POLLO

VENUE BAR & LOUNGE

MIGUEL M CASTILLO

POLITUR

JARAPAN

CARIBE EXPRESS

BUS TO LA VEGA

JOSE DURAN

PELEGRINA HERRERA

JARABACOA SUPERMARKET

COLON

LA TINAJA

FRESCO BISTRO

MELLA

AV INDEPENDENCIA

MERCADO PUBLICO

SANCHEZ

AROMA DE LA MONTAÑA

DUARTE

LUPERON

BANCO POPULAR

PLAZA RAMÍREZ

MARIO NELSON GALAN

MIRABAL

Parque Central

CALLE EL CARMEN

16 DE AGOSTO

© MOON.COM

enough distance. Locals have been known to hop the fence for photo ops.

**Salto de Jimenoa Uno** is a lot steeper, tucked inside a ravine with water cascading 75 meters (246 feet) on the way to Constanza. You can't see the waterfall from the road, only the sign indicating where to begin your hike down. It reads *"El gran salto proyecto comunitario,"* on the left-hand side after about 7.25 kilometers (4.5 miles) along the Constanza Road. You'll hike a steep hill down to the bottom. Wear good shoes, and keep in mind that you'll have to come back up.

Which of the two waterfalls is better? It's really hard to say—if you're intent on swimming, head to Jimenoa Uno. Jimenoa Dos is more of a scenic ride and hike, and you'll get to see one of the most beautiful neighborhoods of Jarabacoa.

## Salto de Baiguate

My favorite place in Jarabacoa is **Salto de**

**Baiguate,** tucked inside a gorgeous canyon. It's an easy place to reach and a refreshing place to swim, and the vibe is very local: kids often climb the dark rocky cliffs under the 25-meter-tall (82-foot) waterfall and leap into the deep pool below. But it's also the views of this impressive flow of water against a lush, rocky landscape towering over you that will make you want to stay longer. The water is clean and crisp, as expected in Jarabacoa, and it makes for a fun and easy two-hour break. You can reach this place by motorbike (US$10). The 15- to 20-minute ride is an absolute blast, as it takes you down the narrow, lush trail directly to the steps leading down to the fall. You can also ride horses here with **Jarabacoa Eco Adventures** (tel. 849/917-7638, http://jarabacoamotoadventures. blogspot.com, US$15 pp). There's no entrance fee, as it's not a national park. If you drive your own rental here, take Avenida Pedregal south from town, which leads you to the entrance. You'll have to leave the car by the big Salto de Baiguate sign, then hike the trail for about 10-15 minutes to the steps.

## ★ La Confluencia

One of the most relaxing spots in Jarabacoa, **La Confluencia** is a spacious park where the Baiguate, the Jimenoa, and the Yaque del Norte rivers converge. Locals flock to this family-friendly place, especially on the weekends. On the weekdays it's quiet and even more blissful.

There are picnic tables and a small local bar shack, and locals bring their coolers and pots and plates, just like they do at the beach. It's a great place for swimming—there are various mini pools amid the rocks where you can sit and relax in refreshing water, just like a natural Jacuzzi spa, while enjoying a *trago* (drink) or two. There are even horses for rent (US$7/ hour) if you want to go on a ride along the river, along the back of La Confluencia.

Finding the park is easy—from the center of town, Avenida La Confluencia will lead you directly toward the park, which is at the end of the road.

## Café Monte Alto

Jarabacoa's **Café Monte Alto** (Carretera Belarminio Ramírez, Altos del Yaque, tel. 809/574-2618, www.ramirezcoffee.com, 8am-6pm Mon.-Fri., 8am-4pm Sat., US$3.31 or RD$150) is a hit in the Cibao region—and their coffee is only sold in this particular part of the country. Founded in 1943 by the Ramírez Coffee Company, the factory oversees 350 hectares (865 acres) of coffee in the Cordillera Central. They produce two types of Arabica ground coffee: Monte Alto, a regular coffee brand, and Café Monte Alto Orgánico, which is harvested at the highest altitude on their farm (793-1,494 meters [2,600-4,900 feet]) and guaranteed to be chemical-free.

If you're a coffee lover, take a short ride from Jarabacoa to this family-owned coffee factory for a one-hour tour of the facility, where you'll see their cleaning, roasting, and grinding machinery. You'll learn about the coffeemaking process from bean to cup and even get to taste the final product at their on-site café. You can purchase the various coffee brands (including certified organic) there as well. The guided tour is in Spanish only, unfortunately, so you'll have to bring along a bilingual guide or friend if you're not fluent.

## SPORTS AND RECREATION
### Tours

**Rancho Baiguate** (tel. 809/574-4940, www.ranchobaiguate.com) and **Rancho Jarabacoa** (tel. 809/222-3202, www. ranchojarabacoa.com) are the most complete adventure tour operators in town. Both offer similar excursions such as river rafting, canyoning, and horseback riding to waterfalls. Rancho Baiguate has plenty of English-speaking guides. Other independent tour guides offer similar services and usually attract smaller crowds, or will customize trips for you. I highly recommend David Durán of **Jarabacoa Eco**

1: Jarabacoa's lush, natural setting; 2: Salto de Baiguate; 3: Salto de Jimenoa Dos

Adventures (tel. 849/917-7638, http://jarabacoamotoadventures.blogspot.com), a young Dominican guide who knows the area well and offers reasonable prices. He can take you to all of the well-known places but also to off-the-beaten-track ones—including secret waterfalls (I've sworn not to tell about the one I experienced). Some activities only require that you have transportation, which could be a cheap motorbike taxi, a regular taxi, or your rental car.

TOP EXPERIENCE

## ★ River Rafting on the Río Yaque del Norte

Besides being Jarabacoa's signature activity, river rafting is a fun way to enjoy the beautiful scenery along the DR's longest river, the Río Yaque del Norte. **Rancho Baiguate** (tel. 809/574-6890 or U.S. tel. 646/727-7783, www.ranchobaiguate.com, US$50) offers river rafting trips that will take you to the put-in, about a 30-minute drive, and then give you basic rafting training and tips (you will also watch a safety video at the ranch before departure). From there, it's directly in the raft and onto the river. Toss and tumble and paddle your way down the river while your guide shouts out instructions as you go over rapids and small falls. The ride isn't too crazy, but it will get your adrenaline pumping.

The river is flanked by cliffs and lush vegetation. *Garzas* soar overhead, cows graze along the banks, and ramshackle huts are perched dangerously high above the river. There are a couple of stops along the riverbank: one for snacks, another for picking mangoes. Rancho Baiguate's tireless guides make it a lively trip. Bring a change of clothes and shoes and leave your things at the office, unless you're staying at the ranch itself. Wear what you wouldn't mind getting wet. Long pants are recommended in case you fall into the river (take it from me).

The gift shop at Rancho Baiguate sells water shoes, but you can wear your sneakers if you don't mind getting them wet. Just be sure to wear closed-toe shoes.

## Hiking

The hiking opportunities are numerous in Jarabacoa. Getting close to nature comes as easily as walking along the roads or veering off into local villages. The only question is, how much vacation time do you have to spare?

You can climb the mighty **El Mogote,** the second-highest peak in the DR after Pico Duarte. It is an extremely steep hike to the 1,163-meter (3,815-foot) peak and not for the faint of heart. The summit can be reached in about 2.5 hours; if you're not an experienced hiker, double that estimate. En route are breathtaking views of the pine-covered mountain range and Jarabacoa below. You'll pass lots of vegetation as you get higher, such as coffee trees and blackberry bushes (you can snack on the blackberries). The last 30 minutes are the toughest, but once at the top by the caretaker's cabin, you can climb yet another 9 meters (30 feet) up a steel lookout tower to take in 360-degree views of the surrounding valleys and mountains, all the way to Constanza. Every ache or pain will disappear. An even better experience, if you have the time, is to camp there overnight so you can witness the most glorious sunrise before making your way back to town.

Contact David Durán of **Jarabacoa Eco Adventures** (tel. 849/917-7638, http://jarabacoamotoadventures.blogspot.com) to take you on this hike. Your guide will bring plenty of water, but make sure you have snacks as well, especially as you'll need more strength when you prepare to hike back down. Remember it's as tricky going down as it is going up. Wear long hiking pants, solid sneakers that fit well around the toes (or you'll end up bruising them), a hat, and sunscreen.

## Mountain Biking

Ride a mountain bike to the area's falls with **Rancho Baiguate** (tel. 809/574-4940, www.ranchobaiguate.com, US$25-40 pp). You can bike to either Salto Baiguate or Salto Jimenoa, or a combination of both, depending on your fitness level.

## Horseback Riding

You can ride to many of the town's main sights, including to Salto Baiguate or Salto Jimenoa, with **Rancho Baiguate** (tel. 809/574-4940, www.ranchobaiguate.com, US$10-15 pp). There are also horses for rent at **La Confluencia** (about US$8/hour or RD$350), allowing you to ride around the park.

## Paragliding

There are two paragliding operations in town. **Flying Tony** (tel. 809/848-3479, www. flyindr.com, US$60 pp, US$800/course) is the longer-running of the two. Tony takes you on a 25-minute drive up to the Paso Alto area on the scenic highway between Jarabacoa and Constanza to the takeoff point, where you're outfitted with equipment and prepped to fly in tandem with your paragliding guide (ask ahead for guidelines on body positioning and paragliding technique, as I received little instruction beforehand). The feeling of floating and flying above Jarabacoa's breathtaking scenery is unlike any other you'll have during your time here. If you've never done it, I

highly recommend it. Liftoff is easy and returning to ground is gradual, requiring you to land on your butt, legs straight out, but there's nothing to worry about—the guides have over 30 years of combined experience.

The other recommended operation is **Hawk Paragliding** (tel. 849/867-3212, www. hawkparagliding.com, US$60). It offers tandem gliding (with photos and video of your experience included), or lessons so you can eventually fly solo.

## Motorbike Tours

Negotiate with a motorbike taxi and go on a ride through some of the most gorgeous scenery in Jarabacoa. One route begins just off the Carretera Jarabacoa-Manabao. From the highway, turn right onto the backcountry road running along the back of the Río Yaque in Vera del Yaque. There are views of wide pasturelands dotted with cows, sheep, piglets, and donkeys, all set against a perfectly green background and Mogote Mountain in the distance; you won't want to leave. You'll get to pose next to footbridges leading to wooden shacks, contrasting against the green river beneath. Make sure you look for the mango trees. There are usually dozens of mangoes on the ground, waiting to

Paraglide over Jarabacoa's mountains and waterfalls.

be enjoyed. You might even spot kids floating down the river in their own homemade tubes. Other scenic motorbike rides are through El Pinar Dorado and along the road leading to Salto Jimenoa Dos.

**MotoCaribe** (Calle Las Palmas 3, Pinar Dorado, tel. 809/574-6507, US$1,795) organizes a six-day motorbike excursion around the North Coast and the Cibao, starting with exploring the central mountains in Jarabacoa for one day before continuing on to Samaná. Dates are set well in advance.

## Golfing

If you're intent on golfing, head to **Jarabacoa Golf Club** (Piedra Blanca, tel. 809/782-9883, www.jarabacoagolf.com, 8am-7pm daily)—the only mountain golf club in the Caribbean! Surrounded by pines and boasting cool temperatures year-round, it has nine holes on 43 acres. It's a membership course but visitors are able to sign up at special rates. After you play, take a ride down to Salto Jimenoa Dos, or just enjoy a drive around this gorgeous neighborhood.

## ENTERTAINMENT AND EVENTS

Jarabacoa isn't exactly known as a party town. It does have its corners, of course, where locals hang out and booze, especially as Thursday rolls around and announces the weekend. But in comparison to Constanza, it's surprisingly quiet during the week. There are few spots where you can have drinks and mingle with the mountain crowd.

### Bars and Clubs

**Parque Central** is the liveliest part of town, and as in most Dominican towns, it's surrounded by casual sidewalk bars and *colmados*. **D'Chano,** across from the park, seems to attract beer lovers throughout the day.

**Downtown Jarabacoa Lounge & Grill** (Norberto Tiburcio or Av. La Confluencia, tel. 809/365-8746) has a sidewalk terrace and quite possibly the iciest-cold beers in town,

## Bonao Carnival

East of Jarabacoa and Constanza in the Cibao Valley, the scenic city of **Bonao** is known for hosting one of the most original, lively, and well-organized Carnivals in the Dominican Republic, having done so since the 1930s. The main character is the *diablo cojuelo* or limping devil—with a face resembling a monstrous animal. Its unique costume is made of satin, shining with lamé and sequins, and ringing with miniature bells and whistles.

You'll see various devil-masked groups during the Carnival parades, which take place every Sunday from the last weekend of January through the second weekend of March. Head to Parque Duarte and anywhere along the main drag of Calle Duarte. Although Bonao Carnival had humble beginnings, it's been the fastest growing of all Carnival celebrations in the country, bringing together individuals from all walks of life. It's a fun, intimate Carnival experience, much more so than the bigger, commercialized ones in La Vega or Santo Domingo.

including imported options. The vibe is trendy but laid-back. Latin hits play loudly all day and evening, with occasional DJs on the weekends. You can dance the night away on the weekends only at **Venue Bar & Lounge** (Av. La Confluencia, 10pm-1am Fri.-Sun.).

### Festivals and Events

The annual **Rancho Baiguate Horse Rally,** or **Rally a Caballo,** takes place on Saturday during Easter weekend. It's a fun day of food, music, and watching hundreds of participants compete in horse races.

Every year during the last week of June, Jarabacoa hosts the **Festival de las Flores** (Flower Festival). Expect horseback parades, folkloric dances, food, art, merengue and *bachata* concerts, and, of course, a flamboyant flower-decorated truck parade! There are fun contests for best flower-decorated hat, umbrella, and horse. The event lasts four days.

## SHOPPING

**Plaza Ramírez** (across from Parque Duarte) has several shops, including a coffee counter where locals quickly sip and go, an Internet center, a hair salon, and fashion clothing stores.

**Calle Duarte,** the main drag in town, is lined with a variety of stores, from fashionable Chinese apparel to pharmacies and *colmados*. Jarabacoa's **Mercado Público** is a small and friendly local market filled with all the vegetables and fruits and chicken and pork counters found in most Dominican outdoor markets. A block past the market, on the main drag, is **Jarabacoa Supermarket** (Av. Independencia or Duarte, tel. 809/574-2780, 8am-10pm Mon.-Sat., 9am-1pm Sun.).

## FOOD

**Jarapan** (next to the police station and Esso gas, Calle Independencia, 7am-10pm daily, US$3-5), smack in the middle of town, offers a nice range of pastries, cakes, croissants, and chocolates to nibble on. Wash it all down with a cup of gourmet coffee. It can get hot inside, with just two ceiling fans, but there's limited shaded outdoor seating if you don't mind the traffic bustle.

The small, outdoor **El Carrito de Moshe** (corner of Calle Mella and Calle Paseo de los Maestros, 809/574-7750, 8am-3am daily, US$3) is the perfect stop for that postadventure burger, burrito, or taco fix. It's tasty, and affordable. They also deliver, like many of the area's restaurants. Next door, pizzas are excellent at **Pizza and Pepperoni** (Calle Paseo de los Maestros, tel. 809/574-4079, 11am-11pm daily, US$5-10), with a large casual dining room and a playground for kids at the back. **El Taíno** (Av. la Confluencia, tel. 809/574-6620, noon-5pm daily, US$3-5) is an excellent and cheap Dominican cafeteria, serving homemade dishes. It's a mere 100 pesos for a plate of rice and your choice of meat at lunch or dinner. The later in the day you stop by, the fewer the options.

The long-standing, recently renovated **Super Cafetería La Tinaja** (Av. Independencia, tel. 809/574-2311, 8am-11pm daily, US$4-10) is a popular option for a range of Dominican dishes, as well as over 20 flavorful sandwiches (including choice of pita or whole-wheat bread) and burgers when you tire of rice and beans. They also offer a Dominican breakfast of *mangú*, as well as local desserts, *batidas* (milky fruit shakes), and cold local or imported beers and wine.

★ **Fresco Bistro** (Calle Mario Nelson Galan, corner of Calle Mella, tel. 809/574-7744, 8am-11pm daily), offers a more intimate, quieter space with a modern setting and tasty dishes that range from breakfast omelets to burgers, salads, and wraps.

There's no missing **Helados Ivon**'s (Calle Hermanas Mirabal, tel. 809/906-2724, noon-5pm daily) homemade ice cream when in Jarabacoa. Pick the coconut flavor; it's so fresh that you crunch on coconut bits in between bites. Numerous other natural fruit flavors include pineapple, passion fruit, mango, and tamarind, served in plastic cups. Expect a line on the weekends.

Late nights are good for a stop at **Fritura de Augustin**—a seemingly simple stand serving delicious fried chicken on a roadside corner, with a shared wooden picnic table for those who stay to eat.

Do *not* miss treating yourself to a sunset dinner at ★ **Aroma de la Montaña** (Jamaca de Dios, between Palo Blanco and Pinar Quemado, tel. 829/452-6879, www.aromadelamontana.com, 11am-10pm Sun.-Thurs., 11am-11pm Fri.-Sat., US$9-35). Whether you come here for a cocktail or stay on for a fantastic meal, this mountaintop restaurant is a gem in Jarabacoa and even the whole DR. You'll understand as you wind up the mountain roads and enter the property and see the view from the terrace after passing the gorgeous fountain and lobby. All of Jarabacoa sits below as you enjoy one of the most romantic dining spots and table views in the entire DR. The food is no less impressive, nor the service. Try the eggplant parmesan or goat or steak dishes, all of which are excellent. It's hard to come by a place such as this.

Only one warning: their credit card machine is known to be faulty due to the altitude and Internet connections, so bring sufficient cash to avoid any inconvenience. A taxi ride to the restaurant averages US$7 one-way for up to four persons.

On the main road to Jarabacoa just outside of town are a string of *paradas,* restaurants specializing in grilled meats. You can smell the delicious aroma as you drive past. Stop at **Parada Corazon D'Jesus** (Carretera Jarabacoa-La Vega Km 9, tel. 809/757-4811, US$5-10) for a T-bone steak or other grilled flesh of your choice.

## ACCOMMODATIONS
### Under US$50

If you have time to spare, spend a night or two at **Sonido del Yaque** (Carretera Manabao Km 10.5, tel. 829/727-7413, sonidodelyaque@gmail.com, US$22 pp, includes three meals a day), run by a local women's cooperative and offering six charming wooden cabins tucked into lush gardens amid a gorgeous hilly backdrop. The property is an inspiring green initiative—it runs off the grid, using renewable energy and water sources. They have a riverfront restaurant that provides organic, locally sourced meals and they also provide local excursions.

**Hotel California** (Carretera Jarabacoa-Constanza 99, tel. 809/574-6255, www.hotelcaliforniajarabacoa.com, US$26.50, fan only) will do just fine if you're on a budget and passing through town. Rooms include fan, cable TV, and dated bathrooms, but linens are clean. There's a swimming pool and a nice outdoor relaxation area. Service is friendly, and there's a convenient *colmado* down the road.

Don't be duped by the name or the incredible rates at Molly and Rudolfo's ★ **Jarabacoa Mountain Hostel** (Calle de los Pintores 2, close to Rancho Ruiseñor, tel. 809/574-6117, www.jarabacoahostel.com,

US$32-36). Molly and Rudolfo's guesthouse is a plush, gorgeous place to stay. Off the beaten track, yet a stone's throw from Jarabacoa's bustling center in a neighborhood known as La Joya, two olive-colored villas set in a gated compound offer self-catering units that share a living room, dining room, and fully equipped kitchen. It's by far the best value in Jarabacoa, with an interior of wood and leather furnishings, and perks so great you might not want to leave: Tempur-Pedic mattresses, flat-screen TVs with Netflix in each room, free local calls and wireless Internet, laundry facilities, and hot water. Because the kitchen and living areas are shared, you'll feel as if you are staying with friends, always meeting fellow travelers when not mingling with the owners and sharing in their longtimers' knowledge of the area. If you're able, ask for the room with the en suite bathroom, complete with a soaking spa tub as well as a large rain shower.

Next door is another great choice: **Casa de Tia Yesi** (Calle Los Pintores 5, tel. 809/661-2220, US$40-50). The warm and bubbly Aunt Yesi—whose husband is a renowned Dominican painter—has four bedrooms available with a variety of beds (2-3 per room) in her home turned hostel, great for traveling groups of up to 14 people. Couples should ask for the newly built, romantic stand-alone wooden bungalow (US$50), which is fully furnished with kitchenette, sitting area, flat-screen TV, and a bathroom with hot/cold shower. It's adorable. There's also a 2nd-floor two-bedroom apartment (US$40), and a wooden tree house cabin was being completed at the time of my visit. Wi-Fi, a large garden with barbecue grill, and outdoor seating are available.

It's a five-minute motorbike taxi ride from the hostel to town, unless you're up for walking 20-30 minutes. It's well worth the comfort of returning here after a long day out exploring Jarabacoa's great outdoors. Molly also provides an extensive list of activities with plenty of details, including driver and guide info that allow you to plan your stay easily. Their

1: delicious food at Aroma de la Montaña;
2: furnished cabin at Casa de Tia Yesi

on-site guide, **David Durán** of **Jarabacoa Eco Adventures**, knows the area inside out and is able to take you anywhere on his motorbike or in your car.

## US$50-100

**Rancho Baiguate** (off Avenida Pedregal, tel. 809/574-4940, www.ranchobaiguate. com, US$80, includes all meals) is one of the most well-known resorts in town, particularly with foreign tourists. It offers a large number of trained guides and outdoor adventures, the most popular of which are the river rafting down the Río Yaque del Norte and the expedition to Pico Duarte. The property's 27 rooms range from standard to bigger, newer suites at the back, with glass showers, fans, screened windows, and either double or king-size beds. They're rather simple for the price you're paying. There are cheaper dormitory rooms; if you're a backpacker, inquire about those. The property's nicely landscaped acres allow for hiking or relaxing by a large pool area (though unshaded). There's a macadamia farm, kids' playground, horses, pisciculture ponds, and shaded trails. The restaurant serves up average meals buffet-style, enjoyed on open-air shared picnic tables.

★ **Jarabacoa River Club & Resort** (Carretera Jarabacoa-Manabao Km 4, tel. 809/574-2456, www.riverclubjarabacoa.com, US$44-65, breakfast included) looks like a big, bright amusement park as you approach and first see the children's park on the left, followed by the lodge's mini soaking pools and larger swimming pools, all perched over the river. The views are gorgeous! Opt for the junior suites, which offer all the basic amenities, with a view. The restaurant also faces the river, and there's a bridge you can cross to find more relaxation areas. It's popular with locals, and the merengue blasts as couples randomly dance along the river or soak in one of the several bathing spots. You might even see the river rafting tour groups descend as they pass under the river club's bridge on the tail end of their adventure.

The brown-brick, one-level **Hotel Brisas**

**del Yaque** (Calle Independencia, corner of Calle del Carmen, US$45-53, includes breakfast) has 19 ground-floor guest rooms with double beds and white and green bedding, air-conditioning, TV, mini fridge, and a small bathroom. There's not much to see or do here, so the price isn't justified; it's essentially a place to rest your head. The parking lot is disproportionately huge compared to the small hotel. There's a restaurant on-site serving meals throughout the day.

**Hotel Gran Jimenoa** (off Av. La Confluencia, tel. 809/574-6304, www. granjimenoahotel.com, US$62-100) is the fanciest of the lot in Jarabacoa, although it's also one of the older properties. Its setting impresses with the gushing streams of the Río Yaque del Norte crossing the heart of the hotel. Its dining room has particularly exciting river views. Rooms range from deluxe to suites. The atmosphere is family-friendly, with breakfast buffets offered with the rate. There's a small swimming pool, open wireless Internet, and plenty of seating areas around the river.

## INFORMATION AND SERVICES

In the center of town, **Ecofarma** (Av. Independencia, tel. 809/365-9595 or 809/365-9500) is available 24 hours for any medication needs you might have. You can call the pharmacy and order for delivery if you prefer (delivery hours are 6am-11pm).

**Nynet Café** (Plaza Ramírez, across from Parque Duarte, tel. 809/574-7972, www. nynetcafe.com, 8am-11pm daily, US$0.81 per hour) provides Internet on tightly spaced desktops in a nicely air-conditioned room.

The **Jarabacoa Tourist Information Center** (tel. 809/574-6810, 8am-noon and 2pm-6pm Mon.-Fri., 8am-1pm Sat.) has information on the town as well as hotels and excursions, but no handouts; maps of Jarabacoa cost 150 pesos or US$3.30. They sell a few random artisan gifts, including ceramics and fruit wines.

An office of the tourist police **CESTUR** is

near Clínica Los Rios, and can be reached at tel. 809/574-2412. The **police station** (tel. 809/574-2540) is across from the Esso gas station smack in the center of town.

**Plaza La Confluencia** (Av. Norberto Tiburcio, tel. 809/365-9391) is a bit of an oddity with its modern concrete buildings dating from 2012. It is not much to write home about, but here you'll find a **Banco Popular,** as well as a couple of pizzerias and Italian eateries.

## GETTING THERE AND AROUND

Across from Punto del Arte Bar and the Panadería, you'll spot numerous **motorbike taxis** waiting to whisk you away. As is the custom, they will call out to you as you walk to see if you want a ride. In that same area, a few steps from the bakery, is the **Expreso Jarabacoa** (tel. 809/574-6464) bus terminal for heading to nearby La Vega, as well as the **Jaraba Taxi** stand (tel. 809/574-6464).

**Sindi-Taxi** (Calle Jose Duran 2, tel. 809/574-4242 or cell tel. 829/285-4243) can get you from point A to B in town, with 24/7 service. Ask for the price before they pick you up; rates are set.

The **public** *guaguas* or **minibuses** for Constanza leave across from the Shell station. If you want to head there for a day trip, be sure not to miss the last *guagua* back from Constanza at 3pm. Still, there are worse things than to get stuck in that gorgeous mountain town.

**Caribe Tours** (Calle Jose Duran, tel. 809/574-4796, www.caribetours.com.do, RD$270 or US$5.88) offers daily trips to and from Santo Domingo, leaving Jarabacoa at 7am, 10am, 1:30pm and 4:30pm. Check their website or call for the latest schedules.

# Around Jarabacoa

## ★ MANABAO AND LA CIÉNAGA

Take a dreamy trip to the gateway villages to Pico Duarte, **Manabao and La Ciénaga.** Manabao—meaning "water springs" in Taíno—is approximately 27 kilometers (17 miles) south of Jarabacoa, or about an hour away, and La Ciénaga is another 7 kilometers (4.3 miles) or 15 minutes southwest from Manabao. The road was newly repaved through this region, which has attracted new vacation homes, as well as roadside lunch *comedores* and *colmados*, in an area that was once deserted. If you've rented a car, head out of Jarabacoa via the Manabao Road as it crosses through town (Highway 28 going south) and take it all the way until you reach Manabao. Continue on that same winding road to La Ciénaga. Otherwise, contact local guide David Durán of **Jarabacoa Eco Adventures** (tel. 849/917-7638, http://jarabacoamotoadventures.blogspot.com, US$25 pp), who will take you on a splendid, slow motorbike ride (or drive) along the Carretera Jarabacoa-Manabao. The ride will take you higher and higher on the winding roads bordering the rolling hills and peaks of the Cordillera Central. Expect to stop multiple times.

Along the way you'll pass **Balneario La Cortina,** a vertical freshwater pool and cascade right off the road. A dip in the water is very refreshing. You will then pass a coffee farm—stop at Finca Altagracia if you'd like a closer look—and the landscape will turn to pine and majestic *grayumbo* trees. Soon you'll be riding alongside the Río Yaque del Norte next to cows and horses relaxing on riverbanks, by shacks lining colorful bridges, and through fields of trees growing guava, banana, avocado, and green *tayota*, or chayote— the main vegetable crop here. This is the real Dominican *campo*.

The ride alone could take up to two hours, stops included. Once you reach Manabao, feel free to pull over and hike your way down the side of the road (it isn't steep) for a swim in the river sourced from Pico Duarte. Nearby is the new **Comedor Mari** for a lunch of the day (rice and beans, with stews), and at least a couple of surrounding local *colmados* or neighborhood stores (one directly opposite) with more snacks and beers. After you're done in Manabao, continue on to La Ciénaga, where you'll see a big entrance sign for the Parque Nacional Armando Bermúdez. Veer left, rather than enter the park, and go to a spot at a bridge leading to another public river-bathing spot known as **Balneario Boca de los Ríos.** There are benches where you can leave your belongings before walking a couple of steps down to the river. It's an ideal place to cool off one more time before heading back to Jarabacoa or on to Pico Duarte. All in all, this trip makes for a blissful day in the countryside.

## PARQUES NACIONALES BERMÚDEZ Y RAMÍREZ

Established in the 1950s as the country's first national parks, Parque Nacional Armando Bermúdez and Parque Nacional José del Carmen Ramírez encompass 1,500 square kilometers (579 square miles) of the mountainous heart of the central Dominican Republic. This area is often described as "the Dominican Alps" for being home to the tallest peaks in the country and the entire Antilles. More importantly, you'll find the highest point in all of the Caribbean here: the infamous **Pico Duarte,** which has outdoor adventure travelers flocking to the region in order to summit its 10,128-foot peak.

At 767 square kilometers (296 square miles), **Parque Nacional Armando Bermúdez** (tel. 809/974-6195, www.ambiente.gob.do/ambienterd/eco-parque/parque-nacional-armando-bermudez, 8am-5pm Mon.-Sat., US$2.18) is the larger of the two, extending from La Ciénaga de Manabao province to the bottom of Parque Nacional Maco and to the Artibonite River basin in the north. This protected park has several rivers and streams sourcing within its limits, including the Yaque del Norte and the Mao Bao and its tributaries. Aside from Pico Duarte, it's home to three more of the Caribbean's highest peaks: La Pelona (3,085 meters [10,120 feet]), La Rucilla (3,038 meters [9,967 feet]), and Pico Yaque (2,760 meters [9,055 feet]). Here you'll find a humid subtropical forest filled with endemic *criollo* pines. Spring-like temperatures range from 12°C (53°F) in the early morning to -8°C (17°F) at night with the

The views from Manabao make it worth a day trip.

occasional frost. Fauna include numerous species of birds, such as the Hispaniolan parrot, the palmchat or *cigua palmera* (the DR's national bird), and the Hispaniolan woodpecker. **Parque Nacional José del Carmen Ramírez** (8am-5pm Mon.-Sat., US$2.18) is south of Parque Bermúdez and covers 764 square kilometers (295 square miles). It also harbors rivers such as the Yaque del Sur, Mijo, and San Juan in a similar humid subtropical forest. Most enter the park in the north, from Jarabacoa via Parque Nacional Armando Bermúdez.

Spending time in these parks with a guide (guides are mandatory) will show you the Dominican Republic's mountainous side, lush flora and fauna, and mountain *campo* lifestyle, which not many visitors get to see. Hiking here requires that you allot at least 2-3 of your vacation days, but the adventure is well worth it.

TOP EXPERIENCE

## ★ Pico Duarte

The tallest peak in the Caribbean—once renamed Pico Trujillo by the eponymous dictator—is one for the bucket list traveler. Even if you don't keep tabs, accomplishing the hike to the highest summit of the Antilles earns you lifetime bragging rights. Should you do it? That will depend on your level of fitness, as well as how many days you have to spare on your trip. You'll need at the very least two full days for Pico Duarte (and possibly a third full day to rest your bones from the hike). While there are several hiking routes to the peak, it's easier to take the one that departs from La Ciénaga or Mata Grande, through the entrance of Parque Bermúdez, simply because the climate is cooler on this side, with more rain and breezes likely, and there are several river sources that run through it. Day one of the hike usually goes from La Ciénaga to Compartición (18 kilometers [11 miles], up to 2,438 meters [8,000 feet] elevation), and day two, from Compartición to Pico Duarte and back.

The latest official per diem rates for guides and mules are listed outside the **Bermúdez park office in La Ciénaga.** The national park entrance fee is RD$100 (US$2.18), a guide costs RD$800 (US$17.44) per day, and mules RD$400 (US$8.82) per person and RD$450 (US$9.81) per carrier mule. Two mules per person are mandatory, as you might tire or need help, and provisions need to be carried separately. It's much simpler and safer to hop on an arranged expedition with one of the tour companies and individual guides listed below.

Last but not least: if you've never attempted such a hike, be prepared in terms of knowing what to pack. It goes without saying that you should be in good health before embarking on this journey. It's not a super-technical hike, but it does require endurance and good fitness. Do your research and ask your hotel or guide for advice. The two most important elements are proper hiking boots and proper clothing to accommodate for the cold nights, which sometimes reach below freezing. You should also remember to bring a waterproof bag and gear, swimwear, sunscreen, toilet paper, and bug repellent. Stay hydrated and keep your own pace—don't kill yourself trying to achieve the hike in a shorter time than allotted. You'll be on your feet for at least eight hours in one stretch on the first day. But the evening spent next to the bonfire and under the stars is as unforgettable as reaching the summit itself.

### TOURS

If you're an independent traveler looking to save a buck and not leave your vacation fortune on a single hike (it's incredibly pricey to hike Pico Duarte), contact the young **David Durán of Jarabacoa Eco Adventures** (tel. 849/917-7638, http://jarabacoamotoadventures.blogspot.com). He's one of the most reasonably priced tour guides. David grew up in Jarabacoa and knows the mountains and their hiking conditions like the back of his hand. Through his company, and through working with guests of Jarabacoa

Mountain Hostel, he has guided numerous visitors to Pico Duarte and back, as well as to other peaks in the area. David takes care of all your arrangements, including transportation to the park entrance, mules, meals and water, and tents for the two-day expedition. The journey up to Pico Duarte takes two days and one night at a minimum. If you choose to space out the hike, it will cost more—just discuss your needs with the guide beforehand.

**Rancho Baiguate** (tel. 809/574-6890 or U.S. tel. 646/727-7783, www.ranchobaiguate. com, US$255/3-day, 2-night pp) is the other major organizer of hikes to Pico Duarte, for hotel guests as well as anyone wishing to join their groups. They have a minimum of two nights, and an expedition stretching up to five days and four nights if you'd rather space it out that long.

From Cabarete, **Iguana Mama** (tel. 809/654-2325, www.iguanamama.com, 9am-5pm Mon.-Sun.) offers a three-day, two-night excursion to Pico Duarte (US$425,

all-inclusive). Note you are on your own getting to Jarabacoa. You can easily reach town via public transport or a rental car.

## GETTING THERE AND AROUND

Most who visit Pico Duarte choose Jarabacoa as their base. Due to the number of organized tour operators here; you'll also have more luck finding groups to join in high season. The drive to the visitors center at **La Ciénaga de Manabao** to reach Parque Bermúdez and the hiking entrance to Pico Duarte on this side is one of the most spectacular rides in the Jarabacoa area. It's even more enjoyable by motorbike, if you've got time to spare and can spend a half day here—bathing in the Río Yaque del Norte along the way—before beginning your hike the next morning. There are overnight bunk beds at the park office, or you can inquire there for cabanas to rent (call park ranger Herman, tel. 809/271-8929, US$10 for four).

# Constanza

If you thought Jarabacoa's hills were stunning, brace yourself for mountainous, lush Constanza, just 38 kilometers (23.5 miles) south of Jarabacoa and 90 kilometers (56 miles) from Santiago. Named after a 16th-century Taíno chief's daughter, Constanza is where you'll revel in the most breathtaking countryside views in the DR—blessed with mountain range-hugging farmlands everywhere your eyes look, made even prettier with fields of flowers.

A relatively young municipality founded in the 19th century, it saw its first inhabitants arrive in the 1750s. In the 1950s, former dictator Rafael Trujillo brought Japanese immigrants to the country to help build and design the farming community in Constanza, and the rest, as they say, is history. Agriculture is the primary industry here. In addition to Japanese immigrants, Spaniards and Hungarians also

came here, and each culture brought international flair to the small town. You can see this reflected today in the fun bistros and restaurants. Aside from its farming, Constanza is the country's most vital nature conservation zone—the rivers Nizao, Constanza, Las Cuevas, Tireo, and Yuna have their sources here and provide more than 70 percent of the water needed for farmland irrigation in the DR.

Cabins sit atop verdant hills and laborers work in fields of cabbage, strawberries, corn, carrots, and potatoes. It's an image you won't see anywhere else in the country, let alone the Caribbean. The same goes for the cool average temperature of 18°C (64°F) year-round; it falls to -5°C (23°F) in the mountains from December to April. Constanza, which locals call Valle Encantado, or the "enchanted valley," is also a nature lover's and adventurer's

# Constanza

paradise, being home to four national parks, including two scientific reserves, which protect the untouched, biodiverse environment of this area. Parque Nacional Valle Nuevo alone boasts over 400 river sources, as well as cloud forests and pine groves where the hiking is unparalleled. Birders can spot at least 80 species. Trujillo himself owned a cabin in Valle Nuevo and a hotel in Constanza (the old Hotel Suiza).

Navigating the interior roads of Constanza is no small undertaking: you'll need an all-terrain truck to explore this mountainous terrain, particularly the parks. You will also require clothing suited for the cooler temperatures, as nights in the valley require chimney

fires. The effort is worth it for Constanza's incredible charm. Its downtown is filled with buzzing bars, which get packed on the weekends with city dwellers. Its *colmados* offer fresh strawberry shakes. Its mist-filled skies arc above fragrant fields of cilantro and garlic, and the song of the *cigüita de Constanza* (rufous-collared sparrow) accompanies exploration of its pine forests. An effort is being made to expose more visitors to agri- and ecotourism activities around Constanza's gorgeous natural sights, so get here while it's still unknown to outsiders.

A trip to Constanza, also known as the ecological sanctuary of the Antilles, shows you a community that embraces visitors, even though little English is spoken here. This is a place where you'll be granted access to someone's home, despite being a stranger (a good thing to know if you're on the road and dying to find a bathroom—take it from me).

If you're planning on spending time in Jarabacoa, don't leave without at least spending a day in Constanza.

## SIGHTS

Constanza's downtown sights are easily accessed and explored on foot. If you're heading out of the town for sightseeing or other adventures, however, you'll either need your own vehicle or to plan your trip with one of the adventure companies. Sights are plentiful, but when it comes to tour activities, note that this area isn't as commercialized as the more popular tourist zones in the DR, so a little patience goes a long way. Renting your own vehicle is by far the best option at this time. Still, for those who'd rather not drive, try one of these two outfitters based in Santo Domingo during the week: **Constanza Extreme Adventures** (tel. 809/567-6300, constanzaextremeadventure@gmail.com) specializes in four-wheel ATV rides through Valle Nuevo to Aguas Blancas and El Divino Niño Monument, and **Ecoturismo Constanza** (tel. 809/786-3681 or cell tel. 829/801-7199, www.ecoturismoconstanza.net) takes you to thermal pools, canyoning, paragliding, and horseback riding through parks and to other off-the-beaten-track locations. Be sure to contact the tour company in advance.

### Parque Central

For a small town, Constanza's **Parque Central** is quite a sizable and lively square-shaped landscaped expanse. People and pigeons gather here daily, and young shoeshine boys roam looking for their next customer. As in most Dominican towns, the nights are more alive, when locals bring their own beverages and music and socialize on corners with their friends. Set across from the town's most popular bar—La Esquina—as well as the church, this area is your best bet to hang out with the locals. Annual events are often staged here as well.

### El Divino Niño Monument

**El Divino Niño Monument** (El Gajo de Maiz, tel. 809/585-3080 or cell tel. 809/910-0101, mdivinonino.blogspot.com, amcamilocamilo@hotmail.com, 10am-5pm Sat.-Sun. and holidays, no fee) is worth the stop, not least for its spectacular view over the entire Constanza valley. The backstory of this monument, which pays tribute to Jesus and the power of faith, is as moving as it gets. Facing death from two bouts of advanced cancer, Antonio Manuel Camilo, a former vice minister of agriculture and longtime civil servant who traveled often to Constanza for work, had a dream that his deceased mother advised him of the following: "Son! Hold on to El Divino Niño, and he will cure you." He was an atheist, but after failed surgery attempts to remove the tumors and a determination to live, he decided to have faith and listen to his mother. He was miraculously healed, and lives today without a trace of cancer. In gratitude, he decided to build a monument paying tribute to Christ in a town he loves deeply, despite being originally from Salcedo.

The construction of the 15-meter-high (48-foot) and 12-ton El Divino Niño at the hands of Dominican sculptor Ramón Osorio began in January 2011 and ended in October 2011. At the foot of the monument is an offering chamber, where candles burn and photos of loved ones are left with a prayer or two. There are bathroom facilities, and a spacious gift shop where you can purchase souvenirs with El Divino printed on them, as well as books authored by Camilo himself on how the monument was built and how cancer brought him peace. Along the side wall of the gift shop is a pharmacy, La Botica Divina, where free medicine is handed out to those who need it in the

1: cattle feeding in Constanza's hills; 2: El Divino Niño Monument; 3: El Tireo; 4: Aguas Blancas Waterfall

community, courtesy of Camilo's cardiologist brother.

There's a mass at El Divino Niño the last Sunday of every month at 11am, and it often fills up fast. There's now lodging offered below the monument, at a guesthouse/hotel called La Posada Divina (call ahead if you want to use the pool, and they will fill it). You can imagine what waking up to those views will be like!

Getting to the monument is quite simple but will require, again, a solid truck until the planned road paving takes place. Drive along Avenida Gregorio Luperón, the main road as you enter town, and continue straight up until you come across an open residential gate that says "Hacienda Ecológica." Pass through and head to the top of the hill, where you'll end up at El Divino Niño.

## El Tireo

Constanza is a dream for scenic drives around the villages and agricultural and flower fields. Take a turn through **El Tireo,** one of the most breathtaking *pueblos,* and nicknamed "the Switzerland of the Caribbean," to cruise by cabins and homes lining vast fields of potatoes, garlic, and cabbage. Prepare to take plenty of photos of the spectacular views along these bumpy dirt roads. You'll see the laborers at work, many of whom are Haitian immigrants, harvesting or cleaning weeds.

## Aguas Blancas Waterfall

About 10 kilometers (6 miles) from Constanza, **Salto de Aguas Blancas** (or Agua Blancas Waterfall) is one of the town's principal sights and sources of pride. You'll see various artistic renderings in restaurants and hotels around town of the 83-meter-tall (272-foot) waterfall. At 1,676 meters (5,500 feet) it's the highest-altitude waterfall in the Caribbean. The drive to the falls is picturesque, soaring above sweet corn and carrot fields and hills blanketed in pine, hugging local villages and farmers' shacks. Some of the pine appears to be dark maroon, evidence of a recent fire that devastated a portion of the plains. Once at the top, it's an easy walk over from the parking lot to a couple of footbridges that will take you to a main platform where you can observe the gushing falls in all their glory. It is not advisable to swim here, due to the cold temperature of the water and the risk for hypothermia. It's enough to pose for photos and admire the scenery. There's no fee to enter, and there are a couple of bathroom facilities that will hopefully be improved soon.

The bad news is that the road leading to the falls, particularly the last 30 minutes, is incredibly rough and steep, a winding edge-of-the-cliff type of ride with gaping holes and rocks that require a very sturdy, all-terrain truck (not even a 4x4 will do) and a good driver to get to the top. The better news is that there are imminent plans to begin improving this path, and you can get here by *motoconcho* (US$20 for two, round-trip).

If you're taking your own truck, you'll drive the main road going south from Constanza (Route 41) through Colonia Japonesa village. The road will split about a half-mile past the village; take the left fork toward Salto Aguas Blancas. Keep driving for about 30 minutes and you will see a big sign for the waterfall road on the left. This is a really tough road that will put your tires to the test. Go slow. And if you get lost along the way, don't hesitate to stop and ask locals.

## Reserva Científica Ébano Verde

The **Reserva Científica Ébano Verde** (tel. 809-574-7287 or 809-567-4300, areas. protegidas@ambiente.gob.do, no fee, permission required) is about an hour's drive from Jarabacoa on the way to Constanza, sandwiched between two towns and tucked in the heart of the Cordillera Central. There are virtually no signs to this protected reserve established in 1989, and for good reason: it's not generally accessible to the public. You'll need to obtain a permit or announce your visit, at the very least, ahead of time from Santo Domingo. The majority of those who come here are scientists from around the country and the world, as the reserve is used for active study of the country's more than 600 species of flora and fauna. If you do venture here, you'll be one of the lucky few to enjoy one of the greenest and most protected areas of the DR, even if all you get to do is drive to the entrance and its adjacent river. At an altitude of approximately 914 to 1,524 meters (3,000 to 5,000 feet) and covering 29 square kilometers (7,100 acres) in one of the most humid areas of the country, its habitat includes broadleaf cloud and riparian forests, home to the sources of the Camu, Jimenoa, and Jatubey Rivers.

The reserve is named after an endemic tree growing only in this northwestern central area of the Dominican Republic and subsequently endangered due to felling: the Ébano Verde, or *Magnolia pallenscens* species, found only in broadleaf cloud forest and producing valuable wood. There's a small but interesting museum on-site (all in Spanish, I'm afraid), displaying the reserve's rich life, including various plants and over 100 bird species, some endangered. Other endangered species that have a home here are frogs such as the giant tree frog and lizards like the *Anolis insolitus*. Among the flora are 81 species of orchids.

Adjacent to the park office, within the gated grounds, is a well-kept garden where various Ébano Verde species are on display and labeled. Ask the caretaker to show you the tree he planted 18 years ago when he started working here. After you've explored the museum and the garden, head out the gate and hike left toward the end of the path, where you'll find an entrance to the emerald-green **El Arroyazo,** a gorgeous bathing spot where streams cascade down from the Río Camú (it's cold!). The pool attracts locals who swim here on weekends.

When you make your way to the reserve from Jarabacoa, you'll head down the Constanza Road, and about an hour later, turn left at a small sign that says El Arroyazo, just past a green building that says Panadería La Palma. Continue uphill through the Las Palmas community, past fields of tomatoes and flower outlets followed by lush forests lining the dirt road. Continue all the way down until you end up at the entrance to the reserve's office. Note that hiking within the reserve requires permission from the main office in Santo Domingo, but if you ask nicely enough, you can at least see the museum and the grounds by the park office, before proceeding to the river.

## Las Piedras Letreadas

Northwest of Constanza, after the village of La Culata and a steep hike through forests, you'll find the largest Taíno carvings in the Caribbean—essentially gargantuan rocks with petroglyphs of Taíno faces (presumably gods) all over them. It's an impressive sight, if you have the time to spare. Contact **Constanza Extreme Adventures** (tel. 809/567-6300, constanzaextremeadventure@gmail.com) to arrange for an excursion; call them at least a week ahead because this tour doesn't take place as frequently as most tours.

## ★ Parque Nacional Valle Nuevo

If you only make it to one spot in Constanza, it should be the **Parque Nacional Valle Nuevo** (or Parque Juan B Perez Rancier, areas.protegidas@ambiente.gob.do, 100 pesos or US$2.18 pp), one of the most impressive national parks in the DR. Stretching across four provinces—La Vega primarily, Monseñor Nouel, Azua, and San José de Ocoa—the park is southwest of the Cordillera Central, and at 1,981 to 2,134 meters (6,500 to 7,000 feet), atop the highest plateau in the region. The park is known as Madre de las Aguas, "mother of the waters," for being home to over 500 sources of freshwater. Major rivers like Río Nizao and Río Constanza, which supply the country with vital water, have their sources here. Average temperatures during the year hover between 14°C (57°F) and 22°C (71°F) in the park, but in December you can expect temperatures below freezing, as well as ice.

Outside of its importance as a watershed, the biodiversity of Valle Nuevo cannot be

# Saving the Golden Swallow

These nesting boxes were created to help save the endangered *golondrina verde*.

Established in 2010, the **José Delio Guzmán Foundation** (tel. 809/334-6935, www. fundacionjdg.org) was launched by the owners of Villa Pajón Eco-Lodge, longtime landowners in part of what is now Parque Nacional Valle Nuevo. The organization aims at raising conservation awareness in local communities. This includes preservation of forests, rivers, and mountains, as well as contributing to the scientific research and education of rural zones when it comes to Dominican flora, fauna, and endangered species.

Enter the **Golden Swallow Project** (www.thegoldenswallow.org) to save the *golondrina verde* or golden swallow (*Tachycineta euchrysea*), an endangered, endemic species. This bird has an iridescent crown and a metallic blue-green back, its long wings allowing it to stay in the sky for extended periods of time, where it also feeds. But it is at risk from rats and limited nesting locations—this bird doesn't have the ability to build its own nest cavities. The foundation collaborated with Cornell University to build and place approximately 172 wooden nesting boxes at various locations along 31 kilometers (19 miles) of Valle Nuevo. You can spot these boxes as you explore the park. They are fixed to metal posts and stand at head level above the ground. Thanks to this project, each year the swallows have not only nested but also returned in greater numbers. Surrounding communities are now more educated on the importance of bird conservation, and interest in birding has increased as a tourism activity.

A female can lay from one to four eggs, and incubate them with her body heat within 18 days. If you do spot a nesting box that's occupied, try not to disturb it under any circumstances. Do not touch, get too close, or tamper with the box or its contents.

The José Delio Guzmán Foundation has offices both in Santo Domingo and in Constanza. Contact them directly if you are interested in volunteering or bringing volunteer groups to Valle Nuevo.

overstated. The park's 902 square kilometers (348 square miles) are mostly covered in *criollo pine*, king of this landscape, but also include savannas, river forests, cloud forests, and highland plains. Over 531 species of plants have been identified, of which 138 are endemic to Valle Nuevo. Of fauna, there are 17 amphibian species, 27 species of reptiles, over 70 species of butterfly, and between 66 and 72 species of birds. You'll hear the sharp alarm-like whistle of the *jilguero* bird and possibly spot many colorful species like the Antillean siskin.

Hop on the **Sendero de los elechos** for a short but eye-opening walk through *criollo* pines and a humid cloud forest. Seeing the trees from the car and walking among them are two entirely different experiences. A second hike, **Sendero de la Cañada,** continues to the right as you exit the first trail, taking you deeper into the park.

Going farther you'll find a small bust of Colonel Francisco Alberto Caamaño Deño, who hid in these mountains while fighting President Joaquín Balaguer's regime. The statue marks the spot he was shot dead in 1973. Camaaño was actually also buried there for many years before anyone knew, and his body was only later moved to the National Pantheon in Santo Domingo. Just beyond this, you'll find the DR's very own pyramids. Well, sort of—local communities built the two conical stone structures known as **Las Pirámides** in gratitude to Trujillo in 1957 when he built the Constanza-Ocoa Highway linking the two areas. Some say it's the geographical center of the country, and I'm not sure they are wrong—particularly if you look on the map of the Dominican Republic. The

office behind the monument provides a small museum-style display with information on Valle Nuevo. Better yet, take a seat and watch an informative 10-minute video describing the park and its environment, in English or Spanish. A few miles south of the pyramids, the scenery changes to fern trees—some call this area Jurassic Park—dotted with stunning, vibrant bromeliads.

There were devastating forest fires in Valle Nuevo in April 2014 and May 2015. Fortunately, surrounding villages had received training on how to fight a major fire, but tens of thousands of acres of pine were burned—hence their current maroon hue.

The beautiful **Villa Pajón Eco-Lodge** is tucked inside the park—hikers, wildlife and nature enthusiasts, and anyone interested in ecotourism should consider spending a night here.

## SPORTS AND RECREATION
### Mountain Biking

Hop on a bike loaned or rented from your hotel and ride the **Ruta Bicicleta** through El Valle community. It starts behind the airstrip and passes the vegetable fields filled with carrots, potatoes, cabbage, and onions

The Villa Pajón Eco-Lodge is tucked inside the Parque Nacional Valle Nuevo.

that wind along the road. The route will lead you to the entrance of La Sabina community, for more scenic views. The ride is fairly flat and of moderate difficulty. You'll take a left at the Polytechnic School Deligne and end up past Las Auyamas, all the way to the Colonia Japonesa. Feel free to stop along the way to snap photos.

### Paragliding

**Ecoturismo Constanza** (www.ecoturismo constanza.net, US$55 pp) can take you flying over the Constanza Valley for more spectacular views of the villages and fields.

## ENTERTAINMENT AND EVENTS

### Nightlife

Constanza comes alive at night from Thursday straight through Sunday. From the corner bars with karaoke to liquor stores with a sidewalk audience to disco lights, it's all here.

The **Parque Central** is a favorite meetup spot at night, and locals gather here with their speakers, rum bottles, and mixers. Some are happy just hanging out outdoors and enjoying the cool air with their friends. Across the park, **La Esquina** (Calle Miguel Abreu, corner of 27 de Febrero, tel. 809/539-1711, laesquinard@gmail.com, 4pm-midnight Mon.-Thurs., 4pm-2am Fri., 11am-2am Sat., 11am-midnight Sun.) is the busiest and funkiest bar. There's no dancing here, but plenty of eclectic Euro-Latin music. It's more of a mingling and people-watching spot—a great place to start the evening. Over at the indoor **Moe Cafe Bar** (Mueblería Hernández y Sánchez, corner of Salomé Ureña, 8pm-2am Thurs.-Sun, no cover), you can twirl the night away, but some locals don't like its smoky atmosphere. Those who want to club the night away instead head to **Alcoholegio** (tel. 809/991-8036, 10pm-2am Thurs.-Sat., no cover) after midnight, for a mix from merengue to house, including hookahs for the trendy. Feel like laughing hard? Head to karaoke at the ultra-local **Mi Drink** (7pm-midnight Sun.-Thurs.,

7pm-2am Fri.-Sat.). You can hear the off-tune singing a block away.

### Festivals and Events

The annual town fair or *fiestas patronales* are held the third weekend of September, usually in the Parque Central facing the church. Events range from sports activities for kids to live merengue concerts, and there are local food vendors. It's a lively time to be in Constanza.

## SHOPPING

The good news about most of the purchases you'll make in this agricultural town is they will be mostly edible and sweet. Also, what you invest directly supports the local communities who produce the goods.

If you're into coconut sweets, stop by **Dulces de Doña Benza** (Av. Jimenez Moya 13, tel. 809/924-8902, 10am-5pm daily) on the way out of town. Dominicans often stop here on their way back to their respective cities. She's been making *dulce con coco* for the past 75 years out of her small kitchen.

Pick up some strawberry or guava liqueur at **La Montaña de Chenco** (Av. Antonio Duverge, corner of Salomé Ureña, tel. 809/539-3538, 8am-noon and 2pm-6pm Mon.-Fri., 8am-5pm Sat., 9:30am-2pm Sun., from US$5), as well as numerous other locally made products, at this lovely all made-in-Constanza store, including strawberry vinegar, coffee, guava or pear puree, and macadamias. Contact **Villa Pajón** (Valle Nuevo, tel. 809/334-6935, www.villapajon.do) to pick up some jars of locally made strawberry marmalade (US$5.50).

## FOOD

Perched on a hilltop, right as you get on the highway from Jarabacoa to Constanza, **Don Cesar's** cozy wooden tavern begs for a pit stop before continuing the journey. Stop for coffee or drinks with a view on its small veranda with stools, or enjoy a full lunch plate of the day's local specialties. There's free Wi-Fi.

On the route to Constanza is another

roadside stop: right after Palo Alto sits **Parador Aire Libre** (across from the police station, 8am-9pm daily) Ask the owner Juan for a coconut from the pile sitting by the entrance, waiting to be chopped and juiced. It's a great way to get reenergized for your road trip. There's also a shop with snacks, drinks, and ample seating.

In downtown Constanza, head to **Rincón Gourmet** (across from the central park, Calle Gratereaux, tel. 809/539-2440, 9am-5pm daily) for toasted sandwiches, washed down with fresh-made strawberry batidas or milk shakes.

Grab a cup of coffee or hot chocolate and dessert at **A Punto de Nieve** (on side street after Dilenia's, tel. 809/539-3645, 10am-5pm daily)—a darling, vintage-feel café tucked away from the town's noise yet a stone's throw from its center. It's inside a garden casita with a pink interior set in the owner's outdoor garden with distant mountain views—you can see her house in the back. The shop serves up sweet Latin treats, from churros to *tres leches*, and fresh fruit juices and smoothies. Salsa music plays lightly in the background as you sip from porcelain cups and step back to the 1950s.

You will find flavorful home-cooked food at a super-affordable price at the immaculately clean **Pura Leña Comedor** (Calle Antonio Garcia, across from D'Ruth salon, noon-3pm daily, US$3.31). Try the meatballs with a choice of rice, grilled chicken, or any of the other daily specials displayed on a chalkboard. Dishes can be ordered to go or enjoyed at one of just five tables. It's a small joint, but the food is delicious.

★ **Aguas Blancas Restaurant** (Calle Rufino Espinosa 54, 809/539-1561, aguasblancasrestaurante@gmail.com, 9am-10pm daily, US$3.30-11) is easily the best pick in town for a fine-dining experience. Set in a cozy all-wood interior with a mountain tavern feel right in the middle of town, the menu serves up various options from seafood to steaks (oh so tender) and pasta, including a tasty "criollo corner" with Dominican

dishes like *sancocho* and *chivo picante*. The service is top-notch. You must not leave here without trying waiter Manuel's homemade hot sauce (a rare find in the DR and the best I've tasted here). Last but not least, the strawberry flan is a must for dessert, made fresh from Constanza's strawberries, including the coulée.

★ **Antojitos de Lauren** (Calle Duarte 15, tel. 809/539-2129, 11am-10pm daily, US$4-13) is virtually synonymous with Constanza. This locally owned restaurant is run by a well-known family whose parents emigrated from Lebanon to the mountain town many moons ago. Their specialty is pizza. You can watch it being made through the glass counter. Order the Pizza Constanza, the only all-vegetarian pizza in town, topped with all things green grown right here.

Owned by the Ferrer family, who are Spanish and Dominican, ★ **La Esquina** (Calle Miguel Abreu, corner of 27 de Febrero, tel. 809/539-1711, laesquinard@gmail.com, 4pm-midnight Mon.-Thurs., 4pm-2am Fri., 11am-2am Sat., 11am-midnight Sun., US$5-10) reflects a surprisingly Euro-cool vibe but retains its Dominican spirit. This cozy "gastro bar" is the most popular hangout in town and attracts a laid-back, trendy crowd from Santo Domingo on the weekends as well as locals who stop here after a long day of work for a cold beer or a burger. There are sidewalk benches for those who want to watch the buzz around the central park or interior seating hugged by walls with sketches of popular Dominican and Spanish singers. The music is diverse and not so loud you can't hear each other. Last but not least, they brew their own beer, Ferringer—ask for *una negra* like a local and indulge in the dark ale. On Sundays, everyone flocks here for the Spanish-Dominican buffet, with paellas the primary attraction.

The colorful **Miguelito Grill and Tapas** (tel. 809/539-2442, 8am-11pm Tues.-Sun., US$3.25-10) might be harder to find because there's no outdoor sign and it sits below a *ferreteria* or hardware store run by the same place. But this diner-style restaurant

decorated in New York and Paris prints earns its popularity with a wide-ranging menu, including excellent steaks and one of the best burgers in town. It's quite modern for a small town like Constanza—but again, this place is full of surprises.

## ACCOMMODATIONS

Perhaps thanks to it being a popular city-dweller's getaway, Constanza offers some of the best accommodation value in the country. Options vary: You can stay right in town, where there is more noise but basic rooms have amenities such as TV, hot water guaranteed (rare in other parts of the DR outside of resorts), and wireless Internet; or stay in a mountain lodge and enjoy the remoteness, cool weather, and stunning landscape that the area offers. Rates listed are for double occupancy.

It's pricey for the town, but **MON Hotel** (Av. Luperón 59, tel. 809/539-2559, US$67-95) surprises with its modern chic interior and spacious rooms with all the amenities, including coffeemaker, iron, TV, safe, mini fridge, and balcony. It's tucked off a side street in the middle of downtown Constanza, and there's an adjacent restaurant.

### Under US$50

The pink-and-white ★ **Hotel Vista del Valle** (Calle Antonio Garcia 41, in front of Comedor Luisa, tel. 809/365-7273, hotelvistadelvalle@hotmail.com, US$19.90) is a budget hotel that offers the best value in town for its cleanliness, inviting and leafy lobby, and tastefully decorated rooms. There are 12 that are split across three floors, offering all the amenities you'd need: hot water, closets, TVs, and cheerful linens. Rates go up to US$33 on the weekend (Fri.-Sun.), as with most hotels here.

**Hotel Bohio** (Calle Rufino Espinosa, tel. 809/539-2696, US$25-30) is another budget option if the Vista del Valle is booked. Its location across from the excellent Aguas Blancas

Restaurant and around the corner from a bus line to Santiago is probably the only advantage here. Rooms are dated (you might even find the seat missing from your toilet), and service is average at best. If you're just looking for a place to crash for a night, this could work.

### US$50-100

★ **Altocerro** (Colonia Kennedy, tel. 809/539-1553 or 809/530-6192, www.altocerro.com, US$54-120, breakfast included) offers self-catering villas sitting atop the hills of Constanza with gorgeous balcony views over the town. The buildings—including bathroom facilities—are a bit dated but under renovation. The service is warm, and the restaurant offers equally delightful views. You'll need a car or a bike to get into town, unless you're up for a long hike. Wireless Internet, hot water, and cable TV are offered. Just pick a villa closer to the ground if you must use the Internet or if you'd rather not walk too far to and from the restaurant. Altocerro is a favorite of city dwellers, so be sure to book in advance if you're visiting on the weekend.

**Hotel Constanza Villas & Club** (Carretera Constanza-Valle Nuevo Km 1, Las Auyamas, tel. 809/563-5048, http://hotelconstanza.net, US$90, breakfast included) is smaller than its name sounds, with 10 self-catering villas, which can be split as needed, and a total of 25 rooms. It's a cozy alternative that's a five-minute drive from town. The rooms are comfortable and spacious with raised ceilings, wireless Internet, cable TV (though spotty due to the mountains), mini fridges, and a separate sunroom with views onto the Constanza vegetable fields and the mountain range in the distance. It can get a bit rowdy on the weekends when the locals fill the place up or when a wedding takes place, but noise usually dies down after midnight. It's pricey for what it is. Decide whether you'd rather be right in town or outside of it.

★ **Villa Pajón Eco-Lodge** (Valle Nuevo, tel. 809/334-6935, www.villapajon.do, US$66-77 for two, higher on weekends) has been recognized as a "Dominican Treasure." You'll

---

1: roadside strawberries; 2: Pura Leña Comedor

understand why if you stay here. Twenty kilometers (12.4 miles) from Constanza and 2,286 meters (7,500 feet) above sea level, this lodge feels like the remotest, lushest, and most untouched corner of the country. Tucked inside the lush and biodiverse Parque Nacional Valle Nuevo, amid its mix of cloud forest, pine forest, and vast savannas of alpine grass hugged by rocky mountains, this longtime family-owned land—the Guzmáns have owned 40,000 acres of it since 1955—used to be the site of a sawmill and then a flower plantation before the area was deemed protected in 1994. The business eventually turned to ecotourism and cabin lodging on 28 hectares (70 acres).

The lodge is named after a type of spiky bush you'll spot all over the ground at the feet of the pine trees. The fragrant grounds are perfectly landscaped with vibrant hortensias, agapanthus, and daisies surrounding seven self-catering cabins named after the area's birds. These range from one bedroom to three; all are equally enchanting. It's all brick and stone design, with chimneys and wood fires that are started for you in the evening. There are front porches with rocking chairs and outdoor grills. Warm home-cooked meals—often Dominican specials—can be served in your cabin if you order in advance, but you are also free to bring your own groceries and utilize your fully equipped kitchen. The lodge runs on solar power; electricity is available from 7pm until about 10am.

On-site, you'll find a central dining room with a porch for relaxation, an organic garden with lettuce and, cooking herbs, and tea. You'll also spot various farm animals roaming the grounds—usually a favorite with kids—and more than 70 bird species, including the year-round *ciguera de Constanza,* fluttering about in the flower and fruit bushes.

Two trails are currently offered that take you directly from outside the lodge into the park. You can also choose a horseback ride or a trip to local farms.

To get to the lodge, you'll have to first pass

through the entry gate for the national park, where they will collect 100 pesos (US$2.18) per passenger in park fees (bring small change) before you proceed straight up the long, winding road to the lodge. The trip itself from Constanza town up to Valle Nuevo is one of the most scenic drives in the DR and one you won't forget.

## INFORMATION AND SERVICES

Rent wheels right in Constanza from **Hidalgo Rent A Car** (Av. Antonio Abud Isaac 3, tel. 829/204-5290).

Within the local airport compound, the Tourist Information Center run by the **Cluster Ecoturístico Constanza** (Av. Comandante Jímenez Moya, Aerodromo Expedición 14 de Junio, tel. 809/539-1022 or 829/741-2535, clusterecoturisticoconstanza@gmail.com) has useful maps, flyers, and information, and the pulse of the latest and greatest things to do.

For a pharmacy, contact **Farmacia Constanza** (tel. 809/539-2880) or **Farmacia San Jose** (tel. 809/539-2516).

You'll find a **Banco Popular** (tel. 809/544-5000) right at the entrance of town. For emergencies, the **Politur** has presence here (tel. 809/539-2485), and the local **police** can be reached at tel. 809/539-1000.

## GETTING THERE AND AROUND

From Jarabacoa, take the scenic mountain highway known as the Carretera Jarabacoa-Constanza, which will carry you along glorious vistas of the Cordillera Central and through the various villages. When you reach a fork in the road after a 1.25-hour drive, you can go left to head to Las Palmas village and eventually reach the Reserva Científica Ébano Verde, or take a right and continue to the scenic El Tireo village, Constanza, and Valle Nuevo. If you're looking for a driver from Jarabacoa to Constanza, negotiate a rate with **César of Sindi-Taxi** (cell tel. 829/285-4243 or tel. 809/574-4242).

1: the villas at Altocerro; 2: Villa Pajón Eco-Lodge

Public bus services abound to connect to various big cities. If you're coming from Santiago or La Vega, contact **Línea Junior** (Calle 14 de Junio, tel. 809/582-2134 in Santiago, tel. 809/539-2177 or 809/539-2777 in Constanza, 400 pesos or US$8.72), a private bus service that departs daily at 5am and 2pm from Santiago. They'll pick you up right from your front door. Just arrange the day prior by leaving your name, phone number, and location in person at the office or by phone in case you miraculously get an answer. For Constanza to Santiago, the bus also departs daily at 5am and 2pm. The journey each way is around 3.5 hours long, including all the individual pickups.

If you're heading to or from Santo Domingo, contact **Expreso Constanza** (tel. 809/539-2134) or **Caribe Tours** (Calle Duarte, next to Antojitos D'Lauren, tel. 809/539-2554 or 809/539-3180, www.caribetours.com.do) which has daily departures to the capital at 7am and 5:30pm and the same departure times from Santo Domingo to Constanza.

Getting around downtown Constanza is easy on foot, but if you're heading out of the center of town and on excursions, you will definitely need your own all-terrain vehicle. There are no taxis here. Negotiate with a motorbike taxi (ask your hotel or locals), which you'll have to call because they don't generally congregate on corners as in other parts of the DR. Constanza is still developing its tourism infrastructure, so take a strong dose of patience with you; the experience will be worth it.

# Barahona and the Southwest

## Journeying to this isolated region just to visit

Bahía de las Águilas is worth it—it's the number one rated beach in the Dominican Republic—but there's much more to explore in the DR's "pearl of the south."

Rarely a first- or even second-timer's choice, this region offers the remotest, least developed, and most breathtaking landscape in the country. Over 70 percent of its land is protected by national parks: the *sur profundo,* or deep south as it's known, is the greenest, most biodiverse area of the country. It's home to the DR's first UNESCO Biosphere Reserve, stretching 5,770 square kilometers (2,228 square miles) across the Barahona and Pedernales provinces. A surprising panoply of ecosystems coexist within this one region, where temperatures can reach

# Highlights

Look for ★ to find recommended sights, activities, dining, and lodging.

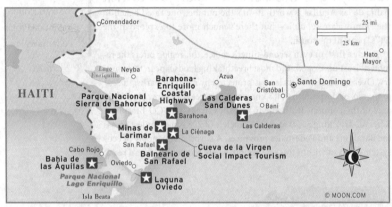

© MOON.COM

★ **Las Calderas Sand Dunes:** Climb a series of tall sand dunes and take in views of the Caribbean Sea on one end and the Bay of Las Calderas on the other (page 322).

★ **Barahona-Enriquillo Coastal Highway:** Drive down Barahona's stunning shoreline and marvel at mountains, sea, and forests while passing through Dominican *pueblos* and fishing towns (page 327).

★ **Minas de Larimar:** Visit a mining area where over 200 men work daily to extract larimar, a unique blue stone found only in this region of the country (page 328).

★ **Cueva de la Virgen:** Hike to a huge cave at the foot of the Bahoruco mountain range, swim in the cavernous chambers, and learn about the mysterious legends surrounding this mystical place (page 330).

★ **Social Impact Tourism:** A local cooperative arranges unique river hiking, cacao farm

visits, and snorkeling excursions near the beautiful coastal town of **La Ciénaga** (page 334).

★ **Balneario de San Rafael:** Bathe in this river's multilevel emerald pools and cascades or grab a table for a cold beer and a plate of seafood and admire the scenery (page 335).

★ **Parque Nacional Sierra de Bahoruco:** Hike amid cloud forests and experience the best birding in the country at this untouched national park (page 340).

★ **Laguna Oviedo:** Get up close and personal with flamingos on a boat ride along the largest saltwater body in the country (page 344).

★ **Bahía de las Águilas:** This beach, frequently referred to as the best in the DR, lives up to all the superlatives with 8 kilometers (5 miles) of brilliant white sand and clear turquoise waters (page 345).

below freezing in the Sierra de Bahoruco and rise to sweltering heat in the dunes of Baní or Jaragua Park. It's a world of abundant rivers, interior lagoons teeming with crocodiles, coral reefs, mangrove-lined shores, coastal estuaries, pebble beaches, pine trees in cool cloud forests, and dry, desertlike landscapes.

It's the wild, wild west: this peninsula is very far from the stereotypical image of the DR. One scenic fishing and agricultural municipality leads to the next on the Barahona highway, winding along the coastline dotted with cactus and views of the *balnearios,* or natural swimming holes, where rivers run to meet the sea. Barahona's pebblestone beaches are no less magnificent, and towering bluffs hug this spectacular natural landscape so close they seem to almost collapse into the sea. Deeper in the countryside and up into the mountains, nature lovers are enthralled with the birds of the Bahoruco Sierra, the flamingos gliding on Laguna Oviedo, and the Lago Enriquillo, a giant saltwater lake where rhinoceros iguanas and alligators roam. Banana fields add to the verdant scenery—the *plátano barahonero* is known to be the best in the country. In Polo, coffee thrives at the cool temperatures over 610 meters (2,000 feet). Take a tour and hike through coffee trees into the cloud forests of Cachote.

History isn't thin in these parts, either. It starts with the mystery of thousands of petroglyphs inside El Pomier's caves. This is also where Taíno cacique Enriquillo (Guarocuya) fought the Spanish for decades. It encompasses the Afro-Dominican heritage of music and dance through Casandra Damirón and, in San Cristóbal, the dismal memory of former dictator Rafael Leonidas Trujillo.

The pace is at its absolute slowest in arid Pedernales—you'll feel a million miles away from the rest of the country.

## PLANNING YOUR TIME

Get a car (you'll need it) and begin your travels from Santo Domingo. If you're strapped for time, head straight to your guesthouse or hotel in Barahona—it's a three-hour drive to Barahona province. The highways are good on this side of the country. Travel should be relatively smooth, as long as you watch for cows and motorbikes. Aside from a couple of difficult-to-reach areas like the larimar mines, you'll be set with a solid truck.

Your drive down the Barahona province is along a scenic highway that passes various municipalities that hug the sea. You can see the southwest's main sights in a couple of days. Spend a few homestay nights with the local cooperative COOPDECI as a base. Visit the larimar mines with the cooperative's guides. Quemaito and San Rafael are must-stops to enjoy the river and sea. You could spend all day surfing Playa San Rafael or hiking in the Sierra de Bahoruco. Cruise the bay of La Ciénaga and take a boat ride across the Lago Enriquillo.

Aside from Barahona's seaside municipalities, save at least half a day for a trip up to Polo—not just to visit the coffee plantations, but also to see this scenic mountain town and enjoy its cool air and friendly people. Organize a hike with local tour guides and explore Polo's hills on foot. Plan an entire day for Bahía de las Águilas—it's a long trip that takes you all the way to edge of the southwest, past Cabo Rojo and onto La Cueva, where boats depart.

---

**Previous:** scenic outlook over Barahona; Barahona's coastal highway; Bahía de las Águilas.

# Barahona and the Southwest

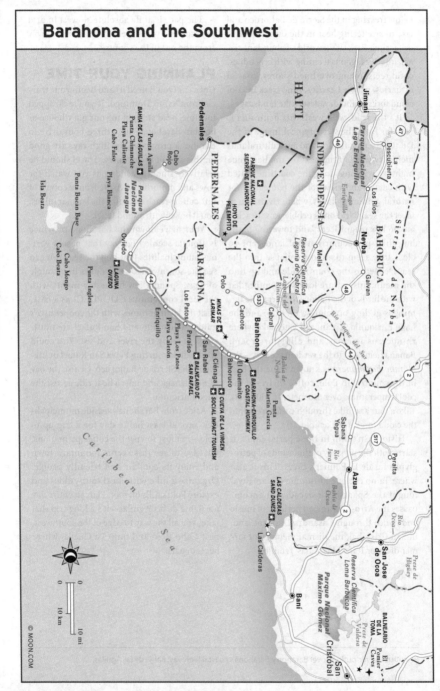

HAITI

Jimaní

Parque Nacional
Lago Enriquillo

La Descubierta

Los Ríos

Lago Enriquillo

Neyba

Galván

BAHORUCA

Sierra de Neyba

INDEPENDENCIA

47

46

48

Pedernales

PEDERNALES

PARQUE NACIONAL
SIERRA DE BAHORUCO

HOYO DE
PELEMPITO

Reserva Científica
Laguna de Cabral

Melia

Laguna del
Rincón

Cabral

Polo

Galván

533

Punta Aguila

BAHÍA DE LAS ÁGUILAS
Punta Chimanche
Playa Caliente

Cabo Falso

Cabo
Rojo

Parque
Nacional
Jaragua

Playa Blanca

Punta Bucan Base

Isla Beata

Cabo Mongo
Cabo Beata

Punta Inglesa

Oviedo

LAGUNA
OVIEDO

44

Enriquillo

Los Patos

Playa Los Patos

Paraíso

Playa Caletón

BARAHONA

MINAS DE
LARIMAR

Cachote

Barahona

La Ciénaga

San Rafael

BALNEARIO DE
SAN RAFAEL

El Quemaíto

Bahoruco

BARAHONA-ENRIQUILLO
COASTAL HIGHWAY

CUEVA DE LA VIRGEN

SOCIAL IMPACT TOURISM

Punta
Martín García

Bahía de
Neyba

Río Yaque del Sur

44

2

Sabana
Yegua

Río
Jura

Bahía de
Ocoa

517

Peralta

Azua

2

Río
Ocoa

San José
de Ocoa

Presa de
Higüey

Reserva Científica
Loma Barbacoa

Parque Nacional
Máximo Gómez

Presa de
Valdesia

BALNEARIO
DE LA
TOMA

El
Pomier
Caves

San
Cristóbal

LAS CALDERAS
SAND DUNES

Las Calderas

Baní

Caribbean

Sea

N

0        0

10 Km    10 mi

© MOON.COM

# West of Santo Domingo

A few towns that you'll pass as you drive from Santo Domingo to Barahona are worth a pit stop.

## SAN CRISTÓBAL

Approximately 28 kilometers (17.3 miles) west of Santo Domingo, San Cristóbal is the town whose primary claim to fame (or shame) is being the birthplace of Dominican dictator Rafael Leonidas Trujillo Molina, who terrorized the country for 31 years from 1930 to 1961. On a more positive historical note, the first constitution of the DR was drafted here in 1844. Today, you can visit Trujillo's decaying old homes if you want: the three-story, seafront La Casa Caoba, which he used to meet his lovers and has since been vandalized, and the extravagant Castillo del Cerro, which he built but never moved into. San Cristóbal also offers beaches, Taíno caves, and swimming holes.

### El Pomier Caves

A 1.5-hour drive from Santo Domingo, the anthropological reserve of **El Pomier** (9:30am-5pm daily, RD$100 or US$2.18 for entrance, additional RD$300 or US$6.54 for a guide) is said to contain the highest number of petroglyphs in the Dominican Republic—across 55 caves, though only a handful are accessible—and indeed the Caribbean region. Don't expect it to be overrun by tourists, however, because few venture to the southwest of the DR. A welcome center and a landscaped park are on the hike to the cave entrance. Petroglyphs of birds, animals, and other mysterious geological formations can be seen in the three linked caves, including lots of bats. The first cave has railings and is easier to explore. It is estimated there are more than 600 animals represented in this one. To get here solo, you could catch a motorbike taxi from the central park up to the cave entrance. If you're driving from Santo Domingo, take

Autopista 6 to the *cruce de La Toma*, turn right at the crossroads, and continue until you reach a bridge, where you'll then turn left and continue straight until you hit the entrance. You can also sign up for an organized tour to the caves through **Viator Travel** (www.viator. com, US$159).

South of San Cristóbal are beaches, black or grayish in color—Palenque, Najayo, and farther south, Playa Cocolandia, which is safer and better for swimming. These beaches are popular with locals who day-trip from the capital.

### Balneario de la Toma

A favorite spot to cool off in the area is La Toma of San Cristóbal, a jade-colored, riverfed pool about 6 kilometers (4 miles) north of the city, sitting at the foot of a rocky hill. There are ladders, as well as toboggan slides for the kids that drop directly into the swimming hole. You'll find food and drinks for sale as well, and multilevel terraces with plenty of seating overlooking the pool. The entire scene looks like a giant water park on the weekends. It's a good spot to visit after your trek at the Pomier caves.

### Playa Palenque

This scenic black sand sits on the southern edge of the province, just a half hour from San Cristobal's town and a mere hour from Santo Domingo. It's a well-kept secret from visitors who rarely venture here, yet you'll find the tastiest beachfront seafood this side of the DR. There are restaurants with huts all along the stretch serving drinks and food, but the western side—also known as Cocolandia— is nicer for some fish and a swim post-lunch.

## AZUA

The town of Azua is hot and dusty, and not much happens here to make you stay long— unless you head east of town to the gorgeous

# Castillo del Cerro: Trujillo's Home

In the city of San Cristóbal, the Castillo del Cerro looks like a dull government building from the outside. But it is actually a five-story home built in 1949 for Rafael Leonidas Trujillo. The dictator didn't fall in love with it or use it, and today it serves as a training center for penitentiary guards. The rooms are a display of opulence in the baroque style, including imported green and rose marble from Italy, granite staircases, and marble floors. There are also "salons" similar to those of the Palacio Nacional in Santo Domingo. On the top floor is a museum with displays on Dominican history, including replicas of some chilling items like the electric chair the dictator used to torture his opponents. Take Avenida Luperón going west from the central park, and turn south at Isla Gasolina.

**Bahía de Ocoa in Palmar de Ocoa,** a bay area that is set to develop in the future with more hotels and real estate projects as folks start paying attention to the stunning landscape in these parts. Wine is being made here, for the first time in the DR (www.ocoabay.com.do), as part of an agritourism project. Stroll by the scenic docks for a quick photo op. And perhaps swim in Playa Chiquita before you hit the road again.

## BANÍ

Birthplace of 19th-century Dominican hero Generalissimo Máximo Gómez, revered for his role in the Cuban independence movement, the town of Baní—meaning "abundance of water"—is mostly known for its salt mines, an important naval base in Las Calderas facing a gorgeous bay with adjacent sand dunes (generally known as Dunas de Baní), and the country's sweetest mangoes (known as the *mango banilejo*), of which it produces hundreds of species, enjoyed during an annual mango festival or "Expo Mango" in the summertime (June or July).

TOP EXPERIENCE

### ★ Las Calderas Sand Dunes

Have you ever seen a desert in the Caribbean, or a landscape of sand dunes overlooking the sea, towering over you while an intense heat wave envelops your body? You'll find just such a surprising landscape in Las Salinas, a half hour outside Baní. Head out of Baní

going west to the naval base of Las Calderas. You'll actually go through the gates of the base—it's fine, just don't take any pictures—to get to the small village of Las Calderas and splendid views of the bay to your right. Keep an eye out for the main entrance to the sand dunes. You'll pay a small entrance fee (RD$100 or US$2.18) before proceeding to explore the dunes. Make sure you first head to the lookout point behind the main office to get a gorgeous porch view of Las Calderas Bay.

Once you're ready to brave the heat, head down and begin your hike to the sand dunes—walk to the left, past goats in the bush, and climb up the sandy hill. Just when you're almost out of breath, the sea reveals itself before you on the other side. It's a gorgeous scene, even if you can't swim in the strong currents at Las Salinas beach.

Getting there by public transportation is quite easy. Take the Expreso Baní minibus or *guagua* from Parque Enriquillo in Santo Domingo (US$2.86 or RD$130); it leaves pretty much every 15 minutes on the hour starting at 7am (ask the cab driver to drop you at the Baní stop). Note that you can also catch this same express bus right off Santo Domingo's Malecón as it runs down the boulevard—technically, you could flag it down from outside your hotel there. Once you approach Baní, 1.5 hours away, ask the driver to drop you at the *guagua* stop for Las Salinas,

---

1: Playa Palenque; 2: Las Calderas Sand Dunes

which is on the way. This second bus ride to Las Salinas (US$1.21 or RD$55) is just about 20-25 minutes; be sure to remind the driver to drop you at the national park/the sand

dunes so he doesn't forget. The minibuses are air-conditioned and comfortable. Bring plenty of small change for the buses and park entrance fee.

# Barahona Province

## BARAHONA CITY

There's Barahona *province*, made up of various municipalities, and then there's Barahona city—a dusty, polluted urban hub. The municipalities, or small towns and fishing villages that begin outside of the city, on the other hand, are the chief attractions in this area.

### SIGHTS

There are no major sights in the city of Barahona. For visitors, this is mostly an area to pass through on the way to the region's more blissful coastal and pebblestone beach scenery, rivers, fishing villages, and national parks.

### EL MALECÓN

The city's waterfront remains in a sad state—partially abandoned in the daytime, part polluted on the beach side. Still, locals hang out at sunset along its bars and on the small stretch of sand under the shade. If you happen to be stuck in town, go to a cleaner and prettier beachfront at Hotel Costa Larimar to grab a cocktail or meal and enjoy the shore.

### Entertainment and Events
#### NIGHTLIFE

Most of the nightlife around Barahona and especially in its various towns and fishing villages consists of roadside bars and the typical thatch-covered *terrazzas* blasting merengue and *bachata* so loud you won't need directions to find them. In Barahona city, the bars and dance spots line the Malecón and filter back on its side streets. Popular picks are the **Big Tree Sports Bar** (Malecón, tel. 809/524-1010, 7pm-2am Thurs.-Sun.), which occasionally hosts live concerts, and a block up from its

corner, **La Fábrica Liquor Store** (Av. Bahía, off Malecón, no phone, 9am-midnight daily, later close on weekends), which fills up thanks to its outdoor veranda and flat-screens showing sports and other entertainment. Enjoy your drinks on-site or take them to go. Also on the waterfront, you'll find pool tables at **Club de Billar La Casita.**

### Festivals and Cultural Events

**Barahona's Carnaval** (February) takes place every Sunday afternoon in February along the seafront boulevard. This is probably the liveliest you'll ever see this city. Expect plenty of colorful devil costumes, as well as the award-winning Pintaos de Barahona—a group easily recognized for their painted bodies, representing the maroons who fought against slavery and persecution. The parades begin around 4pm and last into the early evening.

The oldest carnival in the southwest is the **Cabral Carnival** (March), one of the most African-influenced in the DR and also known as Carnaval Cimarrón, spanning three days at the end of Holy Week. It's the last of all the carnivals to be celebrated in the country, as it's held during Easter. Expect to see the Cachuas of Cabral, the main characters wearing a mask made out of vibrant crepe paper and flapping bat-shaped wings, as they roam all weekend starting at midnight on Holy Saturday. They crack their whips—look out!—and it all ends with a big, loud folkloric ceremony on Monday after Holy Week, when they burn Judas in effigy in the village cemetery.

The **Feria Nacional de la Uva** or **Neyba Grape Fair** (end of August) takes place over a

# Barahona City

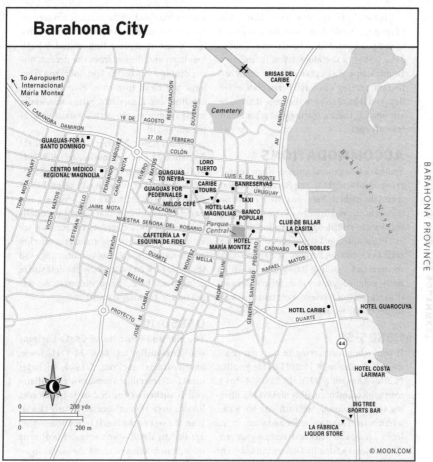

To Aeropuerto Internacional Maria Montez

BRISAS DEL CARIBE

Cemetery

AV CASANDRA DAMIRON

16 DE AGOSTO

RESTAURACION

DUVERGE

AV ENRIQUILLO

27 DE FEBRERO

COLÓN

GUAGUAS-FOR A SANTO DOMINGO

CENTRO MÉDICO REGIONAL MAGNOLIA

FERNANDO VASQUEZ

CARLOS MOTA

SUERO

J. MATOS

LORO TUERTO

GUAGUAS TO NEYBA

LUIS F. DEL MONTE

CARIBE TOURS

BANRESERVAS

URUGUAY

GUAGUAS FOR PEDERNALES

MELOS CEFÉ

ANACAONA

HOTEL LAS MAGNOLIAS

TAXI

BANCO POPULAR

TONI MOTA RICART

VICTOR MATOS

ESTEBAN CUELLO

JAIME MOTA

NUESTRA SEÑORA DEL ROSARIO

Parque Central

CLUB DE BILLAR LA CASITA

AV LUPERON

CAFETERÍA LA ESQUINA DE FIDEL

DUARTE

HOTEL MARÍA MONTEZ

CAONABO

LOS ROBLES

BELLER

MARIA MONTEZ

MELLA

PADRE BILLINI

PEGUERO

RAFAEL MATOS

GENERAL SANTIAGO

PROYECTO

JOSE M. CABRAL

Bahía de Neyba

HOTEL GUAROCUYA

HOTEL CARIBE

DUARTE

44

HOTEL COSTA LARIMAR

BIG TREE SPORTS BAR

LA FÁBRICA LIQUOR STORE

0   200 yds
0   200 m

© MOON.COM

weekend in the town of Neyba, known for its delicious grapes. You can find them on sale in the town's central park, along with the wines and marmalades and juices made out of the fruit. Aside from all things grapes, the festival includes music, local food, and grape grower exhibits. If you're not in town in August, you can always buy some grapes from the central park on your way to or from an excursion to Lago Enriquillo.

## FOOD

Unless you're eating at your hotel or resort where there might be restaurant, don't set your expectations high when it comes to

dining out. Remember that tourism in the southwest is still very much a work in progress. Aside from the few decent selections in the city, you'll mostly find few and far between local restaurants along the highway after leaving town and plenty of fresh seafood shacks by the beaches and rivers outside the city.

For cheap eats, a block behind the central park is the diner-style **Cafetería La Esquina de Fidel** (US$1.74-5.45), the most popular sandwich spot in the city. It dishes out various types of meat fillings in toasted baguettes. Come early if you don't want a long wait. Also available are fresh juices and fruit milk shakes or *batidas*.

**Melos Café** (across from Hotel Las Magnolias, Calle Anacaona, 8am-2pm and 6pm-9pm Mon.-Wed., lunch only Thurs.-Sat., US$5) is the closest you'll find to a Dominican-style local *comedor* or small restaurant, serving a rice and beans plate of the day. You'll have to buzz the front door to be allowed in; there's seating and it's a clean, friendly spot.

## ACCOMMODATIONS

You have two general options when considering an overnight in the Barahona region: spend the night in Barahona city at one of the budget hotels and drive to and from the sights you want to visit along the coastline, or stay in one of the municipalities outside of Barahona, such as Quemaito, Paraíso, or Bahoruco. I'd recommend avoiding Barahona city—it's a noisy, polluted gateway to an otherwise beautiful region. But if you do, note that prices are higher on the weekends.

### US$25-50

If you're bent on staying in the city, you'll find solid value at ★ **Hotel Las Magnolias** (Calle Anacaona 13, tel. 809/524-2244, magnolia.cdm@hotmail.com, US$26), offering air-conditioning, full bath with hot water, wireless Internet, free coffee and water in the lobby areas, and daily housekeeping service. The owner is a friendly Dominican lady. The location is close to a local cafeteria and supermarkets and the central park. If you're just passing through, it will do just fine.

A popular pick for location despite the unjustified price, the no-frills **Loro Tuerto** (Av. Luis Del Monte, tel. 809/524-6600, www.lorotuerto.com, US$42) has nine rooms that are set back from an otherwise busy city street, motel-style, facing a backyard. They have air-conditioning (a perk in these hot parts), wireless Internet, an old TV, and a bath. There's a bar and plenty of tables in a former restaurant space where guests can relax.

Across from Barahona city's Malecón, the four-story **Hotel Caribe** (Av. Enriquillo, tel. 809/524-4111, www.hotelcaribe.do, US$50)

and its blue and white exterior covered in bougainvillea offers simple and clean rooms that come at a price that includes both breakfast and dinner from the decent, on-site dining room on the 2nd floor. You'll get basic but clean furniture, blue walls, air-conditioning, fans, dated bathrooms, and a small swimming tub with a partial view of the boulevard.

Directly across the street is the larger **Hotel Guarocuya** (Av. Enriquillo, tel. 809/524-4121, guarocuyahotel@gmail.com, US$29-44), set in from the road. It still keeps the feel of days gone by, but with a new, spacious, and pastel-colored lobby that leads to ground-floor rooms and an outdoor terrace with sea views. Rooms are simple and clean, offering queen-size beds, TVs, air-conditioning, and showers. Pick an ocean-view room if you're going to stay here. The on-site restaurant was not up and running at print time.

### US$50-100

The blue and white **Hotel Costa Larimar** (Av. Enriquillo, tel. 809/524-1111, www.hotelcostalarimar.com, US$90, includes breakfast) resembles a condo tower in Miami and is tucked at the end of the Malecón. Rooms here are not necessarily any fancier than the rest of the hotels in the zone—they are slightly dated—but the resort is directly on a clean beach and offers the city's largest pool. The sea-view rooms are the better bet, with newer showers and connections to living room suites if you need the space. The beach is a nice, small stretch, but don't wander off the grounds alone, as there are bushes at the back of the beach adjacent to the hotel and robberies have occurred.

## INFORMATION AND SERVICES

Stock up at the **Jacobo Supermarket** (Calle Padre Billini, corner of Calle Anacaona, tel. 809/524-2645, supermercadojacobo@hotmail.com) in Barahona city before you head out of town, especially if you're a picky eater. It can be a bit noisy outside the supermarket with rows of motorbike taxis hollering at passersby, but just ignore it all and shop away. There's an ATM inside the supermarket, though it's been known to be out of service.

Across from the city's central park, you'll find a 24-hour ATM at **Banco Popular** (tel. 809/544-5555, www.popularenlinea.com). There are two machines and on Friday it can be supercrowded; try to go at off hours or during the weekdays.

For medical care, head to **Clínica Magnolia**, also known as **Centro Médico Regional** (Calle José Francisco Peña Gómez, tel. 809/524-2470). You'll find medicine at **Farmacía Méndez** (Calle Jaime Mota, tel. 809/524-2318). The tourist police **CESTUR** can be reached at tel. 809/754-3003.

## GETTING THERE AND AROUND

**Caribe Tours** (tel. 809/524-4952, www.caribetours.com.do, US$6.85 one-way) offers daily departures from Santo Domingo to Barahona, at 6:15am, 9:45am, 1:45pm, and 5:30pm. It's a three-hour trip, with enough time for a coffee stop when the bus unloads at Azua. Bring a cardigan or scarf because the air-conditioning can get super cold on the bus. You'll get dropped off at the Caribe Tours office in the heart of Barahona city, close to many of the smaller guesthouses. Check the website for the latest schedule in case of changes.

You'll need to rent a car, however (from Santo Domingo), if you want to get around at your leisure in the southwest, especially because the chief activity in these parts is exploring up and down the coast and taxis are stupidly expensive as in the rest of the country. There are local buses or *guaguas* running up and down the highway, but they don't always run frequently and you'd be losing a lot of travel time waiting around. It all depends on your schedule and patience level. Getting around Barahona city itself, if you must stay there, is easily done on foot. There are also tour operators that offer pickups from your hotel.

## SOUTH OF BARAHONA

The beauty of Barahona province is in the various scenic fishing towns dotting the highway. Stop along the way, as these spots are sights in and of themselves, in addition to the natural attractions you'll find across the area. Your ride will take you to the following in this order: Quemaito, Bahoruco, La Ciénaga, Paraíso, San Rafael, Los Patos. How often you pause and take in the views is entirely up to your schedule, but you won't want to miss the sights that make the southwest stand out from the rest of the country.

There are only two main bodies offering excursions in this region. One is **Guanaventuras** (La Ciénaga, tel. 829/560-3560, www.guanaventuras.com), part of a local and majority women-run cooperative in La Ciénaga and made up of two Dominican tourism-licensed guides. They offer an exciting and affordably priced catalog of their own off-the-beaten-track tours, as well as jaunts to the more well-known sights. The second is **Ecotour Barahona** (tel. 809/243-1190, www.ecotourbarahona.com), a private French-owned tour operator with slightly higher prices and the advantage of having one fluent English-speaking guide. You will have just as great a time with either, but the cooperative's guide can take you to some lesser-known sites and your dollars would go directly to supporting the local community of La Ciénaga.

## ★ Barahona-Enriquillo Coastal Highway

If ever there was ever a highway that constituted a sight in and of itself, it would be the Barahona-Paraíso, or **Barahona-Enriquillo Coastal Highway 44,** which offers breathtaking views of mountains, sea, and green forests while passing through Dominican *pueblos* and fishing towns. As soon as you depart from the chaos that is Barahona city, you'll find yourself immersed in a landscape unlike any other in the DR. The sea and dramatic cliffs fill your eyes all the way down the coastline. It gives a whole new meaning to a scenic drive, and it's best enjoyed if you rent a car and drive at your own pace. Just watch out for motorbikes, which are easy to miss, and cows; they occasionally like to sit in the road as if they are themselves admiring the scenery.

## El Quemaito
### PLAYA EL QUEMAITO

About 10 kilometers (6 miles) from Barahona, **Playa El Quemaito,** stretching 2 kilometers (1.2 miles), is the safest public beach for swimming and not just wading. It has lovely Caribbean Sea views as you descend into the parking lot from the main highway—you'll see a big turquoise sign for Playa El Quemaito—and you'll immediately spot the great expanse of white rocks against turquoise seas. A damaged wooden walkway (no doubt a result of storms) and, unfortunately, the sight of plastic and Styrofoam litter here and there, has changed this once stunning beach into a rustic one. There are still thatch-covered seating areas, and kiosks serving drinks, fresh catch, and rice and beans.

### ACCOMMODATIONS

Ten kilometers (6 miles) outside of the city, **Hotel Casablanca** (El Quemaito, tel. 829/740-1230, www.hotelcasablanca.com.do, US$70, includes breakfast) is a funky, cozy hotel tucked at the end of a stony path off the main highway and perched over the Atlantic with stunning views of the cliffs and crashing waves below. Rooms offer queen beds, white linens, and tasteful pastel furniture. There's a lounge to relax in and wireless Internet. It's a half-mile to the nearest swimmable (pebble-stone) beach, Playa El Quemaito. Note that there are no stores around, so be sure to shop in town before heading here. If you're looking for a simple oasis in the southwest, this is fine, but rent your own car to get around easily. Dinners are an additional US$30, but most rave about them.

Unpretentious **Hotel Panorámica Barahona** (Carretera Barahona Paraíso, tel. 829/636-7040, www.hotelpanoramica barahona.com, US$70-210, includes breakfast) has a lovely cliff-top setting, with a large swimming pool facing the sea and immaculate, spacious grounds. It's adjacent to Playa La Meseta and tucked away from the highway for the ultimate vacation respite. Rooms range from deluxe to presidential suites and include all the amenities, from wireless Internet to air-conditioning to mountain or sea views. The suites have balconies.

## Bahoruco

Aside from being known for its waves that draw pro surfers, Bahoruco is the site of the world's only larimar mines (the precious stone is found only in the DR). Along with neighboring La Ciénaga, it's a good base for excursions around the region. It's also home to a couple of boutique hotels, and new megaresort Perla del Sur is currently under construction in La Ciénaga.

### PLAYA DE BAHORUCO

Bahoruco's main beach is a surfer's haven and has hosted surf championships. It's not a place for swimming and there aren't any facilities, but the views of palm trees and distant hills are gorgeous—great for a photo op. And it's a pretty stretch to visit and enjoy watching anglers at work or chill with locals hanging out along the pebblestone beach. Look for an eastbound exit sign from the main highway leading you to the beach.

### ★ MINAS DE LARIMAR

The semiprecious blue stone known as *larimar* is unique to the Dominican Republic. It can *only* be found here, in the hills of Bahoruco—part of La Ciénaga municipality of Barahona, about 21 kilometers (13 miles) south of Barahona city. Larimar is believed to be a type of pectolite, a rock made up of acid calcium silicate hydrate and sodium. Its uniqueness comes from the fact that it's a blue not found in other pectolites around the world. Its benefits? Dominicans believe it's a feminine stone that brings healing, calmness,

**1:** Bahoruco's fishing coastline; **2:** Cueva de la Virgen

and equilibrium to one's environment, as well as love, serenity, and creativity.

Although larimar stones were spotted by locals as early as 1916, legend has it that around the mid-1970s a man known as El Ciego—some say his name was Miguel Mendez—from Bahoruco, alongside a Peace Corps volunteer, picked up blue stones along the beach and later in the river. It led him to follow the stream to the mountains, where he found the source. His daughter's name was Larissa, and he decided to call the stone *larimar,* with *mar* referencing its sea-blue color.

Larimar remains Bahoruco's primary economic activity, alongside fishing. You'll spot various larimar workshops as you drive around Bahoruco—including a recently opened official **Escuela Taller Museo Larimar** on the main highway in town. It is a government initiative in sustainable income-producing activities where locals or students work the stone to your liking.

More interesting is a visit to the actual larimar mines, where the stone is extracted from the Bahoruco hills. You'll need a guide as well as their excellent truck for the off-roading required to get there. **Guanaventuras** (La Ciénaga, tel. 829/560-3560, www.guanaventuras.com, US$110/1-5 persons) are the only ones with a truck sturdy enough for the adventure. **Ecotour Barahona** (tel. 809/243-1190, www.ecotourbarahona.com, US$119) offers a tour as well, which includes a stop at Villa Miriam and a larimar workshop. If you can understand Spanish and want to support the local cooperative, sign up with Guanaventuras.

A visit to the mines is fascinating. There are up to 200 miners working here daily, both Haitians and Dominicans (no minors allowed), starting around 8am until usually the end of the day, sometimes late into the night if the production is spectacular. There are up to 80 holes up to 46 meters (150 feet) deep, a portion of which are government-owned; the rest are privately owned. You can walk into some of the horizontal openings, and go deeper if you choose, to watch the men.

Beyond being able to hike alongside hardworking miners into this gritty, unpolished scene, you can also see how they live in their makeshift mining community. Many overnight on-site in shacks rather than commuting back to the village every day. You'll spot everything here—*colmados,* hardware stores, *comedores,* and men cooking outdoors,

You can buy the rock straight from the source (US$11/just under one pound), but stick to the miner recommended by your tour company to ensure you get a high-quality piece. Word is that the amount of larimar available is decreasing and the stone is becoming more expensive in the stores, and no one knows what will happen if it were to run out. You might as well get your stone while you can.

★ **CUEVA DE LA VIRGEN**

Immersed in the subtropical forests of Bahoruco, the hike to **Cueva de la Virgen** (Guanaventuras, local guide Aurelino, tel. 829/560-3560, info@guanaventuras.com, US$88 pp for 1-5 persons, including transport, or US$44 pp with own car)—or the Virgin's Cave—begins from La Ciénaga's riverside. Other outfitters offer this tour, but be sure to contact the Guanaventuras cooperative instead to book—they were the first ones who knew of this trail and deserve the support. This stunning cave, originally called Hell's Gorge or Garganta del Diablo (they changed the name to make it more attractive), is blessed with small cascades and rivers emanating from the Bahoruco range. It is a sight that was known to the members of the cooperative of La Ciénaga and local residents, and with much effort and collaboration with the local tourism body, they transformed into a tourist attraction and official trail in early 2015.

The adventure begins with a 30- to 35-minute drive down a woodsy, bumpy riverside path to the beginning of the hike, and this pre-hike journey is certainly part of the attraction. You'll enter a humid forest and pass dairy farms, colorful foliage, and flowers with butterflies fluttering about against the backdrop of the Bahoruco mountain range. The terrain is part flat and part rocky, making for a fun, bumpy course (especially on a motorbike). Guide Aurelino Feliz of Guanaventuras grew up visiting this area and will explain all of the flora (at least seven species of ferns, avocado trees, yaorumbo trees, passion fruit, mango, and fig trees) and fauna (grass snakes, centipedes, 49 species of birds such as the *cigua palmera*—the national bird of the DR—white-crowned pigeons, white-winged ciguita, and hummingbirds) along the hike. It takes about four hours total or a half day. The hiking trail is well indicated in both English and Spanish.

The area surrounding the Cueva de la Virgen consists of a series of 33 falls as yet unexplored due to dangerous heights, but you can see the last three up the cave via two chambers connected by a ladder. The flow will also depend on the time of year and rainfall. The legends behind the Cueva de la Virgen are haunting, told to you while you stand at the mouth of the cave staring at its dark chambers and listening to the rush of the water.

There are two legends—though one is perhaps more real than the other. The cave was discovered years ago, and, according to the elders, it was during the time that dictator Rafael Trujillo ordered the mass murder of Haitians in 1937 to remove them from the country. Many Haitians refused to leave, having families and homes in the DR, and were afraid for their lives so they hid in this cave. They were the first to discover it. Unfortunately, they were eventually found by Trujillo's guards, who showed up with machetes—and women were raped, men killed, and their bodies left in the open. Many locals believe their souls continue to roam in the cave. The more fictional legend tells of the appearance of a woman with long hair around the largest rock in the first chamber. She was feared because she could seduce you into approaching her, and if you fell into her spell and touched her, you'd turn to stone. When locals came to collect water along the slippery

and rough terrain, they were afraid of ending up stuck here.

The size of the cave is impressive. Sit in a corner and take it all in before or after you take a swim, and imagine what must have happened years ago.

## BALNEARIO LA PLAZA

If river hiking and swimming sound tempting to you, it doesn't get any more stunning than doing it along the crystalline, turquoise waters of the Bahoruco River. The excursion begins from La Ciénaga (Guanaventuras, tel. 829/560-3560, info@guanaventuras.com, US$50 pp for 1-5 persons, including transport), followed by a bumpy 20-minute all-terrain truck ride up into the riverside forests between Bahoruco and La Ciénaga. Past the forest views you'll spot the iridescent turquoise waters you're about to hike through and alongside. There are parts that are shallow, while others require swimming. The two-hour expedition ends at a stunning waterfall and canyon. Bring water shoes and a waterproof camera.

## MOUNTAIN BIKING

You can hop on a bike and explore the southwest's great outdoors when staying at **Casa Bonita Tropical Lodge** (Km 17 Carretera de la Costa, Bahoruco, U.S. tel. 800/961-5133 or tel. 809/540-5809, www.casabonitadr.com).

## FOOD AND ACCOMMODATIONS

★ **Casita Bonita Tropical Lodge** (Km 17 Carretera de la Costa, before La Ciénaga U.S. tel. 800/961-5133 or tel. 809/476-5059, www.casabonitadr.com, US$176-280) is the only luxury resort in these parts and attracts a crowd who wants plush accommodations and facilities, like the infinity pool and lounge-like restaurant overlooking Bahoruco's Caribbean waterfront in the distance, when they're not venturing out during the day. Twenty-three years ago, the resort was the dream of a former Dominican government official from Santo Domingo who was in love with the southwest. There are 12 deluxe double or king rooms with private balconies and ocean-view suites with kitchenettes and open-air showers. Sixteen new suites have been added, and there are currently plans to expand into luxury villas adjacent to the hotel. If you can afford it, it's worth splurging for a stay here.

There's an on-site outdoor spa, **Tanama Eco Spa,** set in the woodsy grounds below the hotel under a thatch *palapa,* accessed by golf cart. Two steps away from the massage bed is a post-massage Jacuzzi filled with bubbles. The **on-site restaurant** (US$9-18) is available to guests and the public. It uses farm-to-table ingredients from the property's organic garden and offers a range of excellent dishes for all meals, from pastas to seafood to steaks and sandwiches. The trendy, open-air, all-white setting, with a wooden dining platform, adds to the romance of the place.

**Casas del Mar Lodge** (Carretera Barahona-Paraiso Km 16, tel. 829/330-3395, www.casasdelmarlodge.com, from US$157) boasts gorgeous sea and pool views from its four thatch-roof villas, set in a tropical garden and perched over the coastline. The villas contain 20 tastefully appointed "eco-suites" that run on solar energy. Rooms range from double deluxe to two-bedroom suites. Private pools and Jacuzzis and a restaurant-bar add to the cozy boutique vibe along this wild coastline. Close to Casa Bonita (for a second meal option), it's also a great base for exploring the area's multiple river pools, coffee plantations, and national parks.

## La Ciénaga

Not to be confused with La Ciénaga in Jarabacoa, this La Ciénaga is a small coastal and fishing town that neighbors Bahoruco to the south and is tucked at the foot of the eastern slope of the Sierra de Bahoruco. It has splendid views and a tight-knit community known for its local cooperative COOPDECI (Cooperativa para el Desarrollo de La Ciénaga), which has the tour-operating arm Guanaventuras, as well as a local comedor or restaurant called **Delicias de mi Siembra.**

### PLAYA LA CIÉNAGA
Fishing canoes, kids splashing along the shoreline while adults idle in the shade: La Ciénaga's beach is a sight for sore eyes when you approach the hill and take in its view from the Malecón above. Walk down the steps and you'll notice litter on the beach, but the water is a clean, beautiful turquoise, especially nice for a morning swim. Grab a snorkel mask and explore the white sea urchins underwater. During the rainy season and with increased climate change, it's not unusual to see a blanket of sargassum washing in from the Atlantic, but it quickly moves on.

### EL MALECÓN
As small as La Ciénaga is, there's still a Malecón (waterfront boulevard), and the views going down the highway and approaching this town are breathtaking. At sundown, locals descend on this area to take in the breeze, have drinks, or play games (including teens taking part in local boxing matches). It's a great place to get a feel for La Ciénaga's community.

### SPORTS AND RECREATION
With **Guanaventuras** (tel. 829/560-3560 or 809/461-3424, www.guanaventuras.com, US$88/1-5 persons), you'll hop into a fishing canoe for a boat ride along La Ciénaga's gorgeous bay, and jump into the waters off the beach to explore corals as well as white sea urchins. Those who want to can fish the traditional Barahona way, with a string (yarn and hook). The views of the shore and village behind it are as memorable as the feel of the Caribbean Sea.

### NIGHTLIFE
La Ciénaga nights get lively starting on Thursdays along the town's small waterfront and at the surrounding bars, with many folks hanging out in the street. Head to **La Bodeguita de la Esquina,** a local bar and *colmado* right off the Malecón, on Calle Duarte. Classic merengue and *bachata* blast through its open wooden doorways, attracting

a hilarious cast of neighborhood characters. Locals tend to sit across from the bar on the street corner with their drinks. It's a typical Dominican weekend scene that begins as early as 5pm and lasts through the night.

### FOOD AND ACCOMMODATIONS

★ **Delicias De Mi Siembra** (Carretera La Ciénaga, La Ciénaga, tel. 829/560-3560, 8am-3pm daily, US$3), run by the friendly ladies of La Ciénaga's local cooperative COOPDECI, serves daily Dominican breakfast and lunch for a great price. Anyone is welcome to come and dine at their casual open-air eatery right off the highway. The location used to be ideally seafront on the town Malecón, but the building was sold by its owner and the restaurant relocated to its current spot. There's a fresh juice of the day, and while you're there, pick up a couple of bottles of their artisan marmalade—with flavors like soursop, passion fruit, and guava, among others.

Save a few bucks and get a cultural experience by signing up for a homestay or *hospedaje en casa de familia* in the fishing town of La Ciénaga with the women of ★ **COOPDECI** (tel. 829/560-3560 or contact guide Aurelino Feliz at 809/461-3424, www.guanaventuras. com, US$15 pp, includes breakfast). You get a basic guest room to yourself, with private bath and fan, at one of the cooperative member's homes, ideally located within a short walk to La Ciénaga beach and off the main highway in a wonderful and typical Dominican neighborhood. Don't expect a lot in terms of the housing; it's a chance for cultural exchange. Breakfasts are served daily and you're welcome to mingle with your hosts or just relax on the porch when you're not off on sightseeing tours with the co-op. Keep in mind that like most rural towns, electricity comes and goes on occasion (though your host will have an inverter in the house).

## San Rafael
### PLAYA SAN RAFAEL

Make a leisurely stop at **Playa San Rafael,** just five minutes south from Paraíso. You'll hit its towering views as you take the curve on the Barahona-Paraíso highway and see its towering green bluffs contrasting against a stunning turquoise sea. There are various entry points for enjoying the San Rafael River. The most popular is the first, where the river cascades down into the sea through a series of multilevel freshwater pools. You can choose to bathe in cold water or head over to

Delicias De Mi Siembra

# Social Impact Tourism in La Ciénaga

Visiting the beautiful *balnearios,* beaches, cliff-front hotels, and national parks is awe-inspiring, but staying with a Dominican family and spending time with the women of La Ciénaga's local cooperative will be the most memorable part of your trip to the southwest.

The COOPDECI, or Cooperativa Para el Desarrollo de La Ciénaga, began as a mothers' club with 35 members from La Ciénaga. They had the idea of developing their club into a micro enterprise and community tourism initiative in order to help contribute to the development of their community and empower themselves economically. They decided to focus on sustainable agriculture, capacity building, and environmental protection. This grand idea turned into reality in 2008, with funding help, in part, from the Taigüey Foundation and the French Embassy.

La Ciénaga's cooperative collection of offerings reflects the cooperative's idea of a better "all-inclusive"—and is a one-stop shop ideal for the visitor seeking immersion.

- Eat at a local restaurant that serves Dominican specialties. Delicias De Mi Siembra (www.demisiembra.com), adjacent to the cooperative's office, serves a daily lunch for just US$2.25 and attracts plenty of locals in an area otherwise lacking in *comedores* along the highway.

- Buy artisan marmalade, produced and sold at De Mi Siembra. The marmalades are made from fruits collected in the nearby Sierra de Bahoruco, and the members rotate days when they make mango, soursop, guava, or orange. The marmalades are their primary income producer; the cooperative signed a two-year contract to produce for a national supermarket chain in Santo Domingo, which was a huge success for them.

- Arrange a homestay, or *hospedaje en casa de familia.* You'll get a basic room and small en suite bathroom at the modest home of a cooperative member, usually less than a 10-minute walk from the beach. Breakfast is included in the fee (US$14.31 or RD$650 per night). To arrange a homestay, call the cooperative at tel. 829/560-3560 or 809/461-3424. They speak a little English—enough to get by and for you to arrange your stay.

- Take a tour through their excursion arm, Guanaventuras, which offers unique and popular tours. You can go snorkeling at La Ciénaga's gorgeous bay, hike to the Cueva de la Virgen on a trail created by the cooperative, go river hiking and swimming to Balneario La Plaza and its sparkling turquoise waters, or visit the larimar mines. To contact Guanaventuras, call head guide Aurelino Feliz at tel. 809/461-3424 or visit www.guanaventuras.com.

Every dollar you spend goes directly into the cooperative and toward sustaining and empowering its members financially, and helping an entire community continue to thrive. It doesn't get any better than that. To reach La Ciénaga from Barahona on public transportation, hop on a *guagua* from Calle Colón and ask to get dropped off at *"donde la cooperativa de la Ciénaga."* The cooperative's headquarters is on the highway in La Ciénaga, a short drive south of Bahoruco (and south of Casa Bonita Lodge).

the seaside where you'll find folks dipping in along the edges of the pebblestone Playa San Rafael. Don't swim on the beach side if you're not a strong swimmer—it's deep and there are strong waves.

The entire scene is one of the prettiest in this southwest region with natural infinity views. You'll find a convivial ambience with plenty of food vendors (US$7 a plate of fish and sides) and seating areas around the river and beach. Expect lots of crowds and music on the weekends when locals and out-of-town travelers head here to relax. To have it nearly to yourself, come early in the week. Expect to pay a small fee to the parking attendant if you're driving, otherwise there's no fee to enjoy this sight—but note that there are no changing facilities.

# Afro-Dominican Roots in the Southwest

The country's African heritage remains strong in Barahona, which borders Afrocentric Haiti and was once home to brave maroons who successfully rebelled against slavery. At the various carnivals in the region, including during Holy Week, Afro-influenced dances and rituals prevail. In Cabral, the Cachúas appearing during Semana Santa are characters wearing colorful masks, armed with whips, and performing rituals and dances from midnight on Holy Friday all the way to Monday, when they burn Judas in effigy in the cemetery.

Another significant event is the Gagá—both a ritual and a dance influenced by Haiti—celebrated in Polo, the western border province of Elias Piña, but mostly in the *bateyes* of the southwest because they were often linked to sugarcane production. It's a celebration of productivity and harvest coinciding with the start of spring. The celebrations begin at midnight on Holy Thursday and last through Resurrection Sunday. The dances are circular, and the chants are in Creole and Spanish to the beat of the *tambu* and *catalie*—different types of traditional Dominican drums—accompanied by a specially made 1.2-meter-long (4 feet) bamboo trumpet for bass. The women wear white, and the elders don colorful garb. The Gagá represents sacrifice, protection, baptism, and blessing. The Máscaras del Diablo from Matayaya, in the province of San Juan, and in Elias Piña province perform a land fertility ritual by burning their masks and scattering the ashes on fields.

## ★ BALNEARIO DE SAN RAFAEL

One of the most popular sights in this region is the stunning emerald cascades and pools of the San Rafael River tumbling down to meet the Caribbean Sea. The **Balneario de San Rafael,** located in the eponymous town, is set up like a giant outdoor natural spa escape, and you'll want to stay all day. Dip in one of the tiered freshwater pools, stand against one of the mini falls for a back massage, or cool off along the edges of the river where it meets with the pebblestone San Rafael Beach. There are numerous fish vendor shacks and bars dotting the site and plenty of plastic chairs and tables spaced out enough that you don't feel crowded (but avoid Sundays).

There's a second, smaller spot to enjoy San Rafael's river pools less than a half-mile up from the first on the right-hand side of the road. Here you can bathe and relax with seating and a couple of food shacks. A third location is the private, gated **Villa Miriam** (tel. 809/524-4141 or 829/868-8828, US$2.20), another block up on the right, where the small entrance fee assures you more privacy and access to bathroom and changing facilities.

## Paraíso

Of all the stops along the southwest, Paraíso is among the most pedestrian-friendly areas and provides opportunity to meander down its seafront as well as through its neighborhood streets. There are fast-food vendors and *colmados* all around (which blast music on the weekend nights). Paraíso's weeklong **Fiestas Patronales** (mid-January) are for the hardcore partiers, with plenty of music, dancing, and boozing, of course.

## PLAYA PARAÍSO

Like most beaches in this coastal area, this is where anglers take off at sunrise to hunt for their catch. It's a striking turquoise-against-white scene, good for a breezy stroll in the morning or at sunset.

## EL MALECÓN

The waterfront is just a block facing a small central park and adjacent to Hotel Piratas del Caribe. Nonetheless, it's the gathering spot for locals, particularly anglers who relax here between their runs and kids who dare to play close to shore (the currents are dangerous to swim in).

## FOOD AND ACCOMMODATIONS

★ **Hotel Piratas del Caribe** (Calle Arzobispo Nouel 1, tel. 809/243-1140, www. hotelpiratasdelcaribe.com, US$99-179) is a darling, five-room villa turned boutique guesthouse. It is tucked beside the town's small Malecón and park facing the Atlantic and Paraíso's pebblestone beach (even if you can't swim there due to the currents). The intimate, luxurious waterfront suites behind a tall gate feature four-poster beds with mosquito nets, flat-screen cable TV, air-conditioning, spacious bathrooms with showers, and private balconies. Meals can be ordered ahead, and breakfasts are served on your terrace. Throw in a swimming pool in the verdant courtyard and it's hard to find a better pick in this area, which has few accommodation options. If you're a light sleeper, keep in mind that there's a local bar across the park that blasts music on the weekends.

In the mountains northwest of Paraíso is ★ **Rancho Platón** (Paseo de los Locutores, www.ranchoplaton.com, US$120-140, all-inclusive meals), a hydro-powered eco-lodge and a good pick for families. Surrounded by rivers, falls, and various mountain-fed pools, its tastefully decorated cabanas—including tree houses—offer cozy accommodations with air-conditioning and hot water, but no TV. Food is decent and all meals are included at an additional cost. The highlight is the on-site activities, including a waterslide ideal for kids, hiking, tubing on the Nizao River, and horseback riding. The road getting there is only for sturdy pickup trucks, so you're better off getting a ride.

## Los Patos

### PLAYA LOS PATOS

Much like Playa San Rafael, **Playa Los Patos** offers a river-and-sea combo. The river is probably more popular than the beach for reasons of safety and temperature. The view is beautiful from the highway, even if the river isn't as deep or fun as San Rafael's. Expect a small parking fee (US$1.10) and options for seafood and drinks. You'll spot ducks—*patos*

in Spanish—and egrets around the river. At time of my visit, the village of Los Patos was experiencing water shortages in homes, and as a result some residents were actually soaping up and bathing in the river.

### LOS PATOS RIVER

Another popular *balneario* (swimming hole) along the coast is at Los Patos, located in the village of the same name about 34 kilometers (21 miles) south of Barahona city. The large freshwater pool, which stretches all the way to the Caribbean Sea, is also the world's shortest river, at just 500 meters or 0.11 miles long. The river is fed by Paraíso's mountains, making it cold and clear. You'll find various species of fish swimming alongside you as well as ducks (*patos*). Ask about the nearby Taíno cave, home to bats and petroglyphs. A handful of newly built shacks here serve typical Dominican fish plates and drinks. There are public bathroom facilities. Expect to pay a couple of bucks for parking. At the time of my visit, residents of Los Patos were in facing water shortages in their homes due to an unrepaired aqueduct and were bathing in the river.

### FOOD

There are multiple vendor shacks surrounding the Patos River attraction, offering fresh fish, chicken, rice and beans, and plenty of rum or beer.

# WEST OF BARAHONA CITY

The options are endless with the numerous national parks that cover more than half of the southwest region. Many are home to endemic flora and fauna. Hike at Parque Jaragua, home to Taíno caves. Look for birds and dry flora at Laguna Oviedo. Explore the cloud forests of Cachote. If you're up for more challenge, walk from Polo to Paraíso with local guides and test your mountain endurance. Another gorgeous site to hike is the Parque Sierra de Bahoruco,

---

**1:** Los Patos; **2:** the Parque Nacional Sierra de Bahoruco

# Polo's Coffee Trail

Polo's coffee is said to be the best in the DR.

The best coffee of the Dominican Republic is produced in the magnificently verdant mountain and birding haven of Polo, a town over 762 meters (2,500 feet) above sea level and approximately 35 kilometers (21.7 miles) from Barahona. Polo's economy once relied on sugarcane, thanks to its fertile and cool lands, but eventually those same conditions allowed for coffee to thrive. Today, aside from agricultural produce including beans, citrus, and pumpkin, Polo's dark and fragrant organic coffee is the number one product to come out of these hills. Polo is responsible for at least a third of all the coffee exported from the Dominican Republic.

To fully appreciate the community of Polo, you'll want to drive up slowly, taking in the winding, scenic views of one the most beautiful areas of the southwest, riding past yellow flowers or *flor*

offering a blend of ecosystems and overnight camping options.

To weigh all of these hiking options, contact **Guanaventuras** (tel. 829/560-3560 or head guide Aurelino Feliz at tel. 809/461-3424, www.guanaventuras.com), run by the local COOPDECI cooperative of La Ciénaga, and with licensed guides who know these woods like the backs of their hands. Their latest tour catalog is available in the office; the one online is accurate in descriptions but the prices are out of date. Other hiking opportunities are offered with **Ecotour Barahona** (tel. 809/243-1190, www.ecotourbarahona.com) or **Tody Tours** (tel. 809/686-0882, www.todytours.com, US$200/hour), which specializes in

birding in the region and takes you on hikes through the Sierra de Bahoruco.

## Polo
### POLO MAGNÉTICO

Turn the engine off and the car rolls uphill by itself—that's what draws visitors to the **Polo Magnético,** or Magnetic Hill, barely a couple of feet long where the phenomenon occurs. Some say it's an optical illusion, while others swear by the magnetic fields in this particular part of the DR. You'll see a sign for it as you head toward the mountains of Polo. To be honest, it's only worth coming here to experience it if you're also headed to Polo for the coffee experience.

*de campo* spilling slightly over the road, not to mention orchids, colorful wooden shacks, and tranquil, cool air year-round.

Once in Polo, you have various alternatives for exploring the coffee trail. One is to head to **Café Toral** (tel. 849/858-1231, www.cafetoral.com, calidad@cafetoral.com, call ahead to arrange a free tour), located at 702 meters (2,303 feet) above sea level, where you can experience **La Ruta del Café**, a comprehensive one-hour tour of the Spanish family-owned coffee plantation. You'll visit the various coffee plants and learn about the origins of coffee, the production process, and the seven types of coffee they produce. The trail is in both English and Spanish, and Jose Miguel Medina, manager of product quality control, will accompany you. Your second option is to head into the village to visit the Dominican-run cooperative **Cooperativa Simona Esmeralda Feliz** (Calle Duarte, tel. 809/993-2811, sucreperez@gmail.com), who produce their own coffee and own their own machinery. Their headquarters are at the *"colmado de la cooperativa"*—they run the convenience store as well—and at the back of it is their coffee machinery. The cooperative counts 286 members, and is a mix of women, men, and adolescents. The pleasant Señor Sucre Perez, manager of the cooperative, is usually at the store; you can watch the coffeemaking process from November through January.

If you'd like to experience another, local coffee trail, such as that at Cafeto Madre on La Lanza farm, contact the **Asociación de Guías La Plataforma Juvenil de Polo** (head guide Brulee, tel. 829/719-3603, US$20 with transport). They can also take you on hikes down various coffee trails, including the Ruta del Café at Café Toral (US$13.25/up to six people or RD$600). The guides can also conduct hikes through nearby Cachote.

If you're lucky enough to be in the Barahona area in late September, look out for Polo's annual **Festicafé** (www.festicafe.org). This coffee festival celebrates the end of the harvesting season and brings together more than 200 coffee producers to celebrate the region's blends. Hundreds of Dominicans from around the country head this way for this colorful festival, held at Polo's baseball field (*el play municipal*) during the last weekend of September. The festival began in 2003. You'll want to come here to get your share of Polo's organic coffee; they sell out soon after the festival. Polo's coffee is also exported to the United States and Europe.

If you're tempted to stay overnight to enjoy the temperatures and views of Polo, the cooperative has one private room with bath, and shared rooms with bunk beds and shared bathrooms for up to 40 people (US$7.75 pp).

## Laguna del Rincón

Although it has suffered through droughts in the last couple of years, **Laguna Cabral** or **Laguna del Rincón**—tucked behind the community of Cabral about 20 kilometers (12 miles) from Barahona—is a scientific reserve and the DR's largest freshwater lagoon at 65 square kilometers (25 square miles). It's home to a variety of marine- and wildlife and surrounded by dry subtropical forest. As a source of water, its importance cannot be overstated; it feeds from the Yaque del Sur and spills into Enriquillo Lake. Among flora and fauna spotted at Laguna Rincón are red mangroves, rhinoceros iguanas, frogs, ducks, and white herons. Communities used to subsist on the fishing the lake provides, but that has led to overfishing.

## Cachote

In the mountains 25 kilometers (16 miles) above Paraíso and La Ciénaga is one of the southwest's ecotourism and biodiversity jewels, a spot few tourists or even Dominicans get to see: the protected area and community of Cachote. Set in a cloud forest at 1,097 meters (3,600 feet) above sea level, approximately 30 families live on the outer limits of Padre Miguel Fuertes Natural Monument. It is here that most of the region's rivers begin, including the Cortico and Nazito.

A welcome center, **Canto del Jilguero**

(Ecoturismo Comunitario Cachote, tel. 829/721-9409 or 809/524-6609, ecoturismocomunitariocachote@yahoo.com, US$55/1-3 persons for two nights, includes three meals per day and hiking; no hot water), is run by the Cachote local cooperative. It provides visitors info on the area as well as two basic wood cabins. This is the departure point for hiking trails and excursions. Birders will be delighted with the opportunity to spot at least 31 species endemic to the island. The five trails (US$33 pp/1-3 persons, includes lunch) range from 30 minutes to an entire day; there's a coffee trail in addition to the bird-watching and nature hikes.

The reserve is also an important home to species of the precious *ébano verde* tree. It can get chilly, so bring warm clothing, as well as extra blankets and a rain jacket. To get to Cachote, look for the sign on the right-hand side of the main Barahona-Paraíso highway. The drive is about 1.5 hours, and you'll need a four-wheel-drive truck. Don't attempt it on your own if you're not an experienced driver.

## ★ Parque Nacional Sierra de Bahoruco

**Parque Nacional Sierra de Bahoruco,** together with Parque Nacional Jaragua and Parque Nacional Lago Enriquillo, constitutes the Jaragua-Bahoruca-Enriquillo Biosphere Reserve, the first UNESCO Biosphere Reserve in the Dominican Republic.

This park west of Barahona in Duvergé has a total surface area of 1,225 square kilometers (473 square miles) and encompasses a variety of ecosystems from pine forests to broadleaf, thorn, and cloud forests rising to 2,286 meters (7,500 feet) above sea level. The Sierra de Bahoruco actually carries over into Haiti, where it's known as the Massif de la Selle. The average temperature in these hills is 19°C (67°F).

Birding is the primary activity here, thanks to the presence of 112 species. You can spot 32 of the DR's 34 endemic birds. Among them are about 14 endangered species such as the Hispaniolan parrot, the Hispaniolan

parakeet, the western chat-tanager, Bicknell's thrush, the white-fronted quail-dove, the golden swallow, the Hispaniolan trogan, the white-winged warbler, the palm crow, and the Hispaniolan crossbill.

There are over 10 species of endemic, endangered amphibians, not to mention more than 1,100 plant species, among which are at least 180 types of orchids, at least 10 percent of which are endemic to the park. The rhinoceros iguana is represented here as well as a few snakes. **Tody Tours** (Calle José Gabriel Garcia 105, Colonial Zone, tel. 809/686-0882, www. todytours.com, US$200/hour) offers birding trips to the reserve at Puerto Escondido and runs a bird-watching base camp within the reserve at **Villa Barrancoli** (US$25/pp, includes dinner). Six screened cabins sit at 400 meters (1,312 feet), offering single beds and a bathhouse with hot water, as well as a shared living, dining, and kitchen facilities. Independent travelers are welcome to book the cabins when there are no scheduled tours. Inquire ahead, and know that you'll have to supply your own breakfast and lunch. To get there on your own, from Barahona you'll head toward Duvergé, south of Lago Enriquillo. In Duvergé, look for a left turn marked by a colorful mural of birds. The road will take you to Puerto Escondido in 20 minutes, where you'll find the park office (RD$50/pp), before continuing to a T-intersection indicating a left toward Rabo de Gato. Continue right at the ensuing intersections until you reach the campsite.

## Hoyo de Pelempito

The main reason you should come all the way out to **Hoyo de Pelempito** (the Pit of Pelempito), if you have the time to spare, is for the spectacular views over the Sierra de Bahoruco. This pit is a geological depression at 700 meters (2,296 feet) below sea level and now a flora and fauna sanctuary.

The hole formed from the collapse of a cave millions of years ago due to the energy released along the fault lines in this region. At night temperatures drop and it gets quite chilly. There's an observation deck from which to take in the vistas. The road to get here is poorly indicated and requires a solid truck; you're better off taking a local guide with you, unless you're traveling in a group. Contact guide Aurelino Feliz with Guanaventuras (La Ciénaga, tel. 829/560-3560, info@guanaventuras.com).

## Parque Nacional Lago Enriquillo

**Parque Nacional Lago Enriquillo** (tel. 809/815-8162, 8am-5pm daily, RD$100 or US$2.21) is home to the largest lake in the Caribbean region. The lake is approximately 260 square kilometers (100 square miles). To give you an idea, that's a little more than the size of Manhattan! The park is part of the trio that constitutes the country's first UNESCO Biosphere Reserve (along with Parque Nacional Jaragua and Parque Nacional Sierra de Bahoruco). You'll quickly notice the park's most famous resident: the rhinoceros iguana. You'll find them roaming around as soon as you enter the park limits, and even on the stretch of road before the park. If you can, get a snapshot of the iguana crossing road sign.

Tucked between the Sierra de Neiba to the north and the Sierra de Bahoruco to the south, **Lago Enriquillo** is 40 meters (130 feet) below sea level. The lake is named after the valiant Taíno chieftain whose rebel forces fought the Spanish. It's the only remaining home for the American crocodile in the DR (they used to be found in the northwest as well, but no longer) thanks to the water's hypersalinity. You'll spot numerous crocs of various sizes as you cruise across the part of the lake known as "*los borbollones*," to the left of the main dock. They tend to get out on the banks during the winter mating season; hiking in this area is now avoided during this time, after an incident in which a croc chased a guide.

The lake's water levels have risen dramatically over the years, nearly doubling in an eight-year span and thus reducing the lake's salinity, which is normally more than two times that of the sea. Some say the shift is due to climate change and increased humidity in the region, though other scientists say deforestation is the likely culprit. So serious is this expansion that you'll immediately notice the hundreds of palms now partly submerged, their tips sticking out of the water and giving the entire lake an eerie, prehistoric feel, as living creatures crawl beneath and above the shimmering surface in the hot sun. These rising levels have also taken over hundreds of acres of land once used for crops—sugarcane, potatoes and plantains—thus taking away from the livelihood of surrounding villages.

Flora around the lake include various cactus species and mangrove shrubs. At least 62 bird species soar above, including sandpipers, roseate spoonbills, white-cheeked pintail ducks, and glossy ibis. There used to be flamingos, but they left when the water level began to rise, and can now be found over on Laguna Oviedo at Parque Nacional Jaragua. In addition to the rhinoceros iguana, Ricord's iguana lives here, as well as other wildlife such as the Hispaniolan slider turtle, Hispaniolan brown racer, and Hispaniolan yellow-mottled frog. Beneath the surface, the primary fish to be found is tilapia and other smaller tropical species. When cruising the lake, you'll spot a few anglers hanging on barely-there wooden planks, hunting away.

At the heart of this lake is **Isla Cabritos** (Goat Island), home to more iguanas and cacti. Visitors are finally allowed to visit this plot again following a five-year closure. Invasive species had occupied the island prior to that time—including cats, donkeys, and cattle—and caused chaos in both the ecosystem and in the population of iguanas, who had previously laid their eggs and lived on the island. The island was thus closed to study how to reinstate its ecosystem; in 2017, the island was finally restored through international collaboration with the DR Ministry of Environment. All invasive species were removed, and iguanas are now seen roaming freely again.

The drive from Barahona or Paraíso to

Parque Enriquillo itself is a beautiful and culturally interesting experience, beginning with the statue of valiant chieftain Enriquillo himself. You'll pass through various villages including Villa Jaragua and Los Rios, where Dominican scenes unfold, including vendors selling grapes in Neyba, ladies sitting in the shade while getting their hair done, and reforested road tunnels like the Tunel Ecológico and one in Río Postrer village. Just before getting to the park, panoramic views of the lake unfold before you as you drive.

To arrange for a boat ride, head into the park, and after paying your entrance fee, go with local guide and passionate conservationist **Manuel Medina** (tel. 809/815-8162, US$77.40/1-10 persons with Isla Cabritos when open, but negotiable for one). Make sure you wear plenty of sunscreen and a hat, closed-toe shoes, long pants, long cotton sleeves, and sunglasses. This is the most intense heat you'll ever feel in the DR, even by Caribbean standards.

On the way back from Enriquillo, a popular stop is **Las Caritas de los Indios**, right off the main highway. A series of wooden stairs allow you to climb to the cliff-top platform, where you can observe impressive petroglyphs carved centuries ago. The view of the lagoon and the surrounding landscape is spectacular.

# Pedernales Province

## PEDERNALES

Pedernales town is at the border, the last frontier of the southwest before you reach neighboring Haiti, with a crossing at Anse-a-Pitres about 1.5 kilometers (0.9 miles) from the town center. The eponymous province is where one of the major natural parks—Parque Nacional Jaragua, which includes Laguna Oviedo—is located, though it is most often visited from Barahona because that town is a better pick as a base and it can be done as a day trip.

The road journey from Barahona to Pedernales town can only be described as excruciatingly long. This is where the coastal highway ends; it's at least a 2.5-hour trek to this region on a straight road. Of course, if you're heading to Bahía de las Águilas or one of the natural sights most visited from Barahona, you'll have something to look forward to and it won't matter that the drive is uneventful, dry, and lined only with cactus. But that's also what's unique about Pedernales: its unusual desert landscape allows you to see a completely different side to the DR. Expect to stop at a handful of military posts along the way; this is mostly

because you're so close to the Haitian border and surveillance is tight.

If you're taking a *guagua*, which don't run up and down this route often due to the distance, you're in for an even longer ride. Aside from the glorious beaches, there's really not much reason to overnight in Pedernales town—unless you're in need of a place to crash as you come in from the Haitian border, want to peek at the Monday-and-Friday Haitian market (not as popular or safe as it used to be), or want to linger for much longer at the national parks without setting up a base in Barahona.

## PARQUE NACIONAL JARAGUA

Undoubtedly among the country's most significant and largest natural reserves, **Parque Nacional Jaragua** (Juancho, tel. 809/601-7979, www.ambiente.gob.do/parque-nacional-jaragua, 8am-5pm daily, US$2.20 or RD$100), at over 1,295 square kilometers (500 square miles), is part of the first UNESCO Biosphere Reserve in the Dominican Republic, the Jaragua-Bahoruco-Enriquillo Biosphere Reserve. Named after a Taíno chief, Parque Jaragua has been comanaged

---

**1:** Lago Enriquillo; **2:** the road to Pedernales

by the Dominican nonprofit **Grupo Jaragua** (www.grupojaragua.org.do) since 1987, and it encompasses a handful of Barahona's and Pedernales's most breathtaking features. Driving through the park on the highway linking to Pedernales reveals just how much of an ecotourism hot spot this area is.

The landscape ranges from towering limestone seafront cliffs to desertlike landscapes to cays—including the isles of Beata and Alto Velo. Bahía de las Águilas runs 5 kilometers (3 miles) northwest of the Jaragua and harbors manatees, turtles, conch, lobster, and colorful Caribbean critters. Pristine white sands and lagoons such as Oviedo surround the bay. Other beaches include Playa Mongo (a surfer haven), San Luis, Beata and Lanza So isles, and Mosquea. The park's total sea surface is 905 square kilometers (349 square miles).

The varied ecosystems found inside the park include subtropical dry forest, thorn forest, wetlands, white and black mangroves, cays, beaches, seagrass, and coral reefs. The flora numbers over 400 species, many of which thrive in desert environments. Bird lovers will find over 130 species, of which 10 are endemic and 47 migratory. They are large populations of American flamingos at Laguna Oviedo, as well as little blue herons, sooty terns, white ibis, belted kingfishers, ospreys, black-crowned night herons, and the showy roseate spoonbill. The park is also known to have the biggest Caribbean population of the white-crowned pigeon. Endangered reptiles such as rhinoceros and Ricord's iguanas call this haven their home. You may also spot the shrew-like, insect-eating Hispaniolan solenodon or the Hispaniolan hutia, a large rodent.

Last but not least, four species of sea turtles make their presence known here: the hawksbill, the loggerhead, the leatherback, and the green sea turtle.

Parque Jaragua is home to several caves—La Colmena, El Guanal, La Poza, and Cueva Mongó—with petroglyphs that reveal the presence of Taíno as far back as 2590 BC.

## ★ Laguna Oviedo

The largest saltwater body in the Dominican Republic at 27 square kilometers (10.4 square miles) of surface area and 1.5 meters (4.9 feet) deep, **Laguna Oviedo** marks the beginning of Parque Nacional Jaragua and is the main reason visitors come to the park. This hypersaline lagoon has a salt level three times higher than the sea; it even crystallizes during the dry season from January through March. It is a major nesting site and refuge for endemic and migratory birds, including American flamingos, West Indian whistling ducks, and the roseate spoonbill.

While the lagoon is protected, there's a co-management plan to allow the families who live around the lagoon to sustain themselves; as such, the lagoon is divided into various zones, each with its own stipulated use or nonuse. Pupfish, snook, and tilapia are taken by local fishers.

If you sign up through the main tour operators in town, you'll likely just do the boat ride down the lagoon with a swim. But if you get here with your own car, the possibilities widen. The entrance to Laguna Oviedo is well marked; there's a giant sign along the highway on the left. There's also an informative makeshift museum-type display at the park entrance, all in Spanish. This is also the main Parque Jaragua office and the base for local community guides who are well versed in the area's flora and fauna and can take you on excursions from the nearby pier or on foot. Note that many speak only Spanish. Ask for the park's licensed tour guide, **Juan Carlos Santana** (tel. 809/601-7979); he is often at the main office if he's not out giving a tour. A visit to the lagoon is often included in other organized tours on the way to Bahía de las Águilas.

Bird-watching is a great here, but there is much more to be enjoyed. Three main hiking trails traverse the area and lead to sulfur water pools. There are several excursion options. Boat rides go out to smaller isles and caves. You'll have to decide among them based on how much time you have. A complete tour of the lagoon by boat can take up to 2.5 hours (US$78 for 1-5 people, plus park entrance fee). A one-hour option is available for less (US$55). Solo travelers should not be afraid to bargain with the guides. A complete list of prices is posted at the park office. The sunrise at the park is spectacular, so ask about camping here.

You can also hike along the shores to view the flamingos on a **Paseo Flamencos** walk (US$20/pp). It takes about an hour. The turtle-nesting season within the park is from March through September, with egg observation possible from April 1 through July, usually at 8pm and 6am.

## ★ BAHÍA DE LAS ÁGUILAS

Touted as the most beautiful beach in the entire Dominican Republic, this beach has nearly 8 kilometers (5 miles) of ultra-fine, powder-soft white sand and heavenly Caribbean turquoise waters so clear you can see your toes. Sitting inside the protected Parque Nacional Jaragua, you can't imagine anyone else has been here, where a magnificent rocky karst landscape hugs the beach and sea.

The road to get to the jumping-off point of La Cueva, where the boats depart, is long—at least two hours from Barahona province—and reveals a surprising landscape of cactus against bright skies with the sea in the distance. The road veers to Cabo Rojo, down a path that's a dark rust color due to the controversial bauxite mine in the area. After the port of Cabo Rojo and the small airstrip for private planes, another left turn takes you to La Cueva, where the departure beach—another pristine stunner—and a couple of restaurants await. The boat ride across the Bay of Eagles is one of the most beautiful you'll experience in the DR. The towering cliffs, dozens of birds, and the sheer magnitude of this body of water lined with white sands are dreamy.

You can also reach Bahía de las Águilas beach by car. There's a rough road that lets you drive up to La Cueva and continue down to the beach past Rancho La Cueva Restaurant. You'll only need to pay the park entrance fees and drive about 40 minutes down a dirt path. The only downside to this alternative is that you'll only get as far as the main beach strip, which is where most people hang out (you'll notice a sort of lookout tower by it). By boat, leaving from either of the two restaurants on the beach, you can go farther into the bay and take in its real splendor, not to mention find more private swimming spots away from the crowd. Note that there is no shade here, but there are often constant breezes. Still, bring an umbrella and plenty of sunscreen.

### Sports and Recreation

Because most of the excursions to the national park are out of Barahona town or province, there aren't many organized tours in these parts and no public transportation to the sights. If you're carless, you can contact **Jopaka Tours** (Hostal Doña Chava, Calle Segunda 5, tel. 809/524-0332, www.donachava.com) to arrange for outings to Hoyo Pelempito and Bahía de las Águilas or fishing trips. If you're into cave diving, contact **Golden Arrow Technical Dive Center** (Calle Victor Garrido Puello 12, Santo Domingo, tel. 809/566-7780, denis@cavediving.com.do, from US$50/nontechnical dive), in operation since 1999 and offering dives off Pedernales at Cabo Rojo, Bahía de las Águilas, and Cabo Falso.

### Shopping
#### HAITIAN MARKET

Haitians are authorized to sell goods at the border of Pedernales, on the Dominican side, every Monday and Friday under a covered space. It really isn't anything so unusual you'd need to make your way here. If anything, it's as chaotic as any other vegetable or thrift market you might encounter in a bustling Dominican town. Given the recent heightened immigration conflict between the two countries, check ahead on the latest situation to make sure it's a good idea to even stop here.

## Food

When you're heading this way, you might as well veer off to Cabo Rojo and enjoy some fresh seafood at one of two restaurants facing Playa La Cueva. **Rancho Típico La Cueva de las Águilas** (tel. 809/753-8058, 11am-10pm daily, US$10-20) is the longest-running restaurant and a jumping-off point to Bahía de las Águilas where you can enjoy the best of Pedernales's seafood, including a delicious *paella de mariscos* or a plate of fish with *tostones*. This restaurant now offers on-site camping.

The adjacent, Italian-owned **Eco del Mar** (tel. 809/576-7740, www.ecodelmar.com.do, 11am-10pm daily, US$10-15), sitting on a breathtaking stretch of Playa La Cueva, offers a delicious menu of fresh-made pizza, risotto, and numerous other options if you're looking for something other than the usual Dominican fare. The owners are friendly and will even let you get behind the bar to mix your own drink if it's the kind not found here; the bar carries premium liquor of all sorts. If you have time, hop on a boat from either of these restaurants and enjoy the renowned Bahía de las Águilas.

Another excellent spot for seafood that's actually in Pedernales town and close to the main beach is the contemporary **King Crab Café** (Calle Fernando Dominguez, formerly Duarte, tel. 809/256-9607, kingcrabcafe@restaurante.com.do, US$10-15). Try the seafood soup or grilled lobster. It's a nice spot (probably the best in town) for a romantic dinner. A more casual but solid option in town is **Comedor Perla Negra** (Calle Central, off Av. Duarte, tel. 809/750-0241), also serving the area's renowned seafood dishes, as well as chicken and goat options.

## Accommodations

Your best bet in Pedernales town is **Hostal Doña Chava** (Calle Segunda 5, tel. 809/524-0332, www.donachava.com, US$22), an immaculate, colorful guesthouse with a charming setup that makes you feel like you're a world away from the concrete jungle. Think thatch-roof corridors, wooden railings, a leafy courtyard, simple and colorful rooms with single beds, cable TV, air-conditioning from 8pm to 8am, wireless Internet, private baths, and shared lounge areas. There's a generator for the frequent power cuts. It's centrally located, while also just 15 minutes from Bahía de las Águilas, and great value for independent travelers.

Up for a little more adventurous and memorable stay? Camp out on gorgeous Playa La Cueva at **Eco Del Mar** (tel. 809/576-7740, www.ecodelmar.com.do, US$10/night), a restaurant and bar offering good value for those who want to enjoy the great beaches of the Pedernales for a little longer. The tents are set on the beach, with a reasonable distance to the back of the public restaurant, and have single beds; new luxury beach houses have also been added. The separate outdoor bathroom facilities are clean and have hot water. The food is decent, and the service impeccable (expect potentially noisier nights on weekends, with beachside bonfires). The advantage is getting to stay overnight after your boat trip to Bahía de las Águilas (also offered through Eco Del Mar) and taking in the sunset and the stars rather than hitting the long road back to Barahona.

Locally owned, adjacent **Glamping Eco Lodge Cueva de las Aguilas** (US$45, includes breakfast) offers camping with either basic tents or slightly larger glamping options with one or two double beds next to its popular, local-favorite La Cueva restaurant. The larger tents have beds and a wooden mini-terrace; bring your own towels and expect outdoor baths that could be distant from your tent. If you're a partier, this would be your spot; music blasts on weekend nights. There's no Wi-Fi.

## Other Beaches

If there's one thing Pedernales has, it's gorgeous, pristine beaches where you're not likely to see another soul—even aside from

1: flamingos on Laguna Oviedo; 2: Bahía de las Águilas

# Wind Energy in the DR

Parque Eólico Los Cocos

It's an unmistakable sight as you venture deeper down the highway into Pedernales province: gargantuan white wings, turning slowly in the distance, towering over green farmland and adding to the already-mesmerizing coastal views. What you're looking at is one of the most groundbreaking privately funded renewable energy projects in the country, if not the Caribbean. Sited on an elevated ridge between 10 and 100 meters (33-328 feet) above sea level, the **Parque Eólico Los Cocos** is the country's first wind energy producer connected to the national grid. Located in the community of Juancho, up to 40 wind turbines provide electricity to the region and the country, displacing approximately 160,000 tons of carbon dioxide emissions per year and generating an annual 220,000 megawatts of clean energy.

The Dominican Republic has suffered through frequent power outages due to a rise in electricity demands over the past 20 years, coupled with high generation costs, poor management, and rising fuel costs. In 2007, the government approved a renewable energy law giving tax exemptions to renewable energy projects in an attempt to encourage infrastructure that would lessen dependency on fossil fuels. A study by the National Renewable Energy Laboratory of the U.S. Department of Energy revealed that the Dominican Republic's wind capacity could produce up to 30,500 megawatts, mostly in the southwest region and in the northwest. But the strongest source is in the region of Pedernales. EGE Haina, behind the Parque Eólico Los Cocos, began operating in the DR in 2009, acquiring four power plants and investing over US$83 million in maintenance and upgrades. Construction of the wind farm in Los Cocos began in March 2010. Transporting all of the wind turbines and substations to such a remote area as Juancho proved to be a challenge, and thus began the million-dollar renovation of the nearby port of Cabo Rojo.

The first installation of 14 wind turbines at Los Cocos, injecting 25 megawatts into the national power network at an investment of US$100 million, took place in February 2011, with official inauguration in October 2011. The project was expanded in 2012, tripling generation capacity to 77 megawatts. To say the park and its turbines are an impressive sight as you drive through one of the poorest areas in the country is an understatement. The website for Los Cocos (www.egehaina.com/plantas/loscocos) has a fun interactive screen explaining how the wind transforms into energy.

Bahía de las Águilas. One of the prettiest is on the way to the bay: **Playa Cabo Rojo.** The long stretch of fine white sand is a great place to stop and swim before you take that left turn to head to La Cueva (de Los Pescadores) and Bahía de las Águilas. The dismal view of the bauxite plant ahead will evaporate from your mind once your eyes fixate on the phosphorescent turquoise water. The beach departure point for all boats to Bahía de las Águilas at **Playa La Cueva** is also gorgeous with its powdery stretch. You can enjoy it while munching at Rancho La Cueva facing the beach or at Ecomar Restaurant, which received a permit to build a controversial 228-villa resort on La Cueva Beach within the park. Closer to the city is the eponymous **Playa Pedernales.**

## PEDERNALES CITY

Pedernales town is at the border, the last frontier of the southwest before you reach neighboring Haiti, with a crossing at Anse-a-Pitres about 1.5 kilometers (0.9 miles) from the town center.

## Getting There and Around

After reaching Barahona from Santo Domingo via the local bus leaving from Parque Enriquillo throughout the day, **Caribe Tours** (tel. 809/524-4952, www. caribetours.com.do, US$6.85 one-way, 6:15am, 9:45am, 1:45pm, and 5:15pm), or with your own car, expect an additional 2.5 hours south to reach Pedernales. Again, there's really no reason to overnight in Pedernales town proper. Many of the excursions to this province depart from the neighboring Barahona province.

Getting around is difficult without your own car, unless all you want to do is hop on a few organized excursions. These will be expensive and leave you to see a lot less than you might on your own. There are local *guaguas* that run up and down the coast, but they might not always show up when you need and you might be waiting a while on the roadside (not to mention they don't run after sundown). Those renting a car should do so from Las Américas airport in Santo Domingo.

Eco Del Mar offers overnight glamping on Playa la Cueva.

# Background

## The Landscape

### GEOGRAPHY

The Dominican Republic is blessed with the most diverse topography of any country in the Caribbean region. It's the entire region in miniature: warm sun and beaches, cool mountain climates that drop below freezing at night, desertlike sand dunes and regions with cactus sprouting out of the roadside, and both the highest and lowest points in the Caribbean in Pico Duarte and Lago Enriquillo, respectively. Throw in subtropical and cloud forests, hypersaline lakes, rivers, and

# The Caribbean

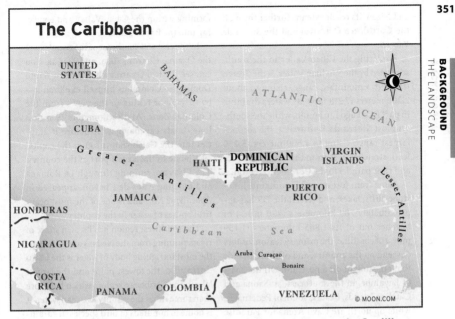

waterfalls, and you could experience the entire Caribbean landscape in a single weeklong visit.

Occupying the eastern two-thirds of Hispaniola Island at 48,442 square kilometers or 18,704 square miles (about half the size of Portugal), the DR is the second-largest country in the Caribbean after Cuba and sits in the middle of the region. To the north are the Bahamas; Jamaica and Cuba lie to the west; there's a 388-kilometer (241-mile) border with neighboring Haiti to the east, with Puerto Rico beyond; and South America is, well, south. The northern coast faces the Atlantic Ocean, while the south basks beside the Caribbean Sea.

There are 31 provinces, plus a National District (comprising Santo Domingo). The country is essentially demarcated by its five major mountain ranges. These mountains are not only part of what makes the Dominican landscape so stunning, they help blunt the impact of major storms.

On the North Coast is the **Cordillera Septentrional,** rising above the coastal plains from Monte Cristi to Nagua. It slopes south to give way to the Cibao Valley, which runs from Manzanillo Bay in the northwest to the northeastern Samaná Peninsula. Swampy lowlands separate the Samaná Peninsula from the Septentrional, but the peninsula is made up of mountains as well, with elevations of up to 579 meters (1,900 feet).

Below the Septentrional, running through the center of the Dominican Republic like its solid spine, the **Cordillera Central** dominates as the biggest and most rugged mountain range. It's home to the tallest peak in the region, Pico Duarte, and has elevations ranging from 1,829 meters to 3,170 meters (6,000 to 10,400 feet), starting at the Haitian border and running south to Constanza Valley, and down to the southern Sierra de Ocoa. Home to additional prominent peaks, such as La Rucilla, it's the source of major rivers such as the Yaque del Norte, Yaque del Sur,

**Previous:** Many Haitians in the DR sell fruit, sweets, and other goods.

and Nizao. Its reach extends further through the **Cordillera Oriental** and the Sierra de Yamasa.

Bordering the Cibao Valley to the south, separated by the San Juan Valley, is the **Sierra de Neiba** mountain range, rising to about 2,200 meters (7,218 feet), its waters draining in part into Lago Enriquillo, while the southernmost **Sierra de Bahoruco**, the second-largest range rising to 1,600 meters (5,250 feet), stretches east from the Haitian border and runs parallel to the Cordillera Central.

Aside from forests and mountains, limestone cliffs, lakes, and rivers, the DR has approximately 789 kilometers (490 miles) of beaches out of its 1,865 kilometers (1,159 miles) of coastline, the primary reason visitors descend on the country, and offshore islands that are straight off a postcard. Off the coast of Bayahibe, in the southeast, sit Saona and Catalina Islands. Beata is south of Pedernales, while up north are Cayo Arena (or Paradise Island) and the Cayos Siete Hermanos, off the Monte Cristi shoreline.

### Rivers and Lakes

The Dominican Republic has *ríos* running in the mountains and over the plains, with seven major drainage basins—six of which are out of the Cordillera Central. Wherever you go, there always seems to be a river and its tributaries nearby for one's swimming enjoyment. The longest of them all is the **Yaque del Norte**, at 298 kilometers (185 miles) with a basin area of 7,044 square kilometers (2,720 square miles), in the central Cibao Highlands. It rises out of the tallest peak of the Caribbean—Pico Duarte—and runs north through Santiago, then winds its way west into the mountain retreat town of Jarabacoa, where river rafting is one of the attractions. The relatively shallow Yaque empties into the Bahía de Monte Cristi of the Atlantic Ocean at the northwestern edge of the country. It's an important source of irrigation for rice farming and agriculture in the central region. The **Yuna River** is the second largest and most important, at 210 kilometers (131 miles),

forming within the Cibao Valley and emptying into the Bay of Samaná.

In the east and southeast of the country are the Ozama, Chavón, Soco, and Magua. You can see the **Río Ozama** when visiting Santo Domingo—Columbus himself explored it—by driving or taking in the views from the Colonial Zone. At 15 kilometers (9 miles) long, boats can navigate it before it empties into the Caribbean through the capital city, home to the largest port of the country. The **Chavón,** running through La Romana and hugging Altos de Chavón, appeared in *Apocalypse Now* and is one of the most beautiful bodies of water in the country.

The southwest region has its own share of rivers running from the Neiba Valley. Perhaps the most intriguing body of water is the **Lago Enriquillo,** the lowest point and the largest lake in the Caribbean region, which has more than three times the salinity as ocean water. It is home to hundreds of bird species. Its drainage basin includes 10 river systems covering an area of over 3,000 square kilometers (1,158 square miles). Up north, you'll find gems such as the **Laguna Gri Gri,** in Río San Juan, teeming with birds and mangroves that are delightful to explore at sunset.

Rivers are popular gathering spots for families on the weekend thanks to the cooler water temperatures they offer in hot weather. Groups come out with large pots and cook riverside while the children splash around and couples hug or dance in the shade.

## CLIMATE

The Dominican Republic's motto should be "365 days of sunshine." For the most part, the country's tropical climate is as ideal as it gets for a vacationer: the average annual temperature is 25°C (77°F), with warm and sunny days for most of the year. The only slight variation comes in the "winter" months—November through April—when temperatures cool off slightly in the evenings (20°C [68°F]) and early mornings, and rainfall is more frequent. In the interior, up in the mountains of the Cordillera Central and the hills of the southwest, it gets a lot chillier—dipping below freezing at night, with frost-covered mountain peaks. If you're heading this way in the summer months, brace yourself: It is uncomfortably hot and humid, but sunny nonetheless, with average daily temperature of 31°C (88°F). Rain has been rather unpredictable during the summer and even year-round the last four years, with more rainfall in December and January than usual, due to climate change.

The Cibao Valley enjoys an eternal spring that makes it an attractive place to live. The area is blessed with constant breezes such that it never feels unbearably humid. If you're staying in the twin towns of Jarabacoa and Constanza, you'll need a jacket and pants for nights—especially in the winter months.

Over in the northwest around Monte Cristi or southwest in Barahona and Pedernales, burning-hot weather awaits and desertlike temperatures can rise up to 28°C (100°F) or more. Rain is frequent from November through April on the North Coast, while other areas are supposed to get precipitation from May to November. Most rainfall comes in unexpected bursts and doesn't last all day or night. The southwest is the driest, hottest part of the country, as evidenced by the cacti shooting up from roadsides in Barahona and Pedernales.

Of course, no place has perfect weather and you could stumble on a couple of days with gray skies, but even that is rare! Blue skies, sun, and glorious days abound in the Dominican Republic.

## Hurricanes

The hurricane season generally runs from June 1 through November 30, although there's a small chance one could form outside of those dates. The Dominican Republic has been hit with approximately 11 hurricanes over the span of the last century—in other words, not that many—and most have had an impact on the southwestern or eastern coast. Hurricane Georges struck in September 1998 as a Category 3 and was one of the most devastating. It hit the capital of Santo Domingo and the Punta Cana coast, causing over 300 deaths and billions of dollars in damage, particularly to agricultural lands. It was the worst storm since Hurricane David, a Category 5 storm that made landfall in 1979 and killed at least 2,000 people. The twin Category 5 hurricanes Irma and Maria that struck several Caribbean islands in 2017 missed the DR, causing only some flooding and road damage in the northern part of the country.

Hurricanes that hit the DR usually begin in the Atlantic off the western coast of Africa as tropical depressions or tropical storms, with the possibility of progressing into hurricanes as they make their way slowly to the Caribbean. It can take up to two or three weeks for a storm to form into a serious hurricane, so there's plenty of time for evacuation if needed. While the possibility exists in the summer months and the Dominican Republic is located in the storm belt—September tends to be the peak period—the chances of a hurricane hitting are minimal and certainly shouldn't affect your trip planning. Hotels and airlines are well prepared by now with contingency plans, so they will be informed before you are. Summer is also a great time for hotel specials and flight discounts.

You can keep up with weather conditions at all times by following the National Hurricane Center (www.nhc.noaa.gov) on social media, and sign up for the State Department's SMART Traveler Enrollment Program to receive notifications in case of extreme emergency situations.

## NATIONAL PARKS

Revealing a growing consciousness of the country's rich biodiversity and the need to preserve it for future generations, the Dominican Republic now oversees 18 national parks, 9 natural monuments, and 6 scientific reserves. The first UNESCO Biosphere Reserve was established in 2009, combining three of the country's most biodiverse national parks—Jaragua, Bahoruco, and Enriquillo—in the southwest region. The protection of all this land was in part the result of the government stepping up to the plate after environmentalists warned in the 1970s that much of the DR's forests would vanish by the 1990s if no changes were made due to illegal forestation, fires, and pollution, among other causes. Challenges and abuses have not gone away in certain national parks in the southwest, particularly Parque Nacional Jaragua, which has been severely damaged by illegal agriculture on what is otherwise protected land. But for the most part, the country is learning to become a staunch protector of its natural resources, recognizing their vital role in ecotourism.

You will be able to explore a handful of the most diverse and unique national parks of the Dominican Republic during your visit, whether you're headed north, south, east, or into the heart of the country. The government manages the parks and entry at each location usually costs RD$100 (100 Dominican pesos) per person, or about US$2.21.

Two of the most important parks protect the mountains and pine forests of the Cordillera Central, the country's most rugged landmass: **Parque Nacional Armando Bermúdez,** founded in 1956 and home to the 3,088-meter-tall (10,128-foot) Pico Duarte, and the adjacent **Parque Nacional José del Carmen Ramírez,** founded in 1958. Many come here to hike the tallest peak of the Caribbean and check that item off a bucket list, but the parks offer plenty for birders and those who want to take in some of the most spectacular views of the DR.

The crown jewel of the DR's parks is in the southwest region, where the greatest numbers of endemic flora and fauna are found, including over 50 species of birds and up to 166 species of the country's orchids, at **Parque Nacional Sierra de Bahoruco.** Within the park the dry forest transitions to cloud forest and Hispaniolan pine forest at high elevations. It is one of the most fascinating parks for scientists because of its limestone subterrane. While it is currently under threat due to illegal farming and felling in the southern portion, there's hope that the damage done is being identified and stopped before it's too late.

On the southern tip of Pedernales, **Parque Nacional Jaragua** provides a habitat for the cute pink flamingo, among other species. It also encompasses mangroves, beaches, Taíno caves, and the Oviedo Lagoon.

**Parque Nacional Isla Cabritos,** also in the southwest and a popular excursion from Barahona province, is a tiny island within Lago Enriquillo, the largest lake in the Caribbean. The lake and park are home to the largest population of American crocodiles, endemic iguanas, and over 60 bird species.

The east coast of the DR, off the Samaná Peninsula, is home to the mystical **Parque Nacional Los Haitises** and its rich variety of mangroves and the giant rock formations jutting out of the water, best explored by boat. It is home to populations of frigates and brown boobies. Along its shores, some tucked away and others seafront, are Taíno caves with expansive chambers filled with petroglyphs and bats.

Equally impressive on the southeastern tip of the DR below the Punta Cana region is the **Parque Nacional del Este,** starting in Boca de Yuma and stretching out to Bayahibe. It consists of dry, flat terrain with tropical forests and limestone bedrock. There are Taíno caves to explore on foot or underwater. The park also comprises the stunning offshore islands of Saona and Catalina and their coral reefs, supporting frigate populations, the endangered *paloma coronita* (white-crowned pigeon), and the country's most important turtle-nesting site, Isla Saona.

Along the northwestern coast of the country is the **Parque Nacional Monte Cristi,** a range of subtropical dry forest with towering cliffs rising dramatically over the Atlantic. The most impressive is El Morro, a limestone mesa towering 213 meters (700 feet) above sea level and facing a gorgeous stretch of beach. The park also counts offshore islands, including Cayos Siete Hermanos, which protect colonies of brown pelicans, great egrets, and frigate birds, coastal lagoons with mangroves, and freshwater pools. Coral reefs stretch from El Morro to Punta Rucia. It's one of the least visited parks despite its uniqueness. Northeast of Monte Cristi is another of my favorite protected areas, the **Estero Hondo Marine Mammal Sanctuary,** with the largest population of manatees. You can observe them from a lookout tower or go paddleboarding on the lagoon. For even more off-the-beaten-track national parks, look into **Parque Nacional Saltos de La Jalda** in Miches, protecting stunning waterfalls, and **Parque Aniana Vargas** in Cotuí.

Just 12 miles east of Santo Domingo, adjacent to the international airport, is one of the first and smallest national parks. **Parque Nacional Submarino La Caleta** is a popular dive excursion from Boca Chica for its marinelife and shipwreck—though not better than the diving you'll find off the coast of Bayahibe within the Parque Nacional del Este.

## ENVIRONMENTAL ISSUES

Today, the Dominican Republic faces a range of environmental issues, including deforestation due to illegal felling, illegal farming in protected areas, soil erosion, water shortages, and serious droughts.

Approximately 25 percent of Dominican Republic land has been designated as protected area, and since 1967 the law has prohibited commercial tree cutting. However, some national parks have proven to be preserved on paper only and are under serious threat from illegal actions—some say from the government itself—including illegal farming and sale of protected lands, with issuance of permits to private individuals. These abuses have been brought to light in the last couple of years in the Parque Nacional Sierra de Bahoruco. They have led to the destruction of southern portions of the most biodiverse park in the country, affecting endemic fauna and birds.

In the summer of 2015, the government decided to begin looking into these violations by creating a technical committee to draw up a plan to address the park's issues. A group

was sent to tour the park and its surrounding communities for fact finding, along with the help of the U.S. Fish and Wildlife Service as observers and Dominican conservation body Grupo Jaragua (www.grupojaragua.org.do). Overpopulation and need have drawn mostly Haitian sharecroppers working for Dominicans who claim to have title to lands within the park. They have been planting avocado while simultaneously destroying the soil when they burn the land to clear it. Sadly, the situation continues today.

Forest fires are another unfortunate issue for the DR's forests, particularly in the pine forests of the Cordillera Central, where arson has taken place in the recent past. Farmers and communities have now been trained to fight fires to minimize destruction when disaster strikes.

Another major source of concern is the increasingly dry weather and lack of water—as in much of the Caribbean region. The nation has faced some shortfalls in the last three years, with the most serious droughts occurring in 2015. Some river basins and streambeds have gone dry. Certain waterfalls that once gushed away are smaller or thinned out (even at El Limón and Damajagua Falls). Homes and farms are facing water shortages. The change in weather is blamed on El Niño, while others point to environmental abuse of riverbeds, by removing sediments and other important natural resources from them. On the flip side, rising sea levels are evident, causing beach erosion in many parts of the Caribbean.

A growing tourism industry also means a need for additional monitoring to prevent pollution and damage, and thankfully governmental efforts have increased to raise awareness among visitors about their own environmental impacts. There are also more eco-conscious travelers and Dominican resorts than in past years, and while there is a passion for showing the rich "nature" of the country away from resorts, care needs to be taken to prevent overvisitation of natural sites and destructive impact on these fragile ecosystems.

# Plants and Animals

Travel outside of any major city and venture inland to take in the country's impressive richness in flora. The Dominican Republic is home to 5,600 plant species, of which 1,800 are endemic. The country's fauna counts 166 species of reptiles (144 endemic), 74 species of amphibians (71 endemic), and over 300 bird species, of which 10 percent are only found right here in the DR. And that is not even counting mammals and land and marine invertebrates. This makes the country an important site for scientific studies and a potentially great destination for ecotourism.

## PLANTS

### Trees

The most common type of vegetation in the country is the subtropical forest. It is what you will find in the Cibao Valley, the Bahoruco range, and on the Samaná Peninsula, for instance.

Subtropical forests are home to the West Indian mahogany (*Swietenia mahagoni*), or *caoba* as they call it here. It is native to the island of Hispaniola but not endemic to the DR. These can grow up to 11 meters (36 feet) tall. Mahogany was used to build the first cathedral in Santo Domingo. Other common trees are the West Indian cedar, the wild olive, the ceiba (silk cotton tree), the bija, and the mammon tree. The Taíno cultivated the *higuero* or calabash tree, which they used to make their utensils and ceremonial masks.

Palm trees of various species are impossible to miss. A signature of the DR, tall coconut palms originally from Africa tower above its diamond-white sands or fill entire forests. The royal palm (*Roystonea borinquena*) is found in deeper soil, but has also been planted along boulevards in big cities. Other types of palm include the sabala, the cana, the guano, and the yarey, all native to the island and often used for making furniture. The Spanish introduced several trees such as the African tulip

and the *poinciana*, also called the flamboyant tree, which blooms in the summer and looks spectacular along country roads.

In the highlands, pines dominate the mountainous landscape. The Creole pine is the most common species. Many trees are festooned with bromeliads and orchids.

Mangroves proliferate in coastal and estuary areas in all varieties and constitute an important barrier against hurricanes and erosion, and they support populations of marinelife and birds. You'll find these in Parque Los Haitises, Parque Monte Cristi, and Parque Jaragua. However, because the DR coastline also includes cliffs and rocks, there aren't as many mangrove spots as in the other Caribbean countries.

### Flowers and Fruits

The array of flowers and fruits encountered is mind-boggling, thanks to the diversity in environments and altitudes across the country, from the highest in the Cibao Valley to the lowest on Isla Cabritos in the southwest.

You're never far from fresh fruit in the DR, and passion fruit in particular is as common and affordable as an orange. Dominicans love to drink fruit smoothies blended with sugar and condensed milk into *batidas*. In Santo Domingo, fruit carts are a dime a dozen, and they'll even cut and slice your chosen produce on the spot for a to-go snack or breakfast. The country is blessed with pineapples, passion fruit, oranges, melons, guavas, papayas, mangoes, bananas (called *guineo*), and grapefruit, among others.

Vegetables are equally ubiquitous, grown mostly in the Cibao region. Avocados are a common find, as well as cabbage, onions, eggplant, plantains, and sugarcane. The indigenous Taíno were the first to cultivate and use *yuca* (cassava), an important ingredient for many Dominican dishes, including the traditional *sancocho* soup.

# La Rosa de Bayahibe

La Rosa de Bayahibe

The country's national flower is the *Pereskia quisqueyana*, the rose of Bayahibe. This gorgeous, delicate pink bloom is actually a species of cactus that grows only in the Dominican Republic, in the Altagracia province and mostly in Bayahibe on the southeastern coast of the country. It's one of the few cacti to carry leaves—the flower's petals can reach up to 2.2 centimeters (0.87 inches) in length. Sadly, it's also in danger of extinction. As a result, the Bayahibe community, as well as several regional hotels, has made efforts to replant and grow this flower. You can find plenty of it planted by the church on the edge of Bayahibe town, known as La Punta de Bayahibe.

Flower lovers will be thrilled to see all the blooms that surround them. Over 300 species of orchids grow in the DR. You can view them at Santo Domingo's Botanical Gardens, the largest in the Caribbean, or at Punta Cana's Scape Park. Even more gorgeous blooms are grown in Constanza, where entire fields are as vibrant as a kaleidoscope. Japanese immigrants helped grow these flowers back in the late 1950s during the Trujillo regime. Over 50 percent of endemic orchids are found in the Sierra de Bahoruco in the deep southwest. You can also spot bromeliads in Valle Nuevo. With the rise in cultivation of cacao, coffee, and other products and the accompanying illegal felling of trees, several floral species are now critically endangered, including the *Pereskia quisqueyana*—the country's national flower—which you can only spot in Bayahibe.

## ANIMALS
### Land Mammals

Almost all of the mammals you'll see in the Dominican Republic are nonnative, initially brought in by the Spaniards centuries ago. The two that are the exception are in danger of extinction: the **solenodon** and the **hutia.** The solenodon is a weird-looking, furry shrewlike creature with an elongated snout and a long, scaly naked tail. It can grow up to 30 centimeters (one foot) in length, not including that tail, which can add 25 centimeters (10 inches). It feeds on insects and worms, as well as roots and vegetables. This is actually one of the rarest and oldest mammals of North America. There are only two living species of the solenodon; the other is the Cuban solenodon (*Solenodon cubansus*). Because it is mostly nocturnal, it's hard to spot this creature, and when it's on the go, it runs in zigzags. Last but not least, the males have spurs on their ankles that release venom, which they use against prey. The hutia is a small rodent, also nocturnal, and roams around tree trunks and in caves. Aside from these, you'll spot an abundance of pigs, cows, goats, horses, chickens, and way too many cats and dogs.

## Marine Mammals

Of the 1,668 kilometers (346 miles) of coastline in the Dominican Republic, including offshore islands, 1,264 kilometers (785 miles) are protected. And the stars of the Dominican Republic's coastal waters are the **humpback whales,** drawing thousands of visitors every year during their mating season, mid-January through mid-March, when about 3,000 of them faithfully return to the Bay of Samaná. The humpback whales can weigh up to 60 tons and measure up to 15 meters (49 feet). They bask in the Caribbean waters simply to mate; they do all their feeding the rest of the year while in the Arctic Circle, building up to 20 centimeters (8 inches) of fat to sustain them.

The **West Indian manatee** is another precious marine mammal, spotted along estuaries and coastal areas. In the DR, the largest population of manatees can be seen at Estero Hondo Reserve on the northwest coast. These endangered herbivores, also known as "sea cows," are as gentle as you can imagine, despite their gargantuan size. Outside of the reserve areas, they remain at risk from hunting and interference from tour boat excursions.

Last but not least, **four species of turtles** roam the reefs of the Dominican Republic: the green sea turtle, the leatherback turtle, the loggerhead, and the hawksbill turtle. Major turtle nesting sites are Isla Saona—where you'll find an active turtle conservation center on Mano Juan—and Parque Nacional Jaragua, where they come ashore at night to lay eggs from May through October. The hawksbill is the most endangered because of demand for its shells, which are illegally sold in jewelry and other accessories. Please always be aware of what you are purchasing.

## Coral Reefs

The growing threats to the country's reef systems from overfishing, agriculture, tourism, and coastal development have caused the government to create marine protected areas, including at Parque Monte Cristi, Los Haitises, Parque Nacional del Este, and Parque Jaragua. Despite over 60 percent of the reefs being protected, the problems continue, and some areas, particularly Punta Cana where tourism is thriving, have begun to implement coral reef gardening systems to help regrow healthy coral.

The largest reef formation in the country is in the northwestern Monte Cristi region, stretching 64 kilometers (40 miles) from El Morro to Punta Rucia. Along this coastline are extensive seagrass beds and red mangroves. Off Punta Rucia are coral keys, teeming with marinelife. Additional reefs are found in Sosúa, off the north shore of the Samaná Peninsula, off Las Galeras at Cabo Cabrón, off the Bávaro-Punta Cana-Macao region, in the islands of Parque Nacional del Este, at Boca Chica, and in Parque Nacional Jaragua.

Diving and snorkeling are popular activities—cave diving in particular—but in the most touristed regions, overuse of sites and lack of monitoring has led to serious reef damage from careless visitors. This is particularly evident in Sosúa and the surrounding areas. Make sure you heed all instructions on how to position your body properly and not touch anything with your fins or hands, potentially hurting yourself in the process. Look, appreciate, and keep it moving.

## Birds

Birding enthusiasts are increasingly drawn to the DR, and rightly so—it is a home to a whopping 300 plus species, of which 27 are endemic. Frequently spotted endemic birds you should look out for include the national bird *cigua palmera (Dulus dominicus)* or palmchat, the black-crowned tanager *(Phaenicophilus palmarum),* the Hispaniolan amazon *(Amazona ventralis),* the vervain hummingbird

(*Mellisuga minima*), the Hispaniolan lizard-cuckoo or *pájaro bobo (Saurothera longirostris)*, and the Hispaniolan parakeet *(Aratinga chloroptera)*. Top birding and conservation sites include the Parque Nacional Los Haitises, the Sierra de Bahoruco (where up to 27 endemics are present), Parque Jaragua, Lago Enriquillo, and Parque Nacional Valle Nuevo.

## Reptiles and Amphibians

Among the DR's well-known reptiles—there are 1,411 species—are the **American crocodile**, the **rhinoceros iguana,** and the **Ricord's iguana.** The rhinoceros iguana, so named because of the horns on the male iguanas' snouts, can reach lengths between 61

and 127 centimeters (24 and 50 inches). You can spot all three creatures in abundance in the southwest region of the country at Lago Enriquillo. There are no poisonous snakes in the country (good news), and frogs are plentiful—coming out at night in the bushy areas, including the hills of Puerto Plata and around coastal areas like Las Galeras where they seem particularly huge and are horrendously loud. **Lizards** are a common sight, of which up to 21 species exist in a variety of bright and dim colors. It's fun discovering a new kind every time you're out hiking or sitting on the porch of your mountain lodge. They're very territorial and inflate their throats when they feel threatened.

# History

To know the history of a country is to understand a place and its people—and nowhere is this truer than in the Dominican Republic. It took many years for the country to reach the democratic system it now enjoys. Independence only came in 1844, after 22 years of occupation from neighboring Haiti and decades of a mix of foreign intervention, despotism, and terror lasted until 1961. Eventually, the democratic process improved along with the country's economic boom. But to understand why the DR stands where it is today in relation to its neighbors as well as in the world, you'll need to understand its tumultuous history.

## PRE-COLUMBIAN PERIOD

As we all know, Christopher Columbus wasn't the first visitor to the island of Hispaniola or the present-day Dominican Republic. Thousands of years before he arrived, various groups of Amerindian origin moved to and occupied the Antilles. They are believed to have traveled from the Caribbean coasts of Central and South America. Various groups lived here over

thousands of years, one replacing or mixing with the others.

The first believed to have settled in the current DR are the Ciboney (*ciboneyes or barreroides*). Their utensils and remains have been discovered in the southwest in Azua. Originally from Central America, they settled in Pedernales, Barahona, and Azua. They didn't practice agriculture or know much about it, but rather survived from fishing and hunting small animals. They lived near coastlines in transient settlements, particularly near river mouths and mangroves. Other Amerindian groups known as the Banwaroides originated in Trinidad and migrated to San Pedro de Macorís and to the north and east of the DR.

Centuries later, two new tribes immigrated to the island. One is believed to be from the Yucatán (the Caribs); the other, the Arawak from the Amazon in South America, essentially became the ancestors to the Taíno people.

### The Taíno

The Taíno were the most advanced of all the groups to settle on the Dominican portion of the island. They practiced complex agriculture, built ceremonial plazas, and were sophisticated in their rituals, art, politics, and entertainment. They planted yucca (cassava), of which they made bread, as well as corn, sweet potatoes, and garlic. They also harvested fruits—papaya, guava, soursop— and lived by hunting and fishing. They didn't write but spoke a common language. In the caverns they used, they drew symbolic images as rock art or petroglyphs, which can be seen today around the country, including inside the Parque Nacional del Este and at El Pomier.

Their homes, known as *bohíos*, were nearly circular with a cone-shaped, thatched roof with palm leaves. The rectangular *caney*, however, was where the cacique lived and would receive his guests. Hammocks can be attributed to the Taíno, too, who called them *hamaca*; other words they used were *barbacoa, tobacco,* and *canoe,* which were later incorporated into Spanish and English. Chances are, you've used and said them all without knowing their origin.

The Taíno had their own hierarchical structure and maintained a peaceful relationship among the various tribes. The cacique was at the top, and servants at the bottom, but none of this caused conflict. Instead, everyone had their assigned roles: women made pottery vases, cups, and spoons, while men built canoes and utensils for fishing, hunting, or fighting. As seen in various caves and archaeological sites in the DR, the Taíno were talented artists and craftspeople. They also made amulets made out of stone, conch, or wood. In ceremonies, they wore gold crowns, and dressed in fine cotton belts and collars.

They believed in a variety of gods, and the cacique communicated with them through the Rito de la Cohoba, a ritual whereby the chieftain would first induce vomit with a wooden or manatee-rib spatula to purge impurities, then inhale a hallucinogenic substance—made out of the ground seeds of the *Anadenanthera peregrina* tree—while participants adorned and painted his body. They believed this state of semiconsciousness gave

them visions and insights into matters of political importance, disputes, or predictions of agricultural yield. The Museo del Hombre Dominicano, in Santo Domingo, has a nice visual display on this ritual. Other respected figures were the *behiques*, who organized religious rites and cured the ill.

Caves were sacred to the Taíno; they had numerous beliefs related to them, including making offerings to the spirits before entering one. Perhaps the most notorious Taíno contribution is tobacco—which they rolled and smoked like the cigars that are a prime Dominican product today.

It's unclear how many lived on the island. Estimates range from 200,000 to millions by the end of the 15th century, and there were five Taíno kingdoms when Columbus arrived. Their peaceful life took a sad turn with the arrival of the Europeans. Between diseases such as smallpox, genocide, and suicide to avoid slavery, it's believed that the Taíno of the Dominican Republic were completely extinguished. But their culture and heritage isn't forgotten and remains preserved in the museums, caverns, forests, agricultural fields, musical or home instruments, and festivals of the DR.

# COLONIALISM: COLUMBUS'S ARRIVAL

Christopher Columbus set sail for the "New World" from Spain on August 3, 1492, on behalf of the Spanish crown, in the hopes of discovering new riches in Asia. Instead, with his men and three ships—*Santa Maria,* captained by the admiral himself, *La Niña,* and *La Pinta*—he stumbled on the Bahamas first, followed by Cuba, before eventually arriving and settling on the north coast of the Dominican Republic on December 5, 1492. He named it "Española," and thus the Dominican Republic became the first Spanish settlement in the Americas and the launchpad for more conquests in the Caribbean region. The term "colonialism" was even coined after Columbus (*Colón* in Spanish).

Enamored of the beautiful land of

mountains, sea, rivers, and valleys before him, Columbus also took note of the warm welcome of the Taíno, the gold they were wearing, and their lack of weapons, and decided to stay on to exploit the land for more gold. By December 1492, Columbus and his men were preparing to return to Spain to report their findings. Their relationship with the Taíno was still peaceful at this point. The eve of their return to Spain, however, the *Santa Maria* hit a reef and sank (other accounts say it was stuck and they dismantled the ship). The Taíno helped the stranded sailors, and Columbus decided to build a fort right along that north coast, leaving his 39 sailors there to hold it down. The settlement was called La Navidad, to mark the Christmas Day they ran aground. La Navidad is believed to have been on the north coast of present-day Haiti, though the original fort site has yet to be uncovered.

During the admiral's absence, tensions arose between the Taíno and the Spanish sailors who began to abuse the natives, forcing them into service or killing them and raping their wives. Cacique Caonabo led an attack against the Spanish, and by the time Columbus returned in 1493 with over a dozen ships and 1,200 men to expand the settlement, La Navidad had been abandoned and burned to the ground. Determined to keep chasing after the gold deposits of the Cibao Valley, Columbus and his men settled 115 kilometers (71 miles) east of their previous location on the north coast in a new enclave which Columbus named La Isabela, after the queen of Spain. But again, there were numerous challenges there—including droughts and disease, which affected both Spaniards and Taíno—and Columbus decided to abandon the area. By this time, in the mid-1490s, the Taíno were already enduring hard labor, having been forced to work in mines. You can visit the ruins of La Isabela and what remains of Columbus's home, now a protected site and with a comprehensive museum, while in Puerto Plata.

The Spaniards headed south where it was reported that gold was found, eventually settling along the west bank of the Río Ozama, in what is now the Colonial Zone of Santo Domingo.

## MASSACRE OF THE TAÍNO

Nicolás de Ovando, governor of Santo Domingo, was considered the mastermind behind the extermination of the Taíno (ironically, there's a luxury hotel named after him in the Colonial Zone). Ovando instituted the *encomienda* system in 1503, per the Spanish crown, whereby all land was considered Spain's property and the Taíno were its tenants. The land would be granted to Spanish settlers or *encomenderos*, along with some Taíno for labor. Their owners were entrusted with educating the natives about Catholicism and paying them wages. But that didn't happen; instead, the Taíno were abused for work, went unpaid, and were stripped of their possessions.

As if this weren't enough, Ovando was determined to get rid of the Taíno and orchestrated a mass murder by tricking Anacaona, cacique and wife of the former Caonabo, into gathering all Taíno chiefs, at least 80 of them, and meeting him for a feast. The house was set on fire and those who escaped, including Anacaona, were hanged. With no leaders left, the Taíno became weak from hard labor, the inability to feed themselves from their own agriculture, and disease. Some also committed suicide. It's believed that the smallpox epidemic in 1518 finally wiped them out.

## THE SLAVE TRADE

The extermination of the Taíno had profound consequences. This period coincided with the decline in Santo Domingo's prestige—more exciting was the conquest of Mexico by Hernán Cortés in 1521 and the discovery of more gold and silver in Latin America. Many Spanish colonialists left for these destinations, and the population of Santo Domingo dwindled.

The shortage of Taíno needed for labor,

particularly in the development of the sugar industry, meant that the Spanish turned their eyes toward Africa. In a continuous quest to regain riches, they began the importation of African slaves in 1503. The colonialists set out from European ports to West Africa's coast with the goods they used to trade for people. They captured a half million slaves who were then brought to Hispaniola and sold. African labor was used exclusively between 1520 and 1801. All the horrors of the transatlantic slave trade are part of the history of the Dominican Republic. African men and women chained in the galleons of ships in horrifying conditions made a three-month voyage to the Caribbean. Many died from disease and despair, and those who survived were no better off at the hands of the Spanish once on Hispaniola. They suffered and were denied the practice of their culture and language, while the riches were transported back to Spain in ships filled with coffee, tobacco, rum, rice, and sugar.

Thus the mixing of populations began in the 16th century, leading to the majority *criollo* population in the DR today.

It wasn't long before the enslaved began to revolt. The first rebellion took place in December 1521 under Diego Colón, and was quashed. But much defiance continued to occur, along with attempted escapes, which were cruelly punished. The movie *Roots* sums up the experience of enslaved Africans on the island. Groups began to form, known as maroons, fighting the Spanish from the mountains. The most famous of these was led by Enriquillo in the Bahoruco range of the southwest.

Aside from slave rebellions, the late 16th century saw French and English pirates attacking ports in the Spanish side of the island, which led Spain to fortify Santo Domingo. But in 1586, the buccaneer Sir Francis Drake captured the city, which he occupied and pillaged for a month while demanding a ransom for its return to Spanish control. He took refuge in the cathedral, and once he was paid, he burned it, Colón's home, and a third of the city to the ground before leaving.

## TUGS OF WAR AND INDEPENDENCE

Over on the western end of the island, neighboring Saint-Domingue—under the Treaty of Ryswick, Spain had ceded the western third of the island to France—was actually the most productive agricultural colony for France and thus brought in the most riches, also through use of enslaved Africans. It had a huge impact on the economy of France, and for this reason, there were at least three times as many slaves in Haiti than there were in Santo Domingo, a smaller colony with little influence on Spain. French landowners had enriched themselves by the end of the 18th century, unlike their counterparts in Santo Domingo, who exported less and had less demand from the market and thus fewer slaves. Spanish law also allowed the enslaved to purchase their freedom for a small fee. This resulted in many obtaining their freedom by the turn of the century, and freed Africans made up a good portion of the population, unlike in the neighboring French colony.

Inspired by the French revolution of 1789, Saint-Domingue (present-day Haiti) saw the biggest African slave rebellion in the Western Hemisphere in 1791, whereby the enslaved formed their own armies and slaughtered the French slave masters. This rebellion shook the institution of slavery throughout the Americas. Over in Santo Domingo, news of this rebellion led many Spaniards to flee the island. The Spanish crown saw it as an opportunity to invade the western end of the island, only to be met by the forces of Toussaint L'Ouverture and General Jean-Jacques Dessalines, who quashed the invasion. Napoleon Bonaparte dispatched forces in 1802 in an attempt to end Toussaint's rule as general of Haiti and reinstate slavery, and the French were again met by Toussaint's forces.

The Haitian Revolution continued under Dessalines and Jean-Pierre Boyer. France had lost two-thirds of its men fighting, not to mention to disease. In January 1804, Haiti became the first independent black nation. Dessalines ordered the death of all the surviving French in Haiti. To distinguish them from the Creoles, they were subjected to a test requiring them to say *Nanett alé nan fontain, cheche dlo, crich-a li cassé* (Nanette went to the fountain, looking for water, but her jug broke). Ironically, a century later, Haitians would be subjected to a similar language test before meeting their death under Trujillo.

Many Spaniards returned to Santo Domingo and sought to regain control of eastern end of the island and reestablish Spanish sovereignty. With the help of the British, Spanish rule was restored in 1809. Meanwhile, Spain's economy was on the decline under Ferdinand VII. With weakened Spanish rule and interest, in 1821 Spain announced the colony to be independent. But within just a few weeks, Haitian troops under President Jean-Pierre Boyer invaded Santo Domingo and declared the entire island to be Haiti.

The 22 years of Haitian occupation of the DR began to shape the complex relations between Haitians and Dominicans that run so deep today. One of Boyer's first actions was to abolish slavery on this side of Hispaniola, leading to freedom for many enslaved Dominicans—a fact that is often lost today in the immigration feud between the countries. These people were the first to receive redistributed plots of land to farm and feed and sustain their families. But the Haitian president grew unpopular among the elite because he seized land belonging to exiles and the Catholic Church, forced the official language to be French, and invited freed blacks from the United States to settle in Santo Domingo (most of them moved to present-day Samaná). Land was also given to members of the military and government officials. Churches were closed and priest salaries suspended.

Another aspect of Boyer's legacy was the agreement he signed with France in 1825, under military duress and desperate to regain access to European markets, stating that France would recognize Haiti as an independent country if it paid a fee of 150 million francs within five years, a sum ultimately reduced to 90 million francs. This was the beginning of the end for Haiti's economy, despite the fact that it had defeated French forces. Boyer borrowed the first amount from France itself and during his rule of the island attempted to force Dominicans to help in paying the debt. Boyer's economic vision focused on increasing agricultural production and replacing the Dominican focus on livestock, while shutting down the cockfights that took the men away from laboring. This was seen as an attempt to change Dominican culture and caused additional friction.

In 1838, an organized movement began against Haitian rule of the DR, at the center of which was a young man from a prominent Santo Domingo family who had returned home after studying abroad: Juan Pablo Duarte. After capturing Santo Domingo and claiming the country's independence from Haiti in 1844, Duarte was forced into exile by General Pedro Santana. Yet another period of turbulence began, with various factions fighting to obtain control of the government under Santana and General Buenaventura Baez. The era of *caudillos* began simultaneously—"strongmen on a horse" who ruled their own areas internally with armies made up of peasants. The Dominican economy was in shambles as Baez left the country and General Santana declared himself president and sought annexation from Spain.

Spanish rule was reinstated in 1861. However, a *Guerra de la Restauración* (War of Restoration) led by Dominican rebels with the help of Haitians pushed Spain out again in 1865. The border town of Restauración, in the province of Dajabón, was named to recognize Haitian's help in the War of Restoration.

But this wasn't the end of Dominican troubles. In 1882, a dictator by the name of General Ulises Heureux came along, brutalizing his people before he was assassinated in 1889. He had also borrowed money from the United States and Europe to finance the army and build up the sugar industry. The United States entered into a debt repayment treaty with the DR, and political instability continued to rock the country until 1916, when

U.S. president Woodrow Wilson sent troops to Santo Domingo to take control and occupy the country until 1924. The occupation was resented on all sides, both Dominican and American, and turned out to be a double-edged sword: it brought stability to the country, but also played a part in bringing to power Rafael Trujillo, dictator from 1930 to 1961. He got his start in the U.S.-trained Dominican National Guard in 1918 and rose to become head of the armed forces after the United States pulled out.

## THE TRUJILLO ERA

The Trujillo era is one that remains firmly planted in Dominican's minds. There isn't one tour you can take without hearing a reference to the former dictator. Rafael Leonidas Trujillo Molina terrorized the country and ruled with an iron fist during his oppressive 31-year reign. Some say he also developed and built up the country unlike any other leader, and that crime rates were low in this day, despite the fact that he also expropriated property and the country's riches for himself and his family. In fact, many of the architectural structures still standing today, and that you'll likely visit, were his doing.

The Trujillo Era was a period of persecution and suppression of civil rights, when anyone who dared oppose "El Jefe"—one of his numerous nicknames—would disappear, along with their families, never to be found again. The dictator renamed buildings and cities after himself—including Santo Domingo, which became "Ciudad Trujillo," and Pico Duarte, as "Pico Trujillo." Worse, households had to carry his portrait, stating their allegiance to El Jefe (the chief), children had to greet him with "Papa," as if he were their father, and his secret police and spies were everywhere. Speaking ill of him was a very dangerous proposition.

Besides being a giant womanizer—he could choose and demand any girl he wanted, and those who resisted suffered retaliation—Trujillo was also known for being a racist. He hated that Haitians were growing in number in the DR, and thus "diluting" the Spanish race. He wanted to "whiten" the Dominican race, and many of his actions were driven by this, including the most atrocious of them all: as part of his *blanquismo* or "whiteness" policy he orchestrated the massacre of an estimated 20,000 Haitian sugarcane workers in 1937, coinciding with a slump in the sugar economy during the Great Depression. In distinguishing them from dark-skinned Dominicans, Trujillo's soldiers would ask the victims to pronounce the word *perejil*—parsley in Spanish—difficult for those who are French Creole speaking. Their bodies were then dumped in the Massacre River.

Trujillo's reputation was tarnished by these shameless murders, and he attempted to make up for it in 1940 when he offered asylum and land in Sosúa to 100,000 Jews during World War II. But few were fooled by his actions, once again suspected as an attempt to whiten the Dominican race. Trujillo's demise began when he had the three popular, revolutionary Mirabal sisters murdered in 1960 as they returned from visiting their husbands in prison. It was made to look like a car crash, but their bodies had been beaten. On May 30, 1961, he was assassinated by members of his own regime who had grown resentful. Some say the CIA had a hand in it as well, with the United States fearing the dictator turning into another Castro in the Caribbean region.

## POST-TRUJILLO AND THE U.S. INTERVENTION

After Trujillo, Joaquín Balaguer came to power, but was a puppet and not an elected president. General unrest and strikes led Balaguer to share power with a seven-member council in 1962. The council led the country into the first free general elections in the DR in a long time. Juan Bosch Gaviño became president, a liberal scholar and poet who supported workers and students. He made numerous changes that conservatives disliked, including crafting a constitution that separated church and state and legalized divorce, enforcement of civil and individual rights, and distribution of Trujillo's estates to peasants. After just seven months, Bosch was toppled from office. But he didn't give up, and with the help of Constitutionalists and Colonel Francisco Caamaño Deño he attempted to take back the National Palace and radio stations and reinstate his presidency. Mayhem and a civil war ensued. U.S. president Lyndon Johnson intervened by sending in 23,000 U.S. Marines on April 24, 1965, to restore peace and hold elections. The occupation lasted until September 3, 1965. The April War—la Guerra de Abril—is celebrated in the DR on April 24; you can head to the Colonial Zone to see official parades, and there is usually an official mass held at the cathedral which the president attends but isn't open to the public.

Balaguer was put back in power and won successive elections (some say through intimidation) such that he was president for 22 years over six presidential terms. A protégé of Trujillo, he was known as a strongman and also ruled with an iron fist, though not quite as brutal, and repressed opposition, particularly in the first decade of his rule. He continued to work until he was well in his 80s and turning blind. It was Balaguer who saw fit to develop the tourism industry in the DR, set up the industrial zones, and also squandered a lot of the country's money—he was the one who built the widely criticized (to this day) million-dollar lighthouse shaped like a cross in Santo Domingo, at a time when the country was suffering from electricity shortages and high unemployment. After Balaguer, the Constitution was amended to bar the successive reelection of presidents.

In 1996, Leonel Fernández, born and raised in the United States, won the election. He focused on squashing corruption, but he wasn't hugely popular. In 2000, businessman and agronomist Hipólito Mejía Domínguez became president. The economy worsened—a massive bank fraud undermined confidence in the government and the country took a turn for the worst financially, with the peso falling to RD$52 to the dollar. Fernández returned to the presidency in 2004, and later in 2008—ironically, thanks to a constitutional amendment made during the Mejía administration, once more allowing the successive reelection of presidents. The country also entered into a free trade agreement with the United States and Central American nations, and economic conditions improved.

## THE DOMINICAN REPUBLIC TODAY

In 2012 a new era was ushered in for the Dominican Republic, with a new president from the same party as outgoing Fernández (the DLP): Danilo Medina Sánchez, former secretary of state for two terms under Fernández. He was also the party's presidential candidate in 2000 but had lost to Hipólito Mejía. This time around, he promised opportunities for all Dominicans, with more trickling down of wealth, and on the campaign trail vowed to spend 4 percent of the country's GDP on education as the key to lifting people out of poverty.

For the past four years, President Medina has come through with his 4 percent investment promise. Schools have been sprouting up like mushrooms, but the quality and availability of teachers remains a problem. Initially, his popularity soared for being the first Dominican president to have ever spent so much on the country's educational system. He also was known for paying surprise visits around the countryside—well documented on social media and online—interacting with all levels of Dominican society, to support and fund local cooperatives in communities and assist with job creation programs. The country's fiscal deficit was reduced, with a steady GDP growth of 5 percent. These achievements made Medina popular among Dominicans. After he first took office, he was named the most popular Latin American leader in 2014 in various media outlets.

But Medina's popularity has suffered since in the eyes of his people, even though he is likely to get reelected in 2016. In 2015, accusations of corruption and inefficiency were leveled against high-level officials in his government, including the courts and judges as well as in the police force. The country has seen increased crime levels and frequent power outages, which have further tarnished Medina's image. And this is despite his being the first president to tackle and face the growing Haitian immigration crisis—particularly, the status of Haitians born in the DR—and propose a solution. After a controversial 2013 court ruling stripped citizenship from Dominican-born Haitian children of illegal migrants, Medina attempted to remedy the issue by allowing illegal residents to apply for residency permits, including those who had been in the country since before 2011.

## THE DR AND HAITI: AN INTERTWINED FATE

Ask about the Haiti-DR immigration situation while you're visiting the Dominican Republic and the response usually begins with: it's *complicated*. Indeed, to understand the evolution of the Haitian illegal migrant worker crisis and get a good feel for present-day relations between Dominicans and Haitians, you'll need to know about the history of and between the two countries, as well as the politics and economics of the DR and its neighbor. Two nations sharing an island, yet separated by a once easily crossed border as well as major cultural differences, has made for a precarious relationship. Both have bloody trails in their past, thanks to politics and power-drunk leaders—from Haiti's 22-year occupation of the DR that sought to suppress the Dominican way of life to the tragic massacre of over 20,000 Haitians under the Trujillo regime. And then there's the fact that the DR obtained its independence in 1844 not after fighting Spain, but rather its neighbor Haiti (making it the only Caribbean nation to have obtained independence from another Caribbean nation). Last but certainly not least, the United States played its part in the mess that exists today—it occupied both countries twice, and Haitian cane workers began arriving in the Dominican Republic en masse in the early 20th century to work in the U.S.-created sugar industry. The United States also meddled in political affairs and supported the selection of presidents according to what served U.S. economic interests best.

It's a difficult situation for both populations, one that the DR and Haiti will be grappling with for years to come. To go so far as saying that Dominicans are racist or believe the U.S. media propaganda that spread in 2015 is erroneous—the majority of Dominicans are rational and hospitable people, and certainly not xenophobes. When you visit the country, you'll realize this for yourself. At the population level both groups have been known to help each other in times of dire need. The Dominicans were the first to rush to help Haiti during the devastating earthquake of 2010. Many also risked their lives hiding their Haitian friends during Trujillo's massacre hunt. The Haitians were the ones who abolished slavery in the DR, a fact often lost on the masses.

An easy read and excellent resource to begin to understand the historical background and events that shaped the relations between Haiti and the DR is *Why The Cocks Fight: Dominicans, Haitians, and the Struggle for Hispaniola*, by Michele Wucker. She explains that "Even now, it is nearly impossible for Dominicans and Haitians to think of each other without some trace of the tragedy of their mutual history."

There's no clear number on how many undocumented workers live in the DR, but it was estimated at about 500,000 in 2013, and they comprise the majority of the DR's total immigrant population. They worked in sugarcane fields as the U.S.-created sugar industry boomed, in what is known as *bateyes*, and others followed to work in construction—all hard, poor-paying jobs that Dominicans avoid. Still others, particularly after the 2010 earthquake, hopped over in desperate search of food and survival—selling fruit and other small items on the streets, hustling to survive day by day.

The Haitian illegal immigration crisis in the DR isn't new. Nor are politicians' tactics of using fearmongering among Dominicans—that Haitians are always plotting to invade the DR again and unite the island—as well as addressing the Haitian immigrant issue to distract from domestic issues. After Trujillo, President Balaguer—clearly anti-Haitian but diplomatic—eventually went after Haitian workers in 1991. As retaliation against Haitian president Jean-Bertrand Aristide for denouncing the slave-like conditions of Haitian migrant sugarcane workers in the DR and painting the country in an ugly light with international bodies abroad including the UN, Balaguer issued a decree that Haitians over the age of 60 and those under 16 had to be deported. His soldiers went through cane fields and villages to find them. It's estimated that over 50,000 fled or were expelled, and some months after, Aristide was overthrown by military coup.

President Danilo Medina's attempt to tackle the immigration crisis is also, some say, politically motivated with Dominican presidential elections ahead of him in 2016. The main argument thrown to the masses is that one poor country (DR) can no longer bear the needs of a poorer country (Haiti) nor support illegal immigrants who are essentially availing themselves of resources (including better health care) without paying taxes.

The issue came to light again and landed in international media in 2013, when the Dominican Republic's highest court ruled to retroactively revoke the citizenship of children of illegal Haitian migrants born after 1929, whose births were never registered in the DR. It relied on a constitutional clause stating that citizenship is determined on the mother's nationality. This decision, on its face, essentially rendered over 200,000 people stateless—many of whom had lived in the Dominican Republic their whole life and had never since returned to Haiti. After an international outcry, a new law was introduced to soften the blow: the National Plan for the Regularization of Foreigners (or PNRE in Spanish). This plan allowed those Haitians who are undocumented but born in the DR to apply for the *cédula,* the Dominican residency card/national ID, so they can legally remain in the country. They were given until July 6, 2015, to file for regularization. Those who did not have a *cédula* by that date would be deported back to Haiti, but the date was extended.

In the spring and summer of 2015, lines were long outside governmental offices. Hundreds of Haitians waited to discover their fate. It's hard to say what really happened or how, but over 25,000 packed up and "voluntarily" returned to Haiti on their own, in fear of being thrown out into the streets by the police when the deadline expired. Many have simply set up camp close to the border, having nowhere else to go, as refugees in their own country. Haiti's government can also be blamed for its failure in providing its citizens with documentation and lacking a way of providing for them.

By mid-September, an estimated 289,000 applications had been received, about 27 percent of which were denied. What the future holds is anyone's guess, as immigration woes and deportation of illegal Haitian workers continues. In the end, it's a sad situation with two poor nations struggling to find a solution for a decent life, and yet at the mercy of political maneuvering.

# Government and Economy

## GOVERNMENT

The DR has a democratic government, with three branches: executive, legislative, and judiciary. The president is the head of the executive branch, appoints a cabinet, and also serves as the country's commander in chief. Both the president and vice president hold four-year terms, with possibility to run again for a nonconsecutive term. In 2015, an amendment to the Constitution was made specifically to allow President Danilo Medina to run for a second consecutive term in light of 2016 presidential elections. He was reelected, and history seems to be repeating itself: as the 2019 presidential elections loom, rumor has it he might modify the Constitution again to allow him to run. As of 2018, the majority of the population has denounced corruption at all levels of his government and his popularity has tanked.

The National Congress consists of the Senate, with 32 members, and a Chamber of Deputies, with 150 members. The country's Supreme Court has nine judges who are elected by the Senate.

The country's three political parties are the Partido Revolucionario Dominicano (PRD), the Partido de la Liberacion Dominicana (PLD), and the Partido Reformista Social Cristiano (PRSC). Medina is a member of the PLD.

Governors are presidential appointees and run the 31 provinces and the National District. The provinces consist of municipalities, with each municipality electing its own council and holding a little autonomy.

## ECONOMY

The Dominican Republic has long depended on agriculture, mainly sugarcane in the country's early years. In the 1970s it began diversifying its economy by increasing mining (gold, silver, ferronickel, and bauxite), manufacturing, and tourism. The cigar production industry, along with coffee and cacao, has grown significantly in the last few years with nearly 60 percent of all exports going to the United States.

In 2003, the country faced a major banking fraud scandal that led to the collapse of the Banco Intercontinental (BANINTER), the country's second-largest commercial bank, and a loss of confidence in the government and the country's economy. Losses amounted to over US$2 billion. The Dominican peso tumbled, the country's credit rating was downgraded, and poverty levels worsened.

It's extraordinary then, that over the past decade-plus, the Dominican Republic has made a comeback from ruin to become one of the fastest-growing economies in the Latin America and Caribbean regions, with GDP growth averaging around 5.4 percent annually between 1992 and 2014. Tourism has played a large role in this rise—revenues from tourism have surpassed sugar earnings for the first time in 1984. A boom that has continued under President Danilo Medina has placed the country as the undisputed king of Caribbean travel. Tourism revenues in 2014 were US$5.6 billion, and are predicted to continue rising.

The country has diversified its exports as well, and "industrial free zones," or manufacturing plants, have been set up to make goods solely for the U.S. market, primarily textiles, tobacco, and medical products. In 2005, the DR ratified the CAFTA agreement with the United States and its Central American neighbors. The free zones now bring in billions in annual revenue. On the other hand, they've been criticized for using cheap labor and for the benefits of trade not reaching the workers.

Public services have improved, in particular education and health. A budget consisting of 4 percent of the GDP was committed to the educational system under President Medina, a first in Dominican history, which has allowed for the construction of schools and

# The Dominican Flag

The Bible sits in the heart of the Dominican Flag.

The flag of the Dominican Republic was adopted in 1844. A thick white cross, representing salvation and the struggle for a free Dominican people, divides the flag in four rectangles. The ultramarine quarters stand for progress and liberty, the vermillion for the blood shed by the country's heroes. At the center of the flag is the Dominican coat of arms, and therein lies a unique element: this is the only flag in the world featuring the Bible. The Bible is flanked by six spears with a golden cross above it. If you're at the restaurant and see "Dominican flag" or *bandera dominicana* on the menu, don't be alarmed! It's also the name of the national dish, consisting of a plate of rice, beans, and chicken stew.

classrooms, and children now attend full-day school. With near 30 percent of the population under the age of 15, this is good news indeed. Last but not least, banking practices have improved alongside the growth driven by the country's largest private and capital bank, Banco Popular Dominicano. Dominicans living abroad support the economy by sending more than US$3 billion a year to their relatives.

Despite this all-around improved performance, poverty remains higher today than ever; according to the World Bank, the DR's poverty rate soared from 32 percent in 2000 to 41 percent in 2013. Basic services remain out of reach from the poorest, and the gap between rich and poor continues to widen, in part due to stagnant wages.

## Tourism

It might be difficult to believe, but the Dominican Republic is relatively new in the tourism game, even if it is now the undisputed top destination of the Caribbean. It wasn't until 1971 that the government began promoting tourism, and only in 1984 that tourism replaced sugar as the country's leading foreign-exchange earner. During this time, the country reaped the benefits of being close to the United States and the general boom in Caribbean tourism tied to a strong U.S. economy.

The DR became and continues to be seen as the king of the budget all-inclusive vacation, in large part thanks to Punta Cana's worldwide fame. This has attracted the type of traveler who would remain confined behind resort walls, with on-site access to food and drinks and an exhaustive number of pools and beaches. In the late 2000s, the tourism game started shifting, with more visitors interested in an upscale experience that included destination weddings and honeymoons. Luxury travel has since risen in the DR, from Punta Cana to the revived North Coast, where swank hotels continue to sprout. The first Aman Resort in the DR opened in November 2015.

The potential for DR tourism continues to grow. There's increasing interest in ecotourism—lesser-known corners of the islands such as Samaná and Jarabacoa are coming to light—educational and volunteer travel, adventure and sports travel, and immersive experiences. Sustainable community tourism groups have started to develop in various parts of the country, in an effort to empower communities while also providing the authentic experiences that visitors now crave.

## Agriculture

Agriculture and *campo* life were the backbone of the Dominican Republic for centuries, until its slight decline in the 1980s when tourism, mining, and manufacturing took on important roles. While you might have images of resorts and beaches swirling in your head, the truth is that a significant number of Dominicans are still farmers. The country is blessed with rich soil and high elevations, and grows its own rice, vegetables, tropical fruits, and flowers—unlike many countries in the Caribbean. Up to a third of the land is used for cultivation. It also supplies its needs for chickens, eggs, dairy products, and beef. Agriculture was the main driver of the economy for centuries, particularly through sugarcane. But when sugar prices fell in the 20th century, coffee, cacao, and tobacco took a more prominent place in the industry. Making a living is tough for farmers, who may be forced to supplement their income with other trades such as making crafts.

# People and Culture

## THE PEOPLE

The Dominican Republic population is a diverse mix of various ethnicities: Taíno, African, and European. This melting pot of cultures and backgrounds makes for a fascinating destination with various influences showing up in cuisine, music, dance, and religious ceremonies. The majority of the population is considered *criollo,* a mix of African and Spanish, but there are also many Dominican Haitians, as well as those of a more Spanish descent (usually in the upper echelons economically). Perhaps it's this multi-continental blend that makes Dominicans such a warm, hospitable people with a zest for life I haven't seen anywhere else.

Dominicans believe in courtesy, hospitality, and kindness to strangers. The more you travel into the countryside, the more evidence of this you'll see. Folks will welcome you into their homes. I was once desperate for a bathroom while driving in the hills of Constanza and stopped at a Dominican home to ask if I could use their toilet and their answer was, of course! Life for Dominicans is about making the most of every day, no matter how little you have, and giving thanks to God. It's about smiling, enjoying, dancing the days and nights away, and loving with all they have—they are die-hard romantics. You'll always hear music playing and people laughing or joking around. And if you think Parisians have perfected the art of sidewalk people-watching, then you need to come to the Dominican Republic. Sitting on the corner and watching the world go by with a cup of rum or a Presidente is the number one activity (which many criticize as laziness, but you have to appreciate their ability to be "in the now"), perhaps followed closely by playing dominoes.

# Things You Might Not Know About Dominicans

Dominicans have their own way of interacting and doing things, some of which might surprise you and others that will make you chuckle.

- They often call others "*mi amor*" (my love) or "*cariño*" (darling).

- "Dominican time" is real—*ahorita* might translate into "right now" but it could mean tomorrow or some point in the future.

- Whenever entering a public space, Dominicans greet everyone with "*saludos*" or "*buen día*," whether it's a bus, a taxi, a restaurant, or a clinic. Not to do so would be considered rude.

- Sunday is the noisiest day of the week and the biggest for partying and drinking. It's also family day.

- Dominicans often use facial expressions in lieu of words—they will move their lips forward to point to a place, or wag their index finger to say no.

- Whatsapp is king—phone credits cost money, so most Dominicans use their smartphones with Wi-Fi.

- It's never loud enough—big speakers are popular in the shops, at home, or even placed in the back of the car.

- Dominicans love their beaches as much as you do. And they have legal access to all of them because all beaches are public.

- Superstition runs deep—certain things you do or don't do can cause bad luck, including opening the fridge while ironing, putting your purse on the floor, or not saying "God bless you" to a newborn.

Family is the core of Dominican life. At any chance they get, Dominicans will tell you it's all about *la familia* (and they show grave concern if you say you don't have children or a spouse). On the weekends, especially Sunday, it's on full display with everyone flocking to the beach or the river, cooking together, playing, and enjoying their time off. Nothing is ever done "solo"—that's just a foreign concept. Sticking together, through thick or thin, is second nature for Dominicans. The mother is the glue that keeps the unit together. Her children worship her, and she would do anything for them.

While Dominicans are all about sharing their plate of food or drinks, watching their neighbors' kids, or running to the aid of a friend who calls in need, it's not all roses all the time—there are issues of race and class,

and many upper-class folks don't mix with anyone who isn't in their circle, as judged according to their family's history and wealth. That's true of most of the once-colonized Caribbean.

Dominicans are often criticized for being too focused on race and color. They call people by their skin color, for instance, and it is considered completely normal here. While it isn't usually intended in a discriminatory manner, it can be surprising and even offensive to foreigners, especially from the United States. If you're darker skinned, you'll hear folks calling out to you with "negro" or "morena," and if you're lighter skinned, "rubio." And there are a dozen other words for all the shades in between. Many Dominicans, however, recognize the beauty in their mixed heritage and will invite you to do the same.

# THE CULTURE

## Language

The official language of the Dominican Republic is Spanish. If you're traveling to tourist areas such as Punta Cana, La Romana, and Puerto Plata, you'll find plenty of other languages are understood or spoken a little by hotel employees and tour guides. But for the majority of the country, Spanish is it—more precisely, Dominican Spanish, which can be difficult to understand. That's because Dominicans have their own colloquialisms. They're also known for speaking fast—really fast—swallowing syllables and not pronouncing the "s" at the end of a word. For instance, you'll hear *Como tu ta?* instead of *Como tu estás?* The more pronunciation, the more foreign you'll sound. If you don't understand, just ask them to speak slowly—*más despacio por favor*—or flat out tell them you don't speak Spanish. They'll gladly try to help how they can (even pulling out a piece of paper when necessary). Dominican phrases can be filled with innuendos and double meaning, and the more you learn about the culture, the more you'll understand how to speak or what is being said to you. Review the phrasebook in the Essentials chapter and you'll be set for your first trip.

## Religion

Dominicans are a people of faith—all you have to do to pick this up is listen to them speak. Their sentences are always accompanied with a *Si Dios quiere* (If it is God's will) or *gracias a Dios* (thanks to God). The majority of Dominicans are Roman Catholic, as a result of the Spanish colonial days. But that's been changing, with other denominations growing in popularity, including evangelicals and Jehovah's Witnesses.

On the other hand, most Dominicans from the countryside—but even those from the city—practice a form of syncretic religion, blending African traditions with Christianity. They consult *curanderos* or folk healers, who "open the way" to any life difficulties faced, and they wear charms. You'll notice the numerous *botánicas* or herb shops inside markets, carrying tons of obscure-looking potions and bottled concoctions, candles, and herbs for sale. Ceremonies involve African-inspired spiritual dances and drums.

## Merengue and *Bachata*

Music and dance—more precisely, merengue and *bachata*—are at the core of Dominican life every day, in every neighborhood, in every corner. They top all the other DR cultural elements including cockfighting and baseball. It's no exaggeration to say that there is no life without twirling your body to music coming from either deafeningly loud speakers or from a live band. Sometimes it seems as if every day is a party in the DR. You'll be hard pressed to find a Dominican, male or female, who doesn't know how to dance merengue or *bachata*.

Beyond the party aspect, merengue and *bachata* have a deeper cultural significance. Lyrics reflect social aspects of life and can talk about love, sex, politics, humor, and everyday struggles. Romance tops it all, though, as Dominicans are as poetic as it gets.

**Merengue** is the national music and dance of the Dominican Republic and has become a word and worldwide genre that is synonymous with the country itself. Merengue is the essence of being Dominican, and its instruments reflect the mixed heritage of the country: an accordion (European), a two-sided drum (African) placed on one's lap, and a *güira* (Taíno), a sort of metal cylinder with holes, with a brush that is run up and down across its surface. The accordion was brought over by the Spanish, but it was later tuned to play merengue notes.

Some say the word originated during the colonial period, from African dances. Merengue's 2/4 beat is danced as a couple and has an intoxicating rhythm that can range from moderately fast to really fast. That's because there are various types of this genre. The folkloric, traditional kind is known as *Perico ripiao* or *merengue típico*. It is believed to have originated in the Cibao region (others say it might have come from Cuban influences) at the end of the 19th century, and can be considered the "country music" of the DR. One well-known, award-winning *perico ripao* performer is Facundo Peña, from the village of Guananico in the Puerto Plata province, birthplace of generations of *merengue típico* performers and instrument makers. If you're lucky to be in this area in late November, contact the UMPC (tel. 809/696-6932, local tourism network for Puerto Plata) for information on the annual *merengue típico* festival.

Ironically, merengue was rejected by the upper classes at first, as it was considered music of the masses with vulgar movements (the same was later considered of *bachata*). But Trujillo arrived and changed all of that, putting merengue on center stage at many of his events and parties.

How do you dance the merengue? The man leads—holding the woman's waist with the right hand—and the couple dances by swaying their hips sensually left and right, but without swinging the torso. They turn, step side to side occasionally, but never release hold of both hands—only one at times. If you're a woman, your job is simply to follow the cues and keep swaying your hips while maintaining the steps and your posture. If anything, it's a great workout. It's relatively easy as well. You can take lessons in various parts of the country if you'd like to practice before you brave the dance floor.

Juan Luis Guerra, today one of the greatest Grammy-winning and world-renowned Latin artists, is perhaps the biggest merengue figure of the 1980s and 1990s. He took the genre and mixed it with the modern sounds of pop and jazz. One of his classic songs is *Ojalá que llueva cafe* (I wish it would rain coffee). Other typical merengue songs include *La dueña del swing* by Los Hermanos Rosario, *Dominicano Soy* by Fernando Villalona, and *Vamo' hablar inglés* by Fefita La Grande.

While the younger generation is leaning toward a more modern merengue with guitars and saxophones or toward the "dancehall" version of Dominican music—known as

*dembow*—*merengue típico* continues to be appreciated and to vibrate in the Cibao region's cities and villages along the *rancho típicos*, as well as in the capital of Santo Domingo.

*Bachata* grows more popular every year and was recently declared the national patrimony of the DR. *Bachata* is a more sensual, slower genre that was long popular among the working class before it received fuller recognition. *Bachata* was influenced by the Cuban bolero, but originated in the DR and is unique to this country. It was looked down on by the upper class for a long time, considered the music of bars and brothels, with lyrics about romance, sex, and poverty. Plenty of double entendre *(doble sentido)* and sexual connotations are hallmarks of *bachata,* which took shape in the 1980s, and for this reason it is culturally entrenched. It's the music of love and heartbreak.

Instruments used in *bachata,* a three-step dance with a fourth tap step, are numerous: guitars (lead, electric bass, rhythm), bongos or drums, and the *güira*. The dance takes two partners, with the man leading as always. They stay close together when they move their hips, as if forming a square or box with their feet, then engage in a push and pull with the hands, depending on one's style. Artists credited for taking *bachata* to the international stage are Juan Luis Guerra, with his album *Bachata Rosa*, and more recently, Romeo has been blazing his way up the charts. Other famous *bachata* artists are Aventura, Raulín Rodríguez, Frank Reyes, Anthony Santos, and Luis Vargas.

Other genres you'll hear in the DR include salsa, son (especially in Santo Domingo), *dembow*, the popular reggaeton, and even Dominican jazz—often at the Dominican Republic Jazz Festival on the North Coast. A great way to experience all the various folkloric dances of the DR, in a historical timeline and one sitting, is to watch the two-hour performance by the Ballet Folklórico del Ministerio de Turismo. The group performs a free dance show, complete with live instruments, twice a week in the Colonial Zone (Fri.

# Carnivals and Festivals

## JANUARY

In San Pedro de Macorís, the first day of the year kicks off with the Guloya Festival, when Afro-Dominican revelers–descendants of late-19th-century migrants from British-speaking Caribbean islands—dressed in vibrant Junkanoo-like costumes dance their way through the streets, to various drums and flutes. The Guloyas' dance is classified by UNESCO as a Masterpiece of the Oral and Intangible Patrimony of Humanity.

## FEBRUARY

An absolute cultural treat is a visit to the DR during this most festive month of the year: Carnaval celebrations take place in major towns and cities across the island every Sunday afternoon of the month, including Santo Domingo (east and west), Santiago, La Vega, Bonao, Río San Juan, La Romana, Punta Cana, and Puerto Plata. Each of these regions has their local carnival personality and traditional devil costumes—such as the Lechones in Santiago or the Taimáscaros of Puerto Plata—as well as *comparsas* and Dominican folklore characters. You could literally hop around the country all month and experience the carnival revelry every Sunday. The season culminates at the end of the month, sometimes the first Sunday of March, with a big national parade on Santo Domingo's Malecón featuring the winning carnival groups from each region competing for the grand prize while entertaining spectators.

## MARCH

Santo Domingo's Ciudad Colonial is where Easter Semana Santa parades take place every evening (starting at 5pm) during Holy Week—including a national evening mass at the cathedral on Easter Saturday. Semana Santa is a celebrated time for Christians around the country, although these days it's also a reason for Dominicans to skip the cities, head to the beach, and party. It's a good time to be in Santo Domingo if you want to see the religious processions and the Saturday evening mass.

Easter Week in Cabral displays the DR's surviving syncretic religion and African traditions with the Cimarrón Festival, when the *cachuas* come out with whips and devilish multicolor masks with horns, impersonating the colonial master as well as the abused slave.

## JUNE

Glimpse the Dominican Republic's Afro-Caribbean pulse at various festivals and ceremonies around the country. Samaná's annual outdoor summer harvest festivals, hosted by the local church, is where African American descendants continue their ancestors' 19th-century celebrations of thanks for crops, rain, and earth with the beat of drums, chanting, and traditional foods like johnnycakes, ginger beer, and coconut rice.

Puerto Plata's annual cultural festival is a great time offering folk music, traditional African tribal dances, salsa, and merengue. There are also many crafts exhibits by local artists.

## JULY

Puerto Plata's gorgeous outdoor amphitheater grounds host the annual Dominican Rum Festival, worth attending for free samples of the country's top rum brands, as well as international visiting rum houses, along with food trucks, cocktails, and some live music featuring major artists from around the Latin American region.

## AUGUST

The **Merengue Festival/Festival del Merengue y Ritmos Caribeños** takes over Santo Domingo's Malecón at Plaza Juan Barón park, with over 30 or artists performing during a weekend-long fest of all things Dominican.

## SEPTEMBER

Puerto Plata hosts its own annual **Festival del Merengue**–usually at the end of the month–with a range of the best of Dominican artists.

**Cattle festivals** are a more authentic expression of the DR's still dominant agricultural and countryside spirit, when cowboys and their families descend on the town and festivities include horseback riding for all ages and games with plenty of music. Puerto Plata's **Feria Ganadera El Cupey** is a great example.

## OCTOBER

The biggest concert in the country, **Festival Presidente,** is an all-out party till the wee hours of the morning at the Olympic Stadium, where the beer flows and Dominican fans dance in the aisles, screaming out lyrics under the stars and occasional fireworks. The event takes place every two years over three nights, from around 6pm to 3am.

## NOVEMBER

The annual **Dominican Republic Jazz Festival** (www.drjazzfestival.com) attracts local Dominican as well as international artists with incredible jazz performances across various cities over the course of five days. From Santiago to Sosúa to Puerto Plata city to Cabarete, it's a nice time out. Book your rooms in advance because hotels sell out quickly.

**Colonial Fest** (www.colonialfest.org) is a celebration of arts, crafts, cuisine, and all things Dominican, and takes place in Santo Domingo's Colonial Zone. Nights are filled with outdoor concerts on Plaza de España or at Parque Colón. They can be late in posting schedules, so don't miss out on rooms while waiting on that.

In November, an annual **Merengue Típico Festival** takes place in the heart of Guananico. It's an authentic insight into Dominican culture.

## DECEMBER

**New Year's Eve** (December 31) is just as big in the DR as other countries: Dominicans take to the streets and celebrate on the Malecón and in local bars with all-night music and dancing.

## YEAR-ROUND

The *fiestas patronales,* or patron saint festivals, are held at various times of the year in the various towns, and are a great expression of the modern side of the DR's Latino culture—from foods to live music, drumming, and all-night partying. These parties last a little over a week (known as the *novena,* the nine days prior to the actual patron saint day). Barahona's are held in January, for instance, while Constanza's take place in September.

and Sat. starting at 7pm), by Plaza de España, and it goes over all of the dances and music of the DR—including African—in colorful costumes. You'll even get to dance with the group members at the end.

For an album with a mix of merengue, *bachata*, and other Dominican genres, a good pick is Latin Hits 2015 Club Edition. For *merengue típico*, look up *El Mero Merengue—Lo mejor del perico ripao* (1995).

## Literature and Film

Perhaps as a result of all the strife in their history, coupled with their eternal romantic spirit, Dominicans have great skill with the written word. The earliest writers came from within the church. Friar Bartolomé de las Casas was among the first, with his accounts in *Historia de Las Indias* of the Spanish atrocities committed against the Taíno, pleading to the crown to intervene. Early poets include Leonor de Ovando—recognized as the first poet in the "New World—and Salomé Ureña, who was revered for championing women's education in the late 19th century by opening the first women's higher education center in the country.

Félix María del Monte is considered the father of Dominican literature in the independence era. He worked alongside "the Trinity"—the three Fathers of Independence—and he was also a journalist, poet, and playwright. Some of his famous works include "El banilejo y la jibarita" and "Las Vírgenes de Galindo." The harsh Trujillo days gave birth to a new wave of creatives and poets, including Juan Bosch Gaviño, who eventually became president of the DR in 1963.

On the contemporary side are award-winning artists like Junot Díaz and Julia Alvarez, who immigrated to the United States and earned worldwide renown. Alvarez's *In the Time of Butterflies* tells the tale of the Mirabal sisters, and Díaz won the 2008 Pulitzer Prize for *The Brief Wondrous Life of Oscar Wao*.

The DR has its own decent film industry—one of the most renowned movies is *Sanky Panky* (2007)—and more movies are being made now than in the past. Pinewood Studios also built one of the largest filming studios in Juan Dolio in 2011, valued at $70 million, and as of 2013 it is home to the world's second-largest water tank for underwater filming.

Internationally, the country has been a favorite backdrop of Hollywood movies and reality series, particularly of the *Survivor* kind. Movies that were filmed in the DR include *Apocalypse Now* (1979), *Jurassic Park* (1993), *The Good Shepherd* (2006), and *Miami Vice* (2006).

# Essentials

## Transportation

### GETTING THERE
#### Air

The Dominican Republic is blessed with 10 international and domestic airports (www.aerodom.com) in key areas of the country. You're never too far from a flight. When planning your trip, be sure to consider the most convenient arrival and departure point according to your itinerary and budget. Sometimes people forget how big the island really is.

The most affordable airport to fly into is usually Santo Domingo's **Aeropuerto Internacional de Las Américas** (SDQ, tel.

809/947-2225). It's the largest of the lot, and because it is just outside the capital city, it is well connected in terms of public transportation to various parts of the country, including Samaná and Punta Cana by bus.

**Aeropuerto Internacional Punta Cana** (PUJ, tel. 809/959-2376) receives nearly two million passengers a year and serves Punta Cana and Bávaro, where the bulk of visitors to the DR end up.

If you are headed to the Puerto Plata, opt for **Aeropuerto Internacional Gregorio Luperón** (POP, tel. 809/291-0000), just a 15-minute ride from downtown Puerto Plata town and the best pick for Playa Dorada, Cabarete, Sosúa, and visits to the North Coast. Some also opt to fly into the Santiago area, at **Aeropuerto Internacional del Cibao** (STI, tel. 809/233-8000)—just remember that the airport is at least a 30-minute ride to downtown Santiago, and from there it is another hour to Puerto Plata. That would mean an expensive cab ride to Puerto Plata, depending on your arrangements and itinerary.

For the southeastern DR, those heading to La Romana (including Casa de Campo) or Bayahibe and Dominicus beach areas can fly into **Aeropuerto Internacional La Romana** (LRM, tel. 809/813-9000). Over on the Samaná Peninsula is **Aeropuerto Internacional El Catey,** also known as **Aeropuerto Internacional Presidente Juan Bosch** (AZS, tel. 809/338-5888), outside Samaná town and ideal for stays around the peninsula. **Aeropuerto Arroyo Barril** (ABA, tel. 809/669-6100) and **Aeropuerto Constanza** (COZ, tel. 809/539-1022) are for domestic charters.

A host of airlines fly to the DR, including **American Airlines** (tel. 809/542-5151, www. aa.com), **Delta Airlines** (tel. 809/200-9191, www.delta.com), **Air Canada** (tel. 809/959-0200, www.aircanada.com), **British Airways** (tel. 809/959-0254, www.britishairways.com),

**Spirit Airlines** (tel. 809/549-0200, www. spirit.com), and **JetBlue** (tel. 809/200-9898, www.jetblue.com). Flights out of the DR (especially from Santo Domingo) head not just the United States but also directly to other Caribbean islands and Latin America. Find affordable tickets online, and stay tuned to airline websites and social media for any special deals.

## Ferry

An overnight ferry service between Santo Domingo and Puerto Rico (San Juan or Mayaguez) is offered by **America Cruise Ferries** (Puerto Don Diego, tel. 809/688-4400, http://ferriesdelcaribe.com/, US$180). The 12-hour journey begins at the port in Santo Domingo, across the Fortaleza Ozama.

# GETTING AROUND
## Air

If you want to save time or are traveling in a group, it might be a good bet to charter a flight. There are domestic airports and airstrips around the country that can get you from, say, Punta Cana to Puerto Plata. Contact **Air Century** (tel. 809/826-4333, www. aircentury.com) or **Dominican Quest** (tel. 809/523-9630), which offer charters as well as shuttle services.

## Bus and *Guagua*

The bus service in the DR is impressive; there's always a bus or *guagua* that will take you to your destination, even if you have to connect. There are three general types of bus service in the Dominican Republic: 1) the large and comfy coach buses that travel long distance between key cities; 2) privately owned and run minivan services that offer express runs to and from destinations; and 3) the in-city or in-town, usually beat-up white minivans that cram in as many people as possible. The last two are usually known as *guaguas*.

Previous: local on a motorbike.

The major coach bus companies are **Caribe Tours** (tel. 809/221-4422, www.caribetours.com.do), **Metro Tours** (tel. 809/227-0101, http://metroserviciosturisticos.com), and **Bávaro Express** (tel. 809/682-9670, www.expresobavaro.com). Caribe Tours offers the most destinations and departures. You can expect comfortable seats, air-conditioning (often uncomfortably cold), wireless Internet, and bathrooms on board. Tickets can be reserved in advance and purchased at the counter at least an hour before departure.

The more local private bus services are decent, with comfortable minivans holding about 25 (no being squashed here). They offer the same perks, along with some colorful curtains and Dominican music playing. All you have to do is ask the locals, and they will tell you which service is best from your destination if you are in a small town.

The local buses—the real definition of a *guagua*—are probably the least comfortable and offer the most chaotic yet interesting social scene, which makes it fun even if you only do it a couple of times. The merengue beats on, above the interior chatter, while the driver stops anytime someone hollers or stands on the side of the road, while the conductor leans halfway out the door calling out for customers and collecting fares. Unless it's an express, they'll stop anywhere along the road to pick up or drop off passengers, so you're often in for a longer ride than in a taxi. More than likely, you'll be squeezed like sardines (if you're claustrophobic, this could be a problem!). The only local *guaguas* I don't recommend are the ones in Santo Domingo—unless a local accompanies you.

When riding on public transportation, always have small change ready for your rides. Drivers might not have change for large bills. Also ask about fares ahead of time from anyone, including other passengers, so you don't get ripped off.

## Rental Car

Be warned: driving in the Dominican Republic is doable if you have experience driving in the Caribbean, but even then it's tricky. The roads and highways are some of the best in the Caribbean, but you will need to drive defensively and constantly be on the lookout for obstacles—motorbikes, cattle, dogs, pedestrians, or anything that could leap from the side, back, or front! And many times, road rules don't apply. Aggressive driving and speeding lead to a high number of road accidents, one of the highest rates in the world.

If you are unsure, this option isn't for you. But if you do decide to rent a car and explore the island—and it is the best way to enjoy its great outdoors and the countryside at your own pace—you will find that all the international rental companies such as Hertz, Alamo, and Dollar have outlets here. They have offices at the international airports, as well as in the tourist areas. Your best bet is to rent a sturdy four-wheel drive, and get full insurance coverage for the duration of your rental. A good map and knowing Spanish go a long way when you are lost (likely to happen the more you go off the beaten track).

## TAXI

Taxis abound all over the Dominican Republic, and you will soon realize that not all taxis are created equal. Some are shiny vans, and others are beat-up Toyota Corollas. To be safe, hop into one that is tourism certified, particularly for airport rides. Locally that won't always be possible. The most important thing when it comes to taxis is to know the rate to your destination and agree on a fare before you board, because there are no meters. If you're in Santo Domingo or Santiago, you can use the ride-share app **Uber**—it works perfectly and you don't have to speak Spanish.

In-city taxis are generally affordable at under US$5 a trip—with rates slightly higher after 5pm—and there are general taxi dispatch numbers you can call in each area. In Santo Domingo, they run 24-hour dispatches (Apolo Taxi, Santo Domingo, tel. 809/537-0000, www.apolotaxi.com). Many times, local rates within cities are set by the taxi association. But when it comes to longer distances, you can openly barter and negotiate. Drivers are usually decent folks, but there are plenty trying to abuse the system and overcharge. Knowing some Spanish and the fare will save you some bucks.

### Carritos (Shared Taxis)

Shared taxis, which are four-door cars usually of the Toyota type, operate like *guaguas*. They stop anywhere along their routes to pick up or drop off. Fares are only slightly higher than the bus, and they cram a maximum of 4-5 people in the back and two in the front, not including the driver. Carry small change and announce your destination as you hand the money over to the driver (while he is at the wheel) shortly after you enter the car.

### Motoconchos (Motorbike Taxis)

They are all over the Dominican Republic, parked on street corners, by bus stations, along *guagua* stops and near major intersections: *motoconchos,* or bike taxis. They'll take you to the same destinations as taxis for far less. Of course, it's a lot more dangerous. Riders don't carry helmets for their passengers (and don't wear any themselves—despite it being a law). Don't hesitate to tell the *motoconcho* to slow down if he's going too fast for your liking. You can have two passengers on the back of the bike, and it's common to see Dominicans squeezing in their entire family. It's simply one of the most affordable ways for them to get around. The countryside roads are safer to explore on motorbike taxis because of lighter traffic. It is nice enjoying the landscape this way, but you will be riding at your own risk.

# Travel Tips

## VISAS AND IMMIGRATION

All arriving tourists will need a passport, valid for at least six months and with sufficient pages for entry and exit stamps. As of April 2018, there is no longer a need to purchase a US$10 tourist card upon arrival or in advance—the fee is rolled into your airline ticket. A tourist's stay is valid for 30 days. Should you overstay that limit by a few weeks or months, you will face a scaled exit charge at the airport when you leave, at the immigration booth past security.

The customs line can be a pain or easy, depending on the airport. Santo Domingo usually has the longest lines, but they usually don't go through your things if you are traveling light and are a short-term tourist. Those who arrive on a visa and overstay will have to pay a fee—check with your embassy if this is a concern.

## CONDUCT AND CUSTOMS

Dominicans love to laugh, joke around, and spend time with their families and friends on the water. They celebrate life through music, dancing, and plenty of drinks (but they can handle their liquor). Sharing is an important aspect of Dominican culture. Always begin a conversation, even if just a question, by greeting the person and asking how they are. Greeting people by saying *Buen día* or *Buenas noches* when entering a public space, even buses, is considered polite and a must. Learn all the courtesy words. Decline an offer you do not want by saying *No, gracias.*

If you'd like to take photographs of people, always ask first. Dominicans are generally fine with this and will indulge you, but you must request politely first. Do not photograph military or police officers for fun; it's prohibited unless you ask nicely and they agree (the Pantheon guards in the Colonial Zone seem to be an exception to this). When tipping, be generous. Wages are incredibly low for Dominicans, and the 10 percent service fee added to restaurant bills, for instance, might not reach their pockets at all. If you receive excellent service or even if it is basic, feel free to tip. At the market, haggling for clothing and other items (besides produce) can be fun, but keep it reasonable.

## VOLUNTEERING ON VACATION

You may want to travel, but feel a nudge to give back to the communities you're visiting, or to immerse yourself and learn more about the culture. One of the best ways to do this is to share what is most valuable: your talent and time. There are plenty of organizations offering voluntourism opportunities. Just be careful in selecting the ones that are a good fit for your skills as well as reliable. Wherever you end up volunteering, your expenses should be affordable. The key is to obtain as much detail as you can.

One that I highly recommend is the local tourism cooperative **Red de Turismo Comunitario de Puerto Plata** (tel. 809/261-2993), which has various communities and opportunities to choose from. You can contact the network and custom design your volunteer time and interests. At the same time, you'll get to enjoy the great outdoors of the North Coast. For more information, see the Puerto Plata chapter. Another great option, out of Cabarete, is the **Mariposa DR Foundation** (tel. 809/571-0610, www.mariposadrfoundation.org). It works with local adolescent girls to educate and empower them economically. They welcome volunteer help in various aspects of their operations ranging from teaching to gardening. Submit their online form for more details.

The DR is challenged in its educational system, above all else, and there's always a dire need for English teachers. One organization that would be interested is **COOPDECI—Cooperativa para el Desarrollo de La Ciénaga,** the local co-operative of La Ciénaga, in the Barahona province. Those heading to the Punta Cana region can volunteer in environmental and sustainable programs with the **Puntacana Ecological Foundation** (tel. 809/959-9221, fepc@puntacana.com). Contact them in advance for a current list of opportunities and matching.

## TRAVELING WITH CHILDREN

Children will need a valid passport. As a general precaution, if a minor is traveling to the DR without one parent, carry a notarized document from the absent parent. It is generally fine for children to travel with nonparents as long as the children return with the same adults, but it is better to be safe and carry an authorizing document from the parents there as well.

With a myriad of all-inclusive resorts at all budget levels, the DR can be an easy family vacation. When selecting a resort, make sure you look into the activities offered and whether there's a special Kids Club or a Preferred Family Club for additional fee. The perks are usually worth it. But don't stay cooped up in resorts either—Dominicans love and understand the family concept, and getting out and about to see how they enjoy themselves is a great way to share time with your kids. In Samaná, Puerto Plata, or Jarabacoa, families like swimming together at the beach, at the river, and by waterfalls, while cooking out and listening to music. There are plenty of water sports for teenagers, especially on the North Coast. If you're visiting in winter, you can take the kids to a baseball game at a number of professional stadiums in Santiago, La Romana, or Santo Domingo. Cultural experiences also abound when you visit the countryside, usually a favorite for kids, where there are plenty of fresh fruits and hiking trails. If you are relying on taxis, use one of the referrals in this book (according to where you are staying) and ask ahead whether the vans have working seat belts.

# Responsible Travel

To travel responsibly is to travel not just to enjoy a place but to realize that your presence has an impact on every person, thing, and place you encounter or visit and to want to make as positive an impact as possible. This is particularly key when traveling in developing countries with heavy tourism, such as the Dominican Republic, where the majority of the population lives in poverty and tourism wealth doesn't trickle down far enough.

So how can you travel responsibly while in the DR? Here are a few suggestions:

- **Pick Dominican-owned businesses**—from local restaurants to guesthouses—as much as you can.

- **Shop at the neighborhood** *colmados.* These Dominican-owned corner stores/bars/ snack shops are the crux of Dominican culture and help sustain entire neighborhoods. They are also fun to hang out in with a cold beer and merengue or *bachata* blasting. Look for what you need here, whether snacks, rum, or a phone card, before heading to the supermarket.

- **Learn a few phrases of Spanish** and interact with Dominicans. They are hospitable people and will gladly interact with you.

- **Tour with local community tourism organizations** (such as UMCP in Puerto Plata, www.popreport.com/turisopp) or licensed Dominican tour operators. The various chapters mention options. Not only will you get a more authentic look at life in the Dominican country-side, but your tourism dollars will go directly to the communities you're visiting.

- **Shop from local artisans and artists** and purchase handmade products. Be careful not to buy any prohibited products such as turtle shells or red coral.

- **Use public transportation** where feasible, or hire a local driver. I've recommended names in each chapter of this book.

- **Attend local festivals,** where you'll get insight into the culture as well as find shopping options for local food and arts.

- **Make your stay as green as possible.** Recycling has a long way to go in this country, but you can try not to contribute to the issue by reducing the amount of plastics and other such containers you use. Eat inside the restaurant rather than taking food out, and try to use one refillable water bottle.

- **Be conscious of your electricity and water usage** in your hotel room or otherwise. Be reasonable, even if it is available to you without limit. Turn off the lights and air-conditioning while you are out exploring. Stay in hotels that are eco-friendly and environmentally conscious.

- Last but not least, **appreciate the people** who are receiving you and **respect their culture.**

## TRAVELING WITH PETS

To travel with your dog or cat, you'll need to bring a recent health certificate from your veterinarian, certified by the Agriculture Department of your state and apostilled by the state government. You must also show a rabies certificate. For up-to-date information and more details, contact the Embassy of the Dominican Republic in the United States (www.domrep.org) or in your country of residence. The website http://hispaniola.com can also provide more details.

## WOMEN TRAVELERS

Ladies, the good news is that it is safe to travel the Dominican Republic solo or in groups. I did it myself multiple times countrywide and have not encountered any issues. Of course, I

# Getting Married in the DR

It's difficult to top the DR's gorgeous scenery, not to mention the array of all-inclusive or boutique hotels offering bridal and honeymoon packages, often with an on-site coordinator. Packages usually include all you need, including judge, license, flowers, cake, champagne, and music, in addition to accommodations. Popular destinations are La Romana and Punta Cana, but you'll find plenty of more secluded options in Puerto Plata and Samaná. Before the fun begins, you'll need to comply with the formalities. To marry in the DR, the bride and groom need to bring a notarized statement of their marital status certified by the Dominican consulate in their respective countries. Valid passports and birth certificates for the couple and copies of any divorce decrees will be needed where applicable. You'll need two witnesses, and all of the relevant documents will need to be translated into Spanish once in the DR. Church weddings are a possibility—imagine the riverfront backdrop of the gorgeous St. Stanislaus Church at Altos de Chavón, or the colonial buildings in Santo Domingo. For an up-to-date list of the complete requirements, inquire with the resort that interests you.

stay as vigilant as I am at home and don't take unnecessary risks (such as walking alone at night). Travel during the day, whether on public transport or on excursions, so you're not isolated. Staying at independently run hotels and guesthouses is also an excellent way to meet fellow travelers and get local tips from owners who will have more time for their solo guests than a massive all-inclusive. That said, all-inclusive resorts also often have an entertainment crew who are more than willing to accompany the solo female.

Look out for the *sanky panky*—a term used for local men who go after foreign women of any adult age and romance them (through selfless acts of generosity and love) for the sole purpose of getting money or, better yet, a visa and a way out of the country. They are often good-looking, well groomed, and display plenty of muscles. They roam the beach or work at hotels on the entertainment crew. This phenomenon is common in many tourism-driven destinations. Just be smart and realistic about whom you are befriending. The only major nuisance for female travelers in the DR is the machismo displayed by Dominican men in the streets. Hollering, ogling, and whistling are common practice. But it is just talk and considered normal (from the men's point of view) to admire and gawk at women, particularly foreign ones. Ignore it and keep moving.

## SENIOR TRAVELERS

Senior travelers love the DR for the well-rounded variety of activities it offers—particularly in terms of sports. The North Coast, for instance, is a dream for its hiking, kayaking, and sailing opportunities, as well as plenty of golfing. Regularly ranked as the Golf Destination of the Year by the International Association of Golf Tour Operators, golfers will find plenty of options on top-rated courses around the country, including world-renowned Teeth of the Dog at Casa de Campo. Seniors are also welcome at all-inclusive resorts, some of which offer preferred club options for more privacy and luxury. Samaná is ideal for senior travelers as well, thanks to its less crowded, powdery beaches and affordable fine-dining options.

## GAY AND LESBIAN TRAVELERS

The Dominican Republic is surprisingly more tolerant than most other Caribbean countries when it comes to gay and lesbian travelers—a world apart from Jamaica or Grenada. Hotels all welcome gay couples. Gay bashing or violence is rare, and you will find many openly gay Dominicans, both male and female. The current U.S. ambassador to the DR, James Brewster, is gay and lives here with his

# Traveling on a Budget

Budget travelers will love the DR: it can be incredibly cheap to explore if you know how.

- **Planning your vacation:** Schedule your vacation in the off-season from mid-April through October. You'll find hotel rates discounted, even at all-inclusive resorts. For local guesthouses and hotels, just showing up often gets you an even lower rate, and unless it's a public holiday, you won't have trouble finding rooms.

- **Getting around:** Take public transportation. Taxis are prohibitively expensive and tend to overcharge tourists. Catch the local shared taxis (*carritos*) or buses (*guaguas*) in small cities and towns to get around like Dominicans do. There's always one going to popular sights, beaches, or shops. Long-distance bus companies **Caribe Tours** (tel. 809/221-4422, www.caribetours.com.do) and **Metro Tours** (tel. 809/227-0101, http://metroserviciosturisticos.com), as well as smaller private bus lines (depending on your destination) charge under US$5 per person for comfortable, air-conditioned vans, often with wireless Internet.

- **Eating:** Eat at the local *comedor* (cafeteria), where the dish of the day is under US$4 with sides. If you're vegetarian, you can stick to the avocado salads or the rice and beans. Fruits sold street-side on carts or at the market—RD$10 (US$0.21) for five bananas, depending on the area—and fresh-squeezed juices are equally cheap. Another solid spot for a quick fill is the *pica pollo* (fried chicken joint); there's always one on the main drag in your town. *Colmados*—the corner stores—also offer a daily dish; you'll need to speak a little Spanish to ask.

- **Sleeping:** Stay in locally owned guesthouses or hostels. Backpackers will find hostels in various areas such as Samaná, Santo Domingo, and even Bávaro. Superaffordable local hotels that are the equivalent of hostels sometimes even provide an amazing bang for your buck (with wireless Internet and hot water). Camping is not a big (or safe) thing here in the DR compared to other Caribbean and Central American destinations like, say, Belize. But there are the occasional locations—in the southwest, for instance—offering beachfront camping. Sleeping al fresco is also popular in the mountains of Jarabacoa on hikes of Pico Duarte or El Mogote.

- **Getting the lowest price:** Bargaining is an art form in the DR. Learn a little Spanish and haggle away—whether when hiring local taxis for a private ride or shopping at the markets.

partner. Still, public displays of affection are not acceptable, and you should be conservative while out and about as a couple. Do not hold hands or kiss outside in order to avoid unwanted attention.

Santo Domingo has the most gay-friendly options for bars, clubs, and hangout spots in parks, especially in the Colonial Zone—check out www.gaytravel.com.

## TRAVELERS WITH DISABILITIES

As in most of the region, independent travel (getting around on public transport for instance) for those who are disabled is extremely limited. If the goal is to relax at an all-inclusive resort, these are well equipped with elevators and usually have special rooms for travelers with disabilities. The DR is a welcoming destination, so don't be afraid to ask for what you need. If going on tour excursions, check that they offer appropriate vehicles and can meet your requirements ahead of time.

# Food and Accommodations

## FOOD

The Dominican national meal is called the Dominican flag or *bandera dominicana*: a plate of rice and beans, with a stewed meat sauce and a side salad. Also called the *plato del día* at the local restaurants (special of the day), it is the most affordable meal aside from fried chicken and, well, anything fried roadside. Cafeterias or *comedor* abound in towns and cities, and offer delicious buffets of Dominican and international foods (ordering alone is a cultural experience) for an incredibly low price (usually under US$5). On the weekends, you will notice more street foods, including chicken and pork being grilled roadside. One advantage of many European expats living in the DR is a greater variety of cuisines than on other Caribbean islands, though not all are created equal. Wherever you end up, you're never too far from an Italian or French restaurant. Cafés and pastry shops are popular, too, given that Dominicans have a super sweet tooth.

If you are staying at an all-inclusive resort, the food will be predominantly non-Dominican, but some have Dominican restaurants à la carte on the list. When that happens, you should make a reservation for it. Be sure to step out and try the local food in town as well.

## ACCOMMODATIONS

The hotel choices in the Dominican Republic are as varied as it gets, from luxurious all-inclusive resorts with preferred club perks to nature lodges, guesthouses, and local by-the-hour "cabanas."

High-season rates are higher (prices listed in this edition are for double occupancy in high season, unless otherwise noted), and you will need to plan ahead for the busiest times of the year, namely Christmastime and Easter. Keep your eye on websites and hotel social media channels for deals.

Although the DR is best known for its wide choice of all-inclusive resorts facing powdery beaches, there are lots more options all over the island to fit every budget. You should give these a try whenever possible. It's the best way to get a feel for the country and its incredible people, rather than staying trapped in an all-inclusive. There's a rise in luxurious accommodations, particularly boutique hotels and luxury, condo-style resorts. But there are also charming, affordable lodges offering the best of the DR's great outdoors. Look into Puerto Plata or Jarabacoa, for instance. My recommended best picks are indicated in each chapter. Camping is not common or recommended in the DR, except when clearly organized for overnight hikes or on the beach through kitesurfing schools or as part of a trip to Bahía de las Águilas, for example. Take your time in researching your chosen accommodations so you get not only a great deal but also good food, service, and location for your buck.

# Dominican Drinks:
# Beers, Rum, and Mamajuana

Dominicans love their **Presidente** beer, made by the national brewery Cervecería Nacional Dominicana since around 1935. It is the iconic brand of the island, pretty much synonymous with being Dominican. The name and the green bottles pop up everywhere: at concerts, the local *colmados*, restaurants, and even on plastic chairs on the beach. The custom is to purchase a "grande" or big bottle and share it with friends—more importantly, it must be served and consumed really cold to the point that the bottle has a light white frosting. The lightweights can opt for a Presidente Light. The latest brand in the Presidente family is the Presidente Black, a thicker-bodied beer with 6 percent alcohol. Aside from Presidente, other brands are popular, such as **Bohemia,** a pilsner with 5 percent alcohol but made in Mexico, and **Quisqueya,** made by the Cervecería Vegana in the DR, a pilsner at 6 percent alcohol. If you find yourself in Constanza, you'll also find a popular thick, dark craft beer made and sold at La Esquina bar called **Ferringer,** a play on the owners' family name.

Equally as popular, and as expected in the Caribbean, is *rum*—or *romo* as they like to say here. The DR produces several popular brands: **Brugal, Bermúdez, Barceló,** and **Macorix.** Brugal 1888 has ranked on many a list of top Caribbean rums. When you head to a local bar, it's customary to buy a bottle (of any size you choose) and your mixer and enjoy with your group. Cuba libres, Santo libres, Brugal Añejo (a popular pick) or Extra Viejo, or on the rocks—everyone has their preference.

Perhaps the most Dominican of all drinks is **mamajuana**—and almost every souvenir store will pounce on you to sample and buy a bottle. Sample away but beware: this concoction is a potent, fermented mix of cured tree barks and herbs soaked in red wine and rum. The herbs and barks could include canelilla (*Cinnamodendron ekmanii*), marabeli (*Securidaca virgata*), bojuco caro (*princess vine*), and *clavo dulce* (whole clove), among other ingredients. There are as many varieties of mamajuana as there are makers of this local drink. Dominicans like to say it's an aphrodisiac or a liquid Viagra. Whatever it is, the right mamajuana is tasty, strong, and makes for an excellent aperitif (some restaurants offer it free post-meal), if you can handle it. If you plan on taking a bottle home, make sure you are purchasing from a reputable store, keep the receipt, and only bring back liquid mamajuana because the tree or bark-only packages are considered plants and not allowed into the United States. Last but not least: Don't consume more than a couple of shots at a time. It's super powerful and there's a danger of alcohol poisoning if you overindulge.

# Health and Safety

## SAFETY
### Emergencies
Use 911 in an emergency. Dispatchers can connect to ambulances, firefighters, and the police. Depending on how remote you are, it may be better not to wait for assistance. Head to the nearest emergency room when possible. Clinics with 24-hour ERs include **Centro Médico Bournigal** (Calle Antera Mota, Puerto Plata, www.bournigal-hospital. com, tel. 809/586-2342), **Clínica Corazones**

**Unidos** (Calle Fantino Falco 21, Ensanche Naco, Santo Domingo, tel. 809/567-4421, www.corazonesunidos.com.do), **Hospiten Bávaro** (Carretera Veron-Punta Cana, tel. 809/686-1414, www.hospiten.com.do), **Centro Médico La Romana** (tel. 809/523-3333, www.centralromana.com.do), and **Centro Médico Regional Barahona** (Jose Francisco Pena Gomez 71, tel. 809/524-2470). Note that in the Dominican Republic, you have to pay before receiving clinical care.

## Crime

Leave valuables at home and remember some commonsense rules: don't walk around flashing expensive clothes, jewelry, or accessories, and keep your wits about you. Petty theft and robberies by passing motorcycle or scooter do happen. Staying aware and low-key will help prevent that.

For crime emergencies, contact the nearest **CESTUR** (Cuerpo Especializado de Seguridad Turistica) office—the specialized tourist police corps assigned to each major area. They are trained in handling visitors and often speak or understand more than just Spanish. You can also grab a glossy copy of *La Cotica* handbook from airports, hotels, or tourism offices for all the latest emergency numbers and tourist information countrywide. The emergency number is 911, just as in the United States. Numbers for regional CESTUR offices at publication time are:

- Santo Domingo: 809/685-0508 or 809/689-6464
- Bávaro: 809/754-3082
- Bayahibe: 809/754-3012
- La Romana: 809/754-3033
- Puerto Plata: 809/754-3101
- Cabarete: 809/754-2992
- Sosúa: 809/754-3274
- Las Terrenas: 809/754-3042

## HEALTH

Carry a small medical first aid kit with you; it could come in handy for minor injuries. Good-quality sunscreen and mosquito spray are a must, along with your preferred painkillers. Other personal necessities you are used to could be hard to find, including birth control. Bringing a pack of wipes wouldn't hurt, particularly since public bathrooms don't always carry toilet paper.

## Water

You cannot drink the tap water in the DR. Always go for filtered, bottled water, even to brush your teeth—better to take these precautions than invite illnesses. Whether on or off the resort, limit the amount of ice cubes in your drinks or salad consumption if you feel unsure that the hotel or restaurant is using tap water for these and depending on your stomach sensitivities. Bottled water is cheap and available at local stores and supermarkets, in the rare case that your hotel doesn't provide it or you need more. Stay hydrated throughout the day—the intense sun and high humidity, particularly in the summer, can cause serious dehydration.

## Diarrhea

Avoid traveler's diarrhea by avoiding tap water, and being aware of the raw fruits and vegetables you are consuming. Stay hydrated with lots of water for flushing the toxins from your body. If it persists beyond a day, go to the nearest clinic and see a doctor.

## Dengue

A rise in dengue cases has caused concern for several Caribbean countries in the second half of 2015, and the DR is no exception with 1,251 dengue-related deaths so far in 2018. This mosquito-borne virus causes fever, severe headaches, and serious joint and muscle pain.

## Malaria

There's little risk of malaria in the DR, especially if you are heading to tourist areas. You only need to be concerned and prepared if you are headed to the border areas of Dajabón or San Juan and are staying there. In the latter case, get prescription malaria pills from your doctor. Treatment often begins before departure and continues for up to a month after your return.

## Women's Health

The local pharmacies and supermarkets carry most women's products in major brands you recognize, from plastic tampons to panty liners. For other medical needs, such as creams or remedies for yeast infections, you'll have to go to the pharmacy and request them (no prescription needed) because these are not sold over the counter. Your best bet is to see an ob-gyn at the nearest clinic.

### Pharmacies

The DR has a host of **pharmacies** across the country, and you're never too far from medication when you need it. Most big resorts have their own first aid kits and pain relievers for basic aches and pains, but you can look to the nearest city for more options. The added bonus is that most pharmacies in the DR also offer a delivery service. Twenty-four-hour pharmacies include **Farmacia Trizza** (Higüey, tel. 809/554-4242), **Farmacia Los Hidalgos** (Santo Domingo, tel. 809/338-0700), and **Farmacia Carol** (Las Terrenas), among many others in various major towns and cities, such as Jarabacoa, Santiago, and Puerto Plata.

# Information and Services

## MONEY

The currency of the Dominican Republic is the Dominican peso (RD$). Its value fluctuates, so you'll have to check it before your trip, but it is currently RD$49 to US$1 dollar. The peso is divided into 100 cents; coins run into 1, 5, 10, and 25 pesos. Bills come in 20, 50, 100, 200, 500, 1,000, and 2,000 pesos. You'll find major banks and 24-hour ATMs in most areas—including Scotiabank branches and Banco Popular. These last two tend to work best with American cards. When using ATMs, do it in busier areas and during daylight; avoid the weekends when lines tend to be longer. The maximum you can withdraw with each transaction is RD$10,000 or about US$220.

While the American dollar is accepted in major tourist areas, shops and supermarkets in smaller towns and cities might not, so ask ahead. If they do, you will need to know the currency exchange rate to check on what you're getting back and paying. Major department stores and restaurants generally accept debit or credit cards, but try to limit your usage of plastic and stick to cash where possible unless at a major resort, shopping mall, or fine-dining spot.

## TIPPING AND TAXES

An 18 percent sales tax is tacked on to food and drinks in restaurants, plus a 10 percent service charge by law. The latter is supposedly the waitstaff tip, but it is unclear whether they always receive it. Some diners choose to throw in an additional 10 percent tip in case. So when you're eating out, look for that extra 28 percent added to your check (on rare occasions it is already included). Avoid using your credit or debit cards wherever possible and use cash, especially in smaller cities or towns. Expect sales taxes of 28 percent on hotel bills and 16 percent in shops. Don't forget to tip the hotel maid (at least US$1-2 a day).

## COMMUNICATIONS

**Wireless Internet** and computers are ubiquitous in the DR and easily used for Skype or FaceTime calls. But if you are in an all-inclusive, you might find that they charge exorbitant prices for usage per hour—avoid this ridiculous fee by researching where you stay ahead of time and ensuring that wireless Internet is included or at least free in common areas. Cybercafés and restaurants or coffee shops with wireless Internet are everywhere in the big cities and tourist areas. The only places that are a bit challenged with connections are the mountains of Constanza. Mac users might find it handy to know that there is an Apple authorized retailer in the DR, I-Zone (tel. 809/955-3237, www.izone.com.do), with various locations island wide and carrying various Apple accessories as well as electronics.

For news on the DR, you will find daily articles and travel information in English on **Dominican Today** (www.dominicantoday.com). **Newspapers** include *Listin Diario* (www.listindiario.com), *Diario Libre* (www.

diariolibre.com), and *El Nacional* (www.
elnacional.com.do).

Forget about the **post office**—it just
doesn't function well at all for important
packages or documents. Your best bet is to
pay for DHL or FedEx if you really need it.
You can also receive packages from North
America through private shipping services
like Caripack, depending on your location.

## MAPS AND TOURIST INFORMATION

The Ministry of Tourism has various offices
in the main tourist destinations around the
island. It also has a useful website (www.
godominicanrepublic.com), in various languages, with background and activity information on each region that you can
download and save. All relevant local tourism office locations are indicated in the respective chapters of this book. If you can,
however, I recommend you grab free tourism publications and maps when you spot
them in hotels, tour operator offices, and at
the airports when you arrive. You will find
additional useful websites and sources in the
Resources chapter.

# Resources

## Glossary

*Avenida:* Avenue.
*Ballenas:* Humpback whales.
*Buen provecho:* Enjoy your meal/drink.
*Calle:* Street.
*Carnaval:* Carnival.
*Cerveza:* Beer.
*Chicharrón:* Deep-fried pork.
*Chivo:* Goat.
*Colmado:* Corner store/neighborhood grocery store.
*Conuco:* Plot of farmland.
*Fiestas patronales:* Patron saint festivals.
*Freiduras/frituras:* Fried-food shacks/vendors.
*Guagua:* Bus.
*Hostal:* Guesthouse.
*Cuba libre:* Rum and Coke.
*La capital:* The capital/Santo Domingo.
*Limpiabota:* Shoeshine boy.
*Malecón:* Seafront boulevard.

*Mamajuana:* A traditional, potent herbal drink.
*Merengue:* The DR's national music and dance, along with *bachata*.
*Merengue típico:* The original (folkloric) merengue genre.
*Mofongo:* A mashed plantain dish.
*Motoconcho/concho:* Motorbike taxi.
*Museo:* Museum.
*Parada:* Stop (bus/taxi).
*Parque central:* Central park.
*Peso:* DR currency.
*Plato del día:* Dish of the day/special of the day.
*Playa:* Beach.
*Presidente:* The most popular Dominican beer.
*Santo libre:* Rum and Sprite.
*Sendero:* Hiking trail.
*Una fría:* A cold one (beer).

## Spanish Phrasebook

Learning a few words of Spanish will make your stay much more enjoyable (and less frustrating). If you're planning on traveling independently around the island, then it's a must to know a few words. Few Dominicans outside of the cities and tourist zones understand English, especially when it comes to public transportation and basic needs.

### BASIC EXPRESSIONS AND GREETINGS

Greetings are important in the DR! Walking into a public space without saying *Buen día* or approaching someone without saying hello first can be considered rude. Keep in mind also that Dominicans tend to chop words and leave out the "s." So it wouldn't be strange to hear *Pa'tra* for *para atras* or for the use of expressions in unexpected ways (*te llamo pa'tra* for I'll call you back.) When in doubt, ask them to speak slowly: *más despacio, por favor!*

For pronunciation, plenty of free online resources allow you to listen to and get a sense of basic Spanish grammar and vocabulary. A solid one is www.studyspanish.com.

*Hola*  Hello.
*Buenos días / Buen día*  Good morning.
*Buenas tardes*  Good afternoon.
*Buenas noches or "Noches"*  Goodnight.
*Como está usted?*  How are you?
*Muy bien, gracias*  Very well, thank you.
*Bien*  Good.
*Todo bien?*  Everything good/cool?
*Todo bien, gracias*  Everything is good, thanks.
*Mal*  Not good, bad.
*Y usted?*  And you?
*Gracias*  Thank you.
*Muchas gracias*  Thank you very much.
*De nada*  You're welcome.
*A la orden*  You're welcome (a Dominican way of saying it).
*Adios*  Goodbye.
*Hasta luego*  See you later.
*Por favor*  Please.
*Sí*  Yes.
*No*  No.
*No sé*  I don't know.
*Momentito por favor*  One moment, please.
*Disculpe/Con permiso*  Excuse me please (when trying to get attention or trying to pass someone).
*Perdon/Lo siento*  I'm sorry/Excuse me (when you've made a mistake or bumped into someone).
*Mucho gusto/Un placer*  Pleased to meet you/It's a pleasure.
*Encantado/a*  Charmed/Thrilled to meet you.
*Como se dice...?*  How do you say...?
*Como se llama usted?*  What is your name?
*Me llamo...*  My name is...
*Usted habla inglés?*  Do you speak English?

*Hablo poco español*  I speak little Spanish.
*Quisiera usted...?*  Would you like...?
*Quieres...?*  Do you want...? (informal)
*Ven conmigo/Vamos*  Come with me/Let's go.

## PEOPLE

*Yo*  I.
*Tu*  You (informal).
*Usted*  You (formal).
*El*  He/him.
*Ella*  She/her.
*Nosotros*  We/us.
*Ustedes*  You (plural).
*Ellos*  They/them (males).
*Ellas*  They/them (females).
*Señor*  Mr.
*Señora*  Mrs./Madam.
*Señorita*  Miss.
*Esposo/esposa*  Husband/wife.
*Amigo/amiga*  Friend (male/female).
*Novio/novia*  Boyfriend/girlfriend.
*Hijo/hija*  Son/daughter.
*Hermano/hermana*  Brother/sister.
*Padre/madre*  Father/mother.
*Abuelo/abuela*  Grandfather/grandmother.
*Sobrino/sobrina*  Nephew/niece.
*Primo/prima*  Cousin.
*Nieto*  Grandchild.
*Chica*  Girl.
*Chico*  Boy.
*Mujer*  Woman.
*Hombre*  Man.

## TIME

*What time is it?*  Que hora es?
*It's five o'clock in the afternoon*  Son las cinco de la tarde.
*It's four in the morning*  Son las cuatro de la manana.
*For one hour*  Por una hora.
*Seven thirty*  Siete y media.
*At what time...?*  A que hora...?
*How many hours?*  Cuantas horas?

## DAYS AND MONTHS

*Lunes*  Monday.
*Martes*  Tuesday.

*Miércoles* Wednesday.
*Jueves* Thursday.
*Viernes* Friday.
*Sábado* Saturday.
*Domingo* Sunday.
*Hoy* Today.
*Mañana* Tomorrow.
*Ayer* Yesterday.
*La próxima semana* Next week.
*El próximo mes* Next month.
*Enero* January.
*Febrero* February.
*Marzo* March.
*Abril* April.
*Mayo* May.
*Junio* June.
*Julio* July.
*Agosto* August.
*Setiembre* September.
*Octubre* October.
*Noviembre* November.
*Diciembre* December.
*Una semana* A week.
*Un mes* A month.
*Después* After.
*Antes* Before.

## TRANSPORTATION

*Guagua* Public bus in the DR (white minivans).
*Carro-concho/Carrito* Shared taxi.
*Motoconcho* Motorbike taxi.
*Vehículo/Carro* A car.
*Jeepeta* An SUV.
*Donde está...?* Where is...?
*A que hora sale...?* What times does the (bus/taxi/etc.) leave?
*A cuanta distancia está...?* How far to...?
*Cuantas cuadras más?* How many more blocks?
*El camino para...* The road/way to...
*La parada de...* The stop for...
*El barco* The boat.
*El muelle* The dock.
*La lancha* The speedboat.
*El aeropuerto* The airport.
*La boletería* The ticket office.
*La entrada* The entrance.

*La salida* The exit.
*Está lejos?* Is it far?
*Está cerca?* Is it near?
*A la derecha* To the right.
*A la izquierda* To the left.
*Derecho/todo derecho* Straight ahead.
*Al lado de* Next to.
*Frente a* In front of.
*Atrás/Pa' tra* Behind/At the back.
*En la esquina* In the corner.
*En el semáforo* At the traffic light.
*Una vuelta* A turn.
*Dale* Give it some gas! Speed up.
*Aquí* Here.
*Donde pueda, chofer* Pull over where you're able, driver (especially in a local bus/taxi).
*Por allá* Over there.
*Calle* Street.
*Punte/Cuota* Bridge/toll.
*La carretera* The highway.
*Kilómetro* Kilometer.
*Cual es la dirección?* What's the address?
*Norte/Sur* North/South.
*Este/Oeste* East/West.

## ACCOMMODATIONS

*Hotel* Hotel.
*Cabaña* A motel, can be luxury or basic (rooms by the hour, if you know what I mean).
*Hay cuarto?* Do you have room? Is there an available room?
*Necesito un cuarto por ___ noches* I need a room for ___ nights.
*Habitación sencilla/doble* Single room/double room.
*Puedo verlo?* Can I see it?
*Cual es el precio?* What's the price?
*Hay más económico?* Is there anything cheaper/more affordable?
*Con baño* With bath.
*Ducha* Shower.
*Hay agua caliente?* Is there hot water?
*Televisión* TV.
*Con aire* With A/C.
*Con abanico solamente* With fan only.
*El desayuno incluido* Breakfast included.

*Toallas* Towels.
*Jabón* Soap.
*Papel higiénico* Toilet paper.
*Mantas* Blankets.
*Sábanas* Sheets.
*La llave* The key.
*El gerente* The manager.

## HEALTH

*Estoy enfermo/enferma* I'm sick (male/female).
*Como se siente?* How do you feel?
*En que le puedo ayudar?* How can I help you?
*No me siento bien* I don't feel well.
*Ayúdame, por favor* Help me, please.
*Llame un doctor* Call a doctor.
*Emergencia* Emergency.
*Sientese y espere* Take a seat and wait.
*Donde está el hopital/centro medico?* Where is the hospital/clinic?
*La farmacia* Pharmacy/drugstore.
*Fiebre* Fever.
*Me duele...* My ___ hurts.
*Dolor de cabeza* Headache.
*Dolor de estómago* Stomachache.
*Quemadura* Burn.
*Medicina* Medicine.
*Antibiótico* Antibiotics.
*Pastilla* Pill.
*Algodón* Cotton.
*Pastillas anticonceptivas* Contraceptive pills.
*Condones* Condoms.
*Crema dental* Toothpaste.
*Dientes* Teeth.
*Dentista* Dentist.
*Dolor de muelas* Toothache.

## COMMUNICATIONS

*Tarjeta de crédito* Credit card.
*Efectivo* Cash.
*Teléfono* Telephone.
*Quisiera llamar a...* I'd like to call...
*Una carta* A letter.
*Correo aereo* Airmail.
*Registrado* Registered.
*Paquete/caja* Box/package.

*Un giro* A money transfer.
*Paquete internet* An Internet package.

## AT THE BORDER

*Frontera* Border.
*Aduana* Customs.
*Migración* Immigration.
*Tarjeta de turista* Tourist card.
*Inspección* Inspection.
*Pasaporte* Passport.
*Cédula* Dominican ID card or used to mean ID card (can be your driver's license for non-Dominicans).
*Licensia de manejar* Driver's license.
*Título* Title.
*Profesión* Profession.
*Estado civil* Marital status.
*Casado/a* Married.
*Soltero/a* Single.
*Divorciado/a* Divorced.
*Viudado/a* Widowed.

## AT THE GAS STATION

*La bomba* The gas station.
*Gasolina* Gas.
*Lleno, por favor* Full, please.
*Goma* Tire.
*Gomeria* Tire repair shop.
*Aire* Air.
*Agua* Water.
*Aceite (cambio)* Oil change.
*Batería* Battery.
*Radiador* Radiator.
*Alternator* Alternator.
*Generator* Generator.
*How much do you charge?* Cuánto cobran?

## DOMINICAN EXPRESSIONS

*Que lo que?* What's up/What's going on? (Also abbreviated as "klk" or KLK.)
*Pana!* Hey buddy/bro.
*Tiguere* A slick man/hustler (in other words, look out for anyone described this way). Can also be used among friends when teasing each other. Can be used in feminine *tiguera*.
*Mi Loco* Hey buddy/my friend.

*Como tu'ta?* How are you? (The Dominican way of chopping words).

*Tranquilo* Everything cool (I'm fine).

*Que chevere/Que chulo!* How cool/wonderful/great.

*Ya tu sabe* You know it/That's right.

*Dímelo* Tell me/Talk to me.

*Está bien* That's fine/OK.

*Entonces?* So?

*Que fue?* What happened? What's wrong?

*Mi amor* My love (used for anyone and everyone).

*Cariño* Darling.

*Que vaina!* What a thing! (In surprise or in lament; vary your tone accordingly).

*Coño!* An exclamation expressing surprise or disgust similar to "Damn!"

*Maleducado, déjame tranquila/dame banda!* Rude man, leave me alone!

*Carajo!* Hell or damn! Can add emphasis by saying, "Coño, carajo."

*Sanky panky* Term used to describe men who go after tourists (usually white women) for money/green cards, etc. They often work at hotels and hang in the tourist beach areas.

# Suggested Reading

## HISTORY

Roorda, Eric Paul, and Lauren Derby. *The Dominican Republic Reader: History, Culture, Politics*. Durham, NC, and London: Duke University Press, 2014. A unique compilation of the most important aspects of Dominican history and culture, this book examines various themes through excerpts from reliable sources. It also provides interesting background and history on some of the country's cultural symbols from baseball to bachata.

Wucker, Michele. *Why the Cocks Fight: Dominicans, Haitians, and the Struggle for Hispaniola*. New York: Hill and Wang, 2000. An excellent, easy read that examines the history of both Haiti and the DR, the evolution of their relationship, and the cause of friction between the two nations. It also gives an excellent historical recap in an engaging manner even for those who are not history buffs. If you pick just one history book for background, make it this one.

## CULTURE

De Feliz, Lindsay. *What about Your Saucepans?* Summertime, 2013. A British expat tells the tale of moving to the DR to make a change from her life in the UK, taking on a dive master position, and meeting and then marrying a younger Dominican man who eventually goes into local politics. The book is a page-turner for sure, an easy read with plenty of humor and excellent depictions of Dominicans, their culture, relationships, and way of life.

## ECOLOGY

Latta, Steven, Christopher Rimmer, et al. *Birds of the Dominican Republic and Haiti*. Princeton Field Guides, 2006. This is the go-to guide for all the bird species on Hispaniola island.

## FICTION

Alvarez, Julia. *In the Time of the Butterflies*. Chapel Hill, NC: Algonquin Books, 1994. Alvarez recounts the life story of the famed "Mariposas," the three Mirabal sisters who rebelled against Trujillo and were eventually murdered on the dictator's orders. The movie based on this novel is also excellent.

Alvarez, Julia. *How the Garcia Girls Lost Their Accents*. Chapel Hill, NC: Algonquin Books, 1994. This truly enjoyable, award-winning read tells the tale of four daughters from a wealthy family who fled their native DR under the Trujillo regime to take refuge in the United States. The stories weave the past with the present and cultural identity issues with immersion in a new culture.

Díaz, Junot. *The Brief Wondrous Life of Oscar Wao.* New York: Riverhead Books, 2007. The Pulitzer Prize-winning novel tells the tale of a Dominican family in the United States through the eyes of a nerdy, overweight teenager growing up in New Jersey. The

novel offers interesting DR historical context through the lives of the various generations within Oscar's family.

Vargas Llosa, Mario. *The Feast of the Goat.* New York: Farrar, Straus and Giroux, 2001. Weaving various story lines from both past and present, this novel tackles the tumultuous days of General Rafael Leonidas Trujillo and his brutal three-decade rule over the Dominican Republic.

# Internet Resources

### Access DR
**www.accessdr.com**
An excellent English-language resource and travel blog with visitor tips and articles on sights, hotels, and things to do around the country. It's also a solid source for tourism-related news. They produce a print version you can pick up in many tourist locations, including airports and hotels.

### Active Cabarete
**www.activecabarete.com**
A website for all water sports enthusiasts heading to Cabarete, with information on lodging, weather, events, and more.

### Caribe Tours
**www.caribetours.com.do**
Though in Spanish, this website for one of the main long-distance bus companies in the DR has an interactive map that's easy to use and understand, allowing users to quickly view routes with departure points, schedules, and ticket prices. You can also email them via the website to reserve a spot.

### Colonial Zone DR News Blog
**www.colonialzone-dr.com**
A handy website on all things Colonial Zone in Santo Domingo. It also has a super news

blog frequently updated with details on monthly events taking place in the Colonial Zone and other relevant news.

### Discover Puerto Plata
**www.discoverpuertoplata.com**
The Puerto Plata private tourist cluster's website on the best of the North Coast, including hotel, food, and nightlife information.

### Dominican Today
**www.dominicantoday.com**
An English-language news resource on Dominican current events and the latest happenings around the country.

### DR Ministry of Tourism:
### Go Dominican Republic
**www.godominicanrepublic.com**

### DR1 Dominican Republic
### Travel Information
**www.dr1.com**
An old go-to resource for all English-speaking expats, with everything from news to travel information. Its most useful feature is the forums organized by region where you can ask for travel advice as well as find a gazillion useful tips. The travel section has useful general information on the DR.

**Embassy of the Dominican Republic in the United States**
**www.drembassyusa.org**

**Go Samana**
**www.gosamana-dominican republic.com**
The private tourist cluster's website providing information on member hotels, restaurants, tour guides, and general history and activities on the Samaná Peninsula.

**Guia Constanza**
**www.guiaconstanza.com**
The private tourism cluster for Constanza offers a colorful website filled with information on sights, restaurants, and member hotels for those exploring this lovely mountain town in the central DR.

**Hispaniola.com**
**www.hispaniola.com**
A website on all things tourism and travel around the DR, including general information on flora, fauna, and history.

# Index

## QR

# List of Maps

# Acknowledgments

I want to express my sincere gratitude to the wonderful friends and contacts in the DR who offered their support and assistance with my work on this book. Your willingness to assist and share your expert insights—on tourism, the environment, politics, wildlife, cultural anecdotes, and more—on your respective regions, pueblos and on your country is deeply appreciated.

Thanks go to the team at BvK and Go Dominican Republic, Tim Hall, Molly and Rodolfo Cruz, and David Durán. I also want to thank all the those individuals who looked out for me on the road, the tour guides went out of their way to make sure I had the information I needed, the locals who showed me their favorite spots in each part of the country, and the small business owners and women's cooperatives who showed me their community initiatives and are making a difference in the DR.

Last but not least, a big thanks to my publishing family at Avalon Travel, for their constant encouragement and hard work—Grace Fujimoto, Kimberly Ehart, Crystal Turnau, Darren Alessi, Kat Bennett, and the rest of the team.

# MAP SYMBOLS

| | | | | | | | |
|---|---|---|---|---|---|---|---|
| ▰▰▰ | Expressway | ○ | City/Town | ✈ | Airport | ⚲ | Golf Course |
| ▭▭▭ | Primary Road | ◉ | State Capital | ✕ | Airfield | 🅿 | Parking Area |
| ─── | Secondary Road | ⊛ | National Capital | ▲ | Mountain | ⛰ | Archaeological Site |
| ┄┄┄ | Unpaved Road | ★ | Point of Interest | ✚ | Unique Natural Feature | ⛪ | Church |
| ─── | Feature Trail | • | Accommodation | | | ⛽ | Gas Station |
| ----- | Other Trail | ▼ | Restaurant/Bar | 🌫 | Waterfall | | Glacier |
| ·········· | Ferry | ■ | Other Location | ▲ | Park | | Mangrove |
| ═══ | Pedestrian Walkway | Λ | Campground | ⬛ | Trailhead | | Reef |
| ▮▮▮ | Stairs | | | ⛷ | Skiing Area | | Swamp |

# CONVERSION TABLES

°C = (°F - 32) / 1.8
°F = (°C x 1.8) + 32
1 inch = 2.54 centimeters (cm)
1 foot = 0.304 meters (m)
1 yard = 0.914 meters
1 mile = 1.6093 kilometers (km)
1 km = 0.6214 miles
1 fathom = 1.8288 m
1 chain = 20.1168 m
1 furlong = 201.168 m
1 acre = 0.4047 hectares
1 sq km = 100 hectares
1 sq mile = 2.59 square km
1 ounce = 28.35 grams
1 pound = 0.4536 kilograms
1 short ton = 0.90718 metric ton
1 short ton = 2,000 pounds
1 long ton = 1.016 metric tons
1 long ton = 2,240 pounds
1 metric ton = 1,000 kilograms
1 quart = 0.94635 liters
1 US gallon = 3.7854 liters
1 Imperial gallon = 4.5459 liters
1 nautical mile = 1.852 km

## MOON DOMINICAN REPUBLIC

Avalon Travel
Hachette Book Group
1700 Fourth Street
Berkeley, CA 94710, USA
www.moon.com

Editor: Kimberly Ehart
Acquiring Editor: Grace Fujimoto
Series Manager: Kathryn Ettinger
Copy Editor: Brett Keener
Graphics and Production Coordinator: Darren Alessi
Cover Design: Faceout Studios, Charles Brock
Interior Design: Domini Dragoone
Moon Logo: Tim McGrath
Map Editor: Kat Bennett
Cartographers: Austin Ehrhardt, Kat Bennett, Brian
    Shotwell
Proofreader: Kelly Lydick
Indexer: Greg Jewett

ISBN-13: 978-1-64049-046-8

Printing History
1st Edition — 1997
6th Edition — September 2019
5 4 3 2 1

Front cover photo: Laguna Dudú, Cabrera © Lebawit
    Lily Girma
Back cover photo: Tropical beach in Punta Cana ©
    Valio84sl | Dreamstime.com
Interior photos: © Lebawit Lily Girma except page 9
    © (top) Giuseppe Crimeni | Dreamstime.com;
    page 14 © Gerold Grotelueschen | Dreamstime.
    com; page 15 © (bottom) Jedynakanna |
    Dreamstime.com; page 16 © (top) Kit Korzun |
    Dreamstime.com page 26 © (bottom) Radoshitzky
    | Dreamstime.com; page 30 © (bottom)
    Giuseppe Crimeni | Dreamstime.com; page 31 ©
    Donyanedomam | Dreamstime.com

Printed in China by RR Donnelley